Hong Kong,
December '94.

THE OTHER HONG KONG R[EPORT]

Related Titles Already Published

The Other Hong Kong Report (for 1989)
Edited by T. L. Tsim and Bernard H. K. Luk

The Other Hong Kong Report 1990
Edited by Richard Y. C. Wong and Joseph Y. S. Cheng

The Other Hong Kong Report 1991
Edited by Sung Yun-wing and Lee Ming-kwan

The Other Hong Kong Report 1992
Edited by Joseph Y. S. Cheng and Paul C. K. Kwong

The Other Hong Kong Report 1993
Edited by Choi Po-king and Ho Lok-sang

THE OTHER HONG KONG REPORT
1994

Edited by Donald H. McMillen ▪ Man Si-wai

The Chinese University Press

© **The Chinese University of Hong Kong** 1994

All Rights Reserved. No part of this work may be
reproduced or transmitted in any form or by any means,
electronic or mechanical, including photocopying and
recording, or by any information storage or retrieval
system without permission in writing from
The Chinese University of Hong Kong.

ISBN 962-201-633-2

The Chinese University Press
The Chinese University of Hong Kong
Sha Tin, New Territories
Hong Kong

ACKNOWLEDGEMENTS

To Government Information Services for illustrations on the cover and on pages 10, 124, 430.

To New China News Limited for illustration on the cover.

To *Overseas Chinese Daily News* for illustrations on pages 40, 266, 350, 366.

To *South China Morning Post* for illustrations on pages xxxvi, 24, 60, 76, 102, 150, 166, 188, 210, 224, 252, 298, 316, 332, 388, 470.

Printed in Hong Kong by Regal Printing Co., Ltd.

Contents

Calendar of Events in 1993–1994 ix

Preface xxvii

Introduction xxix
    DONALD H. McMILLEN

1. Constitution and Administration 1
    NORMAN J. MINERS

2. The Legal System: Are the Changes Too Little, Too Late? 9
    JOHN D. HO

3. Independent Commission Against Corruption 23
    SONNY S. H. LO

4. Civil Servants 39
    JANE C. Y. LEE

5. The Implementation of the Sino-British Joint Declaration 61
    CHRISTINE LOH

6. Politics, Politicians, and Political Parties 75
    MICHAEL E. DeGOLYER

7. Public Opinion 103
    ROBERT T. Y. CHUNG

8. The Economy 125
    TSANG SHU-KI

9. Labour and Employment 149
    WING SUEN

10. Immigration and Emigration: Current Trends, Dilemmas and Policies 165
    RONALD SKELDON

11. The Property Price Crisis 187
    LAWRENCE W. C. LAI

12. Infrastructure 209
    KWONG KAI-SUN

13. Transport 223
    STEPHEN L. W. TANG

14. The Environment 253
    HUNG WING-TAT

15. Public Housing 265
    LAU KWOK-YU

16. Education 297
    ANTHONY SWEETING

17. Elderly in Need of Care and Financial Support 315
    HENRY T. K. MOK

18. Social Welfare 331
    CECILIA CHAN

19. Medical and Health 351
    ANTHONY B. L. CHEUNG

20. Women 367
    IRENE TONG

21. The Media 389
    FRANCIS MORIARTY

22. Sexuality in Hong Kong 415
    NG MAN-LUN

23. Hong Kong's International Presence 429
    BERNARD H. K. LUK

24. Culture and Identity 443
    CHAN HOI-MAN

25. China–Hong Kong Integration 469
    GEORGE SHEN

Index 485

Contents vii

ILLUSTRATIONS

Members of the United Democrats of Hong Kong march to Xinhua agency carrying posters along with their petition urging a fair political system. xxxvi

The Chief Justice, Sir Ti-liang Yang, addresses at the 1994 Legal Year. 10

Sacked Independent Commission Against Corruption official Alex Tsui testifies before the Legislative Council. 24

Anson Chan, who replaces Sir David Ford as the Chief Secretary, bids him farewell at the airport. 40

The political sub-group of Beijing's Preliminary Working Committee meets Hong Kong affairs chief Lu Ping at the villa in Stanley. 60

Anthony Cheung joins hands with Martin Lee to announce their political alliance. 76

In January this year, Elsie Tu and Emily Lau were the most popular legislators. But Lau surpasses Tu, who in turn ranks out of the top-ten, in the middle of this year. 102

Kwai Chung Container Port, the world's busiest port. 124

More than 4,000 people make their way to Government House to serve a petition demanding a retirement protection plan. 150

Thousands of people crowd the halls of Immigration Tower in Wan Chai to lodge applications for passports under the British Nationality Scheme. 166

Should I or Shouldn't I? ... Would-be buyers looking at the Laguna City development and wondering whether to buy. 188

The two towers of the Tsing Ma Bridge start to be joined together by cable. 210

Concerned bus passengers make their point about keeping fare increases to a minimum. 224

Farmers parade through Central in protest over new regulations providing tighter control over the disposal of livestock waste. ... 252

Parents and children protest against the Housing Authority's present rent increase policy. 266

Students of St. Joseph's Anglo-Chinese School and their parents protest the switch of the medium of instruction to Chinese. 298

Two elderly women join a protest outside the Legislative Council building. 316

A local residents' group calls for an increase in pensions outside the Legislative Council building. 332

Some concerned people protest against the linkage between medical fees and costs. 350

Women's groups support Christine Loh's bill on gender equality in land inheritance rights in the New Territories. 366

A crowd of Xi Yang's supporters makes its way to Xinhua. 388

Are Hong Kong people getting progressively liberal or permissive sexually? 414

The Financial Secretary Hamish Macleod joins world leaders at the first APEC Economic Leaders Meeting in Seattle. 430

Movies are one of the most popular entertainments among Hong Kong people. 442

Zhou Zhenxing, general manager of Bank of China's Hong Kong Branch, shows some of the new Hong Kong banknotes to be circulated by the bank. 470

Calendar of Events in 1993–1994

1.7.1993   Elsie Tu and Emily Lau are voted the most popular legislators in the University of Hong Kong Social Sciences Research Centre's poll of 574 citizens.

2.7.1993   British Home Office is criticized for reneging on a promise to give sanctuary to 3.2 million Hong Kong British Nationals in a post-1997 worst case scenario.

3.7.1993   Women's groups cross swords with Heung Yee Kuk in a bid to gain land inheritance rights for New Territories women in cases of intestacy and are told by Lam Kwok-cheung — "you should not force a person to have a Western breakfast if he chooses to have a traditional one."

4.7.1993   *South China Morning Post (SCMP)* poll of 574 indicates overwhelming Hong Kong support for Beijing's bid to host Olympics 2,000.

6.7.1993   The appointment of Executive Councillor, Rosanna Wong Yick-ming, as Chairman of the Hong Kong Housing Authority on the sudden resignation of Sir David Akers-Jones is criticized by housing activists.

7.7.1993   Hong Kong and Macau Affairs Office deputy, Wang Qiren, warns against speeding up democratic development in Hong Kong after new "Full Democracy in '95" group demands 60 directly elected seats in the Legislative Council (Legco).

9.7.1993   Patten says it is better for Britain to take unilateral action on constitutional reforms in Hong Kong than surrender on principles following "whirlwind visit" of the Secretary of State for Foreign and Commonwealth Affairs, Douglas Hurd, to Beijing.

12.7.1993   The Finance Branch accepts Commissioner of Police, Li Kwan-ha's view that the sale of his car registration plate No. 1 would lower the morale and pride of the Royal Hong Kong Police Force notwithstanding legislator Chim Pui-chung's argument that the Commissioner's car should be No. 4.

14.7.1993   The Financial Secretary, Hamish Macleod, reveals that Hong Kong's Exchange Fund at end 1992 was the world's tenth biggest foreign currency reserve at US$35.2 billion.

16.7.1993   Chinese Foreign Minister, Qian Qichen, formally inaugurates a 57-member Preliminary Working Committee (PWC) for the Hong Kong Special Administrative Region (SAR) Preparatory Committee but suspends implementation until the second plenary meeting in December.

20.7.1993   China Light and Power Company Limited (CLP) files a writ in the Supreme Court seeking an injunction to restrain barrister Michael Ford and damages in regard to privileged information relating to an explosion at

	the Castle Peak power station on 28 August 1992 in which two engineers died.
23.7.1993	Deacons withdraw offer to act for legislators Martin Lee Chu-ming and Szeto Wah in a libel case against former Appeal Court Judge, Li Fook-sean, now a prominent member of the Beijing-appointed PWC, arousing widespread concern.
29.7.1993	Patten, in London, refuses to give deadline for conclusion of Sino-British talks on electoral reforms due for the ninth round on 16 August in Beijing.
30.7.1993	Legco's Service Panel contests the government's decision to allow expatriate civil servants to acquire local status and alleges failure to consult.
3.8.1993	Coroner Warner Banks recommends reopening inquest into the deaths of workers in the Castle Peak power plant explosion after reading documents filed in the District Court of Jim Wells County in Texas.
5.8.1993	Huge explosion at a dangerous goods store in Shenzhen kills 70 and is seen from Hong Kong.
5.8.1993	The Secretary for the Civil Service, Anson Chan Fang On-sang, defends the policy of allowing expatriate civil servants to opt for local status.
6.8.1993	Hong Kong broadcaster Pamela Pak Wan-kam's popular Beijing phone-in show is suddenly shut down by the Chinese authorities.
9.8.1993	The Director of Audit, Brian Jenney, seeks to have government-funded corporations put under his value-for-money scrutiny.
10.8.1993	High Court grants CLP an interim injunction restraining *SCMP* and *Sunday Morning Post* from publishing the contents of "Report of the Advisory Board Concerning an Explosion at Castle Peak B Power Station on 28 August 1992."
11.8.1993	The Consumer Council criticizes property agents' commission charges on both vendors and purchasers of residential properties.
13.8.1993	Sincere Company directors agree to repay special bonus of HK$66.68 million on sale of Sincere House after widespread criticism.
15.8.1993	China labour activist Han Dongfang is evicted from the Mainland to Hong Kong and given a seven-day temporary visa but vows to re-enter his home country.
17.8.1993	The ninth round of Sino-British talks on the 1994 and 1995 electoral arrangements ends without signs of agreement but Douglas Hurd and Qian Qichen plan further discussions in New York on 23 September.
19.8.1993	Hang Seng Index reaches 7,605.26 on turnover of HK$4.64 billion in fifth day straight rise on aggressive overseas buying giving a 37.9 per cent increase since the start of the year.

Calendar of Events in 1993–1994 xi

20.8.1993	Elsie Tu, in an end of session interview, severely criticizes Patten for stirring up political controversy and accuses Britain of introducing too much democracy to Hong Kong too late.
22.8.1993	The Alliance in Support of the Patriotic Movement in China protests outside New China News Agency (NCNA) over China's revocation of Han Dongfang's passport.
25.8.1993	Baron Kadoorie dies, aged 94, and is widely praised for his contribution to Hong Kong's development by British, Chinese and Hong Kong notables.
30.8.1993	*Express Daily*'s Hong Kong reporter, Leung Wai-man, is expelled from China, but NCNA's Wu Shishen who allegedly sold her an advance copy of Jiang Zemin's speech at the 1992 Fourteenth Party Congress was secretly tried and sentenced to life imprisonment.
1.9.1993	NCNA's Zhang Junsheng criticizes Hong Kong government officials for interfering in China's internal affairs by commenting on the expulsion of Han Dongfang from China.
2.9.1993	Lu Ping personally guarantees freedom of movement of Martin Lee Chu-ming and Szeto Wah to and from the Hong Kong SAR after 1997 and criticizes Sir David Ford for making irresponsible remarks on the Han Dongfang case.
5.9.1993	Liberal Party's Lau Wah-sum and Ngai Shiu-kit fail to push their party's proposal for a ministerial system in Hong Kong at the Political Sub-group of the PWC in Beijing.
7.9.1993	Patten is accused by China of "trying to create chaos" by advocating a functional constituency for the Hong Kong civil service.
9.9.1993	Two armed robbers are killed in a shoot out at the Chase Manhattan Bank in Cameron Road, Kowloon.
10.9.1993	China's Xu Liugen, in a general statement of policy, makes it clear that ethnic Chinese from Vietnam should be repatriated to Vietnam "in accordance with international practice."
11.9.1993	Dickson Concepts is reported to be pushing ahead with HK$800 million plan for thirty-one "luxury outlets" and two department stores in China in the next seven months.
12.9.1993	Malaysian tycoon, Robert Kuok Hock Nien, buys 34.9 per cent stake in the SCMP Publishing Group for HK$2.7 billion from Rupert Murdoch's News Corporation.
13.9.1993	Hong Kong deputies of the National People's Congress are divided on Ms. Liu Yiu-chu's view that they should form a sub-committee to monitor the work of the PWC.

Calendar of Events in 1993–1994

14.9.1993 China frees Wei Jingsheng six months before the expiry of his 15-year sentence for "passing military secrets and spreading counter-revolutionary propaganda and incitement" but denies that the release is related to the Olympic Committee meeting on 23 September.

15.9.1993 The Secretary for Recreation and Culture, James So Yiu-cho, avers that freedom of the press will survive Hong Kong's return to China without the need for legal protection and that "laws to protect it, or laws to prohibit it would not be desirable."

16.9.1993 Baptist College's "Hong Kong Transitions Project" poll of 1,109 Hong Kong households finds that 78 per cent believe the SAR government will be plagued by corruption and 63 per cent had no trust or slight trust in China's adherence to the terms of the Basic Law.

17.9.1993 Anson Chan Fang On-sang is appointed to be the first Chinese Chief Secretary, designate, on the retirement of Sir David Ford. But Secretaries Yeung Kai-yin and John Chan Cho-chak are to retire early.

23.9.1993 Hong Kong is disappointed as Beijing loses the 2,000 Olympic Games to Sydney.

25.9.1993 NCNA releases Deng Xiaoping's speech of 24 September 1982, warning of possible Chinese takeover of Hong Kong before 1997.

29.9.1993 Legco's House Committee decides to introduce a private member's bill to block the government's policy of allowing expatriates to transfer to local status.

1.10.1993 Legislator Simon Ip urges Hong Kong businessmen not to cooperate in corrupt practices when engaging in business in China and supports Hong Kong General Chamber of Commerce's call for a body like Hong Kong's Independent Commission Against Corruption (ICAC) for China.

3.10.1993 Civil servants are reported to be resentful regarding Patten's performance pledges which are seen as a move to gain personal support from the community at their expense.

4.10.1993 At the World Press Freedom Conference in Hong Kong, Patten urges press to defend freedom of speech and of the press, and Chairlady of the Hong Kong Journalists Association, Daisy Li Yuet-wah, warns of China's intimidating treatment of *Ming Pao*'s reporter Xi Yang.

6.10.1993 Patten, in his annual address to the Legco, challenges China to conclude discussions on electoral arrangements and Hong Kong to support democracy. Hang Seng Index moves through 8,000 to close at 8,041.57 on turnover of HK$6.63 billion.

8.10.1993 Poll of 605 adults indicates 78 per cent agree with Patten's call to stand up for democracy but of these 16 per cent would leave it to others to take the stand.

Calendar of Events in 1993–1994 xiii

11.10.1993 The thirteenth round of Sino-British talks in Beijing on electoral arrangements has an acrimonious start as Minister of State for Foreign and Commonwealth Affairs with special responsibility for Hong Kong, Alastair Goodlad, in Hong Kong, rises to great heights in inaugural ride on the world's longest escalator to Mid-Levels.

13.10.1993 International Maritime Organization claims that action against piracy by Chinese patrol vessels is impeded by the withdrawal of a Hong Kong government report on the attacks.

15.10.1993 Hang Seng Index hits 8,763 in HK$9 billion buying frenzy by overseas investors oblivious to Sino-British political dispute.

17.10.1993 Moody's says that the lack of disclosure of Hong Kong banks is damaging their credit rating.

18.10.1993 House of Commons Foreign Affairs Committee (FAC) delegation visits Hong Kong to solicit the views of legislators, officials and organizations and Chairman, David Howell, calls on Zhou Nan at NCNA headquarters.

19.10.1993 Lu Ping repeats Beijing's warning to Britain that Hong Kong should not be turned into a political city.

20.10.1993 Patten's address on 6 October gets a heavy mauling from legislators at the start of a two-day debate.

21.10.1993 Agriculture and Fisheries Department moves to combat trade in rhino products in response to Convention on International Trade in Endangered Species (CITES) ultimatum.

24.10.1993 Wuhan blames unscrupulous Hong Kong and Macau businessmen for sharp increases in economic crimes involving more than Renminbi 1 million per case.

29.10.1993 Nobel Prize laureate, Milton Friedman, on visit to China, warns against excessive bureaucratic involvement in the market economy and praises example of Hong Kong businessmen.

30.10.1993 Survey Research Hong Kong poll of 1,011 suggests confidence in Hong Kong's future has slipped because of over-long and inconclusive Sino-British talks on the political system.

1.11.1993 Chinese Premier Li Peng, in interview with *Wide Angle* magazine, accuses Britain of violating past Sino-British agreements on Hong Kong and calls for the PWC to speed up its work so as to advance the operation of the Preparatory Committee scheduled in the Basic Law for 1996.

1.11.1993 China's consent is not yet given to the Hong Kong government's nominations for new members of the Airport Consultative Committee.

Calendar of Events in 1993–1994

2.11.1993   Human rights lobbyist John Kamm reports Lu Ping as saying that after 1997 China will modify Hong Kong's Bill of Rights to match the Basic Law.

3.11.1993   China's Maanshan Iron and Steel Corporation shares, newly listed on the Stock Exchange of Hong Kong, rise from HK$2.27 to HK$3.65 on the first day of trading and against a falling market.

4.11.1993   China Airlines Boeing 447–400 with 296 passengers skids into harbour whilst landing in tropical storm Ira. No fatalities but 27 passengers are injured.

5.11.1993   The University of Hong Kong's Professor Edward Chen says that the Asia-Pacific Region has proved it can maintain growth momentum despite slowdown in the world's major economies.

6.11.1993   PWC member and former Executive Councillor, Rita Fan Hsu Lai-tai, attacks Patten for unrepresentative views and high-handed undemocratic conduct.

8.11.1993   Cable and Wireless Chief Executive, James Ross, after discussions with Lu Ping, refutes rumours of sanctions against British firms because of Sino-British dispute over political reforms.

9.11.1993   Thomas Fok, son of Hong Kong billionaire, Henry Fok, pleads guilty in New York Court to smuggling 15,000 AK47 rifles from Holland to the United States (U.S.) but is fined and then freed after a plea bargain.

10.11.1993 The Secretary for Security, Alistair Asprey, rejects a motion tabled by Emily Lau Wai-hing and supported by 36 legislators, seeking assurances of right of abode in Britain for British National (Overseas) passport holders if expelled from Hong Kong after 1997.

12.11.1993 Professor Arthur Li Kwok-cheung and Dr. Paul Morris resign from the Education Commission on grounds that "the Commission now lacks a clear sense of direction and purpose."

13.11.1993 Hong Kong police remove Han Dongfang from "no man's land" between Shenzhen and Lo Wu after his third unsuccessful attempt to re-enter China.

15.11.1993 Dr. Guo Shiping, Wuhan University Professor of Economics, suggests that the 3rd Plenum of the Chinese Communist Party's Central Committee, just concluded, could be interpreted as a statement of China's intention to follow Singapore's lead in reforming China's economic and political structures.

18.11.1993 Legislators Anna Wu and Christine Loh question the accountability of the 450 government advisory committees but a Home Affairs Branch official argues that "because their members do not possess any decision-making powers the issue of accountability does not arise."

Calendar of Events in 1993–1994

19.11.1993 At the re-opening of the inquest on the Castle Peak power plant explosion, ordered by the Attorney General, it is disclosed that two reports concerning faulty equipment were not made available to the Coroner at the original hearing.

23.11.1993 In a farewell speech to the Legco, Sir David Ford warns legislators against meddling in senior civil service appointments as this "could lead to the politicization of the civil service."

29.11.1993 Hang Seng Index closes down 240 points at 9,012.77 on failure of the seventeenth round of Sino-British talks, concluded on 27 November, to produce agreement.

1.12.1993 Legislators vote 33 to 14 to use their powers under the Legislative Council (Powers and Privileges) Ordinance for the first time to investigate allegations of wrongful dismissal by sacked ICAC Deputy Director of Operations, Alex Tsui Ka-kit.

1.12.1993 Wan Chai police prepare for Wo Hop To and Sun Yee On triad gang war after the gunning down of triad leader Andely Chan and associate Tse Chun-fung in Macau.

2.12.1993 Patten tells the Legco why the first part of his electoral reforms is to be gazetted on 10 December and introduced on 15 December. Hang Seng Index drops by 100 points.

3.12.1993 Investors ignore "Beijing's sabre-rattling" over political reforms in Hong Kong and raise index 56.15 points to close at 9,294.35 as anticipated panic selling fails to materialize.

5.12.1993 Sir Percy Cradock, former Foreign Affairs Adviser to Prime Minister Thatcher, again publicly attacks Patten's reforms and predicts dire consequences for the people of Hong Kong.

6.12.1993 The Secretary of State for Foreign and Commonwealth Affairs, Douglas Hurd, in a statement to the House of Commons, supports Patten's constitutional package which, he says, "will bequeath to Hong Kong an open and democratic system offering the electorate a genuine choice."

7.12.1993 The twenty-eighth meeting of the Sino-British Joint Liaison Group (JLG) opens in London to light-hearted banter, with defence lands, civil service, investment promotion and visa abolition agreements on the agenda.

9.12.1993 Hong Kong delegate to the National People's Congress (NPC), Ms. Liu Yiu-chu, is "in constant flood of tears" at the presence of Sir S. Y. Chung and other former pro-British dignitaries at a plenary session of the PWC in the Great Hall of the People.

10.12.1993 Chinese officials slam gazettal of the first-stage electoral bill but Hang Seng Index soars to 10,228.11 on record turnover of HK$11.94 billion.

Calendar of Events in 1993–1994

12.12.1993 Legislators question the effectiveness of the committee for monitoring the employment of retired civil servants but chairman, Sir Roger Lobo, defends its performance.

13.12.1993 *Guangming Daily* deplores China adolescents' blind adulation of Hong Kong and Taiwan singers and actors who, the paper says, enjoy cult status in China.

17.12.1993 China protests BBC showing of the television programme "The Secret Life of Chairman Mao" for its frank, though brief portrayal of Mao's liking for young women.

18.12.1993 Guangdong governor, Zhu Senlin, says Sino-British economic and trade ties would be bound to be further harmed by the dispute over political reforms in Hong Kong as British companies are excluded from participation in the development of the Guangzhou underground railway project.

23.12.1993 Institute of Personnel Management survey shows that Hong Kong's competitive salaries and sluggish overseas economies are drawing Hong Kong immigrants back to the territory at a higher rate than before.

26.12.1993 The government is devising a scheme to draw in professionals from China over and above the increase in the daily quota from the Mainland on one-way permits which is about to be increased from 75 to 105 per day.

27.12.1993 Hong Kong and Macau Affairs Office of the State Council issues formal notification of China's intention to dismantle Hong Kong's three-tier system of government in 1997 and reorganize the SAR government in accordance with the Basic Law.

28.12.1993 Former appointed legislator Andrew So Kwok-wing is appointed to be Commissioner for Administrative Complaints to succeed Arthur Garcia whose contract was not renewed.

29.12.1993 At the inauguration of the giant Tian Tan Buddha at Po Lin Monastery on Lantau Island, Head of NCNA, Zhou Nan, quotes Buddhist texts on three violations and three accords for the benefit of Governor Patten who also attended.

30.12.1993 Hang Seng Index ends 1993 at a lucky 11,888 — 115 per cent up on the year.

2.1.1994 Civil Service union leaders criticize a government directive asking them to decline invitations from the PWC to discuss transitional matters.

3.1.1994 The ICAC warns Hong Kong businessmen not to offer bribes in China.

4.1.1994 The PWC opposes the appointment of legislators to the Airport Corporation.

5.1.1994 Security Branch official says that the right of abode in the Hong Kong

Calendar of Events in 1993–1994 xvii

SAR for 300,000 to 400,000 Hong Kong Chinese citizens holding foreign passports is still undecided.

9.1.1994 The NCNA is reported to be preparing for active participation in the elections of 1994 and 1995 notwithstanding China's vow to dismantle the system after 1997.

10.1.1994 The Chief Justice, Sir Ti-liang Yang, at the formal opening of the Legal Year, sidesteps controversial issues and causes irritation by breaking with precedent and disallowing all speeches but his own.

11.1.1994 Lu Ping criticizes the Hong Kong government for seeking funds from the Finance Committee for airport construction without waiting for Chinese consent and for allegedly stopping Secretary for Economic Services, Gordon Siu Kwing-chue, from attending a meeting of the PWC sub-committee studying the Airport Corporation Bill.

15.1.1994 Three Italian luxury yachts, stolen from Hong Kong, are discovered in China operating tourist high-speed ferry services between Ha Chuen and Sheung Chuen Islands and Guangdong.

16.1.1994 Liberal Party legislator Selina Chow Liang Shuk-yee joins Laguna City residents in march to Government House to protest a day centre for former mental patients operating in the estate, allegedly established without proper prior consultation.

17.1.1994 The ICAC reports the highest year-on-year increase in corruption in Hong Kong since the Commission was set up, at 1,806 cases, up 52 per cent on 1992.

21.1.1994 Sir David Akers-Jones accuses Patten of making a cheap joke at his expense at the FAC hearing by quoting out of context his remark "the Chinese style is not to rig elections, but they do like to know the results before they are held."

21.1.1994 Patten is reported to be launching a business-funded campaign in February for a voluntary code of business ethics to combat corruption to be adopted by all Hong Kong listed companies.

23.1.1994 Both Hong Kong and China-appointed groups concerned with matters affecting the rule of law after 1997 complain at delays caused by the JLG and call for its work to be speeded up.

24.1.1994 The Commissioner for Administrative Complaints says that the government acted improperly in failing to consult the public before approving a golf course and landfill in the Pat Sin Leng and Clearwater Bay Country Parks.

25.1.1994 China threatens to invalidate legal and financial commitments relating to the new airport if Beijing's prior endorsement is not given and drops the

Hang Seng Index 251.37 points to 11,239.57 on a turnover of HK$7.91 billion.

27.1.1994 Legislators support Christine Loh Kung-wai's proposal to initiate a private member's bill on public access to information in view of the Hong Kong government's refusal to enact a Freedom of Information Act.

28.1.1994 Lu Ping questions the right of outgoing Secretary for Constitutional Affairs, Michael Sze Cho-cheung, to speak for Hong Kong at FAC hearings and remarked "How many people in Hong Kong regard this 'loyal' follower (of Patten) as a Hong Kong person?"

31.1.1994 British business firms are reported to be concerned at the damaging effects of rising Sino-British tension on trade after China's Wu Yi warns that "Britain's unfriendly and uncooperative attitude will affect normal trade with China."

1.2.1994 China shows positive reaction to British proposal to raise the government's capital contribution to airport construction to HK$60 billion with Patten commenting "I hope that China will find this an excellent Lunar New Year present for Hong Kong, for China, for everyone."

2.2.1994 Hong Kong Customs Officers make a record-breaking seizure of cigarettes, television sets and air-conditioners, valued at HK$198 million in a Tsing Yi godown awaiting shipment to Shantou on a Panamanian-registered vessel.

5.2.1994 Chinese Premier, Li Peng, formally opens the Daya Bay Nuclear Power Station although Hong Kong's contingency plans against accidents are not yet agreed with Mainland officials. Hong Kong officials reassure by saying that they "are keeping their fingers crossed."

5.2.1994 Executive Councillor, Baroness Dunn and husband, former Attorney General, Michael Thomas, buy prestigious HK$9 million holiday home deep in rural England.

8.2.1994 Larry Yung Chi-kin of CITIC Pacific is reported to have acquired a C$10 million home at Point Grey, Vancouver as well as the country home of former British Prime Minister, Harold Macmillan in Sussex, for £5 million.

12.2.1994 China's Ambassador in London, Ma Yuzhen, officially informs the FAC that China will definitely dismantle the government system of Hong Kong in 1997 whatever the British or the international community may feel about it.

13.2.1994 British Minister of State for Foreign and Commonwealth Affairs with special responsibility for Hong Kong, Alastair Goodlad, in a letter to the *Times* on 11 February, rejects the grant of right of abode to Hong Kong

Calendar of Events in 1993–1994 xix

citizens on the grounds that "successive governments and parliaments have taken the view that it would not be feasible to give such an undertaking. Nor is it necessary."

14.2.1994   Patten, in Sydney, challenges the view that the concept of universality of human rights is not applicable to the Asia-Pacific Region.

15.2.1994   Media tycoon Rupert Murdoch threatens to drop BBC World Service Television from the STAR network unless it addresses China's complaints about the screening of "The Secret Life of Chairman Mao."

18.2.1994   A new Sino-British row erupts over Britain's publication of its account of the unsuccessful seventeen rounds of talks on electoral arrangements for Hong Kong's 1994 and 1995 elections.

19.2.1994   Professor Wu Jianfan, a legal expert of Beijing University, warns that legislator Anna Wu's proposed private bill setting up a Human Rights and Equal Opportunities Commission, would be in breach of the Basic Law and be abolished by China in 1997.

21.2.1994   *Eastern Express* reports a Beijing decision that there must be an organization in Hong Kong, separate from the NCNA, to oversee the work of the SAR government after 1997, even though this would contradict Beijing's declared policy of "Hong Kong people ruling Hong Kong."

23.2.1994   The Legco approves overwhelmingly the first part of Patten's constitutional package, lowering the voting age to 18, adopting the "single seat, single vote" system for all elections, abolishing appointed members from district and municipal councils and allowing Hong Kong delegates to the NPC to stand for election.

25.2.1994   Dr. Helmut Sohmen is appointed Chairman of a high-powered committee of nine to review the powers of the ICAC but the failure to appoint even one directly elected legislator to the committee is criticized.

1.3.1994   The Chief Justice, Sir Ti-liang Yang, urges establishment of the Court of Final Appeal, as agreed by the JLG in 1991, even though he expects strong opposition from Hong Kong's legal profession.

2.3.1994   Sir Hamish Macleod unveils his "pretty historic" budget which, though slashing taxes, promises to leave reserves for the SAR government at no less than HK$269 billion.

2.3.1994   In a rare admission of error, the Secretary for the Treasury, Donald Tsang Yam-kuen, accepts the Director of Audit's criticism of former Director of Building and Land's handling of the sale of a Garden Road site to Hutchison Whampoa as valid.

4.3.1994   In a ceremony at the China Resources Building, Beijing announces the names of 146 new Hong Kong Affairs advisers on district matters making a total of 274 to date.

Calendar of Events in 1993–1994

6.3.1994 Businessman Vincent Lo Hong-sui, prominent member of the Beijing-appointed PWC, warns that the Hong Kong government's unwillingness to allow officials to cooperate with the PWC will create a second nucleus of power in Hong Kong.

7.3.1994 Legislators express concern at possible government tampering with sensitive government files in the run-up to 1997 if administrative guidelines are not backed up by legislation to protect public records.

8.3.1994 The Chief Secretary, Anson Chan Fang On-sang, replaces Governor Patten as figurehead in Hong Kong's campaign in support of unconditional grant of most-favoured-nation (MFN) status to China, to avoid Patten being seen as an apologist for China's flawed human rights track record.

9.3.1994 Hong Kong delegate to the NPC, Ng Hong-min, speaking in Beijing, says that "a high-level body should be set up to combat corruption in China in view of the inadequacy of anti-graft organs."

9.3.1994 Hong Kong lawyer, Liu Yiu-chu, also a Hong Kong delegate to the NPC, protests a Chinese official ban on contact with Hong Kong journalists in her Beijing hotel and changes her hotel room remarking "I'm not here to serve jail."

10.3.1994 Chinese Premier Li Peng, in an address to the NPC, tones down intemperate anti-British rhetoric of his 1993 speech and stresses, instead, the important role of the PWC in the transition of Hong Kong to Chinese rule.

11.3.1994 Lord MacLehose, former Governor of Hong Kong, again attacks Governor Patten for spoiling the "cooperative relationship" between Britain and China over Hong Kong and adds "such mindless political polarization cannot be in Hong Kong's interest."

13.3.1994 NCNA Hong Kong branch director, Zhou Nan, says that China can maintain Hong Kong's prosperity and stability beyond 1997 without British cooperation and will not tolerate attempts to turn it into an "international asset."

15.3.1994 Swire Properties raise the asking price of a new tranche of flats in Hong Kong Mid-Levels from an average of HK$4,400 per square foot for May 1993 tranche to HK$9,728 per square foot, but buyers abound.

17.3.1994 Lu Ping warns of detrimental social and economic consequences of soaring property prices and says that Mainland-funded property companies are partly to blame for speculation.

21.3.1994 STAR TV announces replacement of BBC World Service programmes on its northern beam by Mandarin movies but will continue the BBC programmes on its southern beam until 31 March 1996.

25.3.1994 Violence and rape threat made by Heung Yee Kuk elders against liberal legislator, Christine Loh Kung-wai, should she dare to campaign for equal

Calendar of Events in 1993–1994 xxi

land inheritance rights for New Territories women in the leased territory, leads to massive security precautions by the police.

31.3.1994   Last minute rush for passports in the final stage of the British Nationality Scheme draws 36,014 applicants for 13,160 passports, not including those already mailed.

2.4.1994   400 parents of St. Joseph's Anglo-Chinese Primary School protest at the decision to teach core subjects in Chinese, rather than English, in the secondary stream.

3.4.1994   NCNA steps up its efforts to assess the suitability of senior civil servants for filling principal official posts after 1997 through social contacts arranged with the help of former civil servants.

5.4.1994   *Ming Pao* employees and the Hong Kong Journalists Association protest at the NCNA headquarters over the 12-year sentence passed upon Hong Kong journalist Xi Yang after a secret trial in Beijing on charges of spying and stealing state secrets.

7.4.1994   500 prisons officers and 750 police officers, in full riot gear and with use of tear gas, make successful dawn swoop on the Whitehead Detention Centre and move 1,456 Vietnamese internees to High Island.

10.4.1994   Hong Kong Journalists Association presses for a more precise definition of "state secrets" in Hong Kong law after criticism that Chinese law allows the authorities too much scope for criminalization of media gathering of much routine official data.

11.4.1994   Beijing strengthens its United Front for Hong Kong by appointing 50 more Hong Kong Affairs advisers, increasing the total to 141 and "widening the spectrum of views." One more non-ethnic Chinese, Mrs. Elsie Tu, accepted appointment.

12.4.1994   Hong Kong is hit by Taiwan's decision to ban tourist visits to China following an official cover-up of the causes of the deaths of 32 tourists, 24 from Taiwan, in a pleasure boat fire on Qiandao Lake, Zhejiang Province.

13.4.1994   The FAC's 110-page report on Hong Kong strongly supports Patten's constitutional package and also calls for a Human Rights Commission to avoid any repetition, after 1997, of China's human rights abuses in Tibet.

13.4.1994   Former top civil servants, led by Nicky Chan Nai-keong and including Arthur Garcia, Chan Wa-shek, Wilfred Wong Ying-wai, John Chan Cho-chak, Yeung Kai-yin, form a group to advise Beijing on the Hong Kong Administration.

14.4.1994   At a second formal hearing under the Legislative Council (Powers and Privileges) Ordinance, sacked ICAC Deputy Director of Operations, Alex Tsui Ka-kit alleges that the ICAC tapped the telephones of Executive

Councillor, Rita Fan Hsu Lai-tai and former Secretary for the Treasury, Yeung Kai-yin.

15.4.1994 Hong Kong journalists express outrage at the swift and secret rejection of journalist Xi Yang's appeal against conviction and 12-year prison sentence for spying and state secrets offences and plan further mass protest at NCNA.

18.4.1994 Recently appointed Beijing Hong Kong Affairs adviser, Anthony Cheung Bing-leung's political party, Meeting Point, announces merger with the United Democrats of Hong Kong (UDHK). Chairman Cheung remarked "I hope my relationship with China will not be affected."

21.4.1994 Rupert Murdoch sells 15.1 per cent stake in *SCMP* to Malayan United Industries tycoon, Dr. Khoo Kay Peng, for HK$1.036 billion.

21.4.1994 Sir Percy Cradock, on a business trip to China, warns the Legco that it will be signing its own death warrant if it supports Patten's constitutional reforms.

22.4.1994 CITIC Hong Kong teams up with Swire Properties in HK$1.4 billion project for retail and office complex in Shanghai. CITIC and other Mainland interests to hold a 90 per cent interest and Swire Properties 10 per cent.

23.4.1994 Dissident Wang Juntao is released by China for medical treatment in the U.S. just ahead of the decision on MFN and is told to stay out of politics and never forget he is a Chinese citizen.

26.4.1994 Hong Kong General Chamber of Commerce votes its Legco Representative, J. D. McGregor, off the General Committee in a suspected pro-China coup.

28.4.1994 Patten is not invited to the Bank of China's note issue celebrations which Lu Ping will attend on 2 May.

30.4.1994 PWC's Social and Security Sub-group's briefing on the training and techniques of the People's Liberation Army, in Guangzhou, is declared a fiasco.

1.5.1994 Lu Ping on his first official visit to Hong Kong for two years, evades protesters lying in wait at Kowloon–Canton Railway station but Chinese officials later claim the Hong Kong police told him to.

3.5.1994 International Press Freedom Day report says press freedom in Hong Kong is worse than last year and that the press in China is one of the world's most repressed.

4.5.1994 Conference of 300 top Hong Kong executives on business ethics favours a "broad blueprint" for self-regulation based upon a code of ethics for dealing with business in China.

Calendar of Events in 1993–1994 xxiii

5.5.1994	Hong Kong journalists who signed a protest over the treatment of *Ming Pao* reporter Xi Yang are refused entry to China to cover the visit of a Taiwan delegation to the site of the Qiandao Lake tragedy.
6.5.1994	In a major statement Lu Ping warns against "any foreign government or Hong Kong people trying to exert pressure on China." He also warned that China will not tolerate a Human Rights Commission in Hong Kong which had the power to conduct independent investigations and take action on violations of human rights.
8.5.1994	Former Secretary for Lands and Works, Nicky Chan Nai-keong, urges increased contact between PWC and civil servants "to make a smooth transition more likely."
8.5.1994	Asian Commercial Research telephone survey of 400 indicates that Lu Ping's visit substantially reduced public confidence in China's handling of the transition.
10.5.1994	Furious truck drivers block Lok Ma Chau border crossing in protest against Chinese-side customs delays in clearing trucks at Huanggang checkpoint.
12.5.1994	China announces 13 appointments to the PWC, 8 from Hong Kong and 5 from China. The new Hong Kong members include former senior civil servants and distinguished academics and the Chinese members includes Mr. Guo Fengmin, leader of the Chinese team on the JLG.
13.5.1994	The Secretary for the Treasury, Donald Tsang Yam-kuen, strikes back for the Hong Kong government's embattled executive empire in his "Silence of the Lambs" speech seemingly directed at the supposed spend-thrift mentality of some legislators.
14.5.1994	Patten decides to disallow a move by legislators to block the Financial Secretary's proposal to raise rates.
17.5.1994	Hopes rise for an early agreement on airport funding as the Sino-British Airport Committee is reconvened on 20 May after a lapse of nine months.
18.5.1994	Armed robbers kill one and injure three in afternoon raid on a jewellery shop in Swire House, Central.
19.5.1994	China drops Meeting Point Chairman, Anthony Cheung Bing-leung, as a Hong Kong Affairs adviser following the party's proposed merger with the UDHK, and is criticized for "narrow-mindedness."
19.5.1994	Lord MacLehose and Lord Wilson, in a House of Lords debate, add their voices to criticisms of Patten's "mistake" in making China feel "deliberately tricked" over political reform in Hong Kong.
20.5.1994	Lord Howe, in an American Chamber of Commerce lunch address, drops his 1989 "precious Ming vase" metaphor for Hong Kong and substitutes "living plant to be cherished," but few turn up to listen.

24.5.1994	Posts of Solicitor General and Director of Public Prosecutions are to be filled by Hong Kong Chinese Daniel Fung and Peter Nguyen in a move to localize the upper ranks of the Legal Department.
26.5.1994	Beijing is cool to the Liberal Party's bid to craft a more China-friendly political package of electoral reforms than those proposed by Patten.
26.5.1994	Hong Kong is relieved at U.S. President Bill Clinton's renewal of China's MFN status but is shocked by the ring buying, at HK$2 billion below expected market price, by a consortium of real estate developers, of residential sites at a government land auction.
2.6.1994	The Chief Secretary, Anson Chan Fang On-sang, in a new verbal formula indicative of capitulation to Chinese pressure, says that the Hong Kong government will only support an independent Human Rights Commission if it is "durable."
3.6.1994	Students have a minor scuffle with the police outside NCNA in 4 June 1989 commemoration protest.
4.6.1994	An illegal factory at Longgang, near Shenzhen, built by Hong Kong businessmen, collapses, killing 11 workers in dormitory and injuring 27. The collapsed building was bulldozed after 24 hours giving rise to concerns that some of those still trapped may have been buried alive.
5.6.1994	The Secretary for Home Affairs Michael Suen Ming-yeung's comments on the scope of a private member's Equal Opportunities Bill reveals internal differences over policy-formulation within the executive.
7.6.1994	China lambastes foreign-funded enterprises for "barbaric" means in dealing with workers and unions in the 47,000 joint ventures which employ six million workers on China's booming eastern coast.
9.6.1994	CLP is fined HK$6,000 in Tuen Mun Court after pleading guilty to "failing to provide and maintain a hydrogen generation plant and system of work that were safe and without risk to the health of all persons employed." The prosecution is related to the deaths of two workers in an explosion at its Castle Peak power plant on 28 August 1992. The derisory fine draws editorial criticism of Magistrate Ernest Lim and CLP in *SCMP*.
9.6.1994	China issues its first code of conduct for journalists which stresses, *inter alia*, that all reporters must pledge their loyalty to the Communist Party and socialism.
9.6.1994	Portugal issues passports to Portuguese nationals living in Hong Kong who are not already registered in Macau or Lisbon.
12.6.1994	The government informs expatriate civil servants that their opportunities for promotion will be limited by the requirements of the localization policy.

Calendar of Events in 1993–1994 xxv

13.6.1994　Lu Ping criticizes the Hong Kong government's proposals to curb spiralling property prices but without specifying the shortcomings or suggesting alternatives.

13.6.1994　One hundred representatives of British firms are reported to be organizing a delegation to China in September to counteract Patten's adverse influence on Sino-British trading relations.

15.6.1994　An injury into the Whitehead Detention Centre raid on 7 April by JPs Andrew Li Kwok-nang QC and Professor David Todd criticizes the authorities concerned but fails to identify those who should be held accountable.

17.6.1994　A Chinese Foreign Affairs Ministry spokesperson attacks the Hong Kong government's proposals for a code of practice covering public access to official information on the grounds that it violates the Sino-British Joint Declaration and "involves major changes to the operation of government departments in Hong Kong which are detrimental to smooth transition."

19.6.1994　Guangzhou and the Pearl River Estuary are hit by the worst floods in 50 years.

20.6.1994　Legislators criticize the Secretary for the Treasury for seeking HK$15 billion funding without revealing the fourth packet for airport funding still awaiting China's approval.

21.6.1994　The Secretary for Health and Welfare designate, Katherine Fok Lo Shiu-ching, offers to relinquish her British passport and nationality if Beijing selects her to be a principal official in 1997. However, she neglects to say whether she will be eligible to retain the right of abode in the United Kingdom secretly promised to all Hong Kong Chinese Administrative Officers by the British government in 1981.

24.6.1994　The University of Hong Kong's Social Sciences Research Centre poll of 6,000 shows that 90 per cent are ignorant of the significance of Patten's constitutional reforms.

30.6.1994　Patten's electoral reforms are passed into law after a 17½ hours' debate on a third reading vote of 32 to 24 and with only minor amendments.

Preface

The publication of yet another volume of *The Other Hong Kong Report* may seem to some a matter of course now. This could be due to their acceptance of the publication of "alternative accounts" of trends and development of the society as a well-ingrained part of the Hong Kong cultural heritage, which is a positive token. Nevertheless, hopefully it would not be a sign of oversight regarding the increasing strain on those chapter authors working in local academic institutions which place emphasis more and more on publications that are more restricted. What is meant here is that apart from the usual challenge of having to produce a lucid and well-researched piece of writing while avoiding the recycling of professional jargon and the use of massive footnotes, scholars in tertiary institutions writing for this volume also have to work under the currently strong pressure to publish almost exclusively in "internationally refereed journals." It is therefore hardly surprising to find that many of the chapters here, being written by those individuals from the academic and other professions who have braced the tide of narrow professionalism to undertake the project, actually embody their authors' deep sense of concern about the enigmas and dynamics now embedded in the social fabric of Hong Kong.

The special training of the twenty-five writers and their subject foci do not just result in an equal number of book chapters being produced. Very often they also lead to the revelation of different outlooks, or *Weltanschauungen*, which underpin the different analytical approaches to the events and policies concerned. For example, in the chapter on the Property Price Crisis (Chapter 11), Lawrence Lai evaluates policies with full regard to Hong Kong's prevalent welfare economics ideology as well as city-planning imperatives. Tsang Shu-ki, on the other hand, identifies and discusses crucial issues in Hong Kong's economic future with reference to its political economy context which includes not only the structural order but also the potentialities effected by other existing and future agencies of change. Besides the ideological frame, the time frame is also well represented in many of the chapters. For example, authors of chapters on "Medical and Health," "China–Hong Kong Integration," "Immigration and Emigration," "Legal System," "Constitution and Administration," "Politics, Politicians, and Political Parties" and "Implementation of the Sino-British Joint Declaration" have all traced the development trends in recent years to yield the relevant matrices for focusing the more current events of July 1993 to June 1994. Another common feature of many of the chapters is that different sectors of the community or the community as a whole are depicted as agents of change in the social, moral, political, or cultural landscape of Hong Kong. For example, the youths' ideas on sexuality, the medical professionals' and the bureaucrats' views on medical reform, the choice of entertainment as an exercise of self-expression by the general public, and the women's perspective in the age of political equality and anti-discrimination have been given due regard in the respective chapters and weave together into rich contours of a Hong Kong narrative. In general, the people's and the community's aspirations and frustrations in various circumstances are well recognized and documented in this volume.

As "acts in defiance" (of narrow professionalism), the discourses found in the present volume are quite naturally inclined to manifest a notable degree of humanistic concern alongside high scholarship. These qualities have also become a force motivating us to venture through the sometimes extremely mundane and wearisome months of editing. Yet for the readers to be able to share the joy of reading the products of these discourses, the conscientious efforts of the staff of The Chinese University Press and the power of judgement of Mr. Fung Wai-kit (which sometimes has gone beyond the call of editorial duty) have played an essential role. And, thanks must go to T. L. Tsim, now in absentia, who mentored *The Other Hong Kong Report* as Director of the Press. Finally, our gratitude goes to those closest to us for their support and for the time they allowed us to steal for this volume.

Man Si-wai
Donald H. McMillen
October 1994

Introduction

Donald H. McMillen

> We always think of the Japanese as the egotists, but the Chinese got him licked on it. The Chinese has books to show that he has been educated for thousands of years. I don't mean he is distant, like a strange Englishman. No, the Chinese are the most friendly folks and you can't help but like 'em. But back in that nut of theirs, they feel that all this modern junk you are lording over them will pass in time, and they will be in command.
> And the rascals might be right at that!
>
> Will Rogers (1934)

The year ending 1 July 1994 witnessed the further emergence of the "other Hong Kong." It was a year of contradictions — of economic prosperity but political gridlock; of attempts to further internalize the territory into the "Chinese scheme of things" alongside an intense international activity in the local stock and property markets. In the government's annual review, *Hong Kong 1994*, the former Chief Secretary, Sir David Ford, described Hong Kong not so much a place as a people. He traces the territory's spectacular material success to a "rare alchemy" — albeit but one which he says "resists analysis." He speaks of the importance of its maturing sense of community tempered by constant risk and crisis, which he says is conditioned by "not imposing the will of an individual or an administration, but by allowing the naturally evolved, in-built machinery of consensus to take its natural course." Concurrently, he argues that a respect for the individual,

---

Donald H. McMillen is Professor of Asian Studies at the University of Southern Queensland, Australia. Previously, he was Director of the Hong Kong Transitions Project at the Hong Kong Baptist College.

within the social context, has flowered; although he adds that "we need to balance the public good with the private need, the will of the majority with the protection of the minority." Unfortunately, little is said about the importance of the "rule of law," and its "enculturement," in this context.

The Other Hong Kong Report, now in its sixth year, celebrates a treasured tradition of responsible and informed academic freedom to analyse events and processes in Hong Kong on an annual basis and to articulate them openly to the community. The editors believe that this alternative to the "official report" prepared by the Hong Kong government is of vital importance in the prevailing environment where, to date, the present authorities and the future sovereign have shown a reluctance to develop or entrench a system within which a broader freedom of information is underpinned by institutions and processes protective of human and civil rights and constantly — and consistently — dedicated to achieving a significant accountability and incorruptibility of all who wield power.

But, this celebration continues to be muted by the memories of recent historical events and uncertainties, subtle pressures from within and from outside the political economy, and a detectable tendency of uncertainty and self-censorship as 1997 approaches. Coping successfully with these will, of course, be measured not only by the degree to which Hong Kong remains the dynamic and internationally connected society which Sir David has extolled, but one which indeed preserves and fosters the "soul," the "humanity" of the place.

The Other Hong Kong Report, once again, seeks to identify the most significant happenings and issues of 1993–1994 and to analyse them from a variety of viewpoints. It is not expected that readers will, or even should, agree or disagree with the interpretations in this volume. There always are those who, for whatever reasons and rightly or wrongly, will be identified as "pro-this" or "anti-that" or will be accused of having ulterior motives. The important point is that a constructively critical environment not only be preserved but be augmented; and one within which meaningful and responsible dialogue can be stimulated — and stimulating!

Within the broader conception of "*the* Hong Kong," there are, after all, many "other Hong Kongs" seeking identity, striving for expression or searching for form. The year 1993–1994 particularly has been one in which events have been flavoured by them. There are those who will ever only want Hong Kong to be their "home place." There are those whose circumstances allow them a choice of whether to stay or leave, and at another time perhaps return. There are those — call them the "Hong Kong

Introduction

diaspora" — who are from here but who are not here now, and whose "exported Hong Kongs" scattered around the world always seem somehow less than the real place. There are those, largely of common ancestry, who have never been here but who wish to be, or at least wish to experience in their own place a replicated Hong Kong-like lifestyle. There are those from other places who are guest workers or itinerant revellers. And, there are those who have ruled, who wish to rule, who intend to rule, or who have their own rules.

A reading of this year's "Calendar of Events" reveals a downside trend in the happenings of Hong Kong as its transition to formal Chinese rule proceeds (in what amounts to a major "historical rectification" of the modern Chinese experience). What stands out most prominently is the contradiction between economic optimism and political pessimism, although even the former was dampened by difficulties in the Chinese economy. For Hong Kong, the die was cast for the year when, on 9 July 1993, Governor Christopher Patten said it was "better for Britain to take unilateral action on constitutional reforms in the territory than to surrender on principles." One week later, Chinese Foreign Minister, Qian Qichen, formally inaugurated a 57-member Preliminary Working Committee for the Hong Kong Special Administrative Region (HKSAR) Preparatory Committee, although its implementation was suspended until a second plenary meeting later in December. This was an obvious move by China to further discredit the Patten-led Hong Kong government and, implicitly, to marginalize the partially democratized Legislative Council (Legco), which in any event it did not recognize as a legitimate body, and other lingering and popular democratic groups.

As Sino-British talks on electoral arrangements fruitlessly dragged on in this climate of political "stand-off," the environment was further poisoned by the eviction of labour activist Han Dongfang from China to Hong Kong in August. This immediately raised local fears that if China could selectively deny the freedom of movement to its present citizens, the same could apply to Hong Kong people after 1997 — despite what appeared to many as Beijing's promises to the contrary and regardless of the concept of "one country, two systems."

In late September, the New China News Agency fuelled these worries by releasing Deng Xiaoping's speech of 24 September 1982 warning of a possible Chinese take-over of Hong Kong before 1997 "should disorder there demand it." The following month, after the arrest in China of Hong Kong *Ming Pao* journalist Xi Yang and the resulting local outcry in defence of the freedoms of speech and press, Lu Ping, Head of the State Council's Hong Kong and Macau Affairs Office, repeated Beijing's earlier warning to Britain that the territory "should not be turned into a political city." Oblivious to these developments, the Hang Seng Index and the property market continued to rise in a buying frenzy fuelled by overseas investors seeking opportunities in hot spots away from their own sluggish economies.

At the edges of these headline-grabbing events, of course, there were other significant issues ranging from the resolution of financing arrangements for major infrastructural developments in the territory such as the new international airport at Chek Lap Kok and the building of Container Terminal No. 9. Sino-British talks over military lands also moved slowly, with progress only being achieved late in the period thanks to London's largesse. But, also of importance were such "local" issues as the importation of labour, localization of the civil service, the operations of the Independent Commission Against Corruption in light of the Alex Tsui Ka-kit affair, incidents of smuggling and piracy in territorial waters, and such social welfare problems as care for the elderly, a universal pension scheme, and inheritance rights for women in the New Territories.

At the end of 1993, China felt compelled to decree the end of the so-called "through train" by giving notification of its intention to dismantle Hong Kong's three-tier system of government in 1997 and to reorganize the HKSAR government in accordance with its interpretation of the Basic Law of the HKSAR. Subsequently, Chinese officials first warned, then denied that British economic interests in China would be damaged as a result of London's "unfriendly and uncooperative attitudes" concerning Hong Kong. When Sino-British talks relating to 1994–1995 electoral arrangements failed after seventeen rounds, the Legco, on 23 February, overwhelmingly approved the less contentious elements of the constitutional package framed in Governor Patten's October 1992 Legco address. These included lowering the voting age to 18, adopting a "single seat, single vote" system for all elections, abolishing appointed members from district and municipal councils, and allowing Hong Kong delegates to the Chinese National People's Congress to stand for election. Almost immediately, Beijing proceeded to extend its own political infrastructure in the territory (the so-called "second stove") by announcing additional territorial- and district-level China "advisers."

The capstone to the political wrangle was put in place on 30 June when the more contentious elements of the Patten electoral reform package were passed into law with only minor amendments after nearly eighteen hours' debate on a third reading vote of 32 to 24. However, in the months preceding this vote, there were indications that the British authorities sought by subtle measures to minimize the negative effects of such a decision on broader Sino-British relations. Governor Patten himself was criticized by local democracy and human rights activists for his refusal to put into place processes and institutions which might provide greater guarantees that the post-1997 executive-led regime would honour a range of freedoms. Many felt such rights were left susceptible to the whims of China's highly unpredictable and overly personalized political system. In any case, the Hong Kong government's "minimalist" approach ran counter to public opinion favouring more safeguards against future government abuses.

It is generally accepted that any authority in Hong Kong must henceforth strike some kind of balance between the preservation of governmental power on the one hand and the enhancement of its accountability, and hence its legitimacy, on the other hand. As Hong Kong society has become more politically astute and generally more liberalized and even democratized as a result of such activities as direct elections, civic education through the schools and the media, the continued development of political groupings ("parties"), the extension of cosmopolitan connections with and experiences in participatory and open societies elsewhere, and the counter-productive actions of both the Chinese and the British authorities, the traditional bureaucratic subculture — including the oft-proclaimed system of "bureaucratically absorbed politics" — has become unpopular and outdated.

In fact, it can be argued that because the natural pace, not to mention the (British) "managed pace," of political development and expectations in Hong Kong have increased significantly over the past decade, Beijing's besieged Party leadership had no choice but to torpedo any democratic reforms that might spill-over into the larger Chinese body politic. Arguably, Governor Patten's proposals were based upon the broadest interpretation of and aimed at achieving the optimum amount of political reform within the perimeters set by the Sino-British Joint Declaration of 1984, the Basic Law of the HKSAR and other Sino-British "understandings." As such, they were simply unacceptable to Chinese authorities desperate to maintain some semblance of management over their own reforms and retain at least a modicum legitimacy.

Some, however, would argue that the key factor affecting the future prosperity of the territory is not politics but the fortune of the Chinese economy. Accordingly, Hong Kong will be an "economic hostage" of Beijing after 1997. One author even suggests that Hong Kong may suffer a "political backlash" then, but in the end the economic "golden goose" that lays the golden eggs would be carefully looked after! The argument over whether or not it is better for Hong Kong to become "politically congruent" with China in order for continued economic integration to occur harmoniously is worrisome so far as the otherwise naturally evolving political culture of the territory is concerned. Certainly, although it would never admit it, China would like to preserve as much of a colonial-like political structure in Hong Kong as possible — much the same as the British themselves have done until only the last decade before retrocession — but of course devoid of the "British-ness" of the system. The difficulty any administration will face is the erosion of public trust and confidence in authority generally and the increasing expectation that the government must efficiently, and inexpensively so far as the tax-paying public is concerned, "deliver the goods" in social service and social welfare terms.

The sociopolitical aspirations of the Hong Kong people, if left unaddressed, unfulfilled or held hostage to Sino-British relations at other levels, could well enhance a range of volatility that could further undermine the population's sense of personal and family security and erode the confidence and economic dynamism of the place. Any "policies of dampening or denial" in this regard would be foolhardy and, in effect, contrary to longer-term Chinese interests. Likewise, unfettered, poorly managed or non-redistributive capitalism in Hong Kong would slowly exacerbate income gaps and livelihood expectations. Economic prosperity must be for all *in* Hong Kong, and not just the privileged few. This requires continued socioeconomic and political freedom of opportunity and choice, and demands managers and politicians, institutions, and processes operating accountably in a system of the rule of law which is not only efficient but which is constantly in touch with the reasonable aspirations of its constituent public.

As some contributors to this volume argue, guaranteeing that these elements will persist is subject to interpretations of the moment, often by authorities who are not *of* Hong Kong or who do not understand or "feel" its "ground truths." Moreover, the fact that the territory's fledgling legislative institution, the Legco, could take the government to task and even reprove the Governor over the issue of rates in early June 1994 shows that it is no longer a rubber stamp of the government and as such is a worry to future administrators. And, there are concerns that greater welfare and

Introduction

service demands by an articulate political public and its elected representatives will lead to pressures to raise the levels of taxation.

In the meantime, the people of Hong Kong, like their cousins in the Greater China, must deal with what may be called a "culture of historical denial" which some would suggest includes the following, seemingly contradictory, attributes:

— a denial of the Confucianist (or British colonial) heritage, except as it suits contemporary political struggles;
— a denial of the imperialist and colonialist experience, except as now, practised within its own borders;
— a denial of the student-led 1989 June Fourth Movement and what it stood for, and, implicitly, of its precursors such as the 1919 May Fourth Movement;
— a denial of Chinese "hegemonistic" intentions externally, behaviour to the contrary;
— a denial of the Marxist/Leninist-cum-Maoist path (and, for others, a denial of the "Dengist detour," which advocates the "socialist market economy" and "opening" to the outside world);
— a denial of the regime's mass base through an adoption of an elitist patriarchism and policies which engender socio-regional inequities; and
— a denial of Chinese nationalism through the schizophrenic "one country, two systems" concept.

Many in the Chinese Communist Party leadership, as well as many aligned with it (for their own reasons) in Hong Kong, must feel trapped between the early idealist hopes of communism and Chinese nationalism and the more promising present realities of capitalism and globalism. For the same group, China's population size and its lingering ethno-cultural and historical diversity necessitates a strong nationalism and a "control culture." In this light, Hong Kong — like any other peripheral region of China where geoeconomic and geosocial "development" has advanced rapidly and sufficiently far — looms large and even threatening to many at the older geopolitical centre. Perhaps this is why one might worry, so far as Hong Kong is concerned, that the "rare alchemy" denoted by Sir David Ford may be, after 1997, one in which gold is turned into lead. Should this happen, for some — perhaps many — the "other Hong Kong" would be either no more, or no less, than a fading memory or a recurring and unfulfilled dream.

1

Constitution and Administration

Norman J. Miners

☐ Arrangements for the 1995 Elections

Only one constitutional amendment to the Letters Patent and Royal Instructions has been made in the past year. In July 1993, the Queen formally approved changes to Article VI of the Letters Patent so that the Legislative Council (Legco) should in future be composed of 60 elected members, 20 of whom shall be returned by geographical constituencies, 30 by functional constituencies and 10 by an election committee. This amendment exactly follows the wording of the "Decision of the National People's Congress on the method for the formation of the first Legislative Council of the Hong Kong Special Administrative Region" which is published as an annex to the Basic Law. Similar care to follow exactly the wording of the Basic Law had previously been taken in 1991 when Article VII of the Letters Patent was amended to incorporate the International Covenant on Civil and Political Rights into Hong Kong's colonial constitution. Unfortunately, it appears unlikely that this careful attention to the wording of the 1993 amendment will persuade China to allow the legislature elected in September 1995 to continue after the transfer of sovereignty in 1997. China has already announced that the electoral arrangements passed by the Legco in June 1994 violate the Sino-British Joint Declaration and the Basic Law.

The amendment to the Letters Patent was not officially published in Hong Kong until after the Governor's electoral reforms had been enacted into law by the vote of 32 to 24 of the Legco on 30 June 1994. This was

---

Norman J. Miners is a reader in the Department of Politics and Public Administration, the University of Hong Kong.

probably because Governor Christopher Patten had previously promised that the final decisions on the arrangements for the 1995 elections would be taken by the Legco. When the Governor's electoral reform bill was being debated, Emily Lau had proposed that all 60 seats should be returned by direct elections. If her private member's bill had been passed, the Governor could not have signed it into law since it contravened the new Article VI of the Letters Patent. In the event, Emily Lau's bill was defeated by one vote and so the Governor was spared this constitutional embarrassment.

☐ The Legislative Council

During the 1993–1994 session of the Legco, members made further efforts to extend their influence over the policies of the government. The powers of the Legco are laid down in the Letters Patent and Royal Instructions, the Legislative Council (Powers and Privileges) Ordinance of 1985 and the Legislative Council Standing Orders. In the past, members were restrained from using these powers to the full by the presence of a pro-government majority made up of officials and members appointed by the Governor. But since the 1991 elections, 39 out of the 60 members are elected and the 18 remaining appointed members no longer feel obliged to pay attention to the wishes of the government.

In October 1993, members voted to amend Standing Orders to make the unofficial panels into full committees of the Legco. These panels have existed since the 1970s as groups of unofficial members which met from time to time to discuss particular policy areas and be briefed on current issues by the secretaries or department heads concerned. These panels have now been made full committees of the Legco. When authorized by a resolution passed by the full Legco, a panel may compel any person to attend before it to give evidence or produce any document in his possession. In May 1994, the Legco decided that the Chairman of a panel should be empowered to determine whether a witness could claim public interest immunity when called upon to answer any question. The government had proposed that this power should be exercised by the President of the Legco rather than by the Chairman of a panel, but the Legco voted otherwise.

These powers to compel witnesses to attend were exercised for the first time when the Security Panel summoned the Commissioner of the Independent Commission Against Corruption (ICAC), Bertrand de Speville, to give evidence on the circumstances which led to the dismissal of Alex Tsui, the deputy director of operations and the most senior Chinese member of staff of the ICAC. Mr. Tsui was eager to appear before the panel, but the Commissioner was unwilling to give evidence until compelled to do so. The proceedings of the panel were held in public and were extensively reported in the press. This publicity was most unwelcome to the government. The Security Panel also held public hearings into the police raid on the Whitehead Detention Centre for Vietnamese refugees, despite the fact that the government had set up its own commission of enquiry by two Justices of the Peace. The Information Policy Panel held a hearing on the alleged censorship of news programmes by Asia Television. These and similar enquiries conducted in public by other panels focused the spotlight of publicity on the deficiencies of government operations and put pressure on it to improve its performance.

In November 1993, members for the first time made use of their power to introduce and pass a bill despite the opposition of the executive. Non-government members have always had the right to present private members' bills, but until 1991 this was only done to incorporate a charity, club or other private institution. Such ordinances were uncontroversial and were easily passed into law without any debate. The Public Officers (Variation of Conditions of Service) (Temporary Provisions) Bill was totally different. Its object was to freeze for six months the implementation of the policy of allowing certain expatriate officers employed on contract terms to transfer to local terms of employment when their contracts expired. The bill was introduced at the request of a civil service trade union, the Senior Non-expatriate Officers Association, who objected to any expatriates continuing to serve after their contracts expired, since this would tend to reduce the prospects of promotion for local officers. Government officials opposed the bill claiming that the legislature was encroaching on matters that were the prerogative of the executive. Hints were dropped that the Governor might veto the bill if it passed its third reading. Members of the legislature were undeterred by these threats. The bill was passed and signed into law by the Governor. The Civil Service Branch was forced to revise its policy, and proposed that an expatriate should be allowed to continue on local terms only if he was prepared to accept demotion to a lower rank. This new policy was accepted by the Senior Non-expatriate Officers Association and the Legco has now allowed the law freezing transfers for six months to lapse. Unfortunately, the new policy has been rejected by the expatriate officers and is now being challenged in the courts as an infringement of the Bill of Rights.

Other private members' bills have been proposed, but they have not all been so successful. Hui Yin-fat objected to the large proportion of the Lotteries Fund deducted as taxation and the small amount left for social welfare causes. He threatened to introduce a bill to remedy this, but this was anticipated by the Financial Secretary who proposed a new division of the Lotteries Fund in the 1994 budget. The Governor has announced that he will not give permission for the introduction of a bill by Anna Wu to set up a Human Rights Commission and by Christine Loh to secure access to official information. Instead, the government intends to introduce its own bill to outlaw discrimination, and to allow the public greater access to information by executive order. These government initiatives fall short of the private members' legislation, but it is unlikely that the government would have made any move at all if it had not been put under pressure by the publication of the private members' bills.

No government bills have been defeated, but many have been subjected to considerable delays in the bills committees which conduct a detailed examination of the text of the government draft before the bill returns to the Legco for the resumed second reading debate. The Organized and Serious Crimes Bill has been held up for two years since July 1992 until the administration produces a scheme for the protection of witnesses which the bills committee considers to be adequate. On other bills, the policy secretary in charge of a bill has found himself obliged to accept changes supported by the bills committee because he knows that the government does not have the votes in the full Legco to successfully oppose these amendments.

The Finance Committee of the Legco has to approve all new spending proposals which were not included in the annual budget. In the past, members have occasionally criticized particular items and forced the government to withdraw a proposal and resubmit it at a later date. These forced withdrawals are now more frequent when members are dissatisfied with the documentation produced by civil servants to justify the proposed expenditure. In July 1993, the Finance Committee rejected a request for funds for information technology which would help to reduce the waiting time for trials in the District Court. The expenditure was not approved until June 1994 when the new Judiciary Administrator was able to convince the committee by producing detailed figures on the computerization programme and the staff needed to implement it. In May 1994, the committee very reluctantly approved the payment of $650 million in compensation to a steel plant which had been forced to relocate its operations because the government needed the site. The Finance Committee at first rejected the proposal but the Financial Secretary later informed the committee that the government had entered into a binding contract and would be liable for legal costs and damages if the money was not paid. The government promised to consult the committee in future before any such agreement was finalized.

On 8 June 1994, the Legco passed a motion to reprove the Governor for refusing to permit members to table an amendment to the Rating Bill. Some 21 members voted in favour and 11 against. No such motion critical of the Governor has ever before been passed by the Hong Kong Legco. If a similar motion of "no confidence" is passed in the British parliament, the Prime Minister would be obliged to resign. This does not apply in a British colony where a governor can remain in office so long as he continues to enjoy the confidence of the Crown, that is, of the British government. However, if a majority of the members of the Legco are still angry with the Governor next year, they have the right to vote against the Appropriation Bill to reduce the Governor's salary or eliminate it altogether. There is nothing in the Letters Patent or Royal Instructions to prevent members acting in this way. They are entitled to reject any item in the Estimates of Expenditure. Indeed, they could vote against the entire budget and refuse to supply the government with any money whatsoever.

The behaviour of the Legco over the past two sessions has led some commentators to exaggerate its effective power in relation to the government. There has been talk of the "subservience of the executive to the legislature." One appointed member stated in a debate, "We probably have the weakest government in Hong Kong's history in terms of influence in the legislature." Such views ignore the checks and restraints upon legislative power which have been built into the colonial constitution. Since December 1992, the Legco has passed a large number of motions directing the government to change its policies. Officials have politely agreed to reconsider their plans in the light of the views expressed by members, but there are few if any instances where the Executive Council has been seen to change its course in response to motions passed by the legislature. According to calculations made by Martin Lee, 40 per cent of the motions passed by the Legco in the 1992–1993 sitting have been completely ignored by the administration.

Clause 24 of the Royal Instructions forbids any member to introduce any ordinance, motion or amendment the object of which is to dispose of or charge any part of the government's revenue, unless expressly authorized by the Governor. The President of the Legco, John Swaine, has recently interpreted the meaning of this clause in a broad sense as forbidding any amendment which would have the effect of reducing the government's expected future revenue. This ruling prevented members from proposing an amendment to the Rating Ordinance which would have had the effect of freezing the government's revenue from the rates at the 1993–1994 level, so that it did not rise in line with the increase in property values. Members are only entitled to oppose any specific increases in taxation proposed by the government. The same clause of the Royal Instructions empowers the Governor to prevent the presentation of any private member's bill which would require any increase in staffing levels in the civil service in order to implement it. This clause was used by the Governor to forbid the introduction of Anna Wu's bill to set up a Human Rights Commission and Christine Loh's Access to Information Bill. There is no bar upon private members' bills which seek to repeal existing legislation, but so far no member has introduced a bill of this sort.

The Legco is also weakened by the government's power to deny it the information it needs to effectively criticize policies and monitor the operations of the government. Policy secretaries have refused to answer questions on the grounds that the matter concerns security, that it is under discussion with China, that it is commercially sensitive information that has been communicated in confidence, or generally that disclosure would be contrary to the public interest. All these excuses may be valid, but the inevitable consequence of government secrecy is to weaken the ability of the legislature to challenge the government and expose its mistakes and inefficiencies.

The government is still able to exercise considerable influence over the way in which legislative councillors vote. Most of the appointed members and the members elected by functional constituencies are sympathetic to the concerns of the business community, so normally a majority can be found in support of government policy on issues where the interests of management are in conflict with those of the workers, such as the import of labour from China. Apart from the United Democrats of Hong Kong and the Liberal Party, there are at least four other parties represented in the legislature and many independent members. This enables the government to cobble together a majority on most crucial issues by energetic lobbying. The only issue where the government would be certain to face defeat is any proposal to raise taxes. Since 1991, the Financial Secretary has been fortunate in accumulating large budget surpluses and ample reserves so that no tax increases have been necessary.

In the 1993–1994 Legco session, legislators have taken a responsible attitude towards the routine adjustment of government charges to take account of inflation. These changes are normally imposed by regulations which can be amended by a motion passed in the Legco. Two such regulations were amended to reduce charges in the 1992–1993 session, but members did not repeat this action in 1993–1994.

It appears that the administration and the legislature are learning to adjust to the new situation brought about by the 1991 elections and have achieved a reasonably satisfactory working relationship, within the limits set by Hong Kong's colonial constitution.

☐ The Right of Women to Inherit Property in the New Territories

When Captain Elliot took possession of Hong Kong in 1841, he promised that "the natives of the Island of Hong Kong and all natives of China thereto resorting shall be governed according to the laws and customs of China, every description of torture excepted." When the New Territories were occupied in 1898, the Governor, Sir Henry Blake, issued a proclamation promising "Your commercial and landed interests will be safeguarded and your usages and good customs will not in any way be interfered with." These two proclamations have in themselves no legal or constitutional significance, but they have been regarded as setting down a standard of conduct to which all government officials should conform. In the New Territories the ancestral custom that only male descendants of indigenous inhabitants at the time of the British occupation should have the right to inherit rural land and property was enacted into law by the New Territories Ordinance 1910. This discrimination against women remained undisturbed until 1994. When the Bill of Rights Ordinance was enacted in 1991, the question was raised whether Article 22, which prohibits any discrimination on grounds of sex, would repeal this section of the New Territories Ordinance. The matter was left for the judges to decide but no case came before the courts in the following three years.

The government had no intention to legislate on this issue when it introduced the New Territories Land (Exemption) Bill in 1993. But a member of the bills committee proposed an amendment to the bill which would have the effect of allowing women to inherit land when an indigenous rural inhabitant died without making a will. This proposal provoked furious demonstrations and petitions organized by the Heung Yee

Kuk who claimed that the government was overturning their ancestral customs and constitutional rights. Despite these protests the bill was amended and passed into law. Spokesmen for the Heung Yee Kuk have complained that the legislation is also contrary to the Basic Law, Article 40, which protects the lawful traditional rights and interests of the indigenous inhabitants. The head of the Hong Kong and Macau Affairs Office, Lu Ping, has stated that if this is so the law will be repealed by the Standing Committee of the National People's Congress in 1997.

Whatever the constitutional status of Governor Blake's proclamation may be, the Hong Kong government has never regarded it as protecting all the customs and traditions of the New Territories without exception. In 1925, the colonial government legislated to abolish the traditional custom of *mui tsai* whereby unwanted female children were sold into richer households to serve as unpaid domestic helpers. In 1970, traditional Chinese marriage customs were reformed by ordinance. In 1959, the Heung Yee Kuk itself was reorganized and transformed into a statutory corporation. All these reforms were enacted in the face of vehement objections by opponents who claimed that the colonial government had no moral right to overturn traditional Chinese customs.

2

The Legal System: Are the Changes Too Little, Too Late?

John D. Ho

With less than three years to go in the countdown to 1 July 1997 when Hong Kong reverts to China, the shadow of the future is looming larger and larger over the legacy of the past in all aspects of Hong Kong life. The legal system is no exception.

Under the principle of "one country, two systems," Article 8 of the Basic Law declares that "[t]he laws previously in force in Hong Kong, that is, the common law, rules of equity, ordinances, subordinate legislation and customary law shall be maintained, except for any that contravene [the Basic Law]...."

However, that does not seem to prevent questions being raised about the continued existence of the legal system as we know it today in the future Special Administrative Region (SAR). Duanmu Zheng, vice-president of the Supreme People's Court in Beijing, was reported as predicting that Hong Kong's common law system would be gradually absorbed by the mainland system after 1997, as there is a need "for Hong Kong to get rid of the shadow of colonial rule in its legal system."

There is no doubt that for the present legal system to continue, many changes are necessary. Whether the changes that are made will be sufficient to preserve the system for the SAR or whether Duanmu's prediction will come true remains to be seen.

But the race against time is formidable. Besides having to deal with the perennial issues of organization, structure, efficiency and ethics, the legal

---

John D. Ho is a university lecturer in the Department of Law, City Polytechnic of Hong Kong.

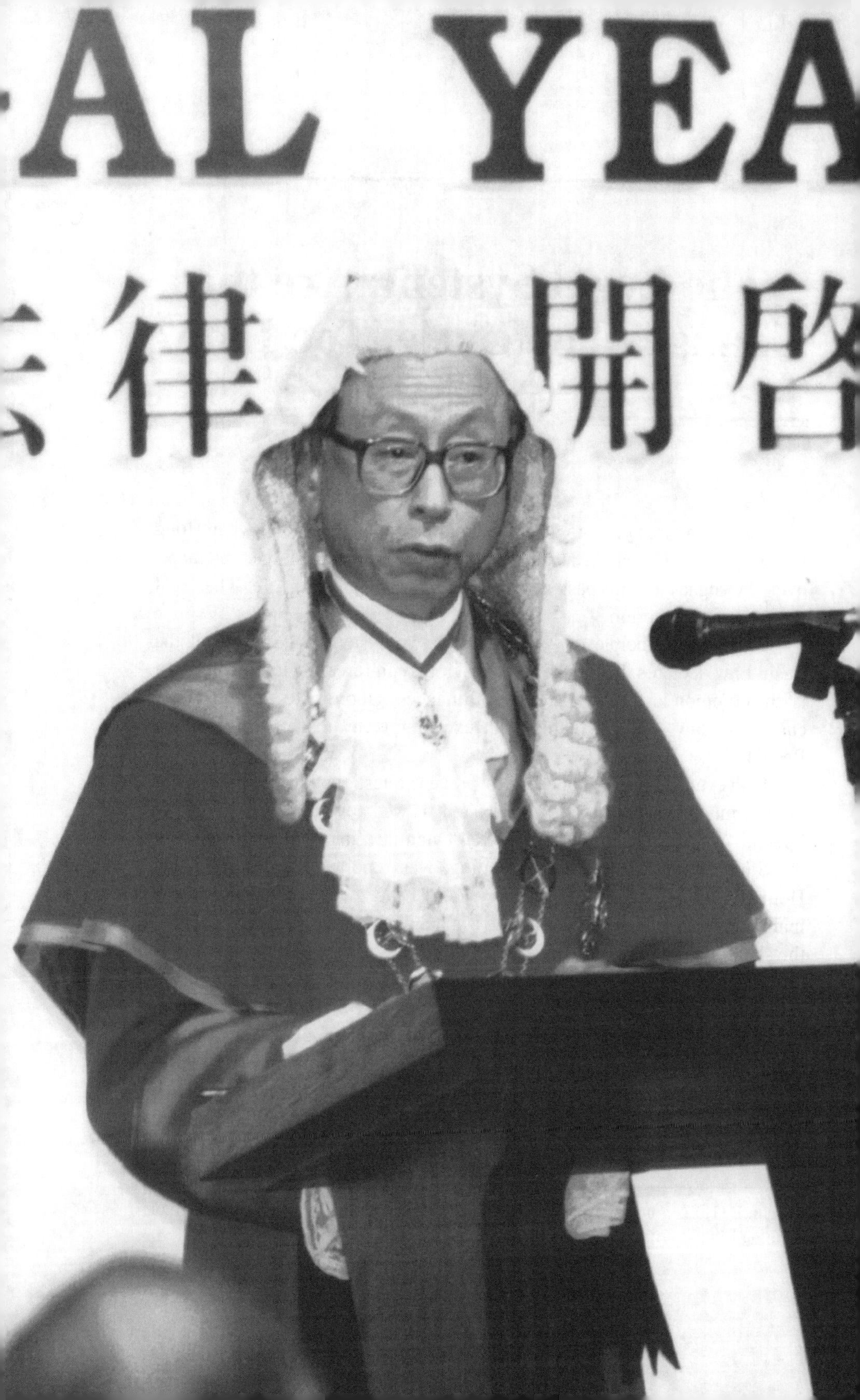
AL YEA
律 開啓

system must make changes in order to comply with the requirements of the Basic Law upon the reversion of Hong Kong to China. A Court of Final Appeal has yet to be set up, and arrangements will have to be made for the abolition of the right of appeal to the Privy Council, the disposal of pending appeals and the transfer of undisposed cases from London to Hong Kong. Laws will have to be localized and adapted so as not to contravene the Basic Law. Even though English may still be used, Chinese will have to be made a language of the law. Legislation will have to be bilingual and Chinese will have to be permitted in court proceedings. In turn, this will mean the Judiciary will need more Chinese-speaking judges.

☐ Localization and Adaptation of Laws

There are some 600 ordinances and 1,000 items of subsidiary legislation under scrutiny for adaptation, and about 300 United Kingdom enactments for localization.

Most of the ordinances would require adaptation in varying degrees to ensure their consistency with relevant provisions of the Basic Law. At the simplest level, all references tainted with any colonial flavour must be removed from the legislation. The Application of English Law Ordinance, which declares the extent to which English law is in force in Hong Kong, for example, will have to be repealed.

Among the 600 ordinances, about 300 are extended from Britain — 200 multilateral and 100 bilateral treaties signed by Britain and other countries — dealing with important areas that help make Hong Kong an international financial centre, like merchant shipping, private international law, civil aviation, international arbitration, extradition and customs cooperation. At present, Hong Kong is automatically covered by those treaties, being a British colony. China is a signatory to only about a third of these treaties.

Whether the SAR can continue to be a member of the multilateral treaties to which China is not a signatory is a complicated question. In some cases, it is possible for the SAR to join the treaties in its own right. In others, it is possible for China to ratify a treaty on behalf of it. But in still others, the SAR may not remain a member unless China becomes one. Many of these treaties are still under study by the government or discussion by the Joint Liaison Group.

Insofar as bilateral treaties are concerned, new agreements must be entered into with the other contracting parties. Although some progress has been reported in the area of aviation, in other areas such as extradition and enforcement of foreign judgments, progress has been slow.

☐ Bilingual Legislation and Translation of Laws

Up to 1987, all ordinances were enacted and published in English only. Since the enactment of the Official Languages (Amendment) Ordinance 1987 (now s.4(1) of the principal Ordinance), all new principal ordinances (that is, ordinances which do not merely amend existing ordinances) are to be enacted and published in both English and Chinese.

In parallel with the production of bilingual legislation is the task of producing authentic Chinese texts of ordinances already in existence. The Bilingual Laws Advisory Committee (BLAC) has been set up since October 1988 to do the tedious work of scrutinizing the translated texts produced by the Law Drafting Division of the Legal Department before they are promulgated. The BLAC has found it necessary to coin phrases and expressions to add to the currently rather lacking Chinese common law vocabulary.

It is hoped that the translation of the existing laws can be completed by the end of 1995 and the authentication completed before July 1997. By the end of March 1994, about 5,400 of the 22,000 pages of legislation had been examined and approved by the BLAC.

☐ Use of the Chinese Language in Court Proceedings

Under s.3 of the Official Languages Ordinance, English and Chinese are to be the "official languages of Hong Kong for the purpose of communication between the Government or any public officer and members of the public," and both "possess equal status." Since Chinese became an official language in 1974, it has been widely used in meetings of the Legislative Council (Legco), the Urban Council, the Regional Council and the District Boards.

However, the situation is different in the court system. Under s.5 of the same Ordinance proceedings in the Court of Appeal, the High Court and the District Court must still be conducted in English alone, although that restriction does not apply to parties or witnesses. Only proceedings in the Magistrates' Courts, any inquiry by a coroner, any Juvenile Court, any Labour Tribunal, any Small Claims Tribunal and any Immigration Tribunal may be conducted in either English or Chinese as the court thinks fit.

The Legal System: Are the Changes Too Little, Too Late?

In the District and higher Courts, criminal indictments and civil pleadings are filed in English. All Chinese documents which are to be produced in court must be translated into English although in a civil case, the judge can dispense with the translation. At the trial, the judge and all the lawyers have to speak in English and what is said is interpreted into Chinese if necessary for the accused or the parties. If the accused, parties or witnesses choose to testify in Chinese, what they say is interpreted into English for the judge and the lawyers (even when they understand Chinese). The judge keeps a note of the proceedings in English, which will be the official record for the purpose of an appeal. The judge's Reasons for Verdict and Sentence or Judgment is written in English and is usually interpreted into Chinese to the accused or parties as it is read in court. But there is no interpretation when the written judgment is simply handed down.

Thus, there is no direct communication between the judge and the accused or the parties if the latter can only speak and understand Chinese. They can only understand what is going on in court through the interpreter and/or their lawyers.

The requirement to use English only in the District Court and above will conflict with Article 9 of the Basic Law, which states that "[i]n addition to the Chinese language, English may also be used as an official language by the ... judiciary of the Hong Kong Special Administrative Region."

More immediately, the English-only requirement reinforces the image of the legal system as an alien one and inhibits its accessibility to the vast majority of Hong Kong's population whose first, and for many the only, language is Chinese. It may also violate the mandate under the Bill of Rights Ordinance that guarantees equality before the courts and tribunals for all persons. Translation and interpretation of original Chinese evidence into English often lead to distortions, affecting the administration of justice.

The need to allow the use of the Chinese language in courts had been highlighted in a Judiciary-ordered study in 1988 but little has been done in the past six years. Last year, Justice Patrick Chan was asked to carry out a study on the use of Chinese in the District Court, and Appeal Court judge Justice Litton was appointed to conduct a wider study on the use of Chinese in law. Justice Chan has completed his study and Justice Litton has submitted an interim report.

The Chief Justice has now proposed amending the Official Languages Ordinance to allow the optional use of Chinese in the District Court and above, initially in areas like matrimonial, labour and tenancy cases in the District Court, and later in simple criminal and civil cases as well. It is also proposed that appeals from magistracies and tribunals in the High Court should be heard by Chinese-speaking judges so that they can be done in Chinese. The earliest possible time for these changes to take place is the middle of next year.

Initially, judges will have to make their own translation of the proceedings until a recording system is provided. A request for funding has been lodged to employ an extra thirty translators and calligraphers to transcribe recorded proceedings in case of appeal. Retraining is recommended for crown counsel and judges to help them adjust to the proposed change.

However, the use of the Chinese language in court proceedings will not be brought about simply by legislative fiat. The practice must be allowed time to take root, and it will not take root without corresponding changes in the attitude and training of judges and legal practitioners, and above all the development of an authoritative and adequate Chinese legal vocabulary.

The laws of Hong Kong consist largely of the statute law and the English Common Law. As mentioned above, not all existing legislation has been translated, and it is extremely difficult if not impossible to translate into Chinese all the Common Law case precedents. Compounding the problem is the current non-existence of authoritative Chinese equivalents to some of the legal principles, concepts and expressions. The City Polytechnic of Hong Kong is attempting to produce a digest of the common law in Chinese, but only the volume on Contract Law has been completed.

Since most of the legal materials are in English, judges and lawyers have been, and are still, trained in English. Many will have difficulty in conducting court proceedings in Chinese without proper training and it will take time to retrain them. While it has been observed that the frequency of conducting trials in Chinese in the Magistrates' Courts has increased and junior lawyers are more willing to use Chinese in trials, the difficulties are exacerbated by the fact that only a minority of District and Supreme Court judges are Chinese-speaking.

Following the announcement by the Chief Justice, the Hong Kong Bar Association has called on the Judiciary to set up a special court to test the use of Chinese in the legal system. The Law Society of Hong Kong has proposed conducting training for judges and lawyers in using Chinese in court as it sees that not just magistrates but many Chinese-speaking barristers and solicitors are also facing tremendous problems in expressing legal terms in their mother tongue.

☐ The Judiciary

Localization of the Judiciary

The past year or so saw the appointment of several Chinese to important positions in the legal arena, including the Solicitor-General and the Director of Public Prosecutions. The University of Hong Kong made news when the first Chinese to become Head of its Department of Law was elected. Now the City Polytechnic has also appointed a Chinese as Dean of its Faculty of Law.

Yet the localization of the Judiciary itself will be more difficult. As mentioned above, only a minority of the District Court and High Court judges are Chinese, and there is currently no Chinese among the Justices of Appeal. The traditional practice of appointing judges from the Colonial Legal Service was not challenged until the late 1960s and early 1970s. It was not until recently that private practitioners were appointed to the Judiciary. But the search for suitable candidates will not be easy. Some potential judges are worried about the security of the job after 1997. Others are doing so well financially in private practice that to join the Judiciary is to take a pay cut.

The Judiciary is considering appointing solicitors directly as High Court judges to speed up the localization programme — an idea that the Law Society has been pushing for a few years. Such a change will entail the amendment of the Supreme Court Ordinance which governs the appointment of High Court judges, and will likely face resistance from the Bar.

Departure of Judges

Just as vexing as the issue of localization is the problem of the departure of judges. At least eight judges from the High Court and Court of Appeal, effectively one quarter of those presently serving, are said to intend to leave within the next twelve months, and many Justices of Appeal may also retire by 1997. There are growing uncertainties as to how the Judiciary will manage to find enough replacements.

Administration of the Judiciary

The 1986 Robinson Report outlined a blueprint for the efficient and effective management of the Judiciary. Most of the recommendations in that report for computerization, and the setting up of a system for the reporting of court proceedings by court reporters or a recording system, rather than having judges take down verbatim in longhand all the evidence, have not been implemented. Judges in the District and Magistrates' Courts are still required to write a longhand note of proceedings, hampering their ability to observe the demeanour of witnesses and to control the proceedings in court.

There are complaints among the judges of "institutionalized apathy and inertia," particularly in the administration of the District Court, and "an increasing tendency of judges to allow almost every request from counsel for adjournments, whatever the reasons, contributing to a reduction in the sitting hours of a court and the amount of work it gets through." The "institutional lethargy" has led to worsening delays in the delivery of justice for defendants and victims, causing undue distress, inflated legal costs and prolonged incarceration for those who are remanded in custody awaiting trial. Reportedly, about 60 people have been on remand for more than a year and 170 for more than six months. In a notorious case, two teenage female illegal immigrants were detained in custody without charge as prosecution witnesses for nine months, while two teenage males charged with using them as sex slaves were released on bail.

A judicial administrator was appointed this year and her task is to introduce a "modern management culture" to the Judiciary and address the thorny issue of how to reduce the waiting time for cases to come to trial in both the High Court and District Court, as well as deal with problems posed by the localization of the Judiciary and greater use of the Chinese language in the courts.

The Court of Final Appeal

The Joint Liaison Group agreement regarding the Court of Final Appeal has been vehemently opposed by the Legco and the legal profession because of the restrictions it places on the number of overseas judges. The joint accord, struck in 1991, stated that the court should comprise four local judges and one overseas judge. China's attitude is that the government should just set up the Court in accordance with the 1991 agreement, as the Legco is "just a consultative body to the Governor." It is unclear whether in this context a local judge must be a Chinese citizen who is a permanent resident of the SAR with no right of abode in any foreign country — a requirement which will apply to the Chief Justice of the SAR, who will be a member of the Court of Final Appeal.

The Bar Association has sent a mission to Beijing to discuss the issue of the Court of Final Appeal and will conduct a poll of its members to see if its opposition to its composition will be reversed.

☐ The Lawyers

Defeat of the Fusion Proposal

Last year, the Law Society put forth a proposal to fuse the two branches of the legal profession, by allowing those currently practising as barristers to conduct the legal business of solicitors while giving solicitors the opportunity to practise in areas that were within the sole remit of barristers. Under this proposal, all lawyers would practise within a newly created legal profession with the right to provide all legal services and appear in all courts. All lawyers would be permitted to enter into partnership with any other lawyer. The Society also suggested that the public should have direct access to barristers, instead of having to retain them through solicitors acting as middlemen. The Society argued its proposals would make legal services more accessible, efficient and effective and would reduce legal fees by as much as half.

The proposal was overwhelmingly rejected by the Bar, on the grounds that it is vital to maintain an independent Bar where barristers are not affiliated to any particular commercial or political interest and can furnish more detached advice. They also argued that a fused system would also likely spell the end of the "cab rank" rule, which ensures barristers are available to any client through any firm of solicitors.

The barristers countered that solicitors already enjoyed rights of audience in the majority of court proceedings heard in Hong Kong, including Magistrates' and District Courts, in all interlocutory proceedings in the High Court and the Court of Appeal and in appeals to the High Court from the Magistracies. Solicitors are only restricted from appearing in High Court civil or criminal trials and before the Court of Appeal in open court, which only constitute a small proportion of court proceedings heard in Hong Kong in any given year.

Besides rejecting the fusion proposal, the Bar Association members voted marginally in favour of the retention of the two-counsel rule — that a Queen's Counsel has to be accompanied by a junior when appearing in court. They were in favour of making solicitors accompanying barristers in court a voluntary rather than compulsory matter. But they voted in support of a proposal to allow professionals other than solicitors, such as accountants, as the middlemen to instruct barristers on behalf of clients — a proposal that the Law Society opposed without fusion.

The disagreement between the Law Society and the Bar Association will likely keep the two branches of the profession divided for the foreseeable future.

New Law Society Code of Conduct Regarding Political Cases

The argument that solicitors are not independent because they are linked to commercial and political interests appears to be borne out by the incident in which allegedly at least eighteen law firms refused to take on the libel suit of Martin Lee, chairman of the United Democrats of Hong Kong, and fellow activist Szeto Wah against Simon Li, a former Appeal Court judge and now a leading adviser to China, over remarks Li allegedly made in Beijing about the behaviour of Lee and Szeto during the Hong Kong pro-democracy protests of 1989.

The incident led to an amendment of the Law Society's code of practice. Under the amendment, those refusing cases on political grounds would be subject to investigation by an internal tribunal with the risk of sanctions being brought against them. But solicitors would still be entitled to refuse cases without giving reasons in situations where disclosure would breach confidentiality, cause bias, embarrassment or offence.

Touting

According to the Bar's current code of conduct, sharing of fees directly or indirectly by paying a commission or otherwise to any person including the barrister's clerk is prohibited. The Law Society has a similar code for law clerks and legal executives. But touting in the legal profession, especially in criminal and conveyancing cases, has been described as "appalling." It has been reported that middlemen who referred cases to solicitors and barristers could charge commissions as high as 70 per cent of the legal fees clients paid, and clients were usually deceived as the sum of legal fees would first go to the lawyers who reimbursed the commission to law clerks in cash, making it difficult for the Independent Commission Against Corruption (ICAC) to obtain sufficient evidence to prosecute.

The legal profession has taken further steps to curtail illegal commission-taking and touting after the problem was revealed by a nine-year ICAC study. The ICAC found that some legal clerks had touted for business and demanded payment from solicitors or barristers, while others had forged solicitors' signatures on bills to get more money from clients.

In an effort to reduce kick-backs, the Bar Association will amend its code of conduct to require its members to accept only cheques drawn on solicitors' firms. This would enable a complete audit trail to be conducted to prevent clients from being defrauded by ensuring the fee itemized in the customer's invoice is the same as that in the cheque paid to the barrister and that on the receipt issued to the solicitors' firm.

Foreign Lawyers

The Legal Practitioners (Amendment) Bill was passed by the Legco in July 1994, providing for the registration for practice of foreign law and the admission of foreign lawyers.

Under the previous system, foreign law firms which were "well established" and had a "substantial reputation" in their home jurisdiction could set up their offices in Hong Kong upon the undertaking, among others, that they would not practise Hong Kong law. Under the new law, registration will be required of all foreign law firms, foreign lawyers in private practice in Hong Kong, and foreign law firms in association with local law firms. Once registered, the foreign law firms and lawyers will be subject to the same professional rules of conduct as their Hong Kong counterparts.

As before, a foreign lawyer will still be precluded from practising Hong Kong law and from employing or forming partnerships with Hong Kong solicitors. But foreign lawyers may be employed as foreign legal consultants in Hong Kong firms so long as the number of foreign lawyers to Hong Kong lawyers does not exceed the ratio of 1:1.

Previously, admission as a solicitor in Hong Kong is restricted to those who are qualified by passing the PCLL (Postgraduate Certificate in Laws) and successfully completing two years of traineeship, or are admitted as a solicitor in England and Wales.

Under the new system, lawyers from both common law and non-common law jurisdictions will be eligible for admission as Hong Kong solicitors if they fulfil entry requirements relating to educational qualification and practice experience, are of good standing in their jurisdiction of admission and have successfully completed or are exempted from all or part of the Overseas Lawyers Admission Examination, the first of which is expected to be held in late 1995.

Legal Aid

The need for legal aid to be run by an authority truly independent of the government has been urged for many years. Without legal aid, the fundamental right of access to the courts will remain only theoretical in most matters. Many applicants for legal aid stand in opposition to the government one way or another. The natural inclination, in such cases, is for the public to be sceptical as to whether and how far the Legal Aid Department, being a government department, would give them the necessary financial assistance to resist or challenge another government department.

There is also the enormous economic factor. Since the Legal Aid Department assigns the greater number of its cases to solicitors and barristers in private practice, leaving only a small portion to be handled directly by lawyers on its staff, its power over the legal profession can hardly be overestimated. Legal aid work forms a substantial part of the practice of many lawyers. The distribution of legal aid work may be seen as a means to quell or punish those members within the legal profession who dare to exert their independence too vigorously against the government.

To monitor the Legal Aid Department and the Duty Lawyer Service, the Executive Council (Exco) decided to set up a Legal Aid Services Council rather than going for a fully independent legal aid authority. The Council will comprise a non-official chairman and four members from outside the legal profession, four members from the legal profession, the Director of Legal Aid and the administrator of the Duty Lawyer Service. The decision was strongly criticized as being cosmetic and inadequate to safeguard the independence of legal aid, as the Council would have only an advisory role and not the power to review individual applications.

The government also announced a set of changes in legal aid policy, including extending the Director of Legal Aid's discretionary power to waive the means test in some human rights cases. The scope of the supplementary legal aid scheme, which mainly serves the "sandwich" class, would be expanded to include medical and dental negligence claims.

Rejection of Recommended Human Rights Commission

A report published in April by the House of Commons Foreign Affairs Select Committee recommended setting up a human rights commission in Hong Kong to safeguard against possible violations of human rights. The recommendation was immediately attacked by China's National People's Congress as an infringement of its internal affairs, bringing into doubt whether such a commission would survive beyond the 1997 handover.

In order to avoid a confrontation with China the Exco rejected the recommendation but instead earmarked $20 million over the next three years for the development of human rights education, and voted for the formation of a human rights sub-committee under the auspices of the ombudsman, which will have powers to investigate government violations of human rights.

☐ The Consumer Legal Action Fund

The current law provides remedies for consumers who suffer loss from sharp business practice. However, the remedies are frequently rendered ineffective as a result of consumers' ignorance or lack of resources to pursue their rights.

The Consumer Council will set up a Consumer Legal Action Fund with an initial $10 million capital grant from the government to provide greater consumer access to legal remedies. Emphasis will be on cases in which there are common defendants and circumstances or where public interest is involved. It is also envisaged that the Fund will pursue representative actions whereby one consumer can sue the same defendant on behalf of a number of consumers in order to have similar complaints determined at one time, and joint claims where one or more consumers can join together to bring claims arising out of the same transactions or series of transactions with a common question of law or fact.

It is intended that the Fund complements the present Legal Aid and Supplementary Legal Aid schemes by providing assistance in cases which would not qualify for those schemes.

☐ An Equal Opportunities Ordinance?

In July, Legislative Councillor Anna Wu's Equal Opportunities Bill, said to be Hong Kong's first comprehensive private member's bill covering an entire area of law, was gazetted. If passed, the law will prohibit discrimination on the basis of a person's sex, marital status, pregnancy and family responsibility, sexuality, race, national or ethnic origin, disability, religious or political beliefs, age, spent criminal conviction and trade union membership or activities.

The government has so far declined to adopt the Bill, but is only committed to legislating against sex discrimination and discrimination against a person's physical or mental disability. The latter was prompted by the harassment by some residents at Laguna City of mentally handicapped patients using a clinic there.

☐ Conclusion

The gravity of some of the issues raised above can be appreciated more readily if one asks a series of "What if" questions. For example, what would happen to the development of the law and legal system if there is no Court of Final Appeal on 1 July 1997? What would happen to Hong Kong's status as a business and financial centre if legislation is not adapted and localized and international treaties renewed in time? What if the use of the Chinese language in court proceedings does not take root? What if judicial vacancies are not filled with people of the right calibre?

The spectre of a "legal vacuum" has been raised by some commentators if a viable system is not in place by 1997, but that notion has met with scorn from China. Beijing will no doubt step in and change the system as it sees fit should Hong Kong's efforts to ensure the survival of the present system fail. As former Attorney-General Michael Thomas put it, "English law will become discredited and will be supplanted by Chinese law, politically driven from Beijing and grounded in Mandarin." The question, then, is whether Hong Kong can maintain its "way of life" and its "status as an international financial centre" as mandated by the Basic Law.

3

Independent Commission Against Corruption

Sonny S. H. Lo

Since its birth in 1974, the Independent Commission Against Corruption (ICAC) had never been severely criticized until 1994, a year of political bombshells for the anti-corruption agency. This chapter will first review how the ICAC responded to environmental changes in the last year, when corruption in the private and public sectors soared and the debate over political democratization reached its zenith. It then will examine the case of Alex Tsui Ka-kit and explore its political, legal and managerial implications for the ICAC. The chapter will conclude with an analysis of the problems and prospects for the anti-corruption agency.

☐ Environmental Challenges to the ICAC

There were numerous corruption cases involving Hong Kong civil servants, who have been regarded as clean, honest and efficient since the mid-1970s. These corrupt civil servants included, for example, two engineers who were charged with receiving bribes from executives of private companies. Meanwhile, four customs officers stationed at the Man Kam To and Lok Ma Chau border posts were found guilty of accepting bribes for arranging unimpeded clearance of luxury cars and electrical appliances smuggled from Hong Kong into China. In another case, five customs officers were charged with conspiring with an illegal immigration syndicate to manufacture forged passports and identity cards, making arrangements for illegal

---

Sonny S. H. Lo is an assistant professor in the Division of Social Science, the Hong Kong University of Science and Technology.

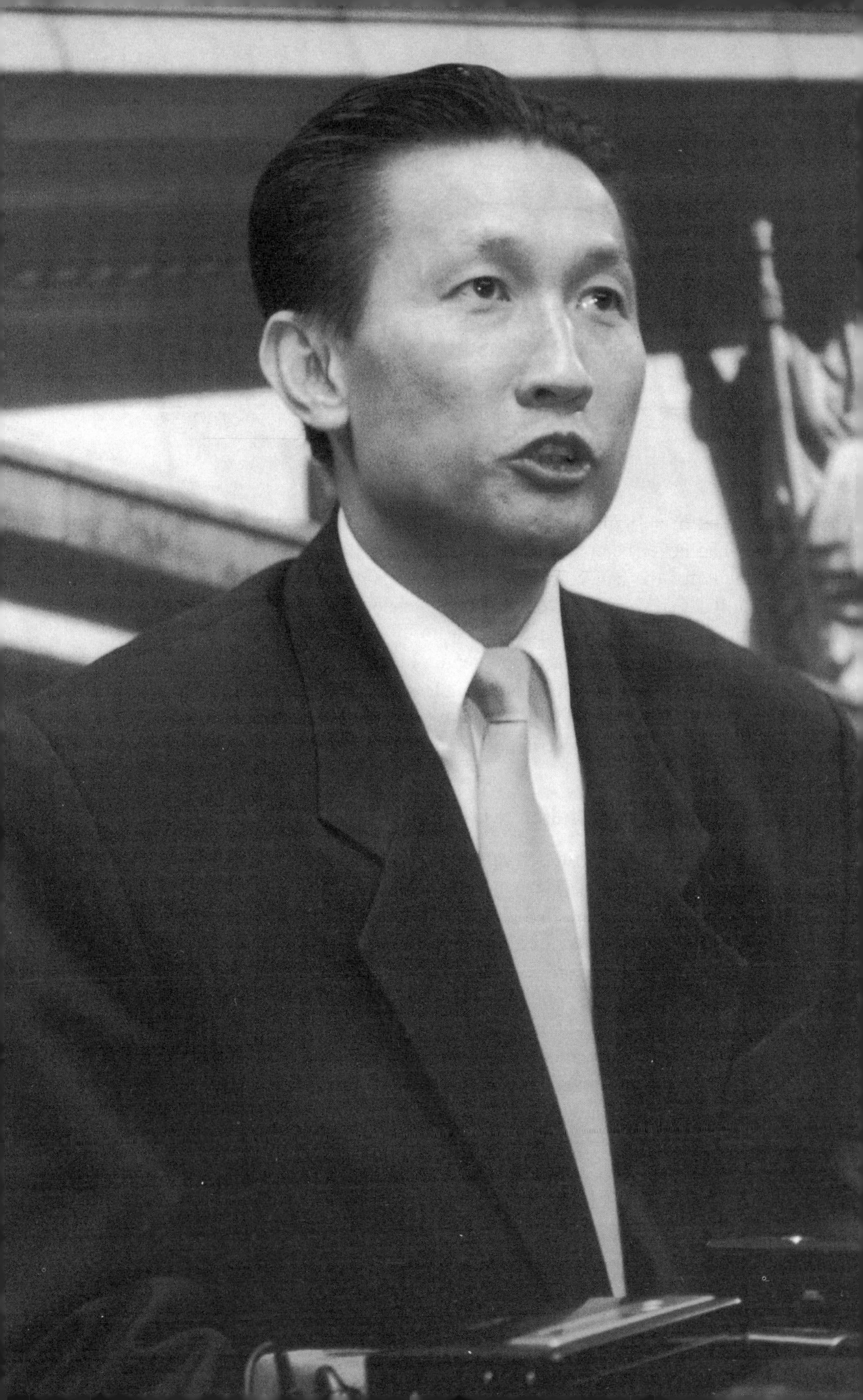

immigrants from China to enter Hong Kong, and allowing them to leave the territory for Canada. Although the public sector was by no means experiencing a crisis of integrity parallel to the situation in the 1960s and the early 1970s, the recent upsurge in corruption cases involving civil servants has been alarming.

There also was a rapid increase in corruption cases in the private sector. Reports of graft there rose 52 per cent in 1993 to 1,806, forcing a 42 per cent increase in overall reports on private and public sector corruption to 3,284. Even the Royal Hong Kong Jockey Club was affected by graft. In January 1994, ICAC officers arrested some staff members of the Jockey Club, and it was reported that young *mafoos* hired by the club might pay up to $300,000 to secure work with popular and successful horse trainers. Although the chief executive of the Jockey Club, Major-General Guy Watkins, denied that large-scale race-fixing syndicates existed in Hong Kong, he remarked that the biggest menace to honest horse-racing were the rich and powerful people who paid bribes for inside information on horses. One track professional even claimed that syndicates paid cash advances to some jockeys and trainers, who were later paid for the successful outcomes of fixed races. If horse-racing — the most popular sport in Hong Kong — has been deeply penetrated by corruption, there are grounds for believing that the ethical standards in society have been gradually deteriorating.

Another environmental challenge to the ICAC was the spillover effect of rampant corruption in China. Some Hong Kong companies investing in China tend to view corruption as a necessary instrument by which they can facilitate their business transactions with the Mainland authorities. On the other hand, it is an open secret that some Mainland companies operating in Hong Kong are corrupt; neither the central government in Beijing nor the local New China News Agency seems to be able to control the corrupt cadres in the territory. Tony Scott, the Director of Corruption Prevention at the ICAC, warned publicly that corrupt Mainland officials might abuse their power in Hong Kong after 1997, a threat that would be greater than Hong Kong people becoming corrupt. Given the get-rich-quick mentality of many Hongkongers and the lack of integrity on the part of some Mainland cadres, it is not surprising that Governor Christopher Patten regarded corruption as "the most worrying feature of our present life." In the event that corruption in Hong Kong from now to 1997 cannot be effectively controlled, there will be a real danger that corruption in post-1997 Hong Kong will be as serious as the period prior to the birth of the ICAC.

☐ The ICAC's Response

In response to these environmental challenges, the ICAC made a greater effort than ever before to curb corruption in the private and public sectors. First, a campaign was launched to institute voluntary codes of conduct to combat corruption in the business community, including Chinese-funded enterprises. The campaign was organized by the ICAC's Community Relations Department and business associations, such as the Hong Kong General Chamber of Commerce, the Hong Kong Chinese Enterprises Association, and the American Chamber of Commerce. Governor Patten was reportedly hoping that all publicly listed companies and about 2,000 corporations which employed more than 100 staff members to adopt the codes of conduct. Therefore, the ICAC was determined to inculcate business ethics into the private sector.

Second, the ICAC took measures to improve its efficiency in an endeavour to deal with a record number of corruption cases. An extra Deputy Director of Operations was created; the recruitment of 40 additional investigators in the 880-member Operations Department was approved; advice from the government, including the Efficiency Unit, was sought; and a consultant from the Coopers and Lybrand Company, Nigel Knight, was asked by the ICAC to study ways to enhance the agency's efficiency. Knight suggested that more computerized files and less paperwork would streamline the ICAC's operation. At the same time, the ICAC acquired from the government more money to subsidize its increased resources and manpower.

Third, the ICAC strengthened its links with People's Republic of China (P.R.C.) officials responsible for controlling China's corruption. On the one hand, ICAC officers sought advice from them to understand Mainland anti-corruption laws for Hong Kong business people investing in China. The Guangdong People's Procuratorate cooperated with the ICAC to produce a booklet on anti-corruption laws for Hong Kong businessmen. Clearly, the ICAC was trying its best to cope with the cross-border corruption cases, which if not handled properly would sooner or later have a spillover effect on Hong Kong.

Overall, the ICAC's swift response to various environmental challenges illustrated its deep concern about the resurgence of corruption cases and the threat of uncontrollable corruption in post-1997 Hong Kong. Enhancing the ICAC's efficiency could be viewed as an inevitable internal reform during the Patten administration, which has been implementing public sector reform with an emphasis on efficiency in various government departments. Meanwhile, the launching of the anti-corruption campaign in the private sector and the strengthening of communications with P.R.C. anti-graft organs could be regarded as progressive external moves to prevent and combat corruption in the long run. The ICAC became so aggressive in its action to fight corruption that it alienated some mysterious opponents, who resorted to a violent response in launching an arson attack on the headquarters of the Operations Department in February 1994.

☐ The Case of Alex Tsui Ka-kit

Although the ICAC responded swiftly to external challenges, the case of Alex Tsui Ka-kit revealed some internal problems within the ICAC. Tsui had been the Deputy Director of Operations before he was sacked by the ICAC Commissioner, Bertrand de Speville, in November 1993. De Speville had invoked Section 8(2) of the ICAC Ordinance under which he did not have to give any reason for sacking any staff member. In the wake of his dismissal, Tsui filed a complaint with the police, alleging that the Director of the Operations Department, Jim Buckle, had "perverted" the course of justice during an internal investigation of an expatriate officer in the department, Michael William Croft, who had sexually harassed female staff members. Following the ICAC's internal investigation, Croft was transferred to a different department and his contract was not to be renewed. In the wake of the police investigation into Tsui's complaint, in January 1994 the Attorney General, Jeremy Mathews, announced that there would be no prosecution brought against Buckle over the charge that the latter had perverted the course of justice.

Tsui also appealed to members of the Legislative Council (Legco) to investigate whether Buckle had perverted the course of justice. Before the police looked into Tsui's complaint, the Legco's Security Panel had decided that in order not to prejudice the police investigation, it was better to defer using the legislature's authority under the Legislative Council (Powers and Privileges) Ordinance to request ICAC officials to answer questions concerning Tsui's dismissal. Two months after the police completed their investigation in January 1994, the Legco's Security Panel decided to call de Speville and Tsui to appear at public hearings in April.

The Legco's move was influenced by Tsui, who wrote a letter to the legislature and offered to attend any session which would hear his complaints. In his letter to legislators, Tsui alleged that members of the ICAC

Operations Review Committee, a watchdog body overseeing the anti-corruption agency, were not given genuine reasons underlying his dismissal. He urged the government to reveal the number of female ICAC employees who had been sexually harassed and to explain why the Legal Department had decided not to prosecute Buckle. Mainly because the Legco was operating in a political atmosphere that emphasized governmental responsiveness, openness and accountability, Tsui took advantage of this democratizing climate and succeeded in demanding that the legislature should look into his dismissal.

Originally, the ICAC Commissioner de Speville resisted the efforts by Legco members to force him to disclose the reasons for sacking Tsui. It was reported that he might use national security as a justification to avoid answering questions from legislators. But in January 1994, when Legco members voted in favour of establishing a committee to review the ICAC's powers, it became clear that sooner or later the grounds for Tsui's dismissal would have to be revealed. Projecting an image of an accountable government, the Chief Secretary of the Hong Kong government, Anson Chan Fang On-sang, remarked in a Legco session that the ICAC should not be immune from the changes in the past twenty years. Indeed, Chan's desire to make the administration more open was consistent with Governor Patten's emphasis on the continual development of a responsible government in Hong Kong.

In an obvious departure from his previous stance, de Speville in March 1994 vowed to reveal all the reasons for dismissing Tsui, and he said that it would be no longer operationally necessary to keep those reasons confidential. Partly because of the decision to make the ICAC more open to the public, and partly because the ICAC's public image had already been undermined to some extent by the open complaints and lobbying activities of Tsui, de Speville had no choice but to defend the ICAC by revealing the details of the Tsui case.

The public hearings of the Tsui case in April 1994 were politically significant. As the final years of British rule have put much emphasis on democratization and liberalization, the ICAC was inevitably forced to be more transparent in its operation and to justify its exercise of power to the public. For the first time in Hong Kong's history, Legco members utilized the Legislative Council (Powers and Privileges) Ordinance to summon people to testify at the Legco. These events represented an experiment with democratization, making the ICAC answerable to the legislature.

More importantly, the hearings raised many questions regarding both

Tsui's behaviour and the ICAC's operations. On 14 April, de Speville listed under oath several reasons behind Tsui's dismissal. First, Tsui failed to report a meeting with the Vice-president of the Hong Kong Boxing Association, Henfrey Tin Sau-kwok, in Macau after Tin had been interviewed by ICAC officers about a loan to a triad suspect. De Speville said that Tsui, who was the Executive Chair of the Boxing Association, had concealed his supposedly severed relationship with Tin, albeit Tsui had already been warned of his attempt to obtain a loan for Tin in 1986. At that time, Tin was charged with armed robbery but was not prosecuted. According to de Speville, Tsui wrote a letter to his superior, claiming that his friendship with Tin ended in the early 1980s as he felt that Tin's life had undergone some changes. However, Tsui later concealed his interactions with Tin, thus breaching the trust of his superiors who then became doubtful of Tsui's integrity and credibility. Tsui's close and undeclared association with his friend who was suspected of participating in criminal activities not only infringed the ICAC's internal standing orders but also sounded the death knell to his career in the anti-corruption agency.

Second, de Speville asserted that Tsui wrote a memo which diverted investigators' attention from looking into Hung Wing-wah, the President of the Boxing Association. According to de Speville, Tin and Hung were involved in cigarette smuggling activities, but Tsui's memo described Hung's company as a well-established distributor. Tsui's memo apparently alarmed his superiors in the ICAC, who believed that Tsui was not honest enough to expose the criminal activities of his associates in the Boxing Association.

Third, de Speville disclosed that he and Governor Patten had received an anonymous complaint letter, which was lodged in July 1993 and which revealed Tsui's questionable involvement in an effort to obtain a letter of support for a boxing tournament from a consular official. According to de Speville, the anonymous letter alleged that Tsui had offered a bribe to forge the signature of a consul-general in a letter pledging support of the boxing tournament to the Television and Entertainment Licensing Authority. Initially Tsui denied that he had knowledge of the letter acquiring support for the boxing tournament. When a copy of the letter was shown to Tsui, he acknowledged that it was his, although Tsui consistently denied that he had offered any bribe to the consular official. De Speville asserted that if Tsui had candidly admitted this letter in the first place, he would not be suspicious of Tsui's honesty and integrity. Moreover, de Speville revealed that Tsui breached protocol by not informing the ICAC that he wrote a letter to a consul-general, which accused the consular official of being involved with triads and being a deceiver. Apparently, Tsui's action went too far, thus resulting in his dismissal by the ICAC without giving any reason.

The Legco's public hearing of the Tsui case reached a climax on 15 April when Tsui himself gave testimony. Objectively speaking, Tsui did not really give sufficient evidence in addressing the points raised by de Speville. Instead, Tsui made several shocking claims during the hearings. First, Tsui alleged that his superior, Buckle, was preparing a list of political targets for use after 1997. According to Tsui, Buckle had told him that they would have to compile a list of persons involved in corruption and political activities. He also revealed that Group G in the Operations Department was responsible for collecting all kinds of information about the targets. During the Legco's hearing on 5 May, Tsui claimed that the ICAC's "target list" included two senior officers in the disciplinary forces, one councillor, politicians and executives of Mainland-funded companies.

Second, he declared that a top ICAC official had inflated statistics concerning corruption in order to win more resources from the government. He also hinted that figures regarding the increase in police corruption, which rose from 450 cases in 1988 to 614 in 1993, were inaccurate. According to Tsui, although staff members in the ICAC increased, prosecution figures actually declined. He also maintained that many cases investigated by the ICAC included fraud, blackmail and conspiracy which could have been managed by the Commercial Crime Bureau of the police force.

Third, Tsui claimed that the ICAC had carried out "political vetting," which was originally the responsibility of the Special Branch of the police force. He named Yeung Kai-yin, the former Secretary of the Treasury and Secretary for Transport, and Rita Fan Hsu Lai-tai, an ex-member of the Executive Council, as "targets" who had been bugged by the ICAC. Tsui said that because Yeung and Fan had close relations with Mainland officials, the ICAC began to monitor their activities through bugging.

Fourth, Tsui claimed that it was "racism" within the ICAC which led to his dismissal. According to Tsui, Buckle abused his power and made judgements in favour of Michael Croft. Moreover, after an expatriate investigator erred in searching a wrong flat, Buckle refused to punish him in defiance of a suggestion by the ICAC Operations Review Committee that the expatriate officer should be sacked. Although Tsui highlighted the internal managerial problems within the ICAC, the charge of "racism" remained unconvincing and unsupported with evidence.

Tsui appeared to be unable to defend his questionable behaviour described by de Speville on 14 April. Adopting a strategy of refraining from discussing the reasons for his dismissal as elaborated by de Speville, Tsui chose to arouse public attention by exposing the possible action of the ICAC to compile a list of "political" targets. However, he failed to elaborate why or how such list, if it existed, was used for "political" purposes. In regard to his claim that the ICAC manipulated the figures on corruption, Tsui also failed to analyse in detail those "falsely inflated" statistics released by the ICAC. Even if these statistics were really fabricated, it was not surprising that the ICAC did so, given the aggressive instinct of the anti-corruption commission. In theory, every government department may pursue empire-building activities, for the desire to expand manpower and acquire more resources is arguably a hallmark of any bureaucratic organization. The ICAC is, theoretically, no exception to this rule.

By accusing the ICAC of politically vetting some Hong Kong people, Tsui helped the public to caution against any clandestine activities of the anti-corruption agency. Although de Speville and Buckle were quick to deny that the ICAC conducted any political vetting, unfortunately none of them could explain publicly what they meant by political vetting. De Speville merely said that the ICAC had been carrying out "integrity checks" on behalf of the government since 1974. Yet, if these checks involved not only the honesty but also the political outlook of civil servants, such checks amounted to political vetting. Given the fact that the Special Branch has been winding down its activities and transferring its functions to the ICAC, there are grounds for suspecting that the anti-corruption commission may be responsible for sensitive political work originally done by the branch. In any case, neither de Speville nor Buckle could allay public anxiety by specifying the meanings of, or any distinction between, integrity checks and political vetting.

☐ Implications for the ICAC

The Alex Tsui case had managerial, legal and political implications for the ICAC. Managerially, the case exposed administrative problems within the ICAC. Although Tsui's claim of "racism" was not fully substantiated, his complaints reflected a degree of tension between expatriate superiors and local subordinates in the ICAC. Being a secretive agency, the ICAC has seldom revealed its progress in staff localization, unlike other government departments such as the Legal Department and the police force. During the last four years of British rule, the Patten administration should realize the urgency and importance of localizing the top echelons of the ICAC. Without promoting more competent and qualified locals to high-ranking positions, the ICAC's leadership would probably experience a vacuum after 1997. Moreover, the Basic Law stipulates that the future anti-corruption commissioner will be a local person without the right of abode in any foreign country.

Apparently, the detrimental impact of the slow pace of localization of the ICAC's upper stratum was shown in the Tsui case. As the most senior local officer in the ICAC, Tsui himself abused his power when he concealed his contacts with his informant, Tin. The fact that Tsui was the top local officer had appeared to make his superiors, Buckle and de Speville, trust him to a considerable extent until his questionable behaviour was discovered. Ironically, had the ICAC's top levels been more speedily localized, it is doubtful whether Tsui would have been so strongly trusted by his superiors in the first place.

In addition to localization, another managerial problem within the ICAC was the insufficient internal checks on relationships between informants and senior officers. During his testimony to the Legco, de Speville admitted that it was "unusual" for an officer of Tsui's rank to have dealings with informants. While all other records used by the ICAC to corroborate the correctness of the officer-informant relationship were regularly examined, this surprisingly was not the case with Tsui's relationship with Tin. As de Speville explained:

> [T]he requirement for an annual review ... applies to the file when it is opened in a normal, regular way. Namely, you have the principal investigator with a number of informant particulars in his safe and he calls for the informants' files which are in his group and sees what the position is. Here, it was different because it was Mr. Tsui himself at assistant-director level who had the information about the informer and the record of contacts with the informer with him on the same file. Nobody else had access to that file though the Deputy Director and the Director of Operations had seen the file and indeed had noted each of the entries made in it. But there was no annual review of that file.[1]

Clearly, the ICAC must tighten its internal checks on all files concerning the interactions between informants and top-level officers. If this is not done, high-ranking officers, as with Tsui, will still retain the administrative discretion of not reporting their contacts with any informant.

---

[1] *South China Morning Post*, 15 April 1994, p. 6.

Legally, the case of Tsui highlighted the extraordinary powers enjoyed by the Governor in approving the ICAC to bug corrupt suspects and, possibly, political targets. Under the Telecommunication Ordinance, all wire-taps must be approved by the Governor who can delegate the responsibility of phone-tapping to other officials if he believes that it is in "public interest." However, since the term "public interest" is open to the chief executive's interpretation, wire-tapping may degenerate into a tool misused by the authorities, especially after 1997. Although the Law Reform Commission has been exploring the criteria for authorizing telephone tapping, any legal constraints on wire-tapping will have to be recognized, tolerated and observed by the post-1997 authorities. Otherwise, wire-tapping will remain a hidden and controversial instrument which the ICAC may misuse easily.

Politically, the Tsui case revealed that the ICAC had not been adequately accountable to any watchdog body for its action. Specifically, the existing advisory committees which review the ICAC's work are relatively weak. For one thing, members of these committees have traditionally been appointed by the government. As some critics of the administration have pointed out, these committees are not really accountable to the public so long as there is no member directly elected by citizens. The dilemma, however, is that appointing directly elected members to these committees may have the unintended consequence of politicizing some corruption-related issues that must be kept confidential at the investigatory stage. While some directly elected Legco members have stressed the way in which members of the ICAC's monitoring committees should be selected, one must not turn a blind eye to Tsui's reference to Buckle's remark that the Operations Review Committee could only review information "fed" by the ICAC. If Buckle did make such a remark, it showed that top ICAC officials had the administrative discretion of filtering any document and information passed to the Operations Review Committee. In reality, stipulating precisely the areas in which the Operations Review Committee can examine the ICAC's work is as important as considering the question of how members of the advisory committees should be chosen.

In April 1994, it was reported that the ICAC's vetting files on top civil servants would not be submitted to the Operations Review Committee, an arrangement different from the normal practice whereby the committee examines every investigation file opened by the ICAC. Under the new practice, these files would probably be submitted directly to the Civil Service Branch and Government House. As long as all the investigation files, including those concerning top bureaucrats, were not circulated to the Operations Review Committee for examination, the ICAC would not be fully accountable to its advisory bodies, particularly the Operations Review Committee.

After the Tsui case had been publicized, the Hong Kong government attempted to improve the mechanisms that review the ICAC's work. In February 1994, a nine-member committee chaired by a former Legco member, Helmut Sohmen, was formed with the responsibility of reviewing the anti-graft agency's powers. The committee called for public submissions and also held public hearings to listen to opinions from citizens about the ICAC. In addition, the committee looked into the controversial Section 8(2) of the ICAC Ordinance that empowered the commissioner to dismiss staff members without giving any justification. The committee will publish a report including recommendations that will impinge on the post-1997 administration. If so, such a report should be sent to Mainland officials and members of the Preliminary Working Committee, who should study those recommendations that will undoubtedly address the issues of ICAC's powers and accountability.

Another political implication of the Tsui case for the ICAC was the danger that the highly secretive nature of the agency's work could be turned into a body that would deviate from its original objectives and functions. Tsui alleged that the ICAC's Technical Services Division, which designs and builds surveillance equipment for operational use, spied on some prominent Hong Kong people for Britain. According to Tsui, he shared the information gathered by a covert bugging operation about Rita Fan with the Special Branch, a secretive body which detects the political activities of the underground Chinese Communist Party and the Kuomintang, and which will be dissolved in 1995. So far, Tsui's claims cannot be substantiated.

In May 1994, it was disturbing to learn that the ICAC wanted to recruit some officers from the Special Branch to manage a unit that would check the integrity of top-level civil servants, and that from July onwards the ICAC would assume the vetting functions originally performed by the Special Branch. If integrity checks of senior civil servants involve the question of their political orientations or affiliations, such checks in practice constitute political vetting. Given the easily blurred borderline between integrity checks and political vetting, there are strong grounds for worrying that the ICAC may sooner or later perform some political functions.

Therefore, it is of utmost importance for the Patten administration to ensure that the ICAC's work should not go beyond its duty of combatting corruption. It is also questionable whether the ICAC should take over the Special Branch's responsibility of vetting senior civil servants. While government officials contend that the ICAC is the most suitable body to vet top civil servants, such vetting by the commission should be confined to the issue of corruption. Although the Patten administration pledges that no political element will be involved in the ICAC's vetting of top bureaucrats, and that it is against the law for the agency to investigate matters other than corruption, the very vague borderline between integrity checks and political screening is constantly played down. The government should realize the danger that integrity checks, if handled without self-restraint, could become investigatory activities unrelated to corruption.

Above all, such activities would have the far-reaching repercussion of transforming the agency into a secret police. Although Governor Patten maintained in May 1994 that the ICAC did not have any target lists and that it operated within the law, the ICAC should also critically review its own work and regularly put forward some constructive proposals that can prevent itself from being distorted or utilized by any post-1997 authorities for political motives.

In February 1994, the ICAC reportedly suggested the establishment of a system similar to the Legco's functional constituencies, allowing various community and professional groups to elect or nominate representatives to monitor the ICAC's work. This move was indeed a positive development as it at least demonstrated the willingness of the ICAC to subject itself to an institutionalized system of scrutiny.

The third political implication of the Tsui case for the ICAC was the agency's relationship with the Legco. Undeniably, the case gave an opportunity for the Legco to comprehend the ICAC's internal operations. During a closed session on 19 May 1994, the Legco's Security Panel screened a videotape of an interview conducted by Buckle on Tsui's questionable behaviour. After this meeting, the panel announced that it would summon Tsui's boss and friend, Buckle and Tin respectively, to give evidence in the Legco in June. These were unprecedented events signalling the ability of the legislature to check the ICAC's power. While the ICAC's public image was to some extent tarnished by Tsui's allegations, Tsui himself appeared to fail to prove that his dismissal had been due to racial and/or political grounds. Arguably, only the legislature became the beneficiary of the entire episode, because for the first time the traditionally secretive ICAC was subject to the Legco's scrutiny. Yet, one should not view this triumph of the Legco as a zero-sum game that jeopardized the ICAC's powers to combat corruption. The entire hearings had positive implications for the commission in the sense that it will be forced to be more cautious than ever before in exercising its powers from now to 1997.

The final political implication for the ICAC was the inevitability of instituting some checks on the power of the anti-corruption commissioner. Prior to the Legco's examination of the Tsui's case, the head of the ICAC had been answerable to the Governor only. The Tsui case raised a fundamental question whether it was justifiable for de Speville to dismiss Tsui without giving any reasons. Even if it was justifiable, de Speville could have actually pre-empted Tsui's action to publicize the issue by disclosing the reasons in the first place. Being an anti-graft colonial administrator who had not been trained to be accountable to the public, de Speville initially chose to keep the reasons secret, thus unnecessarily projecting a conservative image of the ICAC in an era which put heavy emphasis on the transparency of governmental operations.

Since Article 57 of the Basic Law states that the ICAC "shall function independently and be accountable to the Chief Executive," it is likely that the anti-corruption commissioner will remain powerful after 1997. In view of this and given that the post-1997 Chief Executive will be as powerful as the Governor under British rule, the current Hong Kong government must consider whether it should take the initiative to amend the existing ICAC Ordinance, making the commissioner accountable not simply to the Governor but also to other institutionalized bodies such as the Operations Review Committee and the legislature. Paradoxically, it can be anticipated that some critics of the government may maintain that such amendments would breach the Basic Law.

Regardless of any opposition to attempts at increasing the accountability of the anti-corruption commissioner, the ICAC's head should voluntarily account for his action to the public in the democratizing environment. On 24 January 1994, de Speville warned publicly that there was a point at which accountability would cease to become a "virtue." It was understandable that the anti-graft leader tended to put more emphasis on retaining the ICAC's powers than on strengthening its political accountability. But as Hong Kong's sovereignty will be returned to a motherland where political accountability is extremely deficient and where corruption is spreading like a disease, the current emphasis on the ICAC's accountability is actually a virtue. The crux of the problem is how to strike a balance between preserving the ICAC's powers on the one hand and enhancing its political accountability on the other.

☐ Problems and Prospects

The ICAC did take remedial action in response to the Alex Tsui affair. Apart from preparing proposals that can consolidate its accountability, the ICAC has also organized meetings of the Citizens Liaison Group, trying to improve its links with the public. Moreover, journalists have been invited to the ICAC for drinks and chats, trying to create a new image that the agency is not so secretive and inaccessible as conventional wisdom assumes. While these measures are worthwhile, ultimately the ICAC has to develop a more open and democratic style of operation externally and internally.

The problem of the ICAC is that as the society is liberalized and the polity democratized, its traditionally closed bureaucratic subculture becomes outdated. Top officials of the ICAC must learn how to cope with the increasingly politicized environment in which the Hong Kong government is encountering unprecedented criticisms from politicians and pressure groups. The ICAC is no exception to this phenomenon. Alex Tsui acted just like a politician who publicized and lobbied against his dismissal, while the ICAC initially reacted like a conservative-minded colonial machinery which lacked adequate political acumen and finesse in dealing with outside criticisms. In the Alex Tsui case, the ICAC could be seen as a victim of Section 8(2) of its Ordinance, which had been absolutely necessary during the 1970s but which has to be urgently revised in the 1990s. While managerial, legal and political reforms are indispensable to rejuvenate the ICAC, its leaders must realize the ordeal of behaving publicly like politicians defending and promoting their policies skilfully while at the same time remaining as bureaucrats fighting corruption effectively. In addition to managerial, legal and political reforms, there must be a fundamental change in the administrative culture of ICAC leaders.

Another problem for the ICAC is the China factor. Although the Patten administration seems to have the political will to make the ICAC more open and accountable than ever before, it is crucial for Mainland officials to realize the necessity and urgency of reforming the ICAC. Such reforms should not be perceived as sinister moves made by the British to perpetuate its influence in Hong Kong after 1997. What the Patten administration should do is to communicate and discuss with Chinese officials about the recommendations which will be suggested by the nine-member committee reviewing the ICAC's powers. It is crucial that any reform enhancing the ICAC's accountability but retaining its power to curb corruption effectively will have the blessing of China.

In the final analysis, the Hong Kong government should explain in detail to P.R.C. officials why reforms of the ICAC should be allowed to survive in the post-1997 period. So long as some Chinese officials do not fully understand the logic behind such reforms, there is a likelihood that the ICAC would probably abuse its power after 1997. One day after Tsui alleged that the ICAC collected intelligence about local politicians, Zhang Junsheng, the vice-director of the New China News Agency in Hong Kong, went so far as to state that Britain should hand over everything in Hong Kong to China in 1997. Zhang's response to Tsui's allegation was disturbing. Instead of criticizing the British for using the ICAC for political purposes, he tended to accept the ICAC's role in collecting intelligence about local politicians. In the event that the post-1997 authorities view intelligence gathering as a priority over fighting corruption, the prospects of the ICAC would be gloomy.

Ultimately, reforming the ICAC remains a political issue. Without the support of China, any effort to make the ICAC more accountable to the public may be fruitless. It is hoped that the pro-Beijing or nationalistic Hong Kong people, Mainland officials, and the post-1997 Hong Kong authorities can fully understand the managerial, legal and political implications of the Alex Tsui incident, and that they will realize the importance of striking a balance between maintaining the ICAC's powers to fight corruption and increasing its accountability to the public.

4

Civil Servants

Jane C. Y. Lee

☐ Introduction

Senior civil servants are caught in a dilemma between accountability and autonomy. This is the finding of a recent survey conducted in 1993 with a group of 1,066 directorate grade officers, the most senior-level staff in the Hong Kong government. They are in the process of adjustment towards greater public accountability, at the same time they wish to retain as much autonomy as they used to have in former colonial days.

Civil servants are an important group of political actors in Hong Kong's "executive-dominated" system, who perform both policy-making and policy-implementation functions. In the top-level posts, such as Secretaries and Deputy Secretaries, senior civil servants are responsible for policy formulation and resource allocation. They are a very powerful group in the political elite.

Senior civil servants are the most intelligent and distinguished class of employees promoted from within the bureaucratic hierarchy. They are trained to adhere strictly to regulations and to be efficient in the performance of administrative tasks. They are also trained to orient themselves towards making decisions rationally, impartially and objectively. By doing so they claim to protect "public interests" rather than promote "political interests."[1] By keeping themselves aloof from political controversies, they

---

Jane C. Y. Lee is Director of Burson-Marsteller Hong Kong.

[1] Jane C. Y. Lee and J. Lam, "The Changing Public Administration Issues in Hong Kong's Transition," *Teaching Public Administration*, Vol. XII, No. 1 (Spring 1992), p. 46.

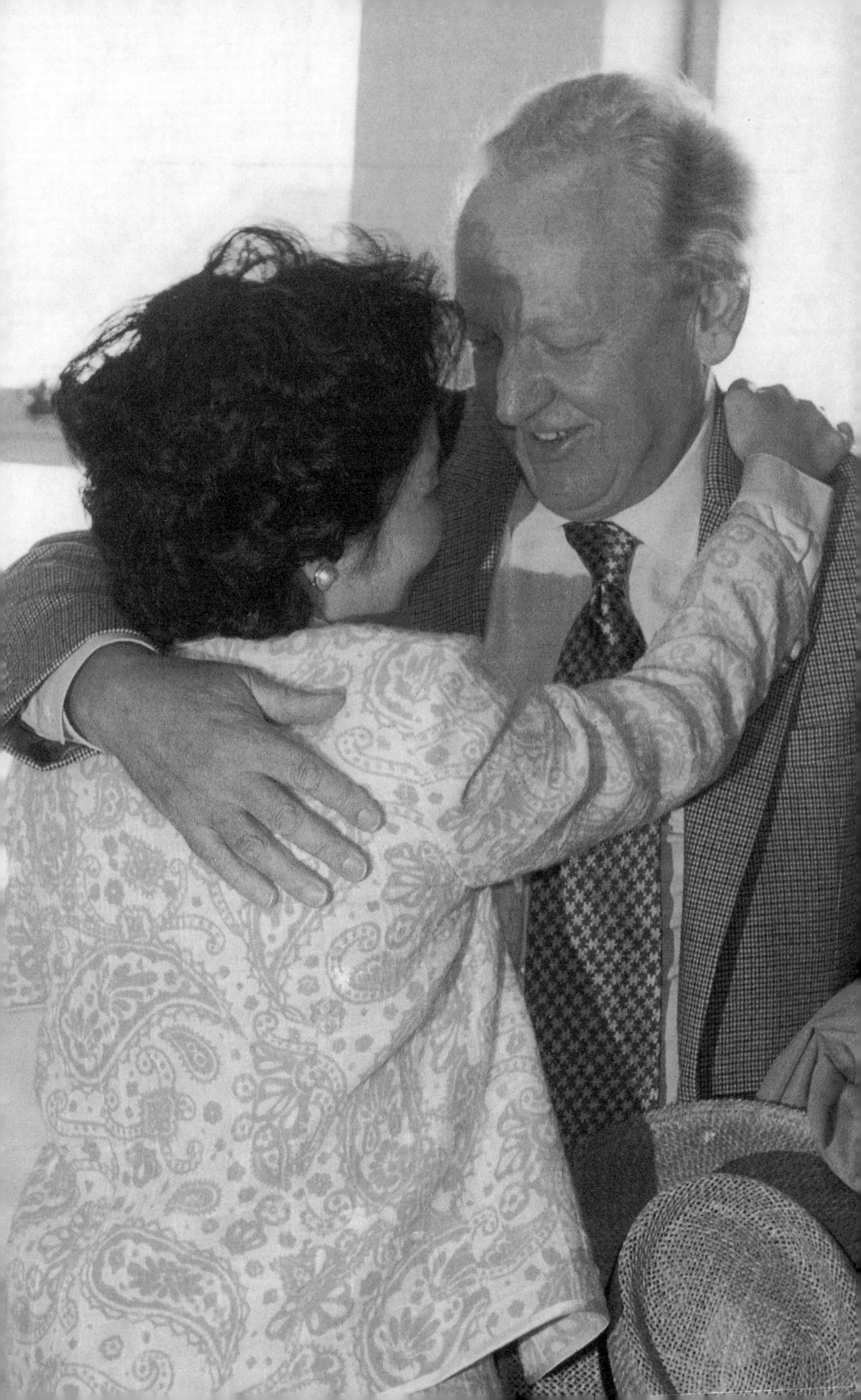

strive to remain autonomous of public pressures. According to the colonial constitution, civil servants are only accountable to their immediate superior, the British-appointed Governor. Structurally, they are not required to be held accountable to an elected legislature or to the general public.

The superior position of civil servants has been under serious challenge during the last phase of the political transition. The activity of civil servants is now vigorously monitored by a partially directly elected Legislative Council (Legco). The government, no matter how reluctant, has to accept greater interference by the legislators in policy-making. Moreover, the Chinese authorities have begun to exert political pressures from above. Hong Kong officials are expected to ultimately comply with commands of the Central People's Government in Beijing. According to the Basic Law, the government of the future Hong Kong Special Administrative Region (SAR) will be accountable to the Legco (Article 64), while the head of the government, the Chief Executive, will be accountable to the Central People's Government (Article 43). Civil servants are thus required to serve inherently two political masters.

Two sets of important questions are to be answered here. First, what should be the relationship between senior civil servants and politicians elected to the Legco? Should senior civil servants retain control over policy decisions or devolve policy-making power to the elected politicians? Second, what should be the relationship between civil servants and the Central People's Government in Beijing? To whom should civil servants be held accountable — the elected politicians in the Legco (and by implication, the people of Hong Kong), or to the future sovereign master, China? In case there is a conflict of interests between Hong Kong and China, whose interests should Hong Kong civil servants first consider?

The discussion here first will focus on the findings of the survey, analysing how these directorate-level civil servants react to the challenges of the Legco and the Chinese authorities. It also discusses how these senior officials adjust themselves to the changed political environment. The second part of the chapter will consider the problems of localization of the twenty-two most senior-level posts within the civil service.

The survey of the directorate grade officers was conducted in two stages. In the first stage, a series of in-depth interviews was arranged between March and August 1993 with fifteen directorate grade officials. The second stage of study was conducted in the form of a mailed survey in October to November 1993. The purpose of using a mailed survey was to ensure that respondents were not identifiable. Given the sensitiveness of the questions being asked, respondents felt more secure in answering a questionnaire that better protected their anonymity. Finally, 608 respondents returned the questionnaire, constituting a completed response rate of 57 per cent.[2]

☐ Relationship with the Legislative Council

The survey revealed that the directorate grade officers have become more open and responsive with the progress of representative government, especially after the introduction of direct elections to the Legco in 1991. A majority of the respondents (59.9 per cent) agreed that they should be held accountable to the Legco (see Table 1). Senior civil servants admitted that they were held accountable to the Legco from a practical point of view. The government is bound by procedural mechanisms to be responsive to the opinions of the Legco because any policy ultimately has to be debated and approved by the Legco in the form of either a bill or financial request.

Table 1. Perception of Directorate Grade Officers towards Accountability to the Legco

Answers	Per cent
a. Should be accountable to the Legco	59.9
b. Should not be accountable to the Legco	24.0
c. Not sure	16.1
Total	100.0

Senior civil servants are prepared to openly explain and argue for their policy and decision, as well as to lobby for the support of the legislators on major policy issues. When asked how they would react to the challenge of a legislator, a majority of respondents (72.1 per cent) answered that "I am prepared to openly defend my decision" (see Table 2). Respondents were also asked: "If you perceive a policy which is not quite likely supported by a clear majority of the Legco, what will you do?" A total of 57.6 per cent

---

[2] The data in this chapter is based on a research report by Joseph Y. S. Cheng and Jane C. Y. Lee, *A Study of the Bureaucrat-Politician Relationships in Hong Kong's Transition* (Hong Kong: City Polytechnic of Hong Kong, February 1994).

Table 2. Reaction of Directorate Grade Officers towards the Challenges of the Legco

Answers	Per cent
a. Would remain quiet	1.5
b. Would be prepared to rebuke the criticism	9.0
c. Would be prepared to openly defend my decision	72.1
d. Would compromise the decision taking into consideration of the view of the Legco	6.7
e. Would demand the resignation from the Legco member	0.7
f. Others	5.8
g. Multiple answers	4.2
Total	100.0

answered that they would "try to win the support of the Legco through persuasion," while only 2.9 per cent said that they would implement that policy in disregard of the feelings of the Legco (see Table 3).

Nevertheless, political accountability in Hong Kong neither operates in the form of parliamentary democracy as in the case of the United Kingdom nor legislative policy-making as in the case of the United States. Senior civil servants are prepared to accept increased monitoring and supervisory powers exercised by the legislators who ultimately have the right to pass or veto government bills and budgets. But they are not prepared to devolve

Table 3. Attitude of Directorate Grade Officers towards Policy Which Is Not Likely to Be Supported by a Clear Majority of the Legco

Answers	Per cent
a. Will try to win the support of the Legco through persuasion	57.6
b. Will not put forward the proposal to the Legco for voting	6.2
c. Will let the Legco discuss and cast votes on it	16.8
d. Will implement the policy decision in disregard of the feelings of the Legco	2.9
e. Will try to get the support of the media	4.9
f. Others	4.0
g. Multiple answers	7.6
Total	100.0

policy-making power to the legislators. When asked who should decide on the major policies of the Hong Kong government, a majority of the respondents considered that the Governor-in-Council (64.7 per cent) and senior government officials (16.2 per cent) should be policy-makers. Only a minority believed that policy-making power should be vested with the legislators (22.5 per cent) or the citizens (8.2 per cent) (see Table 4).

Table 4. Perception of Who Should Decide on Major Policies of the Hong Kong Government before 1997

Answers	Per cent
a. Governor-in-Council	64.7
b. Senior government officials	16.2
c. Legco	22.5
d. Citizens	8.2
e. Chinese government	6.3
f. Others	1.0

Some tensions with the Legco inevitably emerge in this process of adjusting to political change. Tensions relate to the fact that the government has the responsibility and power, but is in need of a demonstration of public support. On the other hand, the legislators symbolize public support but often have very limited responsibility and power. Senior civil servants often have to sell policies to the legislators, but still encounter strong opposition and criticism from one group or another. Consequently, directorate grade officers give a fairly negative evaluation of the legislators. In the mailed survey, 40.1 per cent of the respondents thought that the Legco was "fairly unrepresentative" of the interests of the Hong Kong people and 7.1 per cent indicated "not representative at all" (see Table 5). Moreover 47.7 per cent of them felt "fairly dissatisfied" with the performance of the Legco, while 9.8 per cent considered "very dissatisfied" (see Table 6). When asked to make a judgement about the Legco in general, a majority of them (54.7 per cent) thought that it was "too politicized"; another 23.7 per cent felt that it was "immature" (see Table 7). The data indicates that only a minority of senior civil servants were supporters of open government and democracy. Most of the others, however, considered that comments of the legislators were unreasonable and outrageous, thus feeling that politicians were incompetent, senseless, and sometimes even against the public interest. These civil servants believed that too much criticism was harmful to the

Table 5. Perception of Legislative Representativeness

Answers	Per cent
a. Very representative	0.8
b. Fairly representative	46.9
c. Fairly unrepresentative	40.1
d. Not representative at all	7.1
e. Not sure	5.1
Total	100.0

Table 6. Evaluation of Legislative Performance

Answers	Per cent
a. Very satisfied	0.3
b. Fairly satisfied	37.9
c. Fairly dissatisfied	47.7
d. Very dissatisfied	9.8
e. Not sure	4.3
Total	100.0

Table 7. Comments on the Legislative Council

Answers	Per cent
a. A more democratic and open process	17.6
b. Too politicized	54.7
c. Immature	23.7
d. Others	25.1

efficacy of the governing process. So, in the mailed survey, when respondents were asked to prioritize the basis of the government's legitimacy, a majority of them gave higher priority to "economic performance" and "political stability," but assigned the lowest priority to "popular elections" (see Table 8).

There are conflicting feelings among senior civil servants. The new Governor, Christopher Patten, requires civil servants to "establish more

Table 8. Perception of the Basis of Legitimacy of the Hong Kong Government

Answers	High priority (Per cent)	Low priority (Per cent)
a. Good economic performance	93.1	6.9
b. Stable and non-violent	91.6	8.4
c. Clean and incorrupt	83.7	16.3
d. Comprehensive welfare	22.5	77.5
e. Popular elections	7.4	92.6

creative dialogue" with the Legco,[3] that is to ensure that the government wins the support of the Legco rather than push through unpopular policies. But the legislators are exercising nothing more than a supervisory function. Senior civil servants remain a group of fairly independent political masters who ultimately make final decisions. On many occasions senior officials reiterated their neutrality and impartiality in politics, implying that they would not succumb to pressures from the legislators. An example of this was the government's insistence on increasing property tax in 1994. The government refused to make concessions even when dominant parties in the Legco joined forces to oppose the bill.

China's attitude further discourages senior civil servants from orienting towards greater accountability to the Legco. According to Article 62(1) of the Basic Law, the SAR government, rather than the Legco, would remain responsible for policy formulation, with a Chinese-appointed Chief Executive being responsible for policy-making. China's position is to refuse recognizing the Legco as a representative body, implying that the Chinese government will not let the Council become a major partner in policy-making after 1997. Inevitably, senior civil servants cast doubt on devolving political power to the elected legislators.[4]

---

[3] *Our Next Five Years: The Agenda for Hong Kong* (Address by the Governor, The Right Honourable Christopher Patten at the opening of the 1992–1993 Session of the Legislative Council, 7 October 1992), pp. 34–35.

[4] See Joseph Y. S. Cheng and Jane C. Y. Lee, *A Study of the Bureaucrat-Politician Relationships in Hong Kong's Transition* (Hong Kong: City Polytechnic of Hong Kong, February 1994), pp. 32–33.

Civil Servants

Senior civil servants have had a strong sense of efficacy and superiority. But they are not confident of preserving the existing political authority which they are enjoying. Chinese authorities will become the future political master after 1997. As the following data shall reveal, civil servants are afraid that both the selection of personnel and major policies of the Hong Kong government will be largely controlled by the Chinese authorities in Beijing. The China factor inevitably creates a sense of impotence among the directorate grade officials.

☐ Relationship with China

Senior civil servants are afraid that Chinese officials would exert control over the internal affairs of Hong Kong. When asked in the survey whether or not they were "worried about the involvement of Chinese officials in Hong Kong's policies before and after 1997," 46.9 per cent indicated that they were "fairly worried" and 21.2 per cent said "very worried" (see Table 9). Moreover, 42.3 per cent of the respondents considered that "the Chinese government would become dominant over the major policies in Hong Kong after 1997." Only 6.5 per cent thought that senior civil servants would still remain dominant in policy-making (see Table 10). Such a perception differed sharply from their belief that the Governor and senior civil servants should dominate policy-making.

The data reveals that senior civil servants in Hong Kong do not accept the interference of the Chinese government to the same degree as they accept those of the legislators. A total of 71.8 per cent considered that they

Table 9. Worries of Directorate Grade Officers about the Involvement of Chinese Government Officials in Hong Kong's Major Policies

Answers	Per cent
a. Very worried	21.2
b. Fairly worried	46.9
c. Fairly unworried	21.4
d. Not worried at all	7.5
e. Not sure	2.5
f. Multiple answers	0.5
Total	100.0

Table 10. Perception of Who Would Decide on Major Policies of the Hong Kong Government after 1997

Answers	Per cent
a. Chief Executive	29.3
b. Senior government officers	6.5
c. Legco	11.0
d. Citizens	3.3
e. Chinese government	42.3
f. Others	1.8
g. Multiple answers	5.8
Total	100.0

should not be held accountable to China. Only a minority, 17.1 per cent, agreed so (see Table 11). When asked in what ways should the Hong Kong government be held accountable to the Chinese government after 1997, merely 4.7 per cent said "no way." A majority of them (70.6 per cent), however, believed that accountability to Central People's Government should only be limited to regularly reporting and explaining its policy (see Table 12). A directorate officer, for example, said in an interview that there should only be a very minimum accountability relationship between Hong Kong and the Central People's Government. He favoured to use the word "consultation" which has been stipulated in both the Sino-British Joint Declaration of 1984 as well as the Sino-British Memorandum of Understanding of 1991. He said, "Consultation is consultation. It does not mean that they have a veto." Another officer preferred to use the words "communication and dialogue" because it referred to maintaining a good

Table 11. Perception of Directorate Grade Officers about Political Accountability to China

Answers	Per cent
a. Should be accountable to China	17.1
b. Should not be accountable to China	71.8
c. Not sure	11.1
Total	100.0

Table 12. Perception of the Directorate Grade Officers about the Ways in Which the Hong Kong Government Should Be Held Accountable to the Chinese Government after 1997

Answers	Per cent
a. No way	4.7
b. Senior Hong Kong officials could be removed by the Chinese government	7.1
c. Hong Kong government regularly reports the progress of major policies to the Chinese government	50.9
d. Hong Kong government regularly reports and explains its policies to the Chinese government	70.6
e. Government policies should be endorsed by the Chinese government before being discussed in the Legco	8.0
f. Behaviour of Hong Kong officials should be supervised by the Chinese government	4.1
g. Others	4.2

working relationship with the central authorities in Beijing without being subservient to their commands. Hence the survey revealed that a significant proportion of the directorate grade officers either disagreed (38.5 per cent) or strongly disagreed (12.4 per cent) with the view that "decisions of the Chinese government leaders could override those of the Hong Kong government" (see Table 13).

The practical concern of the senior management is whether the existing administration can retain public confidence and govern the territory effectively before the transfer of power in 1997. The Governor insisted that the

Table 13. Perception of Directorate Grade Officers about the Statement: "Decisions of the Chinese Government Leaders Could Override Those of the Hong Kong Government"

Answers	Per cent
a. Strongly agree	6.9
b. Agree	35.1
c. Disagree	38.5
d. Strongly disagree	12.4
e. Not sure	7.1
Total	100.0

Hong Kong government should have full internal autonomy to decide on its full domestic policies, at least before 1997. The British government, however, failed to settle important issues like airport financing after having consulted the Chinese side a few times since 1992–1993. When China is being consulted, its "approval" is a significant indicator of "friendly dialogue and useful communication" in Sino-Hong Kong relations. China's increased participation in Hong Kong's domestic affairs not only generates a sense of distrust in the community towards the existing administration, but also arouses scepticism among its own staff within the civil service. Thus, when asked in the mailed survey whether or not they were worried about "Beijing governing Hong Kong," 25.3 per cent answered that they were "very worried" while 42.4 per cent replied "fairly worried" (see Table 14).

Table 14. Worries of Directorate Grade Officers about "Beijing Governing Hong Kong People" after 1997

Answers	Per cent
a. Very worried	25.3
b. Fairly worried	42.4
c. Fairly unworried	22.1
d. Not worried at all	7.7
e. Not sure	2.5
Total	100.0

The survey data reveals that directorate grade officers prefer to maintain autonomy in policy-making. They are annoyed by the interference of both the partially elected Legco as well as Chinese authorities. Their resentment is a result partly of their bureaucratic training and culture, and partly of their reluctance to open up the government process to allow greater public participation. Their resentment is also very much related to concerns about their own career in the future. In the survey, 12.9 per cent indicated they were "very worried" about their career in the civil service after 1997, while another 23.9 per cent said they were "fairly worried" (see Table 15).

Early retirement and resignation from the civil service are the methods by which senior civil servants express their resentment towards the changed

Table 15. Worries of Directorate Grade Officers about Their Career in the Civil Service after 1997

Answers	Per cent
a. Very worried	12.9
b. Fairly worried	23.9
c. Fairly unworried	25.5
d. Not worried at all	33.1
e. Not sure	4.6
Total	100.0

political environment.[5] The survey found that 64.3 per cent of the directorate grade officers held British passports; 38.9 per cent of these said that they would not remain in the civil service after 1997 and 27.7 per cent of them were undecided. Another 10.9 per cent held other foreign passports, with 40 per cent of these saying that they would not remain in the civil service after 1997 (see Table 16). Altogether 39.8 per cent of the respondents were aged 51–60 and a large proportion of these answered that they would not stay in the civil service after 1997. The remaining group of directorate grade officers was between the age of 31–50, but 30 to 40 per cent of those in these age groups, however, were undecided whether or not they would remain in the civil service after 1997 (see Table 17). This information is likely to arouse a general worry in the community about the lack of qualified local candidates to take up the top-level posts reserved for "Chinese nationals." As 1997 approaches, the practical problem confronting the Hong Kong government is whether there will be an adequate number of experienced personnel to fill the posts at principal official levels in future. This issue is closely related to controversies over localization.

☐ Localization

Principal officials of the future Hong Kong SAR must suit the requirements

---

[5] See *Ming Pao*, 11 July 1994, p. 11 and *Hong Kong Economic Journal*, 11 July 1994, p. 25. It has been reported that in the two years between 1993–1995, twenty-six senior government officials have left the civil service before reaching the normal retirement age.

Table 16. Perception of Directorate Grade Officers about Remaining in the Civil Service after 1997: By Nationality

Nationality	Per cent who chose the answer			Total
	Yes	No	Undecided	
BDTC/BNO	50.4	21.5	28.1	22.7
British	33.4	38.9	27.7	64.3
Others	23.1	40.0	36.9	10.9
Invalid	46.2	23.0	30.8	2.1
Total	36.4	34.7	28.9	100.0

Table 17. Perception of Directorate Grade Officers about Remaining in the Civil Service after 1997: By Age Group

Age group	Per cent who chose the answer			Total
	Yes	No	Undecided	
31–35	40.0	20.0	40.0	0.8
36–40	54.8	9.5	35.7	7.4
41–45	52.8	18.1	29.1	21.7
46–50	43.8	18.6	37.6	30.3
51–55	23.6	49.0	27.4	27.1
56–60	5.6	90.2	4.2	12.7
Total	36.4	34.7	28.9	100.0

of the Basic Law. Article 61 of the Basic Law defines principal officials as "Chinese citizens who are permanent residents of the [Special Administrative] Region with no right of abode in any foreign country and have ordinarily resided in Hong Kong for a continuous period of not less than 15 years." The Basic Law has clearly stipulated that principal officials have to be Chinese citizens, permanent residents of Hong Kong and having no right of abode in other countries. The Chinese officials seem to give more emphasis to the criteria of ethnic origin, citizenship and nationality. These three criteria, however, do not exist in the Civil Service Regulations of the Hong Kong government.

There are only two terms of appointment in the Hong Kong civil service, namely local and expatriate. Under Civil Service Regulations, a person is employed on expatriate terms if he/she is not habitually resident in Hong Kong, Macau, China or Taiwan; he/she has his/her general background or social ties somewhere other than Hong Kong, Macau, China or Taiwan, and if appointed on local conditions of service, he/she would suffer a material degree of dislocation and uprooting. All expatriate staff are entitled to accommodation provided by the government, longer annual leave, and free passage to and from their home country. The government admits that 90 per cent of the expatriates are Anglo-Saxons in origin, who are predominantly from the United Kingdom, Ireland, Australia, Canada and New Zealand.[6] But there are specific cases whereby some ethnic Chinese are on expatriate terms, and some non-ethnic Chinese (mainly Indians, Pakistanis and Portuguese born in Hong Kong) are on local terms. By early 1994, expatriate staff only constituted about 1.2 per cent of the 190,000-strong civil service establishment. Yet most of these expatriate staff were occupying senior posts at Point 45 or above on the Civil Service Master Pay Scale. Therefore the major concern for localization in the Hong Kong civil service is to prepare senior "local" staff for the transfer of sovereignty who suit requirements of principal official levels as stipulated in the Basic Law. Nevertheless, the government argues that the objective of the localization policy should aim to standardize all existing conditions of service into one set of local terms. In other words, ethnic origins, citizenship or nationality are not the rationale for localization. The government also claims that a local officer will not be given credits for his local status in a promotion exercise. Promotion criteria are to be based on qualification, experience and character rather than terms of appointment.[7]

Localization in the civil service has attracted much public attention since July 1993. Before 28 March 1985, overseas officers were given a choice of selecting expatriate or local terms (generally known as permanent and pensionable [P&P] terms of appointment). Expatriates were then given an opportunity to apply for switching to permanent and pensionable terms. The success of such an application, however, depended on whether a local replacement was available. After March 1985, all overseas

---

[6] Gilbert Mo, "The Localization Policy of the Hong Kong Government: A Practitioner's Viewpoint," paper presented to an International Conference: "The Quest for Excellence: Public Administration in the Nineties" (Hong Kong: City Polytechnic of Hong Kong and Hong Kong Public Administration Association, February 1994).

[7] Ibid.

appointments have been on a contract basis. The government assumed that overseas contractual officers accepted appointment on the understanding that if a local staff was available to replace him/her, their contracts would not be renewed. This assumption was however subject to intensive attacks, particularly from the Association of Expatriate Civil Servants, which represented the interests of overseas employees.

With the enactment of the Bill of Rights in 1991, the debate became more vigorous. The Association of Expatriate Civil Servants threatened that if they were forbidden to apply for a change to local terms, they might sue the government for violating their rights to have equal access to the public service of Hong Kong. The Hong Kong government believed that it would lose the case in a law suit. Consequently, the then Secretary for the Civil Service, Anson Chan, announced in July 1993 an arrangement to allow contractual staff, who have obtained a British Dependent Territories Citizens (BDTC) or who have resided in Hong Kong for more than seven years, to apply for switching to local terms of appointment for one more contract period.[8] Conditions for satisfying contract renewal, including service need, satisfactory conduct, and performance and physical fitness, also applied. From the government's point of view, the new policy did not impose new requirements other than naturalization as BDTC.

The announcement of the new policy aroused strong protests from local staff, who criticized the government as demoralizing the "local" Chinese. The government was confronted with very strong opposition from the Senior Non-expatriate Officers Association. Consequently, a private member's bill was moved by the Convener of the Legislative Council Public Service Panel, Tam Yiu-chung, in December 1993. The bill was passed by the Legco as Public Officers (Variation of Conditions of Service) (Temporary Provisions) Ordinance which served to freeze temporarily the government's new localization policy. Meanwhile the government published a consultation document on "Civil Service Terms of Appointment and Conditions of Service," clarifying that the government would aim to introduce only one set of new terms of appointment and conditions of service. The Ordinance was a compromise which temporarily preserved the status quo and allowed a short period of time to work out more acceptable solutions to these problems.

---

[8] *South China Morning Post*, 8 August 1993, p. 11.

The controversies of 1993–1994 show that the Hong Kong government hopes to define the meaning of "local" based on the requirement of permanent residence rather than ethnic origin. Article 24 of the Basic Law specifies that permanent residents include Chinese citizens born in Hong Kong who ordinarily have resided in Hong Kong for a continuous period of not less than seven years, or persons of non-Chinese nationality who have been born in Hong Kong or have resided in Hong Kong for a continuous period of not less than seven years. Such definition, however, does not resolve the basic issue. Some local officers may have satisfied the criteria of permanent residents of the Basic Law, but they may still be disqualified to become principal officials of the SAR government. The Secretary for Transport, Haider Barma, is an example. He is a third generation Hong Kong-born Indian who has been brought up in Hong Kong and has been working in the civil service for more than twenty-eight years on local terms. Although he has fulfilled all the requirements as a permanent resident in Hong Kong, he is not an ethnic Chinese. The case of Barma suggests that even though the Hong Kong government has standardized the terms of appointment, its policy on localization may not necessarily satisfy the requirements of the Basic Law. By 1994, 34.9 per cent of the directorate grade posts are still occupied by expatriate staff. The Hong Kong government has to promote more ethnic Chinese to the top principal official levels from within the bureaucracy.

Article 101 of the Basic Law specifies that principal official posts must be filled only by "Chinese citizens among permanent residents of the [Special Administrative] Region with no right of abode in any foreign country." Since 1993, the Governor has made important steps to "localize" two most important posts. In July 1993, Anson Chan, aged 54, replaced Barrie Wiggham as the Secretary for the Civil Service. She then was promoted in November to replace Sir David Ford as the first Chinese Chief Secretary. Her vacancy in the Civil Service Branch was filled by Michael Sze, aged 49, in February 1994. Michael Sze immediately took initiatives to identify the twenty-two most senior level Secretary posts for localization. These posts included the Chief Secretary, Financial Secretary, Attorney General, fourteen Policy Secretaries, Director of Audit, Commissioner of the Independent Commission Against Corruption (ICAC), Commissioner of Police, Director of Immigration, and Commissioner of Customs and Excise. As of July 1994, twelve of these twenty-two top posts have been filled by ethnic Chinese. Three expatriate staff, including Elizabeth Wong, Secretary for Health and Welfare, were scheduled to retire at age 57. Others like, Michael Cartland, Secretary for Financial Services, and Alistair Asprey, Secretary for Security, would be compensated for early retirement in 1995 (see Table 18). The posts of Financial Secretary and Attorney General were also expected to be replaced by "locals" before 1996. In the same month, Michael Sze took a further step, specifying that the number of expatriate Administrative Officers ranking immediately below Secretary level, i.e. at Staff Grades A and B1, would be limited to two and four respectively. In other words, the existing Staff Grade B and B1 expatriate Administrative Officers would not be further promoted from their existing rank. Moreover, these expatriate staff would be allowed to switch to local terms only if they accepted demotion. By July 1994, expatriate staff still criticized the government's policy for violating human rights. Yet their protests were much less effective. The legislators now supported the government's policy as an acceptable compromise.

Most importantly, the success of any future arrangements would require the support of the Chinese government. Under the atmosphere in which Britain and China distrust each other, the two powers have not been able to arrive at any agreements on the definitions of "local." There have also been no concrete agreements between the British and Chinese governments regarding the appointment of principal officials in the 1997 handover. After Michael Sze became Secretary for the Civil Service, he actively addressed on a number of occasions the issue of localization. He openly suggested that the Hong Kong government would make efforts to arrive at consensus with the Chinese side on this matter. Sze, however, emphasized that negotiations with China would not mean obtaining endorsement of the Chinese side on specific appointments.[9]

The Chinese side did not feel satisfied with all these arrangements unilaterally planned by the Hong Kong government. First, Chinese officials criticized the Hong Kong government for not allowing civil servants to have direct communication with Chinese officials and the Chinese-appointed Preliminary Working Committee (PWC). Chinese officials therefore argued that the British side did not genuinely intend to bring about discussion on the matter. Second, Chinese officials argued that the future Chief Executive, rather than the existing British Hong Kong officials, would appoint the future principal officials of the Hong Kong SAR

---

[9] *Hong Kong Economic Journal*, 9 February 1994, p. 8.

Table 18. The Top 22 Principal Official Level Posts in the
Hong Kong Civil Service as of July 1994

Post	Name	Age	Years of service
1. Chief Secretary	Anson Chan	54	32
2. Financial Secretary	Hamish Macleod	54	28
3. Attorney General	Jeremy Mathews	52	26
4. Secretary for the Civil Service	Michael Sze	49	25
5. Secretary for Constitutional Affairs	Nicholas Ng	48	24
6. Secretary for Economic Services	Gordon Siu	49	28
7. Secretary for Education and Manpower	Michael Leung	56	29
8. Secretary for Financial Services	Michael D. Cartland (to retire in 1995)	49	22
9. Secretary for Health and Welfare	Elizabeth Wong (to retire in September 1994 and be replaced by Fok Lo Shiu-ching, present Commissioner of Labour)	57	25
10. Secretary for Home Affairs	Michael Suen	50	28
11. Secretary for Planning, Environment and Lands	Anthony G. Eason (to retire in 1995)	56	2
12. Secretary for Recreation and Culture	James So	54	32
13. Secretary for Security	Alistair Asprey (to retire in 1995)	50	29
14. Secretary for Trade and Industry	Tak-hay Chau	51	27
15. Secretary for Transport	Haider Barma	50	28
16. Secretary for the Treasury	Donald Tsang	50	27
17. Secretary for Works	Ronald James Blake (extended until September 1995)	60	3
18. Commissioner of Police	Ki-on Hui	51	31
19. Commissioner of the ICAC	Bertrand de Speville	53	13
20. Director of Audit	Brian G. Jenney	59	25
21. Director of Immigration	Ming-yin Leung	53	29
22. Commissioner of Customs and Excise	Donald McFarlane Watson	54	20

Sources: *Staff List: Hong Kong Government* and *Staff Biographies: Hong Kong Government*, various years.

government. They therefore criticized the existing Hong Kong government for establishing a *fait accompli* before 1997. The pro-China media speculated that all these moves were intended to extend British colonial influence in the post-1997 government. After all, the Chinese government is sceptical about the British Nationality Scheme which qualifies the senior staff with long period of service in the Hong Kong government for British passports. The survey on directorate grade officers, for example, has revealed that by 1993, 64.3 per cent of the respondents held British passports. Members of the PWC Political Sub-group therefore suggested in its meeting of 29–30 March 1994 that civil servants should register before 1997 whether they intend to stay in the civil service after 1997. Such a proposal was, however, criticized by major political parties in Hong Kong as a means of political veting. The Hong Kong government also commented that this was further demoralizing to the civil servants.

Some tensions have been developing within the civil service on the matter of localization. While the Chinese side and some Hong Kong non-expatriate civil service unions saw it as a "sinification" process,[10] the Hong Kong government argued it on the ground of standardizing all appointments into local terms. Both the British and Chinese governments claimed to recognize the need to have dialogue with each other. Nevertheless, the stance of both sides remained harsh. The Chinese side has been developing the PWC as a "shadow" preparatory government. The British side, however, refused to recognize the legality of the PWC. Civil servants would like to see the Hong Kong government preserving its autonomy. Yet they were increasingly uncertain whether their existing appointment would be terminated by China after 1997. They were also ambivalent in their attitude towards the hard-line approach of the British government which was portrayed as a fight to preserve Hong Kong's autonomy and effective rule.

The controversy over localization policy is an example which reflects civil servants' dilemma over autonomy and accountability to the Chinese government. Senior bureaucrats want to protect their vested interests and preserve localization policy as an area of their internal autonomy, but the Hong Kong government is unable to resolve the matter unilaterally without

---

[10] Sonny S. H. Lo, "Localization in Hong Kong and Macau," paper presented to an International Conference: "The Quest for Excellence: Public Administration in the Nineties" (Hong Kong: City Polytechnic of Hong Kong and Hong Kong Public Administration Association, February 1994).

the consent of the Chinese authorities. In the remaining three years, the Hong Kong government needs to develop a working relationship with the future sovereign master, China. Otherwise, senior civil servants will not be able to retain as much internal autonomy as they would like to have. The stability of the civil service system will also be disrupted by the new requirements imposed by the future SAR government leaders.

☐ Conclusion

Hong Kong senior civil servants are policy-makers in an executive-dominated political system. Yet they are increasingly much less capable of doing their job because their positions are challenged by members of an elected Legco as well as officials of the Chinese Central People's Government. The strategy of senior management in the Hong Kong government is to encourage its staff to orient towards greater public accountability, at the same time they claim to retain as much autonomy and control as they previously had. This attempt is partly a response to public demands for attaining a "high degree of autonomy" in the post-1997 SAR government. It also partly reflects a subconsciousness to protect the vested interests of the existing bureaucrats, both expatriates and locals. China's increased involvement in Hong Kong's domestic affairs, however, discourages the process of developing more political accountability and autonomy. Consequently, the attitude of senior civil servants is inconsistent. They want to have a high degree of autonomy with minimum interference from China as well as the Legco. Such an attitude is, however, contrary to their self-proclaimed objective of achieving a more open and accountable government.

Both the elected politicians and the Chinese officials serve to undermine the autonomy civil servants have previously enjoyed. Senior civil servants are losing the confidence which they once developed in their training. The process is frustrating for the ruling elite who have been dominating in the political system for decades. Senior civil servants are in a dilemma between autonomy and accountability. After all they are "servants" as well as "masters" of Hong Kong society. Their continued commitment to good public service is, nonetheless, the key to maintaining the confidence of the general citizenry towards the political system.

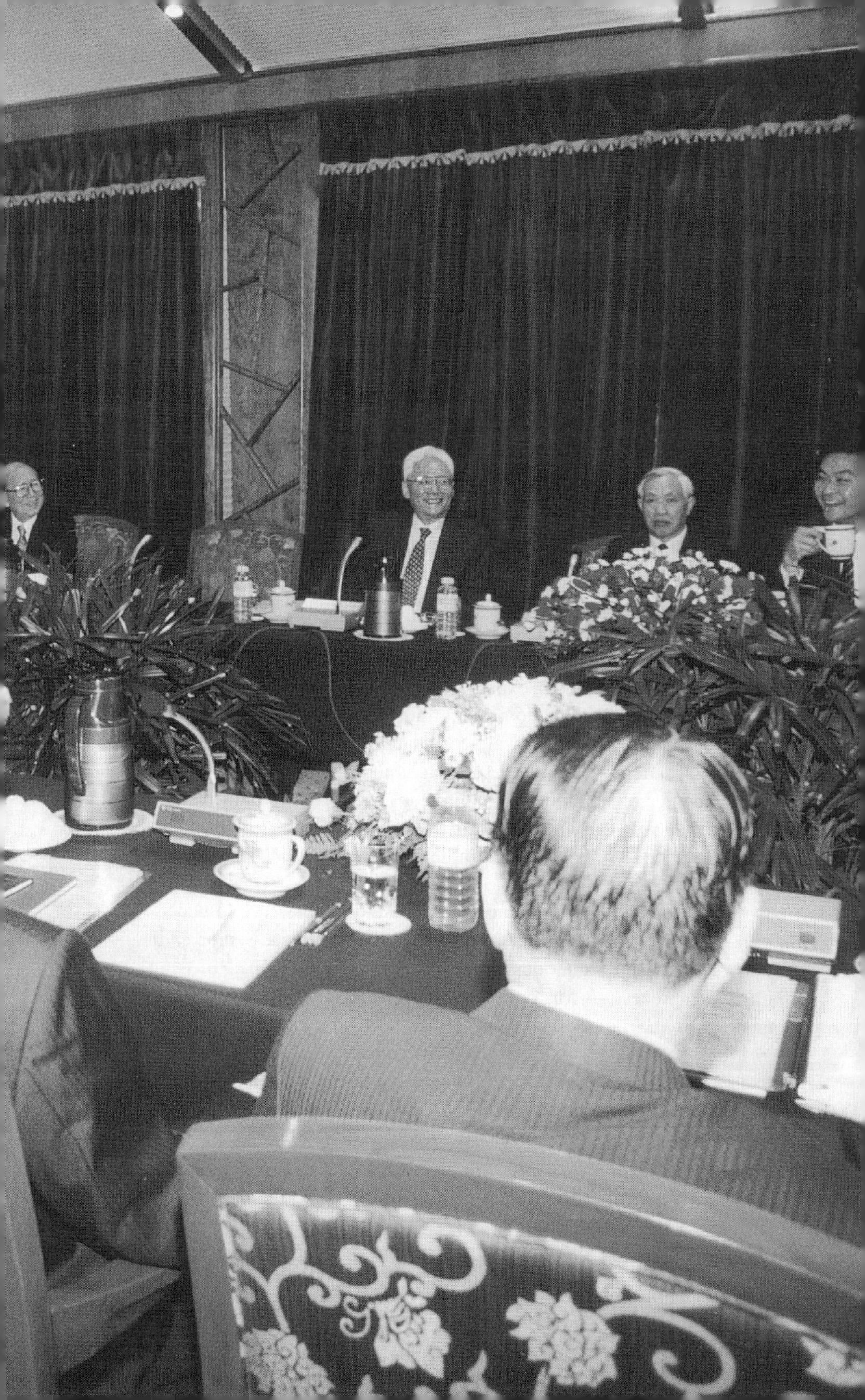

The Implementation of the Sino-British Joint Declaration

Christine Loh

More than a decade has passed since the governments of Britain and China began diplomatic meetings to negotiate the future of Hong Kong. In less than three years the product of those negotiations will be realized. Britain will leave Hong Kong, and yield its power there to China.

Hong Kong was told that the Sino-British Joint Declaration of 1984 set down the terms agreed between Britain and China for the territory's future. Having been denied knowledge of the negotiations while they were proceeding, the people of Hong Kong were issued with only the most grudging of invitations to comment on the Joint Declaration after it was published. They were told no amendments were possible and no referendum was allowed. Instead, they were allowed only a government-sponsored sampling of public opinion, which reported that Hong Kong would rather have the agreement as it stood than no agreement at all.

To the extent that the Joint Declaration commanded the confidence of Hong Kong, it did so because it appeared to make a series of important promises in unambiguous terms. It promised:

1. that Hong Kong would enjoy a "high degree of autonomy" from the Chinese central government in Beijing;
2. that Hong Kong would be invested with independent judicial power, including that of final adjudication;
3. that the legislature would be constituted by elections; and
4. that rights and freedoms already enjoyed would be protected and extended.

Christine Loh is a Legislative Councillor.

In the course of the past year, the political climate between Britain and China deteriorated to the point at which senior Chinese officials openly called into question the future of the Joint Declaration. The atmosphere was in many ways reminiscent of the mood of a decade ago, when the Sino-British negotiations on Hong Kong were passing through their most difficult stages. The arguments of the early 1980s are still echoed in current debate. As 1997 approaches, they have become still more urgent but, regrettably, no easier to resolve. At the centre of them is one key question: How can "two systems" be preserved within "one country"?

☐ Test of Legitimacy

The Joint Declaration represents a political solution to a difficult problem. This agreement, which has the status of a treaty between Britain and China, serves to transfer sovereignty over Hong Kong from Britain to China. Unless China changes fundamentally in less than three years, it will effectively transfer oversight of Hong Kong from a parliamentary government to that of a dictatorial one on 1 July 1997.

A government ordinarily requires the consent of the governed if it is to be regarded as legitimate. It is difficult to argue that any colonial government meets that criterion, because it is not the habit of colonial governments to seek consent through democratic means. A colonial power can at best claim a tacit or passive form of consent, i.e. that it is not overthrown. In Hong Kong's case, that has been made easier because most Hong Kong people preferred rule by the Hong Kong government to the alternative, rule by the Chinese government. Over the years, the Hong Kong government has also developed its own efficient and corruption-free civil service, thereby earning a form of "legitimacy" by proving its ability and capacity to govern.

The existing political structure is still highly autocratic. Power comes from London and is vested almost exclusively in the Governor. Until 1991, when the first direct elections were held for a minority of the seats on the Legislative Council (Legco), the constitutional structure remained much as it had been in the nineteenth century. The Governor still appoints the Executive Council, his top policy advisory body, and makes nominations to other bodies including the legislature. Appointees largely represent business and professional viewpoints. Hong Kong can thus be said to be ruled by an oligarchy not prescribed by formal constitutional rules, but the appointment system co-opts the rich and influential and was created to give the colonial structure a semblance of local involvement.

How legitimate is the Joint Declaration when put to the test of having the consent of the governed? The people of Hong Kong were not allowed to take any part in the negotiation over their future. The Joint Declaration was a *fait accompli*. Essentially, the 3.25 million Hong Kong people who are British subjects at law, will be handed back to China by the British government without having given any formal consent. China regards all ethnic Chinese Hong Kong British subjects as Chinese nationals because China does not regard the unequal treaties of the last century as valid. At best, the people of Hong Kong can be said to have given their conditional consent to the Joint Declaration. If the fundamental promise made to them in 1984, including "a high degree of autonomy," cannot be realized, then any consent must be regarded as void.

☐ Autonomy and Sovereignty

The essence of "autonomy" as a political concept is that the people of a territory within a state can make political decisions affecting themselves. This should entail making decisions on public policies and law within the scope of the autonomy without interference from the central government. It is crucial that a regional government should be able to truly represent the interests of its residents *vis-à-vis* the central government, otherwise the autonomy of the territory will in effect be compromised.

It is in this light that the quest for democracy should be seen in Hong Kong. Without an authentic representative system of government in Hong Kong which can legitimately represent the interests of Hong Kong people, and which will be fully responsible and accountable to them, it is difficult to see how Hong Kong could practise autonomy as a Special Administrative Region within the People's Republic of China after 1997.

Hong Kong's present autonomy from Britain is established through informal political undertakings based on accepted principles, conventions, practices and mutual interests. This is unlike the sort of autonomy which provides constitutional independence secured by legal guarantees, as enjoyed by the states of the United States and of Australia. The Joint Declaration does not expressly state how the "high degree of autonomy" for Hong Kong after 1997 is guaranteed.

However, if Hong Kong is only to enjoy an informal kind of autonomy after 1997 depending merely on Beijing's good faith, that would be wholly insufficient because there is no established political and legal framework within the Beijing–Hong Kong relationship which can operate reliably, as one has within the British Commonwealth. Furthermore, notions of law and politics between the "two systems" are fundamentally different.

Thus, the Joint Declaration only makes sense if the guarantee for Hong Kong's "high degree of autonomy" is written unambiguously into law. A supporting factor is Paragraph 3(3) of the Joint Declaration which provides that the Hong Kong Special Administrative Region (HKSAR) will be vested with independent judicial power, including that of final adjudication over all legal questions arising in Hong Kong, except those concerning foreign affairs and defence. However, when the Joint Declaration is read together with the Basic Law of the HKSAR — Hong Kong's post-1997 mini-constitution promulgated by China in 1990 — it can be seen that the HKSAR will only have an informal political kind of autonomy, although there will be some expressed legal regulation.

Rights and freedoms of citizens contained in the Chinese Constitution, and those in the Joint Declaration and the Basic Law, are subject to the ultimate approval of the National People's Congress (NPC) which represents the sovereign will of China. The legislature is in turn controlled by the Chinese Communist Party (CCP) and reflects the will and the policies of the Party. Sovereignty to the Chinese government is the be-all and the end-all of political power. To have sovereign power, in its view, is to have the right to rule without restriction. China also uses the defence of "sovereignty" as a way of telling its international critics to mind their own business.

☐ Autonomy and Law

The gulf between what passes for law in China, and the legal system now operating in Hong Kong, is correspondingly vast. The Chinese government and the CCP have had a tortuous history with legal reform. In 1959, Mao Zedong abolished the Ministry of Justice. During the Cultural Revolution, law was regarded as a bourgeois form of restraint on the revolutionary masses and legal skills became a positively dangerous thing to possess. With Deng Xiaoping coming to power in 1978, the law in China underwent a gentle rehabilitation. The Ministry of Justice was restored in 1979. The idea of "legality" was affirmed in China's 1982 Constitution. In 1983, provisions were made for the first time in China that judges should possess some professional knowledge of the law.

But the significance of legal developments in China in recent years should not be exaggerated. Judges are still servants of the CCP. Verdicts against the state and the CCP are impossible, unless of course the CCP itself orders them. Since Chinese leaders have long been accustomed to political mastery over courts and judges, they are likely to expect the same from the courts in the HKSAR. The fear in Hong Kong is that Beijing will be liable to see any moves to uphold the autonomy in the HKSAR as moves to circumscribe its sovereign power over the territory, and Beijing is liable to react accordingly.

Hong Kong has already had a taste of this. In the spring 1988 issue of the *Journal of Chinese Law* published by the Columbia University School of Law, Zhang Youyu, the Deputy Chairman of the NPC Legal Committee, professor in the Law Department of the Beijing University and a member of the Basic Law Drafting Committee wrote in an article on the drafting of the Basic Law:

> It is ... clear that the PRC [People's Republic of China] must be able to protect itself. Hong Kong will be a local administrative region of China. The high level of autonomy it will enjoy is conferred on it by the central organ of state power, and this high level of autonomy is not without limits. When exercising its high level of autonomy, Hong Kong will not proceed entirely without guidance, and even necessary intervention from the central government.... If the central government abdicates all power over Hong Kong, then chaos may ensue, damaging Hong Kong's interests.... Under the policy of "Hong Kong people administering Hong Kong" we cannot allow the continuation of British colonial system, wherein foreigners or local scoundrels pandering to foreign interests ruled Hong Kong.... The criteria for determining who is to rule Hong Kong ... must be that patriotic people are the specific Hong Kong people to rule Hong Kong.... Who are "patriots"? The touchstone of a patriot is respect for his own nation, honest and sincere support for the motherland's resumption of its sovereignty over Hong Kong and restraint from harming the stability and prosperity of Hong Kong. So long as they meet these requirements, they are patriots, no matter whether they believe in capitalism or feudalism or even the slave-owning system.

Zhang's line was reinforced in April 1994 by Duanmu Zheng, the vice-president of the Supreme People's Court of China and also a former Basic Law drafter who predicted that the common law system in Hong Kong would gradually disappear. He was reported to have said that judgements based on precedents relied too much on the British system. He thought the Chinese system was simpler, and therefore presumably better.

An area of complication is the setting-up of the Court of Final Appeal in Hong Kong to replace the Judicial Committee of the Privy Council in Britain. There have been on average about ten appeals per year from Hong Kong to the Privy Council. The Joint Declaration and the Basic Law both provide that the Court of Final Appeal "may as required invite judges from other common law jurisdictions to sit" on it. Sino-British discussion on the setting-up of the court began in 1988 and reached agreement in 1991 that the court should comprise five judges, namely the Chief Justice who must be a Chinese national with no right of abode elsewhere, three permanent Hong Kong judges and one non-permanent judge drawn from either a list of serving or retired local judges of appeal or from a list of judges from other common law jurisdictions. This agreement was reached without any consultation with either the judiciary or the legal profession.

Both the legal profession and the Legco rejected the agreement which was seen as a reneging by Beijing on its original promise to allow overseas judges to be added on a flexible basis to the Court of Final Appeal. Instead, with little British resistance, it has imposed a more rigid formula whereby foreign judges would make merely token appearances. The rationale for appointing foreign judges was that they would maintain an organic link between the Hong Kong courts and other common law jurisdictions. The Hong Kong government postponed bringing legislation to the Legco to establish the court because it feared a possible constitutional crisis in the event whereby the legislature threw it out or amended it.

After three years, the issue was raised again in early 1994 when the Hong Kong government felt that the attitude of the opponents might have changed. The Hong Kong government argues that although the Sino-British agreement is not ideal, it is important for the Court of Final Appeal to be set up before 1997 to ensure that Hong Kong can have maximum input on issues such as its jurisdiction, the appeal procedure and the appointment of judges. In April 1994, the Hong Kong government announced its intention to introduce legislation before the end of the 1993–1994 legislative year in July 1994. No bill was introduced in the end and none is expected to be tabled before the end of 1994.

There is nothing to stop the British and the Hong Kong governments from putting in place a Court of Final Appeal which meets the requirements of the Joint Declaration. Indeed, this is what they are legally obliged to do. They have not done so to date because China does not want it done, irrespective of the promise in the Joint Declaration.

☐ Autonomy and the Basic Law

The extent of the HKSAR's autonomy will be compromised because of numerous provisions in the Basic Law. For example, Article 17 empowers the Standing Committee of China's NPC to invalidate HKSAR legislation. This in effect gives a power of veto over Hong Kong legislation to the Standing Committee. Article 160 confers a similar power over "laws previously in force in Hong Kong." These provisions allow a political body in China to strike down any Hong Kong legislation for alleged inconsistency with the Basic Law.

It may be argued that the central government has a legitimate concern with Hong Kong law and that it is reasonable for it to ensure that Hong Kong laws conform with the territory's status as a part of China. But the question of whether Hong Kong law conflicts with the Basic Law is a legal question. It is wrong that it should be determined by a political organ and so, in effect, by the CCP. The Basic Law should say that conflicts are to be decided by the courts of the HKSAR.

Although the Joint Declaration provides that maintenance of public order is the responsibility of the HKSAR, Article 18 empowers the Standing Committee to apply China's national laws if there is "turmoil" in the HKSAR. This provision is obviously open to abuse since "turmoil" can have a very flexible meaning. For example, China's foreign minister, Qian Qichen, described the gazettal of the first electoral provisions bill in December 1993 as "man-made disorder." Will there be "man-made disorder" whenever the HKSAR disagrees with Beijing?

Article 19 exempts "acts of state" of the central government from the jurisdiction of the HKSAR courts and Article 158 gives the Standing Committee the power also to interpret the Basic Law. Article 158 provides that Hong Kong courts may interpret the Basic Law in adjudicating cases before them but that if the case involves affairs which are the responsibility of the central government, then Hong Kong courts must seek an interpretation from the Standing Committee of the NPC.

The power of interpretation is a vital one. The power to interpret the law is in effect the power to lay down the law. This task, assigned to a political organ and not a judicial one, is in effect a power of legislation. Thus, even though Article 17 provides that the HKSAR shall be vested with legislative power, Article 158 has by stealth allowed China's legislature to make HKSAR law.

Furthermore, there will be no institutional mechanisms to enable the

HKSAR's Chief Executive to challenge any such decisions or directions issued by the central government even where they may violate the autonomy granted under the Basic Law. As there is no provision in Chinese law for bringing legal proceedings against the state or its administrative organs, there can be no legal remedies against the state. The courts of the HKSAR will have no more power to question acts of the central government than have the courts of Mainland China.

This is of considerable concern to Hong Kong because the lack of remedy against the possible excesses of the central government could undermine the provisions about "a high degree of autonomy," the legal system and the powers of final adjudication which the Joint Declaration and the Basic Law are supposed to protect. If "acts of state" of the central government are outside the jurisdiction of the HKSAR courts, the effect is to place the central government above the law. Article 19 and other provisions in the Basic Law contradict the assurance in Paragraph 3(3) of the Joint Declaration that the "laws currently in force in Hong Kong will remain basically unchanged" and in Annex I, Part XIII that "Every person shall have the right to challenge the actions of the executive in the courts." The central government could not be legally prevented from infringing the HKSAR's autonomy in any way whatever.

The Foreign Affairs Committee (FAC) of the House of Commons report on "Relations between the United Kingdom and China in the Period up to and beyond 1997" published on 23 March 1994 came close to suggesting that parts of the Basic Law contravene the promise of "a high degree of autonomy" in the Joint Declaration. In the words of the FAC: "Articles 18 and 158 of the Basic Law are grave potential threats to the autonomy of the Hong Kong SAR after 1997 and to the implementation of the Joint Declaration."

Deficiencies in the Basic Law, including Articles 18 and 158, have been pointed out to Britain by many people in Hong Kong since the drafting of the Basic Law began in the mid-1980s. The British government had never wanted to call for amendment to the future mini-constitution. It accepts that the drafting of the Basic Law is an exclusive Chinese affair, even though it is supposed to give substance to the Joint Declaration.

The British government continues to absolve itself from responsibility over the implementation of the Joint Declaration, as in the manner in which it chose to respond to the FAC report. On 1 July 1994, the British government offered this (at best half-truth): "China has often reaffirmed its strong commitment to the Joint Declaration." It claims that the FAC does not have to fear that Article 158 will be used to overrule the Hong Kong Bill of Rights after 1997 because the Bill of Rights is "entirely compatible with the Basic Law. There is therefore no reason why it should not remain in force."

The British government also stresses that the Joint Declaration is an international treaty registered at the United Nations. It is, in fact, no more than a bilateral treaty between Britain and China with no legal recourse for either Britain or Hong Kong should the Joint Declaration be breached. With a track record for avoiding difficult issues, it is unlikely that Britain will jump to Hong Kong's defence after 1997 if autonomy is denied. Throughout the last decade, since the signing of the Joint Declaration, Britain had occasionally proclaimed its commitment to upholding the Joint Declaration but in practice, it has adopted a minimalist attitude towards its implementation.

☐ Autonomy and the Preliminary Working Committee

Mao Zedong described the united front tactic as a "magic tool" of the CCP. The tactic aims to isolate the enemy and then to mobilize other forces to destroy the enemy. The United Front Department is controlled by the CCP's central secretariat. The united front is being used in Hong Kong to win over as many "friends" as possible. China's president, Jiang Zemin, told a group of left-wing trade unionists on 13 June 1994 that patriotism is essential for maintaining stability in Hong Kong in the transitional period. Jiang was quoted to have said that uniting Hong Kong people under the banner of patriotism could guarantee stability and a smooth transition.

Chinese officials have worked hard to woo businessmen and establishment leaders. In 1992, China appointed a group of 44 people as Hong Kong Affairs advisers. They were mainly former members of the Basic Law Drafting Committee and the Basic Law Consultative Committee. In 1993, China appointed a further 49 advisers, this time including conservative legislators, academics, businessmen and three ex-civil servants. The appointees are nominated by the State Council's Hong Kong and Macau Affairs Office and by the Hong Kong branch of the New China News Agency (Xinhua).

An article published in June 1994, written by Huang Wenfang, a retired vice-secretary general of Xinhua, provides interesting insight into who decides on policy over Hong Kong:

> The Foreign Minister Qian Qichen, as a politburo member, handles foreign affairs, Hong Kong and Macau, and Taiwan. As the assistant of Jiang Zemin and Li Peng, Qian helps with Hong Kong. So Jiang and Li are the highest power-holders in respect of Hong Kong. Right now, matters of great importance concerning Hong Kong is first reported to Qian, then Jiang and Li are asked for advice. Jiang and Li divide Hong Kong work between them: Li handles most jobs concerning government departments, while Jiang handles party affairs and decisions concerning the overall situation. It can be said that Jiang handles more than Li ... Xinhua is the top-level overseas post of the Chinese Communist party, while the Hong Kong and Macau Affairs Office is an office of the State Council.

According to Meeting Point chairman, Anthony Cheung, who was a Hong Kong Affairs adviser for a month before China refused to confirm the appointment because of the merger of his party with that of the United Democrats of Hong Kong, the role of adviser entails "no officially stated functions, although whenever Chinese officials talk about Hong Kong affairs advisers, they always emphasize that they will help with the transition. But there was never any terms of reference as to what exactly we would do."

In June 1993, when relations between Britain and China had deteriorated over the government's proposal for electoral reforms, China set up the Preliminary Working Committee (PWC) for the Special Administrative Region Preparatory Committee and appointed 57 members to it. This is a prelude to the Preparatory Committee which, under the Basic Law, will be set up within 1996 to prepare for the establishment of the HKSAR and the formation of its first government.

The PWC has been described as a "second stove," a sort of Legislative Council in waiting, its main task being to advise China on transitional matters. It is primarily made up of an odd assortment of long-time leftists, mixed with recent converts, such as Hong Kong Affairs advisers and the recently dropped Executive Councillor, Rita Fan. A further batch of 13 members were appointed in May 1994, including the recently retired head of the Commission for Administrative Complaints.

The PWC is perceived as China's attempt to have a hand in Hong Kong affairs even before 1997. It started with five sub-groups covering political, economic, legal, cultural and education, and security issues, and added two more in July 1994 covering external economic relations and trade relations with China. The political and legal sub-groups have accepted that the Chinese government will in 1997 disband the three tiers of government elected in 1995, and they are considering how a provisional legislature may be set up or, alternatively, whether to vest powers in the Chief Executive or even to allow the NPC to legislate for Hong Kong. The security sub-group has commented on the issuance of HKSAR passports prior to 1997. The PWC has also demanded that civil servants be made available to brief them directly on current matters, such as funding for the new Chek Lap Kok airport, even though there are other official channels for the two governments to discuss airport-related matters.

The cultural and education sub-group is reviewing school textbooks for after 1997. In a strange and disturbing turn of events, Hong Kong's own director of education, Dominic Wong, announced at the end of June 1994 that history of the past twenty years has not really been sorted out by historians and therefore it is best if educational textbooks remove references to the contemporary period. He instructed a number of publishing companies to remove mention of the 1989 Tiananmen massacre from textbooks. Wong subsequently claimed that what he said to publishers was not binding and the law did not empower him to give instructions on how textbooks ought to be written. The issue was dropped after a public outcry.

During 1993 and the first half of 1994, Sino-British cooperation within the Joint Liaison Group (JLG), the official body set up under the Joint Declaration to discuss transitional matters, has remained erratic. China has a clear responsibility under the Joint Declaration to negotiate in the JLG but it chooses to treat its treaty obligation as an option to be selected only if it feels Britain is being cooperative on Hong Kong matters. Despite all its united front work, China has so far failed to widen China's appeal in Hong Kong. At times, the pro-China lobby has even undermined China's image.

The failure of united front work in Hong Kong is due to its inability to cope with Hong Kong people who hold different views from Beijing's, and who have greater legitimacy than members of the pro-China lobby because they have been elected to office by the people of Hong Kong. In the days when the tactic was used to promote revolutionary work in China, united front was used to win allies by moral and rational appeal. But nowadays, "friends" are attracted to Beijing because it is, and will remain, the political power centre as London's importance recedes. Infighting within the China camp will doubtless intensify as more people with career ambitions post-1997 start jockeying for position. China only has itself to blame if its appointees lacks popular appeal. Unless China is able to respect the views of those who have different ideas about what autonomy must mean for Hong Kong, China will be unable to convince people that it is genuinely interested in helping Hong Kong with its transition and abiding by its promise of giving Hong Kong "a high degree of autonomy."

☐ Autonomy and Human Rights

Part XIII of Annex I of the Joint Declaration provides that "The provisions of the International Covenant on Civil and Political Rights and the International Covenant on Economic, Social and Cultural Rights as applied to Hong Kong shall remain in force." The covenants are United Nations multilateral treaties, and together with the Universal Declaration on Human Rights, which China helped draft, they make up the core documents for upholding human rights internationally by legal and diplomatic means. The very essence of the covenants is a recognition that any infringement on human rights is a breach in international law. A state which has ratified them cannot plead that its human rights infringements are a domestic matter. By ratifying the covenants, the state accepts an obligation of accountability to the United Nations Human Rights Committee (UNHRC). States that violate human rights risk being exposed to adverse publicity and international condemnation. This may not mean very much but when that sort of publicity carries the moral endorsement of the United Nations, it can help to encourage states to change their ways.

By committing itself to full enforcement of the covenants, China is accepting that any human rights violations in Hong Kong after 1997 will be a matter of legitimate international concern. Given the frequency with which human rights of all kinds are violated within China, this should in principle be a source of comfort for Hong Kong. There is, however, a problem here which threatens to make even this very modest degree of comfort illusory. Britain has ratified the covenants but China has not. Unless China ratifies them before 1997, it is hard to see how it can meet the commitment it made in the Joint Declaration. Without ratifying the covenants, China does not engage itself to be accountable to the UNHRC and for Hong Kong, the covenants are stripped of much of their force.

The contradiction is China's to correct but not China's alone. Britain knew in 1984 that the covenants "as applied to Hong Kong" could not "remain in force" until and unless China ratified them. The pledge to uphold the covenants ties the Joint Declaration into the broader structure of international law in an important, concrete way. It may be that discussions have taken place within the JLG but they have probably been fruitless ones since no announcement has been forthcoming about how the covenants will in fact be enforced after 1997.

The British Foreign Office's view about the problem is that by signing the Joint Declaration, China is assumed to have both accepted the terms of the covenants as well as the relevant reporting procedures to the UNHRC. But when the head of the Hong Kong and Macau Affairs Office, Lu Ping, visited Hong Kong in May 1994, he said that Beijing was not obliged to make reports to the UNHRC after 1997.

The FAC's 1994 report reflects the confusion. It recommends that "the UK should seek clarification from the United Nations Human Rights Committee, as to whether it agrees with the UK's interpretation of the Joint Declaration in this regard and whether it would accept reports from a sovereignty not party to the relevant Covenant, and that it was also important that the Chinese side clarify its own position, both with regard to the reporting procedures themselves, and with regard to the location and constitution of the organ responsible for carrying out this task."

The British government does not see such a need. It claims in its response to the FAC report that:

> China's obligations ... are clear, as we have told the Chinese side in the Joint Liaison Group. Since the Joint Declaration is a bilateral treaty between China and Britain, the Government see no need to consult the UN Human Rights Committee on its interpretation. The Government will continue to urge China to become a party to the Covenants, and to discuss how reporting obligations in respect of the Hong Kong Special Administrative Region under the Covenants should be fulfilled after 30 June 1997.

☐ Conclusion

On 4 May 1994, the Legco passed a motion stating that past failures by both the Chinese and British governments to adhere to the Joint Declaration, "led to misinterpretation and violation of the Joint Declaration" and created "grave concerns of Hong Kong people, about the prospects for its full implementation."

If there are breaches to the Joint Declaration, there is unfortunately no mechanism for enforcement. Britain's constant claim that the Joint Declaration is an international treaty, registered at the United Nations, does not offer any comfort for the people of Hong Kong since China does not accept the jurisdiction of the International Court of Justice. If there are breaches of the Joint Declaration, and if Britain does stir itself into action, at most all Britain can do is to try and drag China back to the negotiating table when China has already resumed sovereignty. Past experience suggests that Britain is, in practice, highly unlikely to make any such attempt, whatever the cause; and that if it did, China would ignore it.

A system of representative government firmly rooted in Hong Kong would help Hong Kong to exercise its promised autonomy. But Lu Ping warned on 6 May 1994 that Hong Kong should not be turned "into a political city in order to influence the Mainland in the sense of politics." Two days later, Lu clarified that statement by saying that Hong Kong should not become a base to convert China to democracy. But socialism and democracy are, after all, not mutually exclusive. What Lu really meant is that China is hostile to democracy in Hong Kong because it might spread. Because of this fear, Beijing sees attitudes towards democracy in Hong Kong as the dividing line between friends and supposed enemies.

If the CCP believes that after 1997 it can and will monopolize political power, then its instinct may well lead it to gerrymander Hong Kong's legislature so as to exclude those who say things Beijing does not like. If allowed to pursue those instincts unchallenged, the CCP would soon hollow out whatever institutions of government and justice Hong Kong retained after 1997, turning them into facades and proxies for Beijing itself.

This is a very bleak view of the future. No one in Hong Kong wants to see that happening but it is not an unreasonable view given the history of the last decade. If Hong Kong people no longer feel that their government can represent them, they might well withdraw their consent for the HKSAR government to rule. They will not be able to withdraw consent positively by voting the government out of office because the political mechanisms will not be available to do so. But consent and confidence can be withdrawn passively, with just as much damage to the cohesion of society over time.

6

Politics, Politicians, and Political Parties

Michael E. DeGolyer

Less than three years before the handover date of 1 July 1997, Hong Kong is deep into its transition from British Crown colony to Special Administrative Region (SAR) of the central government of the People's Republic of China (P.R.C.). So far along has the process of handover gone, in fact, that one poll in late June reported that 52 per cent of respondents saw no further useful role for Governor Christopher Patten.[1] All politics in Hong Kong take place within this reality of power flowing from the present to the future sovereign.

☐ The "Through Train" Jumps the Track

Ostensibly, the process of transition to SAR is determined by the Basic Law, the "mini-constitution" spelling out the details of Hong Kong's promised "high degree of autonomy," promulgated by the National People's Congress in April 1990. British policy from the signing of the Sino-British Joint Declaration in December 1984 to early 1994 had been to attempt to insure "convergence" with China's own plans and since 1990, with the specific provisions (such as were actually specified) in the Basic Law. This convergence has been characterized locally as the "through train" provision, modelled on agreements between Hong Kong and the P.R.C.

Michael E. DeGolyer is a lecturer in Government and International Studies, Hong Kong Baptist College.

[1] "Patten 'has no useful role,'" *Sunday Morning Post* (26 June 1994), pp. 1–2.

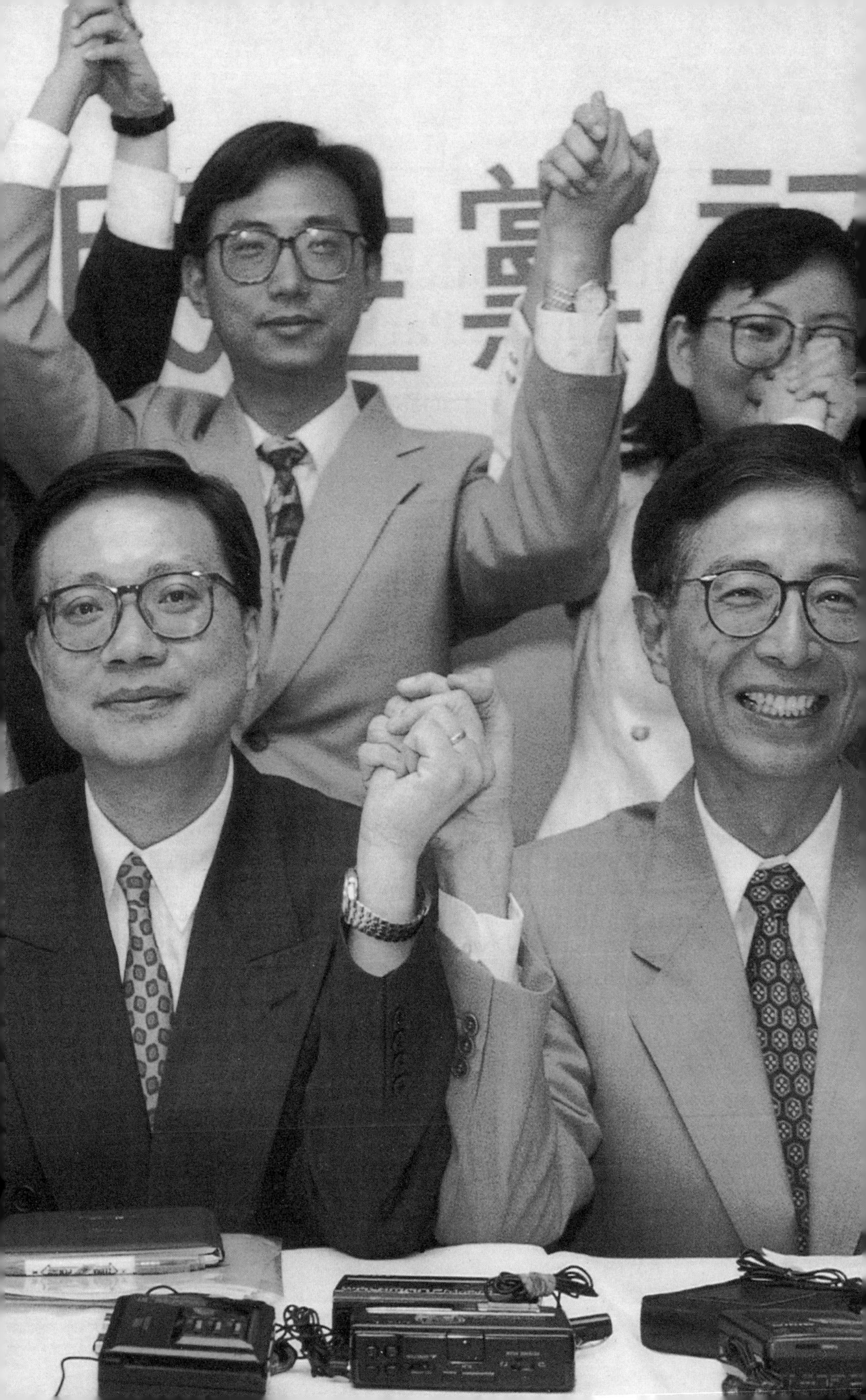

which allow the Kowloon–Canton Railway (KCR) to run its daily trains without border stops.

Governor David Wilson, who left office under a cloud in mid-1992, made great sacrifices both of principle and expedience in hopes to obtain the "through train." One example of those was the Memorandum of Understanding on the Chek Lap Kok airport construction and its signature in Beijing by Prime Minister John Major in September 1991. This marked the first significant Western break in P.R.C. isolation following the 1989 June 4 Tiananmen massacre, and represented major concessions in the construction of the term "local affairs," which according to many experts on the Basic Law, were supposed to be internal SAR matters. Soon after its signature, the Memorandum of (Non-) Understanding, as directorate-level civil servants wryly called it in private, broke down into acrimonious disputes, still ongoing, about the financing and concessionaires for the new airport. This humiliation of John Major, for no effective reason according to insiders, spelled the end for David Wilson and Foreign Office (read Percy Cradock) dominance of Hong Kong affairs.[2] Christopher Patten, a politician "wholly without understanding of Hong Kong and China" as many pro-Cradock and pro-Beijing groups charged, took over the engineer's levers on the laboriously built through train.

As long as specifics could be fudged and British officials appeared suitably appeasing, the through train kept on track. Percy Cradock, in letters to the *Times* of London in December 1993 and in his rather defensive memoirs published in March 1994, characterized this policy as firm but flexible realism, best for both Hong Kong's and Britain's long-term interests.[3] But in October 1992 when, without Beijing's prior approval, Governor Patten publicly proposed specific provisions for the 1994–1995 set of elections, the first elections which would actually comprise bodies on the through train, the weak link in the transition, the trestle of interpretation, began to collapse over the vast gorge of deep differences. By March 1994 the through train appeared irretrievably wrecked.

The derailing began when the Sino-British talks on the 1994–1995

---

[2] Derek Davies in the recently launched English language newspaper *Eastern Express* savaged Cradock and the "mandarins" of the Foreign Office in "Profile, Crawler of the F.O.," *Eastern Express* "Weekend" (12 February 1994), pp. 16–19.

[3] Percy Cradock, *Experiences of China* (London: John Murray, 1994), pp. 161–258.

election arrangements dragged on through 17 rounds during 1993 and early 1994, then broke down in acrimony and public accusations embodied in highly one-sided "transcript summaries" of the "secret" talks both sides released in February and March.[4] The major disputes concerned Legislative Council (Legco) elections. London wanted first-past-the-post provisions for the 20 directly elected seats out of 60 seats. Beijing wanted proportional representation, or one vote, multiple member constituencies. London wanted the 9 new functional constituency seats (making 30 of 60) broadened, with around 300,000 members each and inclusive of all working people. Beijing, and the pro-Beijing Democratic Alliance for Betterment of Hong Kong (DAB) and the pro-business Liberal Party (LP), wanted much smaller franchises, focused on elites and professions, as with the 21 existing functional constituencies. London wanted 10 seats chosen by an election committee comprised of all District Board (DB) members, and all DB members, in contrast to the present two-thirds, to be directly elected. Beijing wanted the DB's untouched and the election committee composed of members appointed on a strict formula by interests. Both sides accused the other of bad faith and poor construction, and both began unilaterally to interpret the Basic Law, insisting that each was preparing its own version of convergence.

Beijing's interpretation, scheduled to take effect *de jure* on 1 July 1997, began to be put into unilateral *de facto* effect in late 1993 to early 1994 with the setting up of the Preliminary Working Committee (PWC), a hitherto unscheduled group slated to turn over to a Preparatory Committee in 1996 as laid out in the Basic Law, and with the appointment of three tiers of "advisers." This was the so-called "second stove," or alternative power, challenging the Hong Kong government and its tiers of (partially) representative bodies. The three Beijing tiers are Hong Kong Affairs advisers, PWC members, and Local Affairs advisers. Beijing began to activate its long-developing shadow government, deciding in March 1994 to replace the Legco, Urban and Regional Councils, and District Boards on the handover. Various subcommittees of the Beijing-appointed, partially Hong Kong resident-comprised, PWC began to work out, in secret sessions, detailed

---

[4] *White Paper on Representative Government in Hong Kong, February 1994* (Hong Kong: Government Printing Department, 1994) and "China Fights Back on Talks," *South China Morning Post*, pp. 1, 11–14 and "China's Record of the Sino-British Talks," *Window Supplement* (4 March 1994), pp. i–viii.

arrangements for such crucial issues as elections in 1997 to the SAR bodies, the continuity of members of the civil service, legal provisions for nationality and subversion, and supervisory provisions for infrastructural developments. Only one party with directly elected members in the Legco, the Association for Democracy and People's Livelihood (ADPL), received an appointment to the Political Consultative Committee, and that was held by a member who had twice been defeated in direct election attempts. The party which held a majority of directly elected seats (11 of 18) in the Legco, the United Democrats of Hong Kong (UDHK), was specifically shunned. This isolation of the UDHK was made very pointedly again when Meeting Point (MP) chairman Anthony Cheung agreed in May to merge his party with the UDHK into a new Democratic Party. The Beijing offer to appoint him a Hong Kong Affairs adviser was angrily withdrawn. In turn, the UDHK and MP refused to allow the ADPL to join the new Democratic Party. Individual members of the ADPL would be accepted, not the organization.

Meanwhile, in tense sessions, the so-called less contentious aspects of the Patten's proposals received their first test in the partially elected Legco in March. The provisions for the direct election of all DB members were finalized and the means of the direct election of 20 of 60 members of the Legco settled as "first past the post." Proportional representation, as desired by Beijing, was firmly rejected. The passage of these measures without amendment and led by directly elected members heartened the Hong Kong government, despite some fractures within that camp from an Elsie Tu proposal to seek one last attempt at agreement with Beijing. Immediately on passage, part 2 of the proposals which mostly concerned the election of 9 new broadly-based functional constituency seats and the composition of the electoral committee selecting 10 members was tabled. Yet the Hong Kong government enjoyed members' support only fleetingly. Patten had stated repeatedly throughout 1993 that the Legco could change these provisions as it wished (a view which was a major reason for the breakdown of the Sino-British talks, in fact) and a lobby group, Full Democracy Now, appeared in late 1993 pushing for direct election of all 60 seats.[5] But in March 1994, newspaper investigations revealed that the Letters Patent had been

---

[5] This debate reached a peak in late June. See *Sunday Morning Post* (26 June 1994), p. 17 where Patten, Emily Lau, and Howard Young all defended their views.

secretly amended and signed by the Queen in mid-summer 1993 to reflect Patten's proposals as originally tabled. Political parties cried foul and Legco members denounced, yet again, secret provisions made without consultation.[6] By late June Patten's proposals appeared in trouble, but after a marathon debate lasting from 9 a.m. on the 29th to 5 a.m. on the 30th of June, exactly three years before handover, they passed by a narrow vote, yet only with the help of the three official members of the Council bound by law and custom to support the Governor. LP members had asked Patten to allow the local members to make the decision without official interference. He refused, winning technically but perhaps losing morally. In the whole affair, neither London nor Beijing really seemed willing to let Hong Kong people have an unfettered say about their future.

☐ From the Wreckage of Convergence

After the collapse of the through train, the Basic Law, which ostensibly insures the principle of "Hong Kong people ruling Hong Kong," came into disrepute, if indeed, as indicated below, there had ever been great trust in its fulfilment. The formal processes of political development (the specification of proportions of Legco members directly and indirectly elected in Annex II through 2003, for example) so carefully spelled out now fell subject to the informal processes of politics, both on the "national" level of influence with Beijing and the "local" level of influence with Hong Kong people.[7] The

---

[6] Another secret held back was the Foreign Office error which calls into question the legality of laws passed with John Swaine as Deputy President of the Legco (since October 1991). See *Sunday Morning Post* (19 June 1994).

[7] A comprehensive collection of documents with an extensive bibliography may be found in Ming K. Chan and David J. Clark (eds.), *The Hong Kong Basic Law: Blueprint for "STABILITY AND PROSPERITY" under Chinese Sovereignty?* (Hong Kong: Hong Kong University Press, 1991). For the Chinese view, see the commentaries following the text and annexes in *The Basic Law of the Hong Kong Special Administrative Region of the People's Republic of China* (Hong Kong: Joint Publishing Co., 1991), pp. 93–146. However, the role of "tradition" and informal arrangements has been less studied. For one of the few examples, see Lisa Skwarok and Robert Wickins, "The Evolving System of Government in Hong Kong: Executive and Legislative Powers and the Basic Law," *Hong Kong Public Administration*, Vol. 3, No. 1 (March 1994), pp. 65–94.

question of London's influence post-1997 became more one of Beijing's accusations and not reality.[8] The reassurances of London and Beijing about concern for the stability and prosperity of Hong Kong which dominated the media from 1982 onwards virtually disappeared by early 1994. Yet the battle for the hearts and minds (and wallets and bodies) of Hongkongese intensified in 1994. It shifted from comforting assurances by both to calls to choose sides.

In this battle, Beijing faces formidable obstacles. Surveys have long shown few Hong Kong people have interest in or knowledge about the Basic Law, and many have deep doubts whether its paper provisions really will mean much. In a survey of 636 respondents in early 1994, when asked the question, "How much do you trust the P.R.C. government to interpret the Basic Law in the best interest of the Hong Kong people?" 42 per cent indicated no trust at all, 31 per cent slight trust, 15 per cent fair trust and a nearly invisible 4 per cent strong trust. A surprisingly low 8 per cent didn't know.[9] The body set up by Beijing to begin determining specific interpretations, the PWC, fared worse. When the same number were asked, "Do you think the Preliminary Working Committee is a suitable (legitimate) body to decide the means to implement the Basic Law?" only 26 per cent answered

---

[8] "Dealing with China, the Barbarians at the Gate," *The Economist* (27 November 1993), pp. 21–23 noted that "foreign attempts to wish pluralism upon China are seen as part of a plot to bring China once more to its knees. Hence, in part, the violence of China's reaction to Mr. Patten's proposals for Hong Kong." Andy Ho On-tat, during a "Newsmakers" programme on Wharf Cable (25 June 1994) noted that Deng Xiaoping had stated that a multi-party system would "never" be introduced in China. Thus why Hong Kong's development of multi-party pluralism and Britain's defence of the same seem so much a plot to weaken China. In reality, Britain has sought to stifle genuine political pluralism in Hong Kong until very recently, even engaging in phone taps and police observation of people like Anna Wu and Rita Fan in the past.

[9] All tables are secured to data collected by the Hong Kong Transitions Project unless otherwise indicated. The Project, beginning in early 1989, has focused on tracking the development of politics in Hong Kong by a variety of measures and with an interdisciplinary and multi-national team. Members include or have included Donald McMillen, Sarah Lau Chiu-wai, Janet Lee Scott, Karen Chai, K. K. Leung, Jane C. Y. Lee, Andy Ho, Sonny Lo Shiu-hing, C. S. Tong, Fang Kai-tai, and this author.

yes, 38 per cent no and a very large proportion, 36 per cent, didn't know. However, the hesitant moves by the Hong Kong government to build up the representativeness of the Legco have also damaged its effectiveness, though it still far outweighs that of the bodies set up by Beijing. In the same survey, when asked, "Which body, the Legislative Council or the Preliminary Working Committee of the HKSAR, best protects Hong Kong people's interests?" 40 per cent chose the Legco compared to 12 per cent for the PWC. However, 7 per cent insisted both were needed and twice that number, 15 per cent, said neither best protects Hong Kong people's interests. A very large 26 per cent indicated they didn't know, a sign in this case as in the other high don't know responses of an increasingly worried populace that the "proper" response wasn't clear, the safety of response wasn't fully assured, or that avenues for truly protecting their interests were simply not apparent.

The Hong Kong government is not currently in danger of losing its ability to attract the toleration, if not the allegiance, of Hong Kong people.[10] Beijing, however, has a great deal of work to woo them. As seen below, satisfaction with the Hong Kong government remained fairly high throughout the fractious talks on election arrangements. However, that of the P.R.C. dropped, and increasingly, as seen in the February 1994 survey results, its actions in China are viewed more favourably than those in Hong Kong (see Table 1).

In the earlier stages of the transition, on the level of formal arrangements such as those in the Basic Law, this battle seemed like that of two large and contentious knights over the rich, beautiful, and helpless damsel in waiting. Hongkongese have long been characterized as politically apathetic, naive, and unnationalistic, either towards Britain or China.[11] London proposes, Beijing disposes, and the Hongkongese repose in the meanwhile. According to popular belief, they have been, are, and always will be interested first, last and foremost in making money. However, in 1993–1994 Hongkongese seem to be changing from passive objects

---

[10] Norman Miners discusses this difference in *The Government and Politics of Hong Kong* (5th ed.; Hong Kong: Oxford University Press, 1991), pp. 32–42.

[11] This characterization, if ever true, may have only been supported by equally undesirable realities faced by Hongkongese between 1949 and 1982. See below.

Table 1. How Satisfied Are You Currently with:

	1993 (Feb.) (N = 615)		1993 (Aug.) (N = 605)		1994 (Feb.) (N = 636)	
	% Satis. to varying degree	% Don't know	% Satis. to varying degree	% Don't know	% Satis. to varying degree	% Don't know
the performance of the Hong Kong government?	60	9	57	15	58	14
the performance of the P.R.C. government in ruling China?	35	16	26	20	29	18
the performance of the P.R.C. government in dealing with Hong Kong affairss?	—	—	25	22	23	21

of dispute between London and Beijing to active participants, if not contenders, over the terms of their present and future.[12] This change in the people themselves is having, and will have, increasing effects on the actual processes of transition over the putative processes spelled out in the contentious provisions of the Basic Law.

☐ Back to the Future: Image versus Realities

The legitimacy of a government rests largely on three things: the image it has in people's minds — preferably, as Machiavelli noted, whether a

---

[12] This change has been noted by worried officials in China according to highly placed pro-Beijing locals confidentially interviewed in the spring of 1994 by The Hong Kong Transitions Project. They fear that polarization has proceeded to such a degree that a confrontation may be inevitable. This growing polarization and its consequences was noted in 1991. See Donald H. McMillen, Michael E. DeGolyer, and Chiu Wai-lau, "Government Administration of the 1991 Direct Elections: A Public Opinion Analysis," *Hong Kong Public Administration*, Vol. 3, No. 1 (March 1994), pp. 95–132, esp. pp. 106–7.

matter of reality or not, a "good" image of efficiency, responsiveness, and righteousness; allegiance — the ability to deliver the goods to its supporters, buying their support through service and benefits; and the toughest of all to achieve, loyalty — the identity of values and shared experiences with those governing. The battle for the hearts and minds of the Hong Kong people is thus largely rooted in differing versions and values of its past, as well as in contentions over present ability to bestow favours, protect interests, and appear forthright and effective.

In early 1994 the Governor weighed in on several occasions regarding protecting interests and forthrightness, criticizing Rupert Murdoch indirectly for dropping the BBC World Service Television from STAR TV over broadcasts the P.R.C. leaders found distasteful or disturbing. This was presented as a continuation and elaboration of one of the themes sounded in his passionate address to the Legco in October 1993, in which he promised, in a rather curious elocution, to support the Hong Kong people's striving for their way of life as boldly as they themselves evidenced courage. This was his attempt to project an image of righteousness and forthright identity with Hongkongese longings for freedom. In March 1994, a group of legislators promptly challenged the image of the government as a defender of freedom of information by calling for its support of an Access to Information Bill. In June, the Executive Council came out against putting freedom of information in the form of law, instead choosing to implement a "code of practice" which would be a civil service guideline. This was promptly denounced as inadequate by the democrats and as pernicious meddling in the ability of the post-1997 government to protect sensitive information by PWC members and China. A similar fate met the campaign for a Human Rights Commission, with a Commission being rejected, and instead the Commissioner for Administrative Complaints was given additional powers. He could now initiate investigations on his own (previously he had to wait for complaints to be forwarded through the bureaucracy), report, recommend, and publicize. He could not, however, directly enforce his findings.

This battle for hearts and minds also involved the media, with the English language *Eastern Express* commencing publication in February 1994, touting itself as "a paper to trust" and promising it would be beholden to no other interest than Hong Kong's. *Media Watch*, a Radio Television Hong Kong production, introduced a welcome element of critique on the media itself. And, in a different sort of media critique, in June five members of the ATV (Asia Television Limited) news team quit in disgust when its managers tried to overrule their decision to broadcast a fifth anniversary commemoration of Tiananmen Square.

While these battles over the images of the Governor, the government, and the media raged, battles over allegiance, by delivering the goods and protecting interests, also took place over the last year. Anson Chan, the first woman and Chinese to be appointed Chief Secretary by the British, took office in a blaze of international publicity and high-profile travel. However, the public benefits of the move soon soured as the speeded-up localization process triggered angry disputes between expatriate civil servants and local Chinese civil servants. The Legco weighed in, favouring the locals who wanted expatriates barred from permanent contracts, or forced to take a reduction in rank and loss of some benefits. But the courts appear to be the avenue of final settlement as the Bill of Rights was invoked by the expatriates in a manner sure to alienate many locals from such interpretations of human rights. Civil servants journeyed to Beijing several times during the year, seeking assurances on everything from adequate funding of pensions to continuity of senior civil servants in office after 1997.

Reports released in late spring from a study conducted at the City Polytechnic of Hong Kong that a large majority of such civil servants planned to leave before 1997 provoked Lu Ping, Director of the Hong Kong and Macau Affairs Office, to retort that the report's conclusions were "impossible" and its methodology flawed. But Lu Ping's own studied snubs of the Governor in his visit to the territory in May rebounded on him as public opinion strongly deprecated his actions. Shortly after, relations between Beijing and London began to assume more reasonableness, though the Governor also took on a much lower profile for several months afterward. By July, after seven years of negotiations, the Joint Liaison Group produced agreements on the airport, on disposal of military lands, and made progress on some of the over 200 laws remaining to be changed to reflect the shift from colony to SAR.

But as important as allegiance garnered by services rendered and agreements achieved, and as disputes about freedom of access to information undoubtedly are, and as critical in this media age as image is, perhaps nothing so defines the mindsets and determines the political loyalties and identities of a people as a common concept of history, for it is out of shared experiences that shared values and common visions grow. In late 1993, this battle began to heat up, with a group of Hong Kong educators and publishers meeting in Beijing to get "guidance" on acceptable texts for the post-handover educational market, and several books, including *The Other Hong Kong Report 1993*, presenting challenging reinterpretations of Hong Kong's past.

☐ Back to the Future: The British Version of Hong Kong's Apolitical History

British writers have asserted an interpretation of Hong Kong's history notable mostly for the absence of politics among the populace. Characterized as a "barren rock," this colony, according to this version, had no people of consequence when first settled. From the beginning, the British intended to protect themselves and their trade from the arbitrary and barbarous "laws" of China where business was despised, corruption rampant, the law arbitrary and severe and the death penalty frequent.

Little has changed in their eyes to this day. Last year half of all the criminal executions in the world took place in China; the Han Dongfang (a union leader excluded from returning to China after a trip abroad) and Xi Yang (a *Ming Pao* newspaper reporter jailed for twelve years for procuring documents concerning interest rates) affairs appear wholly arbitrary if not illegal cases, even according to China's own laws; corruption sparked over 10,000 disturbances in China in 1993 and, at least officially, business is associated with the oft-denounced bourgeois corruption of socialism. The April 1994 Foreign Affairs Committee Report on Hong Kong, the first since 1989, continued this emphasis on British concern with China's human rights record.

According to the British version of Hong Kong's history, and Frank Welsh's *A History of Hong Kong* came out in late 1993 as the latest edition in this line, Hong Kong was kept strictly non-political, subject to the rule of law, with subversives who refused to be apolitical deported (strictly according to the rule of law, however). Hong Kong was primarily a port of trade, with its government legitimized by its efficiency, control of corruption, reasonable rule of law, and provision of a better life in peaceful circumstances. The occasional disturbances to law and order were caused by agitators in the hire of or under the influence of "outside" forces. Typical Hong Kong people simply wanted to be left in peace to pursue their business; they had little or no interest in politics. And thus until 1982 there was no demand to provide extensive formal means for political participation. As long as the proper people were consulted (or co-opted), changes in governance and policy could be made with little "political" activity involved. If it had not been for the ending of the lease of the New Territories in mid-1997, Hong Kong people would have preferred continued British rule.[13] According to the British interpretation, Beijing's promise of no change for fifty years after 1997 and protection of Hong Kong's way of life with its "one country, two systems" formula specifically means to safeguard this version of a largely apolitical past.

☐ Back to the Future: The P.R.C. Version of Hong Kong's Political History

China's version differs. Local mandarins and "better people" were driven by Western force from the imperial outpost of Hong Kong. This contest over territory happened not once, but many times, at great cost to China. To China, Hong Kong represents imposed, not "free" trade, unequal treaties, and protected not honest businessmen seeking the rule of law, but rapacious drug dealers seeking a haven from legitimate Chinese control. It has from the beginning been a hotbed of subversion: subversion of Chinese society by drug smuggling; of Qing Dynasty rule with its well-connected, wealthy triads and the Hong Kong usurper, Sun Yat-sen; of Nationalist rule by providing a haven for Communists and by frustrating Nationalist takeover at the end of the Second World War; of Japanese conquest and rule by providing supplies to both Nationalists and Communists; of Communism by its protection of Nationalists fleeing the P.R.C. and by its large group of China watchers prying into China's affairs and discrediting its government and by the UDHK and other groups which burnt the Basic Law, called for the overthrow of the Beijing government, and which funded, supplied, and encouraged the June 4 protesters.

Hong Kong is and always has been subversive in this version. For example, Dr. Sun Yat-sen, in a commencement address at Hong Kong

---

[13] This has never been sustained by public opinion polls. A total of 79 per cent of respondents in 1984, according to a Survey Research Hong Kong Ltd. (SRH) poll "agreed that sovereignty over Hong Kong should be returned to China." Joseph Y. S. Cheng (ed.), *Hong Kong in Transition* (Hong Kong: Oxford University Press, 1986), p. 11. The question has always been when and how Hong Kong would return to China, not whether, according to most residents. However, a large portion prefers independence or a very high degree of autonomy, but few prefer British rule. See Table 8 below.

University in 1923 asked, "Where did I get my revolutionary and modern ideas from? I got them from the colony of Hong Kong. I compared Huengshan with Hong Kong and, although they are only fifty miles apart, the difference of the government impressed me very much." Dr. Sun then encouraged the students to "carry this English example of good government to every part of China."[14] This is what the current rulers of China, themselves supposedly heirs of Dr. Sun, most fear. To them, it has been not a port of trade, but a port of interference.

In China's version, Hongkongese have been repeatedly restive, and while subjugated by force and the threat of expulsion from their homes and families, have been protected as much as possible by successive Chinese governments. The Hong Kong government has ruled by sufferance, as a matter of mutual convenience in a time of weakness, now decisively past. There have been many protests against colonial rule, many expulsions, and much repression, and what has seemed political passivity to the colonialists was in reality patriotic disdain for participating in colonial government. Only China, they assert, legitimately represents the Hong Kong people, for Hong Kong was, is, and always will be part of China and its people Chinese.

In this version of history, the Basic Law is meant to reintegrate Hong Kong into China, while respecting for a period the differences generated by 150 years of forced separation. Eventually, as China develops, Hong Kong and China will become one system, and the Basic Law is not meant so much to isolate Hong Kong from China as to effectively harness its people and resources into a rapidly changing China. China wants Hong Kong's experience in generating wealth; it does not want its interference in political affairs. In the Mainland's view, the Basic Law is not to keep Hong Kong apolitical, but to provide the means and time to integrate Hongkongese into China's politics by teaching them both local governance and allowing them to participate (with due safeguards against their "subversive" influence) in national government. Meanwhile, they hope China also will learn from Hong Kong, and adapt, where appropriate, those ways suitable to its changing circumstances. Thus the ultimate thrust of the Basic Law, to China, is to protect the economic legacy, respect the cultural and political differences, and allow time for full reintegration by 2047.

---

[14] In William McGurn, *Perfidious Albion: The Abandonment of Hong Kong 1997* (Washington: Ethics and Public Policy Centre, 1992), pp. 27–28.

☐ Future from the Past: A Hong Kong Version of Its Political History?

A less partisan reading of history fully supports neither view. From the perspective of participation in formal politics, and this should be emphasized, formal *colonial* politics, Hong Kong people *have* been fairly passive and apathetic until recently. Formal politics concerns elections and campaigning, representation on political bodies, appointment to political posts, organized political groups and lobbies, and membership in governing bodies with public responsibilities. Until 1982 there was little mass participation in formal politics *per se*, and then only at the DB and Urban and Regional Councils level. This should be no surprise; until December 1990 membership in a political party was illegal, and not until September 1991 could most people even vote for a small portion of the Legco. They have never been able to vote for Executive Council members or the Governor. Overall rule of Hong Kong has never been subject to formal political participation by locals. What shared rule there has been, up until the 1980s, was almost wholly conducted by a tiny colonial elite.

On an informal level, however, Hong Kong has long had considerable political activity. Influence and contacts (face and *guanxi*) have been and remain the coin of everyday life. Much of this revolves around family, clan, or interest contact with civil service personnel bypassing most formal government channels. "Corruption," the procuring of favours, has been a pervasive problem, yet corruption is another name for a type of informal political influence — getting the government to do (or not do) something for someone. There are hundreds of community bodies whose membership assures what can only be characterized as political influence (similar to the Black churches of the United States or the mosques of a number of states), and many of these bodies had their *de facto* political efficacy recognized when the Hong Kong government reorganized itself on a consultancy model following the riots of 1967. There have long been groups such as the various chambers of commerce and unions which wielded considerable power in the past, and membership in "illegal" political organizations such as the Chinese Communist Party (CCP) and Kuomintang (KMT) has been estimated in the early 1980s to be 50,000 and 10,000, respectively. The activism throughout the spring and summer of 1994 of the Heung Yee Kuk shows that considerable political power was always latent.

Nor has interest in political coverage and commentary been lacking. No population of similar size on earth has so many daily newspapers, over

20 in Chinese and five in English, and many are well known for their particular political slant. In surveys conducted by the Hong Kong Transitions Project in August 1993 and February 1994, nearly 90 per cent of Hong Kong people considered themselves informed to one degree or another about government policies related to their livelihood. Around 40 per cent considered themselves informed to a fair or great extent. On China affairs, over two-thirds considered themselves informed or had personal experience of Chinese realities. No truly apathetic people would know so much about government policies, nor make such great efforts to keep themselves abreast of current events.

Not only do Hong Kong people support an amazing number of newspapers and television channels containing information on current affairs (four local channels with several broadcasts daily, two full-time cable news channels and one part-time satellite channel, the BBC, now carried on cable); there have been hundreds of demonstrations and protests in Hong Kong's past, and since 1984, thousands of marches, protests, demonstrations, and petitions, several involving over a million signatures, as in the Daya Bay petition of 1986, or a million marchers as happened twice in 1989. Between 50,000 and 100,000 demonstrators now meet regularly in Victoria Park every June 4 and not a week passes without several demonstrations at Legco meetings.

When history is probed without a particular view to protect, one discovers that far from the passive, business-fixated myth, at least seven times was British rule seriously challenged from inside Hong Kong itself. The first was in 1858–1861, when a large portion of the population left Hong Kong in protest against the Anglo-French occupation of Guangzhou. Again in 1884 a massive dockyard strike and riot finally compelled government concessions. In 1898–1899 open revolt and guerrilla warfare in the New Territories compelled the government to recognize village government, clan councils, and Qing Dynasty rules. These provisions were unchallenged until 1994 when the government backed Christine Loh's proposal to allow New Territories women to be bequeathed land.[15] New Territories men (the Heung Yee Kuk) in their hundreds rioted, attacked and threatened legislators, and "declared war" on the proposal, winning the backing of the

---

[15] The bill was passed in late June by an overwhelming majority of those voting 32 to 2 (out of 60 members). The Heung Yee Kuk vowed to continue its opposition.

nominally egalitarian Communist Party. The fourth time was the 1912–1913 Tramway Boycott, in which the government suspended the common law, using inferred and joint responsibility, punishing whole blocks for boycotting the Trams. The fifth was in 1920–1922 when labour strikes paralysed Hong Kong and the Chinese government intervened, settling the strikes after Hong Kong government concessions. The sixth time was the long General Strike of 1925–1926, when 30 per cent of Hong Kong Chinese left and the economy nearly collapsed. The seventh time was the 1967 disturbances, when bombings and riots shook Hong Kong, and Macau fell to Red Guards.[16]

No one knows what might have happened in 1989 when for two weekends in a row over a million people marched in support of the students in Tiananmen Square, and a General Sympathy Strike was spontaneously held in protest of the massacre. Hundreds of groups and individuals published advertisements supporting the Tiananmen students. One of the left-wing papers, the *Wen Wei Po*, came out against the Beijing government. Millions of dollars were collected by hundreds of organizations for the promotion of democracy in China. Scores of dissenters were spirited out past the People's Armed Police and the Public Security Bureau net by the "Hong Kong/China democracy underground." All here were aware of the very high state of feelings.[17] If the Hong Kong government had dared to forbid the protests, or if the Beijing government had fallen, circumstances in Hong Kong could have differed dramatically.

The record shows that 1949–1979 was a period of abnormally low levels of political activity. Previously, demonstrations and political protest had occurred hundreds of times. Scores of groups with thousands of members contended with the Hong Kong government for loyalty. Even entities like the Tung Wah Group of Hospitals were suspected of being subversive organizations or mediums of influence for China. Formally, however, few Chinese participated in colonial politics; who after all would

---

[16] See for more detail the various chapters in Ming K. Chan (ed.), John D. Young (collaborator), *Precarious Balance: Hong Kong Between China and Britain, 1842–1992* (Hong Kong: Hong Kong University Press, 1994).

[17] The Hong Kong Transitions Project members tracked developments on radio (calls were recorded and transcribed), took photos of marches and marchers, monitored the newspapers and television reports, and even administered questionnaires to participants in demonstrations.

want to be tainted by collaboration with the imperialists? In sum, sensitivity to political and nationalistic urges was high in Hong Kong before 1949 and has become so again. Between 1949 and 1979, however, few desirable options presented themselves. A corrupt, violent regime held dictatorial power on Taiwan; a corrupt, violent regime held dictatorial power on the Chinese mainland. But in the 1980s both China and Taiwan changed dramatically, and Hong Kong returned to its more normal state of affairs as a centre of political intrigue and nationalism. Now, unlike any earlier period, its people can choose relatively freely how to participate in politics and towards what purposes, and they have done so in massive numbers.

When formal politics became acceptable after the Joint Declaration, and as Hongkongese were allowed to assume greater power in self-government, participation in formal Hong Kong politics shot up (see Table 2).

In 1991 the number of campaign workers, polling station assistants, and electioneering assistants totalled considerably over 10,000. Campaign person-days probably exceeded well over 100,000 (number of persons campaigning times number of days campaigning). Nearly every street in

Table 2. Formal Political Participation Index

	1981	1991
Elections during year	1	3
Government bodies subject to election	1	4
Members elected to government bodies	15	338
Polling station days during year	13	937
Registered electors*	34,381	1,916,925
Votes cast during year	6,195	1,591,073
Political parties@	0	8
Party members#	0	3,800

Notes: * Highest number registered for any one election (Legco election September 1991). Current registrations are reported as 2.45 million.
@ Formally established as of 1991 (United Democrats of Hong Kong, Meeting Point, Liberal Democratic Federation, Hong Kong Democratic Foundation, Association for Democracy and People's Livelihood, Chinese Communist Party (CCP), Kuomintang (KMT), New Hong Kong Alliance).
# Does not include CCP and KMT members (approximately 60,000). Includes active, dues-paying members only.
Sources: Hong Kong government; *South China Morning Post*; 1991 Hong Kong Transitions Project Visual Data Surveys.

Hong Kong was festooned with signs, posters, banners, and placards and every mailbox received more than one flyer in 1991. Thousands of store owners put up, or allowed up, campaign posters.[18]

☐ The Present State of Political Participation

Months before the September 1994 elections, on nearly every block, posters have appeared advertising various political groups. As of mid-1994, twelve parties, including two new pro-Beijing groups, the DAB and the Federation for a Stable and Prosperous Hong Kong, one KMT-related group, the 1, 2, 3 Democratic Alliance, and one moderate-to-conservative group, the Liberal Party, joined preparations for the elections. In May, UDHK and MP members voted to merge into the Democratic Party in October, after the DB elections, although they agreed to cooperate during the campaigning. A number of quasi-party groups ranging from the Trotskyite April 5th Action Group to the Business and Professional Federation also indicate they will join the campaigning. According to publicly reported surveys, politicians from the Governor down have become known to a larger portion of Hong Kong people. Indeed, the frequency of published political opinion surveys has risen to, and remains at, an all time high, with at least two appearing every week. Hong Kong has become openly and decisively political.

Despite twenty months of dispute over the conduct of the 1994–1995 elections, when asked about their voting intentions, Hongkongese report a fair degree of interest. The voter registration campaign which ended in early July achieved the highest level yet. Voting intentions always tend to be overstated, but in Hong Kong circumstances, even indicating intent reveals both interest and a belief that voting is a socially acceptable behaviour. Of 636 surveyed in February 1994, 54 per cent indicated they were registered voters, and 73 per cent of those registered intended to vote. Some 17 per cent were unsure and 10 per cent had no plans to vote. The breakdown of the Sino-British talks has had a dampening effect on participation. When registered voters were asked, "Have your plans been influenced by the current breakdown of the Sino-British talks?" 81 per cent said no, 7 per cent

---

[18] This estimate is based on detailed observations by the Hong Kong Transitions Project, including systematic visits to randomly selected DB candidate's offices, intensive photographic surveys of all three elections, particularly the Legco election, and interviews of candidates both before and after the elections.

didn't know, and 12 per cent replied yes. Most of the 12 per cent indicating that they had been affected reported that they would not vote, or would restrict their vote to the DB level. Overall, current formal political participation intentions for 1994–1995 after the breakdown are shown in Table 3.

Table 3. Formal Election Participation Intentions
(February 1994, N = 636)

Not registered to vote*	46 per cent
Registered, will not vote or don't know	15 per cent
Intend now to vote in one election	14 per cent
Intend now to vote in two elections	4 per cent
Intend now to vote in all three elections	21 per cent

* This is before the voting registration drive commenced.

This rise in political participation has come at some cost to peace of mind. Indeed, the only certain thing which can be said confidently of politics in Hong Kong is that they are worrying to most people, most of the time, and the level has risen since 1991. Consistently, the highest levels of worry have focused on personal freedoms and the politics of Hong Kong after the handover (see Table 4).

Reflecting the normal lag in reactions to increased stress, this sustained high level of worry has begun to affect social and personal well-being in 1993–1994. Family breakup, spouse and child abuse, suicide, drug and alcohol abuse, and physical illnesses are all up from previous levels. Suicide, for example, rose from 579 cases in 1989 to 748 in 1991 and 732 in 1992. Total deaths have risen 11.5 per cent from 1988 to the end of 1992 while the population increased nowhere near that amount. Divorce rose from 5,893 cases in 1988 to 8,626 in 1993. The 12,691 people arrested for narcotics in 1993 was the highest ever reported, well over the 8,944 reported in 1989.[19] While the number of people leaving Hong Kong has declined somewhat, the level of commitment to stay in Hong Kong after 1997 remains less than a majority. This lack of commitment is surprising given the many immigrants forced to return to Hong Kong by lack of

---

[19] Figures from the respective appendices in *Hong Kong 1991* and *Hong Kong 1994* (Hong Kong: Government Information Services).

Table 4. Degrees of Worry

Question: At present, do you worry about:

	1991 (Nov.) (N = 902) % Worried to varying degree	1991 (Nov.) % Don't know	1993 (Feb.) (N = 615) % Worried to varying degree	1993 (Feb.) % Don't know	1993 (Aug.) (N = 605) % Worried to varying degree	1993 (Aug.) % Don't know	1994 (Feb.) (N = 636) % Worried to varying degree	1994 (Feb.) % Don't know
personal standard of living after 1997?	40	4	50	5	49	4	48	1
personal freedom in Hong Kong after 1997?*	41	3	51	4	53	4	52	2
your family prospects in Hong Kong after 1997?	38	3	48	5	45	5	45	4
Hong Kong's prospects after 1997?	43	7	56	7	49	9	47	5
the politics of Hong Kong after 1997?	43	13	57	15	52	14	55	11

* "personal security and freedom in Hong Kong after 1997" was asked in the 1991 and 1993 February surveys.

opportunity overseas and given the widespread tales of horror occasioned by joblessness, crime, and discrimination elsewhere (see Table 5).

Despite all the problems abroad, staying does not rest primarily on Hong Kong's continued prosperity. Instead, what concerns most whose commitment to stay is contingent are matters such as personal freedom and Hong Kong's politics (see Table 6).

Of course, if Hong Kong developed economic as well as political problems, the outflow could get quite large. Additionally, once a population has become established overseas, it tends to "pull" relatives towards it, and during the 1980s and 1990s this overseas population of Hong Kong Chinese has become larger than ever. Diana Lary reports that while the number of Hongkongese applications for immigration to Canada has declined from 46,214 in 1991 to 26,299 in 1993, the number of visa requests for family

Table 5. People's Plans to Leave or Stay in Hong Kong after 1997

	1993 (Feb.) N = 615 (%)	1993 (Aug.) N = 605 (%)	1994 (Feb.) N = 636 (%)
1. Will stay under any circumstances	38	42	43
2. Plan to leave	4	5	5
3. Would leave or seek means to leave if changes after 1997 are unsuitable	51	44	46
4. Undecided/Don't know	7	9	6

Table 6. What Is the MAJOR Change Which You Would Find So Unsuitable as to Make You Seek to Leave?

	1993 (Aug.) N = 264 (%)	1994 (Feb.) N = 293 (%)
1. Personal standard of living	25	24
2. Personal freedom	32	37
3. Hong Kong's politics	25	19
4. Family prospects	3	6
5. Hong Kong's economic prospects	6	7
6. Others	6	5
7. Don't know	3	2

visitation and student status has risen from 29,620 in 1991 to 35,233 in 1993 (through November, so the actual annual total is even higher).[20] Hong Kong's international ties as fostered by family are strengthening, and thus whatever happens here will have a consequently larger impact abroad.[21] This Canadian phenomenon can also be expected with the other major immigration destinations.

☐ The Battle over Hearts and Minds

The sources of lack of commitment to Hong Kong are many, including worries about one's accustomed way of life, or expectations about life opportunities which may or may not be fulfillable in Hong Kong, but even these seem to revolve at some deep level around questions of fundamental political/cultural identity and political preferences. Politically, identifying oneself as a member of a "nation" is crucial for matters of loyalty and national cohesion. As Eastern Europe and the states of the former Union of Soviet Socialist Republics have shown, divided identity, ethnic or ideological, can be threatening to national unity. Hong Kong people by and large may identify themselves culturally with China, but the description of themselves as Chinese cannot be read as meaning that they now have a nationalistic identity. In fact, as sampling indicates, while fewer than 30,000 people of six million are of British Anglo-Saxon origins, a full 8 to 10 per cent of adults over 18, meaning around 400,000, identify themselves even at this late date as Hong Kong British. Only 40 per cent see themselves as Hong Kong Chinese, an elocution similar to that used by other Chinese citizens in China (see Table 7).

The relation of the regional aspect to this identity may compromise the nationalistic unity assumed by such questions. The full meaning of regional modifying descriptors among Chinese in the P.R.C. needs research. Clearly, in a number of interviews conducted by the author since 1989, the use of the

---

[20] Diana Lary, *Canada and Hong Kong Update* (Toronto: Canada and Hong Kong Project Joint Centre for Asia-Pacific Studies, Winter 1994), pp. 4–5.

[21] The probabilities of disruption in Hong Kong are developed in detail in the author's "A Collision of Cultures: Systemic Conflict in Hong Kong's Future with China," in *One Culture, Many Systems: Politics in the Reunification of China*, edited by Donald H. McMillen and Michael E. DeGolyer (Hong Kong: The Chinese University Press, 1993), pp. 271–302.

Table 7. Fundamental Identity: "What do you consider yourself to be?"

	1993 (Feb.) N = 615 (%)	1993 (Aug.) N = 605 (%)	1994 (Feb.) N = 636 (%)
1. Hong Kong Chinese	36	34	40
2. Chinese	19	20	20
3. Hong Kong person	37	35	30
4. Hong Kong British	7	10	8
5. British	0	0	1
6. Others	1	1	1

term "Hong Kong person" often deliberately means non-identity with the P.R.C. government and even some lack of identity with Chinese mainland culture.

As disturbing as the above may be, even more are the answers given to a question of fundamental preferences about the future, a future destined, at least according to the Basic Law and the Joint Declaration, to be one of unity with the P.R.C. (see Table 8).

The fundamental preferences and identities above played a crucial role in the 1991 elections and will enter into those of 1994–1995. Those candidates who said they would "stand up for Hong Kong" triumphed at the polls.[22] Many of those same candidates had attacked the Basic Law and supported the overthrow of the Beijing regime in demonstrations. Even pro-Beijing candidates had to downplay campaigning which could be construed as pro-regime. Instead, they emphasized that they supported reform in China and that they could more effectively protect Hong Kong people's interests because of their contacts. In 1991 they generally failed in the Legco elections. The pro-Beijing candidates tried hard to focus on purely local issues, and where they could do so credibly, as in the DB elections, they experienced some success.

---

[22] See Jane C. Y. Lee, "Campaigning Themes of the Candidates in the 1991 Legislative Council Election," in *Hong Kong Tried Democracy*, edited by Lau Siu-kai and Louie Kin-sheun (Hong Kong: Hong Kong Institute of Asia-Pacific Studies, The Chinese University of Hong Kong, 1993), pp. 297–315.

Table 8. Fundamental Preferences

Question: If you could control history, and determine its outcome, which of the following arrangements concerning Hong Kong after 1997 would you choose?

	SCMP* (30 June 1991)		1993 (Feb.) N = 615	1993 (Aug.) N = 605	1994 (Feb.) N = 636
1. Make Hong Kong independent	29	(27)	25	22	24
2. Keep Hong Kong as a British colony	26	(24)	19	21	15
3. Make Hong Kong part of the Commonwealth	19	(17)	8	9	10
4. Join Hong Kong and P.R.C. under "one country, two systems" formula	26	(24)	42	39	44
5. Don't know	—	(7)	6	9	7

* A comparable question was asked in a *South China Morning Post* poll reported on 30 June 1991: "If you were controlling history, what would you most like to happen in 1997?" Figures in parentheses are adjusted to allow for the likely level of don't knows to be factored in for comparability purposes.

☐ Conclusion

True in 1991, and even more so in 1994–1995, Hong Kong's politics are by no means exclusively either local or nationalistic, nor are those politics consensual or majoritarian in the formal sense of elected majorities making policies. Hong Kong politics, in fact, seem to be increasingly in search of an identity and a focus. The nature of the identity and focus which is developing will prove of crucial importance for the candidates in the 1994–1995 elections, for the prospects of the Basic Law, and perhaps even for the stability and nature of the nation-state of China.

The Basic Law currently imposes colonialistic institutions on an SAR which will not be a colony. The sources of legitimacy in the colonial framework among people with a divided loyalty and confused identity will find themselves severely challenged when faced with the changes in the hearts and minds of the Hong Kong people. Citizens are not the same as subjects. Already a nationalistic identity is being forged in Hong Kong, but it differs significantly from that on the mainland. However, at this moment "naive nationalism" on the part of many China advisers and PWC members may lead to overenthusiastic embrace of a rather vaguely defined "mother" China, and they may agree to allow the central government too great a sway over Hong Kong. The regional identity of Hong Kong may tend to get lost in the patriotic haze for a short while, unlike the other regions of China which have clearly determined their interests and know the limits of patriotic appeals. The mainlanders have had to live with slogans and nationalistic politics for many years and know how to separate reality from rhetoric very well. They have proven their loyalty; now they expect the payoff. Not so for Hongkongese, especially many of the long time supporters of a China they really don't know very well in most cases. These people will tend to go too far in compromising Hong Kong's interests in the cause of repudiating the imperialists and embracing the motherland, and will eventually, if not sooner, be condemned for doing so by Hongkongese. The people who have allowed this will find themselves in some real degree of difficulty with the Hong Kong people. But this is not by any means the most dangerous repercussion of nationalism in Hong Kong.

The "Manifesto" of the new Democratic Party proclaimed on 18 April 1994 indicates that Hong Kong nationalism will have two elements which will pose a potent challenge to the present leadership of China. First, "We care for China and, as part of the Chinese citizenry, we have the rights and obligations to participate in and comment on the affairs of China." Second, "Democracy, freedom, human rights, and the rule of law are the foundations for progress and prosperity in a modern society."[23] If a growing majority of Hong Kong citizens feel that they, having already successfully modernized, know the best way forward for China, and that they, as citizens of China who care about its and their future, must play a role in its leadership, then if that participation and leadership are denied, who can say that such patriots will quietly sit back and watch China misled and even destroyed? If the takeover of Hong Kong is bungled, and the corrupt politicians of the mainland sour the tender idealism of Hong Kong patriots, then what is the likely reaction? When patriotism cannot be rejected, it must be reformed. Precisely what that patriotism, that nationalistic identity, will be, and what it will provoke is uncertain; however, clearly, nationalism and its fundamental effects will raise up a challenge to a Basic Law which is

---

[23] *South China Morning Post*, 19 April 1994, p. 6.

interpreted to constrict and restrict participation to the sort of nominal level found untenable in Hong Kong in the 1980s.

Indeed, if Marx was correct in the *Communist Manifesto*, the increasing pace of the transition of dynamically capitalistic Hong Kong colonial subjects into Chinese citizens raises harrowing challenges to "Socialism with Chinese Characteristics":

> The bourgeoisie, by the rapid improvement of all instruments of production, by the immensely facilitated means of communication, draws all ... nations into civilisation. The cheap prices of its commodities are the heavy artillery with which it batters down all Chinese walls, with which it forces the barbarians' intensely obstinate hatred of foreigners to capitulate. It compels all nations, on pain of extinction, to adopt the bourgeois mode of production; it compels them ... to become bourgeois themselves. In one word, it creates a world after its own image.[24]

According to Marx, and the evidence available today, Hong Kong cannot help but be "internationalized" as China fears; that is its nature as a member of the world capitalistic culture and as the homeland of millions of immigrants abroad. It is not just different from China; it is far ahead of China in modernization and different only in that it does not see its own identity clearly, nor the path for that identity to make itself felt on China. Its hand of change on China is currently invisible, the hand of Adam Smith. But, if Marx is right about the nature of the bourgeoisie, and history seems to have borne him out, and Hong Kong is made a part of China and forced to clarify its loyalties and responsibilities, the elections of 1994–1995 may not be the last hurrah of the departing British colonialist; they may instead be the first tocsin of deep systemic change in China, a return to the modernizing, democratizing goals of the 1911 revolution which also began in Hong Kong.

---

[24] K. Marx, and F. Engels, *Collected Works* (Vol. 6; N.Y.: International Publishers, 1976), p. 488.

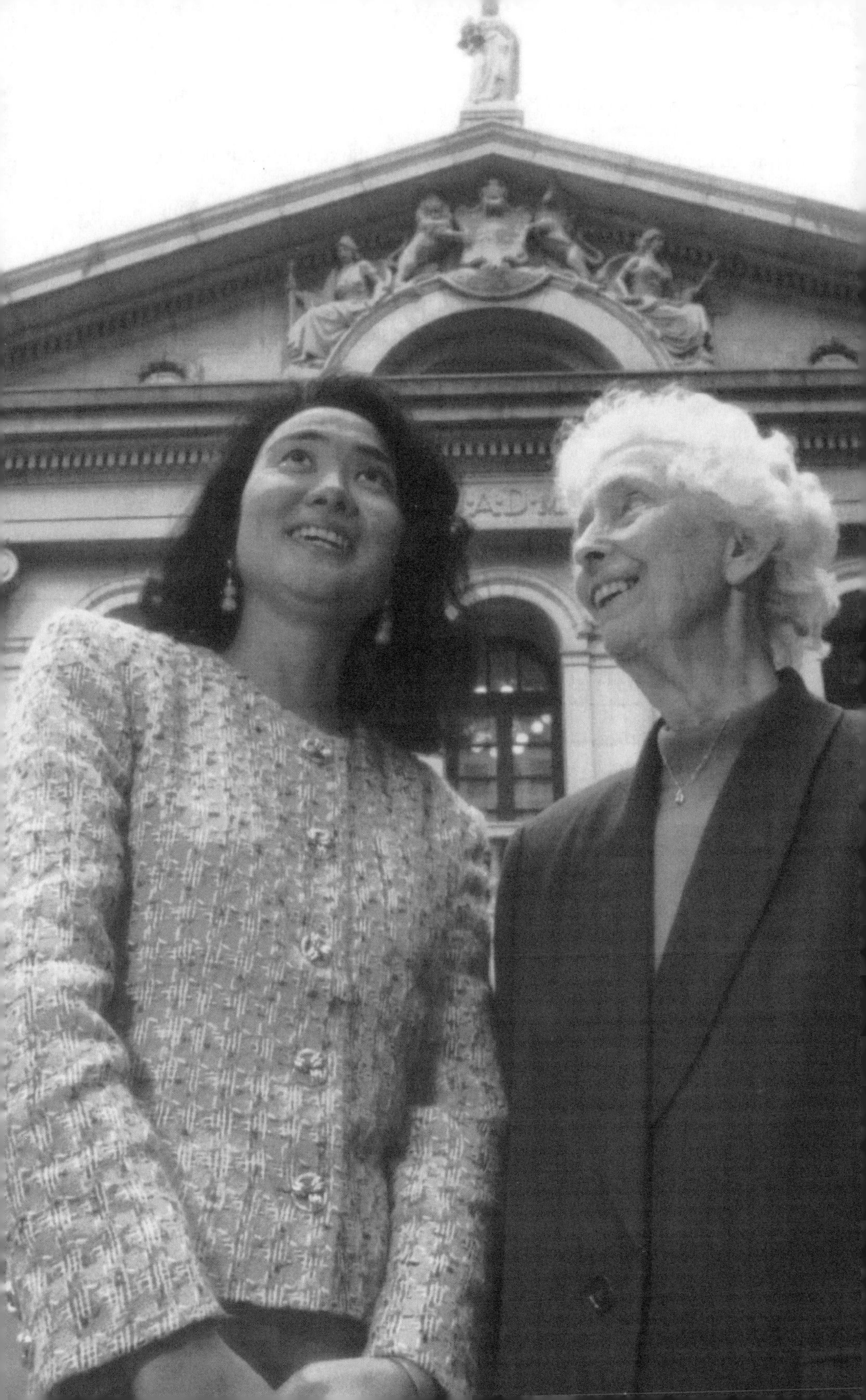

7

Public Opinion

Robert T. Y. Chung

If the year 1992–1993 was "the year of Christopher Patten," in terms of public attention,[1] then 1993–1994 must have been "the year of constitutional debate."[2] This, however, is not to say that Governor Christopher Patten has, in any way, faded away from the public's attention, but rather, that public opinion has become more focused on specific issues like Sino-British talks and constitutional development than on the personality of Christopher Patten. In China's perspective, no doubt, Patten was the invisible hand behind the entire battle between China and Britain over Hong Kong's constitutional development,[3] but in the eyes of the general public, even though the battle has been fought in the name of the Hong Kong people by both sides, it was only a meaningless seven-month

---

Robert T. Y. Chung is a research officer at the Social Sciences Research Centre (SSRC), the University of Hong Kong.

[1] The author made this assertion in his article for *The Other Hong Kong Report 1993* last year, in order to highlight the momentum generated by Christopher Patten in his first year at office.

[2] Sino-British talks on the constitutional development of Hong Kong started on 22 April 1993 and terminated on 27 November 1993, after seventeen rounds of negotiations. The row over constitutional reform, of course, started when Governor Patten delivered his first policy speech on 7 October 1992, and was still going on at the time of writing this chapter.

[3] Pro-China newspapers in Hong Kong, headed by its flagship the *Wen Wei Po*, attacked Patten on an almost daily basis throughout the entire period of the dispute.

scuffle between the sovereign powers.[4] It was only when the talks broke down in November 1993, and Patten's constitutional proposals put before the Legislative Council (Legco) on 15 December 1993 that the issue officially became a local matter (without China's blessing, of course).

Thus, in the first half of 1993–1994, the public's attention was drawn to the progress of the talks, and related issues like the electoral system and the "through train" issue, whereas between January and June 1994 people began to focus on the reform bills and the party politics associated with them.[5] Throughout the year, the Sino-British relationship and constitutional affairs regularly became news headlines, and with this as a backdrop, opinion surveys continued to develop. The present chapter reviews the development of public opinion surveys in 1993–1994, and reports their major findings.

☐ Development of Opinion Polls in 1993–1994

In *The Other Hong Kong Report 1993*, the author reviewed the development of opinion polls in Hong Kong up to 1993, and contended that two "metamorphoses" occurred in recent years: that of 1991 due to the first Legco direct election, and that of 1992 due to the arrival of Patten. If the 1991 election had given birth to popular opinion polls in Hong Kong, and the arrival of Patten had caused their explosion in number, then 1993–1994 was the year when opinion surveys maintained their momentum of development on one hand, but became more structured on the other. Their format was becoming more standardized, and their design more strategic.

In terms of quantity, and counting only opinion polls conducted by

---

[4] Hong Kong people were debarred from sending a representative to sit at the talks, and the Hong Kong Legislative Council was never given the power to endorse or rectify any agreement arising from the talks.

[5] The first part of Patten's constitutional reform package was passed into law by the Legco on 23 February 1994, and the second part was passed on 30 June 1994, incidentally being the last day of the period being reviewed by this volume of *The Other Hong Kong Report*.

Public Opinion

independent professional bodies reported through the media,[6] the number of polls conducted in the year approximated very closely to that of the previous year. According to records kept at the SSRC, the number of such polls has practically remained the same, at about 120.[7] Table 1 breaks down these polls according to the organizations conducting them.

Table 1. Media Polls by Research Organizations, 1993–1994

	Percentage
Social Sciences Research Centre, HKU	42.6
Hong Kong Polling and Business Research	20.5
Survey Research Hong Kong Ltd.	4.9
Asian Commercial Research Ltd.	3.3
Other academic institutions	19.7
Others	9.0
Total	100.0

Source: Social Sciences Research Centre, the University of Hong Kong.

Compared to figures of the previous year,[8] it was found that the share of SSRC polls has dropped over the year, from 53.9 per cent to 42.6 per cent. Polls conducted by the Hong Kong Polling and Business Research also dropped from 24.3 per cent to 20.5 per cent, while the number of polls conducted by other academic institutions rose from 4.3 per cent to 19.7 per cent, indicating increased participation across different tertiary institutions.

If this trend continues, it could be envisaged that more opinion research programmes or centres will be set up across different tertiary institutions in the future, and when that happens, opinion surveys and applied social

---

[6] We exclude surveys released by pressure groups and political parties, government bodies and committees, and non-professional bodies. According to records kept at the SSRC, these surveys amounted to slightly less than one hundred during the period under review.

[7] Approximate figures only. There was no way we could track down opinion polls reported across *all* media, but the figures should be at least 90 per cent accurate.

[8] Choi Po-king and Ho Lok-sang (eds.), *The Other Hong Kong Report 1993* (Hong Kong: The Chinese University Press, 1993), p. 407.

research will be given a new thrust and the infrastructure for opinion surveys strengthened.[9] In the past two years, opinion surveys conducted by the SSRC and other academic institutions together constituted about 60 per cent of all media polls, and were on the increase. It could, therefore, be expected that academic institutions would still be the major source of media polls in the years to come.

In very broad terms, 55 per cent of the media polls counted by the author related to political issues, as against 44 per cent related to social and non-political issues (see Table 2). This was rather similar to the previous year,[10] but non-political polls were on the rise, probably reflecting a public fatigue over constitutional matters.

On the evolution of opinion polls, the year 1993–1994 saw a convergence in the basic design of these surveys. Increasingly, media polls took on standard sample size of about 500, instead of the 300 to 400 in the previous years. Technically, a sample of 500 successful interviews without any

Table 2. Media Polls by Broad Topics, 1993–1994

	Percentage		
Political issues			
Constitutional reform/Sino-British talks	17.2		
Political figures and groups	15.6		
Confidence towards the future of Hong Kong	4.1		
Trust towards governments	3.3		
Other political issues	14.8	*Subtotal*:	55.0%
Non-political issues			
Social issues	35.2		
Other topics	9.0	*Subtotal*:	44.2%
Electoral issues			
Exit polls	0.8	*Subtotal*:	0.8%
Total			100.0%

Source: Social Sciences Research Centre, the University of Hong Kong.

---

[9] The author had in mind the following aspects of opinion surveying: general research designs, sampling techniques, softwares support, hardware configurations, quality control, report formats, data archiving, and research ethics.

[10] Same as Note 8, p. 408.

response bias yields a standard error of about 2.2 per cent for each opinion question, and if we use 95 per cent as the confidence interval, the sampling error would be plus/minus 4.4 per cent, which is quite comfortable for most opinion surveys. The SSRC has adopted "500 plus" as the minimum sample size in all its opinion surveys from the very beginning. The drawback of using 500 instead of 1,000 samples is that more refined analyses like differentiation across demographic factors may not yield meaningful results. In many countries, general opinion surveys usually take on sample size of 1,000 or more. These of course require more input in terms of time and human resources, in return for more useful data. Perhaps when opinion polls become more developed in Hong Kong, and both readers and researchers begin to opt for more powerful surveys, the standard sample size will be expanded.

Another feature of opinion survey development in 1993–1994 was the gradual standardization of measurement. In the domain of market research and social studies, a variety of scales has been used to measure attitudes and general opinion. These ranged from yes-no dichotomy to four-point, five-point, ten-point, and even 100-point scales. Each scale, of course, has its own merits and demerits, and could only be judged on the kind of data warranted. In many democratic countries, the performance of political leaders are often measured in terms of approval rates, which essentially indicate how many people would vote for them *had there been* an election immediately. Responses are usually dichotomized by either "yes" or "no," and a leader's approval rate equals to the percentage of respondents replying "yes."

In Hong Kong, there being no general election to governorship or ministerial positions, approval rates became rather meaningless, perhaps with the exception of Legislative Councillors who came to office through direct elections. As a result, a different kind of support rating has been used to measure the popularity of political figures and organizations. In Hong Kong, the SSRC was the first to introduce the 0–100 scale to measure popularity: respondents were asked to rate their support towards certain persons or organizations using a 0–100 scale, they were explicitly told that 0 stood for absolute no support, 100 stood for absolute support, and the mid-point of 50 stood for neutral. After three years, the community has gradually become familiar with the scale, and a growing number of opinion questions and popularity ratings have been set using this scale. Research findings have therefore become more "portable."

Another development in opinion polling last year was the gradual emergence of "tracking polls" or repeated measures, which was somewhat a natural outcome of opinion poll development. If one poll gives a snapshot of how people think, at one particular point in time, then repeated measures will provide a rolling picture of how opinion changes. Tracking polls therefore give life to opinion development: they provide a dynamic, rather than static, view of opinion formulation and social change. This very important dimension of social research could only be achieved through careful planning and systematic accumulation of research data. Hong Kong pollsters are heading in this direction.

There were, however, negative developments in the year past. Because opinion polls have become increasingly popular, especially those with eye-catching findings, pressure groups and political parties have increasingly used this medium to attract public attention. According to records kept at the SSRC, there were at least 23 "opinion surveys" released by pressure groups or political parties in the past year: once every two weeks on average, and getting more frequent. Many of these surveys were below standard, whether in terms of sample size, research methodology, or questionnaire design. The media has apparently not been able to differentiate proper scientific surveys from mere publicity displays. If this trend continues, the media would soon be flooded by all sorts of "opinion surveys," and the community would not be able to distinguish what is trustworthy from what is not.

Besides political parties and pressure groups, the media themselves were also to be blamed for the flooding of substandard surveys. Because findings from opinion polls often make attractive headlines, and those from instant polls are even more attractive, some media have apparently decided to sacrifice quality for quick or cheap results. Some media used casual telephone surveys of 100 to 200 samples conducted by their own staff as equivalent of opinion polls, some used small-scale street interviews as substitutes, and some employed bias-prone methods like automated telephone interview to collect large sets of useless data. The result was degraded surveys with bias findings, which could be worse than opinion surveys conducted by pressure groups and political parties.

Looking ahead, therefore, it would be very important for the research community to derive a code of conduct to govern the conduct of opinion surveys, and guidelines for the media to distinguish proper opinion polls from casual interviews. Only then can polls maintain their standard and credibility as an unbiased source of information. As the new wave of elections draws near, opinion polls would again attract people's attention, and it would be very important that they are not abused.[11] Tracking polls would continue to grow, and new forms of surveys may emerge. If their development is monitored with care, opinion polls would continue to be an important part of Hong Kong's political culture in the years to come.

☐ Highlight of Poll Findings[12]

Sino-British Talks

Sino-British talks over Hong Kong's constitutional development began in April 1993, more than six months after Governor Patten announced his reform package. The seventeen rounds of talks that followed, spanning over more than seven months, were strictly held behind closed doors. In the midst of frequent rhetoric exchanges, and without the slightest idea of what was going on, Hong Kong people waited patiently for the outcome, and, as usual, with an optimistic outlook.

Table 3 and Figure 1 show that even though Hong Kong people were

---

[11] The year 1994 will be the beginning of another election cycle, with District Board elections in September 1994, the municipal councils elections in March 1995, and the Legco elections in September 1995. The Legco elections would be the biggest, and most complicated, election ever in the history of Hong Kong, because other than the record number of 20 directly elected seats, there will be 30 functional constituency seats practically elected by the entire workforce, on top of 10 seats returned by the electoral college consisting of over 300 District Board members.

[12] Major findings discussed in this section are mainly derived from the SSRC's Public Opinion Programme (POP) Polls, for the following reasons:
   1. There is no fear of infringement on others' copyright;
   2. Table 1 shows that POP Polls constituted 40 per cent of all polls reported by the media in the year past;
   3. Tracking polls are mainly conducted by the SSRC;
   4. Methodologies adopted by other research organizations are often unknown and unreported.

Readers can consult SSRC poll reports for methodological details, like sampling method, response rates, and exact wordings of the questions.

Table 3. Hong Kong People's Optimism about the Outcome of Sino-British Talks

Question: Are you optimistic about the future of Sino-British talks?

	\multicolumn{9}{c}{Date of poll, 1993}
	10/3	14/4	28/4	9–10/6	6–7/7	22–23/7	8–9/9	12–14/10	15–16/11
Optimistic	40.0%	46.2%	62.7%	57.6%	44.8%	47.5%	37.0%	29.4%	32.5%
Half-half	23.1%	37.5%	28.6%	22.1%	36.1%	26.7%	30.5%	25.6%	31.4%
Pessimistic	36.8%	16.3%	8.7%	20.3%	19.1%	25.8%	32.5%	45.0%	36.1%
Total	100.0%	100.0%	100.0%	100.0%	100.0%	100.0%	100.0%	100.0%	100.0%

Note: Add-up discrepancies are due to rounding.
Source: Social Sciences Research Centre, the University of Hong Kong.

Figure 1. Optimism about Sino-British Talks

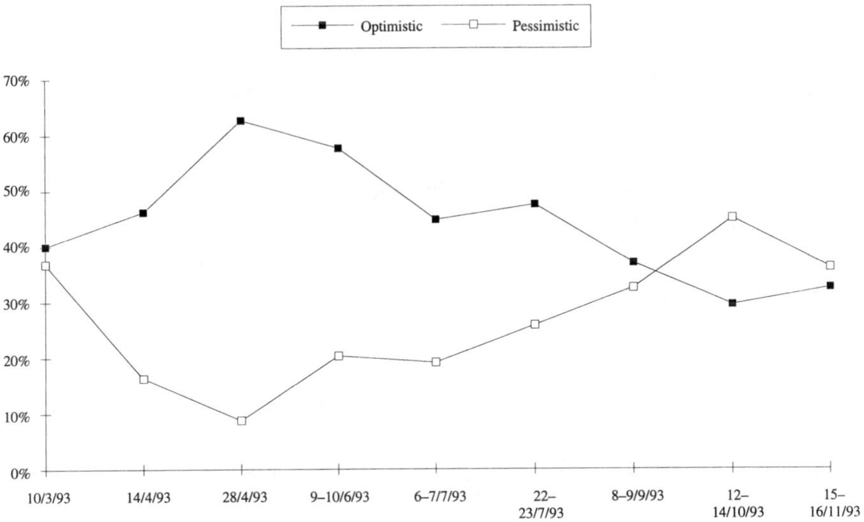

Note: The horizontal scale is spaced according to poll-time, not calendar time.

generally dissatisfied at the progress of the talks,[13] most of them remained optimistic about the outcome of the talks — until the last two months. But even after the "indefinite suspension" of the talks in late November 1993, more people believed in the reopening of the talks than otherwise.[14] This on the one hand demonstrated the tough spirit of Hong Kong people, but on the other hand signalled how disappointed Hong Kong people could have become in the final event.

---

[13] POP Polls conducted between June and November 1993 consistently showed that over half, sometimes as high as four-fifths, of Hong Kong people felt dissatisfied at the progress of the talks.

[14] A POP Poll conducted as late as 17 December 1993, after Governor Patten tabled his reform package at the Legco, registered 49 per cent of the respondents still optimistic about the reopening of the talks, as against 30 per cent who felt pessimistic.

Looking at the chart, it can be seen that Hong Kong people received the reopening of the talks with very high spirit. On 28 April 1993, when the second round of talks began, 63 per cent of the respondents were optimistic that agreement could be reached, against 9 per cent who felt pessimistic. As the talks dragged on, however, people's optimism eroded, until pessimism finally took over in October 1993.

When the talks reached deadlock, in October 1993, 62 per cent blamed *both* Britain and China for not reaching agreement, as against 15 per cent or so who blamed either government. This shows that Hong Kong people were generally pragmatic in outlook: they were more interested in the final result than the pros and cons of the argument. It was probably because of this that they did not have faith in either the Chinese or the British governments. Tracking polls conducted over the past two years consistently showed that only one-quarter of the population trusted either government, as against the 50 to 60 per cent who trusted the local government. The sovereign powers, precisely because of their indulgence in high-sounding principles, and global strategies, have lost the faith of the Hong Kong people who were more concerned with their livelihood and a guaranteed future.

Constitutional Reforms

As Hong Kong's constitutional development in the run-up to 1997 was the focus of the Sino-British dispute, it would be interesting to measure people's actual knowledge of, and support towards, Patten's reform proposals. We start with people's general satisfaction over the Governor's policy speech.

Table 4 summarizes people's feeling towards Patten's policy speeches over the past twelve months,[15] and Figure 2 presents the measurement on a monthly basis, and contrasts them with those of the Patten's first policy speech. It could be seen there was a downward trend of supporters for Patten's second policy speech, among those who expressed an opinion. In June 1993, only 47 per cent, almost a record low, expressed satisfaction over the address, presumably focusing on the constitutional proposals. Compared to the 69 per cent registered in October 1992,

---

[15] Earlier data has been reported in *The Other Hong Kong Report 1993*, pp. 414–15.

when Patten delivered his first policy address, support has clearly dropped significantly.

It could, of course, be argued that satisfaction over Patten's policy address was one thing, support for his reform proposals was quite another. This may or may not be true. According to a series of tracking polls conducted by the author between December 1992 and September 1993, Hong Kong people were generally very ignorant of the content of the reform proposals. At the end of September 1993, 64 per cent of the respondents to a survey replied that they did not understand the first part of Patten's proposals,[16] which was tabled at the Legco about two months later. The second part of the reform package was even worse. On 24 June 1994, about a week before the second and controversial part of the reform package was tabled at the Legco, 89 per cent of the respondents to a poll conducted by the author replied that they did not know the content of the proposal, nor the counter-proposals being hotly debated. People had apparently lost interest in constitutional reforms, and the final outcome of the Legco vote, in support of the original proposals, could hardly claimed to have received people's blessing. In fact, the whole of opinion development in the year past has pointed to a decrease in people's interest over political matters, and it would not be unreasonable to expect that over half of the population of Hong Kong would not like to comment on political issues.

Patten's Popularity

In 1992–1993, Governor Patten was such an unprecedented personality in capturing public attention that the SSRC had to track his popularity first on a daily basis, and then on a weekly basis. As a result, almost 60 polls were conducted in that year to measure his popularity alone.[17] In 1993–1994, however, he became less active, and people's rating for him also became more settled. For this reason, the SSRC began to space out the tracking of his personal popularity on a monthly, rather than weekly, basis, and all previous data was reorganized to facilitate comparison.

---

[16] But there was general support for the expansion of functional constituencies, increasing directly elected seats in the District Boards and the municipal councils, and some other specific proposals, upon prompting and probing.

[17] The weekly data points in 1992–1993 have been reported in *The Other Hong Kong Report 1993*, pp. 410–11.

Table 4. General Satisfaction of Hong Kong People over Christopher Patten's Policy Speech

Question: How satisfied are you with the Governor's policy speech?

	\multicolumn{10}{c}{Date of poll, 1993}									
	6–7 Jul.	14–15 Jul.	22–23 Jul.	28 Jul.	5–6 Aug.	11 Aug.	18–19 Aug.	25–26 Aug.	1 Sept.	8–9 Sept.	16–20 Sept.
Successful cases	511	526	522	550	516	523	617	513	516	529	503
Response %	56.6%	57.5%	51.2%	53.6%	50.7%	52.9%	50.8%	50.0%	56.0%	52.5%	53.9%
Raw data											
Very satisfied	2.9%	3.4%	3.5%	3.5%	2.9%	2.6%	1.3%	1.8%	2.0%	3.3%	2.0%
Just satisfied	22.9%	20.4%	23.5%	21.1%	22.5%	19.0%	20.2%	17.3%	15.9%	18.3%	16.1%
Neutral	6.4%	7.2%	6.2%	5.5%	7.9%	5.7%	9.2%	6.2%	8.2%	17.1%	5.0%
Just dissatisfied	5.0%	7.6%	7.0%	6.3%	6.6%	5.3%	4.9%	4.2%	7.0%	5.8%	5.5%
Very dissatisfied	2.5%	2.9%	0.9%	2.5%	3.1%	2.4%	1.0%	1.3%	0.8%	2.9%	2.7%
Don't know	60.4%	58.5%	58.9%	61.1%	56.9%	64.9%	63.4%	69.2%	66.1%	52.7%	68.7%
Total	100.0%	100.0%	100.0%	100.0%	100.0%	100.0%	100.0%	100.0%	100.0%	100.0%	100.0%

	\multicolumn{10}{c}{Date of poll, 1993}									
	23–24 Sept.	28–29 Sept.	6–7 Oct.	8–14 Oct.	15–21 Oct.	22–29 Oct.	3–4 Nov.	9–10 Nov.	11 Nov.	15–16 Nov.	23–24 Nov.
Successful cases	504	516	1,585	1,070	889	1,363	491	433	523	655	646
Response %	54.8%	53.8%	59.9%	50.1%	68.8%	73.8%	51.0%	51.2%	51.9%	57.9%	53.5%
Raw data											
Very satisfied	3.0%	2.4%	5.6%	6.2%	4.0%	3.0%	2.2%	1.2%	1.3%	2.4%	2.3%
Just satisfied	19.0%	19.2%	37.4%	30.9%	31.2%	25.4%	24.3%	19.9%	22.9%	19.1%	18.1%
Neutral	8.6%	9.3%	10.5%	12.4%	11.8%	12.1%	6.5%	12.0%	10.0%	10.2%	9.3%
Just dissatisfied	7.6%	7.6%	4.6%	9.5%	13.1%	9.9%	9.3%	6.7%	8.3%	5.7%	6.3%
Very dissatisfied	1.9%	3.6%	1.2%	2.7%	1.0%	1.5%	1.9%	1.3%	2.2%	1.6%	0.9%
Don't know	60.0%	57.8%	40.7%	38.2%	38.9%	48.0%	55.9%	58.9%	55.4%	61.1%	63.1%
Total	100.0%	100.0%	100.0%	100.0%	100.0%	100.0%	100.0%	100.0%	100.0%	100.0%	100.0%

Date of poll, 1993–1994

	30 Nov.–1 Dec.	9–14 Dec.	28–30 Dec.	19–21 Jan.	1–7 Feb.	24–28 Feb.	14–15 Mar.	6–7 Apr.	25–27 Apr.	17–20 May	31 May–1 June	22–23 June
Successful cases	530	531	600	513	510	524	500	509	517	504	538	602
Response %	51.1%	51.0%	55.0%	56.5%	50.2%	62.9%	63.3%	60.2%	60.6%	63.9%	59.2%	50.4%
Raw data												
Very satisfied	1.9%	5.7%	1.8%	2.4%	2.8%	1.5%	1.3%	1.5%	1.0%	1.0%	1.1%	0.7%
Just satisfied	13.0%	25.7%	15.0%	16.9%	16.5%	12.4%	17.3%	12.4%	12.1%	15.3%	16.1%	15.9%
Neutral	6.7%	8.2%	7.5%	10.4%	7.2%	6.9%	8.4%	10.7%	5.8%	8.2%	7.9%	10.4%
Just dissatisfied	5.8%	6.3%	8.1%	5.9%	6.4%	6.8%	4.4%	4.3%	5.9%	7.0%	7.9%	7.2%
Very dissatisfied	2.9%	3.5%	2.4%	3.0%	1.7%	2.6%	3.3%	2.2%	2.9%	1.1%	1.3%	1.3%
Don't know	69.6%	50.5%	65.1%	61.3%	65.3%	69.8%	65.3%	69.0%	72.4%	67.4%	65.7%	64.5%
Total	100.0%	100.0%	100.0%	100.0%	100.0%	100.0%	100.0%	100.0%	100.0%	100.0%	100.0%	100.0%

Note: Add-up discrepancies are due to rounding.
Source: Compiled by the author.

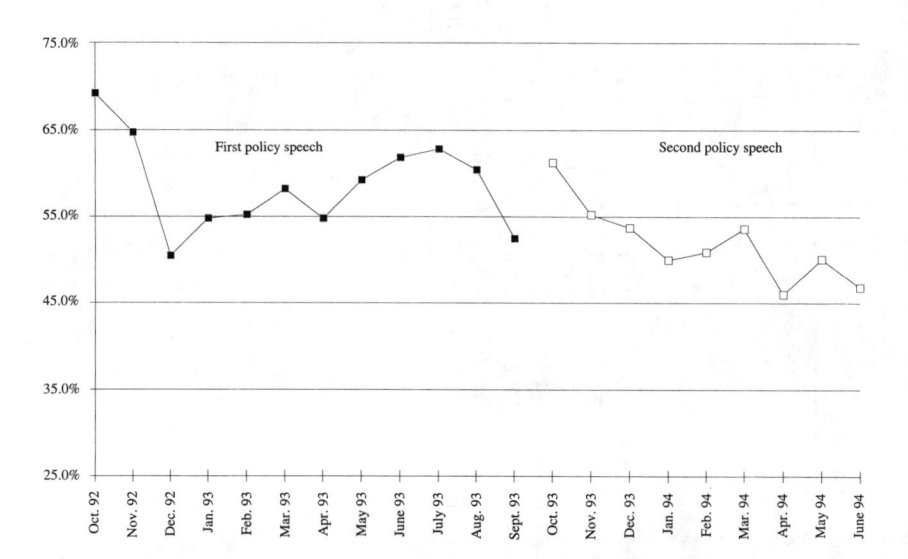

Figure 2. Policy Speech Satisfaction

Source: Social Sciences Research Centre, the University of Hong Kong.

Table 5 tabulates Patten's monthly popularity ratings over the past two years, and Figure 3 presents the change graphically. The ratings were measured on a 0–100 scale described in the previous section of this chapter. From the figures, it could be seen that Patten's popularity rose sharply upon his arrival to Hong Kong, culminated at the time he delivered his first policy speech, and then dropped to a record low in December 1992, after he was severely attacked by the Chinese officials for his constitutional reform. In the year under study, namely, between July 1993 and June 1994, his support rating has remained rather stable, between 55 and 60 points, and gradually settled on the 55 points level at the end of the year. The highest rating he obtained in the year was that of October 1993, after he delivered his second policy address. Thereafter, his ratings were gradually on the drop.

To put Patten's rating in perspective, it should be noted that a rating at 55-point level was far behind the ratings enjoyed by the most popular Legislative Councillors. SSRC's record shows that the rating of the former Governor, David Wilson, was 64.6 in December 1991 and 64.3 in March 1992. Patten's latest ratings were fairly poor compared to these figures.

Table 5. Monthly Ratings of Governor Christopher Patten (from April 1992)

The monthly ratings are obtained by averaging specific ratings obtained in separate polls during the month. The number of raters refers to the total number accumulated during that month.

1992

	Apr.	May	June	Jul.	Aug.	Sept.	Oct.	Nov.	Dec.
No. of raters	622	1,002	574	—	662	—	4,282	1,908	3,552
Rating	53.3	56.1	58.2	60.7	63.1	63.6	64.1	61.6	55.7

1993

	Jan.	Feb.	Mar.	Apr.	May	June	Jul.	Aug.	Sept.	Oct.	Nov.	Dec.
No. of raters	2,328	2,639	3,093	2,135	2,286	2,443	1,823	1,945	2,267	3,983	2,152	1,533
Rating	58.0	57.3	58.0	56.2	58.2	58.6	58.6	58.8	57.6	59.5	57.6	57.2

1994

	Jan.	Feb.	Mar.	Apr.	May	June
No. of raters	473	1,003	419	877	936	993
Rating	55.6	55.3	54.9	55.2	55.0	55.6

Source: Compiled by the author.

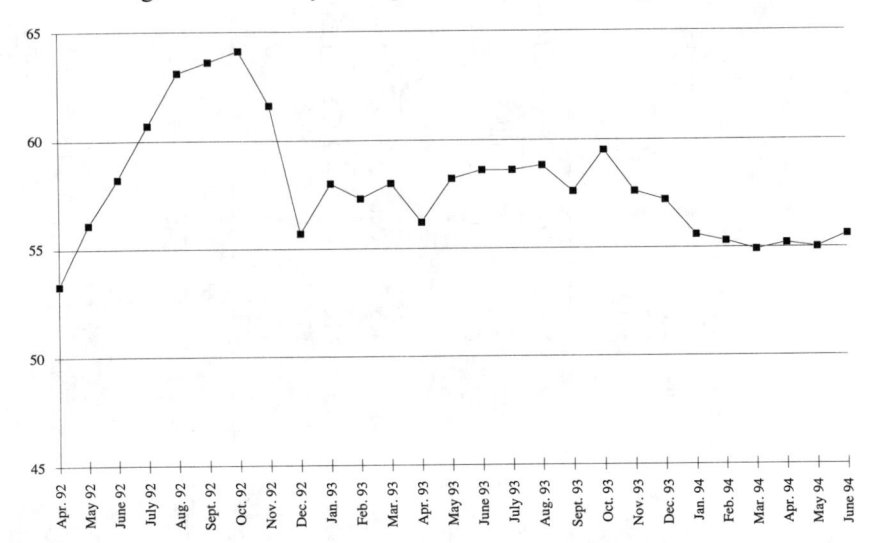

Figure 3. Monthly Ratings of Governor Christopher Patten

Source: Social Sciences Research Centre, the University of Hong Kong

Ratings of Legco Members

Table 6 presents the result of the SSRC's "Top Ten Legco Members" rating exercises conducted within the year under review. The lists are in fact Legislative Councillors who were most readily recognized by the public, ranked by the degree of support expressed by the public. Tracked on a bi-monthly basis, it could be seen that the results were generally very stable. In terms of recognition, Martin Lee, Emily Lau, and Szeto Wah continued to be the most popular councillors, with Selina Chow, Christine Loh, Lau Chin-shek, and Allen Lee trailing behind. In terms of support, Emily Lau, Martin Lee, and Lau Chin-shek continued to be among the top.

Two significant changes occurred in the year: that of the emergence of Christine Loh, and the disappearance of Elsie Tu from the list. Christine Loh entered into the "Top Ten" list in April 1994, probably due to her very firm stand on the issue of gender equality within the indigenous community of the New Territories. At that entry point, she scored 7th in terms of recognition, and 5th in terms of support. In June 1994, she remained 5th on the ladder, but her recognition rate went up to the 5th. Her emergence in Hong Kong politics was the most dramatic one in recent years.[18]

With as much surprise as Christine Loh's emergence in local politics, was Elsie Tu's disappearance from the scene. Ever since the SSRC started rating Legislative Councillors in 1991, Elsie Tu has been on the top of the list. In terms of recognition, she was not the most familiar figure, but she was among the top ten and unfailingly had the highest score of support. From late 1993, however, her recognition rate continued to drop. In February 1994, she was the 7th most familiar councillors, but in April 1994, she became the 10th. In June 1994, she dropped away from the list altogether, and Emily Lau took over the top position.

The sudden emergence of Christine Loh and the disappearance of Elsie Tu in mid-1994 marked a new era of local politics in Hong Kong: both are female councillors, without party background, but with very different personality and political outlook. Tu was sometimes said to be conservative, a characteristic of most veteran politicians, while Loh was more radical and aggressive. In a way, Loh was more like Emily Lau than any other Legislative Councillors. The "replacement" of Tu by Lau and Loh on the Top Ten list probably signified the decline of traditional politics.

Ratings of Political Parties

The year 1993–1994 continued to a year of intensive development on the part of the political parties. The merger between Meeting Point and the United Democrats of Hong Kong (UDHK) was announced, the Hong Kong Association for Democracy and People's Livelihood (ADPL) became somewhat isolated, and the Liberal Party as well as the Democratic Alliance for Betterment of Hong Kong were gearing up themselves for the new wave of elections due to take place in 1994–1995.

Table 7 summarizes the result of SSRC's "Top Five Political Parties" rating exercises conducted in the year. It could be seen that compared to ratings of top Legislative Councillors, political parties scored much lower both in terms of recognition and support. This indicates that people are still sceptical about political parties, and take time to become familiar with them.

---

[18] Excluding Governor Christopher Patten, perhaps.

Table 6. Popularity Ratings of Top Ten Legco Members

	Support	Std. Err.	Total sample	Raters	Recognition
POP POLL 31 MAY to 1 JUNE 1994					
Emily Lau	63.2	0.9	538	413	76.8%
Martin Lee	61.9	0.9	538	435	80.9%
Lau Chin-shek	60.5	1.0	538	385	71.6%
Szeto Wah	57.4	1.1	538	416	77.3%
Christine Loh	57.1	1.1	538	396	73.6%
Fung Kin-kee	55.5	1.0	538	342	64.6%
Selina Chow	54.6	0.9	538	399	74.2%
Allen Lee	50.0	0.9	538	377	70.1%
Andrew Wong	49.4	1.0	538	343	63.8%
Lau Wong-fat	46.1	1.1	538	342	63.6%
POP POLL 25–27 APR. 1994					
Elsie Tu	65.8	1.0	517	327	63.2%
Emily Lau	63.3	1.1	517	390	75.4%
Martin Lee	61.9	1.1	517	415	80.3%
Lau Chin-shek	61.7	1.1	517	358	69.2%
Christine Loh	60.7	1.2	517	357	69.1%
Szeto Wah	59.2	1.1	517	400	77.4%
Selina Chow	59.0	0.8	517	381	73.7%
Allen Lee	51.4	1.0	517	362	70.0%
Andrew Wong	49.6	1.1	517	305	64.6%
Lau Wong-fat	47.4	1.0	517	342	66.2%
POP POLL 1–7 FEB. 1994					
Elsie Tu	66.3	1.0	510	366	71.8%
Emily Lau	62.4	1.0	510	391	76.7%
Martin Lee	61.9	1.0	510	437	85.7%
Lau Chin-shek	61.7	1.0	510	399	78.2%
Yeung Sum	59.8	1.2	510	317	62.2%
Szeto Wah	58.6	1.0	510	432	84.7%
Selina Chow	57.4	0.9	510	416	81.6%
Tam Yiu-chung	55.9	1.0	510	326	63.9%
Andrew Wong	54.9	1.0	510	328	64.6%
Allen Lee	52.3	1.0	510	395	77.5%
POP POLL 9–14 DEC. 1993					
Elsie Tu	62.7	1.0	531	372	70.1%
Emily Lau	62.0	1.0	531	414	78.0%
Martin Lee	61.8	1.1	531	461	86.8%
Lau Chin-shek	59.8	1.0	531	408	76.8%
Yeung Sum	58.0	1.3	531	338	63.7%
Selina Chow	57.3	0.8	531	445	83.8%
Szeto Wah	56.6	1.1	531	447	84.2%
Andrew Wong	53.0	1.0	531	354	66.7%
Tam Yiu-chung	52.9	1.1	531	343	64.6%
Allen Lee	50.2	1.0	531	421	79.3%

Public Opinion

Table 6. (Cont'd)

	Support	Std. Err.	Total sample	Raters	Recognition
POP POLL 12–14 OCT. 1993					
Elsie Tu	64.1	0.9	505	363	71.9%
Emily Lau	62.9	1.0	505	415	82.2%
Lau Chin-shek	58.5	0.9	505	404	80.0%
Yeung Sum	57.1	1.0	505	369	73.1%
Andrew Wong	57.0	0.8	505	378	74.9%
Selina Chow	56.9	0.8	505	420	83.2%
Martin Lee	55.5	1.1	505	440	87.1%
Allen Lee	55.4	0.9	505	437	86.5%
Tam Yiu-chung	55.4	0.9	505	369	73.1%
Szeto Wah	53.9	1.1	505	444	87.9%
POP POLL 18 AUG. 1993					
Elsie Tu	68.6	0.9	617	453	73.4%
Emily Lau	66.4	0.9	617	474	76.8%
Lau Chin-shek	64.1	0.8	617	492	79.7%
Martin Lee	61.9	0.9	617	524	84.9%
Szeto Wah	60.0	0.9	617	528	85.6%
Selina Chow	59.8	0.8	617	495	80.2%
Allen Lee	58.0	0.8	617	513	83.1%
Andrew Wong	57.9	0.8	617	422	68.4%
Tam Yiu-chung	57.4	0.9	617	391	63.4%
Lau Wong-fat	54.4	0.8	617	409	66.3%

Note: All data are weighted by sex of valid raters.
Source: Social Sciences Research Centre, the University of Hong Kong.

Compared among themselves, the UDHK is still the most popular party, both in terms of recognition and support, throughout the entire period. The Liberal Party is the second most recognizable party, but lags behind Meeting Point and ADPL in terms of support. The Democratic Alliance for Betterment of Hong Kong entered the list in December 1993, and is gaining popularity in terms of recognition, but has remained at the bottom in terms of support. The Federation of Trade Unions enjoyed relative stable recognition and support, until it dropped out of the list in June 1994, probably not so much because of its declined popularity but because people no longer consider it as a political party.[19] The vacuum left by the

---

[19] Its membership overlaps substantively with that of DABHK, and the two organizations are closely aligned with each other on practically all political issues. DABHK, therefore, can be taken as the political arm of FTU.

Table 7. Popularity Ratings of Top Five Political Groups

	Support	Std. Err.	Total sample	Raters	Recognition
POP POLL 22–23 JUNE 1994					
UDHK	59.8	1.1	602	380	63.1%
MP	54.8	1.0	602	312	51.8%
ADPL	52.5	1.0	602	291	48.3%
LP	52.3	1.1	602	350	58.1%
DABHK	51.1	1.1	602	289	48.0%
POP POLL 25–27 APR. 1994					
UDHK	61.2	1.2	517	332	64.2%
FTU	58.6	1.6	517	237	45.8%
MP	58.5	0.9	517	239	46.2%
LP	55.4	1.0	517	286	55.3%
DABHK	51.8	1.1	517	239	46.2%
POP POLL 24–28 FEB. 1994					
UDHK	58.2	1.2	524	328	62.6%
FTU	53.9	1.4	524	204	38.9%
MP	52.8	1.2	524	219	41.8%
LP	50.1	1.2	524	291	55.5%
DABHK	49.3	1.3	524	186	35.5%
POP POLL 28–30 DEC. 1993					
UDHK	60.9	1.2	502	345	68.7%
MP	56.1	1.0	502	257	51.2%
LP	54.3	1.0	502	327	65.1%
FTU	52.2	1.2	502	255	50.8%
DABHK	48.7	1.3	502	237	47.2%
POP POLL 3–8 NOV. 1993					
UDHK	58.2	1.2	494	332	67.2%
MP	57.0	1.0	494	238	48.2%
LP	55.8	1.1	494	306	61.9%
FTU	54.6	1.1	494	229	46.4%
LDF	51.3	1.3	494	218	44.1%
POP POLL 25–26 AUG. 1993					
UDHK	60.8	1.1	513	374	72.9%
MP	53.9	1.1	513	258	50.3%
FTU	53.7	1.1	513	280	54.6%
LP	52.5	1.1	513	311	60.6%
LDF	51.0	1.2	513	242	47.2%

Abbreviations:
ADPL = HK Assn. for Democracy and People's Livelihood
DABHK = Democratic Alliance for Betterment of Hong Kong
FTU = HK Federation of Trade Union
LDF = The Liberal Democratic Federation of Hong Kong
LP = Liberal Party
MP = Meeting Point
UDHK = United Democrats of Hong Kong

Note: All data are weighted by sex of valid raters.
Source: Social Sciences Research Centre, the University of Hong Kong.

Federation of Trade Unions was taken up by the ADPL which failed to join the "Top Five" in all previous ratings.

With the prospective merging of the Meeting Point and the UDHK, and the advancing elections to the three tiers of representative government, party development will take on a much faster pace than before. The popularity of different political parties are expected to fluctuate significantly in the near future.

☐ Conclusion: The Way Ahead

After rapid development in the past two years, opinion polls have already become a regular feature of daily life. In 1993–1994, the number of opinion polls conducted by professional bodies was very similar to that of the previous year. More tracking polls have appeared, with the design of such polls becoming standardized.

Poll findings are often eye-catching, but quality surveys are expensive. This encouraged the development of "casual surveys" conducted by political parties and pressure groups to attract press coverage, as well as substandard surveys conducted by the media themselves to generate exclusive news. These developments may have the effect of compressing the growth of professional polls,[20] but with the onset of the 1994–1995 elections, there will be renewed interest in high-quality opinion surveys. One could therefore expect the number of opinion polls to be maintained at roughly the same level, but that is not to say that we should be satisfied with the current standards.

As yet, pollsters in Hong Kong lack a common code of practice, many reporters lack the basic knowledge to digest poll findings, and commentators very often picked on irrelevant questions to discredit polls. What is needed for Hong Kong is better education for the public, and more serious training for journalists. Before that could be achieved, whether opinion surveys would be abused or not depends very much on the conscience and self-control of the pollsters, the media, and the political person.

---

[20] The *Eastweek Magazine*, for example, starting from January 1994, replaced their weekly poll column by casual street interviews. This move alone takes away 52 opinion polls from the annual total.

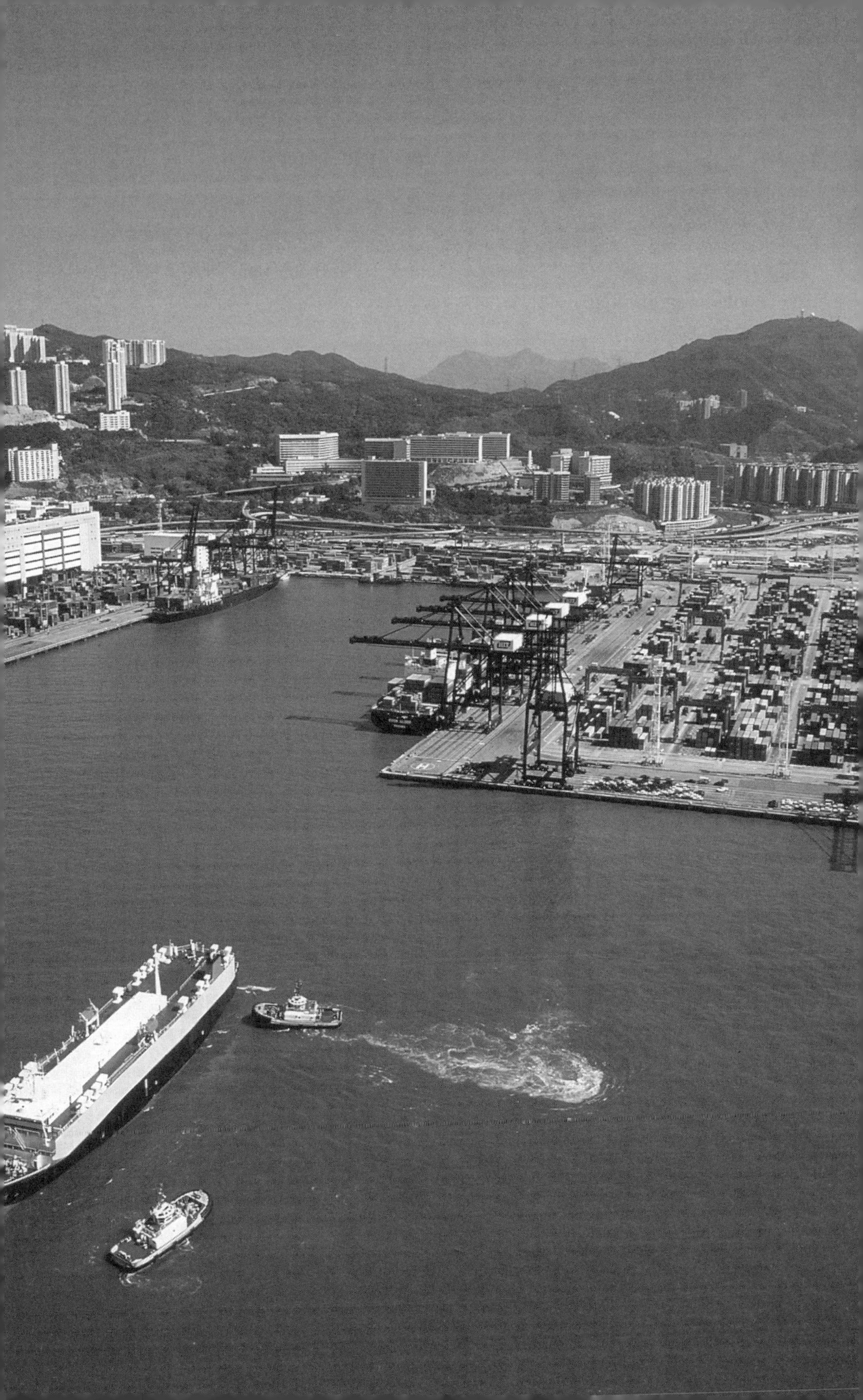

8

The Economy

Tsang Shu-ki

☐ Growth: Boredom, Worries and Waiting

Talking about the short-term macroeconomic performance of Hong Kong, particularly on the basis of statistics, has lately become rather boring. The Hong Kong economy posted a real gross domestic product (GDP) growth of 5.6 per cent for the whole of 1993 — almost right on the trend rate of 5.5 per cent that the government uses for various planning purposes. A cursory review of GDP forecasts by major banks and brokerage firms in the course of 1993 showed a low of 5.1 per cent and a high of 5.8 per cent. As for 1994, the official revised prediction stuck with 5.5 per cent (see Table 1), while the Hang Seng Bank recently lowered its forecast for the year from 5.8 per cent to 5.3 per cent. Other publicized projections differ only to the extent of 0.1 to 0.4 per cent. Some pundits are privately worried that local GDP forecasts may become a dying sport.

That type of pessimism may be premature. Taking a longer view, even the statistics seem more exciting. GDP growth rebounded from the cyclical low of 2.8 per cent in 1989 and rose steadily to 5.6 per cent in both 1992 and 1993. Such a revival was of course much less spectacular than the ones which Hong Kong was used to in the past. For example, GDP growth jumped from 2.7 per cent in 1982 to 9.8 per cent in 1984 and, more dramatically, from 0.2 per cent in 1985 to 14.5 per cent in 1987. The Hong Kong economy has apparently become more stable. The standard deviation

---

Tsang Shu-ki is a senior lecturer in the Department of Economics, Hong Kong Baptist College.

of GDP growth rates in 1980–1989 was 4.24 per cent, while that in 1988–1993 was 1.85 per cent. The normalized standard deviation was, on the other hand, 0.56 in 1980–1990 and 0.37 in 1988–1993.[1]

The major factors behind the recent stability have a lot to do with the changing configuration of Hong Kong's external influences. Being a small open economy where total exports of goods have exceeded GDP in value since about eight years ago, the local economy is very much affected by the welfare of outside markets. In the 1980s, Hong Kong had to deal with its

Table 1. GDP Growth: 1993 and 1994

	1993 Actual	1994 Government revised forecast
Private consumption expenditure	7.7	7.0
Government consumption expenditure	0.9	4.4
Gross domestic fixed capital formation	4.7	5.6
Transfer costs of land and building	−4.7	0.0
Building and construction	9.0	10.4
Private	−5.8	−2.0
Public	39.0	27.5
Real estate developers' margin	−9.0	−2.0
Plant, machinery and equipment	8.5	5.8
Private	7.6	5.0
Public	54.0	35.0
Total exports of goods	13.1	12.0
Domestic exports	−5.1	−5.0
Re-exports	19.9	17.0
Imports of goods	12.8	12.2
Exports of services	7.8	9.0
Imports of services	6.9	8.0
Gross domestic product (GDP)	5.6	5.5
Consumer Price Index (A)	8.5	8.5

Source: Census and Statistics Department, Hong Kong Government.

---

[1] The standard deviation is a common statistical measurement of the fluctuations in a variable around its mean value. Hence the higher the standard deviation, the more "fluctuating" is a variable. The normalized standard deviation, i.e. the standard deviation divided by the mean, has the added advantage that it takes into account the possible changes in the average value of a variable over different time periods.

The Economy

domestic excesses and was forced to ride the roller-coaster with Western economies. The China factor, although gaining increasing importance, was not yet a dominant countervailing force.

Into the 1990s, the importance of the China factor has become clear as it began to make a significant impact on local growth. However, there has been a marked divergence of economic fortunes between China on the one hand and the United States, Western Europe and Japan on the other. The Chinese economy, propelled by the "Deng whirlwind," grew in real terms by 13 per cent and 13.4 per cent in 1992 and 1993 respectively, while the OECD (Organization for Economic Cooperation and Development) economies were in a depressive mode, expanding by an average of only 1.4 per cent per year in 1991–1993. Hong Kong has been caught in the cross-currents, as the China-led boom was offset to a certain extent by Western gloom. Hence, the superficial stability could be deceptive. In the future, if Chinese and Western economic cycles become more synchronized, Hong Kong may witness bigger ups and downs in economic growth.

Another issue worthy of attention is whether a 5.5 per cent GDP growth represents the best average rate that the local economy can achieve. In the 1970s, annual GDP growth averaged 9.2 per cent, and in the 1980s, 7.5 per cent. The decline in Hong Kong's workforce has often been cited as a reason. In the 1970s, Hong Kong's workforce grew by 4.2 per cent per year. The rate fell to 1.7 per cent in the 1980s, and further declined to 1.1 per cent in 1990–1993. These are pieces of *prima facie* evidence, but should not be overplayed. After all, per capita real GDP growth averaged 5.9 per cent in 1980–1989, but fell to 3.8 per cent in 1988–1993. Similarly, per worker GDP growth fell from 5.7 per cent to 4.0 per cent. This may indicate problems in Hong Kong's labour productivity as well.

Another possible explanation is that as Hong Kong's economy becomes more integrated with China's, the accuracy of GDP statistics is in increasing doubt and GNP (gross national product) estimates are necessary. The Hong Kong government, after a lengthy period of feasibility studies and preparation, may release the first batch of GNP statistics in 1995. We can only wait and see whether they would significantly alter the growth picture.

☐ Growth: Shifting Combinations of Momentum

Despite the similarity in overall growth rates in 1993 and 1994, there have actually been some shifts in the combinations of growth momentum, particularly in the twelve months ending June 1994. A slow-down in export growth was experienced, which also affected investment in plant and machinery. Domestic exports fell in real terms by 5 per cent and 7.2 per cent in the third and fourth quarters of 1993, and by 8.9 per cent in the first four months of 1994 respectively, while re-exports, which maintained handsome expansion in volume, saw a real growth rate decline from 22 per cent in the first half to 18 per cent in the second half of 1993, and then further to 12 per cent in the first four months of 1994. Real growth of investment in plant and machinery, on the other hand, fell from the double-digit level seen in the first half of 1993 to only 3.8 per cent in the third quarter. In the fourth quarter, a negative growth of 3.8 per cent was registered, to be followed by a small positive growth of 2.3 per cent in the first quarter of 1994.

On the other hand, though, continued robust consumer spending and a pick-up in investment in building and construction have offset these shortfalls. Consumer expenditure went up by about 7 per cent in the second half of 1993, and by 10.6 per cent in the first quarter of 1994. This trend was echoed by the 11 per cent hike in retail sales volume in the first four months of 1994. Strength in consumer expenditure has actually been quite consistent for the past few years. It grew by 9.2 per cent in 1991 and 8.3 per cent in 1992. Spending on furniture, clothing and transport rose at particularly fast rates of 23 per cent, 9 per cent and 16 per cent per annum respectively. Some economists have attributed this phenomenon to the spending pattern of the baby-boomers, who are now aged between 25 to 44. This age group represented 27 per cent of the total population in 1981, but the proportion increased to 32 per cent in 1986 and to 37.5 per cent in 1991. By 1996, baby-boomers are expected to account for 38 per cent of the local population. As this group tends to have a higher propensity to consume, its larger number would help to boost spending in the territory and change the overall consumption pattern.[2]

Two factors may, however, qualify such a projection: (1) Widening income disparity[3] would constrain local consumption, even among

---

[2] See "Mid-year Review of the Hong Kong Economy," *Hang Seng Economic Monthly*, July 1994.

[3] For an analysis of the long-term trend of widening income inequality in Hong Kong, see Tsang Shu-ki, "Income Distribution," in *The Other Hong Kong Report 1993*, edited by Choi Po-king and Ho Lok-sang (Hong Kong: The Chinese University Press, 1993), pp. 361–68.

The Economy

baby-boomers, as higher-income groups usually have a *smaller* marginal propensity to consume than lower-income groups; (2) Continued high property prices may absorb an increasing share of the incomes and savings of the baby-boomers so that they could not afford to spend much on consumption.

As far as investment in building and construction is concerned, it has largely been driven by expansion in the public sector. A drop of 5.8 per cent in private investment in 1993 was more than offset by a 39 per cent growth in public investment. Other than local factors including bureaucratic red tape and inefficiency which hindered private efforts, one important reason might have been the inroads that Hong Kong construction firms and property developers made into the infrastructure and housing developments in China in 1992–1993, which diverted attention and funds from the territory. In 1994, two conflicting factors are working. On the one hand, the adjustments in China's property market could result in some re-channelling of funds back to Hong Kong. On the other, local private sector building activities have been affected by uncertainties over the outlook for the surging property prices after a year of huge increases, partly due to shortfall in supply.

In contrast, public sector investment has been growing at a rapid pace as works on a number of major infrastructure projects are in active progress. An agreement between the Chinese and British governments regarding the financing arrangements for the new airport as well as the government's plan to provide more public housing may lead to an acceleration in public sector construction activities in the near future. In the first quarter of 1994, total investment in building and construction in aggregate rose by 25.5 per cent over the same period of 1993, but the breakdown between private and public investments is not yet available at the time of writing.

☐ Inflation: Winners and Losers

In 1988–1993, consumer inflation in Hong Kong in terms of the Consumer Price Index (A) [CPI(A)] averaged 9.5 per cent per year, compared with 8.5 per cent for the period of 1980–1989. Asset inflation has actually been more serious. Residential property prices have more than doubled in 1991–1993, underpinned by strong internal as well as external demand. It is apparent that at least for medium and small-sized flats, prices have increased at a faster pace than incomes and become unaffordable for many first-time buyers. Financial assets have also been rapidly inflated as international investors began to "re-rate" Hong Kong in the light of the improving long-term prospect of the Chinese economy, and Hong Kong's special relationship with it. The Hang Seng Index for local stock prices doubled in the year 1993 alone, although it settled at lower levels in the first half of 1994.

Such a spur of high inflation has made Hong Kong one of the most expensive cities in the world. Moreover, as inflation (particularly asset inflation) continues to surge, Hong Kong is in the danger of pricing itself out of the market. Prices and rental rates of office space are approaching the Tokyo levels, and users are loudly complaining that the charges of the container terminals in Kwai Chung are the highest in the world.[4]

While the government seems quite impotent in directly affecting the prices of financial assets like stock shares, it did announce in June 1994 the first part of a package of measures to stabilize residential property prices, which focused on the tightening of pre-completion sales and efforts to increase land supply. The government also made it clear that if these failed to generate real effects, it might consider introducing further measures including punitive taxation on speculation. Judging from the latest reduction in transactions and downward adjustment of prices in residential units, these measures appear to have had the desired cooling impact on the overheated real estate market, although their long-term effectiveness is still a big question.

In theory, there should be a self-adjusting mechanism in a market economy facing inflationary pressure, particularly for a small open economy like Hong Kong. Rising costs will lead to higher output prices, which will undermine the competitiveness of the territory's exports and erode the purchasing power of households. Economic growth would slow, thus dampening further price increases. However, this automatic adjustment mechanism has not been properly functioning in Hong Kong because of the rapidly ascending importance of the China factor. High inflation has not affected the territory's export performance as the relocation of manufacturing to the Pearl River Delta has enabled local exporters to maintain their price competitiveness in the world market. At the same time, domestic spending has not been curbed as earnings generated from a much expanded production base have kept household income growth well ahead of inflation, at least on average.

---

[4] *Wen Wei Po*, 22 February 1994, p. 5.

As I have argued elsewhere,[5] the formation of inflation in Hong Kong is a complex phenomenon. Some of the factors are outside Hong Kong's direct influence, e.g. international investors' perception and "re-rating" of the prospect of the local economy. There is also a limit to what the authority can do to bring inflation down without endangering other policy objectives, e.g. exchange rate stability if the government re-floats the Hong Kong dollar, in the hope that possible appreciation could be deflationary. Nevertheless, there is always a second line of defence. High inflation is socially divisive, as it tends to aggravate income and wealth distribution. Under such circumstances, the government should re-orientate its efforts and devote more resources to helping the less fortunate members of the society, whose income growth fails to catch up with the surge in the cost of living. An informed redistributive policy is particularly important for Hong Kong. I shall have more to say below when I discuss the longer-term future of the local economy.

In any case, it is interesting to note that a clear winner in the inflationary tug-of-war is the Hong Kong government. Thanks particularly to asset inflation, it has been faced with a fiscal bonanza, which proves somewhat embarrassing. It budgeted a deficit of HK$3.36 billion for the fiscal year 1993–1994. The actual balance turned out to be a surplus as huge as HK$19.2 billion and roughly about one-third of the total revenue was derived from the property and the stock markets. Cumulative fiscal reserves stood at HK$140.2 billion on 31 March 1994, which equalled to 14.5 per cent of the projected GDP for 1994. This actually reinforces my argument for the implementation of a redistributive policy in Hong Kong, as the government is in a sound fiscal position to do so.

More specifically, Hong Kong's inflation, as measured by the CPI(A), was 8.5 per cent for the whole of 1993. In the first half of 1994, it hovered at around 7.5 per cent. The slight easing has also to do with the China factor. While the costs of housing, services and transport continued to show the fastest rates of increase, fresh food prices rose only modestly, by about 2 per cent. With China being the main supplier of fresh food to Hong Kong, the depreciation of the Renminbi, in the course of 1993 as well as following the unification of the dual exchange rates at the beginning of 1994, was one of

---

[5] Tsang Shu-ki, "Inflation," in *The Other Hong Kong Report 1992*, edited by Joseph Y. S. Cheng and Paul C. K. Kwong (Hong Kong: The Chinese University Press, 1992), pp. 425–45.

the reasons behind the moderate growth in food prices in the territory. Foodstuffs are the single largest component accounting for over 20 per cent of the weighting of the CPI(A).

The easing may however not last too long. The Renminbi has stabilized, indeed slightly strengthened, after the successful launching of the foreign exchange reforms of 1994, while the U.S. dollar, to which the local currency is linked, has come under pressure. The floods in Southern China as well as the delayed effects of high property prices on rental rates could also put upward pressure on inflation in Hong Kong in the near future.

☐ Industrial Restructuring or De-industrialization?

The industrial restructuring, or de-industrialization, of Hong Kong has continued to proceed with full force, as Table 2 indicates. In 1984, the manufacturing sector employed 898,947 workers. The total number had been halved by March 1994. That the manufacturing workforce of an economy could be trimmed by 50 per cent within ten years must be one of the records in world economic history. Given the very low unemployment and underemployment rates prevailing in recent years, the ease with which employees have switched across sectors is a testimony to the famous flexibility of the Hong Kong economy.

Table 2. Employment by Industry Group

	Persons engaged			
	1992	1993	Dec. 1993	March 1994
Manufacturing	582,199 (–13)	511,415 (–12)	483,628 (–14)	455,853 (–14)
Construction sites	62,232 (–2)	56,226 (–10)	55,852 (–6)	57,955 (–3)
Wholesale/retail, import/ export trades and restaurants & hotels	897,130 (+3)	937,751 (+5)	948,881 (+4)	997,750 (+9)
Financing, insurance, real estate & business services	307,712 (+)7	328,804 (+7)	338,093 (+7)	349,381 (+11)

Note: Figures in parentheses are percentage changes over the preceding year.
Source: Hong Kong government, *Report of Employment, Vacancies and Payroll Statistics*, various issues.

To critics, however, it also reveals that employment in the territory has largely been non-sector-specific in nature. It reflects rather poorly on the skill level that has been required in the major sectors. To put it dramatically, anyone here can be a textile worker in one month, a salesman in another, and a property agent in yet another. This does not augur well for the long-run prospect of productivity enhancement, which requires specialization, professionalization, and accumulation of expertise in specific areas. It adds force to the sceptical view that the Hong Kong economy is still ravelling in the bonanza of the China factor for cost reduction and "re-rating" by international investors and speculators. No serious efforts in industrial and technological upgrading have been made.

☐ Exports: The Chinese and Western Factors

One notable result of the slow-down in exports in 1993–1994 has been the widening of Hong Kong's trade gap, which rose from 2.5 per cent in 1993 to 8.0 per cent in the first half of 1994. It appears that both the China factor and cyclical developments in the Western economies have contributed to that (see Tables 3 and 4).

Table 3. Value of External Trade

(HK$ million)

	1992	1993	June 1994	Jan.–June 1994
Total exports	924,953	1,046,250	99,988	527,028
	(+21)	(+13.1)	(+16.9)	(+10.0)
Domestic exports	234,123	223,027	19,688	98,743
	(+1)	(–4.7)	(+6.4)	(–4.3)
Re-exports	690,829	823,224	80,300	428,285
	(+29)	(+19.2)	(+19.8)	(+14.0)
Imports	955,295	1,072,597	110,753	572,863
	(+23)	(+12.3)	(+24.0)	(+13.1)
Retained imports	264,466	249,373	30,453	144,578
	(+8)	(–5.7)	(+36.8)	(+10.4)
Trade balance	–30,342	–26,347	–10,765	–45,835
Trade gap (%)	3.2	2.5	9.7	8.0

Note: Figures in parentheses are percentage changes over the preceding year.
Trade gap = [(imports – total exports) ÷ imports] × 100
Source: Hong Kong government, *Hong Kong Monthly Digest of Statistics*, various issues.

Table 4. Domestic Exports Value by Major Market

(HK$ million)

	1992	1993	May 1994	Jan.–May 1994
China	61,959	63,367	5,337	22,944
	(+14)	(+2.3)	(–2.5)	(–9.3)
United States	64,600	60,292	4,710	19,886
	(+3)	(–6.7)	(–1.2)	(–3.1)
Germany	15,956	13,969	934	4,363
	(–17)	(–12.5)	(–13.0)	(–12.3)
Singapore	10,360	11,344	975	4,642
	(+18)	(+9.5)	(–2.2)	(+0.9)
United Kingdom	12,541	10,771	763	3,537
	(–8)	(–14.1)	(–4.0)	(–9.9)
Japan	10,997	9,677	786	3,864
	(–6)	(–12.0)	(+10.0)	(–4.6)
Taiwan	6,500	6,261	457	2,341
	(+7)	(–3.7)	(–8.7)	(–5.6)
Others	51,210	47,346	3,743	17,486
	(–6)	(–7.5)	(–2.3)	(–7.1)
All markets	234,123	223,027	17,705	79,063
	(+1)	(–4.7)	(–2.4)	(–6.6)

Note: Figures in parentheses are percentage changes over the preceding year.
Source: Hong Kong government, *Hong Kong Monthly Digest of Statistics*, various issues.

Following the dramatic upswing of the Chinese economy in 1992, the Chinese authorities, still wary of the lessons of 1988–1989, have tried to control the economy through an innovative approach. Top leaders understand that any "across-the-board" retrenchment to cure overheating is very costly. Hence, there is a need for a more gentle approach to macroeconomic control. The ideal solution will be continuous "fine-tuning," perhaps on a monthly or even daily basis. But China simply does not possess the necessary monetary and fiscal instruments and has not established the required institutional framework. Instead, therefore, a "stop-go" approach seems a second-best alternative.

Following such a strategy, Beijing has already implemented two rounds of "tightening" since the "Deng whirlwind," with these coming in the last four months of 1992 and in July–September 1993, in an attempt to tame the roaring economy before it becomes too late. The objective was to break

The Economy

away from the past "make-or-break" cyclical pattern, under which overheating was allowed to get out of control before crude administrative measures were used to overkill. The new stop-go approach has achieved some success. Thanks to it, overheating in 1994 is not as serious as that in 1988. The speculative bubbles in the stock and property markets have also been pinched.[6]

Moreover, the present economic cycle in China has been driven mainly by investment rather than by consumption.[7] In 1993, for example, fixed asset investment rose by 22 per cent in real terms, while the retail sales volume of consumer goods increased only by 11.6 per cent, compared with a real GDP growth of 13.4 per cent.

Consumer demand in China now is mainly restrained by a number of factors: the relative saturation of basic consumption items after a decade of prosperity in the 1980s, at least in the urban areas; income constraints for luxury goods and importables in cities, partly because of a widening in income disparity; and income and infrastructure constraints for some basic goods and many luxury items in the rural areas.

In other words, Chinese consumers are caught in a bottleneck of income and infrastructure. Given, say, five more years of continued growth in incomes (without drastic worsening of income disparity) and infrastructural expansion, the economy may become more consumption-driven than it has been for the present cycle.

The decline in the propensity to consume has been well reflected in slackening market sales. Total retail volume of consumer goods grew by a mere 4.2 per cent in the first four months of this year, the slowest since the resurgence of economic growth in 1991, right at a time when retail inflation was the highest. Accordingly, Hong Kong's exports to China that cater for the country's domestic consumption increased 11 per cent in the final quarter of 1993, down significantly from 45 per cent in the preceding quarter. There are, however, some indications that retail spending in China may pick up somewhat in the second half of 1994, and Hong Kong's exports could benefit from it.

As far as the U.S. market is concerned, the rebound in consumer

---

[6] See Tsang Shu-ki, "Why a Soft Landing Is Possible," *Sunday Morning Post*, 22 May 1994.

[7] Tsang Shu-ki, "So Far So Good for Chinese Economy," *Sunday Morning Post*, 7 August 1994.

spending in the first half of 1994 came in an atmosphere of rising interest rate expectations. Growth was therefore concentrated on durable goods like motor vehicles and furniture, items which were purchased on credit, taking advantage of the as-yet low interest rate charges. As Hong Kong's exports to the U.S. consist mainly of non-durable items such as clothing and footwear, they grew only 9 per cent in the first five months as against 13 per cent in the second half of 1993. However, the inventory for non-durable goods in the U.S. looks low. If the recovery persists and consumer confidence rises, U.S. retailers may have to replenish their stocks. This would translate into stronger demand for Hong Kong's exports.[8]

Hence, both the Chinese and U.S. factors have contributed to a slowdown in Hong Kong's exports. In the near term, though, there is cause for cautious optimism.

☐ 1997: The Political Economy of Transition

Economic integration between Hong Kong and China would necessitate some form of political congruence, which is theoretically possible under the framework of "one country, two systems" that defines the constitutional relations between the central authority and the future Special Administrative Region (SAR) government. In reality, there are difficulties in achieving harmonization in the transition process, given the long history of colonialism in Hong Kong, the territory's changing social profile, as well as political developments in China and Hong Kong's varied reactions to them. The political economy of the 1997 transition seems more complicated than the optimists think.[9]

Despite the Sino-British Joint Declaration, the Basic Law and all the politicking, the concept of Hong Kong as a local government functioning under the sovereignty of China has still not sunk in for a significant portion of the local population. Recent events have only added to their confusion and suspicion. The most important ones were of course the 1989 turbulence

---

[8] "Mid-year Review of the Hong Kong Economy," *Hang Seng Economic Monthly*, July 1994.

[9] A number of the major points discussed below has been covered in Tsang Shu-ki, "Hong Kong's Economic Prospect in a Changing Relationship with China: A Speculative Essay," *BRC Papers on China*, No. CP94004 (Hong Kong: School of Business, Hong Kong Baptist College, February 1994).

The Economy

in China and its aftermath, the collapse of communism in Eastern Europe and the former Soviet Union, and the political row between China and Britain since October 1992. People migrate, castigate Beijing, fight for democracy, or do nothing but earn money, as much and as quickly as possible. All these could be interpreted as signs of unsettled anxiety about "one country, two systems."

This kind of sociopolitical hesitance is in stark contrast to amazing progress on the economic front. China and Hong Kong are now each other's largest "outside" investor. The Hong Kong economy is so integrated with the Chinese counterpart that the latter's boom and bust have a huge impact on the territory. It is estimated by economists of the Hang Seng Bank[10] that 25.7 per cent of Hong Kong's aggregate output in 1990 could be attributed to "the China factor." This compares with only 5.3 per cent in 1980, the first full year after China launched its economic reform. Recent developments, particularly in the light of the "Deng whirlwind" of early 1992 and the subsequent euphoria over the prospect of China becoming the largest economy in the world by the early twenty-first century, would mean that the Hang Seng estimate has to be revised upward rapidly and significantly now and in the near future.

Many fear that the incongruence between transition economics and politics may generate adverse effects on the economy, at least in the medium term. However, the resilience of the local economy even in face of the political row has convinced the optimists who would argue that the negative impact of Sino-British political confrontation and the possible instability of non-convergence has been largely "discounted," as investors get used to the bickering between the two sides.

These optimists reckon that the key factor affecting the Hong Kong economy is not politics but the fortune of the Chinese economy itself. Moreover, Hong Kong's economic importance to China is so great that no matter how the political conflict between China and Britain over Hong Kong evolves, China will try its best to separate politics from economics in the transition. Hong Kong may suffer a political backlash after 1997, but the economic goose that lays golden eggs would be carefully looked after.

Unfortunately, the political economy of the transition is not that straightforward. China might become very uneasy in dealing with an SAR

---

[10] *Hang Seng Economic Monthly* (Hong Kong: Hang Seng Bank, June 1993).

with a significant number of "intransigent" residents, embolden by the last colonial governor who would get away without having to foot any bill (earning indeed huge political capital in "standing up to China"). The central government could feel that it should teach somebody a lesson to ensure longer-term stability. The fact that Hong Kong might serve as a geopolitical leverage for other outside powers after 1997 would only add to the complication.

One scenario, and I stress that it is nothing more than a *possible* scenario, is that China decides to implement a policy of economic absorption and assimilation of Hong Kong, downgrading the territory to an entity of economic dependency, in the hope that the SAR's political bargaining power is as a result commensurately kept within agreeable limits. Any foreign ploy to use Hong Kong as a pawn to destabilize China in the post-1997 era would likewise be frustrated.

In a way, it would even be advisable for China to transfer "portions of prosperity" in Hong Kong inwards, to Shenzhen, Zhuhai, the Pearl River Delta, Guangzhou, or further north. Metaphorically, Hong Kong should continue to be the magical goose that lays golden eggs, but don't let it get too fat, lest it will be stolen. (Or don't let its ego expand too much, otherwise it'll walk or fly away.)

The other side of the coin to this strategy is to let Mainland Chinese capital establish an even more powerful presence in Hong Kong, i.e. to increase the "Chinese-ness" and reduce the "Hongkong-ness" of the local economy. Top-level Chinese institutions and enterprises could use their political as well as economic clout to "buy into Hong Kong." Economically at least, their ability to help any Hong Kong collaborator to tap the Mainland market may mean that they could acquire assets in the territory at a "discount." As to the grassroots, Beijing may find it beneficial to give a freer hand to provincial and local funds in China to flow into Hong Kong. It is less likely for a Hong Kong billionaire with Mainland origin and links to become a political enemy to Beijing.

This is just one of the possible future scenarios, and I do not think that such a strategy on the part of China is the best way to handle central-local relations in the post-1997 era. Some would doubt the ability of Beijing to implement a regional policy with so high a level of sophistication in an era of "economic warlordism." Others would categorically deny that the Chinese government has this kind of intention whatsoever.

But there are other more obvious casualties of the Sino-British political row: the Chek Lap Kok replacement airport, the new container terminals in

Kwai Chung, and *possibly* the recently proposed Old Age Pension Scheme (OPS), to name a few. As commentators have pointed out, even if the first runway of Chek Lap Kok is completed and can be used by 1997, it might already be operating at maximum capacity in the very first month. The two sides should actually be discussing the construction of the second runway. Yet an agreement on the financing of the new airport with the first runway and the other related programmes was still pending by as late as mid-August 1994.

Rather than a deliberate tactic to stall developments in Hong Kong, China's hesitation in reaching quick agreements through generous compromises seems to have stemmed from its lack of trust in the British side, either on its motivation or on the viability of any plans straddling 1997. Conspiracy theory (that the other side has ulterior objectives or is careless in handling one's interests) has become a popular ammunition in Hong Kong's transition politics. Under such an atmosphere, any agreement on major long-term planning with a time horizon beyond 1997 would be difficult. To put it rhetorically, the design and implementation of long-term projects in Hong Kong would in general suffer a delay of four to five years because of the Sino-British political row that erupted in October 1992. And this is to assume that the future SAR government would be in a position to assume a "business as usual" attitude almost immediately after 1 July 1997.

From China's perspective, such delays might mean that some economic costs have to be borne by Hong Kong, but they could at the same time save the future SAR from heavy burdens as a result of failing to properly handle British conspiracies, "irresponsible behaviour" (like "splintering money to the public to gain political capital"), or ill-conceived ideas (a benign interpretation of the OPS proposal). The Hong Kong government, on the other hand, seems more interested in demonstrating who the real boss is in the remaining years before 1997 than helping China to overcome her suspicion, e.g. the final report of the consultancy firm assigned to conduct a feasibility study of the OPS proposal was forwarded to the Chinese side only after it had openly and loudly complained in August 1994. I actually got hold of a copy of the report almost a month earlier.

Moreover, looking at infrastructure developments in Southern China as a whole, some lags and lapses in Hong Kong would not be a serious problem. China is now catching up fast as it enters an "infrastructure-led, heavy-industries-driven" stage of economic development, which is quite different from the mode of growth in the 1980s. The latter was characterized by rapid expansion of light industries that process and manufacture consumer goods.[11] A large number of highly ambitious plans for the construction of airports, ports, railways, highways and telecommunications facilities has been announced by central and local authorities. Those for the Yangtze Delta (e.g., Ningbo and Shanghai) and areas around Bohai (from Tianjin to Dalian) are particularly noteworthy as they may form direct competition with Guangdong and Hong Kong.

Actually, intra-regional rivalry is likely to heat up in the future even within Southern China. Shenzhen already has its own airport (Huangtian) and is building a huge port at Yantian. Zhuhai and Macau are constructing their own airports, while Guangdong is going to have a much larger replacement to the present Baiyun. Even Foshan has had its airfield, which operates commercial flights. Some experts have indeed warned that there are perhaps too many airports in the Pearl River Delta and much better traffic coordination is necessary.

Whether the delay in Hong Kong's infrastructural developments fits with any version of conspiracy theory is left to the readers to judge. One complication is that a number of prominent investors in Hong Kong are involved in those huge infrastructural projects in Southern China, and accusations that they may be betraying local interest have been voiced in some quarters locally. As they are in a "sure-win" situation whether the new facilities are built in Hong Kong or the Pearl River Delta, some commentators have criticized them for not exerting enough of their political influence on China to have the facilities located in Hong Kong, at least not quickly enough.[12]

☐ Futurological Speculation: "Manhattanization"

Any speculation about Hong Kong's economic future beyond 1997 and into the twenty-first century is enmeshed by uncertainty and unpredictability. Nevertheless, the temptation to make a trial run is so great that I am willing to take here the risk of being ridiculed by history later. Let me start

---

[11] See Tsang Shu-ki, "The Chinese Economy Marching onto a New Plateau?" *Ming Pao*, 12–13 February 1993.

[12] See the report by Simon Fluendy, *South China Morning Post*, 31 January 1994.

with something cheerful. Under the most "optimistic" scenario, economic integration is total and Hong Kong would serve as the "Manhattan" of a prosperous China in the twenty-first century. As a result, the demand for assets in Hong Kong would undergo a dramatic change: it will be *internationalized* to an unprecedented extent. In so far as Hong Kong is a stepping stone to a booming China on its way to becoming the largest economy in the world, or a synchronized economic sub-entity, albeit with better facilities and still being more market-friendly, foreign investors would be tempted to establish a base in the territory.

Likewise, an extrovert China would put increasing value on Hong Kong as an outpost to the world, not to mention the formal and informal capital flight to the territory that has been gathering momentum. This would translate into strong demands for financial assets as well as commercial property for business operations and residential property for managerial accommodation. Hence, the observation that property prices are beyond "local purchasing power," which is undoubtedly accurate at least for small-sized and medium-sized flats, would become increasingly irrelevant. The stock market could reach new heights that few could now confidently predict.

Under such a scenario, the Hong Kong urban centre in the twenty-first century would be quite "uninhabitable" for the non-rich, who will be driven out to the cheaper outskirts, or even to Shenzhen and other areas in the Pearl River Delta. A 24-hour customs service at the border between Hong Kong and China and commensurate rapid-transit transport would render it possible for the local white-collar employees, and blue-collar workers as well (if there are any left), to work in Hong Kong but live in the southern part of Guangdong. Economic growth is so robust that most of them can afford to lead such a "schizophrenic" life. Whether they like it or not is another story.

☐ Over-priced, Side-tracked but More Manhattanized?

However, is Hong Kong really so important to China? Will such importance last? On top of the port function that we have already discussed above, most commentators can cite two other major roles that Hong Kong has been playing in China's economic take-off, namely, serving as the country's marketing outlet and financier. It appears that, in the long run at least, Hong Kong may see a decline in its relative importance in these two roles. Such an answer, however, could in my view produce an ironical result: Hong Kong would be "Manhattanized" to an even greater extent!

The concept of Hong Kong serving as China's marketing outlet is a familiar one, as vividly captured in the term *qian dian hou chang* — "the shop at the front, the factory at the back." Obviously, Hong Kong is the *dian* (shop), and Southern China is the *chang* (factory). Such a link has worked well because of two factors: (1) the factory has been making light-industrial goods that the shop previously made itself; and (2) the shop has a large equity stake in the factory through various forms of investment. These could change in the future if Southern China embarks on its own version of development with much greater emphasis on heavy and high-technology industries in which Hong Kong has as yet to establish any comparative advantage.[13] Guangdong would form partners with outside foreign investors who already have their own global distribution networks, hence bypassing Hong Kong. In any case, the territory lacks experience in selling heavy industrial and high-technology products.

Hong Kong has undoubtedly been playing a very important function in providing external financing for China's growth and reforms, not just in being its largest "outside" investor, but also in extending bank loans, listing the H shares of some of its largest enterprises, and housing many of the foreign financial institutions which are keen to go into China but need a modern and convenient base in the territory. The biggest competitor to Hong Kong is Shanghai, which is at the forefront of China's unfolding financial revolution. The city has attracted worldwide attention through its huge developmental plan for Pudong and the openly stated goal of turning the Bund into the "Wall Street of China." The fact that Citibank moved its China Headquarters from Hong Kong to Shanghai in 1993 was a clear warning to the territory not to be complacent about its financial clout.

Some commentators are much more optimistic about Hong Kong's role in China's economic modernization. They point to the fact that Hong Kong's importance as a trade intermediary actually *increased* in the past

---

[13] Guangdong has apparently decided to implement an industrial strategy, and has chosen the petrochemical, automobile, electronics, metallurgy, construction material, textile, and medical drugs industries as the province's "pillar industries." The need for the Special Economic Zones to develop high-technology and new-skill industries is also stressed. See "The Guangdong Economy Marching towards the Twentieth First Century," *Guangdong–Hong Kong Information Daily*, 11 January 1994, p. 6.

decade even as China opened herself to the rest of the world. Various reasons that evoke the theory of economic intermediation are cited. The gist of the arguments is that Hong Kong can continue to offer services that would reduce the transaction costs for foreigners in doing business with China, because of the territory's geographical proximity and cultural affinity to China and its "first-mover" advantages including accumulated experience and economies of scale. Moreover, on the Chinese side, the rise in the heterogeneity of products traded (a result of development) as well as the decentralized mode of open policy, under which local authorities and enterprises have greater autonomy in conducting foreign trade, would increase the transaction costs for foreigners, which Hong Kong with its presumed experience and contacts could help to alleviate.[14]

Such an analysis gives an interesting interpretation of Hong Kong's increased importance to China in the past decade. However, it is dangerous to extrapolate this view into the future without careful consideration of changing dynamics. As an explanation it has neglected the simple technical reason that China's transportation and communications facilities had not been able to catch up with its rapidly expanding volume of external trade, and therefore she was forced to route a good deal of it through Hong Kong. With China entering a period of vast infrastructural build-up and all the ambitious plans for airports and ports, "diversion" (or more accurately "reversion," some would say) of at least a significant portion of trade is inevitable. Moreover, as inflation (particularly asset inflation) continues to surge locally, Hong Kong is in the danger of pricing itself out of the market as a trade intermediary.[15]

Technical factors aside, the economic explanation also warrants closer scrutiny. Hong Kong's connection with China is mainly in the southern part of the country and concentrates on light industries, i.e. it is at best partial. As far as cultural affinity is concerned, investors from Taiwan (who now

---

[14] See Sung Yun-wing, *The China–Hong Kong Connection: The Key to China's Open Policy* (Cambridge University Press, 1991).

[15] In a related development, the Chinese Customs has publicly complained that Hong Kong re-exporters have been obtaining apparently unreasonable benefits by setting mark-ups of more than 30 per cent on imports from China. See "Hong Kong Fetching Stocking Profits in Re-exporting Mainland Goods," *Shanghai Economic News*, 24 June 1994, p. 1.

form the second largest outside source of direct investments for China) as well as overseas Chinese in Asia or the West can claim at least equal advantage. For multinational corporations investing in infrastructure, heavy and high-technology industries in China, Hong Kong could hardly offer them any service that helps to reduce cost significantly. Moreover, in "using" Hong Kong's experience and connection, foreigners need not invest in Hong Kong at all. They can just form partnerships with big Hong Kong companies and pour money directly into China. The impact on the Hong Kong economy could be minimal, unless the profits are massively repatriated by the Hong Kong partners. And then it depends on how the money is spent locally.

It does not mean that Hong Kong would lose all its functions under this much more sobering scenario. Nothing like that is going to happen. These developments do, however, point to the possibility that Hong Kong might get a smaller share of the pie in the future. But if the absolute size of the pie gets bigger, or much bigger, that should not be much of a worry.

What would cause concern is that if significant "diversion" does take place, distributional struggle in the territory could become a problem. Asset inflation is likely to intensify because of factors such as monopoly, international investors' strategy and preference, profit repatriation, and so on. It would also worsen because the same rate of returns can only be achieved through higher prices as demand becomes less robust in line with slower growth. Hong Kong may have to undergo further "structural transformation" to keep ahead of other competing cities and regions in China. In the end, the territory would be forced into a peculiar mould of specialization, under which only activities of a very "high-risk, high-returns" nature find it viable to be based here. Hong Kong might discover that it has absolute advantage only in producing fanciful "financial derivatives." The trouble is that a limited proportion of the local population can engage profitably in these activities. Unemployment may then replace labour shortage as a headache. Ironically, therefore, Hong Kong will be even more "Manhattanized" under such a scenario, as de-industrialization becomes total, financial wizardry dominates, and the ugly reality of poverty in the midst of affluence surfaces. The social consequences could be rather daunting.

☐ Facing the Not-so-distant Future

The future will probably turn out to be a case somewhere between the rosy and the sobering scenarios. The economic integration between Hong Kong and China would go on, and could withstand the 1997 transition and major political upheavals in China, unless they are of the disastrous kind. Even if China decides to contain and assimilate the Hong Kong economy, or if significant diversion occurs naturally as a result of cost and benefit considerations, growth in the future SAR should still be very decent by world standard, at least on average.

Chances are that Hong Kong will increasingly be "Manhattanized." People who do not benefit from the "China boom" will be under great pressure and progressively marginalized, while the rich and the super-rich live in glamorous styles.

We should certainly try our best to maximize the benefits and minimize the costs of such a historical course of development. Overall, for the long-term well-being of the territory, a balance has to be struck between industry and service, prosperity and equity, although the temptation to go for where quick profits can be earned is always great, as testified by the experience of the past decade.

Some would argue that the de-industrialization of Hong Kong is nothing to worry about. To put it bluntly, it is not necessary for Hong Kong to have any manufacturing industries at all. New York does not have such industries, nor does London or Paris. Such a comparison is however misleading, because Hong Kong is supposed to be a separate economic system under the Joint Declaration and the Basic Law. After 1997, Hong Kong will continue to issue an independent currency, keep its fiscal autonomy, and determine its own migration policy. So in theory the Hong Kong economy cannot be *fully* integrated with the Chinese counterpart because there will not be totally free flows of monetary, fiscal and human resources.

Hong Kong residents will not be able to migrate to Guangdong in the same way as U.S. citizens move from New York to California. Hence, any local structural unemployment cannot be easily solved by an expedient transfer of human resources to the north. In the case of a fiscal or a balance-of-payments crisis, Beijing is not supposed to come to our rescue, at least not directly. We also have to look after our own inflation and distribution problems. In a nutshell, Hong Kong is a very special case of regional economics.

For want of a better analogy, I would say that as a case of economic integration, Hong Kong in China is closer to Singapore in ASEAN (Association of South East Asian Nations) than New York in the U.S. or Tokyo in Japan, minus all the politics of course. Moreover, whether New York,

London or Paris represent models of successful development that should be emulated is an open question. We probably could learn more from the experience of city economies that aspire to maintain a balance between industry and service, such as Singapore and Shanghai. So perhaps instead of becoming the "Manhattan" of Southern China, Hong Kong should serve as its "Shanghai." A possible mode of operation for Hong Kong's industries is the combination of China's capabilities in technological research and development with the territory's expertise in design, packaging, and commercialization.

Alternatively, Hong Kong, Shenzhen, Zhuhai, and Guangzhou could serve as a cluster of "southern Shanghai's," with Hong Kong functioning under a special category with a more international outlook. Division of labour among these centres has to be coordinated. Genuine efforts need to be made to climb the technological ladder and to maintain a viable industrial base, which would bring long-run benefits. It is foolhardy to abandon totally short-run comparative advantage. Trading and services sectors should no doubt be further promoted, but not one-sidedly. In any case, a balanced strategy like this can only be implemented through conscious effort by the authorities with regard to macroeconomic and microeconomic policies, as well as cooperation by the state enterprises and the private sector.

As for the appropriate industrial mix, Hong Kong need not duplicate Shanghai's efforts in developing or upgrading heavy industries such as iron and steel, petrochemical, automobile, and machinery. We should concentrate on the lighter, the less "land-intensive," the more "skill-and-design-oriented" industries such as computers, consumer goods based on the new material sciences, audio-visual and optical products, and so on. It will be industrialization with "Hong Kong characteristics."

☐ A Second Line of Defence

Admittedly, it is not easy to pursue such a course of economic development in Hong Kong, as it implies an explicit industrial strategy and related changes in fiscal and other policies. This line of thinking obviously goes against the prevailing mood of fetching easy money by following short-run market trends and requires visionary courage on the part of the authorities and far-sighted entrepreneurs, which may be lacking around the 1997 transition. Sadly, it also seems to be inconsistent with the conservative attitude of some of the top Chinese officials regarding developments in the territory, which has been provoked, or at least reinforced, by the political row with the British. Their stance has apparently become minimalist: the less change in Hong Kong, the better. In reality, of course, Hong Kong is changing all the time. The real question is whether the direction of the emerging changes is desirable. Ruling out *a priori* preventive and rectifying measures is myopic.

While I would urge the adoption of a balanced strategy of economic development for Hong Kong on intellectual grounds, I am prepared to retreat to the second line of defence. Problems such as inflation and income disparity, which have arisen from the so called "structural transformation" of the local economy, need to be seriously addressed. Even a more sensible developmental pattern could alleviate but not eliminate them. Remedial measures by the authorities will be necessary to contain their harmful social consequences. If the primary market trends of "Manhattanization" cannot be reversed, redistributive and protective measures should be activated.

In Hong Kong's case, proactive moves including a public pension scheme with a "pay-as-you-go" mechanism as the core (perhaps supplemented by a component of mandatory provident fund in a two-tier system), capital gains taxes (at least on property speculation), a revamp of the taxation system to introduce higher progressivity and to plug the loopholes arising from the economic integration in Southern China, fair trade and anti-monopoly laws — to name just a few — should have been introduced years ago if the colonial government had paid serious attention to unfolding socioeconomic trends. And even with all these modest systems in place, Hong Kong would still be a long, long way from the social-democratic welfare state of the Western type.

In this regard, the future SAR government in Hong Kong may perhaps be less constrained by the self-imposed *laissez faire* ideology of the colonial authority, which is increasingly out of touch with reality and in conflict with its own practice. Alternatively, things could turn worse should "money politics" replace "sanitized colonialism" in the post-1997 era. The minimalist attitude might also persist beyond 1997, and there is no lack of conservative commentators and parties of vested interests who are only too eager to provide justifications for decision-makers to resist socioeconomic changes. On the other hand, a China that successfully develops a viable model of "socialist market economy" can also be much more receptive to progressive developments in the territory.

The future of Hong Kong is as exciting as it is uncertain. So much depends on our relations with Mainland China and the outside world, and the unfolding patterns of international geopolitics and geoeconomics, which could take unexpected twists and turns into uncharted territories. Nevertheless, there is a real chance for Hong Kong to become a great metropolis of the twenty-first century. Whether it would be one with a human face and one that fits into a rational development framework of a powerful China at ease with itself and the world is not totally outside our control.

Labour and Employment

Wing Suen

The aggregate labour supply in Hong Kong took an unexpected jump in 1993. Following years of stagnant growth, the size of the labour force increased by 2.9 per cent, or 80,000 people. Part of this increase can be attributed to the government's general scheme for importation of labour. In early 1994, the government announced a new scheme that will allow university graduates from China to work in Hong Kong.

Employers' complaints about labour shortage continue to be heard, and labour advocates continue to voice their opposition to importing workers. Yet the public's attention is turning to other labour issues that cannot easily be characterized by the simplistic label of labour versus capital. After prolonged consultation on the merits of a decentralized pension system or a central provident fund, the government unveiled a compulsory old-age security scheme that threw most observers off-guard. Details of the scheme remain to be worked out and approved, but essentially it will require employees and their employers to each contribute 3 per cent of the wage bill to be redistributed to all elderly people in Hong Kong. Call it what you like, the scheme amounts to an employment tax of 6 per cent. Such massive intervention in the labour market is unprecedented in Hong Kong.

Another labour issue that caught the headlines is the ongoing dispute concerning the conversion of expatriate senior civil servants to local terms. Local civil servants claim that such conversion violates the government's professed policy of localization, while expatriate staff are prepared to sue

---

Wing Suen is a lecturer in the School of Economics and Finance, the University of Hong Kong.

民航職工總會
民主建港聯盟
辦事處
九龍西
強烈要求
迅速設立退休保障制度
退休保障 不容緩
拖拖拉拉 何時有
港工會聯合會 民主建港聯盟
強烈要求
退休保障制度
民主建港聯盟 香港工會聯合會
送呈：
港督彭定康先生
台啓

☐ Growth of the Labour Force

Labour shortage in Hong Kong has been a theme mentioned in each of the previous five volumes of *The Other Hong Kong Report*. From 1988 to 1992 the size of the labour force increased from 2.76 million to 2.79 million — an increase of 1.1 per cent in a four-year period. Labour force growth was negative in three out of these four years. In 1993 the size of the labour force rose sharply to 2.87 million. This represents a 2.8 per cent increase from the past year. In fact, the growth of the labour force in 1993 was more vigorous than any other year since 1981. Does it signal the end of labour shortage? Or is it just a temporary aberration in a long period of stagnating labour force growth?

To put things in perspective, it is useful to extend the focus beyond the most recent past. Figure 1 plots the size of the Hong Kong labour force for various years since 1976. The reader can notice a distinct change in the rate of labour force growth before and after 1981. In the period 1976–1981 the labour force grew rapidly at a rate of 5.6 per cent per annum, thanks largely to the influx of refugees from China. In 1980 the government abolished the "touch base" policy that allowed refugees to stay once they reached the urban areas of Hong Kong. Since then, legal and illegal immigration from China continued, but at a much reduced rate. As a result, the growth of the labour force dropped significantly. From 1981 to 1993 the size of the labour force increased at a modest rate of 1.2 per cent a year. Labour force growth was particularly sluggish from 1988 to 1993, when annual labour force growth averaged only 0.8 per cent.

Changes in labour supply depend on two factors: (1) changes in the size and age structure of the population; and (2) changes in labour force participation rates. The overall size of the population is obviously an important determinant of labour supply, as the population is the pool from which the labour force is drawn. The size of the population is in turn determined by mortality, fertility, immigration, and emigration. The age distribution of the population is also important because different age groups are characterized

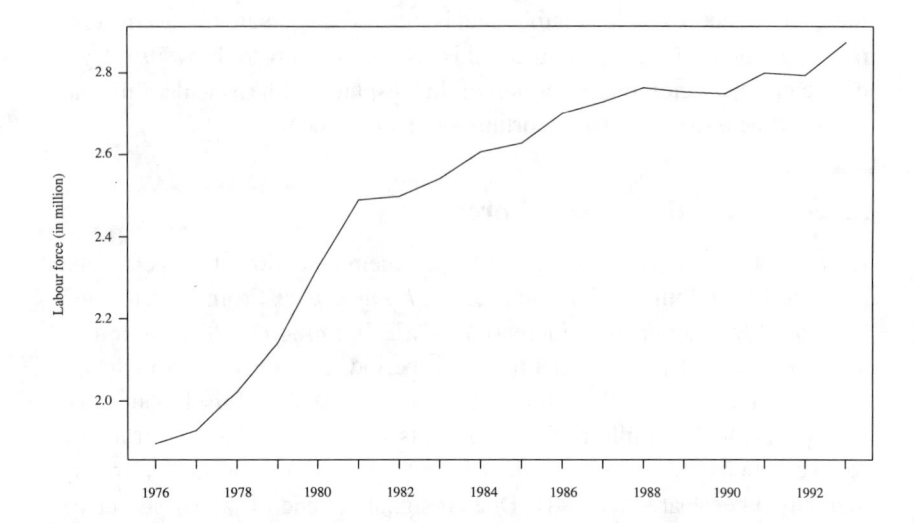

Figure 1. Growth of the Hong Kong Labour Force

by different labour force participation rates. For example, since older people are more likely to retire from the labour force than younger people, the labour force will shrink if the population ages, other things being equal.

The second set of factors (i.e., changes in labour force participation rates) is more directly related to economic considerations. For example, as the general level of real income rises, people would like to spare more time pursuing leisurely activities. The increase in demand for leisure may take the form of shorter work hours, or it may take the form of earlier retirement. Both trends have been observed in the developed countries. As another example, a higher tax rate will reduce the rewards from working. This will adversely affect labour supply.

To see more clearly how these two factors contribute to changes in labour supply in Hong Kong, one can ask two hypothetical questions:

1. If labour force participation rates had remained unchanged, how would changes in population have affected labour supply?
2. If the size and age structure of the population were constant, how would changes in labour force participation rates affect labour supply?

Table 1 presents the result of such an exercise for the period 1988–1993. Columns (1) and (3) of the table show the change in labour force for

Labour and Employment

Table 1. Decomposition of Labour Force Growth, 1988–1993

Age Group	Male (1)	Male (2)	Female (3)	Female (4)	Total (5)
15–19	−6,100 (−5%)	−9,700 (−9%)	−6,100 (−6%)	−14,100 (−13%)	−36,000 (−33%)
20–29	−57,700 (−52%)	−16,100 (−15%)	−22,400 (−20%)	−1,500 (−1%)	−97,700 (−89%)
30–39	75,700 (69%)	−4,000 (−4%)	65,900 (60%)	13,300 (12%)	150,800 (137%)
40–49	95,000 (86%)	300 (0%)	61,100 (55%)	−12,600 (−11%)	143,700 (131%)
50–59	−8,000 (−7%)	−1,600 (−1%)	−7,000 (−6%)	−5,900 (−5%)	−22,500 (−20%)
60+	17,200 (16%)	−25,700 (−23%)	3,900 (4%)	−23,700 (−22%)	−28,300 (−26%)
Total	116,000 (105%)	−56,900 (−52%)	95,400 (87%)	−44,500 (−40%)	110,100 (100%)

Note: Figures are based on author's calculations using data from the General Household Survey. Row and column totals may not add up due to rounding error.

men and women due to changes in population factors alone, and columns (2) and (4) show the change in labour force due to changes in labour force participation rates alone. For example, there was a drop in the population for 15–19 year old males during the period. Even if labour force participation had remained unchanged, the drop in population would have reduced the labour force by 6,100 people. At the same time the labour force participation rate for this group also fell. Even if population had remained unchanged, the fall in the labour force participation rate would have removed 9,700 people from the labour force.

Reading this table carefully, several interesting developments can be discerned. First, changes in population still contributed to a net increase in the labour force. If there were no changes in the labour force participation rates, the labour supply would have increased by 211,400 people, in contrast to the actual increase of 110,100 people. However, notice that the population in the 15–29 age group had fallen. As this cohort advances in age, the population in older age groups will decrease in the future. Thus, barring increased immigration, it is expected that the population base from which the labour force is drawn will eventually shrink.

The reduction in the population of young people in this period is the result of reduced immigration (since new immigrants are predominantly young) and of long-term decline in fertility. The total fertility rate (i.e., the number of live births per thousand women during their lifetime) in Hong Kong fell dramatically from 3,460 in 1971 to 1,210 in 1991. This fertility rate is lower than almost any other country in the world. In the absence of immigration, having 1.2 children per family is not sufficient to keep the population growing.

Second, labour force participation for men had fallen. The reduction in labour force participation rates for men had subtracted 56,900 people from the labour force. This drop may be interpreted as the result of rising affluence that increases the demand for leisure. The drop is particularly pronounced among people over 60 years of age as these people are retiring earlier. Their labour force participation rate fell from 36 per cent to 29 per cent.

Third, overall female labour force participation also fell but there are significant variations across different age groups. As women are marrying at a later age and are having fewer children, they are more inclined to stay in the labour force. Rising education and wages for women also encourage them to work. As a result, labour force participation for prime age women rose sharply. The increase in labour force participation by women in the age group 30–39 alone contributed to 12 per cent of the net increase in the total labour supply during the period.

However, this rise in labour force participation was not shared by women in other age groups. In particular, women over 40 years old showed a decline in labour force participation. One possible reason is related to the transformation of the structure of the economy in Hong Kong. Many women take a few years off from the labour market when they marry or when they raise their young children and then return to the labour market when the children grow up. Because of the rapidly changing character of the local economy, many of the industries (for example, textiles and garments) that formerly hired these women are now in decline, and many women would find that the skills they used to possess are no longer in demand.

Fourth, labour force participation rates for the 15–19 and the 20–29 age groups fell for both sexes, primarily because young people are acquiring more schooling before they enter the labour market. The government's expansion of tertiary education further helps reduce the size of the labour force. One should bear in mind, however, that the quality of labour matters as much as the quantity. While rising education tends to reduce the quantity of labour, it also helps produce a more skilled workforce.

The above analysis suggests that the strong growth of the labour force in 1993 may not be the beginning of a sustained period of growth. Except for women aged between 25 and 40 years, rising schooling and rising income has caused labour force participation to drop. The trend is not expected to be reversed in the near future. During the last year, when the growth of labour force was unusually high, the labour force participation rate rose only slightly from 62.3 per cent to 62.5 per cent. This implies that increased labour force participation contributed to about 9,000 people out of the total 80,000-people increase in the labour force. The remaining increase had come from the sudden surge in population.

Hong Kong's population reached 6 million in 1994. This figure exceeded the official projection made in 1991 by more than 200,000. Since mortality and fertility are very stable during short intervals of time, and since fertility has followed a long trend of decline, the bulk of the growth in the labour force was due to a net migration of people into the territory. Unless such net in-migration can be maintained, the fundamental factors do not predict a near end to the slow growth in labour supply that has been with us since 1981.

Aggregate labour market conditions in 1993 did not change much compared to the recent past despite the sudden change in labour supply. Table 2 shows the growth in real wages, and unemployment, underemployment, and vacancy rates for various years. Real wages seem to have picked up slightly after two years of slack growth. Amid a period of massive transformation of the economy, when the manufacturing sector alone has shed more than 300,000 jobs in five years, maintaining full employment is no small accomplishment. Hong Kong manages to do just that. The unemployment rate in 1993 was 2.0 per cent, which is effectively full employment. The underemployment and vacancy rates also give no special cause for alarm. For good reasons, annual reports tend to emphasize current events. However, the temptation to put every twist and turn in the statistics under a microscope and to interpret every "up" and "down" as significant developments should be resisted. On the whole, the figures in Table 2 do not give an impression that the year 1993 was significantly different from previous years.

Table 2. Selected Statistics for Aggregate Labour Market Conditions

	1989	1990	1991	1992	1993
Growth of real wages					
(a) craftsmen and operatives[@]	1.4	2.4	−1.1	0.0	1.7
(b) non-production workers (to supervisory level)[@]	4.6	2.9	−0.8	0.4	2.6
(c) middle management and professionals[#]	3.7	2.1	−0.3	0.4	0.2
Unemployment rate	1.1	1.3	1.8	2.0	2.0
Underemployment rate	0.8	0.9	1.6	2.1	1.6
Vacancy rates*					
(a) manufacturing	4.4	3.9	3.5	3.0	2.8
(b) services	3.6	3.2	3.2	3.3	3.2

Notes: [@] Figures for 1993 refer to the period September 1992 to September 1993.
[#] Figures refer to June to June changes.
* Vacancy rates refer to the third quarter for 1993 and the fourth quarter for other years.

Source: *Monthly Digest of Statistics*, various issues.

☐ Importing Workers

The decrease in fertility and the decline in male labour force participation rates are two trends commonly observed in developed countries, and it seems unlikely that they can be easily reversed in Hong Kong. The expansion of education also means people will be entering the labour force at a later age. These considerations leave only two avenues for increasing labour supply in Hong Kong. One possible source of labour growth is from married women who work as homemakers. In 1993 the female labour force participation rate for the age group 35–54 was slightly over 50 per cent in Hong Kong; the comparable figure for the United States was above 70 per cent. Part of the reason for the relatively low female labour force participation was that economic transformation had rendered their skills obsolete. The Employees Retraining Board was set up in late 1992 to assist workers to acquire new skills that are valued in the marketplace. It is still too early to assess its effect on the aggregate labour supply. A more immediate source for increasing labour supply is from imported workers.

To ease labour shortage, the government has introduced several schemes for the importation of workers since 1989. Under the general scheme for the importation of labour, a maximum of 25,000 workers at the technician, supervisor, craftsman and experienced operative levels would be admitted to work in Hong Kong at any one time. Under a separate scheme for the new airport projects, another 5,500 construction workers at any one time are allowed. These two schemes are primarily targeted at low- to medium-skill jobs. In early 1994 the government announced a new plan that would allow 1,000 graduates from certain approved universities in China to come to work in Hong Kong. There will be no administered wage provisions for these workers, and those who come and stay here for more than seven years would be eligible to become permanent residents. Although this plan represents a new policy towards professional workers from China, it is little different from the way the government has always treated professional workers from other countries. Hong Kong traditionally has a very liberal policy towards the entry of foreign workers for professional, administrative and managerial jobs. In 1993 alone more than 17,000 people from other countries were admitted for employment in Hong Kong as professional workers.

With an economy that is increasingly intertwined with China, many employers look for people who know about Chinese business practices, who can speak the language, and who are willing to spend part of their time working in China. The new policy to import Chinese professionals will help ease the demand for such workers. In fact, the Hong Kong economy has been shedding low-skill jobs and expanding the demand for high-skill labour. Importing skilled workers makes more sense than importing unskilled workers. Research in Hong Kong and elsewhere generally finds very minor effects of immigration on the overall level of wages. This is understandable, as labour is not a homogeneous factor of production. Increasing the supply of typists, say, will lower the wage of typists, but it will also increase the wage and productivity of their co-workers. If skilled workers and unskilled workers are complementary to one another, importing skilled workers will raise the wages of unskilled workers.

In 1994 there was another change in policy towards Chinese immigrants which has aroused less attention but which will have more long-lasting effect on labour supply in Hong Kong. Starting from January the government increased the intake of legal Chinese immigrants from 75 to 105 persons per day. The purpose of the increase in the immigration quota is to allow more children of Hong Kong residents who live in China to come to Hong Kong. Under the Basic Law, these children are entitled to become

Hong Kong citizens after 1997. Allowing them to come earlier would ease the potential impact of a sudden wave of immigration after 1997.

Although the majority of those who come to Hong Kong under the newly raised quota will not enter the labour force immediately, they will help replenish the potential pool from which our labour force is drawn. From 1981 to 1991 the population of children below 15 years old fell from 26 per cent to 23 per cent of the total population. Given the fertility pattern in Hong Kong, the overall population will shrink in the absence of replenishment from other sources.

Allowing the children to come now rather than after 1997 also has the advantage that they will be exposed to Hong Kong's education system earlier. This will help ease their transition to a new environment and give them more opportunity to learn the skills (such as English language) that are important for labour market success in Hong Kong. Research done by Samuel Lui of Lingnan College indicates that education obtained in China is much less valuable in Hong Kong than education obtained locally. One additional year of education obtained in China increases a person's earnings in Hong Kong by 2.5 per cent. The rate of return to education obtained here, in contrast, is 10.5 per cent. Since the difference in rates of return is 8 per cent, allowing children to join local schools now rather than four years later would boost their future earnings by more than 30 per cent.

Hong Kong is one of the very few places in the world where immigration of direct family members of local citizens is subject to stringent quotas. This has exacted its toll on a lot of local residents. Because of prior waves of immigration, the sex ratio in Hong Kong is highly skewed towards males. Many men in Hong Kong are unable to find a wife here. With the opening of China, some began to arrange cross-border marriages with women in China. According to a special report of the General Household Survey in 1991, there were 95,200 people (mostly men) in Hong Kong who had a spouse in China. Of these, 78 per cent had children still living in China, with an average of 2.2 children per person. Many have to travel long distances to visit their families, and many children can see their fathers only a few times a year. If the spouse and children of local residents who are still in China are allowed to settle in Hong Kong sooner, this would ease the pain and strain present in the cross-border families. Legal and economic considerations aside, the immigration quota for these family reunification cases should be relaxed on compassionate grounds.

Labour and Employment

☐ Old-age Security Scheme

In October 1992 the government issued a consultation paper on retirement protection in Hong Kong. The paper recommended a compulsory but decentralized system in which employers and employees would have to contribute to a pension fund. Benefits would be drawn from the fund at retirement and they are tied to the worker's past contributions. Following a year of heated debates on the merits of a decentralized system versus a central provident fund, the government announced a new Old Age Pension Scheme that bears little resemblance to its predecessor. The new scheme would require workers and their employers to each contribute 3 per cent of the wage bill to the government. The money would be used to pay each person over 65 years old an amount equal to 30 per cent of the then current median earning in Hong Kong. At current incomes, this is about $2,100 a month. Although the Old Age Pension Scheme is called a pension scheme, two features of this scheme makes it a radical departure from a pension system. First, benefits are not tied to contributions. Each and every person over the age of 65 in the community will receive an equal payment without any means test and regardless of their prior history of contributions. Second, it is a pay-as-you-go system. The contributions made now are not invested for the future; rather they are redistributed to finance the payments to the current generation of elderly people.

At the time of writing, the scheme has yet to be approved and many details remain to be worked out. Because a pay-as-you-go social security system was not even on the agenda of the previous consultation paper, it threw most of the leaders of opinion off-guard. It did not take long, however, for many legislators to reach the conclusion that (1) contributions are bad; (2) benefits are good; and (3) government should do more. In a show of their political (if not economic) sophistication, three political parties joined forces to recommend cutting employees' contributions while keeping the benefits. In a world where free lunches abound, they reasoned correctly, we can have our cake and eat it too.

The economics of the compulsory Old Age Pension Scheme is not difficult to understand. Whether contributions are made by employers or employees makes little difference. When there is a tax on the payroll, the demand for labour falls. The fall in labour demand will be translated into a reduction in employment and a reduction in real wage. And if the government foots the bill, that means the pensions are financed by general taxes rather than a payroll tax. In the existing tax structure of Hong Kong, about half of the working population pay the incomes tax. Financing the scheme from the incomes tax would directly affect fewer people than from a payroll tax, but the required increase in the tax rate would be greater than 6 per cent. Again, there would be adverse effects on real wages and employment.

Economic research generally finds that male labour supply is relatively unresponsive to small changes in tax rates. Changes in tax rates, however, affect the relative returns from working at home versus working in the labour market and will therefore significantly affect the employment of married women. Using data from the 1991 Population Census, one can predict a monthly wage for each married woman (even if the woman reports no earnings) based on her place of birth, work experience, education attainment, and English language ability. The predicted wages are then ranked into thirty groups. Figure 2 plots the labour force participation rate against the average predicted wage for each group. The size of the circles reflects the number of observations in each group, and the straight line is the best fit to the data. The reader can see that women who face higher wages are more likely to be in the labour market. In particular, this simple model predicts that a six percentage point increase in tax will reduce the labour force participation rate of married women by about three percentage points. This is not to say that reduced labour participation is bad; it is not. But when people who could otherwise gain by joining the labour market are deterred

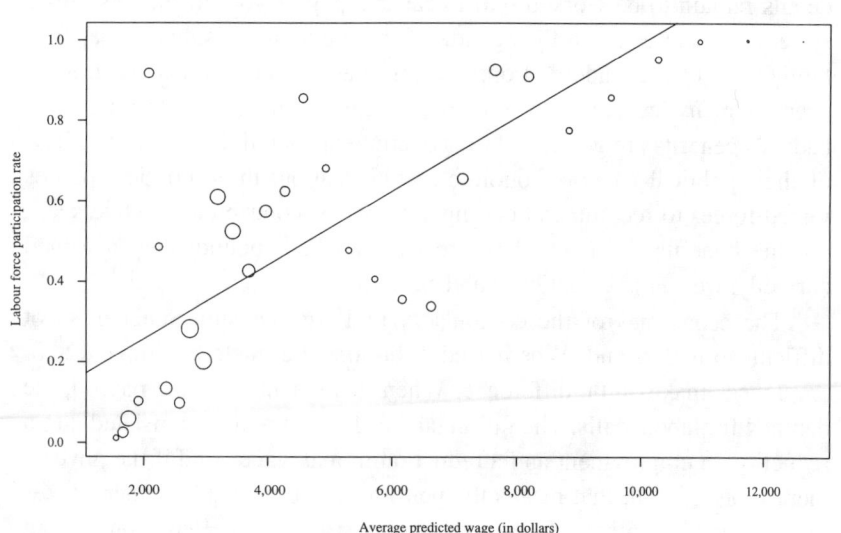

Figure 2. Female Labour Force Participation and Predicted Wage

from doing so by an employment tax, these potential gains are destroyed to no one's benefit. The result is a net reduction in wealth for society as a whole.

The Old Age Pension Scheme is supposed to provide income security to the elderly. However, giving up 6 per cent of wages and salaries every year for a future pension equal to 30 per cent of the median wage is not a good investment. Using labour force participation, wage, and mortality data in Hong Kong, the internal rate of return from the compulsory pension plan for a typical person is calculated to be 1.5 per cent in real terms. This is a dismal return compared to investments in equities or real estate. Moreover, because some people do not participate in the labour force, only about 70 per cent of the population in the relevant age group have to pay contributions. Therefore, people who work and contribute to the fund throughout their life until retirement will get a return which is worse than 1.5 per cent. For example, the real rate of return from the scheme will be −0.4 per cent for a secondary school graduate who works from age 18 to 64. For a male university degree holder who works from age 23 to 64, the expected return is −3.1 per cent.

The calculated rates of return are based on the assumption of zero wage growth. If real wages increase at a rate of one per cent per year, the calculated rates will increase by one percentage point. For any realistic projection of real wage growth, the returns from the compulsory pension plan would not beat most conventional instruments of investment. Several additional considerations make the plan even less attractive than what its rate of return suggests. First, with the looming change of political sovereignty, people in Hong Kong probably have more confidence in private institutions than in the British, the Chinese, and the future Hong Kong governments. There is a distinct possibility of default or an erosion of real benefits. Second, in this period of political and economic uncertainty around 1997, people desire to hold more liquid assets to prepare for emergencies. The compulsory pension plan is extremely illiquid: there is no way to withdraw or to claim any benefits before retirement age. Third, housing prices and mortgage restrictions in Hong Kong have denied or delayed home ownership to a large segment of the population. To many, the security from owning a flat is more important than the security from a relatively meagre pension. A lot of young people are saving as much as they can for the first down payment. Forced saving by the government would only further delay or deny home ownership for these aspiring home buyers.

Demographic trends in Hong Kong are also at odds with the financial viability of the old-age pension system. In 1991 there were eight people between age 15 and 64 to support each person aged over 65. Because of declining fertility and mortality, this ratio is projected to fall to 6:1 by the year 2011. Because the scheme is a pay-as-you-go system, it is politically impossible to dismantle or curtail the system when revenues cannot meet expenses: people who have made contributions but have not yet received benefits would be opposed to such a move. The only alternative then is to raise contributions. What is more, a pay-as-you-go system is subject to the "ratchet effect." When the fund shows a surplus, it is politically very tempting to extend benefits. When current outlays exceed current revenues, on the other hand, it is politically very difficult to cut benefits because people regard their benefits as entitlements earned through past contributions. Thus, short-term surpluses cannot accumulate to cover short-term deficits, and contribution and benefit rates can only go up. In the United States, for example, the combined Social Security tax for employers and employees was 2 per cent when it first started in 1935. Now it stands at 15.3 per cent of the payroll.

The disincentive effects of a payroll tax and the distortionary effects of forced saving are well known to economists. Policy-makers, however, often justify their proposals on equity rather than efficiency grounds. The Old Age Pension Scheme entails a wealth redistribution that cannot be said to be equitable. The absence of a means test implies that it is not targeted to the needy. What is more, the old-age security scheme cannot even benefit old people as a class (with the exception of the current generation of the elderly); it can only bring net benefits to those rare creatures who are old without first being young. The primary redistributive effect of the plan is therefore not from the young to the old, but from those who contribute more to those who contribute less. Since people not in the labour force do not have to contribute and yet will receive the same benefits as people who are in the labour force, the scheme redistributes wealth from those who work for pay to those who do not. For example, the female labour force participation rate is below that of men. The scheme thus redistributes wealth from men to women. Women in wealthy families are less likely to be in the labour force than women in lower-income families. The scheme thus redistributes wealth from poor families with working wives to well-off families where the female household heads stay home. And if contributions are collected through a special levy on the payroll, employers and the self-employed — who are on average richer than employees — are likely to escape the levy on their own earnings.

Hong Kong is famed for its low-tax environment that encourages business and rewards hard work. The Old Age Pension Scheme, if enacted, will impose a tax of 6 per cent on the payroll. This amounts to the largest tax hike in the history of Hong Kong. As the number of elderly people who are truly in need of public assistance is small relative to the number of people who will be adversely affected by the scheme, it is hard to justify such a Draconian measure in the labour market — especially when the tax is inefficient, and possibly inequitable.

☐ The Question of Equal Opportunity in Employment

Since the enactment of the Bill of Rights, various groups in Hong Kong have been advocating legislation against discrimination on the basis of age, sex, or national origin in the workplace. A dispute in the civil service last year brought the issue of equal employment opportunity to the forefront. In July 1993, the government announced its plan to allow expatriate civil servants who are on fixed-term contracts and who have been in Hong Kong for more than seven years to switch to regular staff status under local terms of service. Representatives of local senior civil servants accused the government of reneging on its promise to replace foreign contract staff with local people. Legislators have put a freeze on the government's plan. Expatriate civil servants continue to threaten a law suit for violation of human rights. At the time of writing, the dispute is yet to be resolved.

This dispute directly concerns a small (albeit important) segment of the civil service, but it brings together the many complicated issues that will arise in the wider argument over discrimination in the labour market. In a parallel but unrelated development, Legislative Council member Anna Wu Hung-yuk is preparing a bill that would require equal employment opportunity in the private as well as the public sector. This is not the place to arbitrate a labour dispute, but examining some of the arguments made during the civil service dispute will help illuminate the debate on equal employment opportunity legislation. First, local civil servants contend that expatriates have been unfairly favoured in the past because of colonial rule. The government's localization policy, they argue, is to redress past discrimination against local people in the civil service, rather than to discriminate against expatriates. Even if one is prepared to accept this argument, several questions remain to be explored: To what extent is affirmative action that redresses past discrimination legally and morally justified? Are we prepared to accept its consequences, especially when extended to the private sector? It is highly unlikely that, in the near future, Hong Kong will have a rule that explicitly calls for affirmative action. However, if equal employment opportunity is written into law, affirmative action type of arguments are bound to arise.

Second, expatriate civil servants receive substantially better benefits in housing and in passage allowances than local staff. If there is equal opportunity in employment, should there be equal pay as well? If equal employment opportunity includes equal pay, is the government prepared to interfere with the contractual terms in every private employment relationship?

Third, some legislators propose that Chinese language proficiency should be a prerequisite for those expatriate civil servants who wish to convert to local terms. For some positions, this requirement can be a mirage for discrimination. It is hard to understand why airplane pilots, say, should be able to speak Cantonese to do their job. In fact, it is hard to understand why there should be a localization policy for such staff at all. For other positions, such as those in the police force or in district offices, inability to speak the local language is a severe hindrance to performing the job. Most positions, however, fall into the grey area. In the private sector, some retail outlets for young people's fashion do not hire sales workers who are over 40 years old. One might call it age discrimination. But the age requirement can also be a way for the stores to project a youthful image that helps lure young customers. If it is so difficult to judge whether certain job requirements are discriminatory, how is the equal employment opportunity law to be enforced? Are we prepared to accept statistical evidence to prove discrimination? Will this lead to implicit numerical quotas?

In some ways, the civil service dispute gives a distorted picture of the employment scene in Hong Kong. In the past few years, the number of foreigners who came to Hong Kong to take up employment has increased substantially. Most of them join the private sector, and they have excited little complaint from the locals. Many private companies are beginning to scale back the special benefits they offer to expatriate staff, but they are not giving any special priority to employ locals either. The special benefits would be too expensive, and localization would not always find the best person for the job. In this sense, market forces have solved a problem that the government fails to resolve. Before the government enacts a law to tell the private sector what to do, maybe it has something to learn from them first.

10

Immigration and Emigration: Current Trends, Dilemmas and Policies

Ronald Skeldon

The year 1993 saw Hong Kong's population surpass the six million mark. Population growth during the year was estimated by government statisticians at 2.0 per cent, the highest rate for well over a decade. The numbers of births and deaths have remained fairly constant over the last few years and so the sharp difference in annual growth in 1993 was due to migration. Again, using government estimates, the excess of arrivals over departures was put at 76,500. Natural increase, or the balance of births over deaths in 1993, was only 41,300, which shows the dominant role of migration in affecting the recent trend in Hong Kong's population growth (Table 1).

This author last wrote the chapter on population for *The Other Hong Kong Report* three years ago, when the principal concern was emigration and the brain drain. In 1993–1994, the main population concerns are related to immigration and immigration control rather than brain drain. The reason why there has been such an abrupt change in concern can partly be related to the restless nature of Hong Kong society, ever seeking new issues, and partly to the real situation itself. The general areas of public concern have shifted towards political participation and reform, and relations with China. In terms of population, public concern has shifted from emigration towards immigration, even though the real shift in the balance of these two flows has not been particularly great. This chapter will first consider the recent trends in both emigration and immigration before moving on to examine

---

Ronald Skeldon is a reader in the Department of Geography and Geology, the University of Hong Kong.

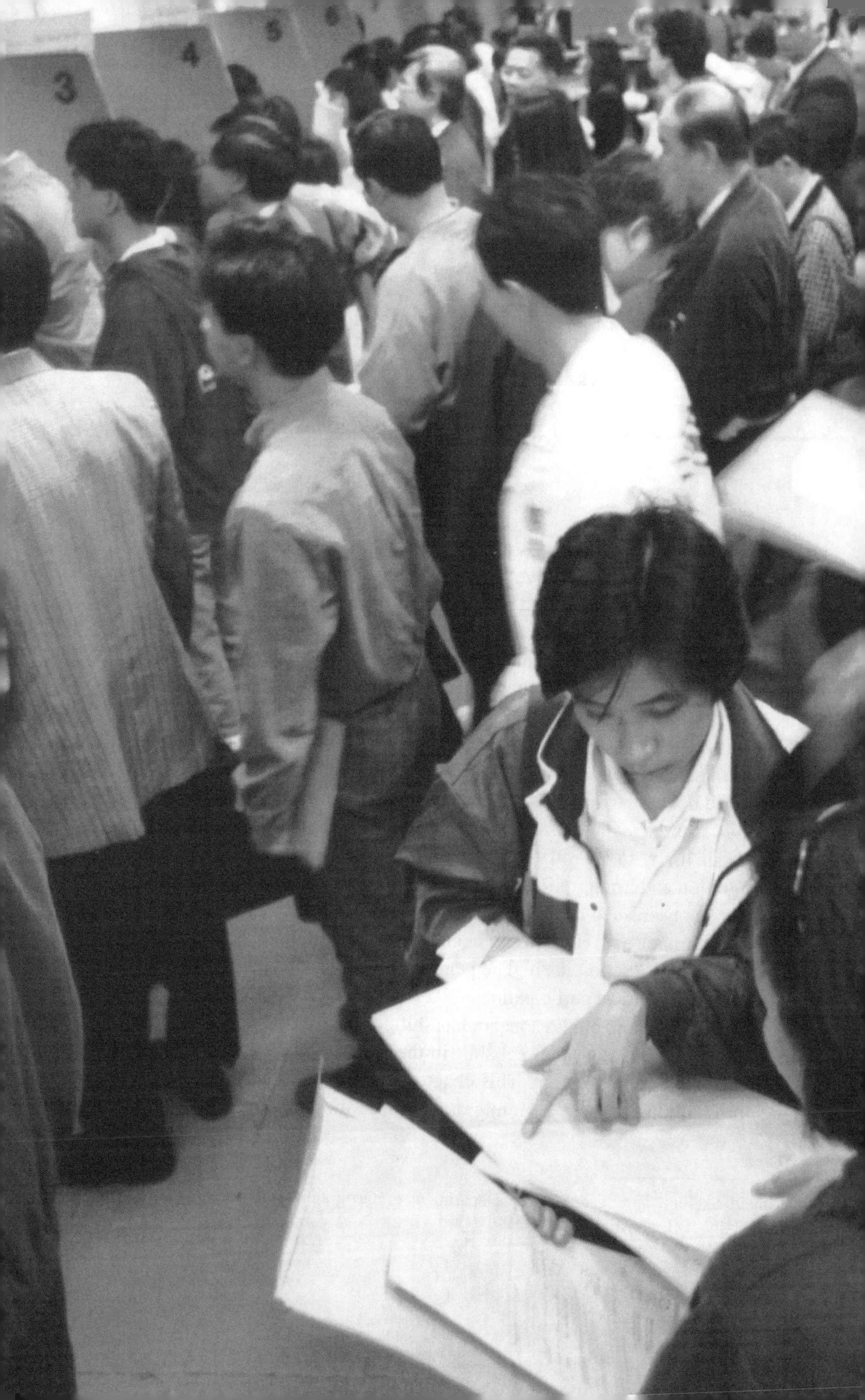
3
4
5

Table 1. End-year Estimates of the Hong Kong Population, including Vietnamese Migrants, 1981–1993

Year end	Population estimate (including Vietnamese migrants)	Annual population growth Number	Annual population growth % over preceding year	Natural increase Births	Natural increase Deaths	Natural increase Natural increase	% of natural increase in population growth	Balance of arrivals and departures
1981	5,238,500	—	—	—	—	—	—	—
1982	5,319,500	81,000	1.5	86,000	25,400	60,600	75	20,400
1983	5,377,400	57,900	1.1	83,800	26,600	57,200	99	700
1984	5,430,900	53,500	1.0	77,800	25,500	52,300	98	1,200
1985	5,500,400	69,500	1.3	76,500	25,300	51,200	74	18,300
1986	5,565,700	65,300	1.2	72,000	25,900	46,100	71	19,200*
1987	5,615,300	49,600	0.9	70,200	26,900	43,300	87	6,300*
1988	5,671,600	56,300	1.0	75,900	27,700	48,200	86	8,100*
1989	5,726,500	54,900	1.0	71,300	28,800	42,500	77	12,400*
1990	5,752,000	25,500	0.4	70,400	29,200	41,200	162	−15,700*
1991	5,822,500	70,500	1.2	70,100	28,500	41,600	59	28,900*
1992	5,902,100	79,600	1.4	72,700	30,400	42,300	53	37,300
1993	6,019,900	117,800	2.0	71,600	30,300	41,300	35	76,500

* Includes an adjustment for Hong Kong residents living in China and Macau.

Source: Unpublished tabulation, Hong Kong government.

emerging areas of concern in the general area of population change in Hong Kong.

☐ Emigration

Unquestionably, numbers emigrating have come down, but emigration remains, by the standards of recent history, at quite a high level. The government estimate of the number of leavers in 1993 is 53,000. This is down from their estimate of 66,000 for 1992. However, we know from figures for landings at the major destination countries of Canada, Australia and the United States (U.S.) that the 1992 estimate was almost certainly on the low side, with probably at least 10 to 15 per cent more having left during that year. To date, 1992 was the peak year of emigration from Hong Kong, although that fact passed relatively unnoticed as public opinion was then focused on other issues.

Emigration in 1993 was considerably lower than in 1992, although the greater part of that decline can be accounted for by the movement to a single destination, Australia. The number of Hong Kong people going to that country dropped from 15,656 in financial year 1991–1992 to 8,111 in 1992–1993. Information on visas issued by the Australian Consulate General suggests that the decline continued during the second half of 1993, although there is some indication of an upturn in the first half of 1994. Applications for visas for Australia received during financial year 1993–1994 were up by almost 20 per cent over 1992–1993, at 3,863 compared with 3,238. These applications are still the lowest since the recent emigration began in 1986–1987 and only a fraction of the 14,029 received in the year following the Tiananmen massacre in 1989. The numbers going to Canada, however, which is by far the most important destination for Hong Kong emigrants, showed only a slight decline in calendar year 1993 compared with the peak year 1992, dipping 38,910 to 36,510 (about 6 per cent less).

The most important reason for the decline in numbers emigrating lies in the nature of the global economy: an economic boom in Hong Kong and southern China and a recession in Australasia and North America. We know that many Hong Kong people who moved overseas after the most recent wave of emigration began in 1986–1987 have taken a drop in income and in working status. Unemployment levels in Australia and Canada in 1992–1993 exceeded 10 per cent of the labour force. Hong Kong is a labour-deficit economy with virtually no unemployment. Hence, this economic reality has pushed into the background in the minds of many potential emigrants, for the moment at least, any worries and concerns about the transition to Chinese sovereignty in 1997. The recession in the developed destination countries has also brought different responses to immigration. Australia has cut its overall targets substantially from around 130,000 per annum in the late 1980s and early 1990s to 76,000 in 1993. The 1994 target was raised by 10,000 to 86,000, but this increase was to accommodate the change in status of Chinese already in the country rather than an increase in intake itself. These Chinese are mainly students and their close relatives who were in Australia at the time of the Tiananmen massacre in 1989 and who did not wish to return to China. Their settler status will be confirmed during 1994.

In contrast to Australia's cut-back in immigration in the face of high domestic unemployment, Canada has maintained its annual immigration target of 250,000. In the first half of the 1980s, Canada did indeed reduce its annual intake from around 140,000 in 1980 to 84,000 in 1985, in response to the economic downturn and high unemployment at that time. In terms of policy response, the current situation is quite different, and Canada is maintaining the targets set down in its five-year immigration plans announced in October 1990. This is partially due to the fact that immigration is not a major political issue in Canada and partially due to the acceptance of the results of a major demographic review which held that immigration at around those levels was necessary for the sustained long-term good of Canada in the face of declining overall population growth as a result of low fertility. Thus, Canada continues to accept settlers at a steady rate both from worldwide sources and from Hong Kong.

The movement from Hong Kong to Canada may, however, decline more markedly in the near future as the number of applications for visas received at the Canadian Commission in Hong Kong has declined markedly. From a peak of 21,934 applications in 1989, most made after the Tiananmen massacre in June, and 18,672 in 1990, the numbers of applications dropped to 9,428 in 1991, to 5,629 in 1992 and to 4,683 in 1993. The figures for these last two years are by far the lowest since 1986, when 9,980 applications were lodged. The figures for applications do not, of course, refer to total numbers of individuals but to principal applicants, which could represent one individual but could also cover an entire family group. Hence, these figures should not be confused with figures of numbers of visas issued. The number of applications received does, however, indicate the future trend in the numbers of visas that will be issued, and these figures clearly show that emigration pressure has subsided in Hong Kong. That there was only a gradual decline in the number of visas issued in 1993 thus represented more a catching-up with the backlog of previous applications rather than any persistent desire for emigration in the Hong Kong population. If the recent recommendations of an all-party committee on Canadian citizenship are adopted, landed immigrants will not be able to leave Canada for extended periods while waiting to qualify for citizenship. Such a policy change might further discourage from applying to Canada those businessmen, and others, who wish to be "astronauts," maintaining activities in Hong Kong while at the same time having access to Canada. Hence, emigration to the most important destination may further slow.

The slowdown in emigration can therefore be explained by spatial differences in the development of the global economy and by different government responses to those same differences. Clearly, though, the pressure to emigrate abated in 1993, with fewer people wanting to leave Hong Kong. The intensity of that pressure should not, however, be exaggerated. Even at the height of concern about the brain drain in 1990–1991, only a relatively small proportion of the total population seriously considered emigration. A mid-1991 survey coordinated by the University of Hong Kong and the Baptist College found that only 13 per cent of the population would "definitely" or "most probably" emigrate before 1997. Then, as now, emigration is considered as a viable option only by the few who are concentrated among the wealthier, more educated and highly skilled groups. About 35 per cent of the total numbers of emigrants from Hong Kong have, since 1990, been in high-level occupations. The proportion of principal applicants would have been much higher. In 1993, some 15 per cent of all emigrants had first degree or postgraduate levels of education. Although the total number of emigrants fell in 1993, the composition of the flow did not change and was still biased towards the educated and the skilled.

Several flows of people are excluded from the official estimates of emigration. Those moving to China or to Taiwan are not counted in the official figures. It is likely that about 20,000 people a year moved to China over the last half of the 1980s. Almost certainly, the majority were retirees going back to their home areas, but others were going to work. No more than a few thousand are likely to have gone to Taiwan over recent years. Precise numbers are not regularly published but, in 1990, a year of considerable nervousness, some 7,000 Hong Kong people moved to Taiwan. If the reduction in interest in emigrating observed for Australia and Canada holds across the board, then one would not expect more than a very few thousand to be moving to Taiwan at present.

Of perhaps more interest among the figures of people leaving Hong Kong who are not included in the emigration estimates are those of students. Students, of course, are not emigrants: under the terms of their visas they are expected to return home after completing their studies. There are no reliable estimates of how many may later have changed their status to that of settler at their chosen destinations, although some data from the United States, the most important student destination, suggest that the number doing so may be quite small. However, the figures themselves on students leaving Hong Kong for overseas studies in Australia, Canada, the U.S. and the United Kingdom do provide an interesting perspective on the overall situation.

The numbers going for study overseas in the four countries mirror, to some extent, the number of emigrants. Prior to 1987, there were fluctuations of between 9,500 to 12,000 per annum. From 1987 to 1990, there was a marked increase to over 21,000 by 1990. Then there was a fall and, in 1993, only 14,483 students left for the four countries (Table 2). Demographic factors, or changes in the number of people in the age group most likely to pursue education, cannot explain this trend. The government's push to expand the number of places at local tertiary institutions from 1990 was one factor. Two other explanations are more likely, though. First, the nervousness of the late 1980s has dissipated somewhat, and parents are now more content to allow their children to pursue senior secondary and university courses locally rather than sending them overseas. Increases in overseas fees are also likely to be a burden on the emerging middle-income groups, who are now amongst those who would be most likely to send their children away for higher levels of education. Secondly, and perhaps most importantly, those who would be most likely to send their children overseas may themselves have left. This point is supported by the sharpest decline, which can be seen in the figures for Canada. As seen above, Canada has been by far the most significant destination for Hong Kong emigration. Thus, those who would have sent their children to study there may now themselves be resident in Canada.

The data on emigration as a whole and on the movement of students do suggest that there may be a specific and relatively small proportion of the population that is particularly likely to emigrate. That number will fluctuate, given particular economic conditions, but it is never likely to represent more than a small and declining proportion of the total population —

Table 2. Students Leaving Hong Kong for Overseas Studies, 1971–1993

	Australia	Canada	United States	United Kingdom
1971	91	1,628	2,746	913
1972	113	2,536	2,420	1,310
1973	91	3,761	2,812	1,352
1974	139	3,909	2,601	1,348
1975	225	2,215	3,121	1,698
1976	249	1,858	2,719	1,669
1977	215	2,061	2,605	2,566
1978	439	2,155	2,560	5,093
1979	155	3,589	2,765	4,255
1980	404	4,803	2,012	4,134
1981	987	4,752	3,264	4,276
1982	757	3,946	2,088	5,547
1983	428	3,284	2,049	5,394
1984	473	2,850	1,820	4,733
1985	564	2,953	1,872	4,158
1986	688	2,930	3,506	4,269
1987	1,877	3,616	3,679	4,232
1988	3,147	3,808	4,215	3,856
1989	4,678	5,096	4,855	4,539
1990	5,258	5,681	5,840	4,349
1991	3,590	4,541	5,866	4,428
1992	2,866	3,583	5,410	4,408
1993	3,153	2,828	5,025	3,477

Notes: 1. 1971–1985 arrivals for study at destination countries are for 1 September to 31 August.
2. 1986–1993 visas granted for study in calendar years.

Source: *Annual Reports* of the Hong Kong government, appendix on education.

declining as, by the end of 1993, the majority of those who fell into this category were likely to have gone. Does this mean that the great phase of emigration is now over as the pool of potential emigrants is slowly drying up? To some extent, this may indeed be the case and would explain the decline in visa applications. Emigration can thus be expected to continue to occur from Hong Kong, but at a slowly declining rate. However, there are other aspects of emigration that are likely to intensify and these, paradoxically, are associated with immigration and return movements. The "pool" of potential emigrants is not just a function of the residual non-migrant Hong Kong population. It is to these aspects that we now turn.

☐ Immigration

The recent upswing in emigration can be traced to 1986–1987, when not only concern about 1997 in Hong Kong was rising but the developed countries of North America and Australasia were emerging from the recession of the first half of the 1980s and increasing their intake of immigrants. From that time, too, can be traced an increase in the annual numbers of immigrants coming to Hong Kong. In 1986, some 56,457 people were allowed to come to Hong Kong to take up residence. This increased to 64,358 in 1987, to 76,063 in 1989 and to 95,425 in 1992. In the first nine months of 1993, almost 90,000 had come in which, if admissions continued at the same rate, would imply a legal immigration of 120,000 for the year.

There are various components to the inflow. Since the abolition of the "touch-base" policy in October 1980, movement from China into Hong Kong has been strictly controlled. There was an unofficial agreement to allow 75 people a day out of China on one-way exit permits. This meant that around 27,000 to 28,000 people, mostly dependants of Hong Kong residents, were granted residence in Hong Kong through the 1980s. From 1 January 1994, the figure of 75 a day was raised to 105 a day. However, it can be seen from the number of those entering on one-way permits from China in 1993 that there already had been a *de facto* increase in that year to around 90 a day. Whether there will be further increases will be discussed below, as it is the migration from China that is emerging as one of the current areas of concern. Other components in the flow include domestic servants, who account for around one quarter of the annual intake, skilled professional personnel and their families, and others, again mainly from China, who have the right to come to Hong Kong.

The reasons for the increased inflow of population, with the exception of the movement from China, revolve around three closely related trends: (1) the shift from a manufacturing towards a service economy, with increasing demands for more high-level skills; (2) the rising educational level of Hong Kong's population, which means that the low-skilled, so-called 3-D jobs (dangerous, demanding and dirty) are increasingly avoided by the local population; and (3) the growing affluence of the population. The increasing participation of women in the labour force is perhaps one of the clearest reflections of these trends. Service economies have heavy demands for female labour and, in order to release educated married women into the labour force, domestic servants are required.

The annual immigration figures exclude part of the inflow of population. There are, in addition, various labour importation schemes, originally set up in 1989 and subsequently expanded, that allow up to 25,000 workers into Hong Kong on temporary (usually three-year) contracts. The supply of these workers is in response to specific demands from employers and, as of 1993, the demand far exceeded the supply by a factor of about two and one half. Other labour importation schemes were set up for the construction work associated with the airport at Chek Lap Kok which will allow the temporary employment of up to 5,500 foreign labourers at any one time. The vast majority of all the labour brought in under these various schemes comes from China.

At the other end of the skill spectrum, the government has introduced a scheme to bring up to one thousand skilled or professional personnel from Mainland China into Hong Kong. The idea is to bring in people who can facilitate the transition in 1997 through their understanding of both China and Hong Kong by that time. The first group of 250 places requested by companies had to be distributed by ballot because of heavy demand. China, however, has so far blocked the implementation of this programme through its insistence that these migrants must be "official." The Hong Kong government's view is that the migrants are ordinary employees recruited for the private sector. As of mid-1994, this issue still had to be resolved.

The result of this recent immigration has been a sharp increase in the number of foreign nationals in Hong Kong — excluding those from China. At the end of 1986 there were some 168,400 foreigners in the city. This number had virtually doubled to 320,700 by the end of 1993 and, in the first four months of 1994, it had increased by more than 10 per cent to 358,700. By far the largest group is made up of Philippine nationals, the vast majority being domestic servants, followed by Americans, British and Canadians. The booming local economy and the recession in North America, Europe and Australasia have made Hong Kong a much more international city in terms of the origins of its population, with around 6 per cent being of foreign origin. It is possible that some of these foreign nationals are Hong Kong people returning on newly acquired passports, although these people are unlikely to account for many of the foreign passport holders. The latter are much more likely to have returned on their Hong Kong documentation and are not classified with the "foreign" population. It is to this group that we now turn our attention.

☐ Return Movements

No accurate means have thus far been developed to measure accurately the volume of return movement to Hong Kong. Returnees do not appear among immigrant figures as the vast majority return on their Hong Kong documents, even if they do possess a foreign passport. Many also return before having completed residence requirements for foreign passports. This particularly applies to those who went recently to Australia and who, under existing regulations, can return to Hong Kong for periods of up to three years before having to take up residence in Australia. Data shows that, of migrants who went to Australia in 1990 and the first half of 1991, at least one-third had probably returned to Hong Kong. Return rates from Canada and the U.S., where residency requirements are both stricter and becoming more rigorously enforced, are likely to be lower. The Hong Kong government estimated that 8,000 returned in 1992, which was only a relatively small proportion of the total number who left in that year.[1] Clearly, many, if not most, of those 8,000 had originally left Hong Kong well before 1992. Others establish families in destination cities and commute across the Pacific at regular intervals. Very large numbers of female-headed households among the Hong Kong-born in Australia and New Zealand attest to the importance of this "astronaut" phenomenon. It is a form of a new extended family and is a product of migration.

The reasons for the return movements, too, are to be found in the nature of the economies of the origin and destination areas. Wives and children, and even children by themselves, are being left in the low-growth economies of Australasia and North America, while the principal breadwinner, or even both parents, return to Hong Kong to take advantage of high salaries, low tax and negligible unemployment. This phenomenon is not unique to Hong Kong but is also common amongst emigrants from Taiwan. The strategy is a hedge against both economic and political risk. The recession in the destination countries will not continue indefinitely; nor can the economic upswing in southern China be maintained forever. To keep residences and a foothold in two economies at different stages of the business cycle makes perfectly rational economic sense over the medium to long term. In addition, this strategy can minimize political risk. Should things become difficult in Hong Kong after the transition to Chinese

---

[1] *South China Morning Post*, 24 May 1994.

sovereignty, those who have their families and residences overseas will be able to move there quickly as access has already been attained.

The bilocality of these new extended families raises sensitive issues. Most of the destination countries wish to attract settlers, or people who will become Canadian, Australian or American, not international commuters who may spend most of their time elsewhere. China has made it clear that senior members of the administration of the future Special Administrative Region (SAR) of Hong Kong will not be able to hold "foreign" passports. Hence, should the transition proceed smoothly, we may have influential people renouncing newly attained foreign passports. Lest this be seen as pure opportunism, it must be emphasized that Hong Kong people are not alone in adopting bilocality. The movement of the highly skilled and the business migrant has become a global phenomenon. There are expatriates worldwide who elect to settle more or less permanently in countries distant from their home nations. Modern systems of transportation and communications and an increasingly interdependent global economy facilitate such movements. Hong Kong migrants are but part of this broader movement towards an internationalization of populations. As we move into the twenty-first century, narrow definitions associating people with just one nation will have to be modified in the face of the increasing fluidity of populations.

One immediate consequence of both the immigration of foreign nationals into Hong Kong and the increasing numbers of returnees is that there is a growing population with the ability to leave for other countries quickly should things go wrong economically or politically. While this population still represents a small minority of the total, perhaps 7 to 8 per cent, it will account for a large proportion of the business and leadership elite of Hong Kong. While some of the more dire assessments of the impact of emigration on the labour force made by Paul Kwong in *The Other Hong Kong Report 1990* have not come to pass, this does not mean to say that they can be discounted for the future. More Hong Kong people now have the networks in place to move faster, if necessary, than was the case a few years ago.

☐ Immigration and the Floodgates Scenario

By far the most evocative migration-related story in the past year has been the case of a six-year-old boy, Hai Ho-tak. This story caught the public imagination through wide coverage in the press and on television and well illustrates dilemmas and contradictions in population issues in the lead-up to 1997. The boy's parents had originally been migrants from China but had become legal residents of Hong Kong, working and living in the territory. Their son was judged by government officials to have been born in China and to have come to Hong Kong without proper authority. He was therefore classified as an illegal immigrant and repatriated amid a blaze of publicity and condemnation. On the one side, it was argued that here was an example of an uncaring bureaucracy tearing a small boy away from his loving parents to put him in a poor household in China where he was neither loved nor wanted. On the government side, the defence was essentially one of population control: that, since 1990, some 2,200 children had fallen into similar categories and had to be repatriated and that there were clear rules and procedures about who could and who could not be a Hong Kong resident. Underlying this argument is what might be called the "floodgates" scenario: that there are hundreds of thousands of people across the border in Guangdong just waiting to pour into Hong Kong if procedures are in any way relaxed. This anticipated wave of immigration could swamp the government's ability adequately to house or to supply basic services and thus threaten the future standard of living and social order in Hong Kong.

The fear of a tidal wave of immigration from China has been virtually a constant aspect of colonial government policy in the post-Second World War era, and the preoccupation with emigration from 1988 to 1991 but a short-term aberration. In the past, Hong Kong has experienced pronounced waves of immigration — in 1945–1951, 1962 and 1977–1979 — when social services were indeed strained. However, the demographic, economic and social conditions have been transformed over the past decades. Fertility has declined to reach levels seen only in the most advanced countries in Europe, and levels of economic prosperity have risen dramatically. What we have now is a curious contradiction of a labour-deficit economy and a government tightly controlling the immigration that might relieve labour shortages.

This situation is certainly not unique to Hong Kong. It is being faced by other East and Southeast Asian industrial economies such as Japan, South Korea, Taiwan, Singapore and, increasingly, Malaysia. The question facing all these governments concerns the extent to which they can relax immigration controls without straining the fabric of society. Hong Kong, sited next to the most populous nation in the world, which is currently experiencing a level of internal movement of its population of staggering numbers, has to be particularly vigilant. There can be no question of abandoning border controls and allowing the free flow of labour. Also, much of the labour that

Hong Kong, as a service economy, needs is skilled and semi-skilled and not the type that is "floating" around coastal China. Few of these "floaters" from inland areas will even have the linguistic skills, either in English or in Cantonese, to be easily absorbed into the increasingly complex Hong Kong economy.

One other factor does, however, have to be taken into consideration lest one becomes totally convinced that the majority of migrants in China will be heading for Hong Kong. Although the numbers moving within China are today many times greater than they were in the late 1970s, when the last major wave of movement to Hong Kong took place, there are, today, a great many more "intervening opportunities" between the sources of movement in China and Hong Kong. In the past, people looking for urban opportunities in southern China, if they could move at all, could look only to Hong Kong. Now, urban opportunities have spread not just to Shenzhen but deep into Guangdong Province itself. Hence, the zone of attraction for migrants is now very much larger than in the past, and unskilled migrants are more likely to be absorbed into the low-wage, labour-intensive, industrial activities on the periphery of the "Greater Hong Kong" urban area than into the core, high-labour-cost, service economy of the future Special Administrative Region. Nevertheless, as stressed above, control of the immigration from Mainland China will still be required in the future in order to prevent the continuation of labour-intensive activities through the illegal exploitation of labour in central urban areas. This is a situation which has clearly occurred in one other global city, New York, where illegal migration from China, amongst other places, has allowed the persistence of sweat shops in the downtown area.

In its justification of control of immigration, the Hong Kong government has focused mainly on the numbers of people in China who will be eligible under the Basic Law to settle in Hong Kong after 1997. These are essentially the children of Hong Kong residents, such as Hai Ho-tak, and wives of Hong Kong residents. A survey taken in 1991 indicated that there were 95,200 Hong Kong residents who had married in China and who had a spouse still living there, and there were some 310,200 children of Hong Kong residents still in China. If all were to enter within a short period of time — as they will legally be entitled to do after 30 June 1997 — then they might indeed strain Hong Kong's capacity to absorb them and to provide all with an acceptable quality of life. However, an examination of the age of those with spouses in China casts some doubt on the numbers who might actually want to come to Hong Kong. Over 40 per cent of those with spouses in China were 50 years of age or older and only 6 per cent fell into the 20–29 years age group. Given the high cost of living in Hong Kong, it would appear that there would be a higher probability of husbands going back to join their spouses in China on retirement than of the wives coming to Hong Kong to join their husbands.

Similarly, according to the survey, the age structure of the children in China of Hong Kong residents indicated that the majority were adults rather than youngsters. Only one-fifth of the number of children were younger than 10 years of age and some 40 per cent were 30 years or older, many of these presumably with spouses and children of their own who would not automatically be eligible for residence in the future SAR. Clearly, many of those eligible will want to come to Hong Kong, but the age structure of the family members suggests that a sizeable minority, even the majority, will not wish to come to live in Hong Kong as they will be well established in China. If there is one universal generalization that can be made about migrants, it is that the vast majority are young adults, and these make up a minority of the close relatives of Hong Kong residents who are still in China.

The Hong Kong government is already making provision to accommodate the increased inflow of dependants from the mainland through the 40 per cent increase in its daily intake from 75 to 105. A gradual, continuous increase in this quota over the last years of colonial administration can be expected. However, there is a basic contradiction here. Hong Kong authorities have no control over who is granted a one-way exit permit from China. Hence, there is no guarantee that Hong Kong dependants will receive priority in the allocation of the additional permits. It is known that quotas for the permit are allocated within China down to county and district levels, and there are substantial waiting-periods in most areas. It is a system in which the implementation may not be entirely free from abuse.

While it would seem unlikely that Hong Kong will be able to exercise much control over who is allowed out of China, it does seem imperative that a more proactive approach should be taken towards immigration in general. Labour deficits are not going to disappear, and it is essential that there is a coherent approach to recruit the kinds of labour that Hong Kong will need through the transitional period and beyond. Once the channels of recruitment are clearly established and institutionalized, there is less chance of an immigration policy that might not be in the best interests of Hong Kong being imposed at a later stage. Some progress has been made towards this goal through the several labour importation schemes described earlier in this chapter, although these seem to be evolving in a somewhat piecemeal manner. Much more needs to be done in this area, particularly in the mid-skill categories and from areas other than China. The protection of workers' rights and conditions will also have to be an integral part of these policies.

One part of any immigration policy will be continued border control. The importance of this is reflected in a rise in the number of illegal immigrants detained. This rose from 15,841 in 1989 to 27,826 in 1990 and then to 35,645 in 1992. The figure for 1993 was 37,517, with similar rates for the first five months of 1994, showing that illegal immigration appears to have stabilized at a fairly high level. Nonetheless, an immigration policy must be much more than border control and should seek the most appropriate skills from around the region, and globally, particularly in the face of increased competition from other industrial economies in Asia.

Two other areas associated with population immigration and emigration require comment. One is an issue on the wane and the other is becoming high-profile. The former deals with the Vietnamese migrants; the latter refers to passports and freedom of movement.

☐ Vietnamese Migrants

The long saga of boat people from Vietnam, which really began for Hong Kong in 1977, at last seems to be moving into its final phases. In 1993, only 101 arrived from Vietnam and, in the first five months of 1994, 210 arrived, half of them in January. These numbers are negligible compared with the arrivals of 1991 (20,206) or 1989 (34,112) and the peak year of 1979 (68,748). The only "blip" was caused by a surge of Vietnamese who left where they had been living in China to come to Hong Kong in mid-1993. These migrants called ECVIIs in official parlance — "ex-China Vietnamese illegal immigrants" — are subject to essentially the same treatment as all illegal migrants from China — deportation. Almost 2,400 arrived and, as their repatriation is a matter between China and Hong Kong rather than involving Vietnam and the wider community, they do not fall into the same category as the majority of people who came directly from Vietnam. By mid-1994, all but 677 of the ECVIIs had been returned to China.

In mid-1994, there were 27,670 Vietnamese migrants in Hong Kong, down from 40,727 a year earlier, and down markedly from the peak month of September 1991, when there were 64,128 in Hong Kong. Only about 7 per cent of the Vietnamese migrant population in mid-1974 were classified as "refugees" and waiting for resettlement. The vast majority of the balance had already been screened out and were to be repatriated to Vietnam. The decline of over 30 per cent over the twelve months from mid-1993 to mid-1994 attests to the continued success of the voluntary repatriation programme. Unfortunately, the steady progress towards the reduction in the number of Vietnamese languishing in closed camps was marred by what can most charitably be called the heavy-handed transfer of migrants from the Whitehead Detention Centre in April 1994. This incident, in which a large number of inmates were injured, in many ways reflects the frustration of the authorities over an issue that has seemed to be without end.

Now that the inflows from Vietnam are negligible, and unlikely to increase significantly, and now that the migrant population is being brought down through repatriation, the end of this phase of Hong Kong's history does indeed appear to be in sight. While voluntary repatriations, which tend to pick up in the second half of the year, will continue to reduce the total number in the camps, there may well be increased difficulties as the Vietnamese migrant population is reduced to the "hard" core of stayers. Many, indeed, fear the return to Vietnam, others earn more in the camps than they would be able to do in Vietnam; yet others are intimidated by those who, through graft and other means, have achieved positions of power and influence and hence local status. However, all non-refugees will have to go back to Vietnam and, at a time when there are clearly more deserving cases in a world exhibiting all the signs of "refugee fatigue," the sooner this occurs, the better for all concerned. This last period of the Vietnamese influx to Hong Kong will have to be handled locally, and internationally, with sensitivity as well as firmness. Despite declining numbers, it is still likely to be a high-profile and difficult issue over the short term.

☐ Passports and Residence

In the euphoria after the signing of the Sino-British Joint Declaration in 1984 and the passing of the Basic Law in 1990, it was assumed that there would be concrete guarantees for the population to travel freely overseas. Those who had been entitled to a British Dependent Territories Citizens (BDTC) passport (which automatically expires on 30 June 1997) would be able to obtain a British National (Overseas) (BNO) passport that would allow them to continue to travel freely after the transition. The latter has been issued to all who acquired the BDTC designation from 1 July 1987 and can be held for the lifetime of the holder. Those who did not meet the residency requirements for a BDTC, or through personal choice, can travel up to 1 July 1997 on a Certificate of Identity which, after that date, will entitle the holder to a passport of the SAR. All permanent residents of Hong Kong will be eligible for a Hong Kong Special Administrative Region (HKSAR) passport after 1997.

The issues revolve around three quite different concepts: right of abode, nationality and freedom to travel. The BNO, and its predecessor, the BDTC, are in effect only travel documents which give right of abode to their ethnic Chinese holders in Hong Kong only. They confer no nationality, and the holder is in practice stateless even if residence rights in the present British colony and the future SAR of China are guaranteed. The HKSAR passport is still an unknown quantity, although it will be issued by the government of the future SAR. It will be a "subspecies" of the Chinese passport and, as such, should convey Chinese nationality as well as right of abode in Hong Kong. The perceived problems with this document will clearly be seen in terms of ease of travel as third countries may indeed treat it as a Chinese passport, and there will be little hope of visa-free travel. This danger is being exacerbated by the Chinese government's refusal thus far to work with the British or Hong Kong governments to achieve visa-free travel for *both* the BNO and the HKSAR passports.

The dispute can only prejudice the BNO passport. While this passport does entitle the holder to British consular protection overseas, it cannot do so in Hong Kong after 1997 as the holders, being Chinese, cannot have this protection against their own government. Also, Britain cannot guarantee to repatriate BNO passport holders to Hong Kong after 1997, should this be required, as Hong Kong obviously will no longer be under British administration, and this is likely to be the main concern of third countries about the BNO. China's attitude seems to be that it cannot see why should it be responsible for people travelling on a British-issued passport, even if this attitude effectively goes against the promise under the Joint Declaration to allow Hong Kong people to travel on BNO passports. Without a visa-free facility, such travel will be inhibited. There is a further complication: the British Overseas Citizens (BOC) passport. This passport is issued in Hong Kong and elsewhere to ethnic minorities who, in Hong Kong, are mainly those of Indian origin. Like the BNO, this passport does not grant right of abode in the United Kingdom, but it does provide the holder with consular protection in Hong Kong as well as elsewhere. This right can be passed down to children for two generations, whereas the BNO is granted only for the lifetime of the holder. However, the BOC passport has very limited visa-free travel compared with the BNO which, at present, gives visa-free entry to some seventy countries. If the BNO were to lose this advantage after 1997, the BOC might begin to seem more attractive. The United Kingdom may find it hard to justify why the allocation of BNO and BOC passports should be on the basis of race, should a concerted effort be made to obtain BOC status by Hong Kong Chinese, particularly in a case where there was mixed Chinese and Indian ancestry.

Ultimately, much of the question revolves around identity — with the departing or with the arriving power. Up to the end of 1993, some 844,000 BNO passports had been issued, representing about one quarter of the eligible population. Numbers can be expected to increase further: the phased allocation started last year to ensure that everyone who wanted a BNO passport was able to obtain one before 30 June 1997. Clearly, no allocation will be made after that date. Levels of uptake are higher than expected. Large numbers are concerned about their future ability to travel freely even though, given the present attitudes, there is absolutely no guarantee that the BNO passport will in future allow them to do so. China, at present, seems not prepared to consider, or is perhaps not aware of, the importance of joint "visa abolition" agreements. So serious has this issue become that a question mark is now hanging over the future ease, if not freedom, of travel.

Ease of travel and the ability to move quickly through international networks will be essential components in the preservation of Hong Kong's future prosperity. While many Hong Kong residents do now have foreign passports on which to travel, this itself poses a dilemma. The post-1997 residency status of Hong Kong Chinese on Canadian, Australian, U.S. or other passports has not been satisfactorily clarified by China. While the Basic Law is clear on the right of abode, this was based on nationality: Hong Kong Chinese are Chinese nationals. However, if a foreign nationality is adopted, then the transition to Chinese sovereignty introduces conflicts with the Nationality Law of China, which does not permit dual nationality as the British law presently does. Article 9 of the Chinese Nationality Law clearly states: "Any Chinese national who has settled abroad and who has been naturalized as a foreign national or has acquired foreign nationality of his own free will shall automatically lose Chinese nationality." Permanent residence in Hong Kong is therefore having to be sought for Hong Kong people on foreign passports under Section 24(4) of the Basic Law, along with other foreigners, and not under Section 24(1) or (2) for Chinese. This means that right of abode in Hong Kong will not be granted automatically to Hong Kong Chinese holders of foreign passports.

Some Chinese officials and advisers are suggesting that, in these cases, right of abode should involve evidence of a clear commitment to Hong Kong, although just what this might involve is not yet itself clear. After 1997, right of abode will almost certainly mean more than it does today and will be related to voting rights, access to certain civil service positions and possibly other, as yet unspecified, areas. Hence, part of the Hong Kong population is caught in a dilemma: on the one hand, having a foreign passport and being able to travel, but with several unknowns associated with residency rights and on the other hand, having either a BNO or an HKSAR passport, being clearly Hong Kong Chinese in identity and residence, but with unknowns hanging over the ease of future travel. Until there is an agreement between Britain and China on the respective status of the BNO and the HKSAR passports and the two governments can both begin to lobby internationally, the prospect of visa-free entry to most countries looks dim indeed.

One indication of the increasing tensions between wanting to remain in Hong Kong, yet holding a foreign passport, is the interest in the British Nationality Scheme. Three years ago, when the scheme to offer 50,000 heads of household and their families full British passports was first opened for application, interest was lukewarm, with few of the categories significantly oversubscribed. The overall oversubscription rate for the first phase was 1.54 applicants for every place available. The category for managers and administrators was even undersubscribed. Now, in the final phase and in the allocation of the last 13,160 places, the overall oversubscription rate has risen to 3.16 for every place and that for managers and administrators is more than four times oversubscribed. The allocation for business professionals is more than fourteen times oversubscribed, compared with a 1.74 rate in the first phase. This scheme to allocate passports was designed to provide an insurance policy for Hong Kong people: a scheme to keep people in the city rather than have them emigrate. While emigration rates are indeed down, as we have seen, the changed attitudes towards the British scheme suggest that underlying tensions are very much on the increase.

Many practical, as well as legal, issues need to be resolved. For example, when will the issue of HKSAR passports begin? It will not be feasible to issue potentially two to three million HKSAR passports within weeks after 1 July 1997. Countries are going to have to be convinced of the integrity of the issuing procedures before granting visa-free access. Without careful planning, there could easily be a significant hiatus when Hong Kong people will not be able to travel easily on their own travel documents. This will have a significant effect on a city that depends upon the high degree of mobility of its population. This very practical issue urgently needs to be resolved and is yet one more factor in the future confidence matrix.

☐ Conclusion

Emigration is slowing from Hong Kong, although it is likely to continue at a gradually decreasing rate as the pool of those who want to, and can, move contracts. This pool of potential emigrants is, however, being continuously replenished, not just by educated Hong Kong-born people moving into the cohorts most likely to move, but also by an increasing supply of immigrants and returned migrants. Should the economic or political climate deteriorate in Hong Kong, very large numbers of people are in a position to leave for overseas destinations quickly, if necessary. Hong Kong people have prepared the way by acquiring foreign passports or attaining permanent residency status at one or more destinations abroad and establishing close family overseas. Immigrants from foreign countries can obviously return to their native countries or move on elsewhere. These numbers, substantial in themselves, represent a relatively small proportion of Hong Kong's total population but a substantial proportion of its business and administrative elite. The rapid loss of this sector of the population would indeed pose problems for Hong Kong and those with responsibility for the future of the city clearly need to keep this potential exodus in mind when drawing up plans for its economic, social and political development.

Thus, emigration and immigration are closely interrelated. There are also other apparent contradictions: between tight immigration control and the existence of a labour-deficit economy. It is argued in this chapter that the fear of mass immigration from China is likely to be more apparent than real under existing circumstances. Nevertheless, border controls need to be maintained. Although immigration restrictions might be gradually relaxed, there is a clear need for an immigration policy to be developed that will allow Hong Kong to import the kind of people that the economy and society require, and find humanely acceptable. Some restrictions on numbers and quality will always be required.

There are other dilemmas associated with future freedom to move and residency status. While foreign passports might guarantee freedom to move, they may raise questions about local loyalties and full residential status. Hong Kong-issued passports, while guaranteeing the latter, may not be widely accepted after the transition to Chinese sovereignty. These issues are clear and pressing and need speedy resolution.

Hong Kong was the creation of population migration. Given its low fertility, population movements into and out of the city — immigration and emigration — will be critical issues in its future development. These flows are difficult to control, being dependent upon global economic conditions and unforeseen political directions. Nevertheless, careful planning through specific policy measures is an important factor in the equation, which requires careful thought.

11

The Property Price Crisis

Lawrence W. C. Lai

The focus of the property market by mid-1994 was on government policy measures regarding stabilizing residential property prices announced on 8 June. This chapter examines, in the context of Hong Kong's land use planning endeavours and commitment, two problem areas: (1) the background, nature and causes of the heavily politicized "property price crisis"; and (2) the effectiveness and implications of adopted policy measures. For the latter, both economic and planning[1] points of view will be utilized.

☐ Has There Been a "Property Price Crisis"?

Background

In 1984, before the Sino-British Joint Declaration on the future of Hong Kong was signed, the average price for small- and medium-sized flats was about HK$600 per square foot. By June 1994, the price had risen to

---

Lawrence W. C. Lai is a lecturer in the Department of Surveying, the University of Hong Kong.

[1] In order to better appreciate the planning issues assessed in this chapter, the reader is urged to read the Hong Kong government's annual report and the following publications of the Planning Department: *Territorial Development Strategy Review — Development Options* (July 1993); *Territorial Development Strategy Review — Foundation Report* (July 1993); *Metroplan: The Selected Strategy* (1990) and the public consultation documents of the Northwestern New Territories and Southwestern New Territories Development Strategy Reviews.

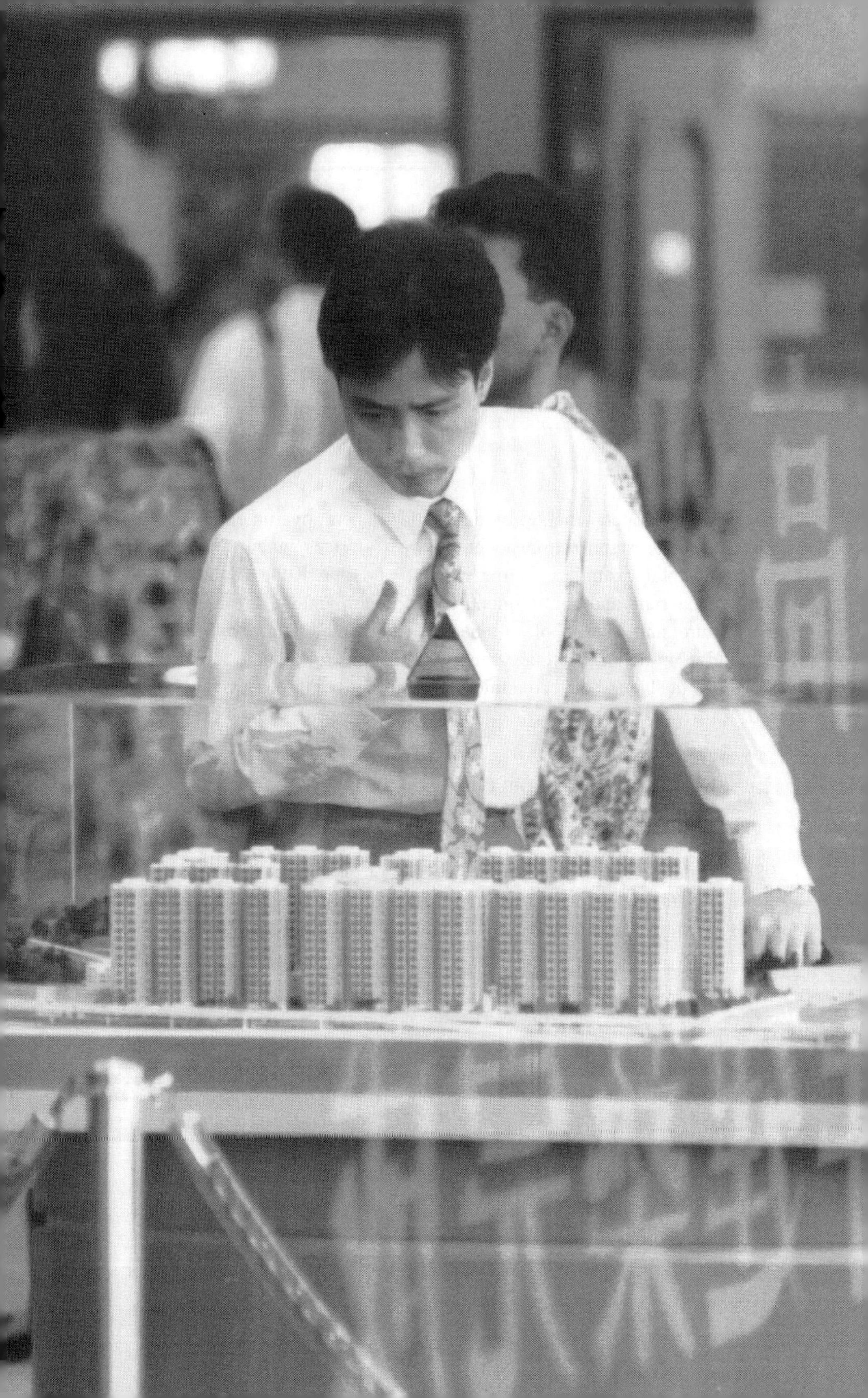

HK$6,000 per square foot. Over ten years, property prices actually rose continuously, apart from a few occasions such as the aftermath of the June 4 incident in 1989 and the Gulf War of 1991. Young working couples have found it increasingly difficult to afford a mortgage for new units, notably those in comprehensively developed private housing estates. At the same time, however, it is not uncommon for estate agents to come across institutional purchasers who buy aggressively in residential property. Before the June 4 incident, Japanese companies were very active in the second-hand market but their leading position was taken over by Chinese enterprises after the event. Individual purchasers spent nights waiting in long queues in order to get the right to buy a pre-sale unit. As triad involvement became apparent, queuing was finally replaced by a lottery arrangement. Soaring private housing prices caused a chorus of outcry within the context of political democratization. Politicians of all persuasions and party affiliations urged the government to intervene. The most vocal demand was directed to the curbing of housing price escalation and speculation, with speculation alleged to be the cause of most property price escalation.

In response, the Governor established an Anti-Speculation Task Force in March 1994. The Secretary for Planning, Environment and Lands announced in late March a four-pronged strategy to tackle the problem. The contents of the strategy are: (1) to achieve an earlier utilization of Tin Shui Wai Phase II; (2) to utilize private sector land holdings in the New Territories, requiring developers to shoulder infrastructural costs if necessary; (3) to speed up urban renewal by assisting the Land Development Corporation (LDC) and private sector in land assembly (application of government resumption powers is the measure to be taken); and (4) to speed up development programmes of the Housing Authority and the Hong Kong Housing Society. Later, the government made a new financial arrangement with the Housing Authority, conferring upon it a new development fund. The Housing Society has also stepped up the process of implementing new lending instruments such as the "sandwich class" housing loan schemes.

These proposals and measures were considered by some politicians as ineffective in bringing about a substantial fall in housing prices. The use of government resumption powers in profit-seeking urban redevelopment projects has also been opposed by affected tenants, politicians and academics on grounds of the violation of private property rights. Meanwhile, the Housing Authority made a controversial move to put up new blocks on sites in housing estates currently used as open space or car parks.

Politicians advocated the use of a capital gains tax and punitive vacant units levy to bring about an immediate fall in property values. After some vacillation, the government resolved to shelve the capital gains tax proposal and decided to adopt, in addition to aforesaid measures, an "action plan." The gist of the latter is twofold. Firstly, to curb "speculation," it contains measures which include reducing the quota for "internal sale" by developers from 50 per cent to 10 per cent, banning the re-sale of uncompleted flats, restricting pre-sales to nine months before completion, doubling the deposit for units to 10 per cent, and raising the forfeiture amount included in an estate contract from 3 per cent to 5 per cent. Secondly, as regards increasing supply, the government would endeavour to plan for the provision of 60,000 more flats in the next six years, expedite redevelopment plans, release 70 more hectares of land over four years, build a land reserve of 50 hectares and accelerate supporting infrastructure development. Other measures are stipulating more information on pre-sale flats, adopting statutory control over estate agents, resurrecting the post of Secretary for Housing and reviewing the land auction process. The last measure is considered by the government as necessary because at the scene of the first land auction of the 1994–1995 financial year, developers apparently worked in collusion and were criticized by the public for attempting to obtain land at "lower than market prices."

The Nature of the Crisis from a Historical Perspective

From the point of view of many developing countries, Hong Kong's housing crisis is actually a rich man's problem. The crux of the issue is not a question of many people without roofs over their heads as in the 1950s and early 1960s, but a question of tenure: the quest for home ownership. In the 1950s and 1960s, a huge influx of refugees fleeing political and economic upheavals in China created a situation of massive hillside squattering. Recurrent fires created an immense dislodgement problem. The government responded after the 1953 Christmas fire of Shek Kip Mei by commencing a low-cost public rental housing programme. The original government perception of the issue was not out of philanthrophy but land economics:

> Squatters are not resettled simply because they need, or necessarily because they deserve, hygienic and fireproof homes; they are resettled because the community can no longer afford to carry the fire risk, health risk and threat to public order and

public prestige which the squatter areas present, and because the community needs the land on which they are in illegal occupation. And the land is needed urgently.[2]

The quality of the first batch of government housing was very basic and not "self-contained." It was

> not high-grade housing: it was emergency accommodation built to meet a grave emergency. A family of five adults was housed in one room measuring 120 square feet and smaller families were required to share a room. Thirty or forty such rooms were required to share one communal water tap and three communal flush latrines.[3]

The government, however, depicted its "decision to accept this type of sub-standard housing as the answer to the overall squatter problem" as "not lightly taken."

Bearing in mind the social conditions associated with the 1967 riot, the MacLehose government utilized fiscal resources provided by rapid economic take-off of the 1970s to adopt a ten-year housing programme which aimed at the provision of self-contained units for every household in Hong Kong. A new town development programme adopting modern planning principles and standards was also introduced. In spite of set-backs to this scheme due to another wave of illegal immigration from China in the late 1970s, the objective of adequate housing, in numerical terms at least, was achieved by the late 1980s. Table 1 and Figure 1 show the number and percentage of living quarters accommodating more than one household. In 1976, the percentage was 26 per cent. By 1991, it had fallen to only 2.7 per cent. This notable achievement was the result of the high rate of production of both the public and private sectors. An empirical study reveals that the productivity of the construction industry has been on a par with the overall productivity of the economy.[4] The contribution of the private sector, often underplayed by academics, would be appreciated if we take a careful look at relevant figures of the past two decades as shown in Table 2 and Figure 2.

The potency of the private sector is due to the rapid economic development of Hong Kong. With hindsight, a number of the predictions of scholars like Hopkins, Drakakis-Smith and Dwyer in this respect deviated

---

[2] Annual Report of Department of Resettlement, 1954, p. 46.

[3] Ibid., p. 16.

[4] Chau Kwong-wing, and Lawrence Wai-chung Lai, "A Comparison Between Growth in Labour Productivity in the Construction Industry and the Economy," *Construction Management and Economics*, 12 (1994), pp. 183–85.

Table 1. Number of Domestic Households in Living Quarters

Year	Number of living quarters with households >1	Total	Percentage
1976	258,760	990,290	26.13%
1981	102,361	1,061,086	9.65%
1986	72,758	1,346,058	5.41%
1991	40,791	1,507,997	2.70%

Figure 1. Percentage of the Number of Living Quarters with Households >1

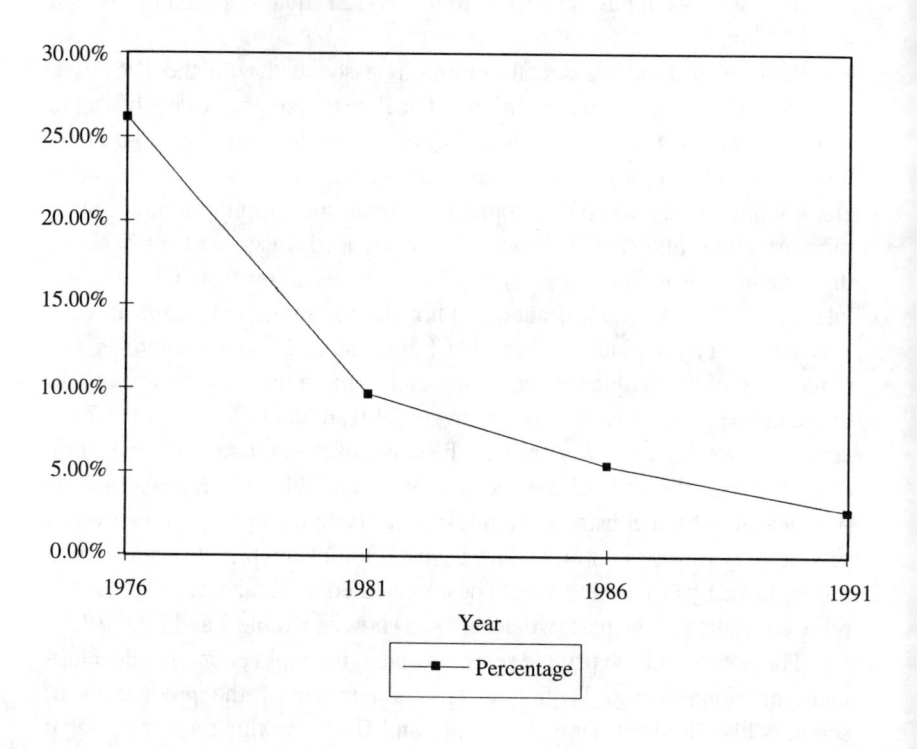

Sources: For Table 1 and Figure 1:
(1) Hong Kong government, *Hong Kong 1981 Census Summary Results* (Hong Kong: Census and Statistics Department, November 1981).
(2) Hong Kong government, *Hong Kong 1986 By-Census Summary Results* (Hong Kong: Census and Statistics Department, October 1986).
(3) Hong Kong government, *Hong Kong 1991 Census Summary Results* (Hong Kong: Census and Statistics Department, November 1991).

The Property Price Crisis

Table 2. Private Domestic Units — Supply and Vacancy

Year	Supply in the year	No. vacant at the end of the year
1972	20,589	7,012
1973	23,733	10,103
1974	18,949	7,784
1975	14,455	4,860
1976	15,425	4,305
1977	20,870	5,545
1978	26,230	5,620
1979	27,795	11,200
1980	24,995	10,405
1981	34,475	18,120
1982	23,900	31,700
1983	23,860	25,530
1984	22,270	22,435
1985	29,875	22,090
1986	34,105	24,665
1987	34,375	22,330
1988	34,470	20,225
1989	36,485	30,295
1990	29,400	26,150
1991	33,380	33,005
1992	26,222	34,069
1993	27,673	32,247

Figure 2. Private Domestic Units — Supply and Vacancy

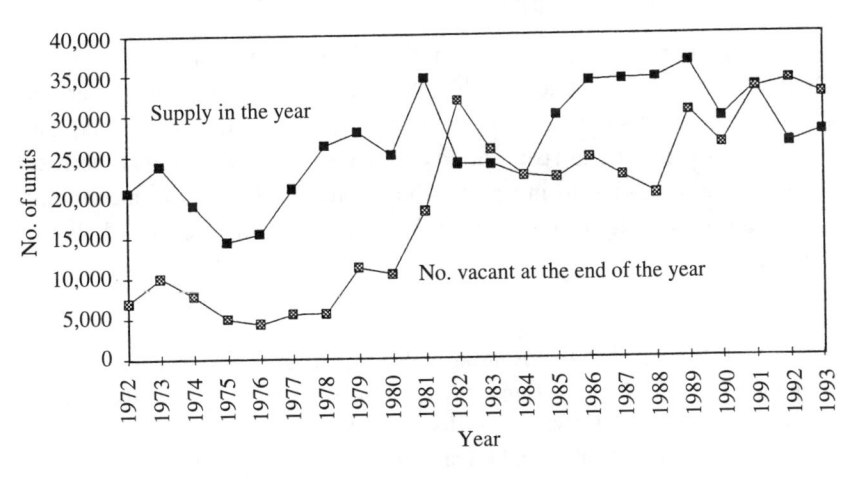

Sources: For Table 2 and Figure 2, see Hong Kong government, *Hong Kong Property Review* (Hong Kong: Rating and Valuation Department, various issues).

from the real situation substantially. It is, however, worth reviewing their views in order to appreciate how drastically the housing drama has changed as a result of rapid and sustained economic growth which has transformed Hong Kong from a manufacturing centre into one of the world's three largest financial centres. The dates quoted in these sources are significant because they signify turning points in the history of Hong Kong. As Hopkins noted:

> Let me sum up. First, the demand for housing will be heavy, for some time to come, because of current overcrowding and the inability or unwillingness of private developers to build for sufficiently low rentals. The main stimulus will be population growth. This is usually measured in terms of natural increase. In Hong Kong, we have an additional problem. A bulge of young people is approaching marriage age ... Secondly, the common expectation that it is Government's job to provide more public housing will be politically unavoidable. Economically, a rise in wages will not be generally sufficient to service the capital required for buying accommodation in the private market.[5]

It seems that the unwillingness shown by private developers was due mainly to political uncertainty and partly to the financial circumstances of the poor. However, Hopkins soon discovered the potency of the private market. Implicitly, he revised his opinion towards the ability of the people to pay for better housing as well:

> During the seven years 1962–1969 there has been a significant increase in owner occupation ... this means that over the last few years owner occupiers have emerged as a new and powerful sector of the market.... It serves as one index of the formation of a new middle class.[6]

In his early formulations, another Hong Kong-based academic, Drakakis-Smith, did not confine his attention to the housing producer but focused on the consumer's willingness to spend. Basically, he believed that there was a general and rising ability to spend on shelter as income rose rapidly. The hesitation to invest was both a result of political uncertainty and a low propensity to consume housing that is typical of Third World countries:

---

[5] Keith Hopkins, "Public Housing Policy in Hong Kong," inaugural lecture from the Chair of Sociology, *University of Hong Kong Supplement to the Gazette* 46, No. 5 (Hong Kong: University of Hong Kong, 1969), p. 11.

[6] Keith Hopkins, "Public and Private Housing in Hong Kong," in *The City as a Centre of Change in Asia*, edited by D. J. Dwyer (Hong Kong: Hong Kong University Press, 1971), p. 207.

Too many minimum shelter units have been provided for rapidly rising income level.... The willingness of the local population to invest in housing is generally low at present and reflects a basic uncertainty as to the political future of the colony.

Hong Kong is in a difficult situation with regard to ownership as the uncertain political future, coupled perhaps with past experience [the local 1967 riot and confiscation of privately-owned means of production by the Chinese socialist government] has discouraged any strong commitments to expensive homes.

The problem is to convince a great proportion of Hong Kong's privately housed population that their extra cash should be spent on housing ... but reluctance to invest in housing has always been a feature of Hong Kong's residential population.[7]

Drakakis-Smith's prescription for Hong Kong and other Asian cities was:

... government stimulation of the market demand and this mainly takes place by attempting to channel savings into house buying. This operation involves several steps, each of which can be encouraged at various levels of economic progress. Firstly there is stabilization of the financial and banking system and the consequent creation of confidence in its institutions. Money is then deposited where it can be made use of, rather than "hidden" in the form of jewelry, cars, etc. or dissipated in consumer spending.... The effect of this is to encourage a much greater commitment from households towards their future home, eventually leading to larger home ownership.[8]

However, he remained sceptical of the likelihood of the expansion in home ownership in Hong Kong, and thus argued that the government had to shoulder the burden of meeting housing needs. While both Hopkins and Drakakis-Smith considered that consumers would be able to pay for better housing (at least in the long run), Dwyer was totally pessimistic. Rapid population growth and the likelihood of a poverty trap syndrome were taken to be the main problems:

If the existing population trends continue, it is expected that by 1986 Hong Kong's

---

[7] D. W. Drakakis-Smith, "Housing Standards and Housing Policy in Hong Kong: Implications for Asian Cities," paper presented at the Nuffield Social Science Seminar held in Hong Kong by the Centre of Asian Studies (University of Hong Kong, 12 March 1971) (mimeographed); and D. W. Drakakis-Smith, "Housing Needs and Planning Policies for the Asian Cities: The Lesson from Hong Kong," *International Journal of Environmental Studies*, 1 (January 1971), pp. 115–28.

[8] Refer to the latter reference of Note 7.

present population of 4.2 million will have increased to 5.8 million ... the crux of the housing problem (in Hong Kong), as elsewhere in the Third World, is the present and anticipated future poverty of the population. It was officially estimated in 1968 that HK$200 a month was the minimum economic rent at which the private developer could build self-contained residential units in Hong Kong. If it is assumed that a poor family can afford to devote only about one-fifth of family income to rent, then a minimum income of HK$1,000 monthly would have been required for accommodation at that date. Approximately three-quarters of the families in Hong Kong were below this level in 1968, and it was not officially anticipated that this proportion could be reduced much below two-thirds over the twenty years despite Hong Kong's growing prosperity.[9]

In retrospect, both Dwyer's economic pessimism and Drakakis-Smith's concern about political uncertainty and lack of investment incentive have proven to be inappropriate. However, Hopkin's prediction about middle class home ownership demand has stood the test of time. Although Hong Kong's population has really grown tremendously since the 1967 riot, its per capita income has grown even faster while household size has gradually fallen. Table 3 shows household income and size during the period of 1971 to 1991. The nature of the current heavily politicized housing price issue is not one of inadequate shelter but of middle class home ownership. Table 4

Table 3. Household Income and Household Size in Hong Kong

	1971	1976	1981	1986	1991
Median monthly household income					
at current prices (HK$)	708	1,425	2,955	5,160	9,964
at constant 1976 prices (HK$)	1,069	1,425	1,969	2,255	2,798
Average household size	4.5	4.2	3.9	3.7	3.4

Sources: (1) Hong Kong government, *Hong Kong 1981 Census Summary Results* (Hong Kong: Census and Statistics Department, November 1981).
(2) Hong Kong government, *Hong Kong 1986 By-Census Summary Results* (Hong Kong: Census and Statistics Department, October 1986).
(3) Hong Kong government, *Hong Kong 1991 Census Summary Results* (Hong Kong: Census and Statistics Department, November 1991).

---

[9] D. J. Dwyer (ed.), *People and Housing in Third World Cities* (London: Longman, 1975), pp. 155–56.

The Property Price Crisis

Table 4. Home Ownership/Rental Ratios

Year	Home ownership ratio (Households)	Rental ratio (Households)
1971	18.1%	81.9%
1976	23.2%	76.8%
1981	27.9%	72.1%
1986	35.1%	64.9%
1991	42.6%	57.4%

Figure 3. Home Ownership/Rental Ratios

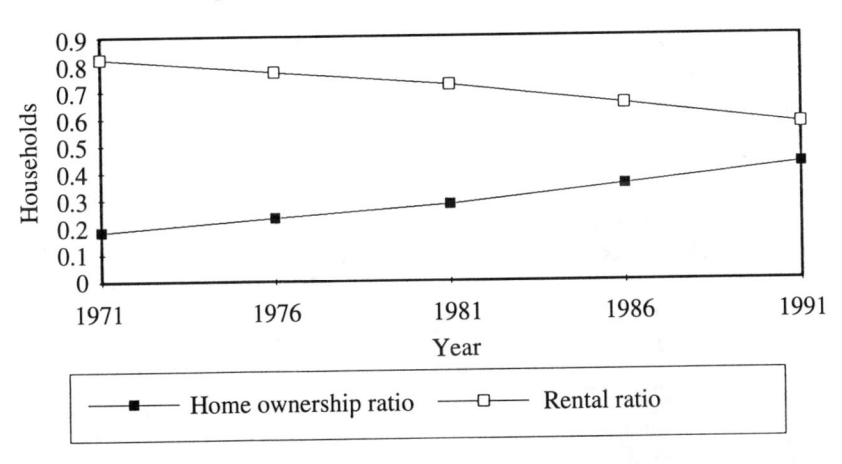

Source: For Table 4 and Figure 3, see Hong Kong government, *Hong Kong Annual Digest of Statistics* (Hong Kong: Census and Statistics Department, 1993).

and Figure 3 show the changes in the home ownership ratio of households in Hong Kong from 1971 to 1991. The ratio has risen steadily from 18 per cent in 1971 to 43 per cent in 1991, reflecting major income growth. The rental ratio has correspondingly fallen from 30 per cent in 1971 to 7.4 per cent in 1991. Indeed, property had become in the 1980s a major store of value for Hong Kong. In April 1989, the total value of property was HK$1,241,760 million (see Table 5)[10] and, by April 1993, it had risen to

---

[10] Anthony Walker, Chau Kwong-wing, and Lawrence Wai-chung Lai, *Hong Kong: Property, Construction and Economy* (1st and 2nd editions; London: Royal Institution of Chartered Surveyors, 1990).

Table 5. Estimate of Total Value of Property at 1989 Market Price

	Value as at 1 April 1989 (HK$ Million)	Value after 4 June 1989 (HK$ Million)
Domestic		
Private domestic		
(A) less than 40 sq.m.	108,870	90,725
(B) 40–69.9 sq.m.	170,467	142,056
(C) 70–99.9 sq.m.	57,864	48,220
(D) 100–159.9 sq.m.	56,424	47,020
(E) 160 sq.m. and over	63,624	53,020
Public domestic	148,617	123,848
Mis. domestic	1,619	1,349
Car parking space, domestic	8,884	7,403
Non-domestic		
G/F shops	137,302	109,841
U/F arcade, basement & U/F shops	61,231	48,985
Commercial premises	82,032	65,625
Offices	154,570	123,656
Factories (urban area)	99,998	79,998
Factories (N.T.)	70,164	56,131
Storage	17,069	13,655
Hotels	35,086	28,069
Cinemas & theatres	7,261	5,809
Schools	32,417	25,933
Recreation club premises	3,873	3,099
Community welfare premises	13,595	10,876
Car parking spaces	14,676	11,741
Others	180,877	144,701
Total	1,526,520	1,241,760

Source: A. Walker, K. W. Chau and L.W.C. Lai, *Hong Kong: Property, Construction and Economy* (1st and 2nd editions; London: Royal Institution of Chartered Surveyors, 1990).

HK$2,834,478 million (see Table 6). In a context where half the population has been accommodated in public sector housing (see Table 7 and Figure 4), the current housing politics is really a matter of home ownership promotion against a background of property prices upsurge and democratization.

Table 6. Estimate of Total Value of Property at 1993 Market Price

		Value as at 1 April 1993 (HK$ Million)
Domestic		
Private domestic		1,057,942
Class A (less than 40 sq.m.)	242,359	
Class B (40–69.9 sq.m.)	453,720	
Class C (70–99.9 sq.m.)	144,173	
Class D (100–159.9 sq.m.)	112,400	
Class E (160 sq.m. and over)	105,290	
Public domestic		331,674
Mis. domestic		21,076
Car parking space, domestic		2,592
Non-domestic		
Commercial premises & shops		405,870
G/F shops	184,264	
G/F arcade, basement & U/F shops	102,925	
Commercial premises	118,681	
Offices		330,922
Factories		205,791
Urban area	112,152	
N.T.	93,639	
Storage		24,726
Hotels		37,613
Cinemas & theatres		6,528
Schools		51,101
Recreation club premises		6,805
Community welfare premises		19,019
Petrol filling stations		6,992
Advertising stations		5,776
Car parking spaces		27,978
Mis. premises		292,071
Total		2,834,476

Source: Same as Table 5 (3rd edition, forthcoming).

Table 7. Percentage of Total Population Living in Public Housing

Year	Population in public housing	Total population	%
1972	1,667,000	4,067,500	41.0
1973	1,669,900	4,164,100	40.1
1974	1,706,000	4,229,600	40.3
1975	1,743,200	4,337,000	40.2
1976	1,799,700	4,437,000	40.6
1977	1,859,400	4,494,000	41.4
1978	1,881,400	4,579,000	41.1
1979	1,909,200	4,779,000	39.9
1980	2,009,700	4,985,600	40.3
1981	1,994,000	5,105,500	39.1
1982	2,100,500	5,207,400	40.3
1983	2,186,300	5,271,700	41.5
1984	2,293,000	5,341,200	42.9
1985	2,336,100	5,396,600	43.3
1986	2,437,200	5,479,100	44.5
1987	2,592,300	5,590,700	46.4
1988	2,630,000	5,629,000	46.7
1989	2,669,000	5,707,100	46.8
1990	2,759,100	5,750,300	48.0
1991	2,688,900	5,636,400	47.7
1992	2,882,100	5,751,000	50.1
1993	2,871,900	5,845,000	49.1

Figure 4. % Total Population Living in Public Housing

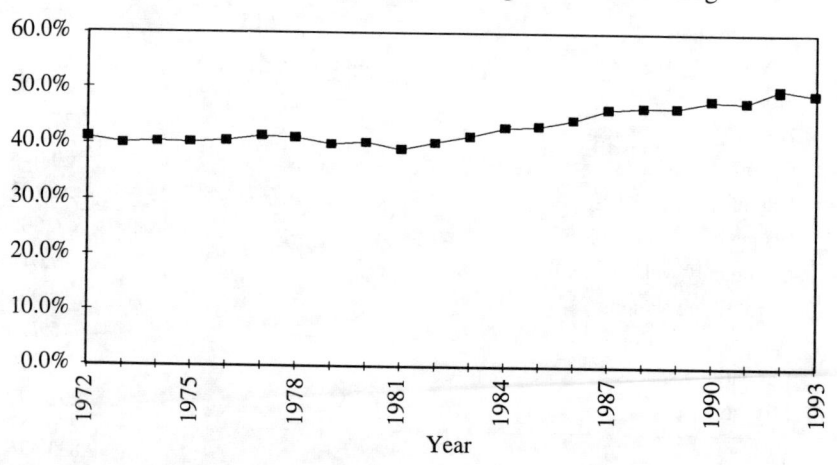

Sources: For Table 7 and Figure 4, see Hong Kong government, *Hong Kong Annual Report* (Hong Kong: Government Printer, various issues).

Demand and Supply Parameters

Contrary to widespread expectation in the mid-1980s that both stock and property prices would collapse in anticipation of the political uncertainty associated with the transfer of sovereignty in 1997, stock and property values have actually escalated since 1984. This caused both the final users and speculators in the housing market to continuously readjust their price expectation upwards, validating the price escalation phenomenon. Housing prices are at any time a result of the interaction of a number of demand and supply factors governed by structurally determined conditions. As regards demand (which comprises effective demand of both the "end users" and "speculators"), the factors are: (1) sustained growth in domestic income and therefore growing desire for improvement in living environment; (2) rapid capital accumulation in China in the absence of reinvestment outlets, resulting in the inflow of cash into Hong Kong; (3) the "linked exchange rate" system[11] which imports a low interest rate regime from America; and (4) the inflow of expatriate labour searching for high-salary occupations and business opportunities. These demand-side parameters are either not amenable to government intervention without serious economic repercussions or are totally out of its control.

On the supply side, the factors are: (1) the 50-hectare new land allocation ceiling (calibrated on the basis of "past trends" a decade ago); (2) development control over urban densities to improve the environment and planned conversion of mixed commercial/residential uses into pure commercial uses (notably of offices and hotels) to accommodate the growth of the tertiary sector; (3) tight and introvert planning controls over change in agricultural land made on environmental and infrastructural grounds; (4) adherence to a numerical balance between the number of households and number of living quarters included in strategic housing planning; (5) a shortage of construction labour; and (6) commodification of housing and the demise of the informal squattering sector due to stringent enforcement measures. These supply-side parameters act as political, policy or operational rules which originated as well-considered though *ad hoc* responses to specific issues at particular moments. Like most policy measures, they are amenable to changes in the face of new circumstances.

---

[11] This is a misnomer because it is actually a money supply and not an exchange rate regulation mechanism.

However, decision-making associated with such changes takes time and might incur other types of cost. The first four factors pertain to land use planning, which largely determines the spatial and temporal distribution of housing supply. The general influence of land use planning upon the supply of housing will be dealt with below. Here, discussion is restricted to the first four factors.

The application of the 50-hectare rule requires the concurrence of the Chinese government. Although a flexible attitude has been adopted in the past, variation of the rule entails time being assigned for negotiation. The second factor is the object of Metroplan, a laudable long-term urban restructuring strategy for Hong Kong Island, Kowloon and Tsuen Wan New Town. Substantial alteration of the content of this package is not desirable from the planning point of view. In particular, urban densities in the Metro Area are far too high and require thinning out. The third factor is conditioned by the fourth one, which may be one of the decisive causes of the price escalation expectation. The quantitative balance approach may not match the choice of households in locational, temporal or tenure terms and may not be able to cope with non-domestic demand, which is some function of economic growth, without pushing up property values. Such mismatches are not uncommon in centrally planned economies. Any mismatch between actual housing preference and planned supply will be reflected in price differentials of different areas and types of housing.

From home ownership ratios, rent profile and rent variance analysis, the following features of existing housing preferences are discernible: (1) a strong preference for ownership; (2) strong preference for accessibility — areas with reliable mass transit service are in great demand; and (3) strong preference for better planned and managed private comprehensive development. However, as the strategy would restrain net addition to the stock of living quarters in the next thirty years, price escalation is a natural market response given strong demand. The Metro Area is naturally the prime area from the home buyer's point of view. In this context one can conceive of the value of housing in Metro Areas which results from keen competition as has been in the upsurge as the price for achieving long-term planning benefits. Alternatively, one can consider that the location of major future housing supply would be in the non-Metro Area. This basic strategic planning consideration is addressed in the Territorial Development Strategy (TDS) Review. And it is noteworthy that the Foundation Report of the Review does recognize some aspects of property market responses to planning constraints:

The 1992 Long Term Housing Strategy Review estimates that up to 2001, 649,000 households would need new housing as against a new flat supply of 635,000 flats. After adjustments to include sharing and vacancies, an outstanding demand of 14,000 flats will remain. Taking into account the shortfall in 2001, the total potential demand from 2001 to 2011 is forecast to be about 516,000 households.

The number of people who come to work in Hong Kong from China and other countries is expected to rise in the medium and long term as a result of increased economic interaction with China. The resultant demands in housing will be addressed in the formulation of TDS options.

Estimates of the potential demand for housing *indicate only the need for shelter*. The provision of serviced land for housing should also take into consideration other aspects including vacancies, second homes, non-domestic use and even a measure of over production to help curb speculation.[12]

The Planning Department will now comprehensively review the nature of housing preference in terms of tenure mix (ownership and renting), local and exogenous demand, and the like.

Land Use Planning and Housing Supply

The government has often been condemned by social critics for monopolizing land supply and adopting a "high land price policy." The government does control land supply and housing in a number of significant ways. First, it controls the means by which a given amount of new land is allocated for housing by coordinating the land sale programme. Second, it controls uses and changes in use of land through the zoning and planning application mechanism. Third, it controls the supply of public rental, the Home Ownership Scheme, and the Public Sector Participation Scheme through coordination done under the Long Term Housing Strategy, as well as the supply of "sandwich class" housing. Fourth, as an employer, it provides staff quarters, private tenancy allowances and housing loans. Besides being seen as problematic in several other aspects,[13] criticism of the government's adoption of a "high land price policy" also is definitely insensitive to

---

[12] Hong Kong government, 1993.

[13] See the author's review on Rosanna Chan's "An Anatomy of the Failure of Hong Kong Government's Announced 10 Years Public Housing Plan in 1972," *Hong Kong Journal of Public Administration*, Vol. 6, No. 2 (December 1984), pp. 227–30.

the fact that all the above control measures are necessitated by land use planning. The location and use of new land need to be determined by town plans before lease conditions can be drafted. Zoning and planning application must take into account many planning considerations. The Long Term Housing Strategy, for example, and the housing provision of the government require prior land use planning. However, land use planning is more than just housing land planning. The apparent rigidity in land supply may be said to be the result of forward planning and development control which are required in a context of major spatial restructuring of Hong Kong to cater for future economic development and integration with China.

Since the mid-1980s, land use planning in Hong Kong has become more comprehensive and rational. This is due to the adoption of strategic and regional planning, which is meant to (1) avoid district planning as *ad hoc* responses to a fluctuating market and (2) coordinate major territorial infrastructure development projects and new growth poles. The latter aspect necessitates a host of major detailed studies such as the Port and Airport Development Strategy (PADS), the Territorial Development Strategy Review, the Rail Development Strategy (RDS), and four Regional Development Strategy studies, namely Metroplan, the Northwestern New Territories Development Strategy Review, the Southwestern New Territories Development Strategy Review, the Northeastern New Territories Development Strategy Review and the Southeastern New Territories Development Strategy Review. Metroplan has been completed and the Development Strategy Reviews for the Northwestern New Territories and Southeastern New Territories are near completion.

The gist of the Metroplan and the Regional Development Strategy Reviews as regards the future supply of housing land is threefold. First, the Metro Area would not have net growth in population or housing units notwithstanding massive reclamation and hill terracing. The objects are to thin out population and allow for expansion of the office and hotel sectors. The mechanisms involved are rezoning, comprehensive urban renewal and reduction in plot ratios. Second, North Lantau (Tung Chung and Tai Ho New Towns) and the Northwestern New territories (notably Tin Shui Wai Phase II) would be the major housing growth foci. And third, the Metro Area would remain as the major territorial employment centre especially for office work.

In this context, the speed of new housing supply expansion would depend on the speed of planning and development for North Lantau and

The Property Price Crisis 205

Northwestern New Territories. Before such new supply materializes, home buyers intending to reside in the Metro Area would need to compete among themselves for a constrained amount of units. The new supply, however, could not possibly be realized instantaneously especially as the community have expressed keen preference for comprehensive planned development, conserving the natural ecology and environmental protection, and easy accessibility.

The considerations involved entail lengthy period of time for political articulation and professional analysis. Comprehensive development normally requires the preparation of Master Layout Plans for planning approval. Ecological and environmental protection, demanded always by the Department of Environmental Protection, implies classifying certain developable areas, such as the Mai Po Marshes, as development no-go areas, as well as the timely provision of sewerage for the selected housing development areas. Easy accessibility for the population requires construction of new highways (like Tsing Ma Bridge, North Lantau Expressway and Route 3) and railways such as those proposed under the RDS, notably the Tsuen Wan–Yuen Long rail link. These transport links need resources and time to build. Expanding the water supply and treatment system is also a major development task. It is simply important to allow for some "waiting time" before substantial amount of new housing units as well as other social objects desired or needed by the public can be built in the strategic growth areas. It needs to be stressed that the potential supply of land in North Lantau and the Northwestern New Territories is more than sufficient to meet the long-term housing needs of Hong Kong. The relevant planning issues involved under the current "crisis," however, is how such land can be developed within a time frame which enables the amount supplied[14] to lead to a fall in the general level of housing price. What could be done is to interject more resources into the Planning Department and Territorial Development Department so that they could expedite their work. The Planning Department has recently been overloaded with work, and the Territorial Development Department also needs extra resources if the Public Works Programme is to be advanced.

---

[14] Tin Shui Wai Phase II, for instance, has been formed with a developable area of 113 hectares, which could accommodate 200,000 to 260,000 people.

☐ Do Government Policies Ignore Price Theory and Planning Needs?

Conditions for a Fall in Property Prices

In all forms of markets, prices are determined by demand and supply. This price theory applies whether or not a market is "perfectly competitive," "monopolistic," "oligopolistic" or "monopolized." Even where an overt market is suppressed and superseded by a "command economy," the theory still operates albeit the ordering of transactions is not predicated on price signals but on other criteria, like rationing, which deal with competition for scarce resources.

In the housing market, property prices would fall if either or both of the following conditions occur: (1) effective demand falls because income and the rate of family formation fall, desire for living environment improvement subsides, and/or mortgage rates and down payment amount increases; and (2) supply expands because the speed of new land formation and redevelopment increases, construction efficiency improves, and costs of housing construction fall. Decrease in demand alone will not only cause a fall in price but also a contraction in market transactions. However, as the public do not look for a price fall based on the shrinking of market transactions, the government logically should not attempt any demand-side management measures. It should increase supply as that would lead to a fall in price while expanding the volume of market transaction. Downward adjustment in property prices would be faster as a result if the cost of price searching (which is a typical transaction cost of a monopolistic market) is reduced. Speculation is a typical price searching phenomenon. In Hong Kong, the cost of price searching is substantially reduced by "pre-sales," which is a form of future option market, an open land auction market and a free-entry estate agent profession. Conversely, if the cost of price searching increases, price responses to changes in demand and supply conditions may become very sluggish.

Relevance of the Government's Policies

As discussed above, government policies can be divided into two categories: (1) those which curb speculation and (2) those which increase supply. From the above price theory analysis, the anti-speculation package, in spite of its equity and emotional underpinnings, would indeed increase the costs of price searching and delay the speed of price adjustment. Unfortunately, the government presumes that speculation is bad right from the beginning. The establishment of the "Anti-Speculation Task Force" reminds historians of the panicking price regulation committees of the French Revolution. The politicians are totally mistaken in criticizing the government for being too modest in this respect. As regards augmenting supply, government policy solutions are correct. The politicians' criticism that the measures would take a few years' time to realize is irresponsible, as overnight changes (as discussed previously) are not possible. The government should be criticized in this regard not because its policies are too weak but because it appears to yield to political demands in (1) sacrificing taxpayer's resources in the "sandwich class" scheme; (2) increasing the costs of price searching and other transaction costs by increasing the cost of speculation, restraining the future option market and conferring monopolistic licensing rights on the estate agents association; (3) sacrificing long-term planning interests by squeezing new housing blocks into already congested housing estates; and (4) thinning out resources which should have been expended on the proper planning for the new supply, which needs to be in compliance with adopted land use strategies and planning policies.

The "sandwich class" scheme which allocates public money to selected income groups on the basis of random chance is inequitable not only because not all members of the groups would get the benefits or income groups are arbitrarily selected, but also because the policy actually augments effective demand, bringing pressures on the market. Furthermore, the middle class is a class possessing human capital which enables them to earn above average long-term income. To subsidize this class is indefensible except for political reasons.

To artificially shorten the period of the units' pre-sale is not only an infringement on the freedom of contract but also constrains the effectiveness of the mechanism in price searching. Indeed, in the presence of policy measures prohibiting re-sale of pre-sale units, this constraint is redundant and would only increase the costs of "genuine end users," as they have to arrange for mortgages in a shorter period of time on the one hand and the liquidity costs of the developers who cannot obtain cash income earlier on the other hand. The latter aspect may, eventually, harm the small developers and reinforce the position of the big ones who have more resources and induce the developers to switch on to office and other commercial development.

Licensing would raise the costs of entry through requirements of training, membership subscription and other qualifications. Usually such costs would be transferred to the consumer. In Canada, the agency cost for a property transaction is seven times those in Hong Kong. In New South Wales, Australia, it is three times. If the Hong Kong licensing system involves the creation of a legal monopoly power debarring private property transaction without an agent, it is likely that the consumer will be victimized.

To squeeze additional blocks into built-up estates is a bad *ad hoc* practice upsetting good local planning according to adopted planning beliefs. Many housing estates have over time experienced an increase in shortages of parking space for private cars and goods vehicles due to growing affluence and export trade. This desperate attempt on the part of the government to provide more urban housing units would create future problems not only for the existing population but also future tenants.

Finally, the government has taken an unduly high-profile commitment dealing with speculation, which is actually price searching behaviour and is incapable of "pushing" prices above the equilibrium price. This misconception is reinforced by the collusion of the developers in the first land auction of the 1994–1995 financial year. The loss of confidence in the prevailing auction arrangement is quite unnecessary so far as entry into the auction market is unrestricted and the auction process is carried out in the open. Any collusion would fail if there is a keen "outside" bidder. The post of Secretary for Housing has been resurrected. The political benefit of this, perhaps, is to relieve the Planning, Environment and Lands Branch of involvement in political confrontation with politicians. However, this expedient administrative response cannot increase supply unless more manpower and financial resources are made available to the Planning and Territorial Development Departments.

Infrastructure

Kwong Kai-sun

☐ Introduction

The future of Hong Kong rests on its emergence as an international centre of trade, finance, business, and tourism. On this, the people of Hong Kong, the Hong Kong government, and probably the Chinese government would have no argument. Yet Hong Kong is not the only city in the region that has these aspirations. Competition is going to be intense. While Hong Kong has the natural advantage in being the gateway to China, competitiveness in other aspects is equally important. This is where infrastructure building enters the picture.

By infrastructure, we mean the capacity to provide road networks, transport, water, electricity, gas, telecommunications and environmental protection services. This is indeed a broad spectrum. Yet, they share a number of characteristics. First, infrastructural services are not tradeables. One has usually no choice but to buy these services locally. Competition is therefore limited. Second, providers of infrastructural services usually enjoy some economies of scale, meaning that unit cost of output decreases with increasing production scale. Once a provider is in business, it is often hard to find a second provider willing to enter the industry. Modern technology may, however, change the situation drastically in some industries. Third, it takes time to build up infrastructure. Because of the long lead time, planning becomes important. Good planning is nevertheless a difficult task,

---

Kwong Kai-sun is a lecturer in the Department of Economics, The Chinese University of Hong Kong.

TRAFALGAR HOUSE
MITSUI COSTAIN

Infrastructure

particularly in Hong Kong where the economy is constantly being affected by local and global changes. If a piece of hardware is built ahead of time, excess capacity appears, hence wastage. If it lags behind demand, then a bottleneck emerges which slows down the economy.

The quantity, quality and price of infrastructural services are therefore of central importance. They would affect the economy's productivity, quality of living, and competitiveness. This chapter attempts to analyse how these needs are being addressed in Hong Kong.

☐ Major Infrastructural Investments

The key infrastructural services in Hong Kong are provided by the government, government-owned public corporations and private enterprises. Plans have been made by each of them to accommodate the future growth of demand.

Of key importance in infrastructural development is the building of the replacement airport at Chek Lap Kok. The plan includes, in addition to the runway and passenger terminals, new highways, tunnels, bridges, railways, and hotels, as well as commercial and residential development. As Chek Lap Kok is a remote undeveloped area, extensive land reclamation and site formation, and building of supporting infrastructure need to be carried out. The cost of the scheme has been estimated at HK$112.2 billion at 1991 prices. Construction began in 1992 and was originally expected to be completed by 1997. Unfortunately, to date the Chinese and British governments have not been able to arrive at a detailed financing package for the entire scheme, and some of the construction tenders have to be delayed. The new airport is now expected to commence operation in 1998.

The development of the seaport is of great importance to the future development of exports and re-exports. Facilities are offered for both mid-stream cargo handling and terminal operations. In terms of total container throughput, Hong Kong is the largest container port in the world. All seven existing container terminals are privately operated. The growth in re-exports from China, however, leads to strains in existing capacity. Even though Container Terminal No. 8 will soon commence operation, if capacity is going to keep pace with demand growth, construction on Container Terminal No. 9 will have to start soon. Unfortunately, as the concession given by the government to build and operate Terminal No. 9 confers a right which extends beyond 1997, the concurrence of the Chinese government is required. Following the conflict over the territory's political reform, negotiation has been dragging on and is still unresolved at the moment. There are signs recently that economic considerations are given higher priorities in Sino-British talks, and it is likely that a consortium led by the Jardine Matheson Group would be given the development rights. The total cost of developing Terminal No. 9 would be HK$10 billion, inclusive of a land premium of HK$4 billion.

Road space shortage is a perennial problem. Traffic congestion is serious in certain parts of the road network. But road expansion is costly, because of the density of urban development and high land prices. In the past, the government has attempted to tackle the congestion problem by improving bus services, expanding railways and prioritizing road usage in favour of public transport vehicles. Nevertheless, the expansion of the road structure is still required to keep up with the development of new towns, the new airport, and to relieve congestion. On the other hand, a larger network also requires more maintenance. As a result, the government is expected to spend some HK$8 billion each year in the maintenance and expansion of roads.

Environmental problems are of increasing concern. The government is prepared to spend HK$18 billion between 1993 and 2002 in building sewerage and drainage facilities, as well as waste disposal and treatment facilities. Financing will follow a "polluter pays" principle. Increased spending on facilities and more stringent control on emission standards would better keep pollution under control. Concurrently, as more industrial production is being moved into China, the amount of industrial waste and emission may diminish slowly.

Railway operations are in the hands of public corporations. The 43 route-kilometres' urban subway lines are operated by the Mass Transit Railway Corporation (MTRC). The Kowloon–Canton Railway and the Light Rail Transit in the New Territories are operated by the Kowloon–Canton Railway Corporation (KCRC). Both are independent enterprises operating on commercial principles and are solely owned by the government. All railway services are heavily used by commuters. In particular, certain segments of the MTR line are saturated during busy hours. The MTRC is planning to install advanced signalling systems to increase train speeds, and to spend HK$8 billion between 1994 and 2000 to upgrade services. In the longer term, the airport rail link, which may commence operation in 1998, would relieve some of the existing congestion. This link would cost HK$34 billion at 1993 prices. Financing would come from bank loans and bond issues. The KCRC also has heavy spending plans. Between

1993 and 1997, HK$6 billion would be spent on maintenance, station expansion and service improvement.

Electricity generation, transmission and distribution are provided by two commercial enterprises, the China Light and Power Company (CLP), and the Hong Kong Electric Company (HEC). Both companies have heavy investment plans for the future. The CLP is going to invest HK$60 billion between 1992 and 1999 to build new generating plants at Black Point and enhance the transmission and distribution systems and reduce air pollution. The HEC is going to spend at least HK$15 billion to build new plants and substations and reduce air, water, and noise pollution. Both companies finance their investment by a combination of depreciation reserves, retained earnings, export credits, and bank loans.

In telecommunications, the Hong Kong Telecom (HKT) provides local as well as international telephone and data services. The company has been investing regularly in buildings, exchange equipment, international and local transmission plants and equipment. In 1993, the company invested HK$3.6 billion. In 1994, the amount would increase to HK$3.9 billion. Despite the liberalization of the local telephone market from 1995, the company is expected to maintain its dominance by aggressively expanding services, especially in the area of multimedia services.

☐ Share of Infrastructure Spending between Private and Public Sectors

The provision of infrastructural services is shared by the government, public corporations and commercial enterprises. Relative to other economies, the share of private enterprises is actually quite large. As a matter of fact, the government has adhered to a "small government" principle, i.e., low tax rate corresponding to low government expenditure. It is therefore necessary that much of the required infrastructural spending be taken up by the private sector.

Table 1 shows the percentage of infrastructural spending by the government in gross domestic product (GDP) and public sector expenditure (PSE). Here, infrastructural spending includes expenditures on land reclamation and development, government buildings, transport, water and environment. Spending refers to both recurrent and capital expenditure. It should be noted that spending by the public corporations is not included. PSE includes government spending (recurrent and capital) on economic services,

Table 1. Public Sector Expenditure and Infrastructural Spending (HK$ million)

	Year				
	1989–90	1990–91	1991–92	1992–93	1993–94
GDP	499,157	558,859	642,930	745,407	847,813
PSE	81,945	95,198	108,422	123,493	158,499
(% of GDP)	(16.4)	(17.0)	(16.9)	(16.6)	(18.7)
Infrastructure by the government	15,113	13,925	16,922	20,613	26,842
(% of PSE)	(18.4)	(14.6)	(15.6)	(16.7)	(16.9)
(% of GDP)	(3.0)	(2.5)	(2.6)	(2.8)	(3.2)

Notes: 1. The railway corporations are not classified as part of the public sector.
2. Infrastructure by the government includes transport, water, environment, land formation, and government buildings.

Sources: Government annual report, various years.

security, social services, education, community and external affairs, support services, housing, as well as infrastructure.

The "small government" principle is illustrated by the rather small percentage of public sector spending in GDP. In the last five years, about 16 to 19 per cent of GDP was accounted for by the public sector. Infrastructure, on the other hand, accounted for about 15 to 18 per cent of PSE, or 2 to 3 per cent of GDP. For comparison, the government has in fact been spending similar amounts on education as on infrastructure. In 1993–1994, for example, HK$25,103 million was spent on education, versus HK$26,842 million on infrastructure. This shows the importance placed on soft infrastructure as opposed to hard infrastructure.

The private sector accounts for a sizeable proportion of infrastructural spending. Table 2 shows the capital expenditure by the key private infrastructural enterprises, including the two public corporations, the MTRC and the KCRC. For the railways, the KCRC had no major expansion in capacity in the last five years and so capital expenditure was relatively small. The same applies to the MTRC, except that the Eastern Harbour Line boosted spending to over HK$1,700 million in 1989 and the new airport rail link boosted spending in 1993–1994 to HK$2,203 million. The electricity and telecommunication companies, by contrast, have been investing heavily throughout the last five years. All three companies are financially

Table 2. Infrastructural Investment by Major Private Organizations (HK$ million)

	1989–90	1990–91	1991–92	1992–93	1993–94
Railways					
KCRC	694	420	609	655	na
MTRC	1,710*	120*	300	887	2,203
Electricity					
China Light & Power	1,892	3,344	3,516	2,982	2,785
Hong Kong Electric	2,433	2,439	2,667	2,970	3,486
Telecommunications					
Hong Kong Telecom	2,387	2,676	3,018	2,204	3,620

* approximate figures
Sources: Annual reports of respective companies.

strong and financing by loans, papers or retained earnings did not pose any problem.

Combining public and private infrastructural spending, around 4 to 5 per cent of GDP could be accounted for by investment in infrastructure. The actual percentage could be slightly smaller because infrastructural spending includes some spending on imports. Nevertheless, this percentage is in line with the situation in other high-growth developing countries. It is important to note, however, that at least 40 per cent of the infrastructural investment is accounted for by the private sector. Most developing countries, on the other hand, have 90 per cent of their infrastructural investment accounted for by their governments. This observation highlights the extent of "privatization" in infrastructure in Hong Kong.

In the next three years, the government would maintain its infrastructural spending outside the Airport Core Programme projects. But since the two public corporations, the Airport Authority and the MTRC, together with private firms would take up the bulk of the airport investment, government's share in infrastructural investment would not increase as a result.

☐ The Chek Lap Kok Airport

The new airport project at Chek Lap Kok is the largest infrastructural project in the history of Hong Kong. It is probably also one of the largest construction projects in the world in the present decade. A project of this scale has a definite impact on the budgetary procedures of the government and the pattern of urban development. In the particular political setting of Hong Kong, it has also become the focus of some hard political bargaining.

The existing airport at Kai Tak took its modern form in the 1950s. In the following four decades, air traffic in terms of passenger and cargo throughput has been growing so rapidly that despite several phases of capacity expansion, it became apparent that land area limitation did not permit further expansion to handle future growth. The key constraint is in the single runway and the geographical setting which does not permit a second runway to be built. The proximity of the airport to dense population settlement further restricts the daily hours of flight operation. Suggestion of a replacement airport has been voiced many times. In the early 1980s, the government came close to making a replacement decision. A commissioned consultancy study identified Chek Lap Kok, near the large outlying Lantau Island, as the suitable site for a replacement airport, together with a crude development plan for a new satellite town. Unfortunately, a decision was to be made at a time when the British and Chinese governments were negotiating over the future sovereignty of Hong Kong. The government therefore decided to shelve the plan. Studies were conducted to find ways to expand the physical capacity of Kai Tak and to use demand management to exploit the capacity more intensively.

Liberalization and openness in China after 1978 certainly led to an increased flow of passengers and cargo through Hong Kong. These increases certainly brought Kai Tak to saturation. The maximum capacity of Kai Tak is 24 million passengers per year and saturation will be reached in 1995. A number of suggestions emerged from the private sector as to the best site for a new airport. A related development was that the seaport was in need of expansion too. During the late 1980s, the government decided that the development of the airport and the seaport should be integrated so that new highways can be shared. Under this premise, Chek Lap Kok was favoured over the alternatives.

There was also a view that questioned the necessity of a new airport. The argument was that the development of Hong Kong should be viewed in the context of the development of Southern China. Given that an airport in Shenzhen would commence operation in the early 1990s, Hong Kong could access it by building highway links to Shenzhen. Proponents argued that this alternative would save enormous costs for Hong Kong. Furthermore, although the land at Kai Tak could be redeveloped under the new airport

Infrastructure 217

scenario, land grants had to come under the constraints set down in the Sino-British Joint Declaration, and therefore could not be added quickly to the government treasury.

It was the June 4 incident in Beijing, 1989, which prompted the government to make the bold decision to build the Chek Lap Kok airport. The decision, known as the Port and Airport Development Strategy (PADS), was first announced in the Governor's policy address in December 1989. At that time, confidence of the public was at the lowest and the general outlook was pessimistic. The government saw the opportunity to use PADS to keep people and capital from leaving. The new airport would have a capacity of 35 million passengers with one runway and 87 million passengers with both runways.

This airport decision may be correct in sustaining Hong Kong as the gateway to China and as an international centre of business. Without the replacement airport, air traffic would be diverted to nearby airports, and while the development of China may not be hurt significantly, the prominence of Hong Kong would in time be lost. Yet the decision, from hindsight, might have been made too hastily. For the Hong Kong government did not think it necessary to seek approval from the Chinese government. It soon appeared that China's approval was necessary in attracting participation from the private sector and in securing foreign loans, for the generation of income and repayment of loans would take place after the transfer of sovereignty.

The government was determined to have one runway open for operation before the transfer of sovereignty, i.e., before 30 June 1997. Therefore, despite China's open opposition to the scheme, the government pressed ahead with detailed planning, the establishment of a Provisional Airport Authority and the construction of the 100 per cent government-financed Lantau Fixed Crossing, which is the only highway access to the airport. In a more favourable political climate, the Lantau Fixed Crossing might have been financed, built, and operated by private interests.

As a result of negotiations between Britain and China, a Memorandum of Understanding was signed in September 1991. Under this Memorandum, China agreed to the need of a replacement airport and the site of Chek Lap Kok. Britain agreed to complete the construction works as far as possible. More importantly, the Hong Kong government would leave at least HK$25 billion as reserves for the future Special Administrative Region (SAR) government and the maximum amount of debt raised would be HK$5 billion unless with the prior approval of China.

The Memorandum did not specify the detailed plan for finance. And this became the main focus of contention between the two governments in the next two and a half years. During this period, conflict emerged over political reforms proposed by Governor Christopher Patten. The airport matter, which is basically an economic matter, became an item on the bargaining table. During this period, four financing proposals have been put forward. In the first proposal, dating from April 1992, the Hong Kong government would inject HK$20.3 billion from fiscal reserves and raise debts of HK$73 billion. In the second proposal, dating from September 1992, the British side proposed injecting the entire land premium derived from the sale of railway land, estimated at HK$40 billion, into airport construction. Half of this land premium should have belonged to a land fund of the future SAR government. In the third proposal, dating from June 1993, the British side reduced the amount of debt to HK$43 billion without further requesting the injection of land premium from the land fund. The Chinese side rejected all three proposals in turn. In the fourth proposal, which is still under negotiation, the Hong Kong government would inject HK$40.3 billion from fiscal reserves, HK$20 billion from land sales, and raise a debt of HK$23 billion.

The source of the problem, dating from 1990, is a lack of trust. From the very beginning, China was suspicious that the British side was scheming to drain the fiscal reserves of Hong Kong by building mega-projects. The British could award contracts to foreign enterprises that they favoured, possibly in exchange for other favours. The setting up of an Airport Authority (later proposed by the Hong Kong government to be renamed the Airport Corporation) as an independent enterprise with the authority to award construction contracts and franchises further added to this suspicion. The Airport Authority would remain independent from the government even after July 1997. Furthermore, the Hong Kong government has in the past occasionally allowed construction cost to overshoot budget. China feared that before the return of sovereignty, there was little assurance over actual construction outlay. In this light, the Memorandum of Understanding of 1991 stipulated that HK$25 billion be left as reserves and a maximum debt of HK$5 billion.

Despite the 1991 agreement, the British side appeared reluctant to inject funds from fiscal reserves and instead proposed huge debts. One reason might be that the Hong Kong government has the tradition of underestimating revenue. This has been the government's budgeting philosophy. Another reason might be the ability to raise cheap loans on the market, and in so doing, vast reserves (setting aside HK$25 billion for the SAR government) would be at the discretion of the government. The pressure to raise taxes would be lower and the room for increasing services would be larger, thus helping the popularity of the government in the last years. On the other hand, China's objective was to indirectly control the actual outlay by limiting debts, forcing the Hong Kong government to control costs, because raising taxes or cutting services would face public opposition.

Rising land prices are going to put the stalemate to an end. Recent Government estimates of land premium to be collected from railway land amounted to HK$100 billion, two and a half times that of the original estimate of HK$40 billion in 1992. Moreover, fiscal reserves at the time of sovereignty change could be as high as HK$120 billion. It seems that the Hong Kong government still has a deep cushion to support its spending-for-popularity drive, and the Chinese government has much less fear of being unable to service debts after taking over.

☐ Privatization and Competition

Relative to other developing economies, private enterprises in Hong Kong assume a much larger role in the provision of infrastructural services. The provision of electricity, telecommunications, fuel gas, container terminal services, and bus transport are provided purely on a commercial basis. The government does not hold any shares in these enterprises. Even the railways, which are entirely owned by the government, follow commercial principles in their operations.

The recent trend in government policy seems to be a further inclination to rely on market forces in the provision of infrastructural services. Operations originally run by government departments have been privatized in a variety of ways, and industries controlled by monopolists have been liberalized to allow new entry. Privatization and competition could lead to improvements in quality and quantity of service as well as lower prices. Such changes would enhance Hong Kong's role as an international centre of trade, finance, business and tourism.

Privatization and competition changes have occurred most frequently in the transport sector. The trend can be traced back to the early 1980s. Before 1982, the Hong Kong section of the KCR was operated by a government department. As a result of the development of new towns in the New Territories, and the government's objective to ease road congestion, the railway was electrified and dual-tracked. A public corporation, the KCRC, was set up by statute, with the government as the single shareholder. The hardware was injected into the new corporation and the debt holding was therefore rather light. The KCRC was intended to be run according to commercial principles. Although it is governed by a board whose members are appointed by the government, its operations and planning are independent from the government. In particular, pricing decisions are autonomous. The KCRC also has engaged in real estate development in partnership with private developers, mostly on sites near railway stations. Such developments were very profitable. The public and the government alike regard the KCRC privatization as a success. Its railway operations have yielded consistent profit and dividends have been paid to the government. Compared with the MTRC, however, the KCRC has been favoured by two exclusive factors. First, the KCRC does not have a heavy interest burden. Second, the boom in China–Hong Kong passenger flow has exceeded original growth expectations.

Privatization of the road structure has taken a different form. While most of the roads are owned by the government, there are in operation three "private tunnels." In addition, all toll tunnels owned by the government are now operated by private firms through management contracts. The three "private" tunnels, namely, the Cross Harbour Tunnel (1972), the Eastern Harbour Crossing (1989), the Tate's Cairn Tunnel (1991), and a fourth one which is under construction, the Western Harbour Crossing, are granted operation rights by build-operate-transfer contracts. The tenure of the contract varies from 25 to 30 years. The overall plan of the project is set out by the government, but the detailed design, construction time and pricing mechanism are proposed by the private developer. The government invites bidders to submit proposals, but even when a winner has been selected, detailed negotiations are necessary before a contract can be signed. The contract normally specifies an arbitration mechanism in case disputes arise.

Container terminals have always been operated by private firms, on land developed by the government. There are in operation seven terminals, and the eighth terminal will be fully opened by 1995. These terminals are operated by four private organizations. Over the years, there have been complaints from shippers that the operators are forming a cartel and are charging them monopoly prices. The terminal companies are not economically regulated by the government and genuine competition among them can hardly be ensured. Nevertheless, the government is trying to introduce a new operator to develop the ninth terminal. The granting of this franchise

Infrastructure 221

is now under Sino-British negotiation. The Chinese side is reported to have queried why the grant has not undergone an open bidding process. The government believes, however, that a private treaty that introduces a new competitor can ensure open competition among the operators.

The Kai Tak Airport is operated by the Civil Aviation Department and owned by the government. The Chek Lap Kok airport is designed and will be operated by the Airport Authority, which is a public corporation modelled after the railway corporations. Setting aside its government ownership, the airport would probably be run as a commercial enterprise. The bottom line will be a required rate of return for investment. This principle would have immediate impact on the pricing of the wide range of services offered, such as the handling of flight operations, cargo and passengers, maintenance of aircraft and other ancillary facilities, even though some of these services will be offered by private firms. One advantage of a public corporation, as opposed to a government department, is that treated as a separate organization, the public can assess more readily the financial performance of the airport. Management also has more clearly identified objectives which should aid efficiency.

All urban transport modes, except railways, are operated by private firms. The operations of large and small buses, taxis, trams, peak trams and ferries are run by private firms with no government subsidy. Their patterns of operation are, however, tightly regulated by the government, with the assistance of the Transport Advisory Committee. Recent developments seem to indicate the government's inclination to introduce more competition. Large buses on regular route service were, until 1991, run by the China Motor Bus Co. (CMB) and the Kowloon Motor Bus Co. (KMB) on the basis of route monopolies. These franchises were granted by the government who has the right to approve fares and development plans, and monitor service quality and quantity. Rate of return was also controlled. In the late 1980s, the government was increasingly dissatisfied with the service of the CMB. In an unprecedented move, the government awarded a route to a new competitor, Citybus, in 1991 and in 1992 took away 26 routes from CMB and awarded them to Citybus as well. At the same time, the rate of return control on CMB was removed. For the first time, the government shows that monopoly franchises are "contestable." If the service offered is unsatisfactory, the privilege could be given to a competitor.

Telecommunications are mostly controlled by HKT. But technological and regulatory changes may soon produce new twists in the industry. HKT holds two franchises, a local telephony franchise which expires in 1995 and an international service franchise which expires in 2006. The government has already allowed Wharf Cable to install a second territory-wide network to offer cable TV service. This network can be used in future to transmit data and voice in addition to video. The second network could therefore compete with HKT after 1995. The government also urged HKT to lower international rates. What would happen after these changes is not easy to predict. HKT is a publicly listed company with the largest market capitalization. Its huge profits from the international services make it very strong financially. The local service, on the contrary, barely breaks even because of very low local rates. It is doubtful whether a new competitor can threaten its dominant position. Furthermore, HKT is aggressively exploring multimedia services such as video-on-demand, leveraging on its all-digital territory-wide network. To this end, HK$4 billion is going to be spent in 1995. The company has also applied to the government for a cable TV license. However, further complications arise from new forms of telecommunications. Pagers and cellular phones are being offered by a number of operators through non-exclusive franchises. In addition, satellite services could open new substitute markets. In view of these rapid changes, the government has formed the Office of the Telecommunications Authority to monitor the industries.

☐ Conclusion

The future development of infrastructure would focus on airport and container port development as well as environmental protection. While these developments are government initiatives, due to public corporations and private participation, they would not diminish the role of the private sector. In fact, changes in the direction of privatization and more market competition are gaining momentum. This should not imply that the government can let the market work without regulation and monitoring. As technology advances and industries become more complicated and diversified, the objective is for optimal regulation. Modern regulation involves much more than rate of return control and price ceilings. It is a delicate task of coordination, contracting, enforcement, motivation of private initiatives and balancing of diverse interests.

13

Transport

Stephen L. W. Tang

During the last year, a number of major transport-related events and issues have taken place. First, after close to thirty months of study by a Working Group of the Transport Advisory Committee (TAC), the Committee finally released the much anticipated *Taxi Policy Review* in March. It detailed the policy recommendations of the TAC to the Executive Council (Exco) for endorsement.

Second, upon the backing of the *1990 White Paper on Transport Policy in Hong Kong*, the Administration had commissioned Scott Wilson Kirpatrick, a transport consultancy firm, to conduct a full-scale study of problems in the freight transport industry. The study, released in April, has proposed a package that comprises twenty recommendations that are intended to enhance the efficiency of the freight transport industry, hence to sustain Hong Kong's global competitiveness as a major freight transport hub.

Third, after years of constant struggles, the Legislative Council (Legco) finally won an endorsement from the Administration that they should be more informed of the public transport fare adjustments. Subsequent to that, all major public transport operators are required to brief the Legco's Transport Panel about the magnitude and rationale behind their application for fare adjustment. Though the Legco's formal endorsement is not required, it helps to set the Legco's eventual, substantive involvement in the public transport fare fixing exercise.

Stephen L. W. Tang is a lecturer in the Department of Sociology, The Chinese University of Hong Kong.

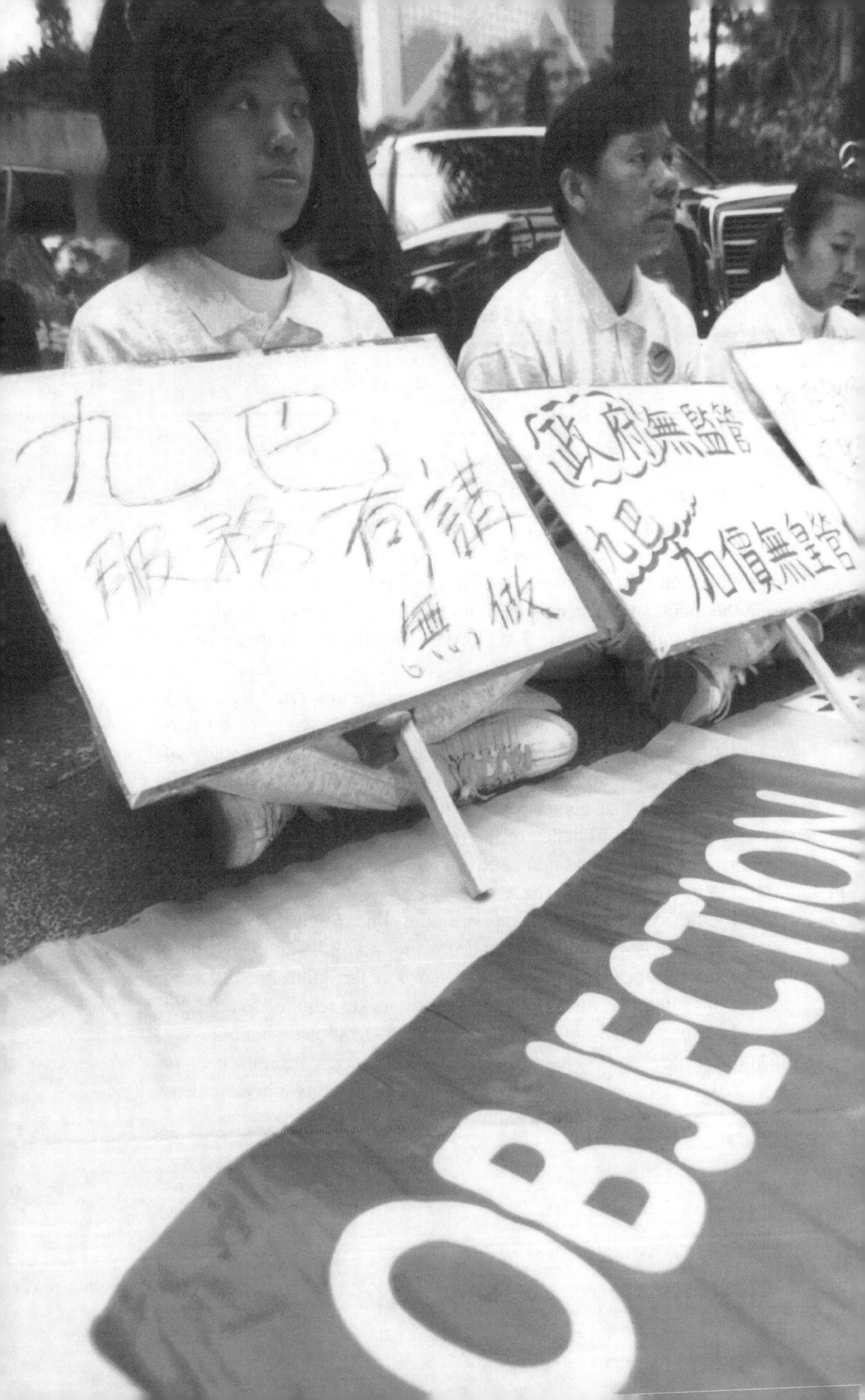
九巴
政府無監管
九巴加價無監管
OBJECTION

Fourth, after more than half a century of *de facto* monopoly of operating bus services on Hong Kong Island, China Motor Bus (CMB) was finally forced to give up part of its network — 26 bus routes altogether — to the Citybus.

Fifth, for a long time, cross-border truck operators have been extremely unhappy with the incessant, corruption-induced inefficiencies on the Chinese side of the border. During the year, they made their angry voices heard by organizing two wildcat strikes that totally paralysed cross-border movement. Each time, senior officials from Shenzhen had to intervene, and make a number of promises designed to increase border control efficiency and penalize the corrupted officials. But once the anger of the truck operators subsided, the previous problems returned.

Sixth, under the direction of the government, some public transport operators had worked out a senior citizen concession scheme that would enable them to enjoy some fare reduction. But the issue of who should pay for the concession has never been settled. When asking for fare adjustment, a few public transport operators claimed the senior citizen concession scheme was one of the contributing factors in their cost increase. This inflamed the whole issue of who should pay for the concession. Politicians claimed that the operators should pay it out of their profits, whereas the travelling public were quite unhappy that they had to cross-subsidize the aged. They object strongly to transport socialism. The Administration claimed that they had made a contribution through exempting the operators from rental charges on temporary depots. Nonetheless, operators were quite reluctant to do so as they insisted on having paid their share through corporate taxes. There has not been any consensus on the issue so far. The issue will be raised once again in the next round of fare adjustment. At the end of the day, the travelling public still has to shoulder the major part of the expenses.

And finally, feeling uncomfortable with the much deteriorated road congestion problem, and its impacts on Hong Kong's long-term economic competitiveness, the Governor directed the Secretary for Transport to form a Steering Committee comprising top ranking civil servants from relevant departments to study the problem, and work out a solution package as soon as possible. It is likely that the package will be announced in his third Governor's speech late this year. The public will closely watch not only the content of the package, but also the determination of the Administration to solve this perennial problem.

All these events and issues are of great importance, and should be addressed at some length. However, given the scope and length of the chapter, it is unrealistic to address each of them in turn. Instead, the author will focus on a few and analyse them in relative depth. Our major attention will focus on the *Taxi Policy Review* and the Freight Transport Study. We will also briefly identify a few issues (i.e., congestion solution package, CMB franchise renewal, the locus of transport decision-making, etc.) that are expected to dominate our discussion on transport field in the year ahead.

☐ Taxi Policy Review: A Much Needed Revisit

In October 1991, the TAC formed a Working Group to review the government's taxi policy and to make recommendations to the TAC in due course. The *Taxi Policy Review* was released in March 1994, and contains some eighteen recommendations. It has been submitted to the Exco for consideration and approval. These recommendations are grouped together under four major categories: (1) taxi licensing system; (2) fare policy and structure; (3) law enforcement; and (4) quality of taxi services.

Taxi Licensing System

The taxi licensing system is unquestionably the most critical issue in any review of taxi policy. The Working Group had looked into the possibility of issuing a seven-year, fixed-term, and non-transferable licence (known as *Type B* licence), and informally tested the responses from the trades. To their disappointment, it attracted drastic, negative responses from both the trade associations and frontline drivers as impracticable. Hence, the TAC decided not to consider this option further. Instead, it made five recommendations under the heading of the taxi licensing system:

1. There should be no pre-set quota on the number of taxi licences to be issued in a given period of time.
2. Taxi licences should be issued as and when necessary, having regard to the demand for taxi services, the financial viability of the trade, and the capacity of our road system.
3. In a public tender exercise for taxi licences, an applicant can bid for only one licence.
4. Procedures for the transfer of taxi licences should be tightened to dampen manipulation.

5. New licences should not be transferable within twelve months after the date of issue.

Capacity of the road network seems to be the only and most critical factor in the determination of the taxi fleet size. Similar to private cars, the government has always held that taxis are an inefficient mode of public transport, hence they should not be accorded a high priority in Hong Kong's public transport hierarchy. This position has been unchanged for close to a decade. The rapid deterioration of road congestion throughout the territory in recent years has further affirmed the government's determination to keep the growth of private or semi-private (e.g., taxis) vehicle under control. Hence, it is very unlikely that the government would be prepared to increase the taxi fleet size.

Thus, taking the first two recommendations together would lead one to conclude that the government is, and will also be, impotent in resolving the issue on exorbitant speculations of taxi licences. This explains clearly why despite the government's threat of increasing the taxi fleet size, the market fails to respond negatively in terms of the current market price of taxi licences. In other words, these two recommendations might be redundant.

The third recommendation, while upholding the public tender exercise for taxi licences as a fair and effective system, makes a significant deviation from the previous mode of tendering. It calls for a system that only allows an applicant to bid for one licence. However, at the end of the day, the market premium for a taxi licence may only be marginally affected. It does not exclude the formation of the cartels in total. If they intend to do so, they could pool together a significant number of individual applicants, and ask each of them to submit the applications separately. Furthermore, given the relatively small number of licences to be issued each time, the cartels could still control the premium through the operation of a taxi trade futures market. They have been doing this for the last decade. In other words, the effect of such a recommendation has yet to be proved.

Among all the recommendations under taxi licensing and structure, there is only one that touches on the existing licences. The fourth recommendation calls upon the Administration to tighten the procedures for the transfer of taxi licences as a way to dampen speculation. In general terms, the TAC wants the Administration to bar the unregistered transfers of ownership of a taxi before a legal transfer is registered. They consider this as an effective measure to curb taxi licence speculation. In specific terms, the TAC asks the Administration to tighten the present transfer procedure by requiring both the buyer and seller to register the transfer in person. They expect this would regularize the transfer of taxi ownership and, therefore, taxi licences. This recommendation may touch on some sensitive issues regarding the operation of the open and futures markets, and inevitably, the Administration may not have sufficient resources to tackle its complexity and enforcement. Hence, it is likely that such a recommendation would be accorded low priority.

In short, the TAC has failed to make any significant policy changes in the taxi licensing system. This is not unexpected as politically feasible, infrastructurally sustainable, and administratively implementable options are rather limited. The TAC warns the trade that if speculative activities are harming the operational efficiency and licence premium stability of the taxi industry, they are prepared to dump the market with a no pre-set quota at an unspecified time. Nonetheless, the warning is practically useless as the capacity of the TAC to issue any new licences would be severely constrained by the capabilities of both the existing and future road infrastructure.

Fare Policy and Structure

The taxi is a form of public transport, but it is more than that. It is a personalized form of public transport that provides a door-to-door service. Moreover, it serves another extremely vital policy function, namely, avoiding the rapid build-up for the needs of private form of transport. This is particularly so in those affluent newly industrialized economies like Hong Kong and Singapore where ownership of a family car has become increasingly more affordable to a large proportion of its population. Easy accessibility and affordability of taxis provides an incentive for most potential owners to defer car ownership, and strengthens a government's bargaining power in taking fiscal measures to dampen the surging demands for private transport. Hence, any price-fixing of taxi fares would have to take into account these policy considerations. Throughout the review, the TAC has not paid adequate consideration to this important policy dimension. Instead, it only highlights five recommendations:

1. The policy of maintaining a fare differential of 5 to 7 times between urban taxis and other modes of public transport and 3 to 4 times between New Territories taxis and other modes should be maintained.

2. Like all other modes of public transport, taxi fares should be frontloaded (i.e., the rate of flagfall charge should be higher than the subsequent incremental charge).
3. There seems to be no justification for increasing artificially the rate of the waiting time charge to deter passengers from taking taxis to busy commercial areas as this would be unfair to many other passengers who may be caught in a traffic jam outside such areas (e.g., as a result of a traffic accident or road works).
4. The number of surcharges should be kept to a minimum. The introduction of a typhoon surcharge should not be pursued.
5. The definition of what constitutes a piece of baggage should be worked out between the Transport Department and the trade.

The first recommendation is a repeated affirmation of the taxi fare policy in the *1990 White Paper on Transport Policy in Hong Kong*. The maintenance of a significant fare differential between taxi and other modes of public transport is based on two presumptions: (1) to discourage the joint use of taxis as a cheap form of public transport; and (2) to regulate the use of taxis for short-distance travels. Basically, the existing fare structure has adequately addressed this issue. It is hardly true that taxi is a cheap form of public transport in Hong Kong. Any further increase in taxi fares may lead to a widening differential, and subsequently induce more incentives for potential owners to shift to private car ownership.

While confirming the needs for maintaining the differentials, the TAC has gone a bit further by proposing a frontloaded pricing strategy (FPS). By making the first two kilometres more expensive, FPS may help to dampen short-distance travel demands. However, in Hong Kong, not all short-distance travels are fully taken care of by an inexpensive community-based feeder service. Therefore, the use of frontloaded pricing would be grossly unfair as it poses a double penalty on the users.

If the Administration accepts the TAC's recommendation without working out a balance between frontloaded pricing and the differentials, taxi fares would become excessively expensive. Subsequently, it may pose a number of problems: (1) taking a taxi may become beyond the reach of a large proportion of wage earners; (2) a taxi's dead mileage may increase substantially as drivers have to move around more frequently searching for customers; and (3) it may increase the incentives of the middle class to own cars as the cost differentials between taking taxis on a regular basis and maintaining a car of their own would become minimal.

Road congestion has deteriorated in recent years. It is not uncommon to find that cars are locked in the traffic for tens of minutes. Taxi drivers are particularly hard hit by road congestion as their incomes depend largely on both the number of trips generated and paid mileage. Yet, the TAC has taken a misconceived view that taxi drivers are taking advantage of the waiting charge while customers are unjustifiably penalized. If refused hire is allowed, the problem could easily be solved. But the situation is not like this, legally, taxi drivers have no options but to take customers wherever they are legally allowed to enter. To put the issue into proper perspective, drivers are being penalized when they are directed to move into the congested corridors and areas. A prudent businessperson surely would agree with taxi drivers that the issue on waiting charge should have been taken seriously. Without that, it is not illogical that drivers are refusing hire or bargaining with customers. This is something which prudent policy-makers ought to take into account when formulating taxi fare policy. But this is not the case when one reads the third recommendation in this section. The presumption behind it seems quite naïve. It reflects a lack of understanding of the trade.

In sum, in the area of taxi fare policy and structure, where there is lots of scope for development, the TAC has failed to offer anything substantive. Their advocacy for the adoption of FPS, though nothing new in itself, is moving in the right direction. But throughout the review, there are very few details on what policy objectives the TAC wants to achieve with the implementation of FPS. In future, the Administration once again may be forced to take a new look into the issue as the problems linger.

Law Enforcement

Taxi malpractice is one of the major items in the Transport Complaints Unit (TCU)'s inventory of complaints. There has been a phenomenal growth in the number of complaints about taxi malpractice since 1986. In 1993, out of 12,793 complaints received by the TCU, there were 3,242 cases relating to taxi malpractice. They constituted 25.3 per cent of all complaints received by the TCU. The complaints about taxi malpractice fall into four major categories: overcharging, refusing hire, misconduct and poor driving manner, and failure to take the most direct route. Complaints at times may be rather subjective. Experiences confirm that other than refusing hire, most complaints about taxi malpractice are usually dropped for a number of reasons. They include: (1) complainants fail to supply adequate information; or (2) preliminary investigations show no further grounds for action.

Transport

Police records have also shown a rising trend of taxi malpractice. The figures over the last five years have fluctuated quite a bit. The figures for 1989, 1990, 1991, 1992, and 1993 are as follows: 1,076, 615, 712, 945, and 1,965. Between 1992 and 1993, there was a phenomenal growth of slightly more than 100 per cent in police action against taxi malpractice. In 1993, out of 1,965 cases of action against taxi malpractice — some 696 cases belonged to "soliciting passengers," and another 542 cases falling into "refusing hire." These two categories represented close to two-thirds of the cases. This differs notably from the proportion in the preceding years. Take 1992 for example, when there were only 57 and 264 actions against soliciting passengers and refusing hire, respectively. They represented only one-third of all cases of action. There may be two reasons for the phenomenal growth in police action along these lines: (1) the situation of taxi malpractice had further deteriorated down the road; and (2) there might be policy reasons that pushed for police action against taxis. Compared with figures in preceding years, the second explanation seems more persuasive. Some hint that police action against "soliciting passengers" and "refusing hire" were stepped up in 1993 to prepare the factual and political grounds for the TAC's recommendations on stiffer law enforcements on taxis. Such a speculation may not be too illogical. In fact, it is strategic for the Administration to do so as a pretext for the announcement and promotion of a new set of policies. Besides, politically, any law enforcements against taxi malpractice are bound to gain public support. It is a totally different thing whether it is equitable and fair to the parties concerned.

Unlike the provisions of the taxi licensing system and fare policy and structure, the provisions on law enforcement are very specific. There are altogether five recommendations under this section:

1. To maintain an adequate deterrent effect, the maximum penalties for taxi offences such as "refusing hire," "soliciting passengers," and "overcharging" should be increased from the present $5,000 to at least $10,000.
2. To facilitate law enforcement, the most prevalent taxi offences (i.e., "refusing hire" and "soliciting passengers") should be brought under the fixed penalty system.
3. Procedures for lodging complaints against taxi malpractice should be simplified to facilitate reporting.
4. Fare receipts should be issued on demand, again to facilitate reporting.

5. The proposed demerit points system for taxi drivers and operators should not be pursued for the time being.

Taxi drivers gave three main reasons against the adoption of the measures recommended in (1) and (2). First, the increase in the maximum penalty would increase the financial burdens of most casual offenders but could hardly deter those who are repeated offenders. A $10,000 fine is around 22 to 24 times an individual taxi driver's daily income or close to a month of his earning. This is considered to be unconscionable. Second, the fixed penalty system is the most convenient, easily implementable administrative measure, but can be quite unfair to most law-abiding drivers. Without safeguards, its convenience can easily be abused by customers. Of course, taxi drivers who disagree can appear before the court to make his case. Yet by doing so, they have to waste at least a working day. Even if they succeed in contesting the case, they still have to forego a day's income. To avoid the loss of a day's income, many taxi drivers have no option but to pay for the penalty instead of appearing before the court. This would be grossly unfair to them. Representatives of taxi drivers have called upon the Administration to seriously consider a compensation scheme that would enable the innocent drivers to claim any losses. Third, most of the offences which the TAC recommends to be included in the fixed penalty system are not clearly defined. The ambiguities could easily become the major sources of many conflicts between customers and drivers.

In response to these two punitive measures which frontline taxi drivers considered as unconscionable, they initially planned to stage some kind of showdown to express their dissatisfaction. Subsequently, owing to the untimely death of Chan Kam-pui, the most powerful representative and speaker of frontline drivers, the plan was stalled. Prolonged factional fights among the key contenders to take over the leadership have further weakened the unity and authority of the Joint Committee of the Urban Taxi Drivers Associations, hence grossly weakening their bargaining power with the Administration. Towards mid-1994, there have been signs that the power struggles among them are gradually settling down. Instead of having one powerful Joint Committee, a few driver associations will be formed. Nonetheless, despite their differences in leadership, they may once again form a united front to take up the issues with the Administration.

Simplifying the complaint procedures against taxi malpractice, and the production of a fare receipt upon request are recommendations in the right direction. They are fair to both passengers and drivers, and have attracted little objection from the trade. Technical problems are the only concerns for drivers, which may not be too difficult to solve. Overcharging has always been one of the major complaints received by the TCU, but cases that deserve further action are rather limited. This has also been confirmed by the police action records. From 1989 through 1993, the police are only taken 187 prosecutions on overcharging. As compared with 624 cases of prosecution on taxi meter offences over the same period, overcharging is a relatively trivial problem. In fact, after the Independent Commission Against Corruption (ICAC) action on taxi meter tampering in 1992, prosecution on taxi meter offences has dropped to a record low of only 18 cases in 1993 as compared with the 161 cases in 1992. The production of fare receipt will surely help improving the public image of the trade, and minimize the potential conflicts between customers and drivers.

In short, the TAC is prudent not to pursue the adoption of a demerit points system at this stage. This helps to reduce the tension between the TAC and frontline drivers. However, their recommendations to increase the maximum penalty and to adopt a fixed penalty system for malpractice offences may have gone a bit far, and lack an in-depth understanding of the problems confronting frontline drivers. Furthermore, their recommendations to simplify the complaint procedures and to issue a fare receipt upon request are in the right direction. Overall, their recommendations in law enforcement are more specific than those in other areas. Perhaps, this reflects the difficulties they are encountering in other areas where the scope for changes is severely restricted.

Quality of Taxi Services

The TAC has briefly touched on the issue of quality of services, but run short of any concrete recommendations on what they intended to achieve. They outline three recommendations under the heading of quality of taxi services:

1. An updated taxi service guide should be made available to the travelling public.
2. A separate booklet setting out a Code of Practice for taxi drivers and operators should be made available.
3. Induction courses for new taxi drivers should be organized by the trade to prepare them for their new career and encourage them to provide a good service.

Updating the taxi service guide can hardly be considered as anything new. In fact, it is the responsibility of the Administration to update it on regular basis. Surprisingly, the TAC has made this as an independent recommendation. The recommendation to produce a separate booklet setting out a Code of Practice for taxi drivers and operators is in the right direction. However, it runs short of any specifics on what the Code of Practice should be. Surprisingly, the TAC advises that the Code of Practice should be observed by both the drivers and the operators. Perhaps, the TAC may have missed the important issue of the lack of common link and interest between the two interested parties. Thus, for anything substantive to be drawn from a Code of Practice, heed must be paid to make operators (in this context, the licence traders) jointly accountable for the problems frontline drivers are facing. It would be a major breakthrough in an industry where ownership and actual operation are in different hands if that is to materialize.

Another naïvety of the TAC is its recommendation that induction courses for new taxi drivers should be organized by the trade to prepare them for their new career and encourage them to provide a good service. As mentioned earlier, in the context of the taxi industry, licence traders/ operators and frontline workers are two totally separate groups. Licence traders are interested mainly in licence premium and rental rate, whereas frontline workers have to cope with the daily problems associated with the actual taxi operation. The former groups, as a cluster of cartels, do have the resources, but have not been keen to plough back a minor part of their profits to ease the operation of frontline workers. On the other hand, frontline drivers are totally preoccupied with the pressure to meet the total operating cost of running a taxi. Driver associations are exclusively run by a small number of activist groups. They lack manpower, professional knowledge, and organizational capabilities to run and sustain a cluster of robust training programmes for new entrants. This was confirmed in an interview the author had with Chan Kam-pui, who felt extremely excited about the idea, and also encouraged the Joint Committee of the Urban Taxi Drivers Associations to run an experimental programme. He ended up advising the Administration to take over the responsibility.

When the TAC calls upon the trade to organize such programmes, it is not clear which groups they are actually referring to. If none of these groups have the resources to do, would the TAC advise the Administration to make it mandatory for them to carry out the jobs? This, of course, would be dubious. Should the TAC have a better understanding of the industry structure, they may opt for advising the government to encourage either the Open Learning Institute or the Vocational Training Institute to offer the programmes.

In short, the TAC is correct that quality of taxi services should be further improved. However, they are quite naïve as to how it should be promoted. Advising the trade to develop a Code of Practice for drivers and operators who have little common interests in the actual operation of a taxi on the road seems quite irrelevant. Likewise, recommending the trade to organize training programmes for new entrants without realizing that there are practically no institutional infrastructure seems unimaginable. Perhaps, it would not be going too far to speculate that these recommendations are unlikely to be implemented.

Conclusion

Concluding our discussions on the *Taxi Policy Review*, it may be too harsh to say that the review is a redundant one. Yet, for most in the industry, this may not be too far from reality. There are surely many pressing problems with the taxi industry, but unfortunately they have not been properly dealt with. In the years ahead, when a new TAC is put into force again, there may be another compelling need to have another taxi review exercise.

☐ **Freight Transport Study**

Since the early 1980s, Hong Kong has benefited substantially from the sustained, rapid economic growth of South China. Currently, the transport system in Hong Kong is not a self-contained one any more. Both the cross-border and the related local backup demands have generated a remarkable growth in the number of goods vehicles in Hong Kong since the mid-1970s. In 1976, a year when China just began to explore the possibility of opening up its economy, there were only 32,582 registered goods vehicles. In 1981, 1986, 1991 and 1993, the fleet size jumped to 52,825, 73,553, 117,592 and 118,757 respectively. Over the period from 1976 to 1993, there has been 2.6 times increase in the number of goods vehicles. This extraordinary growth has imposed tremendous pressures on Hong Kong's limited road spaces and supporting infrastructure. With Hong Kong's further integration with the economy of South China, the trend is likely to be rise.

The *1990 White Paper on Transport Policy in Hong Kong* had recognized the problem, and recommended the Administration to fund a study of freight transport as soon as possible. The objective of the study was to advise the government on how to improve the efficiency of the freight transport industry without posing significant adverse effects on the economy. The study was commissioned to a private consulting firm. Its work commenced in June 1991, and its much expected final report was submitted to the government in April 1994. The final report contains two volumes with mountains of statistical analyses and an executive summary. As this is not the proper place to deal with these statistical analyses in depth, we only intend to briefly outline their main recommendations, and address some of the issues raised therein.

A Freight Transport Policy

At the outset, the consultants hint that there should be two presumed roles of the government: (1) the government should guide and strengthen the development of the freight transport sector in Hong Kong so that the territory can remain a major international port, business and service centre, and together with South China, a major manufacturing region; and (2) the government should also ensure that such development does not jeopardize other standards and initiatives to improve social and environmental well-being. Both involve the macro-management of freight transport. They are not necessarily compatible with each other.

The first presumption calls for government's active participation in providing a framework of development, but the second warns of the needs for a balance so that the development framework should not inhibit well-being in other areas. Past experiences on transport policy formulations (i.e., electronic road pricing, the introduction of mass-carrier-only lanes, etc.) have shown that a stress on balance has always resulted in a total impasse. The real issue is not whether a balance could be made, but whether the government and the politicians have the sufficient vision to realize the critical nature of a policy and the courage to push through a good policy even if there were opposition of different kinds and degrees to it. The construction of a replacement airport at Chek Lap Kok, the adoption of electronic road pricing, and the introduction of some time/direction-specific bus-only lanes are excellent examples of its kind.

The report has called for the development of a freight transport policy. It suggested that measures to develop the freight transport sector in Hong

Transport 237

Kong must aim at achieving financial competitiveness, economic efficiency, environmental acceptability, a good level of safety, and implementability based on public support and commitment.

These recommended visions look absolutely superb, and few would object to them provided that they are devisable. Otherwise, it is just another puff from the knowledge salesmen. At a closer look, each of these objectives represents the very best a highly competitive, efficient and humane society which would be expected to achieve. A vision is nothing but a vision unless the policy-makers are able to devise a well-integrated package of programmes that are achievable within the limits of their resources. The consultants seem to be confident that their vision is achievable. They offer a package of prescriptions, including some twenty-eight recommendations that are clustered around six major issue headings: (1) overnight parking; (2) daytime parking and loading/unloading; (3) container storage; (4) port operations; (5) cross-border freight movement; and (6) impacts on the community. Before a critical review of how innovative and effective these measures are, it may be appropriate to briefly outline them.

Overnight Parking

Lack of parking spaces has always been controversial issue in Hong Kong. This is not only a problem for private car owners, but more so for goods vehicles and taxi operators. Over the years, goods vehicle operators have been seen as the most militant groups in their protests against police enforcement action on illegal parking. They accused the government of using them as scapegoats when politicians and the public are impatient with the illegal parking-induced congestions and road hazards. The consultants are working in the right direction in taking a serious inquiry into the problems surrounding goods vehicle parking. The report differentiates parking problems into two categories, namely overnight parking and daytime parking (together with the issues of loading and unloading).

Under overnight parking, the consultants have proposed nine different recommendations:

1. (R1/2) Reclassify goods vehicles and modify their length limits. This will allow corresponding changes to the dimensions of on-street and off-street parking spaces to permit more efficient use.
2. (R3) Carry out area-specific investigations and revise Hong Kong Planning Standards and Guidelines to ensure that parking standards

are suitable to meet current requirements and to ensure that future developments do not cause similar problems. The implementation of new standards will also help encourage further provision of parking spaces in redeveloped lots and cope with specific demands for parking spaces.
3. (R4) Increase the allocation of on-street parking spaces for goods vehicles so as to reduce illegal parking and double-parking of these vehicles thereby alleviating the consequent congestion of some local streets.
4. (R5) Allocate short-term tenancy sites to provide surface goods vehicles parks on a rolling programme. Formalize the procedure for designating short-term tenancy sites to ensure proper planning in the provision of parking spaces for each district and avoid sudden cancellation of sites without appropriate continency arrangements.
5. (R6) Conduct a feasibility study into the use of landfill sites for goods vehicles parking/holding areas.
6. (R7) Build goods vehicle garages to provide additional parking spaces and help relieve the shortage of parking spaces in the urban area.
7. (R8) Provide light goods vehicles parking spaces at the lower levels of new multi-storey car parks where appropriate.
8. (R9) Increase enforcement of goods vehicles parking restrictions to reduce illegal parking and double-parking of goods vehicles and the consequent congestion this causes.

Anyone who has served a member of the traffic and transport or environment committees in any district board since the early 1980s will find recommendations R4 through R9 being repeated items of discussion in their meetings. Besides, anyone who has made an effort to read the complaints section of local newspapers would laugh endlessly at these recommendations. Any government officials who have ever dealt with district-level transport and planning issues will tell you that by making these recommendations, the consultants probably have presumed them to be idiots. Police officers and housing managers would tell you that if they were given free hands to take enforcement, they surely would do these simple things. They can hardly understand why the public has to pay a substantial consultancy fee for such trivial recommendations. This is no wonder why, when interviewed by the author, some officials who refuse to be named want to distance themselves from the study. They acknowledge

Transport

some novelty in recommendations (R1 through R3), but readily refuted their practicality: what purposes will be served by reclassifying goods vehicles and modifying goods vehicles length limits if there is practically no way they could find additional land in the developed areas for uses like on-street and off-street parking? Likewise, at the demand of individual district boards and the trade, they have already done tens of area-specific investigations in individual administrative districts over the years. To their disappointment, few pieces of land could be set aside for goods vehicle parking purposes. In short, few would agree that the consultants have really offered something in this area.

Daytime Parking and Loading/Unloading

In the freight transport industry, rarely are there cases of working two shifts. There are clearly economic reasons behind it. To cope with the one shift schedule, goods vehicles' operating hours tend to be packed compactly into ten hours. During the operating hours, they are either on the road or in the process of loading and unloading. In very unusual cases would the operators park their cars in the developed commercial and industrial areas. So, with the exception of Sundays and public holidays, daytime parking is a relatively minor issue. On the other hand, queuing, and improper parking for loading and unloading are two major daytime problems for the freight transport industry. The consultants did recognized the seriousness of these problems and also their potential hazards and inconvenience to the general public. In reply, they offered two recommendations to address the problems. First, (R10) carry out investigation and implementation measures towards lot assembly to address problems of on-street goods vehicle activities in older industrial areas. The assembly of larger lots in existing industrial areas, for redevelopment in the long term, is necessary so that these sites can accommodate the proper parking and loading/unloading facilities within the curtilage of the site. Second, (R11) carry out selective re-zoning of sites to non-industrial use to reduce the density of industrial development and associated goods vehicles congestion problems in existing industrial areas in the long term.

At first sight, the first recommendation (R10) looks quite innovative and attractive. Frontline transport and police officers in the administrative districts would remind you that they have always been keen to find assembly lots so that good vehicles don't have to queue on the limited road space waiting for loading and unloading. However, there are a number of problems with such an arrangement. First of all, there are only very little lots available in the developed urban and industrial areas for such purposes. The situation is no better in the new towns where most of the empty lots have either been rented out temporarily or are in the hands of developers. Second, even if lots are available, there are problems with their management. High operating costs may drive temporary operators to charge a high premium for the assembly. Hence, the option may not be attractive enough to the goods vehicles operators. Instead, they may choose to queue on the road unless the police takes strict enforcement. This seems to be very unlikely as the police have become politically more sensitive than before. Third, when lots are available, they may be far away from the loading and unloading areas. That generally creates insurmountable communication problems among the drivers, the goods owners, and the lot management. Consequently, it reduces the option's attractiveness. Finally, because of the high costs of land in nearly every part of Hong Kong, property developers seldom find this kind of management-intensive operation worth their consideration. In short, the consultants may not have acquainted themselves sufficiently with the operating environment, and thus came up with a recommendation that offers little scope for further consideration.

The recommendation (R11) to carry out selective re-zoning of sites to non-industrial use to reduce the density of industrial development and associated goods vehicles congestion problems in existing industrial areas in the long term seems extremely weird. Anyone who has some touch with planning and property development in Hong Kong would know that the property developers have been doing this for a long time in the redevelopment of industrial areas. The trend has further been facilitated by the relocation of the manufacturing industry both across the border and into the new towns since the late 1970s. Most of the redevelopment projects in the urban/industrial areas are in the form of industrial/office or industrial/commercial complexes. Neither of these really need as much loading and unloading as those in the conventional industrial complexes.

In sum, the consultants' lack of an in-depth understanding of actual goods vehicle operation may be one of the reasons why the two recommendations they make under this heading have been taken as trivial. Of course, night-time operation may be an alternative, but the viability of it as an option is severely limited by Hong Kong's severe shortages of labour, the general reluctance of industrial labour to work a night shift, and the one shift operation in the trade.

Container Storage

Over the years, the Administration has been admired by many for its capability to synchronize the planning of Hong Kong's container port facilities with the growth of its export/import/re-export trade. Some suspect that the competition with Singapore for leadership as the region's international port has exerted sufficient drive for the government to carefully watch the needs of our port facilities. On the other hand, there are others who feel the government has failed completely in terms of the provision of basic supporting infrastructures for the freight containerization. The severe shortage of container storage facilities is an excellent example. Perhaps Singapore has offered something extraordinary that deserves the Hong Kong government's attention. In the realm of competence and growth in port and freight transport containerization, Singapore impresses outsiders as having been able to cope with the situation better. Few would find in Singapore the same containerization-induced visual and environmental pollution as in Hong Kong. The lack of adequate provision for container storage facilities has forced many of the container trucks to run an extremely high dead mileage to and from the far away illegal container storage parks throughout New Territories West and Northwest. Consequently, the Tuen Mun Highway and the old Castle Peak Road have been flooded with an unplanned growth of truck traffic. It has severely affected the quality of life in the region. Moreover, every now and then, the transport networks in the vicinity of the Kwai Chung container port terminals are totally paralysed by freight transport.

Putting the problem in proper perspective, the consultants rightly advise that "in the short term, more land should be allocated on the West Kowloon Reclamation for port back-up. This will bring economic benefits due to the shorter travel distance to the Kwai Chung container port and hence reduce traffic congestion. The permanent use of the land on the West Kowloon Reclamation and the Tuen Mun Port Development Area for container storage and container vehicle parking should also be studied in detail since substantial economic benefits are expected." This is very much in line with the demands of residents who live in both the New Territories South and the New Territories West. Since the early 1980s, they have complained incessantly about the abuses of many agricultural lands along the Tuen Mun Highway corridor as container storage and truck parking facilities. Consequently, a massive volume of traffic totally unrelated to the original designs of the Tuen Mun Highway have contributed to the road congestion in region. They call upon the government to take measures to penalize the abusers. In response, the consultants recommend that the Administration introduces legislation/licensing to control non-conforming uses (R13), and conduct a study on how this could be achieved. An investigation of how this could be achieved should be carried out. They presume that upon implementation in the long term, traffic and environmental conditions will be improved.

On the other hand, the freight transport operators claim that they have no intention to abuse the agricultural lands for container storage and truck parking. In fact, using New Territories West as freight backups is not an economically sound strategy. They are also extremely concerned with the high cost incurred by dead mileage, the associated labour costs, and the additional capital outlay. They claimed the inaction and lack of planning by the government was the cause of all these problems. Furthermore, government planners, police and transport officials maintain that they have always been working very hard to find temporary solutions for container storage and truck parking facilities in the vicinity of the container port, but responses from politicians in the district have always been negative. Few politicians would be ready to endorse the proposal of having container backup facilities located in their own constituencies. Officials claim that it is politically very appealing to call upon the government to take action against abuses, yet when solutions are proposed, few would endorse them. Hence, it may be unconscionable to take action against freight transport operators when there are no legally acceptable alternatives provided. The consultants' recommendation may be a bit naïve considering the operational limits.

Port Operations and Cross-border Freight Movement

It was mentioned earlier that as the economy of South China has gradually become an extension of Hong Kong's industrial capital, our transport system has to serve concurrently the needs of the Delta's global trade activities. As there is no direct rail link between the Delta and the container port, cross-border trucking has been the dominant mode of transport. Trucking activities have created serious congestion problems, and at times total chaos, in the vicinity of the Kwai Chung container terminals where it also forms the nerve centre of transport connecting New Territories West and South with the rest of Hong Kong. The situations have been particularly serious both before and after long holidays, and after typhoon. It has not been uncommon for the traffic flows in the vicinity of the container terminals to be turned into a total impasse for hours as a result of container trucks waiting for loading and unloading. That in turn seriously affects the livelihood of ordinary residents in the New Territories South and West.

In response, the consultants recommend a number of measures to the government:

1. (R14) Coordinate with the Guangdong Province to extend the operating hours for at least one of the border crossings to match the 24-hour operation of the container port.
2. (R15) Encourage a container booking system to avoid sudden surges and minimize truck movements to and from the container port.
3. (R16) Review requirements and implement improvements to waterfront facilities to ensure proper planning of waterfront facilities taking account of the associated traffic impacts.
4. (R17) In the long term, build a Port Rail Line to Kwai Chung.
5. (R18) Make the border permits transferable between crossing points so as to make more effective use of the crossing capacity.
6. (R19) Keep the border processing facilities under constant review and expand them as necessary to match cross-border traffic demand.

To the disappointment of many, the recommended measures are not substantively innovative. Most of them have been widely discussed and debated by the public since the mid-1980s. A number of observations could be made with regard to them. Firstly, in the late 1980s when the government was working on the Second Comprehensive Transport Study, as a serving member of the TAC the author had been active in warning the government both formally and informally of the need to operate the Lok Ma Chau crossing around the clock once it was put into operation so as to increase the operational efficiency of the cross-border freight transport industry, and to reduce the daytime overburdened road system. Unfortunately, the proposal was rejected by the Administration on grounds of policy, needs and lack of manpower resources. It took a long time and a lot of public pressure before the government adopted the proposal in late 1991. Happily, the idea had finally been endorsed by both governments, and is in the process of implementation. Secondly, it is unquestionably a good idea to encourage terminal managers to adopt a booking system, but how far can it be extended depends very much on the operational efficiencies of both our road networks and the relevant government departments on both sides of the border. Thirdly, recommendations R16 and R17 have already been fully taken into account in the Port and Airport Development Strategy, and the Railway Development Study. Furthermore, they have also been comprehensively discussed, debated, and endorsed by the community and the Legco. Their inclusion here as major recommendations seems a bit repetitive. Finally, the recommendation to make the border permits transferable between crossing points, and to keep border processing facilities under constant review looks a bit cumbersome to be incorporated as these should be the routines of the relevant government departments.

Impacts on the Community

Throughout the study, the consultants have time and again stressed the importance of balancing the interests of freight transport as an engine of economic growth and the community. They have listed some thirteen recommendations on the impact of freight transport operation on the community. As some of these overlap with the preceding sections, we will focus only those not mentioned before. They include recommendations to:

1. (R19) Extend truck management policies to facilitate goods vehicle movement and to reduce goods vehicle traffic on unsuitable roads and at times when their adverse impacts on traffic flows and the adjacent community are deemed unacceptable;
2. (R20) Coordinate and increase enforcement of goods vehicle weight control measures to improve road traffic safety and reduce road damage;
3. (R21) Strengthen existing goods vehicles inspection procedures to improve road traffic safety and provide environmental benefits;
4. (R22) Review/evaluate goods vehicles engine modifications, monitor the development of new engine/fuel technology and development of exhaust treatment, to minimize the air and noise pollution caused by goods vehicles. This will ensure that environmental concerns, with regard to air pollution and noise in the urban areas, can be minimized;
5. (R25) Introduce a demonstration scheme for dangerous goods vehicle facilities to reduce risks posed by dangerous goods vehicles;
6. (R26) Provide an air cargo landside shuttle service from the

existing air cargo terminal at Kai Tak to reduce the number of goods vehicles taking goods to Chek Lap Kok airport, thereby eliminating excessive journey lengths and travelling times, and poor vehicle utilization;

7. (R27) In the long term, the establishment of new air cargo consolidation centres, other than at Kai Tak, should be given serious consideration; and

8. (R28) The introduction of use-related charging for all traffic should be investigated. This is potentially the most flexible and equitable means of restraining traffic demand within the capacity of the road network.

The set of recommendations listed under "Impacts on the Community," with the exception of R26 and R27, is nothing but a litany of all the "ought to." Quite a few of them (i.e., R20, R21, R25, R22, etc.) have been implemented on a partial scale usually as consequences of some serious road accidents involving goods vehicles or complaints from environment lobbyists. Their inclusion as policy recommendations seems unnecessarily repetitive and crude. Their recommendations relating to the replacement airport at Chek Lap Kok (R26, R27) are clearly ones that deserve the Provisional Airport Authority and relevant government departments to get an in-depth assessment.

The last of their recommendations is surely nothing new except that it is coined in a less controversial manner. They call upon the government to investigate the possibility of introducing a use-related charging for all traffic. The use-related road charging strategy had long been recognized by both the community and the government. This was undoubtedly reflected in the study of electronic road pricing (ERP) and the unsuccessful public consultation following its publication in 1986. Strong opposition to the ERP scheme had led the Administration to stop considering its implementation, thus contributing substantively to the rapid deterioration of road congestion problem in Hong Kong. In 1989, the government had put forward a new round of public consultation on transport strategy which aimed at providing a solid policy to move Hong Kong into the next century. It should have provided an excellent opportunity to test the public's response to use-related road pricing as a strategy to improve the road-use efficiency in Hong Kong. Quite disappointingly, despite their recognition of the seriousness of road congestion problems and its consequences on Hong Kong's long-term economic competitiveness, most political actors (i.e., the TAC, the Administration, and politicians at different levels of our political hierarchy) failed to take any progressive steps to address the problem. They had been over-obsessed by Alan Scott's bitter career failure after his unsuccessful, courageous defence of the government-supported ERP. Their lack of courage and commitment has contributed nothing but to the further deterioration of our road congestion problem. The consultants are definitely correct that the competitiveness of freight transport industry depends critically on the efficient use of our severely limited road networks. Little can be achieved if the problem is not tackled properly. Their backing on the need to assess use-related road pricing seems to logically echo the Patten Administration's latest concern with the deteriorating road congestion problem.

Conclusion

In sum, problems facing the freight transport industry are perennial, and deserve to be addressed with a more focused, in-depth study than this one. Anything less would do the industry a disfavour, and weaken Hong Kong's long-term competitiveness as a global freight hub serving one of the most rapid growing economic regions and the world market.

☐ The Year Ahead

We have critically reviewed two government-published transport studies with one being carried out by an internal working group of the TAC, and the other by a consultancy firm commissioned through public fund. Both studies have involved more than two years of investigation, and are presumed to produce implementable strategies that could enhance the efficiency of Hong Kong's transport system. But, disappointingly, they are far from achieving the objectives. It is not unreasonable to expect a compelling need to engage in similar studies in the near future. Looking to the year ahead, we anticipate the following issues to top the agenda of transport in Hong Kong: (1) the government's strategic package to solve the much deteriorated road congestion problems; (2) CMB's franchise; and (3) the locus of transport-related decision-making.

Congestion Management Package

The efficient use of our limited road network is of critical importance to

Hong Kong's competitiveness as a global transport hub and a commercial centre in the region. Likewise, the quality of life for most people will also hinge on the relative efficiency of our transport system. Being locked up in traffic jams for tens of minutes while travelling to and from work has become the routine for many. Key public transport operators and small transport entrepreneurs (i.e., goods vehicle and taxi drivers) have lost their tolerance, and made their grievances public and loud. They complained that operating costs have soared to the limits due to the jams, and pressed the government to take immediate action. The Administration surely had fully recognized the problem and its seriousness. This could be dated back to the early 1980s. Lamentably, strong political opposition to their adoption of some effective but drastic measures (i.e., road pricing, hefty fiscal penalty on car ownership, etc.) in the mid-1980s had curtailed their capability to take progressive steps in solving the problem. Inaction, however, has contributed to nothing but a further aggravation of road congestion.

To address the problem of this magnitude, strong leadership is a must. Preoccupied with the heart-breaking struggles for blessing from both London and Beijing of his governance, the Wilson Administration surely had failed to provide it. Amazingly, in recent months, the Patten Administration has shown a keen interest in the issue. It has directed the Secretary for Transport to chair a steering committee comprising mainly top-ranking government officials in the relevant branches to work out a policy package to him. Patten, who had direct experience in managing and directing transport matters while serving as a minister in the Thatcher Administration in England, has sensed the urgency of the problem, and promised to produce a package of solutions. It is likely to form a vital part of his third policy speech. The next review will assess not only the effectiveness of the substantive issues raised in his package, but also his determination to push them through. His excellent track record in settling difficult issues will be put under test in tackling this fundamental problem which many top-ranking government officials deliberately have avoided.

CMB's Franchise

Prior to September 1993, other than sharing half of the operating rights over the cross-harbour bus services with the Kowloon Motor Bus (KMB), CMB held a *de facto* monopoly of running the bus networks on the Hong Kong Island. Totally dissatisfied with its performance and commitment to improve service, the Administration had unilaterally terminated CMB's monopoly on the Island network when its franchise was up for renewal in 1993. Deregulation of public transport services has been accepted as a policy in the *1990 White Paper on Transport Policy in Hong Kong*. But at that time, options open to the government were rather limited. Firstly, KMB has always been one of the operators that have sufficient resources and organizational capabilities to run additional service, and has indicated interest in bidding for the Island bus networks. However, on political grounds, the Administration has been quite reluctant to endorse KMB's move. Secondly, there were practically no other operators available in Hong Kong that had sufficient manpower, financial, and organizational resources to take over CMB's networks. Thirdly, the Administration was entirely inexperienced in handling the magnitude of such a scale of changes. Hence, instead of pushing for total deregulation, the Administration had opted for a partial resolution which had to address two practical considerations: (1) getting a reliable operator to run the bus networks in the Southern and Western districts where the mass transit system is not accessible; (2) consolidating and strengthening its bargaining power with CMB over the operating rights on the remaining bus networks on the Island. Subsequently, the Citybus was granted a three-year term franchise to operate 26 bus routes covering most of the Southern and Western districts after the public tender exercise. At the same time, CMB was granted a two-year term franchise to run the remaining networks on the Hong Kong Island. CMB's franchise will expire by the end of August 1995. The Scheme of Control which was designed to protect the maximum rate of returns allowed on the average net fixed asset (ANFA) are not included in both franchises.

The move of the Administration has been taken by some insiders as a doubled-edged strategy. Firstly, by giving Citybus the 26 bus route network covering Southern and Western districts, the government is able to completely get rid of its reliance on CMB to run the critical services in an area where mass transit is not available. In case of CMB's collapse, the Administration only has to concentrate on the bus services along the northern corridors of the Island. Secondly, once the service of Citybus is consolidated, the Administration can step up its bargaining with CMB over the operating rights of the Island's remaining bus networks. The Administration has long felt uncomfortable in dealing with CMB's top management.

With CMB's operating rights up for renewal, the Administration has been strengthened on a number of grounds. Firstly, poorly run CMB services on the Island angered nearly every politician on the Island. Presumably, no political party will be so naïve as to take a sympathetic view about the CMB. This is particularly so in the middle of the 1994–1995 electoral cycle when popular support is crucial. Secondly, Network 26 of the Citybus has been well received despite some problems they had encountered during its initial stage of operation. Quality and reliable bus services have been accepted as a must. CMB may have to prove living up to the standards Citybus has achieved in order to renew its operating rights. Thirdly, some cash-rich property developers in Hong Kong are quite keen to get involved in the running of public transport as a training ground for their future involvement in urban public transport operations in China, and other parts of the Pacific Rim. Fourthly, quite a few experienced overseas urban transport operators (such as the United Kingdom's Stagecoach, Singapore's SBS, etc.) are interested in the operating rights of the remaining bus networks on the Island in case of either CMB's collapse or its failure to obtain renewal of operating rights. Most of these operators share the same vision of the cash-rich property developers that proof of success in managing urban public transport services in Hong Kong will give them a solid competitive edge in their bid for operating services in other parts of the Pacific Rim that need desperately to upgrade their urban public transport services.

With all the advantages, the Administration is in a strong position in its negotiations with the CMB over the renewal of the franchise. There have been signs that the Administration is not totally unprepared to completely abrogate CMB's franchise, and put the remaining bus networks on the Island on public tender. Such a thinking is gaining ground among the public and major political parties. Besides, the Administration would be put into an extremely difficult political position if they fail to consult the public as to whether CMB's franchise should be extended. Once the consultation is put in force, it is likely that the public would press the Administration to require CMB to produce a comprehensive service upgrade plan for the coming years. Failing that, the public may compel the government to invite public tenders for the remaining bus services on the Island. CMB will be put in the same position with other competitors. Of course, there is always the chance that Citybus will be granted operating rights of the remaining bus networks. To do so, the Administration may have to convince the public why deregulation is a better option.

The Locus of Transport-related Decision-making

To the end of 1991, few would question the authority of the TAC. In most cases, the Exco endorsed its recommendations without further queries. Likewise, owing to the partial overlapping of membership between the two, the Legislature seldom confronted the TAC. The media community rarely questioned the authority of the TAC. Transport-related civil servants generally looked to the TAC for direction. In short, the TAC was taken as the authoritative locus of transport decision-making. The situation has gradually undergone some major changes. Firstly, to avoid the unnecessary politicization of the TAC, the Administration decided to sever its linkages both with the Legislature and the Exco. There were signs that some powerful figures of the TAC unidimensionally wanted to transform it into an expert committee.

Secondly, for reasons unknown, the TAC's work has become less and less transparent to the public. Media editors and reporters have complained incessantly about the unwillingness of the TAC's members to entertain their questions. Likewise, operators have voiced similar concerns. The TAC seems to be over-obsessed with its own work, and has kept a distance from the public. In short, few have chances to engage in in-depth discussion sessions with the members and assess their expertise on transport matters.

Thirdly, as transport matters have always been top among the voters' concerns, politicians, especially those who were returned directly to the Legislature through popular votes, have been keen to demonstrate their concerns and competence on any transport-related issues. This contrasts sharply with the TAC's self-imposed isolation.

Fourthly, from the very beginning of their term, most directly elected legislators started taking issues concerned with transport to build up their credibility and political capital. As a group, they have been extremely active in dealing with those issues (i.e., quality, service level, fares of public transport services, etc.).

Fifthly, the Legco's Transport Panel has taken some proactive steps in building its credentials on transport-related matters, and succeeded in turning itself into a public forum for transport policy issues. The positions of individual legislators and the Panel as a whole on certain controversial transport issues (i.e., fare policy, service quality control, etc.) have become more and more apparent to the public. Their expertise on transport matters has ensured.

Finally, an increasing number of transport-related issues have been scheduled for motion debate in the Legislature before their formal tabling in the TAC or for the government's initiatives to take on the issues.

All these changes have undoubtedly led many to question where the

Transport

locus of our transport decision-making is situated. Some civil servants have admitted that those who command political mandates and maintain some expertise on the subject are surely the bosses. Increasingly, they have to spend more time to address issues raised by the Legislature than the TAC. Being fed up with the self-imposed isolation of the TAC, the media has, instead, turned to the Legislature for authoritative views. Being unable to exert influence on the TAC, community activists, pressure groups, and district board members are feeling more comfortable to lobby the Legislature directly. To avoid direct confrontation with populist demands, the Exco has become more ready than ever before to accommodate the resolution of the Legislature. There are hints that the locus of transport-related decision-making has shifted to the Legislature. This is a very important issue which deserves to be dealt with in depth.

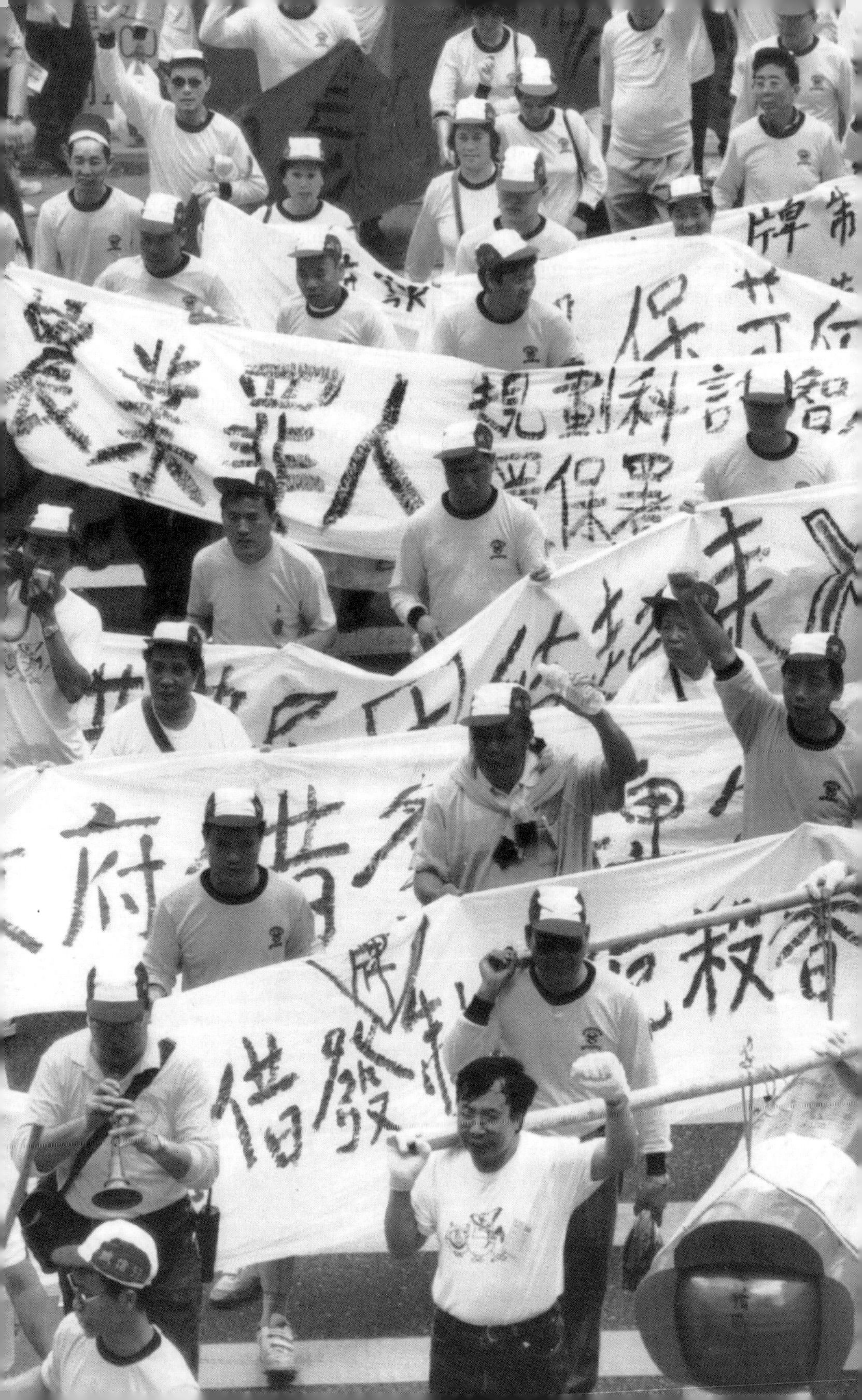

14

The Environment

Hung Wing-tat

☐ Overview

The level of pollution in Hong Kong is particularly surprising ... we cannot escape the accusation that the environment is the one striking failure by Hong Kong's normal standard of success.[1]

Immense construction activities have been going on day and night in Hong Kong as the government presses ahead with the new airport, port and other related infrastructure projects. The ten core projects of the airport, for political reasons, have to be finished before 1997. These projects involved a huge scale of seabed dredging, earth excavation as well as land reclamation, in the order of billions cubic metre of earth work. This size of work sets a historical record both locally and internationally. Finishing these works within a compressed time frame would require extraordinary resources. One consequence would be the massive environmental and ecological destruction.

Development can have adverse consequences. The dredging activities in Victoria Harbour stir up the deposited poisonous chemicals and heavy metals and give rise to the problems of treating and disposing of

---

Hung Wing-tat is a university lecturer in the Department of Civil Engineering, Hong Kong Polytechnic.

[1] Extracted from the address of the Governor, the Right Honourable Christopher Patten at the opening of the 1992–1993 session of the Legislative Council, 7 October 1992.

contaminated mud as well as total eradication of the ecology at the affected spots. The reclamation activities give rise to stagnant dirty waters, odors, dust and other pollution problems.

The adoption of the strategy of creating land for development by reclaiming the sea reflects that land is very expensive in Hong Kong. Indeed, every inch of land is put under the pressure of property development, noticeably, for residential housing and offices. As property price doubles and even triples, there are other activities rigorously competing for land too, such as container storage, car scrapping and golf. These activities produce scars on the land surface in the originally tranquil New Territories. Some ecologically sensitive areas, typically the Mai Po Marshes, are seriously under threat.

Despite the involvement of the Environmental Protection Department (EPD) in all development projects, environmental factors do not appear to be of any importance in determining the implementation of these projects. A prerequisite condition of environmental impact assessments (EIAs), no matter at planning, implementation or operation stages, is to make sure that all the projects must go ahead and finish on time! For example, EIA could only suggest that the contaminated mud arising from seabed dredging be transported for burial underneath another part of the sea with great care to ensure no human health hazard occurred but no due regard for the immediate and long-term negative impacts on the water ecology was being paid. Also, the EPD would only suggest compensation to the fishermen while disregarding the obvious fact that the sucking of sand from the seabed to obtain material for reclamation would totally wipe out the ecology. All the same, residents affected by the construction of the third harbour crossing can receive only minimal compensation.[2]

In general, Hong Kong shares the typical problem of other developing countries, namely, the conflict between development and environment. The United Nations Conference on Environment and Development (commonly referred to as the Earth Summit) held in June 1992 solemnly addressed this problem. Sustainable development was the main theme of discussion. Two international conventions, the Biodiversity Convention and the Climate Change Convention, were concluded. It is unfortunate that the Hong Kong

---

[2] The government only compensates installation costs for double window glazing and air conditioners.

government did not attend this conference. Hong Kong is, nevertheless, a dependent territory of the United Kingdom who has committed to abide by the conventions signed at the Summit. The Hong Kong government, under the pressure of environmental non-governmental organizations, hereafter named "green groups," decided to find ways to respond to the conventions. The implications of the Earth Summit were subsequently addressed in the *Second Review of the White Paper on Environmental Pollution* announced in November 1993.

The year 1994 should be engraved in the environmental history of Hong Kong because of the commencement of operation of the Daya Bay Nuclear Power Station. In February 1994, Hong Kong entered the nuclear era when the Daya Bay nuclear power plant was officially opened by the Chinese Premier, Li Peng, despite strong opposition of the people of Hong Kong. Nuclear power is, for the first time, transmitted to Hong Kong. The opening of the Daya Bay nuclear plant highlights the urgency of addressing the issue of energy use in Hong Kong. However, the government iterates, time and again, that it does not intend to formulate a policy to regulate energy supply and demand. The energy sector is totally manipulated by individual private power companies. This non-intervention policy unfortunately ties the hands of the EPD in controlling the pollution caused by burning fuels effectively.

These events set the backdrop for this year's environmental protection and conservation work in Hong Kong.

☐ Reactions to the Earth Summit

Besides ratifying the Rio Declaration and two conventions, the Earth Summit also endorsed "Agenda 21," a document that lists detailed programmes to ensure the implementation of the conventions. These documents state clearly the obligations of the world's countries to protect the environment.

Only one "green group" from Hong Kong, the Conservancy Association, attended this important conference. The Hong Kong government did not send representatives because of the anticipated opposition from the Chinese government. The Conservancy Association, in order to urge the government to comply with the conventions concluded in the Earth Summit, drafted a document — the Agenda 21 for Hong Kong. The Hong Kong government reacted by incorporating one chapter on the Earth Summit in its *Second Review of the White Paper on Environmental Pollution.* Although sustainability was mentioned in the second review of the White Paper, not much was proposed in terms of pursuing the compliance with the obligations called upon at the Earth Summit.

There are specific targets set in the conventions. For example, the reduction of greenhouse gas emissions to 1990 levels by the year 2000 was stated in the Framework Convention of Climate Change, and the immediate development of an eco-system database to reflect the current biodiversity situation and the formulation of strategies to protect the biodiversity. The Hong Kong government responded to these requirements with minimal commitment. So far, it has done three things: (1) requesting the existing Energy Efficiency Advisory Committee to launch a high-profile campaign to alert the public to the concept of energy efficiency in buildings; (2) adding as a term of reference to the EPD the gathering of information in relation to energy consumption, and (3) offering help to the World Wide Fund for Nature (HK) for the preparation of an ecological map of Hong Kong.

There is no solid programme on how Hong Kong could achieve the year 2000 targets and there is not even manpower diverted to look after the formulation of such a programme. It appears that the government has demonstrated its awareness of the obligations laid down at the Earth Summit but totally lacks the sincerity to commit to them.

☐ Destruction Versus Conservation of Nature

> The most depressing example of the way in which we abuse our natural heritage is the New Territories.[3]

It is really very difficult for the government to substantiate its commitment to preserve the remaining natural environment once it has committed itself to the Port and Airport Development Strategy (PADS) projects. It is easy simply to talk about sustainable development but to really implement it is extremely difficult, especially for an administration which will be departing in three years' time.

In this place of borrowed time and borrowed land, both time and land are money. The faster the exploitation of land, the more ready is the financial return. Admittedly, the fast growing population and economy exert huge pressure on land. Apart from the port and airport, residences,

---

[3] Extracted from the address of the Governor, Christopher Patten at the opening of the 1993–1994 session of the Legislative Council.

The Environment 257

offices, factories, stores and highways all require land. How can we "produce" land? The answer is: either through reclaiming the sea or resuming land from the New Territories. The government resorts to the former answer while private developers the latter. The government exploits the sea and in the process produces a huge amount of contaminated mud, kills all the eco-systems at locations of sand burrowing and dumping, and turns Victoria Harbour effectively into a channel and aggravates the pollution situation.

The private developers, on the other hand, exploit the land. They buy land from the farmers. The small developers, for various reasons,[4] turn the land into temporary open storage for containers, gas cylinders, etc. or car scrap yards. The big developers apply for development through the Town Planning Board. Huge luxury private housing estates such as California Garden, Tai Sang Wai are being constructed. And, these developments even encroach into the Buffer Zone (Zone II)[5] of the natural reserves.[6] The consequences are obvious. The fish ponds which are of significant ecological and environmental value disappear in large scale. The natural life in Zone I and even within the natural reserves is being seriously disturbed.

Apart from these housing development applications, there were a number of applications for golf course development, for example, the Luk Keng and the Sha Lo Tung golf course proposals. These developments involve eradication of tens of hundreds of hectares of country green which could lead to subsequent land and water pollution from chemical residuals of herbicides used on the golfing greens. Furthermore, both developments fall within ecologically sensitive areas. Largely because of these reasons, the Town Planning Board turned these proposals down. The Board, however, cannot stop these applications from being lodged again. In fact, the Sha Lo Tung development proposal has just been revised and re-submitted for the Board's consideration.

While the Town Planning Board declined these golf course

---

[4] It may be owing to either the shortage of capital or that the land is not large enough for any comprehensive scale of development.

[5] In order to protect natural reserves which are of significant ecological value, the government has put buffer zones round these reserves; development in Zone I is strictly forbidden but restricted in Zone II.

[6] There were totally 61 applications for development within the Zone II boundary last year and 19 of them, involving 24.3 hectares of land, were approved.

applications, the government itself, to the disappointment of many, applied to construct a "public" golf course at Kau Sai Chau, another area within the country park. The government explained that interest in this sport is growing, as borne out by the long lists of applicants waiting to join the private clubs and the heavy usage of the existing driving ranges. The "public" courses, therefore, are needed, so that the public will no longer be discouraged from participation in the sport. The government, however, has avoided mentioning that every member of the public can enjoy the country park while only a few people can enjoy playing golf for lack of time and, most importantly, money. Is it, therefore, justified to do irreversible harm to the environment for the enjoyment of a few?

While the government pushes ahead with the Kau Sai Chau golf centre development which is to be completed as soon as possible, it does not show the same sort of efficiency in legislating for a "Ramsar" site[7] in the North West New Territories, which is to include the Mai Po wetland. The designation of Inner Deep Bay and the Mai Po wetland as a Ramsar site may be delayed until mid-1995, a postponement from the end of 1994 which was the date originally scheduled. The main reason given is "the lack of funds."

The low priority that this government gives to conservation seems too plain to need other illustrations.

☐ Energy Conservation and Air Pollution

The continuous high development rate has to be supported by a consistent supply of resources, one of which is energy resources which can be in the form of coal, oil, natural gas, water and even sunlight. The energy consumption growth rate of the past decade is 117 per cent[8] which is in line with the 110 per cent average growth rate in the gross domestic product (GDP).[9] The major sectors of energy consumption are power generation (68.4 per cent), industries (11 per cent) and road transportation (9 per cent).[10] Among the

---

[7] The Hong Kong government is a signatory country of the Ramsar Convention which is an international agreement to protect the natural ecology of wetland.

[8] Extracted from "Hong Kong Statistics 1981–1991."

[9] Extracted from "Estimates of Gross Domestic Product 1966–1990."

[10] Figures estimated by Tromp and Ng in "The Energy — Environmental Equation in Hong Kong" at POLMET '91.

consequences of increasing energy consumption are a demand for land to build more power stations and increasing emissions of greenhouse and other poisonous gases.

In Hong Kong, the responsibility of exploring energy supply has been left totally in the private hands, i.e. the utility companies, the oil companies and the gas company. In the search for energy supply, the main objective of these companies is to ensure cheap and consistently available energy resources. As far as power generation is concerned, Hong Kong has gone through periods of different energy forms. Before the oil crisis in the early 1970s, the energy form used for power generation was largely oil. It was switched to coal in the late 1970s to avoid the situation of uncertain supply of oil. Now, nuclear power is added to the energy mix in Hong Kong. Natural gas will come into use before the turn of this century. The biggest utility company, the China Light and Power Company, is building one of the world's biggest natural gas plants at Pillar Point in Tuen Mun.

In fact, Hong Kong has been planning and constructing power stations throughout the past century. The difficulties in locating suitable land for future power stations is becoming more and more pressing as the land shortage problem aggravates and the government becomes more open.

Another grave concern over energy use is to do with its close relationship with air pollution which leads to the greenhouse effect and direct health hazards. The major greenhouse gas is carbon dioxide. The amount of carbon dioxide emitted from fuel combustion is estimated as 34 million tonnes in 1990, with power generation accounting for over 76 per cent, and industries and road transportation for 8 per cent each. As the government has no intention to change its positive non-intervention policy in this regard, the amount of greenhouse emissions will continue to rise roughly at the same rate as the growth of GDP. If that is the case, how can the administration achieve the target stipulated at the Earth Summit?

The only alternative is to promote energy saving either through improving the energy efficiency of machineries and equipment or good housekeeping practices. The government intends to do this through the Energy Efficiency Advisory Committee. Leaflets promoting energy saving in building were distributed and competition on the best energy-efficient building design was organized this year. The effect, however, is still to be seen. The government, on the other hand, also requests the power companies to promote energy saving practices to their customers. Unfortunately, these practices, in fact, contradict their profit-making objectives. The promotion, if done at all, is expected to be half-hearted.

As for road transportation, oil is the only energy source used by motor vehicles because of the constraints in availability of mature alternative vehicle technology and the government's non-intervention policy. Road transportation alone consumes around 36 per cent of the total oil consumption. The exhaust emissions of motor vehicles is continuously a major contributor to air pollution in urban areas and are a major health threat. The EPD is formulating a policy to discourage the use of cars that contribute most to the pollution, i.e. light-duty diesel vehicles, and to encourage the use of electric vehicles. Purchase of electric vehicles from this year onward can enjoy exemption of first-time registration tax which amounts to 110 per cent of the vehicle price. Unfortunately, one of the drawbacks in promoting electric vehicles is that our electricity is generated mainly from coal; increasing the consumption of electricity means burning more coal and emitting more greenhouse gases! That would mean saving some human lives in the local scene while jeopardizing the earth as a whole. That is a dilemma to be solved.

☐ The Changing Role of the "Green Groups"

Faced with these environmental and development dynamics, the "green groups" have been forced to readjust their positions. Traditionally, "green groups" were pressure groups. The formation of these groups have been the result of the government's neglect of specific environmental issues. And this is the reason why these groups have always been critical of government policies. The pressure exerted by these "green groups" is somehow constructive; in particular, it leads to the formation and flourishing of the EPD. The EPD gradually comes to understand this special relationship and starts to lure these groups to stand on its side. The government has been cautious about appointing representatives of these groups to sit on the related consultative committees such as the Advisory Council on the Environment (ACE) (formerly called the Environmental Pollution Advisory Committee). All appointments were on a personal basis. But, from the year 1993–1994, the EPD appears to have dropped the confrontational attitude and started to allow these members to join in the capacity of representatives of the groups. Now, there are "green groups" representatives on the ACE and the Environmental Campaign Committee (ECC). Communication, consensus and cooperation take the place of distrust, criticism and confrontation. Apparently, the "green groups" have been quieter on environmental issues such as the PADS and the sewage disposal strategic plan in recent years. It

The Environment

may be owing to (1) the draining of manpower by participating in government advisory committees, and (2) attention of the mass media being devoted more to political bodies such as the Legislative Council. Nevertheless, too much care given to maintaining a good relationship with the government may also be a key factor.

The EPD also tries to get all the "green groups" under the umbrella of the ECC, the quasi-government organization, to work together to promote, in particular, environmental awareness. In the early years of its establishment (1990), the government provided the secretariat support only. The ECC had to solicit funds for its activities in competition with other "green groups." There existed some negative feeling towards the ECC among "green groups." The ECC, in effect, competed for funds and activities with other "green groups" and drained manpower resources from these groups. There was constant call for government direct subsidy to the ECC and "green groups." In October 1993, the Governor of Hong Kong eventually decided to use 50 million Hong Kong dollars to set up an Environmental and Conservation Fund. The Fund will support the two quasi-government organizations, i.e. the ECC and the Energy Efficiency Advisory Committee, as well as research and public environmental education activities. "Green groups" are invited to sit on the management board of the Fund.

Partly owing to the opportunities of members meeting in various committee activities and partly because of the need for a united force to put pressure as regards environmental issues relating to major development projects, the "green groups" have come together on a more regular basis. A number of joint statements/submissions objecting to proposals for development such as those of golf course construction at Kau Sai Chau, Luk Keng and Sha Lo Tung were presented to the government.

The objections of "green groups" do sometimes exert influence on government decisions. One typical example is that of a private development proposal at Nam Sang Wai near Mai Po Marshes. The proposal includes a land exchange of Lut Chau[11] owned by the developer with an equivalent piece of crown land adjacent to the Nam Sang Wai development. The developer also promises to preserve and maintain Lut Chau in the future. In pursuing its case, the developer is very active in soliciting the support of the

---

[11] Lut Chau is situated next to the Mai Po Marshes and falls within the Zone I buffer.

"green groups." Some prominent members of the "green groups" have been involved in preparing the proposal for the developer. Their opinions do carry weight on the decision of the Town Planning Board at its final hearing of the case.

Two controversial points have, however, emerged. Should "green groups" accept development projects taking place at the fringe or even inside buffer zones of the natural reserves and make compromises with developers who are willing to offer compensations for the destruction? Should prominent members of the "green groups" act as consultants to developers or should they stick to their role of guardian of the environment? Furthermore, the more fundamental questions of whether there should be a trading of one eco-system for the other, and who has the right to do so should be addressed. These questions are indeed very difficult to answer.

☐ China Link

As it is less than three years before Hong Kong reverts back to China, more and more issues, including those concerning the environment, have to obtain the endorsement of China. The controversial strategic sewage disposal scheme (SSDS) and the Deep Bay pollution abatement plan are projects which fall into this category. Unfortunately, the political dispute between China and Britain has damaged cooperation of the two governments in other areas. The Sino-British Joint Liaison Group (JLG) which deals with matters of the transition period virtually ceased its operation until June 1994. In June, the Hong Kong government, for the first time, put the SSDS on the agenda of the JLG meeting. The Chinese government reacted, rather to the surprise of some people, by asking the Hong Kong government to consult the people of Hong Kong.

The Hong Kong government has, however, never been willing to carry out public consultation on the SSDS despite urging from the "green groups" and legislative councillors. It has been trying, through various ways, to get around public consultation on the plan. First of all, it pushed ahead with the plan by passing legislation to set up a "trading fund" for the management of the sewage disposal plan. This fund will be separated from the government's annual financial and budgetary report and will be operated independently by the future designated authority. It then injected seven billion Hong Kong dollars into this fund to carry out the less controversial Phase I works of the SSDS. It also passed a bill to levy sewage charges from domestic as well as industrial users, which is considered by some to be financially motivated. Throughout, legislators have been put in a difficult position: for if they do not pass these legislations, the water quality in Victoria Harbour will continue to deteriorate until a decision is made. Yet, because of the way that the government has been handling the SSDS, most people are sceptical about it.

The urgency of the matter is all too obvious. Cholera bacteria has been discovered in the sea water and a number of cholera cases thought to be related to eating seafood were reported in July 1994. Some people suspected that the cholera bacteria was carried down the Pearl River to Hong Kong during the flood in southern China while others blamed it on the reclamation works in the harbour. No matter what the real cause is, one thing is certain: the waters around the Pearl River Delta are very polluted. It requires the concerted effort of the governments of Zhuhai, Shenzhen and Hong Kong to fight this pollution. A commonly agreed set of rules for the discharge of pollutants into common waters as well as a joint enforcement team would be ideal in tackling this problem. In view of the current political circumstances, this is quite unrealistic. The only remaining active task seems to be for the academics and the "green groups" to promote information exchange among these places through organizing forums and visits. These activities, however, can never supplant concrete actions taken by these governments.

To date, the only formal link between Hong Kong and China on environmental issues is through the Hong Kong–Guangdong Environmental Protection Liaison Group which was set up in 1990. The only cooperation effort between the governments of Hong Kong and Guangdong which is of any material importance concerns the formulation of a strategic management plan for the Deep Bay catchment area. It is understood that the plan has been under discussion for years, starting with the formation of the Group. Yet it took recent flooding, which seriously affected both Hong Kong (Kam Tin and Yuen Long valleys) and southern China, to alert both governments to consider implementing the plan. Apart from the joint monitoring programme on water quality, a joint cleaning action to be undertaken soon is very much expected by the people of Hong Kong.

☐ Conclusion

In the newly issued EPD report — *Environment Hong Kong 1994*, the Secretary for Planning, Environment and Lands, A. G. Eason, highlights that a great deal of "fresh thinking" about the issues themselves and about the way they are approached are required. This is indeed the case. Simply thinking is not enough; actions are also required. What the government has so far failed most to do is to invest adequate resources so as to comply with the well-pronounced commitments to protect and conserve the environment, especially those related to agreements signed at the Earth Summit. A comprehensive database of living creatures in Hong Kong, which charts animals and plants, on land or in the sea, should be taken up by the government and not be left to a non-governmental organization. Moreover, there should be legislation and proper enforcement effort to protect these living creatures. On the other hand, the government should be able to see the limitations of depending solely on energy saving and energy efficiency improvements to achieve goals of emissions reduction. An energy supply and consumption plan should be drawn up and implemented instead of leaving the matter totally to the private sector. Finally, the impossibility of working without China's partnership on transboundary pollution issues as well as on longer-term programmes is obvious. The government has to be more proactive in initiating joint actions with the Chinese officials across the border.

The task of pressing on with environmental education must, of course, not be overlooked by all parties concerned. Indeed, the situation will remain grim for the environment if the mentality of the Hong Kong people remains anthropocentric and their attitude towards nature is exploitation-oriented, as a survey done a few years ago[12] has indicated.

---

[12] The survey conducted by the Conservancy Association in 1991 shows that a majority of Hong Kong people think that humans have the right to modify the natural environment to suit their needs. For full report, refer to "New Environmental Paradigm Survey 1991."

15

Public Housing

Lau Kwok-yu

While the Hong Kong Housing Authority celebrated its 40th Anniversary (1953–1993), many people in Hong Kong expressed that "housing-related problems" are the number-one problem to be solved. They were concerned that the price of private housing was too high and there was inadequate provision of public rental housing (PRH) and Home Ownership Scheme (HOS) flats.

A report on a telephone opinion poll commissioned by the Government Secretariat Home Affairs Branch in May 1994 shows that "housing-related problems" are perceived to be of most concern to Hong Kong people (33 per cent). As regards problems that were of most concern to the respondents personally, "housing-related problems" (32 per cent) remained on the top of the list, followed by "Hong Kong's future" (18 per cent) and "economy-related problems" (8 per cent).

Regarding the "housing-related problems," only 11 per cent of the respondents considered that the government had handled them well and 78 per cent considered that it had handled them badly. The proportion of the latter group is on the rise from 68 per cent in May 1993 to 78 per cent in May 1994.[1]

Lau Kwok-yu teaches social policy and administration, housing and policy studies at the Department of Public and Social Administration, City Polytechnic of Hong Kong. His current research interests focus on housing and policy studies in Hong Kong and China.

[1] Home Affairs Branch, Government Secretariat. *Report on a Telephone Opinion Poll in May 1994*, Appendix III. Home Affairs Branch, Government Secretariat. *Report on a Telephone Opinion Poll in November 1993*, Appendix IV.

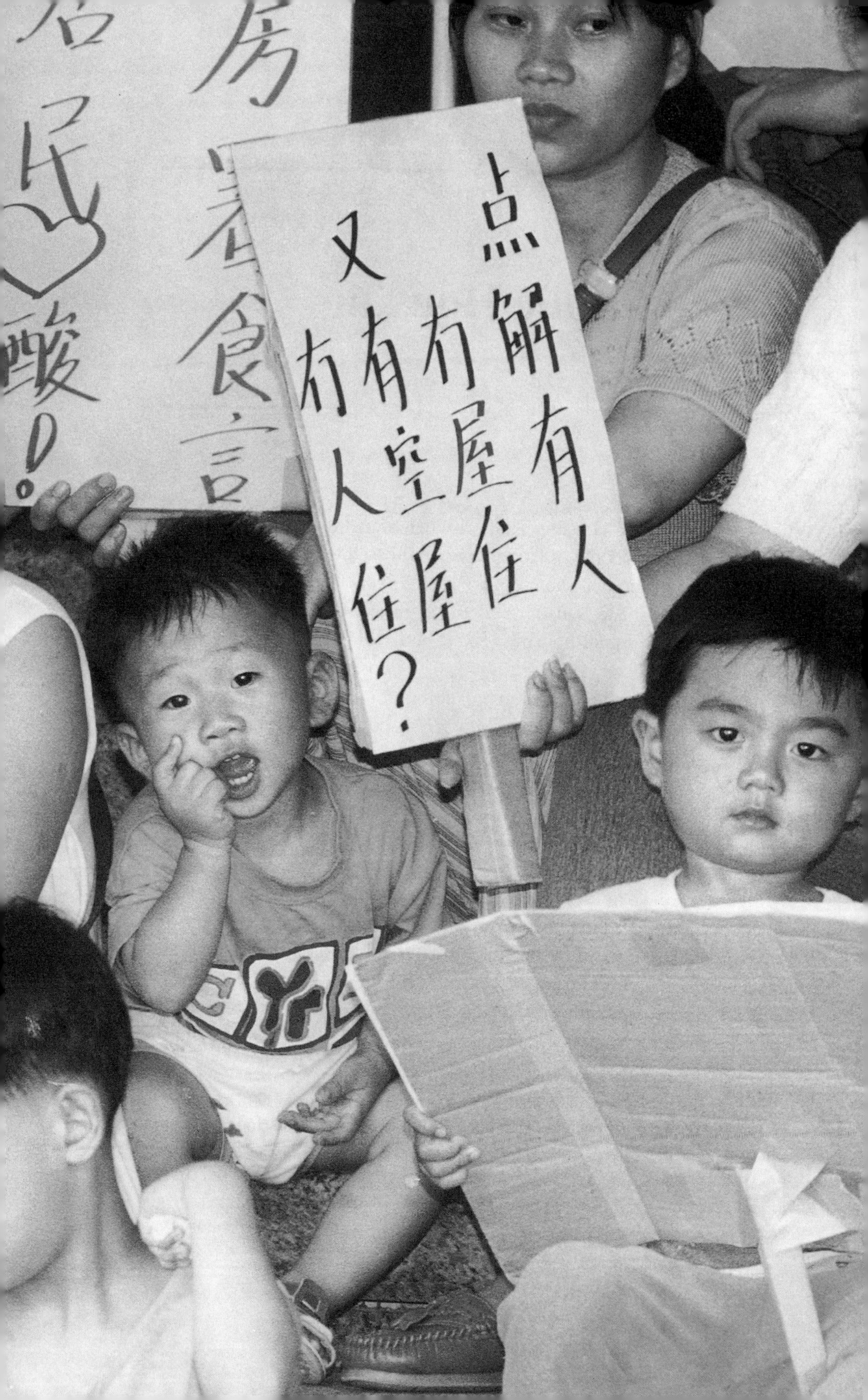
点解有人
冇屋住
有空屋
又冇人住？
房署食言

Public Housing

As another chapter in this volume will examine the property market, this one will focus on issues in public sector housing during the period July 1993 to June 1994.

An attempt is made to answer the following three questions:

1. Is public accusation that there has been inadequate provision of PRH and HOS flats a valid one? If the answer is yes, then what are the likely effects of such inadequate provision on eligible households awaiting public sector housing?
2. Will policy changes made in the review period bring new hope to the inadequately-housed households?
3. What other measures have been introduced for the betterment of living conditions to sitting tenants of public housing estates?

Questions 1 and 2 are to be addressed with a thorough examination of the ways the government defines who is eligible for housing assistance and the outstanding demands at the end of 1993–1994 and 2000–2001. As for question 3, a list of measures will be examined.

During the review period, the most significant event in the public housing sector is the Housing Authority's Mid-Term Review of the Long Term Housing Strategy (LTHS) which identifies the problems the Authority faces and the way forward. Another important development is the agreement reached between the government and the Housing Authority on the new financial arrangements. The third major change relates to the much expanded maintenance and improvement programmes for the PRH estates.

The constraints on housing production imposed by the terrain of Hong Kong have been well recognized. The total land area in Hong Kong in 1993 is about 1,078 square kilometres of which about 14.3 per cent (155 square kilometres) are developed areas. Out of the 155 square kilometres of built-up lands, approximately 52 square kilometres comprise residential areas for private sector and public sector housing. Housing approximately 6.02 million people (about 1.71 million households) in an area of 52 square kilometres renders Hong Kong one of the most densely populated areas in the world.

High density living is a fact of life in metropolitan Hong Kong, many people of the territory also have to face the problem of having to pay extremely high prices for the private sector housing they occupy. Families allocated public sector housing units are considered the lucky ones as rent and price are usually within their affordability.[2] Together with the large-scale public sector redevelopment programme[3] and maintenance and improvement programme[4] as well as being given the privileged priority opportunity to purchase HOS flats (trade-up), public tenants are enjoying a much better living condition at subsidized prices than many eligible households still waiting for their turn of public housing allocation.[5]

Owing to the limitation of space, this chapter will not discuss the impact of governmental measures such as rent control and public sector housing subsidy provisions on the beneficiaries. In the author's opinion, these beneficiaries are in a relatively better position than all those waiting for government assistance in solving their housing problems of affordability and unsatisfactory living conditions.

The main focus of this chapter will be on the review of housing policies for the low- and middle-income households in Hong Kong during the period of July 1993 to June 1994. Part I is to discuss the income eligibility criteria of government-subsidized housing programmes. Part II will discuss the outstanding housing demand in 1994–1995 and by 2000–2001. Part III will include an examination of the new measures and policy changes and their impact on the sitting and prospective residents of public sector housing programmes.

---

[2] The median rent-to-income ratio of public housing tenants was 6.5 per cent in the first quarter of 1985 and was about 7.9 per cent in the first quarter of 1993; the price of HOS flats are set at 52 per cent of the assessed value of comparable private sector flats in 1993–1994.

[3] See Lau Kwok-yu and Kathleen S. K. Suen, *Redevelopment of Public Housing Estates in Kwai Tsing District, Hong Kong: A Study Report* (Hong Kong: Kwai Tsing District Board, 1989), pp. 2–11.

[4] The Housing Authority's recurrent expenditure on estate maintenance and improvement will be increased from $1.3 billion in 1993–1994 to $2.6 billion in 1994–1995. Refer to Speeches by the Chairman of the Housing Authority and its Building Committee Chairman in the annual special open meeting of the Housing Authority held on 2 June 1994.

[5] The median rent-to-income ratio of private sector households eligible for PRH was 21 per cent and 27 per cent in the third quarters of 1985 and 1993 respectively. See Planning, Environment and Lands Branch, Hong Kong government, "Replies to Questions Raised by the Legislative Council Sub-Committee on Property Speculation," 23 May 1994.

☐ Part I: Income Eligibility Criteria of Government-subsidized Housing Programmes

The Hong Kong government basically adopts the producer subsidy approach[6] to supply public sector rental and sale units to almost half of the Hong Kong population (about 3 million). There are about 874,000 flats in 286 estates throughout Hong Kong. Some 2.6 million people live in 688,000 PRH units while some 500,000 live in purchased flats such as the HOS or Private Sector Participation Scheme (PSPS).[7] The public housing programme, launched since the Shek Kip Mei fire on Christmas Day in 1953, is regarded as one of Hong Kong's finest achievements.[8] However, there is much to be done before 2001 if adequate housing is to be provided to all those needy households with housing problems.

Defining Adequate Housing in Hong Kong

Subsidized housing in Hong Kong refers to adequate public sector housing under the Housing Authority and Housing Society rental and sale schemes as well as housing loan schemes. The concept of "adequate housing" is an important starting point for any consideration of housing policy and housing conditions. There is no universally accepted definition of adequate housing. It takes on different meaning in different societies and their governments. Concepts of adequate housing vary over time and according to the resources available and the value attached to housing. In the process of developing the LTHS in the mid-1980s, the Hong Kong government adopted the following definition of "adequate housing" requiring living quarters to be:

1. built of permanent materials;
2. self-contained (a complete unit of residence which has its own

---

[6] For a fuller discussion on the merits and demerits of the producer and consumer housing subsidy approaches, see E. Jay Howentstine, *Housing Vouchers: A Comparative International Analysis* (New Jersey: Centre for Urban Policy Research, 1986).

[7] *Hong Kong 1994* (Hong Kong: Government Printer, 1994), p. 187.

[8] "Message from the Governor," in *Rising High in Harmony* (Hong Kong: Housing Authority, December 1993).

entrance, an internal kitchen/cooking place, a bathroom/flush toilet system and internal piped water supply and electricity supply);
3. occupied on an unshared basis except in the case of very small (one-person) households;
4. not overcrowded; and
5. at a rent or price within the household's means.

The first four criteria are basically concerned with the conditions within living quarters while the fifth is on affordability. A more comprehensive concept of "adequate housing" would include conditions outside the living quarters but which intrinsically affect the quality of life enjoyed by the occupiers. Thus, living quarters should be located in an area with adequate amenities and community facilities so that the residents may have easy access to markets, shops, schools, means of transport, recreational facilities, health and social welfare facilities, and a range of employment opportunities. It is also important that housing should be sited in locations free from environmental hazards such as flooding, landslip or pollution.[9]

For the purpose of meeting the International Covenant on Economic, Social and Cultural Rights (Right to Adequate Housing), seven factors/aspects[10] listed below have been taken into account in determining whether particular forms of shelter can be considered to constitute "adequate housing." These factors/aspects include:

1. legal security of tenure;
2. availability of services, materials, facilities and infrastructure;
3. being affordable;
4. being habitable;
5. being accessible also to people with special housing needs;
6. convenient location; and
7. cultural dimension.

---

[9] See Lau Kwok-yu, "Housing," in *The Other Hong Kong Report 1991*, edited by Sung Yun-wing and Lee Ming-kwan (Hong Kong: The Chinese University Press, 1991), pp. 343–87.

[10] Refer to Habitat International Coalitions Centre on Housing Rights and Evictions, "General Comment No. 4 on the Right to Adequate Housing" (Article 11(1) of the International Covenant on Economic, Social and Cultural Rights adopted by the United Nations Committee on Economic, Social and Cultural Rights) dated 12 December 1991, pp. 4–6.

With the exception of the cultural dimension aspect, it appears that all other aspects listed above have been incorporated in Hong Kong when defining adequate housing.

Public Rental Housing Waiting List Income Limits

Public Rental Housing

Broadly speaking, families are admitted into PRH[11] on account of either demonstration of a definite housing need or compliance with the Waiting List Income Limits (WLIL). To put it in simpler terms, the first group are the Non-Waiting List applicants and the second group the Waiting List applicants. Through the years, about two-thirds of the public rental flats are allocated to the Non-Waiting List applicants.[12]

Waiting List applicants can be considered as the low-income households in Hong Kong. Families admitted into PRH through the Waiting List should comply with the WLIL. The WLIL have been determined so as to limit eligibility of public housing only to those who are likely to encounter difficulties in getting adequate accommodation in the private sector.

The income limits effective from 1 April 1994 for the Waiting List applicants shows that, given the stringent limits, out of 293,100 non-owner-occupier households in private permanent housing and all households in private temporary housing, about 36.4 per cent (i.e., 106,700 households, including 34,800 one-person households and 71,900 two-person and above households) are estimated to be eligible for PRH because they have income below the limits. In other words about two-thirds, that is 186,400 non-owner-occupier households now living in private sector housing are not eligible to apply for PRH through the Waiting List. In the view of

---

[11] As the Housing Society constitutes only a very small proportion of the total public housing stock (4.4 per cent), the discussion on PRH will be limited to those of the Housing Authority.

[12] For a fuller discussion on the reasons about allocating more PRH units to non-Waiting List applicants, see Lau Kwok-yu, "Why Is the Public Sector Housing not Targeting at Helping Low Pay Households?" *Journal of Policy Viewers*, No. 2 (January 1993), pp. 40–44. Also see Leung Wai-tung, "Housing," in *The Other Hong Kong Report 1993*, edited by Choi Po-king and Ho Lok-sang (Hong Kong: The Chinese University Press, 1993), p. 271.

the Authority, these households are not likely to encounter difficulties in getting adequate accommodation in the private sector.

This could be true only if the assumptions and data used in arriving at the income limits have incorporated the housing needs of all those who are financially incapable to rent reasonable accommodation in the private sector. Before judging whether the WLIL set by the Authority is a realistic one or not, we should know the approach adopted in assessing the limits.

Approach in Assessing the Waiting List Income Limits

According to the Housing Authority, the assessment of the current WLIL is based on the "household expenditure" approach which consists of the following two components:

1. the non-housing cost, i.e., the average household expenditure on food and other necessities excluding housing cost; plus
2. the housing cost, i.e., the average rent and rate for reasonable private sector domestic accommodation of a size comparable to space allocation standard in PRH.

It is claimed that this approach of assessing income limits enables a family which financially cannot afford to rent reasonable accommodation in the private sector to qualify for PRH.

The non-housing cost household expenditure is based on the average of that of the lowest one-third of tenant households for each household size in private housing. The housing cost element is the cost of renting reasonable sized flats, based on a "Weighted Average Rentals" method.

A concrete example may assist understanding of how the household expenditure approach is being used. Take the WLIL of the four-person households as an example, the income limit (effective from 1 April 1994) is set at $12,400 per month.[13] It is derived by adding the non-housing cost ($6,050) and the housing cost ($6,300). It is the Housing Authority's belief that those earning more than that limit could find adequate accommodation

---

[13] When dollars are quoted in this chapter, they are Hong Kong dollars. Since 17 October 1983, the Hong Kong dollar has been linked to the U.S. dollar, through an arrangement in the note-issue mechanism at a fixed rate of HK$7.80 = US$1. As at 31 March 1994, HK$100 = RMB112.43.

in the private sector. Comparing this income limit ($12,400) with the four-person (a married couple with two children) salaries tax exemption level of $15,333 (or a total of $184,000 per annum) for 1994–1995, it is without doubt that the WLIL have been set at a very unrealistically low level. Even those not required to pay salaries tax are not necessarily eligible to apply for PRH through Waiting List.

Upon further examination of the data used for the two components of housing and non-housing costs, it is argued that the Authority has ignored the housing needs of many other low-income households. There are two groups being victimized by the stringent income limits. The first group is tenant households of new and fresh lettings.

For tenants of fresh lettings, they need to spend HK$9,000 on rent and rates for a 42 square metres private sector flat (multiplication of proposed size of accommodation and projected unit rent of new and fresh lettings, i.e., 42 × $214 = $8,988, round-off to $9,000)). But the Authority only assumes that the rent and rates per month are HK$6,300 (i.e., multiplication of proposed size of accommodation and adopted unit rent: 42 × $150 = $6,300).

Should the Housing Authority recognize the needs of tenant households of new and fresh lettings to rent a reasonable private sector domestic accommodation of a size comparable to the space standard in public housing and spending $6,050 per month on non-housing items of necessities, the WLIL for four-person households should be revised upwards to about $15,050. This amount is 121 per cent of the adopted income limit of $12,400. Revising the income limits upward would mean a larger number of eligible households for PRH.

Let's further examine the possible impacts of the stringent income limit on the newly formed low-income four-person households (those families with incomes at the officially adopted WLIL of $12,400), which need to rent a private sector flat with HK$9,000. Paying $9,000 would mean that the household has already consumed about 73 per cent of its total household income. After meeting housing costs, a four-person family with $12,400 income would only have $3,400 left for food and other necessities.

Their purchasing power is thus significantly lower than their counterparts who could spend $6,050 per month on food and other necessities. It is most ridiculous to find that such an amount on non-housing cost is even lower than the amount received by the four-person households in the public assistance scheme (renamed comprehensive social security scheme since 1 July 1993). The standard rates of public assistance effective from 1 April

1994 for the four-person poor households (with two able-bodied adults and two able-bodied children) amount to HK$4,290. This amount is exclusive of rent allowance ($2,858 is the maximum rent allowance) and other special grants.

Conversely, if they were to maintain a spending of $6,050 (say $6,100) on non-housing items, they then must be content to rent a much smaller flat. This contradicts with the Authority's assumption that those with income above the WLIL are not likely to encounter difficulties in getting adequate and reasonable private sector flat of a size comparable to the counterparts in PRH.

The second group is tenant households whose non-housing cost is higher than that of the average of the lowest one-third of the expenditure group but lower than that of the 33rd percentile tenant households. Evidence shows that the Authority's adopted non-housing cost for the four-person households is roughly equivalent to that of the 18th percentile expenditure group.[14]

Tenant households whose income enable them to afford spending more than $6,050 (say $6,101) and less than $7,500[15] on non-housing items only belong to the 19th to 33rd percentile expenditure groups. With such level of income and spending $6,300 on housing, they will then be ineligible for PRH via the Waiting List.

The choice of not using the non-housing cost of the 33rd percentile tenant households and rental of the new and fresh lettings as the two components of WLIL is very much related to the self-restrained commitment of the Hong Kong government in meeting the needs of the housing poor.

The administration will not wish to see the insurmountable pressure of increased PRH housing demand. According to official estimate, the total number of eligible households for PRH via Waiting List will be increased from 121,000 to 184,000 (a 52 per cent increase) if the Authority is to use

---

[14] According to official estimate in 1992, the average non-housing cost of the lowest one-third non-owner-occupier households is roughly equivalent to the 18th percentile expenditure group, see *Overseas Chinese Daily News*, 5 March 1994.

[15] It is assumed that the non-housing cost of the 33rd percentile four-person tenant households (i.e., from $7,030 in 1993–1994 to $7,500 in 1994–1995) increases at the same rate (6.5 per cent) as that of the average non-housing cost of the lowest one-third four-person households (i.e., from $5,680 in 1993–1994 to $6,050 in 1994–1995).

the non-housing cost of the 33rd percentile tenant households and the rent of the new and fresh lettings in determining the 1993 WLIL.[16]

Income Limit for HOS, PSPS and Home Purchase Loan Scheme

The eligibility income limit for the HOS/PSPS and the Home Purchase Loan Scheme (HPLS) are the same and will be examined here. Before going into the details, some background information of each of the three schemes is presented below.

Home Ownership Scheme and Private Sector Participation Scheme

The Housing Authority's HOS was drawn up by the government in 1976. This is the first public sector flats for sale scheme. It had been the government's intention to build flats for sale to better-off tenants of PRH estates and to that lower-middle-income section of the general public whose household incomes were too low to afford to buy flats in the private sector but too high for PRH.

The PSPS was launched as a result of the Real Estate Developers' Association's expressed anxiety over the entry by the government into the domestic flats for sale market. Since 1977, private sector developers have participated in this scheme. This is to demonstrate the government's clear intention that a right balance be achieved between production from the Authority's HOS and production by private developers. Under the PSPS, sites are sold by tender to developers for the construction of flats for sale to the Authority's nominees. Under the Conditions of Sale of the site, various requirements are imposed upon the developer including the residential accommodation (e.g., number of flats, flat sizes, etc.), car parking spaces, commercial accommodation, community facilities, open space, and so on. In return, the developer receives a guaranteed price for the flats.

Up to 1993, a total of 191,800 HOS/PSPS flats have been sold to eligible families and about 45 per cent of them were sold to public housing tenants (Green Form applicants, who were required to surrender their rental flats in return). The figure of 191,800 includes 61,500 flats produced under

---

[16] For detailed calculation of WLIL, refer to Lau Kwok-yu, "Defining Income Eligibility Criteria for Government Subsidized Housing Schemes in Hong Kong," *Hong Kong Journal of Social Sciences*, No. 2 (Autumn 1993), pp. 39–64.

the PSPS.[17] The pricing strategy, rules on eligibility, income limit and so on are the same for HOS and PSPS. To the general public, PSPS is considered as part of the HOS. The government considers PSPS a complementary scheme to HOS.

Home Purchase Loan Scheme

The government regards the HPLS an integral part of the LTHS which aims to boost potential demand for private sector housing (so as to encourage private sector to maintain its interest in building domestic units and to utilize its resources), and to help satisfy the growing demand for assisted home purchase by widening the range of choices available. Before the introduction of the HPLS in June 1988, choices available include HOS and PSPS. Since its introduction, eligible applicants may choose to apply for an interest-free loan to purchase a private sector flat of their own choice within their affordability.

The loan is meant to help eligible applicants to overcome the problems of initial financing faced by many families wishing to buy their homes in the private sector.

As a response to the high property prices, the amount of loans has increased to $300,000 since April 1994 (the loan amount of $70,000 was set in 1988–1989; revised to $130,000 in August 1990; and to $200,000 in April 1993). From April 1991, the age limit of the purchased property has been further extended from 10 years to 15 years so that successful HPLS applicants could choose flats of affordable price from a larger pool of domestic properties.

Since October 1991, a new option was introduced to allow eligible applicants to opt for a monthly subsidy of $2,000 (subsequently revised to $2,600 from April 1993) for a period of 36 months (subsequently revised to 48 months from April 1994), which is not repayable. Flats bought under the HPLS are not under stringent resale restrictions like those of the HOS.

The original LTHS assumed that 102,500 private sector flats would be taken up via the HPLS during the period 1988–1989 to 2000–2001. However, response to the scheme so far has fallen short of expectations. The 1993 LTHS review therefore has reduced the assumed take-up to 15,800 for the whole strategy period, i.e. only 15 per cent of the original target. Since

---

[17] *Hong Kong 1994* (Hong Kong: Government Printer, 1994), p. 190.

the start of the HPLS in 1988 until the end of 1993, some 8,090 loans and 250 subsidies have been granted. As a result, 4,550 public housing units have been recovered for allocation to other families.[18]

Assessment of the Home Ownership Scheme Income Limit (HOSIL)

When the income limit of White Form applicants[19] was first set in 1977–1978, it was based on the minimum income required then to afford a private sector flat with a household paying a 10 per cent deposit and taking a 90 per cent mortgage repayable over 15 years, with 40 per cent of household income devoted to repaying the mortgage. From Phase 1 (February 1978) to Phase 3A (March 1981), the income limit has been changed while taking into account inflation, changes in property prices and non-housing expenditure. However, owing to the excessive demand on the limited supply of HOS flats, the Authority has decided not to review the income limit between March 1981 and June 1984. Consequently, fewer households in the sandwich class were eligible because of the tighter income restrictions.

As from June 1984 (Phase 6A) onwards, the Authority decided to change the basis of calculating the HOSIL. The limit had been set at the level required to own an average priced HOS flat, with account being taken of average family expenditure on non-housing necessities. The basis of assessment of the HOSIL between Phase 6A (June 1984) and Phase 13C (February 1992) is similar to that for the PRH's WLIL and consists of two components:

1. the non-housing cost: that is the average household expenditure on food and other necessities excluding housing costs (based on the average of the middle one-third expenditure group of four-person tenant households in private housing); and

---

[18] *Hong Kong 1994* (Hong Kong: Government Printer, 1994), p. 191.

[19] Only those non-owner-occupiers in the private sector (White Form applicants) are required to pass the income test before they are given HOS/PSPS/HPLS assistance. All those public housing tenants and prospective tenants who are about to be allocated public housing via Waiting List or due to government clearance programmes (Green Form applicants) are not required to pass any means/asset tests for HOS/PSPS/HPLS assistance.

2. the housing cost: that is the expenditure required to own an HOS/ PSPS flat at an average price level including mortgage repayment, rates and management fee.

In the review of HOSIL for 1992–1993, the Authority further changed the calculation of monthly housing cost by taking the average between the expenditures required to own an average HOS/PSPS flat of $909,400 with 90 per cent mortgage and repayment period of 20 years at an interest rate of 9 per cent per annum and that of a private sector flat of $1,400,000 with 70 per cent mortgage and repayment period of 20 years at an interest rate of 10.25 per cent per annum.

In 1993–1994, the calculation of monthly housing cost has been further changed, taking only the expenditures required to own a sub-urban private sector flat of $1,650,000 (40 square metres saleable floor area) with 70 per cent and 80 per cent mortgage (the mean was used) and repayment period of 20 years at an interest rate of 8.25 per cent per annum (February 1993 interest rate).[20]

In the 1994–1995 HOSIL review exercise, the private sector flat price is further increased to $1,950,000. Mortgage percentage is kept to 70 per cent minimum and with a repayment period of 20 years at an interest rate of 8.25 per cent per annum (March 1994 rate).

According to the estimate of the Administration, there are around 78,400 households with incomes above the WLIL and within the $22,000 HOSIL in April 1994. This represents 26.7 per cent of 293,100 non-owner-occupier households in private housing.

A closer examination of the basis used in calculating the housing cost required to own a private sector flat in 1994 suggests that the Administration's income limit estimate is still on the low side. This is because the mortgage repayment of $11,630 was worked out by assuming that households have already had enough savings of $585,000 (i.e., 30 per cent of the flat price, assuming that the bank's current 70 per cent limit on mortgage advances; this sum does not include the conveyancing and legal charges of about $60,000) to afford the down payment when purchasing a private sector flat costing $1,950,000. It is very doubtful whether there are that many households with such a substantial amount of savings.

---

[20] For calculation of the HOSIL, see Note 16.

Sandwich Class Housing Scheme Income Limit

Sandwich Class (Short-term and Long-term) Housing Scheme

A new middle-income housing scheme for the "sandwich" class was introduced in 1993, aiming to help families that are neither eligible for public housing nor able to afford to buy their own homes in the private sector. The scheme, operated by the Housing Society, comprises a short-term and long-term programme. Under the short-term scheme, a low-interest loan fund of $2 billion was set up to provide beneficiaries with a one-off loan as part of a down-payment for a private sector flat. The $2 billion fund is estimated to benefit 4,000 families by phases.

In August 1993, the first phase of the loan scheme was launched, offering to 1,000 beneficiaries low-interest loans of 20 per cent of the sale price of a flat, up to a limit of $500,000. Repayment at a low interest rate (2 per cent per annum, decision made in June 1993) over 120-month period would only begin in the fourth year, when the beneficiary's financial position has improved.

The applicants had to have at least seven years' continuous residence in Hong Kong and the total monthly family income had to be within the range of $20,001–40,000, among other requirements. A total of 3,435 applications were received and only 712 applicants were issued with Certificates of Eligibility and 213 certificate holders had successfully purchased units approved by the Housing Society.[21]

As prices for small properties have risen about 10 to 15 per cent during the months from August 1993 to February 1994, the maximum loan amount for Phase 2 beginning April 1994 is raised to 25 per cent of the sale price of a flat, up to a limit of $550,000. The income eligibility limits are also raised by 10 per cent to $22,001–44,000. A quota of 1,500 loans will be offered in Phase 2 which has attracted about 4,500 applications.

Under the long-term scheme, land is to be given to the Housing Society at a concessionary premium to build 10,000 flats for sale to the "sandwich" class at affordable prices before 1997. The first batch of about 1,000 flats is expected to be completed in 1995.

Compared with the official estimate of about 38,500 eligible sandwich class households in 1994–1995, the provision of 1,500 sandwich class

---

[21] Refer to a press report in *Tin Tin Daily News*, 9 May 1994.

housing loan plus 1,000 Sandwich Class Housing Scheme (SCHS) flats in 1995 indicates a very low success rate of 6.5 per cent.

Sandwich Class Housing Scheme Income Limit

Unlike the PRH and HOS, the Administration has set the lower and upper eligibility income limits for the SCHS. As households with income below $22,000 are eligible for HOS, the Administration therefore has taken $22,001 as the lower income limit (effective from April 1994). Household expenditure approach again is used to work out the upper income limit for sandwich class housing scheme. The calculation of monthly housing cost takes into account the expenditure required to own an urban private sector flat of 60 square metres (saleable floor area) with 70 per cent mortgage and repayment period of 20 years. The non-housing expenditure for sandwich class household is assumed to be at least comparable to that of a HOS/PSPS household. The only exception is that sandwich class households are assumed to reserve a proportion of their income on tax, savings and contingent liabilities, etc. To be fair, households with monthly income below $22,000 (HOSIL) should also reserve a proportion of their income (perhaps a smaller proportion) on these expenditures of tax, savings and contingency. When working out the HOSIL and the PRH's WLIL, an additional expenditure group covering savings, tax and contingency should also be included.

A Tenure-bias Public Housing Policy: Promotion of Home Ownership

The decision to provide HOS/PSPS/SCHS and to introduce public sector subsidy in the form of interest-free loan (HPLS) or low-interest loan (Sandwich Class Housing Loan Scheme) to aid eligible households to become home owners reflects the government's tenure-bias position which oriented towards home ownership.

Hong Kong's owner occupation rate rose rapidly, from 32 per cent in 1982–1983 to 44 per cent in 1988–1989 and after a short pause, increased to 47 per cent in 1992–1993. The latest projection made in 1993 indicates that the rate will further increase to 54 per cent in 1997–1998 and 59 per cent in 2000–2001. (Refer to Table 1 for the difference between public and private sector home ownership trends.)

Underlying this home ownership orientation, the government minimizes its cost of public subsidy (see Table 2) despite the fact that sandwich class households as well as those eligible HOS/PSPS/HPLS households are unlikely to experience the same degree of difficulty if they decide to rent

Table 1. Home Ownership Rate in Hong Kong

Year	Private sector (%)	Public sector (%)	Overall (%)
1982–1983 (Actual)	54	5	32
1992–1993 (Actual)	71	20	47
1997–1998 (Projection)	78	27	54
2000–2001 (Projection)	83	33	59

Source: Hong Kong Housing Authority, *A Report on the Mid-Term Review of the Long Term Housing Strategy*, October 1993, pp. 24–32.

Table 2. Estimated Cost of Public Housing Subsidy (as at Sept. 1993)

	Total "cost" to HK govt/Housing Authority	Recipients' perceived value of subsidy
PRH flat	37,000	1,088,000
HOS flat	–650,000	766,000
PSPS flat	–601,000	790,000
HOS transfer flat	–530,000	645,000
HPLS loan amount		
$200,000	83,000	127,000
$300,000	125,000	190,000
$400,000	167,300	253,000
$500,000	209,300	316,000

Notes: (1) Assuming 55 square metres (gross floor area) per flat
(2) Figure with (–) denotes net proceeds
(3) "Cost" includes estimated land premium

Source: Same as Table 1, see p. 55 (Table 10).

similar flats in contrast to purchasing flats. According to the Housing Authority and the Census and Statistics Department's data, the median private sector rent-to-income ratios for the sandwich class households and households with monthly income above WLIL but below HOSIL are 14.8 and 19 per cent respectively. As at September 1993, sandwich class households at the upper income limit of $40,000 and HOS/PSPS/HPLS eligible households with income of $20,000, after spending on housing (rent, rates and management fee) for a private sector flat at urban and sub-urban locations, could still enjoy similar or better living standards (as indicated by the amount of income available for the payment of non-housing expenditures) than that expected by the Administration.

Comparing their situation with those of the newly formed tenant households on the PRH Waiting List (whose housing expenditure constitutes a considerable proportion of the total household income), the latter group obviously should be accorded with a higher priority for public housing assistance if the principle of progressive vertical equity is to be observed in public housing policies.

☐ Part II: An Appraisal of Outstanding Housing Demand, 1994–1995 and 2000–2001

Overall Appraisal

With a total stock of about 1.8 million public and private permanent housing units, which is 5 per cent more than the estimated number of households, there should be no shortage of housing for the purpose of shelter.[22] However, many households are still living in inadequate housing according to government's recent housing assessment exercise.

According to a conservative estimate by the author, the total outstanding demands for PRH, HOS/PSPS and SCHS at the end of 1994–1995 and 2000–2001 are 198,600 and 108,500 respectively. Data also show that there is a greater number of eligible low-income households' PRH demand unmet in 1994–1995 when compared to that regarding the middle-income household's demand for home ownership assistance in the form of HOS/PSPS and SCHS. While in the year 2000–2001, it is projected that the largest number of unmet demand will be from those middle-income households aspiring to become home owners through the HOS/PSPS.

In the 1994 LTHS Review for the eight-year period (1993–1994 to 2000–2001), the potential demand for permanent adequate housing is estimated at 695,000 households.[23] After discounting those not coming

---

[22] The notional surplus is accounted for by the existence of vacancies, second homes, smaller households and a growing tendency for emigrants to retain their properties in Hong Kong. See Planning, Environment and Lands Branch, Hong Kong government, *Report of the Task Force on Land Supply and Property Prices*, June 1994, p. 3.

[23] Refer to *1994 Long Term Housing Strategy Review — Assessment of Housing Demand and Supply: Housing Department's Preferred Scenario (1993–1994 to 2000–2001)*, Hong Kong Housing Authority, May 1994.

Public Housing 283

forward, the effective demand is estimated to be 606,000 households. Despite programmed and assumed high housing production (the programmed public sector housing production and the assumed private sector production total 575,000 housing units during the period), the residual demand at the end of the strategy period remains high (outstanding demand for new housing comes from 31,000 households living in inadequate housing and 44,000 households currently in adequate housing but who wish to change sector in order to improve their living environment).

Outstanding Demand for PRH

Even with the stringent criteria, the Administration has not been successful in providing PRH to eligible households. Information shows that between 1986–1987 to 1993–1994, no more than 15 per cent of the eligible households are provided with PRH through the General Waiting List for PRH.[24] The limited provision and low success rate of Waiting List PRH applicants in turn have deterred eligible households from applying.

By adopting a very low come-forward rate,[25] Housing Department's estimate of housing demand for PRH is around 65,000 and about 13,000 eligible households will be added into the waiting list each year for the period 1992–1993 to 1996–1997.

In other words, by 1992–1993, there should be about 78,000 households in need of PRH and registered on the waiting list. However, according to PRH allocation records, only about 14,000 households on the waiting list would be allocated a public rental flat each year. If the trend

---

[24] See Planning, Environment and Lands Branch, Hong Kong government, "Replies to Questions Raised by the Legislative Council Sub-committee on Property Speculation," 23 May 1994.

[25] Come-forward rates are derived by expressing effective demand as a percentage of potential demand. The major factors influencing the come-forward rate include affordability and the perceived chance of success. The government noted that when private sector flats were in plentiful supply and relatively affordable, households might stretch themselves to buy from the private sector because of choice of location or absence of re-sale restrictions. When private sector prices are high or when public sector supply is perceived to be forthcoming, more eligible households are likely to apply for public housing.

continues, it means that at any year, there would be over 70,000 waiting list households in need of PRH but yet to be allocated a public housing flat.

Outstanding Demand for HOS/PSPS

The Planning Section of the Housing Department estimated in October 1991 that the effective demand (assuming that some households though eligible but not coming forward to apply for HOS/PSPS flats) for HOS which arises from public rental tenants and the private sector (Green Form and White Form applicants respectively) is 85,000 for every year in 1992–1993 to 1996–1997. Comparing this set of conservative estimates with the programmed annual production figure of 16,000 HOS/PSPS flats of the same period, it is obvious that over 69,000 households, though eligible, are not provided with HOS flats.

If we take all private sector households who have monthly income below the HOSIL as the base and compare it with the number of successful applicants, we can be very sure that the chance of getting HOS for most eligible households is not promising at all. Less than 5 per cent of identified households per annum were given HOS flats during the period of 1986–1987 to 1993–1994.[26] Despite the low success rate, many White Form applicants still apply for HOS because it is the only way to satisfy their aspiration for home owning within their means. The over-subscription rates of White Form applicants ranged from 10 to 28 times between 1987 and February 1992.

Application and sale statistics for HOS/PSPS Phases 13A to 13C (a total of 18,620 flats were sold, of which 12,388 (66 per cent) were sold to Green Form applicants and 6,232 (34 per cent) were sold to White Form applicants in 1991–1992) suggest that on average, 1 out of 6 Green Form applicants succeeded in the HOS purchase and only 1 out of 21 White Form applicants succeeded. The most recent sale of HOS (Phase 16A in April 1994) has attracted 25,400 Green Form applicants and 58,400 White Form applicants. In other words, about 1 in 7 Green Form applicants succeeded in the HOS purchase and only 1 in 34 White Form applicants succeeded. The over-subscription rates have demonstrated the obvious need of the applicants for subsidized public sector sales flats. The limited production of

---

[26] Source same as Note 24.

HOS flats each year again has pushed many of the eligible White Form HOS applicants into the private sector housing market, or to be precise, to keep them in the non-public sector housing where they have been residing.

The residual demand for HOS/PSPS remains high at the level of about 70,000 in 1994–1995 and 2000–2001. Without greater determination on the part of the government to build more HOS/PSPS units before 2000–2001, it is very unlikely that the size of the residual demand for HOS/PSPS be reduced and that middle-income households' aspiration for assisted home ownership scheme units be realized sooner.

Outstanding Demand for SCHS Assistance

Housing needs of sandwich class households could be met by resorting to renting and these households would still enjoy a relatively comfortable living standard. With the government's eagerness to promote a higher rate of home ownership in Hong Kong and the consequence of price hike in the private sector property market in recent years, sandwich class households have then become targets for housing subsidy. The residual demands at 1994–1995 and 2000–2001 are assumed to be constant at the level of about 33,500 to 36,000. The actual demand is dependent on the pricing of private sector flats.

Why Set Income Eligibility Limit at Such a Low Level?

The way the Hong Kong government defines who is eligible for housing subsidies is very much predetermined by its covert policy of maintaining "a right balance" between public sector and private sector housing in meeting the housing needs of the people in Hong Kong. Table 3 shows that the forecast proportion of population as well as living quarters in the public sector in the years 2001 and 2011 will be no more than 50 per cent of the total. Delimiting its housing production on the one hand keeps capital expenditure on public sector housing low and on the other hand allows private property market to prosper, which in turn will benefit government coffer through land sales and increased tax revenue from property transaction activities.

The above discussion suggests that the Administration has set the eligibility income limits for applicants of subsidized housing programmes in an arbitrary manner. The basis used in the assessment of income limits of various subsidized housing programmes may change according to the government's interpretation of people's financial ability to solve their own

Table 3. Occupied Living Quarters and Population by Type of Housing, 1991 (Actual) and 2001, 2011 (Forecast)

		Public	Private	Others	Total
1991 (Actual)					
Living quarters	(%)	45.8	49.1	5.1	100.0
	(No.)	690,609	740,220	77,168	1,507,997
Population	(%)	48.0	47.4	4.6	100.0
	(No.)	2,650,105	2,610,376	250,698	5,511,179
2001 (Forecast)					
Living quarters	(%)	48.2	49.9	1.9	100.0
Population	(%)	48.6	45.1	6.3	100.0
2011 (Forecast)					
Living quarters	(%)	46.7–44.7	51.7–53.7	1.6	100.0
Population	(%)	49.1–46.9	46.8–49.0	4.1	100.0

Notes: 1. Public sector includes the Housing Authority's and Housing Society's rental blocks and HOS/PSPS.
2. Others refer to temporary housing and institutions.
3. Population figures exclude persons living on board vessels.

Source: Census and Statistics Department, Hong Kong government, *Hong Kong 1991 Population Census Summary Results* (Hong Kong: Government Printer, 1991), p. 62; and Planning Department, Hong Kong government, *Territorial Development Strategy Review: Development Options* (October 1993). The forecast figures are based on the steady growth scenario.

housing problem. One possible explanation for the existing practice of not including more households into the eligibility pool of public sector housing is that the government has no plan to provide subsidized housing to more than half of its population.

This is consistent with the author's argument that the government has no intention to upset its long-cherished covert policy of "balanced development."[27] In its 1994 LTHS Review the government assumed an annual production of private sector flats at 35,000 throughout the period of 1993–1994 to 2000–2001. This assumed production will exceed the estimated

---

[27] In completing the task of housing most of those in need by the turn of the century, the Housing Authority has been careful to ensure that there is a right balance between private and public sector production. See *Rising High in Harmony* (Hong Kong: Housing Authority, December 1993), p. 50.

Public Housing 287

annual demand of 21,000 flats during the same eight-year period. Pushing more people into the private housing market may help to stimulate more demand for or to consume the excess supply of private housing and hence sustain the interest of property developers to continue a high-level housing production programme.

The over-supply of unaffordable private sector flats in the past years has not pushed the price down. Instead, owing to speculative activities and hoarding of properties, price continues to rise.

Households wanting to improve their living conditions have been frustrated by the high residential property prices and its consequential effects on rents. Over the last ten years (1984–1993), the average price of residential flats rose by 430 per cent. Information shows that the prices of domestic accommodation have been rising ahead of household income since 1990.[28] According to official source, prices for all classes of private domestic properties had risen by an average of 150 per cent between year-end 1989 and 1993. Prices of the more popular estate-type private sector developments have increased by more than 200 per cent.

In the first quarter of 1994, it is estimated that prices in popular developments soared by another 30 per cent. Rental increases averaged 40 per cent between 1989 and 1993 for all classes of domestic properties. Moreover, a sample survey of 10,078 private sector units in large developments completed in 1992 showed that 1,803 units (17.9 per cent) were still unoccupied at the end of April 1994, i.e. more than a year after completion. Furthermore, another sample survey of 17,544 units in large developments completed in 1993 showed that 7,009 (40.5 per cent) remained vacant at the end of April 1994. Nearly half of these vacant units were held by developers or certain individuals who have purchased blocks of flats in the same development. The government considers these prima facie cases of hoarding and speculation.[29]

It is disappointing and frustrating for many public sector housing scheme eligible households to see so many private sector flats unoccupied but with prices still buoyant and the government reluctant to produce more public sector housing units so as to bring the price down.

---

[28] *The 1994–95 Budget: Speech by the Financial Secretary, Moving the Second Reading of the Appropriation Bill, 1994*, p. 15.

[29] Planning, Environment and Lands Branch, Hong Kong government, *Report of the Task Force on Land Supply and Property Prices*, June 1994, p. 28.

What we need in Hong Kong is a more determined government to change its so-called "balanced housing development" policy in favour of the disadvantaged households. The government not taking steps to change the housing policy, those who cannot afford reasonable and adequate housing still have to wait for a very long period[30] and pay a higher price in the private sector market either by cutting their non-housing expenditure or by working longer hours or to continue living in sub-standard housing. Given the fact that the GDP grew by 6.5 per cent per annum in real terms in 1984–1993 and the government's estimated reserve balance stood at $136,130 million on 31 March 1994, is it the right policy for a government with envied growth in economy and a huge surplus to adopt?

☐ Part III: New Measures and Policy Changes

Long Term Housing Strategy Mid-term Review

Under the leadership of Rosanna Wong, the newly appointed Housing Authority Chairperson, a mid-term review on the LTHS was completed in the summer of 1993. While recognizing the achievements since the promulgation of the LTHS in 1987, problems and difficulties have also been identified. The report of the mid-term review[31] was subsequently released for public consultation in December 1993.

The Authority is frank to admit that there are three major problems. The first relates to: (1) a shortfall of rental flats; (2) the reduced production of public rental and sales flats programmed for the period 1994–1995 to 1997–1998; and (3) the difficulties in obtaining formed sites with infrastructural facilities for meeting the production targets. Together they contribute to the government's inability to meet the demand of the housing poor in Hong Kong.

According to the June 1993 Public Housing Development Programme,

---

[30] During 1987–1992, the average waiting period for PRH for Waiting List applicants is 10 to 12 years for urban PRH unit, 6 to 7.5 years for a sub-urban PRH unit, 4.5 to 6.5 years for a PRH unit in the convenient New Territories districts such as Tai Po, Fanling and Sheung Shui, 3 to 5 years for a PRH in remote districts such as Tuen Mun and Yuen Long.

[31] *A Report on the Mid-term Review of the Long Term Housing Strategy*, Hong Kong Housing Authority, October 1993.

only about 34,000 rental and sales flats a year have been programmed for the period 1994–1995 to 1997–1998. In the words of the Authority, "this compares not so favourable with an average of 44,000 flats a year between 1985–1986 and 1992–1993. Shortage is particularly acute in respect of new one-person and two-person units."

The second problem concerns the slow mobility of PRH tenants to home ownership. The review report states that the home ownership rate in respect of public sector will increase at a slower pace in the years ahead partly due to the drop of the Sale of Flats to Sitting Tenants Scheme and partly due to the tenants' and prospective tenants' preference for the rental housing blocks of significant quality improvement and at affordable rent. The Authority also notes that some of the tenants are able to invest in properties in the private housing market — one estimate shows that about 13 per cent of PRH tenants (74,000 households) own private domestic properties, accounting for 12 per cent of all private properties owned by local individuals.[32] The Authority argues that while those public sector tenants who can well afford purchasing will stay put at the expense of families in genuine need of rental housing.

The failure of the HPLS is considered the third problem of the LTHS. However, the Administration after its mid-term review of the LTHS, though it reduced the assumed take-up to 15,800 for the whole strategy period, i.e. only 15 per cent of the original target, it still considered the need to enhance the HPLS in terms of the loan amount and quota, in view of three factors: (1) the important role of the HPLS for clearing the outstanding demand for home purchase under the LTHS; (2) the need to encourage more sitting and prospective tenants to buy flats in the private sector, thereby releasing more rental units; and (3) the HPLS being the cheapest form of subsidized housing compared to PRH and HOS.

The review report lists a number of recommendations:[33] (1) to increase land supply; (2) to reprogramme the redevelopment programme beyond the five-year rolling plan and to make use of retainable and refurbished housing blocks to be evacuated under the redevelopment programme to provide an additional source of supply; (3) to increase the turn-round of flats within the existing stock by encouraging greater social mobility among better-off sitting tenants; (4) to enhance the HPLS by increasing the amount of loans

---

[32] Ibid., p. 9.
[33] Ibid., pp. 66–68.

and monthly subsidies as well as the quota with cautions of its effects on the property market and its financial implications; and (5) to re-examine the housing needs and provisions for the elderly.

Among the various recommendations, the most contentious one is the proposal of transferring more new rental blocks to home ownership and designating these flats as HOS Type II, with a price differential from normal HOS/PSPS flats (to be renamed HOS Type I). These may be sold to certain categories of applicants who are required to move (by redevelopment and clearance) and those whose turn for rental housing is due. Public housing tenants in general welcome this proposal on condition that HOS Type II is sold at cost price and tenants affected by redevelopment or clearance programmes be given a genuine option of either buying HOS Type II flat or renting a public sector housing unit comparable to the converted HOS Type II flat. Unfortunately, the report states very clearly that "those who insist on rental housing may be rehoused to casual vacancies in less popular locations, subjected to stricter tenancy control or different rates of rent increase."[34] This is perceived as an erosion of the existing "rights" of the privileged tenants of public housing redevelopment programmes and a penalty threat to those who have not opted for HOS Type II flats and is therefore fiercely opposed by public housing interest groups. In its final report of the LTHS mid-term review, the proposal of HOS Type II flats is shelved.

Another issue of public controversy raised in the mid-term review is the extent of private domestic property ownership among PRH tenants. The public as well as the Authority members are quite divided on this issue. Some think that tenants owning private domestic property should no longer be eligible for PRH and, therefore, flats recovered from them could be allocated to those with greater housing needs. Others think that it is unreasonable to penalize only those investing in private domestic property and not other things. The Authority then referred the issue to the *Ad Hoc* Committee on Private Domestic Property Ownership by Public Rental Housing Tenants in 1994 summer. The *Ad Hoc* Committee is asked to ascertain the extent of private domestic property ownership among PRH tenants; to recommend to the Housing Authority whether any policies should be introduced and if so, whether the policies were applicable equally

---

[34] Ibid., p. 45.

Public Housing

to sitting and new tenants. The *Ad Hoc* Committee is expected to complete its preliminary report by early 1995.

Other measures such as the development of infill and small urban sites for public housing blocks, maximization of the development potential of some of the sites in the Public Housing Development Programme and additional supply of land from the government all help to increase housing production. As there is lead time for the public housing building projects, the additional flats can only be available from 1997–1998. In other words, households in need of subsidized public sector housing again have to test their patience before they are allocated with a proper shelter in the public sector. As discussed earlier, even with the estimated addition of 40,000 public housing flats for 1997–1998 to 2000–2001, the outstanding demand for public sector housing remains high in 1994–1995 and in 2000–2001. The figures could be even higher if land could not be made available in time to meet the increased demand for public sector housing.

The Chairperson of the Housing Authority in its fourth annual open meeting held in June 1994 was critical of government's assistance in land provision for public housing programme. Her remarks are worthy of a lengthy citation here:[35]

> In our negotiation with the Government for the allocation of land, we encountered difficulties too. Firstly, the Government invariably took quite some time before it could identify the land for development. For example, we requested 49 hectares of land in 1991 and the shortfall rose to 55 hectares in 1992, but it was not until after two years' negotiation when it was already June 1993 did the Government supply us with 49 hectares of land.
>
> Among the 184 hectares of land supplied to us in the past six years, only 47 hectares are formed and are ready for immediate development, while the rest called for preparation works to different extent, including modifications to town planning layouts, land resumption, clearance of squatters, major site formation works, services connection, road works etc. For instance, in 1990, the Government proposed to include the 19 hectares of land occupied by Rennie's Mill Cottage Area into our public housing development programme, but up until now, the Government still fails to arrive at a compensation scheme that is acceptable to the residents of that cottage area.
>
> What is more, either due to the lack of infrastructures or because land resumption procedures are involved, some of the land supplied by the Government just

---

[35] Speech by the Hon. Rosanna Wong Yick-ming, OBE, JP, Chairman of Housing Authority at the Housing Authority meeting on 2 June 1994.

cannot be made ready in time to provide homes to the people of Hong Kong by 2001. Hence on the face of it, we are supplied with sufficient land, but when it comes to meeting housing demand in the reality, we are not able to live up to our expectation of achieving our target by 2001.

The above situation shows that the crux of the problem does not only lie in the amount of land supply. It is regrettable that despite its long-term housing plan, the Government does not have a proper and corresponding mechanism to support its demand-led long-term housing strategy, thus giving people an impression that it only "acts according to circumstances".

Other than being the Chairperson of the Housing Authority, Rosanna Wong is also a member of the Executive Council. It is hoped that her words will carry weight and hence the government will seriously consider her proposal of developing a land bank to provide a reliable guarantee for future housing construction.

The Government's New Financial Arrangements with the Housing Authority

After a lengthy period of one and a half years, the review on the 1988 financial arrangements between the government and the Housing Authority was completed in May 1994 and subsequently endorsed by the Housing Authority. In the press conference, the Secretary for the Treasury said that the new arrangements aimed at enabling the Authority to make better use of its surplus cash to speed up the supply of public housing and upgrade its existing estates. Moreover, the new arrangements will ensure the Authority's continued financial autonomy.

The Authority estimates that it has a positive gross cash balance of $18.2 billion as at 31 March 1994. Of this, it is estimated that the net cash surplus to the Authority's operational requirements is about $9.5 billion. By the end of 1997-1998, this will rise to $17 billion. According to the 1988 arrangements, the government is entitled to take back the huge surplus beyond the Authority's operational requirements and put them into general revenue. But it is politically unwise to do so at the time of property prices escalating and provision of public sector housing for a large number of eligible households is so insufficient. It is therefore in the public interest that the cash surplus from the Authority be left with it to fund more housing and housing-related projects.

In the new arrangements, a Development Fund will be set up with an initial cash balance of $7.5 billion. The establishment of the Development

Fund hopefully could help speed up the production of housing over the next five years. This is done by using the fund to bring forward infrastructural works which have not yet reached their turn of tendering under public works programmes. In addition to the Development Fund, it is also agreed that the remaining part of the surpluses will be used to set up a new $2-billion Improvement Account within the Housing Authority's existing Capital Works Fund. The Improvement Account is set up to provide for the upgrading of the standards and community facilities of existing estates. In other words, these two funds will benefit both existing and prospective public sector housing consumers.

Another key part of the new arrangements is on the restructuring of the permanent capital totalling $26.3 billion. The Authority will cease to repay any interest on the $13.5 billion representing capitalized Development Loan Fund loans to the Authority in 1988. In other words, the $13.5 billion will become non-interest bearing permanent capital, thereby reducing interest payments by $0.7 billion per annum. However, the Authority is required to continue to repay with interest at 5 per cent on the remaining $12.8 billion cash payments received by the Authority since 1988. That is to say, the $12.8 billion will become loan capital bearing interest at 5 per cent per annum. This loan capital will be fully repaid over 14 years compared to the current payment, at the same level, without an end date. The combined effect of the restructuring on permanent capital is that, for the next fourteen years, there will be no change to the Housing Authority's cash payments to the government but thereafter, all cash payments of interest and capital will cease.

Apart from these changes, other arrangements such as requiring the Authority to pay the government 50 per cent of the dividends arising from the Authority's non-domestic operations; and to pay the government the land cost element of HOS flats which is equivalent to approximately 35 per cent of the development costs of a flat.

The new arrangements are regarded as financially more advantageous to the Authority than the existing arrangements. However, critics hold different views. There are worries that the establishment of the Development Fund would be used as an excuse by the government to reduce its commitment in respect of housing and to relieve itself of its overall commitment to provide formed land and related infrastructure for public housing development. The government reiterated that the Housing Authority will be provided with free land for PRH and subsidized land for the HOS. However, the remarks quoted above from the Housing Authority

Chairperson on government's response to the Authority's land request may substantiate critics' worry.

Another major criticism of the new arrangements centres around the high charges on the Authority's coffer: one being the 5 per cent interest on the loan capital of $12.8 billion which is higher than the interest payment given by a commercial bank to its saving depositors; the other being the share of dividends on the Authority's commercial operations. It is argued that if the dividends are not shared with the government, $3.54 billion could be saved for use by the Authority during the period 1988–1989 to 1993–1994. This sum of money is sufficient for the construction of 11,700 flats for the housing poor, assuming that the construction cost per flat is about $300,000.

Furthermore, the government is accused by the housing interest groups that the current calculation on land cost element of HOS flats (equivalent to approximately 35 per cent of the development costs of a flat) is grossly overcharged as the actual land development cost is only about 12 per cent to 15 per cent of the total development costs of a flat.[36]

Increased Budget on Estate Maintenance and Management

The Housing Authority Chairperson has rightly pointed out in its fourth open annual meeting that estate maintenance and management are of close concern to the residents. The provision of good quality housing for those in need should remain the primary concern of the Authority. The Housing Authority's recurrent expenditure on estate maintenance and improvement will be increased from $1.3 billion in 1993–1994 to $2.6 billion in 1994–1995. A total of $19.9 billion has been provided in a five-year forecast (1993–1994 to 1997–1998) for maintenance and improvements. Major new initiatives include improvements of security to entrances of public rental blocks, upgrading the standard of refurbishment of vacant flats and electrical rewiring and reinforcement, lift modernizations and lighting improvements.

That a child accidentally fell to her death through a broken railing on

---

[36] Hong Kong People's Council on Public Housing Policy, "When Will the Negotiation on the Housing Authority's Financial Arrangements End?" *Sing Tao Jih Pao*, 5 November 1993 and Liu Sing-lee, "Housing Authority Robs Public Housing Tenants to Aid the Government," *Ming Pao*, 27 April 1993.

the sixth floor of a Sha Tin public housing building has given an alarm to the estate management over their service on handling complaints. The toddler slipped through a gap in railings caused by a missing bar on 13 February 1994. Residents claimed that complaints had been repeatedly lodged about the damaged railing in 1992 and 1993 but the Housing Department said there was no such complaint on record. Immediately after the incident, the Housing Department started a trial Customer Service Assistance Scheme in four estates. The main duties of the Customer Service Assistants are to receive complaints from tenants and issue acknowledgement receipts. They are also responsible for referring urgent cases to housing officers for immediate action. After a trial period of two months, the Scheme is to be expanded to cover 153 housing estates. The introduction of this Scheme is a positive step to provide remedial measures in handling resident complaints. However, tenants should be properly notified that they are entitled to know the progress/results of their complaints. The current practice is that Customer Service Assistant will only inform complainants about the progress/results of their complaints if residents take initiative to ask for report. On the other hand, the employment of Customer Service Assistants cannot be a substitute for the important task of patrolling the estates by estate management staff. The Housing Officers Association in its June 1994 Newsletter revealed that it have repeatedly voiced its concern over the problem of lack of time in patrolling the estates. It is a contradiction to the claim made by the high-ranking housing officials that they are performing their role and patrolling the estates regularly. The value-for-money study of 1985 has ridiculously classified the task of patrolling estates an unproductive activity. If the Housing Department does not recognize the importance of the patrolling task and provide additional staff for this activity, it is worrying that the passive approach of receiving complaints from tenants through the Customer Service Assistance Scheme will not prevent tragedies such as the one happening earlier in Sha Tin.

The law and order problem prompted by a number of rape cases in the remote housing estates of Tuen Mun has further reinforced the Authority's decision to upgrade the security measures in PRH blocks. The Housing Authority agreed that the costs for providing security installations and their subsequent maintenance be borne by the Authority. About $250 million will be spent on installing security measures in 351 newly completed housing blocks in the next three years. The installation of security gates and closed-circuit cameras in lifts and the employment of security guards will give residents a better sense of security, which is most welcomed by public housing tenants. What we need is to speed up the improvement measures and to extend them to older housing estates built between late 1960s and 1980s.

"Increasing funds alone cannot solve the problem," said the Chairperson of the Housing Authority. Apart from having an effective implementation of maintenance and management service to ensure that money is put to good use, gaining residents' full support and cooperation is of equal importance. The idea of introducing reforms of management at district level mentioned by the Authority's Chairperson in the 1994 open meeting is not a new one. Pressure groups have been advocating this for some years.[37] To ensure management efficiency and to take better care of the needs of individual estates, estate management requires fuller participation from the community.

☐ Conclusion

We have witnessed policy changes in 1993–1994 and there are hopes for those needy households to gain benefits from all the measures introduced. Yet, the magnitude of these changes and the impact of the new policies on public sector housing consumers is to be monitored carefully. From the above discussion, we are quite sure that more people will benefit from changes brought forward in 1993–1994 but many more are still waiting for their turn to be allocated an adequate public sector housing unit and provided with up-to-standard management and maintenance service.

To improve housing services to the low- to middle-income households, what we need is not only an increase of financial support from the government but also its determination to expand and speed up the public housing programme with formed land and adequate infrastructural support facilities and to allow fuller participation of the people.

---

[37] Joint Committee on Review of Housing Policies, *Unofficial White Paper on Housing Policies in the 1990s*, January 1992.

16

Education

Anthony Sweeting

☐ Towards a Review of 1993–1994

The purpose of this chapter is to review developments in the field of education which have taken place in Hong Kong from July 1993 to June 1994. The review is based on an exploration of official documents published in the period and of reports or commentaries appearing in the local press. It focuses upon the clients and agents of educational activity and on the main issues which divided them during the year, attempting to draw conclusions about problems and progress. It does not, however, claim to offer an encyclopaedic description of the educational system.

☐ Clients and Agents

Students

There were about 1.3 million students undertaking full-time courses of study in Hong Kong during the year. If one were to add the students in courses abroad and those undertaking part-time courses, one will gain a clearer impression of the scope of educational activity. Partly because of their numbers, students received close attention in the local press. Much of it was critical.

Students were said to be more interested in livelihood concerns than in current affairs. Their ignorance of and lack of interest in China and more

---

Anthony Sweeting is a reader in the Department of Curriculum Studies, the University of Hong Kong.

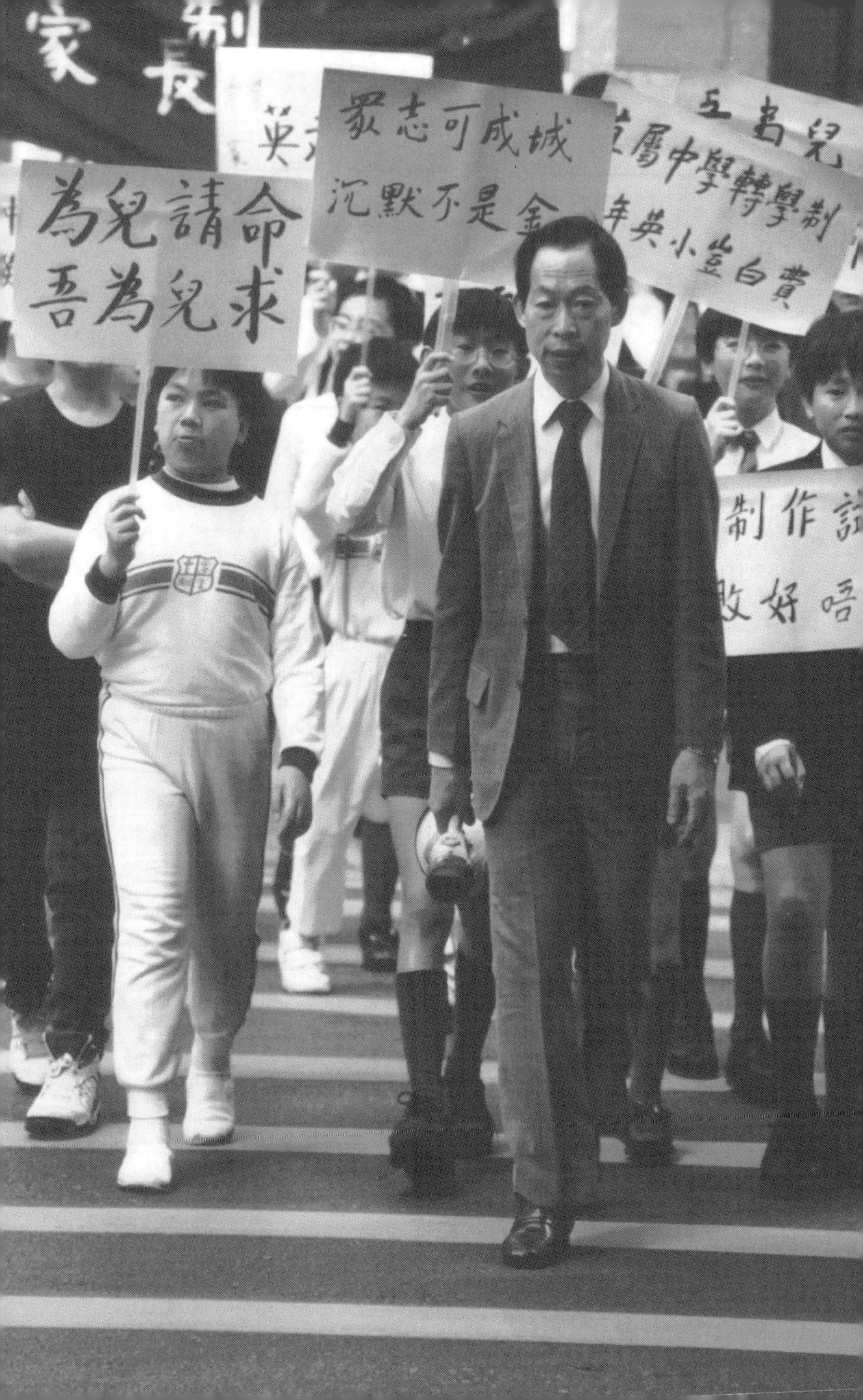
為兒請命
吾為兒求
衆志可成城
沉默不是金
屬中學轉學制
英小豈白費

generally in political issues earned rebuke as well as suggestions for curricular change. Their language standards in Chinese and in English frequently provoked negative comment. The problems of students described either as "academic low achievers" or, from their results in the Secondary School Places Allocation Scheme, as "Band 5 students" continued to excite anxiety, despite the publication in June 1993 of the final report by the working group on "Support Services for Schools with Band 5 Students." Students dropping out of the system aroused concern, especially when a survey of 400 dropouts from junior secondary forms revealed in early 1994 that almost 70 per cent of the 155 respondents blamed the schools, claiming that they had developed no sense of belonging and that teaching methods were unattractive. Commentators called for a full-scale review of the system of nine-year compulsory education and for the government to make available more "alternative" educational opportunities such as could be found in prevocational and practical schools. The suggestion that the dropout problem at Secondary Form 4 level could be solved by extending the scope of compulsory education to eleven years appeared somewhat naïve and received little support. One Education Department official admitted, however, that the concept of "beating the tiger" actually meant scrutinizing the whole education system in order to resolve the dropout problem and that it was essential that educationalists identify clearly students' needs, the role teachers could play, and the strategies suited to acquiring more resources to tackle the problem.

A perceived upsurge in crime involving young people led to calls for greater cooperation between the Education Department, the Social Welfare Department, and the police so that an integrated guidance programme for teenagers could be organized. The activities of triad members in schools attracted much publicity, focusing on stories of intimidation and extortion, together with the news that children as young as five were engaged in drug trafficking. Drug abuse was described as the number one enemy of Hong Kong youth. All indicators suggested a worsening situation, including the rising numbers of students seeking methadone treatment at clinics. Similarly, the press reported an increase in the numbers of young people requesting psychological counselling from student services, which were described as inadequate and uncoordinated. Suicides or attempted suicides of students claimed headlines during every single month of the year under review, blame being attributed variously to the pressures placed on the young by the school system, especially examinations, to lack of attention and guidance by parents or, alternatively, to the role of the family in actually creating stress, to problems of personal relationships, and to the influence of the mass media, including comics.

Newspaper emphasis on the negative aspects of students' behaviour and attitudes may be as much a comment on newspapers as it is on students. To counterbalance possible bias, one should note that the vast majority of Hong Kong students continue to work hard and many achieve impressive results. Numerous students take part in community service activities. Others are active in sports and a range of healthy hobbies. More than a hundred students from four schools volunteered to escort schoolgirls home in a district which had suffered from a spate of sex crimes. The suggestion made early in the year that one way to help deal with children who have serious emotional problems and even suicidal tendencies would be to set up guidance teams comprising senior students shows confidence in their intentions and abilities. The representation of student unions on management committees at the tertiary education level, the call for even greater student union activity at the secondary level, and the establishment in March 1994 of a joint student union for schools in the Tsuen Wan/Kwai Chung district suggests similar faith, as does student representation on the new Education Services Liaison Group, intended to monitor the services provided by the Education Department.

Parents

The role of parents in education was regarded somewhat ambivalently by administrators, spokespersons of pressure groups, and journalists. Their participation in such bodies as the Committee on Home-School Cooperation, the Educational Services Liaison Group, and, at the individual school level, Parent-Teacher Associations was encouraged. Although even its chairman doubted the autonomy of the Home-School Cooperation Committee, during the year it publicized the need for efficient communication between homes and schools by means of a van, a series of leaflets, and surveys of parents' opinions on such issues as the size and weight of school bags, the amount and nature of homework, and the balance between academic subjects and extracurricular activities in schools. It also sponsored research and began to disburse funds to facilitate the growth of Parent-Teacher Associations. The Education Services Liaison Group was produced by random selection from under 90 people who responded to an invitation, three of whom were appointed as parent-representatives and two each to represent students, teachers, schools, and the general public. It began its work of monitoring the services provided by the Education Department and forwarding suggestions to the Board of Education in November.

On the other hand, parents also played their more customary roles during the year — as sources of complaint and as subjects of exhortation, cajoling, and patronization. A recurrent complaint concerned the shortage of schools in certain districts and, especially, the shortage of places in Class 1 of primary schools and in Forms 1, 4 and 6 of secondary schools (i.e., at the transitions from pre-school to primary school, primary school to secondary, junior secondary to senior secondary, and senior secondary to sixth form education). Other complaints from parents centred on the rising cost of textbooks and the methods adopted by publishers to influence purchases (such as the offer of free exercise books and the production of "tied-in" workbooks). Parents were exhorted to pay more attention to the psychological development and the moral education of their children, to place less pressure on them, and to make less noise at home. Many were branded as conservative when they revealed that they preferred their children to be in English-medium schools. At least one school devised its own "educational marketing strategy" to convince parents of the virtues of mother-tongue education. Spokespersons of pressure groups and from the Education Department frequently talked of the need for "parent education" in this field.

Teachers

There are almost 50,000 teachers in all types of schools in Hong Kong. The overall vacancy rate in 1993–1994 was only 1.3 per cent, whereas the overall wastage rate (including retirements) was 11.7 per cent. Vacancies were highest among special school teachers. Whereas most kindergarten teachers who left their posts took up employment outside the teaching profession, most primary and secondary school teachers cited migration as their reason for leaving the profession. Methods adopted by the Education Department to improve the teacher supply position included the reactivation of the Teacher Recruitment Information Office (TRIO), the launching of a new "Be My Teacher" campaign, the re-employment of retired teachers and the reduction of minimal admission requirements for the colleges of education. At pre-school, primary and secondary levels, the ratio of trained to untrained teachers was lower among new recruits than it was among existing teacher-stock, a situation which reinforced the continuing need for in-service teacher education programmes and underlined the problems faced by teacher education institutions attempting to run pre-service courses. Questions concerning teacher qualifications, especially the equivalence of qualifications obtained abroad, occupied the attentions of the Advisory Committee on Teacher Education and Qualifications (ACTEQ), which had been set up in February 1993 as a government response to Education Commission Report No. 5 (ECR5). Among other tasks, ACTEQ supervised the work of the Education Department's Non-Graduate Teachers' Qualification Assessment (NGTQA), which provided one supply source, mainly from China and Taiwan, for additional primary school teachers.

The role, status, and image of teachers attracted a range of comments. The Governor, for example, said how impressed he was with the profession's vitality. Journalists and pressure group spokespersons, however, compared the position and workload of teachers in Hong Kong unfavourably with those of teachers in the People's Republic of China and in Taiwan. Similarly, remarks about the dedication of teachers, their role in improving the quality of education, and how those with a high self-image are able to promote healthier self-images among their students should be balanced against reports of the provision of a "help-line" by the Education Department for teachers under stress, of unimaginative teaching methods concentrating on the promotion of rote-learning, and of numerous errors appearing in teacher-constructed test-papers.

Two measures designed by ECR5 to enhance the status and improve the morale of teachers began to take formal shape during the year. These were the Council for Professional Conduct in Education (CPCE) and the Hong Kong Institute of Education (HKIEd). Both attracted considerable publicity.

In the case of the CPCE, the crucial date was 20 April, election day. Some interested parties complained about an alleged lack of assistance provided by the Education Department. Others remarked on the likelihood that the Hong Kong Professional Teachers' Union (HKPTU), the largest and most vociferous of the teachers' unions, would have a strong influence on the outcome of the elections. An anonymous educator claimed that teachers with heavy workloads would not show great interest in the CPCE elections and this prediction seemed to be borne out by the relatively few nominations of candidates. The two main categories of membership (14 seats nominated by teachers and representing types of schools, 11 nominated by and representing organizations such as schools councils, subject associations, and teachers' unions) were supplemented by nominations from the Director of Education of one person to represent the Education Department and two to serve as "lay members." The complex procedures for the election went ahead. In the event, it was reported that the turnout for teacher-nominated categories was about 90 per cent, though only about 60 per cent of eligible voters cast their votes in the organization-nominated categories. With few exceptions, victorious candidates attended the first meeting of the CPCE on 22 April, when they proceeded to elect their chairman and vice-chairman. Subsequent meetings of the CPCE, in addition to criticizing its lack of resources (especially accommodation), made it clear that the majority of members favoured expanding its remit and campaigning for its elevation into a statutory body. The Director of Education, however, was adamant that the newly elected CPCE should not be regarded as an interim body and that it should concentrate upon the drafting of a new Code of Professional Ethics for teachers, although he did concede that, in three years' time, there would be a review of its status and functions.

By May 1994, the HKIEd had achieved substantive legal status and much more than skeletal shape. The appointment of its Directorate staff, the passing of its Ordinance, and the consequent setting up of its Governing Council were important indicators of progress. During May, it began recruitment campaigns both for students and for lecturers. The autonomy of the HKIEd, its provision of better pay and more generous fringe benefits for teaching staff (including fee assistance for higher degree study), and the prospect of rethinking the nature of courses for kindergarten, primary, and junior secondary teachers ensured that it was rapidly accepted as a major new force in teacher education. The fact that it absorbed the four colleges of education together with the Institute of Language in Education (ILE) helped improve the image of teacher education at these levels, though the contrast in management styles between the ILE and the colleges may cause the HKIEd itself a few "teething problems." Throughout the year, the local Chinese language press gave coverage to anxieties expressed by the Association of Lecturers at Colleges of Education that promotion prospects were threatened by the establishment of the HKIEd. The secondment of college lecturers to the HKIEd, with arrangements for those who wished to transfer back to the civil service to do so as soon as was practicable without detriment to their seniority, also provoked dissension. The other main debating point stimulated by the HKIEd concerned its decision to separate the training of primary school teachers from that of secondary school teachers. Opponents predicted that most prospective student-teachers would opt for training as secondary school teachers because of the higher salary scales and that, as a result, the primary school sector would suffer. By the end of June, however, such problems seem to have faded — at least, from the news — and the HKIEd was concentrating on its recruitment programmes and the planning of its new courses. The latter did not yet include degree programmes, but these continued to be provided by the Faculties of Education at the University of Hong Kong and The Chinese University of Hong Kong, while plans were nearing fruition for the courses to be offered by a consortium of the Open Learning Institute, the Hong Kong Baptist College, and the School of Professional and Continuing Education at the University of Hong Kong.

Administrators and Policy-makers

The other main agents of education in Hong Kong can be described as administrators and policy-makers, although the demarcation between the two on occasions appears to be quite flexible. During the year under review, comments appeared in the local press criticizing the concentration of power in the hands of principals and school supervisors. A particular case which attracted the spotlight of the mass media occurred at the St. Joan of Arc Secondary School. Originally arising from complaints by five students that they had been strongly "persuaded" to withdraw from the school, a saga developed between November 1993 and May 1994, involving accusations from teachers that their dignity was demeaned by the practice of having to "clock-in" each day and adverse comments about the autocratic way staff meetings were conducted, as well as general remarks about the strict discipline imposed in the school. After investigations by the Education Department and the Catholic Diocesan authorities, the school's management committee was restructured, the principal was suspended from duty, and eventually both the principal and the school supervisor were induced to resign.

Efforts to improve the efficiency of the central administration included the reorganization of the Education Department's Administrative Division, the creation of a new Division of Information Systems, and the development of a five-year plan involving an information system strategy intended to strengthen the Education Department's communications with schools. The Education Department publicized its series of performance pledges at the end of August 1993 and a departmental survey plus feedback from the newly formed Education Services Liaison Group enabled it to claim in

February 1994 that it had met 90 per cent of its targets. The Director of Education expressed his belief in the importance of public relations and one newspaper rated his job performance on the whole as B, with an A grade for public speaking. Although the Director's own allegedly strict management style came in for some criticism and was even blamed for an "earthquake" involving the departure of several senior members of the Department's staff, it was quickly defended, with alternative explanations provided for staff movements.

What appeared at the time to be of even more cataclysmic significance was the resignation from Hong Kong's principal policy-concerned body, the Education Commission, of two of its members, both academics. The reasons which they gave for their resignations in November 1993 centred around their belief that the Commission had become a mere "talking shop" which had lost its sense of direction. They argued that critical policy areas such as pre-school and special education had been neglected and the Commission's energies diverted to the consideration of technical matters. Their action and arguments struck a responsive chord. For over a week, the press reverberated with editorials, commentary, and reportage on the significance of the resignations. Much of this was critical of the Commission, which was accused of being dominated by officials, unnecessarily secretive, insensitive to public opinion, and representative of the shortsightedness of a "sunset" government. Several commentators called for a review of the methods of selecting Commission members, suggesting that the appointment system should be replaced by elections. The Commission's chairperson publicly defended its track record and was supported by the remaining members in her denial that a sense of direction and purpose had been lost. The Secretary for Education and Manpower announced that the appointment system would not be changed because the role of members was to give expert advice and this could not be guaranteed through direct elections. In the event, towards the end of December, three new appointments (including a specialist in pre-school education) were made to fill the vacancies caused by the two resignations. For much of the remainder of the year under review, the Commission focused on three basic issues for which three working groups had been formed: language proficiency, educational standards, and the funding of education. Issues which occupied the energies of other policy-related bodies included pre-school education (with important input from an *ad hoc* working group of the Board of Education), a range of curricular matters (particularly those deriving from the activities of the Curriculum Development Institute and from the Target Oriented

Curriculum Advisory Committee), and the development at tertiary education level of "centres of excellence" (as recommended by the University and Polytechnic Grants Committee, or UPGC).

Pressure Groups

Although they do not fit comfortably into a designation as either clients or agents of education, mention should be made also of the activities of education-concerned pressure groups during the year. The HKPTU maintained its customary high profile, responding quickly and usually critically on almost every issue — although, HKPTU endorsement of the introduction of computer systems into schools to reduce the clerical tasks of teachers may rate as one case in which the union was actually supporting the government. The spokespersons of the political party Meeting Point on education were also very active, as were leaders of the Federation of Educational Workers and, on matters related to their special interests, the Association of Lecturers at Colleges of Education, the Hong Kong Council of Early Childhood Education and Services, and various Parents' Concern Groups. These and other groups ensured that all policy proposals and many administrative decisions were subject to debate. Their close links with the mass media, however, and the fact that several of their leaders held positions on important education policy-concerned committees almost certainly prolonged, embittered, and politicized both discussion and decision-making, suggesting to some observers that only the loudest, most strident voices were heard.

☐ Main Issues

Language in Education

Throughout the year, many different minds and voices addressed the complex and often emotive problems concerning language policy. The central (though by no means the only) problem is related to the choice of medium of instruction, especially at secondary school level. Whether measured by yardage of newsprint, by decibel level, or by signs of consensus, the major outcome of the year was a distinct increase in momentum of the campaign in favour of "mother tongue education." The central problem did not concern so much a dispute over whether or not mother tongue education was most suitable for the majority of students. The government, via its "positive discrimination" policy and its sanctioning of the Education Commission Report No. 4 (ECR4 of 1990) had already accepted that it was. During the year many officials reiterated this position and the Education Department even organized a travelling exhibition to publicize the advantages of mother tongue education and the achievements of those who had received it. The crux of the problem was implementation. It involved the persuasion of parents who believed that, whatever the language abilities of their offspring might be, they would benefit later, in terms of either employment or opportunities for higher education, if they attended schools which had, at least officially, adopted English as medium of instruction. Influenced by these parental attitudes, numerous school authorities remained reluctant to switch from English to Chinese. The result was a mismatch between opportunities for Chinese-based education and the numbers of students considered unsuited to benefit from its alternative. This led to doubts about the efficacy of the ECR4-derived exercise known as the Medium of Instruction Grouping Assessment (MIGA), which was linked with the Secondary School Placement Allocation (SSPA) in order to provide data about students' language abilities. Many advocates of mother tongue education favoured compulsion — of the schools, the students and their parents. The government baulked at this, considering that the inducement of schools through additional resources for those willing to change over to Chinese-medium education, the provision of information to parents about the language abilities of their offspring as well as about the language practices of schools in their vicinity, and various other forms of parent education were more appropriate ways of tackling the issue. During the year, the decision of St. Joseph's Anglo-Chinese School and twenty-four Catholic Diocesan schools to switch to Chinese-medium teaching earned the acclaim of many commentators in the local press, but also generated bitter opposition from some parents who complained about lack of consultation.

The establishment of a Language Fund, announced in the Governor's address at the opening of the Legislative Council in early October last year, reflected concern about language proficiencies. With an initial allocation of $300 million, the Language Fund was intended to improve proficiencies in both Chinese and English by upgrading the skills of language teachers through new, intensive courses and through the preparation of new teaching materials, while increasing language learning opportunities both in the classroom and through extracurricular activities. Almost all interested groups and individuals welcomed the setting up of the Language Fund, with several emphasizing the need for at least half of the $300 million to be devoted to Chinese language projects. By the beginning of May 1994, an Advisory Committee had been set up to oversee the disbursement of the Fund.

In the meantime, another body occupied itself with similar concerns. This was the Education Commission's Working Group on Language Proficiency. Established in October 1993, the Working Group consulted language specialists from Hong Kong and overseas, commissioned a survey on perceptions of what helps and hinders language development, and focused on the language situation in schools, including the problems faced by a student progressing through the educational system, in order to suggest policies which would maximize the help, minimize the hindrances, and contribute to the solution of the problems. It also sought to identify topics which would benefit from research. Leaks of its report, due to be published in July, began to appear in the local press from late May onwards and in great detail at the end of June. At this time, it appeared that there would be little public opposition against proposals to improve the existing supporting framework for language learning or against the Working Group's other suggestions about language research and methods of promoting better language learning and teaching. However, the rumoured recommendation that, in usual circumstances, a child should not begin to learn a second language before the age of eight provoked some hostile reactions as being too directive. Perhaps ironically, its reliance on the publication of the outcome of the SSPA and MIGA exercise in 1994, on further research, monitoring actual language use in secondary classrooms during 1994–1995, and a review of the arrangements for bridging programmes, as the basis for a Medium of Instruction policy, was open to criticism as being insufficiently directive.

Quality in Education

Indications that concern over quality in education was increasing during the year were provided by the numerous speeches and press statements attempting to identify its chief constituents. Five other developments were directly linked with such a concern.

The School Management Initiative (SMI), which since its launching in 1991 had attracted strong criticism from pressure groups and some of the more traditional members of school management committees, appeared to be gaining ground. In the first two years, only 34 secondary schools had entered the scheme. This was despite publicity given to its four main aims: to define more clearly the roles of principals, managers, supervisors, and sponsors; to provide for greater participation in policy-making by parents, teachers, and past-students; to encourage more systematic planning and evaluation of the school's activities and fuller reporting of their performance; and, to offer schools more flexibility in the use of resources to meet their pre-defined purposes. Although these aims seemed admirable, requirements that each school produce a proper constitution for its management committee, as well as an annual School Plan and an annual School Profile in detail, ensured that many schools were reluctant to enter the scheme. However, the SMI's Advisory Committee set up various task groups to compile reference materials designed to help schools implement change. The Education Department ran seminars and workshops on the SMI for practising teachers and principals, promised to set up a resource centre of SMI-related materials in 1994–1995, and commissioned The Chinese University of Hong Kong and the University of Hong Kong to conduct training courses for staff from schools joining the scheme. Practical incentives to join were emphasized. These included the provision of a block grant for expenditure unrelated to teachers' salaries, a substitute teacher grant, an additional non-recurrent furniture and equipment grant, and priority in the provision of computer systems for school administration. In September 1993, the scheme was extended to primary schools. The result was that 70 primary schools joined the scheme in September, together with 23 additional secondary schools. Feedback from schools in the scheme was, on the whole, positive and commentary in the local press generally became less critical, although the HKPTU maintained its position that students unions, alumni associations, and Parent-Teachers Associations should be formed before the implementation of the SMI.

Secondly, the Education and Manpower Branch of the Government Secretariat published its *School Education: A Statement of Aims* in September 1993, based on the draft statement earlier produced by the Education Commission. Some commentators criticized the pamphlet on the grounds that it omitted specific mention of nationalism as a valid aim for school education, but others noted and appreciated its inclusion of suggestions about the implementation of the aims and their evaluation by the Board of Education and its new Educational Aims Implementation Sub-committee, the Advisory Committee on Teacher Education and Qualifications, and, for a general overview, the Education Commission.

A third development involved modifications to the ECR4 proposals for

"Targets and Target Related Assessment" (TTRA), which had aroused considerable anxiety amongst teachers, mainly because of its anticipated effects on their workload. The name of the policy was changed to "Target Oriented Curriculum" (TOC) in order to downplay the assessment aspects and emphasize the implications of clearly defined targets for learning and teaching. Documents and reference materials were simplified. Attention was paid to the encouragement of greater teacher participation in the development of TOC policy and materials, improved teacher education programmes, and resource support for teachers, including the promise of a TOC resource centre, a "bank" of learning tasks, and additional funding to enable schools to acquire better resources. The new TOC Advisory Committee advised the Director of Education to restrict initial implementation to "key-stage 2" (or Primary 4 classes) and to the three core subjects of Chinese Language, English Language, and Mathematics and this advice was accepted. In general, the modifications did allay some anxieties, though there were still complaints about over-hasty implementation and a lack of "user-friendliness" in many of the reference and resource materials.

Fourthly, ideas about quality also affected the tertiary level of education. In this field, which some commentators claimed to be over-generously financed, a "research assessment" exercise was piloted to evaluate the productivity of academics in the different institutions, with the intention that, eventually, a significant proportion of funding would depend on the outcome of such an exercise. There were teething problems associated with this exercise but a refined version was promised for 1994–1995 and the prospect of an appraisal of tertiary level teaching quality raised. In November 1993, the UPGC published *Higher Education 1991–2001: An Interim Report* to raise questions about the future direction of higher education in the territory, taking into consideration not only the balance between degree and sub-degree courses and how to cater for the large-scale increase in students and teachers created by the expansion programme announced in 1989, but also a concern for future goals and standards. Among the proposals contained in the report, the one which stimulated most comment and was most clearly associated with the concept of quality in education was the idea of establishing "centres of excellence" within existing tertiary institutions. These would be particularly well resourced so that they could provide "high quality bilingual manpower for both Hong Kong and the hinterland," serve as reference points especially in Business and Social Studies and in innovative science and technology, and, in the view of the

UPGC, help Hong Kong retain a leading position in the economic development of China and the Pacific Rim.

The fifth main development concerned the Education Commission's Working Group on Educational Standards. Unlike the case of its Working Group on Language Proficiency, few leaks appeared in the local press about the workings of this body. An exception was the rumour involving the Education Department's new plan to integrate its procedures for school inspections into what was described as a "Whole School Approach." This was said to overlap with the Working Group's advocacy of strategies designed to ensure high quality for schools to practise which would be monitored by a "Quality Assurance Unit" (QAU). It appeared that the latter would be a small team of expert inspectors, independent of the Education Department, reporting to the Secretary for Education and Manpower. It might be assumed that the draft report will attempt to resolve this overlap and also present a version of Quality Assurance which will coordinate the efforts of Educational Aims Implementation, the SMI, and the TOC in the interests of greater commitment in the schools to the achievement of agreed goals. The limited amount of material published before the end of June 1994 suggested that the QAU would involve itself primarily with a new type of assessment of the quality of schools, reporting its evaluation to concerned parties and making this information available to parents, teachers and school management alike in order to ensure a high degree of accountability.

The Funding of Education

As usual, there were frequent criticisms of the alleged paucity of the funds devoted to education, together with complaints about the amounts provided for specific educational activities such as special education and adult education. Attention was also paid to the methods by which funds were distributed to the educational institutions. This was basically the business of the Education Commission's third Working Group.

The main problems addressed by the group were the unequal distribution of funds throughout the education system and the tight central control of how funds were to be used by individual schools. Although no leaks about the recommendations of this body appeared in the local press before the end of June, it might be assumed that its main message will be compatible with the report on educational standards and with the SMI. This would mean more flexibility given to educational institutions to determine their own needs and to decide on priorities for expenditure, together with greater "transparency" and fuller information passing between the central administration, the educational institutions, and the general public.

Pre-primary Education

Extra funding will be expected for the education of the 3–6 years old if the report of the Board of Education's *Ad Hoc* Pre-Primary Education Working Group is adopted by the government. The remit of this group was wide and, given the green light to look at the overview, members hoped to take advantage of the timing to review all aspects of early childhood education.

The proposal that represented the most significant breakthrough towards improving pre-primary services was the recommendation to upgrade teachers' training from the present short, part-time in-service courses to full-time, two-year courses in 1995 and eventually to make them pre-service in nature. Questions and suggestions about how these improvements would be funded created unease amongst Legislative Council members, educational groups, and even within the Working Group. The idea of government subsidizing what is essentially a private sector as proposed by some pressure groups aroused debate, which, up to the end of June, was essentially unresolved, although, for the time being, advocates of this view seem to be appeased by an additional direct subsidy (calculated with reference to the pay of a Qualified Kindergarten Teacher and 5 per cent of school fees), with private kindergartens receiving a teachers' salary supplement for a period of three years. Larger questions of how to unify kindergartens with child care centres (the former under the aegis of the Education Department, the latter under the Social Welfare Department) and how to achieve quality assurance at the pre-primary level were not fully addressed and certainly not resolved.

☐ Conclusion

There were numerous influences on education policy during the year. Perhaps the most noteworthy were the actions and arguments of individuals and pressure groups within Hong Kong, perceptions about the interests of the Hong Kong economy, the "1997 factor" and the increasingly common practice of "looking over the shoulder at" or even second-guessing politicians and officials in the People's Republic of China, and the desire to keep abreast of international trends and developments. It is possible, for example, that the more urgent approach adopted towards pre-school problems was at least partly an outcome of public reaction to the resignations from the Education Commission as well as to pressures from educational groups. The same factors might well have influenced the decision to produce the three new reports from Education subcommittees as drafts for public consultation before fully-fledged and possibly amended Education Commission Reports Nos. 6, 7, and 8 are published. A concern for Hong Kong's economic development appeared to be at the heart of the UPGC's proposals about centres of excellence, while the concern expressed by employers about falling language standards contributed towards a willingness to spend money on attempts to resolve Hong Kong's many language problems. The increased number of children legally entering Hong Kong from China provoked public discussion about arrangements which should be made to cater for them, including the provision of more facilities for the Putonghua teaching and, perhaps, a specially tailored curriculum. The sharp reaction at the end of June 1994 to the Director of Education's suggestion that events, such as the June 4 "incident" in Beijing and others which had taken place during the last twenty years should not be discussed in textbooks seemed motivated partly by the belief that he was kowtowing to China. The SMI, the TOC, and proposed measures to deal with language proposals were frequently linked with similar developments overseas, often but not invariably in the United Kingdom.

Despite some progress in the areas of teacher education, school management, curriculum development, and plans for pre-school education, problems persisted. In general, debate about education became more obviously politicized and increasingly embittered, while the various innovations in education appeared to lead to greater fragmentation and at least the potential for demarcation disputes between the various agencies and even between the various consultative committees. "Transparency" was one of the buzz-words of the year, but the increased level of transparency may have actually hindered the smooth and effective implementation of some proposals. Inadequate levels of staffing, together with the need to process a whole series of innovations and deal with a very large number of questions from members of the Legislative Council and leaders of pressure groups, contributed towards a demoralized spirit among some officials. This was not reduced by the removal of teacher education responsibilities from the Education Department or by support shown publicly for making the Curriculum Development Institute independent of the Education Department.

On the other hand, the main directions which can be detected from a review of 1993–1994 seem to be towards greater decentralization. Advice from consultative committees (over such issues as the SMI, Language, Educational Aims and Standards, Centres of Excellence, Funding, the Council for Professional Conduct in Education, and even, to an extent, the Target Oriented Curriculum) was in favour of handing responsibilities over to the educational institutions or the agents involved so that they might formulate and implement their own policies on such matters within the guidelines provided by a larger framework and make the effort to "sell" their policies to parents and the wider public. When considered in conjunction with the attention now being paid to quality assurance and the higher level of activism among students, teachers, and parents, this trend provides some grounds for optimism.

Elderly in Need of Care and Financial Support

Henry T. K. Mok

☐ **Introduction**

The speed of population ageing and the need for substantial care and financial support have constituted a burning issue for most countries around the world. Hong Kong is no exception. In 1994, several key studies have been done, which include community care for the elderly[1] and a consultancy report on the Old Age Pension Scheme (OPS).[2] A government working party was also convened and is to publish its report on elderly service planning by December 1994. The aim of this chapter is to review these findings and outline some of the basic issues relating to the needs of the elderly in Hong Kong.

☐ **Demographic Issues**

The publication of the *1991 Census Report*[3] and the report on the 20-year population projection of Hong Kong from 1991 to 2011[4] provide very

---

Henry T. K. Mok is a senior lecturer in the Department of Applied Social Studies, Hong Kong Polytechnic.

[1] Hong Kong Council of Social Service, *Role of the Family in Community Care* (Hong Kong: Hong Kong Council of Social Service, 1994).

[2] Wyatt Company, *Feasibility Study on an Old Age Pension Scheme in Hong Kong* (Hong Kong: Wyatt Company, 1994).

[3] Hong Kong government, *1991 Census Report* (Hong Kong: Census and Statistics Department, 1993).

[4] Hong Kong government, *Hong Kong Population Projection 1991–2011* (Hong Kong: Census and Statistics Department, 1992).

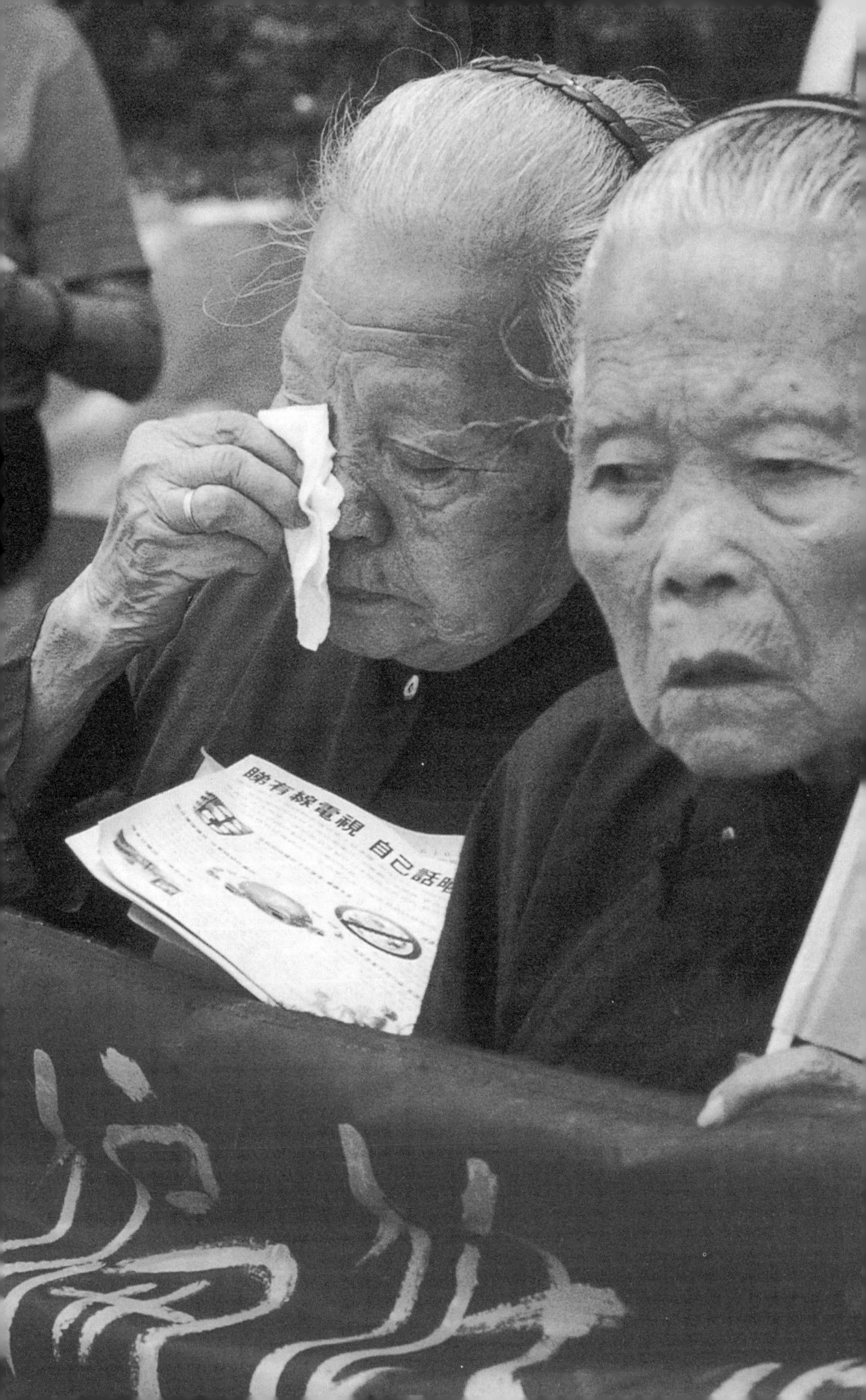
睇有線電視 自己話

important data for understanding the current and future demographic development of the elderly population in Hong Kong.

Facing a Rapid Rate of Ageing

As shown in Table 1, the Hong Kong population will be increasing by around 3 per cent at five-year intervals. But the age 65+ population will increase by more than 10 per cent by 2006. It is clear that the elderly population is growing more rapidly than the overall population in the next two decades. When compared with other countries in Asia, the percentage of old people ranks second to that of Japan, which has the fastest rate of population ageing in the world (see Table 2). In fact, the 1991 Census data

Table 1. Hong Kong Population Projection (in Thousands)

	1991	1996	2001	2006	2011
Total population	5,686	5,885	6,081	6,282	6,486
Rate of increase	2.9%	3.5%	3.3%	3.3%	3.2%
Age 65+ population	500	610	705	762	793
Age 65+ rate of increase	17.9%	22.0%	15.6%	8.1%	4.1%
Elderly ratio	8.8%	10.4%	11.6%	12.1%	12.2%

Source: Hong Kong government, *Hong Kong Population Projection 1991–2011* (Hong Kong: Census and Statistics Department, 1992).

Table 2. Percentage of Age 65+ Population in Various Asian Countries

	1990	2000
Malaysia	3.8	4.4
Indonesia	3.9	5.0
Thailand	3.9	5.0
South Korea	4.7	6.3
Singapore	5.6	7.1
Taiwan	6.1	8.4
Hong Kong	8.9	11.6
Japan	11.4	15.2

Sources: "Asia 2010," *Far Eastern Economic Review*, 17 May 1990, p. 29; Hong Kong government, *Hong Kong Population: A 20-Year Projection* (Hong Kong: Census and Statistics Department, November 1987).

has shown that the Hong Kong population satisfies all the features of an aged population structure, with 9 per cent age 65+ and a median age at 32. Hence, in 1991, Hong Kong's population joins the family of developed countries in having an aged population structure, whereas other Asian countries such as Malaysia, Indonesia, Thailand, South Korea, Singapore and Taiwan still enjoy a relatively younger population (see Table 2).

Aged Suffer from a Low Socioeconomic Status

The elderly population in Hong Kong does not enjoy a high status in social and economic terms. About 85 per cent of them came to Hong Kong from China. About 50 per cent live in public rental housing estates and over 80 per cent of them have a primary education or below.[5] In general, the elderly population is relatively poorer than the other age groups. For instance, in 1990, 6.6 per cent of the aged compared with 1.5 per cent of the total population received public assistance from the government.[6]

Increasing Demand for Social Services

It is understandable that as a person grows old and becomes more frail, he or she would need more social and medical care. This is particularly serious if one considers the increased life expectancy in Hong Kong. It is projected that male life expectancy will increase from 74.9 in 1991 to 77.3 in 2011, and female life expectancy will rise from 80.5 to 83.0.[7] Hence, if the number of old-old people (that is, 80 and over) increases in absolute terms, it is expected that more social services will be needed. It was estimated that the population of the age group 70–79 will increase by 58 per cent from 1991 to 2011. The very old-old will increase by threefold. The future demand for care of the elderly is tremendous.

Under these circumstances, it is important to look at the working population base which will carry the burden of supporting the aged population. Table 3 shows that in 1981, more than seven workers supported one elderly person; in 1991, about six supported one; but in 2011, less than five will support one elderly person. In other words, the demand for social

---

[5] See Note 3.
[6] See Note 3.
[7] See Note 4.

Table 3. Aged Dependency Ratio in Hong Kong (1981–2011)

Year	Age 65+ (a)	Age 15–64	Working force (b)	Aged dependency ratio (a ÷ b)
1981	32.7	342.3	250.4	1:7.66
1986	40.9	374.0	275.4	1:6.73
1991	48.2	388.9	281.1	1:5.83
1996@	61.6	421.1	310.0*	1:5.03
2001@	70.5	438.6	327.4*	1:4.64
2006@	76.2	455.6	342.0*	1:4.49
2011@	79.3	470.6	353.6*	1:4.46

Notes: * = Labour force participation rate is assumed to be 64.3 per cent of 15–64 population group based on 1991 figures.
@ = Estimates

Sources: Hong Kong government, *Hong Kong 1991 Population Census: Summary Results* (Hong Kong: Census and Statistics Department, 1992); Hong Kong government, *Hong Kong Population Projection 1991–2011* (Hong Kong: Census and Statistics Department, 1992).

services for the elderly increases tremendously while the supporting ratio keeps on decreasing. This means that Hong Kong society needs to devise some innovative measures to look after its ageing population in the near future.

☐ Issues of Elderly Care

In Hong Kong, there is great concern for the care of the elderly. Nonetheless, quite a number of the frail elderly have been left unwanted in institutions like hospitals, elderly homes, care and attention homes, and so on. Hence, it is important to assess the current need of the elderly in the community. One way of measuring the caring need is to assess the degree of dependency.

Caring Need of the Elderly

In 1994, the Hong Kong Council of Social Service[8] completed a detailed

---

[8] See Note 1.

study on the role of the family in community care. It was found that 85 per cent of the dependent elderly are capable of self-care. Assistance is needed most in tasks such as cooking, shopping, household cleaning, laundry and money management. On average, the elderly require regular assistance with five tasks, and need daily assistance with two tasks. However, it must be noted that the elderly are not the only ones, nor are they necessarily the ones, who receive such care. The study also reveals that over 80 per cent of the family carers found the dependent elderly eager to help with household chores such as looking after young children. Hence, one should avoid the stereotype of the elderly being dependent on the provision of care from others.

Disadvantaged Elderly Women

Significant sex and age differences were found in many aspects of retirement life by a recent study conducted by the University of Hong Kong.[9] Female respondents had fewer sources of income and were poorer compared with their male counterparts. They were more isolated and had a smaller social circle. Usually, they received less social support from their families as compared with others, particularly when they became older. In the authors' words,

> the cumulative effects of wage discrimination, occupational segregation, unpaid labour in the home, and interrupted workforce participation, coupled with their survivorship, place these women in a financially precarious position throughout old age. In addition, wage and retirement income policies have been based on the assumption that women are economically dependent on a wage-earning male head of household, who will share with his spouse his earnings....[10]

However, the issue of disadvantaged elderly women has not yet received much attention among professionals and policy-makers.

Psychosocial Burden for Family Carers

The aforementioned study of family carers of the elderly[11] also reveals that the care-givers spend on average 8 hours a day caring for the elderly. On weekends, the hours of care reach an average of 9.3. Moreover, half of the

---

[9] I. Chi, and K. W. Boey, *A Mental Health and Social Support Study of the Old-old in Hong Kong* (Hong Kong: University of Hong Kong, 1994).

[10] See Note 9, p. 53.

[11] See Note 1.

carers have spent more than ten years looking after the elderly. All these reflect the extent of the psychological and physical burden on the carers who are usually female members of the family. Furthermore, about half of the respondents in the study have to accommodate the caring roles by either quitting their employment or reducing the number of working hours. Thus, quite a number of them feel stressed, unhappy, depressed and less able to concentrate. Indeed, one-third of the carers feel that their family would be better off financially without caring responsibilities, and another 20 per cent feel they would be happier without these responsibilities. Looking into the future, one-quarter of them expect an increase in care-giving demand and worry about meeting the needs of the elderly. In short, carers themselves need support and services.

☐ Financial Needs of the Elderly

Many policy-makers and scholars do not see the importance of the financial needs of the elderly. They think that the availability of public assistance will provide a safety net for the elderly poor and society does not have to worry about those who are above the subsistence level. However, it has been clearly demonstrated[12] that the rate of impoverishment of the elderly exceeded 40 per cent from 1976 to 1986; that one-third of the elderly has been working up to age 70 and one-tenth up to age 80; that the number of elderly living with their family members was estimated to be halved in the next ten years; and that the financial support and physical care provided by the families to the elderly were found to be heavier, due to the increasing participation of female members in the labour force.

However, there is no social security provision for the retirement of the general public by the Hong Kong government, and the occupational retirement benefits in the private sector were found to be very limited, encompassing only less than 25 per cent of the total working population. A number of studies have shown that many elderly have to work for a living.[13] The

---

[12] H. Mok, "The Demographic Scenarios and the Social Security for the Aged in Hong Kong," *Hong Kong Journal of Social Work*, Vol. 22, No. 1 (1988), pp. 23–29.

[13] H. Mok, "Retirement Protection for the Aged: A Burning Issue in Hong Kong," in *Social Security and Industrial Workers in Hong Kong*, edited by H. Mok et al. (Hong Kong: Joint Publication of 14 Community Organizations, 1986), pp. 34–43.

1991 Census revealed that over 150,000, or about one-fifth, of the elderly population were still working and their median income was less than $3,500 (see Table 4). It is not surprising that the working poor have been striving very hard for the establishment of a public retirement protection system in Hong Kong since the late 1970s.

Because of public pressure, the government did consider various options of introducing a public retirement protection scheme. In 1977, the government proposed a semi-voluntary social insurance scheme, which was later rejected by the Government Secretariat in 1981 under severe opposition from the business sector. The unions and the popular organizations stepped up the pressure for a central provident fund (CPF) scheme in the first half of the 1980s, and succeeded in urging the government to put forward a restricted consultative document on CPF. But the idea was defeated by business representatives in the Legislative Council (Legco) debate in 1987, and was formally rejected by the Governor in the later part of that year. However, the introduction of direct elections in the Legco in 1991 pushed the government and the Executive Council (Exco) to take a

Table 4. Working Population by Age and Monthly Income from Main Employment

Monthly income	Age group (N = 153,385)			
	60–64		65 and over	
	N	(%)	N	(%)
Under $1,000	3,747	(2.4)	4,169	(2.7)
$1,000–1,999	6,722	(4.4)	9,377	(6.1)
$2,000–3,999	35,664	(23.3)	29,687	(19.4)
$4,000–5,999	21,865	(14.3)	11,608	(7.6)
$6,000–7,999	7,247	(4.7)	3,322	(2.2)
$8,000–9,999	2,557	(1.7)	1,201	(0.7)
$10,000–14,999	3,539	(2.3)	2,216	(1.4)
$15,000–19,999	1,202	(0.8)	740	(0.5)
$20,000–29,999	1,167	(0.8)	977	(0.6)
$30,000 and over	1,542	(1.0)	1,202	(0.7)
Unpaid family workers	1,714	(1.1)	1,920	(1.3)
Total	86,966	(56.7)	66,419	(43.3)

Source: Hong Kong government, *Hong Kong 1991 Population Census: Main Tables* (Hong Kong: Census and Statistics Department, 1992), Table C15, pp. 126–27.

proactive stand on the issue. To avoid the policy embarrassment and the constitutional crisis that might occur if the Legco passed a resolution to set up a retirement protection scheme, the Exco endorsed government action to propose a compulsory retirement protection scheme for public consultation in November 1991, two months after the first Legco direct elections in Hong Kong.

The government came up with a proposal for a compulsory private provident fund scheme entitled the "Retirement Protection Scheme" (RPS) in October 1992. The public consultation, however, ended with a unified opposition from the business sector and grassroots organizations, with all of them worrying about the financial guarantee of the scheme should the private financial institutions become bankrupt. The government reconsidered the whole issue and finally decided to propose the OPS in December 1993 with three rationale.

First, OPS provides immediate benefits upon implementation. A CPF or RPS will take at least thirty years to yield meaningful benefits for the retired workers only. Second, OPS provides income security for all eligible elderly citizens including housewives, the disabled and the current elderly population. A CPF or RPS will only cover those who have regular jobs for a long period of time such as over twenty or thirty years, and therefore, leaves the majority of the population unprotected. Third, the contribution rate under OPS would be much lower than that of a CPF or RPS.

☐ Proposal for the OPS

The public response to the proposal was mixed, due to the lack of details and figures for genuine assessment. In January 1994, the government invited the Wyatt Company to be the actuarial consultant for designing and assessing the financial feasibility of the proposed OPS. In July 1994, the Education and Manpower Branch of the Government Secretariat published a consultative paper on OPS with the following details:

1. The qualifying age for pension benefits should be 65.
2. A pensioner must be a Hong Kong resident and continue to reside in Hong Kong up to 180 days without absence a year.
3. No assets declaration is required for potential beneficiaries who have contributed to the OPS for not less than ten years and those aged 70 or above. Non-contributors between the ages of 65–69

must be able to declare that their overall financial resources are less than two million Hong Kong dollars.
4. The pension level should be set at $2,300 a month in 1994 dollars, to be indexed with the Composite Consumer Price Index.
5. Income earners making less than $4,000 a month should be exempted from contributions but their employers will have to pay the employers' share of the contributions. There should be no income ceiling for contribution purposes.
6. Members of civil service pension schemes and voluntary occupational retirement schemes should not be allowed to contract out of the OPS.
7. The cost of the OPS will be funded entirely by the total contributions from the employers, employees, self-employed and the government.
8. The recommended rate of contribution is 1.5 per cent of assessable income each from employers and employees in the case of salary earners, and 3 per cent of assessable profits for the self-employed.
9. The government is prepared to make a one-off contribution of $10 billion to the OPS as a start-up fund.
10. The OPS should be run by a new non-civil service public agency.

☐ Assessment on the Feasibility of the OPS

To embark on an assessment on the feasibility of the proposed OPS, it is necessary to examine the Wyatt feasibility study report.[14] A few scholars challenged the following assumptions on which the actuarial assessment was made:

1. An average annual wage increase over inflation rate after 2001 = 2 per cent
2. An average annual fertility rate after 2021 = 2.1
3. An average annual increase of total population in the age group of around 30 = 1 per cent
4. An average annual unemployment rate = 2 per cent
5. Pension benefit be indexed with inflation

---

[14] See Note 2.

Detailed discussion on these assumptions can be found in the feature article of the August edition of the *Hong Kong Economic Journal Monthly*.[15] But the challenge of these scholars was severely criticized for lacking evidential support.[16] The Hong Kong Affairs adviser, S. K. Tsang, has disputed some of the challenges with substantial evidence on 1 August 1994, and forcefully argued that these assumptions are to a large extent quite realistic.[17] For instance, some scholars misused the wage data and failed to recognize the use of assessable income (which should include all fringe benefits and allowances) in the actuarial calculation. Up to now, there has been no repudiation of Tsang's argument.

However, despite the fact that these scholars did not give substantial evidence to support their argument, there has been an underlying and genuine concern for the lack of projection analysis with the most pessimistic scenario. Lau has made a strong point on the lack of an actuarial assessment with all the estimates of the parameters lower than the core scenario.[18] Indeed, it is important to PREPARE FOR THE WORST in any policy-making and implementation. The consideration of the worst scenario will definitely be useful for developing contingency plans and alternative solutions. To work out the worst situations is urgently needed. An holistic actuarial assessment based on the following parameters would definitely clarify some of the worries in the minds of the people:

1. An average annual growth rate of assessable income after 1996 = 1 per cent
2. An average annual fertility rate after 2016 = 1.6
3. An average annual total population increase after 1996 = 0.5 per cent
4. An average rate of unemployment after 1996 = 6 per cent
5. Pension benefit be indexed with median income

---

[15] "The Issue of Old Age Pension," *Hong Kong Economic Journal Monthly*, August (1994).

[16] P. L. Tsang, "The So-called Scholastic Criticism were Found without Evidence Substantiation: A Commentary on OPS Debates," *Hong Kong Economic Journal*, 21 August 1994.

[17] S. K. Tsang, "China has Retirement Protection Schemes Similar to OPS," *Hong Kong Economic Daily*, 1 August 1994.

[18] C. T. Lau, "An Assessment of OPS," *Hong Kong Economic Journal Monthly*, August (1994).

Indeed, the approach for a holistic assessment for the worst scenario constitutes the basic component of any professional practice of actuarial assessment. In fact, a similar approach was attempted for the Tripartite Old Age Pension Proposal of the Hong Kong Social Security Society.[19]

☐ Public Responses to the OPS

After the consultative paper was released, there was a general support for the proposed OPS. The first opinion poll was done on 15 July 1994 by the Hong Kong Polling and Business Research sponsored by *Ming Pao*. The results of the 607 successful telephone interviews showed that over 80 per cent of the respondents supported the idea of the OPS. The different trade unions, including the Hong Kong Federation of Trade Unions, the Hong Kong and Kowloon Labour Unions, the Confederation of Trade Unions and the Trade Union Congress, declared unified support for the OPS in principle. Christian and Catholic organizations, women's groups and feminist organizations, and the disabled and patient groups all expressed positive support. The proposal was also well-received by grassroots coalitions which were arguing for a universal retirement protection scheme, including labour groups, community organizations, the elderly leagues and professional bodies. All political parties except the Liberal Party, which is supported by the business groups, welcomed the OPS with some minor reservations. Later, they joined hands to strive for a formal statutory government contribution to the OPS.

☐ Debates over Business Opposition

At the time of writing, business communities were the only interest groups which opposed the OPS. Basically, they took the following positions:

---

[19] Hong Kong Social Security Society, Old Age Pension Scheme (Volume 1: Basic Design, June 1991). See also H. Mok *et al.*, "An Actuarial Assessment for the Old Age Pension Scheme proposed by the Hong Kong Social Security Society," *Proceedings for the 1991 International Roundtable for Social Security* (Hong Kong: Hong Kong Policy Forum and the Hong Kong Social Security Society, 15 July 1991).

1. As the population is ageing, contributions will increase and create a financial burden in the near future.
2. The pay-as-you-go method will lead to the problems experienced by Western welfare states.
3. It will increase the cost of business, reduce competitiveness and slow down the economy.
4. It represents another form of payroll tax.
5. Income redistribution will change the ongoing practice of positive non-interventionism.

But many professionals and academics disagreed with all the aforementioned points. First, they thought that there should be no free lunch. The financing of social security for the aged must be faced squarely and shared by the whole community.[20] Even the CPF or RPS are subjected to pressures for a higher rate of contribution. For instance, the CPF contribution rate in some Asian countries, such as Singapore, Malaysia, Sri Lanka, India and Nepal, have increased from 10 per cent to over 20 per cent. The current government proposal estimated an accumulated surplus of over $100 billion in the next fifty years. A conservative re-estimate would also suggest at least an accumulated surplus of over $10 billion (in 1994 dollar value). If the government estimate of 3 per cent contribution rate was to be over-optimistic, for certain the society would not need to contribute more than 10 per cent for the next fifty years.[21]

Second, the pay-as-you-go method does not necessarily lead to welfarism. Assuming there is a stagnant economy for the next forty years, the total expenditure of the OPS in 2036 would only constitute around 6 per cent of the 1993 gross domestic product ($55 billion over $870 billion). As the pension benefit is first tagged on 30 per cent of the median wage, the total annual expenditure will be much lower than in Western countries, most of whose beneficiaries reached 50 per cent of their average wage. Moreover, unlike the three-tier system of retirement benefits, the proposed OPS aims at the first and the only tier of basic flat-rate pension.

---

[20] See Note 15.
[21] Hong Kong Social Security Society, *Social Security Bulletin 1994*, No. 2 (1994).

In this regard, the OPS will not cost more than one-third of those in the West.[22]

Third, there are many countries such as Japan, Germany, China and South Korea, which operate a similar kind of basic pension system. But their economies keep on flourishing. In fact, many Hong Kong business corporations are currently investing in and operating businesses in Asian countries which require an average 6 per cent contribution rate from the employers (see Table 5). Hence, the motive of the business opposition was very much in doubt.[23]

Fourth, the government proposed that the contributions be put into an independent fund, operated separately from the tax revenue. The fund would be solely used for pension payment. Like the CPF, individuals will get back their contributions through their future collection of pension benefits. If the business community supports the CPF, then they should have no objection to the OPS which requires a total contribution rate of less than 5 per cent.

Table 5. Employers' Rates of Contribution in Selected Asian Retirement Protection Schemes, 1991

Country	Employers' rate of contribution (%)
China	18.0
Singapore	18.0
Sri Lanka	12.0
Malaysia	11.0
India	10.7
Nepal	10.0
Japan	7.3
Fiji	7.0
Papua New Guinea	7.0
Taiwan	5.6
Pakistan	5.0
The Philippines	4.7

---

[22] H. Mok, "The Proposed OPS Should Ease the Worries of the Business Community," *The Economic Reporter*, Vol. 30 (1 August 1994), pp. 6–7.

[23] See Note 16.

Elderly in Need of Care and Financial Support 329

Finally, the opposition to income redistribution is even more difficult to understand. The Hong Kong government has been operating social services with income distribution for more than two decades, which include free compulsory education, subsidized public housing, public medical services and subvented welfare services. The OPS design is no different from those of the social services, and helps reduce the widening gap between the rich and the poor in Hong Kong. Indeed, the income disparity is widening from a Gini coefficient of 0.43 in 1971 to 0.48 in 1991 despite the high rate of economic growth. The income disparity ranks the greatest among Asian countries in the 1990s.[24]

In the eyes of the general public, the business community has been irresponsible in meeting the social needs of the society. They had opposed and crushed the proposal for a semi-voluntary social insurance scheme in 1977 and the idea of a CPF in 1987. And in regard to the current debate, they opposed the proposed compulsory RPS of 1992 and supported the idea of a CPF in 1993. But now they have changed their position again and opposed the OPS. As they now have recommended the idea of the private provident fund which they rejected in the first place in 1992, the business people have been perceived by the public as ingenuine and cunning, and as fooling around so that they do not have to contribute anything to any public retirement protection scheme.[25]

☐ Epilogue

At the time of writing, the New China News Agency had just convened a special meeting with a group of Hong Kong Affairs advisers on 3 August 1994. Many of them, including the Director of the Hong Kong Council of Social Service, felt that the government proposal mixed up the retirement protection with social welfare provisions, and were inclined to oppose the OPS. It was interesting to learn that of all the advisers attending the meeting, the union representatives maintained a positive view towards the OPS and supported it in principle. There were a few advisers (e.g., Tsang Shu-ki) who were not invited to the meeting but who spoke openly in

---

[24] H. Mok, "Possible Social Security Measures in Response to Increasing Income Disparity in Hong Kong," *Hong Kong Journal of Social Sciences*, Vol. 2 (1993), pp. 104–23.

[25] *Hong Kong Economic Journal*, 28 July 1994.

favour of the scheme.[26] It was apparent that the social policy debate was now heavily linked with political considerations. However, it is important that the basic social policy principles and their expected impact on the community needs should be clearly delineated and cross-examined before any political decision is made. It is hoped that a healthy debate will finally lead to a proper introduction of the OPS. The provision of the basic financial support will definitely alleviate the poverty of the elderly and form the foundation of public support on which better social services could be further developed and operated in the near future.

---

[26] *Hong Kong Economics Daily*, 1 August 1994.

Social Welfare

Cecilia Chan

☐ Introduction

This chapter will discuss three main social welfare concerns in 1993–1994. The year 1994 is the International Year of the Family, when special efforts are devoted to issues of and services for families. A major Rehabilitation Programme Plan review has been launched in 1994 and the review report will come out in 1995. There is public concern over the low level of social security for the poor, particularly the children among them.

☐ International Year of the Family

The International Year of the Family 1994 helped to focus our attention on issues concerning the family. Families are the building blocks for society that provide an intimate environment for individual growth and development. The Pope sees the family as "the source of peace between individuals and between peoples of the world." However, sometimes family can also be a source of stress.

Families in Hong Kong are being bombarded by rapid changes in social infrastructure due to the economic and political transitions. Domestic violence, incest, extramarital relationships and concubines in China, divorce and separation, discrimination and adjustment difficulties faced by new immigrant families, families on welfare, care of the frail and elderly,

---

Cecilia Chan is a senior lecturer in the Department of Social Work and Social Administration, the University of Hong Kong.

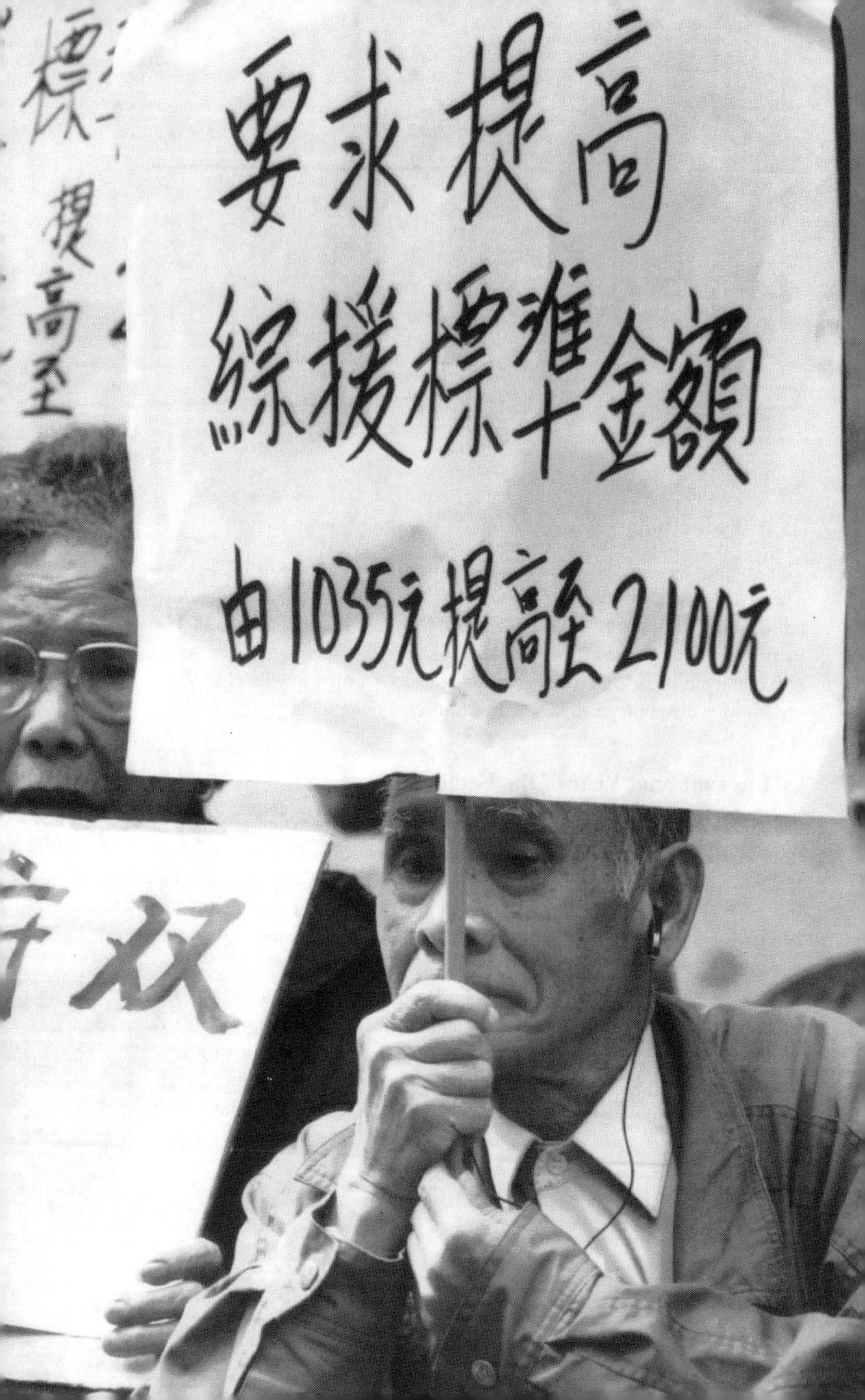
要求提高
綜援標準金額
由1035元提高至2100元

are emerging symptoms of family crisis and breakdown. The actual extent of incest, child and wife abuse in Hong Kong is not known, but there is a growing concern about the use of violence in the family. At present there are few programmes teaching couples how to handle aggression, anger and hostility. Women, children and the elderly are likely to become victims in case of outbreaks of temper and aggression. Needs of these vulnerable families are not being adequately addressed under the present social welfare system.

Family Court and Divorce Mediation

Death of a spouse or divorce is among the most traumatic events in life. Unfortunately, there are increasing numbers of divorce petitions in Hong Kong every year (see Table 1). Marital disputes usually continue after the divorce decrees in the form of fights over custody, maintenance and visitation rights. Children often feel as though they are being torn between parents. They may suffer from severe resentment, frustration and experience a great sense of loss. If the divorce experience is not properly handled, the trauma may result in long-term personality or behavioural problems, or precipitate mental health symptoms for the parties concerned.

Table 1. Divorce Statistics 1983–1992

	1983	1984	1985	1986	1987	1988	1989	1990	1991	1992
Petititons filed*	3,734	4,764	5,047	5,339	5,747	5,893	6,275	6,767	7,287	8,067
Divorce decrees	2,857	4,086	4,313	4,257	5,055	5,098	5,507	5,551	6,295	5,650

* Figures include defended cases.
Source: *Hong Kong Annual Digest of Statistics* (Hong Kong: Government Printer, 1993), p. 20.

The Family Court in Hong Kong is underdeveloped and there is no mandatory mediation service for the couples seeking divorce. Such service could address the emotional need of the divorcees and their children by helping them to face the experience with a positive attitude and continue to live a fruitful life. Overseas statistics show that with mediation, about 20 per cent of the couples dropped the divorce petition, more than half of the couples develop constructive ways of coping with their frustrations and anger, and resolved the divorce arrangements to mutual satisfaction. The government should review the existing Family Court system and implement similar divorce mediation procedures to help local families.

Risks of Split Families

There is a growing concern among social workers in family counselling services over the issue of extramarital relationships and tensions in "split families." Here I shall concentrate on the latter. There are no reliable statistics on the number of split families in Hong Kong. Taking into account the number of persons who work in China regularly (64,200 Hong Kong residents worked in China during mid-1992, i.e., 2.8 per cent of the total labour force) and those who got married in China,[1] Yeung estimated that there are 150,000 split families in Hong Kong, i.e., 9.4 per cent of the total households.[2] As this phenomenon affects almost one-tenth of the households, more attention should be devoted to the needs of the families concerned.

There are increasing numbers of middle-aged male Hong Kong residents who resort to finding a marriage partner in China. The age difference between the husband and wife is often wide. This one-family-two-homes arrangement, with frequent commuting of one or more members of the family across the border, is actually quite stressful for the parties concerned. As family members do not have time together, the husband-wife and parent-child relationships are usually weak.

There were 270,000 applications for "not-married" certificates between 1982–1992. About 240,000 of them reported their intention to get married in China. Assuming half of them still have their spouses and children in China, the Hong Kong government will have to plan for the provision of schools and other social welfare facilities, when an estimated 200,000 children of Hong Kong permanent residents become entitled to settle in Hong Kong in 1997 according to the Basic Law. To put 200,000 children in school, we shall have to build 200 more schools. When they come to Hong Kong as new immigrants, they may encounter difficulties in

---

[1] General Household Survey, *Special Topic Report No. X*, p. 3.

[2] K. C. Yeung, "The Split Families in Hong Kong in the 90's" (paper presented in the Seminar on Hong Kong Family in Focus — the Split Families, 15 December 1993).

adjustment. Also, newly united family members may find it hard to adjust to living together. The government must be prepared for this massive population influx and special services for them need to be planned now.

Community Care and Family Care

One of the key themes of the International Year of the Family is "care." The Hong Kong Council of Social Service conducted a study on the "Role of the Family in Community Care" in 1992–1994 and found that "community care" equals "family care," and "family care" equals "women's care." Women in the family are usually the ones to take on the burden of providing care to the children and the chronically ill in the family. With the reduction in the average household size from 3.9 to 3.4 in the last decade, and the high female labour participation rate of 46.2 per cent, one cannot help notice the urgent need to find someone to take care of the disadvantaged in the families or to share the burden of the women concerned.

The Government Response to the International Year of the Family

The Social Welfare Department (SWD) agreed in 1983 to reduce the caseload of family service workers from 70 to 65, with the eventual goal of reducing the caseload to a more manageable level of 50. Besides counselling services, practical help is also needed. The SWD introduced a category of "family aide" workers and promised to provide each family service centre with one ward attendant to offer practical training on home care, and help with home budgeting and cooking.

Despite the considerable expansion (an additional 12 home-help teams in 1993–1994), the number of home-help teams still falls short of the demand by 35 teams. Doctors express regret that they have to admit sick persons into the hospital because there is no one to take care of them at home. The efficiency of home-help teams can greatly be enhanced if a case manager can be added to each team. A degree level social worker who can act as the case manager, community educator, health promoter and coordinator of volunteers is expected to be a resourceful person.

Table 2 shows that there are significant shortfalls for clinical psychologists, day nursery places, medical social workers, and home-help teams. These shortfalls are already calculated on basis of low service planning standards. The service planning standards need be improved and

Table 2. Planned Provision and Shortfall of Family Services

Type of service	Planning ratio	Provision as at 31 March 1994	1993–1994 Projected demand	1993–1994 Projected provision	1993–1994 Projected shortfall
Family casework service	One family service centre to 150,000 population; one social worker to 70 cases	(32,993 cases) 430 social workers	(34,700 cases) 496 social workers	439	57
Family life education	1:50,000 population	59 social workers	77	67	10
Medical social workers	General beds 90:1; beds for mentally ill 140:1; psychiatric OPD cases 250:1; TB OPD cases 400:1; General Clinic cases 250:1	250 social workers under SWD	505	283	222
Home help	One team to handle 60 to 70 cases at any time and 120 cases per annum	72 teams	119	84	35
Family aide	One ward attendant to each family service centre	4 ward attendants		20	
Clinical psychological service	One clinical psychologist to 1,356 family counselling cases	13 clinical psychologists	51	17	34
Day nursery	100 places to 20,000 population	21,303 places	28,842	22,703	6,139
Foster care		320 places		480	
Small group home	One home to eight children	23 homes		47	
Children's home		1,828 places		1,828	
Occasional child care centre		76 units		76	

Source: *Social Welfare Development Five Year Plan Review 1993* (Hong Kong: Government Printer, 1994), pp. 21–22, 115–16.

the shortfalls rectified. The SWD does not have estimates of demands for services such as family aide workers, foster care, small group homes, children's homes and occasional child care centres. Without such estimates, long-term planning will be hampered.

The Shortfall in Medical Social Work Service

Illness makes one vulnerable. When a person is admitted to hospital, usually for some severe ailments, in addition to coping with the illness, he or she has to learn to handle the associated fear and anxiety. In the cases of life-threatening illness or illness that will lead to permanent disabilities, the patients and their family members are likely to suffer from insomnia, depression, or even suicidal impulses. Under the present manpower planning ratio, there is a shortfall of 222 medical social workers in ex-government hospitals. This shortfall does not account for the shortfalls in ex-subvented hospitals managed by the Hospital Authority. The present manpower does not match the counselling and support needs of the patients and their family members.

The standard of one medical social worker to 90 beds was set in the 1970s and has never been revised in par with the improvement in other service standards and rising expectations of the community. There has never been a keen interest on the part of the government in the needs of patients as they are a group having very limited access to the public forum. The Hospital Authority also seems to be more interested in its corporate image than patients' sleepless nights and strong sense of powerlessness. The development of medical social work service has stagnated. When social workers resign from the hospitals, the Hospital Chief Executive may deploy the resources to more visible items such as public relations.

It is a welcome sign that social workers are involved in the running of the Patients' Resource Centres in major hospitals (e.g., Queen Mary Hospital, Queen Elizabeth Hospital and Tuen Mun Hospital) starting in 1993–1994. The social workers organize patients' self-help groups, new patients' orientation sessions, health promotion for patients, volunteer activities, resource libraries and a whole range of programmes where medical staff are involved in helping patients adjust to their disabling conditions. More hospitals will set up Patients' Resource Centres. These services are complementary to, though cannot replace, the in-depth psychosocial support to patients offered by medical social workers.

☐ Social Security

The SWD is committed to assist all disadvantaged members of society to maintain an acceptable standard of living. The overall objective of social security in Hong Kong is to meet the basic and special needs of those individuals and families in the community who are in need of financial or material assistance. Currently, almost half of the expenditure on social security is spent on old age allowance (see Table 3).

Table 3. Number of Cases Receiving Assistance from the Social Welfare Department as at 31 March 1993

Schemes	Cases	Amount paid ($ million)
Public assistance	81,975	1,408.5
Old age allowance	145,273	2,141.6
Higher old age allowance	282,253	
Disability allowance	65,146	830.4
Higher disability allowance	13,969	
Fee assistance (day nursery)	9,989	77.4
Emergency relief	2,825	0.3
Criminal and law enforcement injuries compensation	686	9.0
Traffic accident victims assistance	4,946	73.6

Sources: *Social Welfare Development Five Year Plan Review 1993* (Hong Kong: Government Printer, 1994), pp. 83–84; *Hong Kong Social and Economic Trends 1982–1993* (Hong Kong: Government Printer, 1993), p. 91.

Totally Inconsistent Policy on Income Protection

While the Old Age Pension Scheme proposed to offer a $2,300 monthly stipend to all elderly persons in Hong Kong irrespective of their income, the SWD is only giving $1,180 to each child and $965 to the mother, who takes care of the children. This amount is hardly sufficient to meet the needs of these children with regard to food and clothing. Paradoxically, if the children are put under foster care or into a children's home instead, the SWD would pay $4,000 to $6,000 a month to maintain the children in care. Proposals to improve social security for the poor were rejected by the

Social Welfare   339

government in September 1994. Disability Allowances have not been revised for many years. Why should welfare recipients be discriminated against? The following case illustrates the detrimental effects of the low level of assistance on children.

> Madam Wong's husband died three years ago in an accident. After the death of Mr. Wong, Madam Wong and her three children had to live on Public Assistance. Each of them was given about $600 a month at that time. She found it hard to swallow the hostile manner of her Social Security Office worker and felt very sorry for herself for not being able to work, and for the loss of her husband. Two years later, Madam Wong developed cancer of the colon. Her children were then aged 14, 11 and 8. As an adult, she receives the lowest level of allowance among all types of Comprehensive Social Security Assistance recipients.
>
> The eldest daughter had been doing very well in school before her father died. Since his death, she had to abstain from all extracurricular activities and social contacts with her classmates as the Public Assistance did not provide her with pocket money to spend. From then onwards, she was often very quiet and unwilling to make friends and developed a very low self-image. She wanted to go to a school camp in the summer which would cost her $200, a sum that the mother could not spare. The Social Security Office said that school camp was not essential spending and therefore no provision was granted.
>
> As growing children or adolescents, all of the three children were hungry most of the time, and the mother was very frustrated for not being able to provide them with more food. The second son often fought with his classmates whenever they teased him for having no father and being welfare dependent. The youngest daughter was very attached to the father. She developed conversion symptoms after the father died and could not speak for two years, until she received counselling service from a voluntary agency.
>
> Madam Wong had to lock the children and herself in the room during the major festivals as they could not afford to go out; Madam Wong did not have the money for red packets for the neighbours' children. Moon cakes were absolutely out of the question. During the summer months when transportation allowances were cut, the children's participation in summer programmes was directly affected.
>
> Madam Wong had a relapse and the cancer had spread to the liver in May 1994. She is now very worried about the custody arrangement of her three children when she dies. She fears that her children may have to live in different children's home under the guardianship of the Director of Social Welfare.

Detrimental Effect of Low Level of Assistance to Children

The lower degree of self-esteem and weaker relationship with parents and the community were apparent among children on welfare when compared with children living in temporary housing areas.[3] The poor self-image and lack of a sense of community can easily precipitate anti-social or socially destructive behaviour. With the present level of provision, the government is depriving these 20,000 disadvantaged children of a normal childhood. The harm to their personality and self-confidence cannot be undone easily. While the government is spending millions of dollars on crime prevention and summer programmes to inculcate social commitment among young persons, money would be equally well spent if the 20,000 children on welfare were provided with a more decent living standard.

Those who seek help from the Social Security Offices are people from families which have undergone traumatic events, such as the death of the bread-winner, ill health, disability, divorce or separation. Yet they are often not provided with timely support and counselling. It is obvious that the Social Security Offices are well-positioned in deploying social workers to reach out to the most disadvantaged individuals and families. To improve service, social workers should be added to social security offices so that families, besides cash assistance, can be provided with means conducive to normal growth for their children.

Cases on Comprehensive Social Security Assistance

Two-thirds of the cases on Comprehensive Social Security Assistance (CSSA) are elderly persons. The numbers will be significantly reduced when the Old Age Pension Scheme is implemented. The second largest category of recipients encompasses those suffering from ill health or disability (see Table 4). A higher payment will not attract more people, as to be qualified for that, one need to be medically certified ill or disabled to the extent that one's ability to work is affected. The existing criteria of disability are also very harsh. Hence, it is unlikely that a lot of people could squeeze into the CSSA Scheme.

Yet, officials of the Health and Welfare Branch have pointed out that an increased level of assistance can be harmful to the work incentive and create welfare dependency. However, it is a plain fact that very few people

---

[3] Cecilia Chan and Wilma Wong. "Psycho-social Impact of Poverty on Children," *Conference Proceedings of the Asia Regional Conference on Social Security* (14–16 September 1993) (Hong Kong: Hong Kong Council of Social Service, 1983), pp. 370–86.

Social Welfare

Table 4. Type of Public Assistance Cases

Public assistance cases	31.3.1983	31.3.1987	31.3.1993	31.3.1994
	Number (percentages)			
Old age	33,910 (66.1)	42,135 (66.5)	53,397 (65.1)	61,026 (64.2)
Temporary disability/ ill health	6,962 (13.6)	7,438 (11.7)	8,889 (10.9)	10,072 (10.6)
Mentally ill	1,166 (2.3)	2,628 (4.2)	4,913 (6.0)	5,687 (6.3)
Single parent family	2,287* (4.5)	3,762 (5.9)	4,897 (6.0)	6,134 (6.5)
Unemployed	985 (1.9)	1,877 (3.0)	2,957 (3.6)	3,876 (4.1)
Physically disabled	1,120 (2.2)	1,262 (2.0)	2,079 (2.5)	2,644 (2.8)
Low earnings	1,655 (3.2)	1,268 (2.0)	1,007 (1.2)	1,407 (1.5)
Blind	768 (1.5)	710 (1.1)	840 (1.0)	946 (1.0)
Deaf	124 (0.2)	138 (0.2)	219 (0.3)	338 (0.3)
Others	2,290 (4.5)	2,148 (3.4)	2,777 (3.4)	2,974 (3.1)
Total	51,267 (100)	63,366 (100)	81,975 (100)	95,104 (100)

* Figures before April 1985 cover only widow(er) with dependent children cases while those from April 1985 onwards are extended to include the deserted, separated or divorced parents with dependent children, which were previously classified under "Others."

Sources: *Hong Kong Social and Economic Trends 1982–1993* (Hong Kong: Government Printer, 1993), p. 92; *Hong Kong Monthly Digest of Statistics*, April 1994, p. 99.

will choose to live on welfare if they can manage to earn an income. The percentage of Public Assistance cases due to low income has actually decreased in the past ten years.

Owing to the import of labour and economic transformation away from the manufacturing industry, the number of available jobs for the working class has actually declined. In 1992, there were 23,600 displaced workers due to businesses closing down or employers moving operations to China,[4] but only a very small portion of these displaced workers have applied for Public Assistance. Unemployment will not automatically entitle a person to CSSA. All of them have to register with the Labour Department for a month and have to accept any job offers if they have working capacity. So it is absolutely out of the question that raising the level of CSSA will reduce

---

[4] General Household Survey, *Special Topic Report No. X*, p. 18.

work incentive. The government should facilitate job creation and job training to help those middle-aged and lowly educated displaced workers, rather than keeping the level of CSSA to a bare minimum to deter new applicants.

☐ Rehabilitation Services

A Green Paper That Has Never Turned White?

It has been two-and-a-half years since the release of the *Green Paper on Rehabilitation: Full Participation and Equal Opportunity*. It is still not clear to date when or whether the White Paper will be published. In the mean time, disabled persons, non-governmental organizations (NGOs) and the government departments are now working on the Rehabilitation Programme Plan review. The first meeting was held on 30 May 1994 and the whole process will take about a year. The Programme Plan is no substitute for a White Paper because a White Paper can introduce new policy directions and programmes, while a programme plan review will only engender incremental changes to what has been decided years ago.

The Governor's Summit Meetings

The Governor, Christopher Patten, has taken a keen personal interest in the issue of disability. In response to the concerns raised by disabled persons, the Governor called and chaired a summit meeting on employment for persons with disabilities on 2 February 1994 and another summit meeting on transportation for persons with disabilities on 16 March 1994. In response to the Governor's initiative, the Mass Transit Railway Corporation will launch experimental projects such as setting up climbers for persons on wheel-chair and tactile paths for the blind in Shek Kip Mei Station. Bus companies will modify the handrails and bells to make it easier for persons with physical disabilities to use bus services.

Unfortunately, as the largest employer, the government is still just paying lip-service to enhancing job opportunities of disabled persons. It cannot be considered a good model when the number of disabled persons being employed in the civil service has actually been on the decline, and the legislation for employment rights for persons with disabilities has been rejected.

Social Welfare

Discrimination Continues

The Tung Tau Estate and Laguna City residents' protest against the setting up of rehabilitation services for disabled persons in the respective housing estates aroused heated public debates. Many were alarmed by the Liberal Party Legislative Councillor Selina Chow's public denouncement of the right of mental health survivors to community rehabilitation. Such open discrimination against disadvantaged members of society was alarming. With the local elections of 1994 and 1995, less principled politicians may decide to campaign against rehabilitation projects in public housing estates. The protest against the setting up of temporary accommodation for post-bone marrow transplant patients by the Queen Mary Hospital at Wah Kwai Estate by a candidate for District Board election could be the beginning of a series of similar events.

The Committee on Public Education in Rehabilitations (COMPERE) is discharged with the responsibility to promote public acceptance of disabled persons in the community. Fun-fairs, gamesdays, and the printing of pamphlets organized by COMPERE do not have the intensive person-to-person contact element. Permanent public education teams should be set up throughout the territory to promote public awareness of the needs of the disabled for effective community integration.

Legislative Protection for Persons with Disabilities

On 15 September 1993, Justice Woo discharged a defendant who was on trial for rape, attempted rape and indecent assault, on the grounds of difficulties and emotional distress experienced by the 25-year-old victim who was born deaf, dumb and with low intelligence. The public and parents groups were greatly alarmed, and saw it as a case of gross injustice. In response to the public outcry, the Chief Justice set up a Working Party to look into the procedures of giving evidence in Court by persons with learning disability in October 1993. The Working Party came up with a series of recommendations in their Interim Report on 18 January 1994.

The key recommendations include: the Court should consider the clinical psychologist's report on the conditions of a defendant or witness with learning disability, the trial be fixed for an early date, and the case be heard in a court room furnished like a juvenile court. Other recommendations include: persons other than those authorized should be excluded and the trial conducted in Cantonese, the judge and counsel should wear ordinary attire, a social worker or teacher be allowed to accompany the witness while the latter gives evidence, and counselling by a clinical psychologist should be tendered before, during and after giving evidence.

In the second report submitted on 25 March 1994, the Working Party recommended firmly that legislation be introduced to make available a video link and that videotaped statements be admissible in court.[5]

Separate legislation for the protection of rights has always been the goal of parent groups of children with mental disabilities. Legislative Councillor Anna Wu proposed a bill on anti-discrimination in 1994 with the aim of eliminating all forms of discrimination on gender, race, age, as well as physical and mental conditions. At the same time, the government is also drafting a bill on anti-discrimination for persons with disabilities. Unlike that which Anna Wu drafted with full consultation of the disabled persons and relevant NGOs, the government's bill is still opaque as far as its content is concerned. Both bills will be debated by the Legislative Council towards the end of 1994. Hopefully, by the end of 1995, discrimination against persons with disabilities will be prohibited by law.

Service Planning and Shortfalls

Rehabilitation services are operated by a large number of NGOs and government departments: e.g., pre-school and school education are under the Education Department, medical rehabilitation is under the Hospital Authority, and social rehabilitation is under the SWD. The Education Department is doing a good job and all disabled children are given schooling. The Hospital Authority offers high standard medical rehabilitation to all who need such services. Unfortunately, social rehabilitation services offered by the SWD (sheltered workshop, day activity centre, hostel, long stay home, social centre) are relatively restricted. The shortfalls of various social rehabilitation services are still very significant.

Despite some improvements in service provision in the last year, large numbers of persons with disability still queued on the waiting list for essential services. Table 5 shows the significant shortfalls in a number of rehabilitation services.

---

[5] "Report of the Working Party on Mentally Handicapped People Giving Evidence in Court," 1994.

Table 5. Planned Provision and Shortfall of Rehabilitation Services

Type of service	Provision as at 31 March 1993	1993–1994		
Shelter workshop	4,535 places	6,630	5,195	1,435
Day activity centre	2,153 places	3,800	2,593	1,207
Half-way house	809 places	1,149	809	340
Hostel for moderately mentally handicapped adults	946 places	1,596	1,146	450
Hostel for severely mentally handicapped adults	1,040 places	2,207	1,340	867
Hostel for physically handicapped persons	339 places	636	431	205
Long stay care home	200 places	474	200	274

Source: *Social Welfare Development Five Year Plan Review 1993* (Hong Kong: Government Printer, 1994), pp. 69–71.

Unable to Meet the Needs Related to Chronic Illness and Death

In his 1993 policy speech, the Governor promised rehabilitation services to persons with chronic illness. This is the first time ever that such promise is made. However, service needs were not clearly defined, and the service structure to serve these individuals was not laid down. The Hong Kong Society For Rehabilitation launched two Community Rehabilitation Networks to serve chronic patients on Hong Kong Island and Kowloon in January 1994. Owing to manpower limitations, they started with services for selected patients groups at the beginning. Problems facing chronic patients are diverse: employment, mood swings, social adjustment and physical rehabilitation. Parents are concerned about the personality formation of their sick children. Family members are concerned about the emotional and social adaptation of their chronically ill members.

There were 30,526 deaths in 1992, of which one-third were caused by cancer, one-third were caused by heart or cerebrovascular diseases, one-sixth due to respiratory illnesses, and 6.5 per cent due to injury or poisoning.[6] The number of casualties by traffic accidents increased from 20,048 in 1990 to 20,904 in 1993. The number of fatal occupational accidents also increased from 246 in 1992 to 287 in 1993.[7] While the government has allocated resources to support a quit-smoking campaign to prevent respiratory illness and lung cancer, there are relatively few resources devoted to public education about other illnesses and injury prevention, such as heart and cerebrovascular diseases and injuries, many of which are largely preventable. Community health promoters should be appointed to educate the public to prevent and deal with life-threatening illnesses and accidents. Without such support, individuals facing health crises could end up in panic and despair.

Few services are concerned with death and dying, for the persons or their relatives. The hospice service in Hong Kong cannot meet the needs of dying cancer patients. Patients dying from illnesses other than cancer are excluded from hospice service. Many of these patients and their family members need no less home care, hospice and bereavement support. Unresolved emotional trauma of the loss of a loved one can lead to long-term mental health problems. However, there is yet no long-term planning for hospice provision.

Services in health promotion, campaigns for public awareness of illness and death, and services for chronic patients or terminally ill patients all fall in the grey area between traditional medical services and social services. It is necessary for the Commissioner for Rehabilitation to take these up and coordinate long-term planning of such essential services in Hong Kong.

☐ Issues in Welfare Administration and Service Delivery

Mass Exodus of High Officials in the SWD

In this past year, a large number of high-level officials in the SWD have retired. In the coming two years, continuous mass exodus is expected. The rapid turnover of key decision-makers means a severe loss of skills and experience. Officials who intend to retire before 1997 tend to play things safe and are reluctant to push for changes or innovation. Lower-level

---

[6] *Annual Digest of Statistics 1993*, pp. 18, 231–32.

[7] *Hong Kong Monthly Digest of Statistics*, April 1994.

Social Welfare   347

officials may be promoted within a short time and feel inadequate in the face of work pressure. Added to the heavy workload of the SWD are the pressures from the performance pledges, politicians and pressure groups, which welfare bureaucrats are not used to tackling.

Career Development and Specialization

In the West, specialization (in probation, child protection, medical social work, family therapy, divorce mediation, and oncology social work) is a must. Specialization fosters professional growth and is conducive to the development of appropriate knowledge and skills in working with a particular target group. In Hong Kong, the SWD is responsible for a wide spectrum of activities (children's homes, probation services, community service orders, medical social services). Social workers are rotated from one service to another for administrative convenience, in the name of "career development," sometimes with notice as short as a few days. Social workers have no say over their job deployment. This uncertainty in job assignment discourages long-term commitment to a service, prohibits specialization and professional development. With the growing complexity of social problems that social workers are faced with, the SWD should seriously consider revamping its manpower deployment policy and move towards professional specialization.

Segregated Service Delivery

The SWD is funding NGOs with project funds allocated according to target groups, e.g., the elderly, children and youth, families, probationers and offenders. Such segregation in funding based on programme areas has led to under-utilization of resources as well as created hurdles for new service development. Currently social centres for the elderly open only during office hours, children and youth (C&Y) centres open mostly in the afternoons and evenings. These centres are closed and left vacant during the remaining time. Family service centres serving underprivileged families do not have resources to run programmes for their target groups while volunteers in community centres have difficulties finding disadvantaged targets to serve. Resources would be put to better use if there is better coordination. The Department of Social Work and Social Administration of the University of Hong Kong worked with three agencies in Shek Wai Kok for two years to develop a community-integrated model where staff providing services for elderly persons, C&Y centres, and services for mentally disabled persons worked closely as a team. All the target groups benefited from the sharing and support offered.

Importance of a Community Work Approach

The Neighbourhood Level Community Development Projects serving underprivileged communities have focused mainly on environmental and housing issues in the past. Their target population is too small to make organization around functional needs meaningful. Agencies serving the elderly, persons with disabilities and other vulnerable populations all too often have operated like isolated institutions with little community contact and focus. However, adopting a community work approach so that community networks and resources can be organized can best serve the clientele. For example, the Christian Service set up a family centre in Tuen Mun to provide both counselling and networking support for families at risk. The experiment was warmly welcomed by the community and very effective. It is high time for agencies to consider abolishing the single modality of intervention and adopt a community approach to all service delivery.

New Mechanisms for Innovation

More resources from the Community Chest, the Royal Hong Kong Jockey Club, and the SWD should be allocated to encourage innovations and pilot projects, including those initiated by advocacy organizations and small interest groups. From experience, new services can be introduced with no experimental phase, such as the introduction of family aides into family service centres. Yet projects proven to be worthy of support should get the necessary long-term funding. Unfortunately, "experimental projects" have been used as a delaying tactic by the government. For example, even though after-school service for children of single-parent families or broken families was found to be serving the needs of these underprivileged children, the projects were terminated at the end of the two years' experimental phase when there were no more funds available. Such practice stifles creativity and innovation. Policy-making and innovation should be better coordinated so that worthwhile projects can be bolstered by timely government funding.

☐ Conclusion

This cursory review of social welfare service development in Hong Kong has highlighted more problems than solutions. Hong Kong is changing so rapidly that social planners have to be on constant alert. It is disappointing to find that the bureaucracy has not been responsive to the new needs and changing demands of the underprivileged population. This chapter contains a number of proposals on what can be done. Readers are invited to join hands in expressing concern about welfare developments in Hong Kong so that improvements and new services can be developed to alleviate hardship and sufferings, and to prevent deterioration in different aspects of the quality of life for the Hong Kong population.

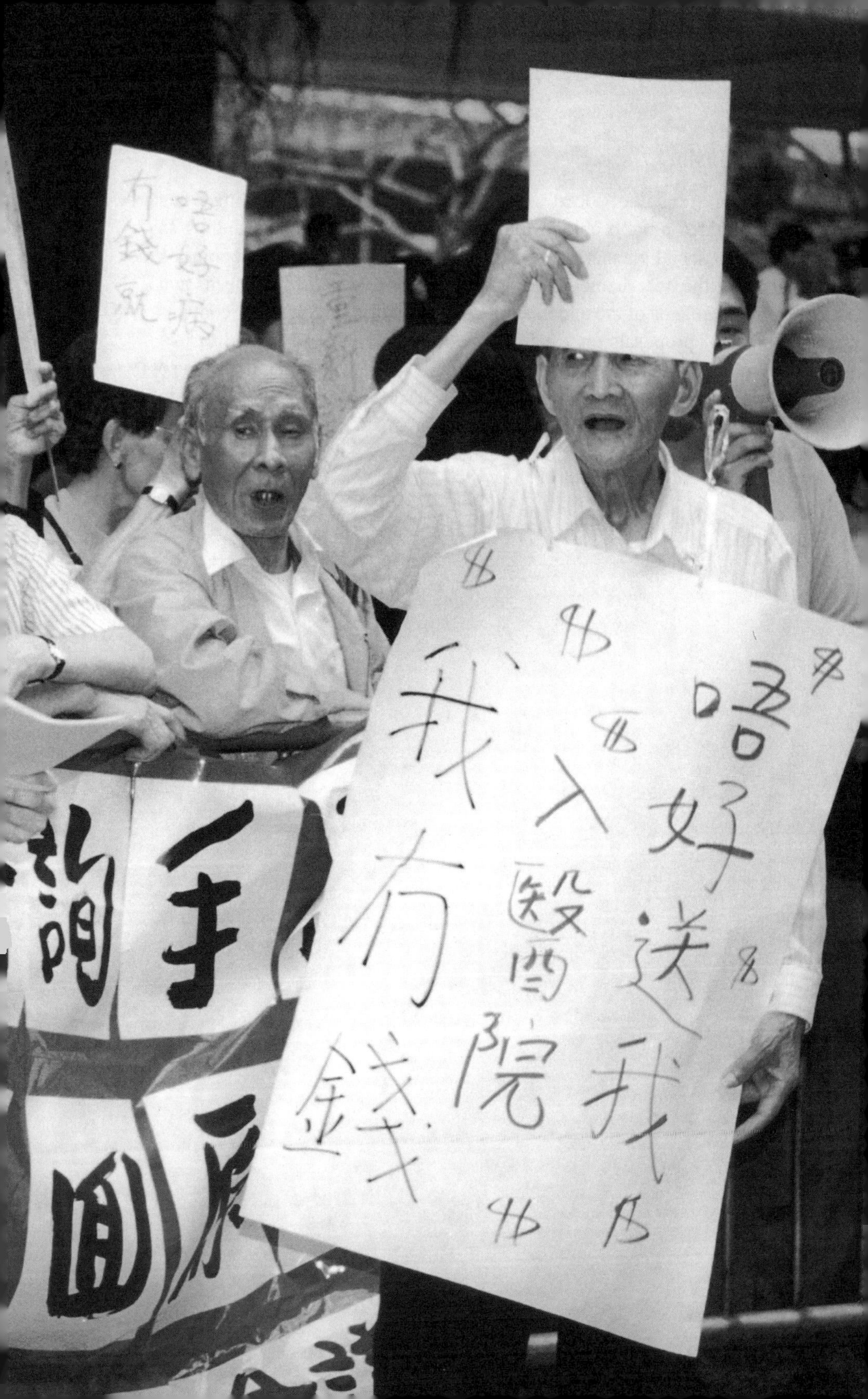
唔好病
冇錢就
唔好送我入醫院我冇錢

19

Medical and Health

Anthony B. L. Cheung

☐ A Decade of Reform — For What?

If one looks at official government reports, one would not fail to be impressed by the rather rosy picture Hong Kong's achievements in health care have been painted in. The first paragraph of the "Health" chapter in *Hong Kong 1994* — the official counterpart of this collection of alternative views — sums it all up:

> Access to affordable health care for all is the cornerstone of the government's health policy. The comprehensive range of health services available, together with improvements in the standard of living, have fostered a good general level of health in Hong Kong.[1]

In this and other officially produced publications, the message repeatedly driven home, supported by vital health statistics, is that Hong Kong people's health compares favourably with that of the developed countries. Indeed, by the beginning of the 1990s, Hong Kong's average life expectancy (for both males and females) has surpassed that of the United States and United Kingdom, while the infant mortality rate has become significantly lower than that in the latter two countries. Hong Kong, on the other hand, spends far less in bringing about such impressive health outcomes. Total health expenditure as a percentage of gross domestic product (GDP) stands at about 4 per cent, compared with 6 per cent in the United

---

Anthony B. L. Cheung is a university senior lecturer in the Department of Public and Social Administration, City Polytechnic of Hong Kong.

[1] *Hong Kong 1994* (Hong Kong: Government Printer, 1994), p. 153.

Kingdom and double that in the United States. Hong Kong thus has a health care system which people should take pride in rather than be worried about.

However, the past decade from 1984 has been one in which "health" was very much treated as being in a state of crisis. If the 1970s can be described as a decade of housing reform (with the then Governor Murray MacLehose launching his famous and popular ten-year public housing programme in 1973 to house 1.8 million people), then the following decade can certainly be seen as a decade of health care reform. Several major reviews and studies were conducted during this period:

1985 Scott Report on the delivery of medical services in hospitals (December)
1989 Report of the Provisional Hospital Authority (December)
1990 Establishment of the Hospital Authority (December)
Health for All: The Way Ahead, Report of Working Party on Primary Health Care (December)
1991 Medical Insurance Study Group studied various options of medical insurance
1992 Health and Welfare Fees and Waivers Review Committee examined principles and approaches to health financing
1993 *Towards Better Health* consultation document (July)

It is an appropriate time in 1994 to evaluate what Hong Kong has actually achieved out of those very intensive review activities of the past ten years. A disappointing fact which will be elaborated below is that practically no fundamental changes have been made to Hong Kong's health care system despite the loud rhetoric about the need for reform (evident in the 1985 Scott Report and the 1993 consultation document) and some structural reorganization in the form of the new Hospital Authority. Some expectations have been raised in the initial stage of the health reform era, but by the early 1990s things have gradually returned to "basics." With due respect to her successor, it may not be unfair to suggest that with the departure of the Secretary for Health and Welfare Elizabeth Wong from the scene during the year, the reform era will have finally come to its end. The momentum for change has outspent itself.

Much of the discourse about health reform in Hong Kong has been couched in terms of rational expectations and adaptations about the health care system which are used to justify as well as to explain changes. Reform-minded medical professionals (as represented, for example, by

Medical and Health

Leong Che-hung, the legislator representing the Medical and Health Care Functional Constituency) have persistently criticized the government for the lack of a proper health policy to supplant the 1974 White Paper which most would regard as being grossly outdated.[2] However, a "policy" is not merely an open statement of intentions; a new White Paper will not in itself solve most of the problems. A policy is a system of practice embedded in specific institutional and procedural arrangements which have their own values, history and memory, and which do not change overnight. There is, therefore, always a health policy as such in Hong Kong, fully exemplified in existing organizations and processes. Whether such a policy suits Hong Kong's current and future needs is of course a different matter.

The health reform decade began with the 1985 Scott Report which is seen to have led to a major restructuring of the hospital delivery system. The government followed up this earlier initiative with a subsequent review of primary health care, and finally with the health finance review. However, none of these three important attempts have been able to fundamentally redraw the extant institutional picture, partly because they each followed different motivations for change, and partly because all along the government leadership has not been particularly keen on comprehensive reform, nor does it have a clear agenda for reform. But the most important reason is that there is an absence of demand for reform from the society at large. Forces for change have come mostly from within the medical community for their own purposes.

☐ The "Basics" of Hong Kong's Health Care System

Historically, Hong Kong has developed what is characterized as a "dual system" in health care provision. While the government and its subvented hospitals together supply some 85 per cent of all hospital beds and about 90 per cent of in-patient days in hospital care, some 65 to 70 per cent of out-patient consultation is provided by private general practitioners. There have always been problems of integration — between the public and private sectors, and between government hospitals and subvented hospitals — within the overall health care system. Such a non-integrated structure

---

[2] See also Leung Man-fuk's account in *The Other Hong Kong Report 1993*, edited by Choi Po-king and Ho Lok-sang (Hong Kong: The Chinese University Press, 1993), p. 232.

underlined basic imbalances in health financing: the public sector on the whole charged a very low nominal fee for its care (most of the expenses being covered by taxation revenue) whereas charges were exorbitantly high in private hospitals or clinics. This means that the majority of the population who cannot afford expensive private care would have to depend on the public system to look after their health, despite complaints from time to time about poor staff attitudes, long waiting lists, insufficient care, and so on.

The gap between the public and private sectors is so large in terms of both the level of supply and prices that there is virtually little complementarity between the two. Each exists for a different purpose and works for a different clientele. The government got the bulk of the health care burden and as a former Director of Medical and Health, Dr. K. L. Thong, remarked upon retirement in 1987, the public system was "always under-financed, under-staffed and certainly overcrowded, simply because it is not possible to provide medical services on such a universal scale without proper allocation of resources." To redress such imbalance demands not only an injection of extra resources into the system, but more fundamentally rationalizing resources put respectively into the public and private sectors.

There was also inefficient use of resources within the public sector. For a long time, subvented hospital staff, though government-financed, had enjoyed inferior pay and conditions than their government hospital counterparts. Promotion opportunities were limited. This resulted in disparity in the utilization of hospital beds, with subvented hospitals being significantly under-utilized because they were unable to recruit and retain medical staff and their standard of service was thought to be second-rate.

Such was the state of Hong Kong's health care system at the beginning of the 1980s when reform was being urged. If comprehensive reform was to be contemplated, then the key questions of integration and finance must be properly addressed. The fact turns out to be that neither was being touched in its essence.

☐ Hospital Authority

The Hospital Authority was formed in December 1990 to take over government and subvented hospitals and to run them on the basis of devolved management and common terms and conditions for staff of both types of hospitals. This followed the recommendations of the 1985 Scott Report and the 1989 Provisional Hospital Authority Report. On the face of it, the very aim of the Hospital Authority is to create a new structure in which more integration and a more efficient resource management system can be facilitated. As Scott put it in 1985,

> overall, there is a feeling that the [old] system lacks the flexibility to be able to cope with the range of problems facing it at the present time. Many initiatives to ease the current situation are precluded on the grounds of civil service wide implications; others which seek to overcome present problems through a greater level of integration between government and subvented sectors are ruled out on the grounds of the independent ownership interests of the private non profit making organizations. Similarly the present arrangements make [a] closer relationship with the private sector, for example in the area of rights of practice in other hospitals, difficult to implement.

In practice, however, the Hospital Authority has done nothing to bring about integration with the private sector within the overall health care framework. What has been achieved through the Hospital Authority is only the amalgamation of the subvented sector with the government sector, by offering staff of the former terms and conditions on a par with those of the latter, in exchange for the former accepting a unified system of management control by a new Authority appointed by the government.

It needs to be remembered that when Scott proposed setting up a hospital authority in 1985, this proposal received a mixed and definitely not enthusiastic response from the community at large. Only eight of the eighteen District Boards welcomed the idea, while only six out of twenty legislators speaking in an adjournment debate on the subject in the Legislative Council expressed full support. Government medical staff were overwhelmingly against the proposal. The management boards of subvented hospitals were lukewarm in their response because they were afraid of losing their autonomy under a hospital authority. Even the Medical Development Advisory Committee, the government's main advisory body on health care policy, was only able to give qualified support. The only group which came out clearly in favour of the change was subvented hospital staff who obviously did so in the hope of having their terms and facilities upgraded. There was, therefore, hardly a consensus outside the government for corporatizing public hospital services as recommended by Scott. The main reservations rested with doubts about a proposed cost-recovery approach to patient charges, government's shrinking of responsibility and commitment to medical services, and whether it would cost more to set up a hospital authority outside the civil service structure.

What drove the government towards the reorganization of the public hospital services delivery system was not so much a concern about cost efficiency. Despite the extensive use of management reform terminology, Scott was conspicuously vague about the cost of the change-over. The main motivations for reorganization were bureaucratic ones. Both the Health and Welfare Branch and the Medical and Health Department at that time were highly dissatisfied with the existing structural arrangements which defined their relationship. The Branch would want to exert greater policy control over the development of hospital medical services but was finding it difficult to do so, partly because of the traditional professional recalcitrance within the Department, and partly because the Department had become by then too huge and too entrenched an organization to be tamed. The Department would want to free itself from policy branch control by opting for a statutory body model under the chairmanship of a non-official with political clout who could claim more resources for the professionals from the government. The subvented sector also demanded change, to improve their facilities and staff benefits in the name of integration. The Hospital Authority idea was therefore already mooted well before Scott was brought into the picture. What the consultant firm has achieved was to justify organizational change in the name of efficient management. It is not a surprise that the change has been cast in doubt by some critics who prefer more "privatization," such as Joel Hay who warns that "the Hospital Authority will maintain a top-down bureaucratic command structure with inadequate incentives to ensure hospital service quality and efficiency."[3]

After the formation of the Hospital Authority in December 1990, there has definitely been a conscious and rather vigorous move to introduce new public management ideas and practices within the new system. This is much evident in the new annual Business Plan process introduced from 1992–1993. More emphasis is now put on performance targets and outcome measurement. A new Patients' Charter was announced in mid-1994. The new executives running the Hospital Authority headquarters, typically represented by their Chief Executive Officer, Dr. E. K. Yeoh, are clearly management-minded reformers whose initiatives for management reforms within public hospitals are being facilitated, if not encouraged, by a private management-biased Executive Committee of the Authority headed by Sir S. Y. Chung, the chairman.

---

[3] Joel W. Hay, *Health Care in Hong Kong: An Economic Policy Assessment* (Hong Kong: The Chinese University Press, 1992), p. 56.

Behind the exhortations for management change and a new corporate culture, there is a restructuring of power within the system. Whereas the pre-reform period was marked by intense rivalry between policy officials who were administrative officers and the departmental medical professionals, the new Hospital Authority set-up has opened the way for a lopsided enhancement of medical professional power which has "captured" the management functions and further expanded their influence through the managerial subordination of nurses and other paramedical professions under the doctors. It remains to be seen whether Hong Kong in this case will follow the example of other developed countries which have undergone hospital management reforms, where the medical professionals are able to counteract "organizational control" imposed by central government managers with their own strategies for "institutional control." Managerial autonomy is used to strengthen rather than to weaken professional control of the system.

What has been achieved by way of the Scott Report and the establishment of the Hospital Authority is so far only the reconstitution of a new unified structure which continues to operate in a top-down fashion. There is clearly a more detached relationship with the government centre, and more autonomy for the managers of the Authority. However, whether this would mean a more participative mode of decision-making structure in which staff of different occupational backgrounds and citizens and patients can all play a constructive role remains debatable.

A preliminary study of four selected hospitals by the author and his colleagues Mark Hayllar and Elizabeth Blower at the City Polytechnic of Hong Kong in mid-1992 suggests there was confusion over just what the new corporate culture in hospital management was meant to entail. Implicit in many of the comments made by staff was a lack of clarity as to whether the reform was meant to be a top-down or bottom-up process. It was also expressed by some staff that the Hospital Authority was as bureaucratic as its civil-service predecessor, only in a different form and repackaged in new management jargons. No doubt the former "officer" titles have now all been replaced by "manager" titles, but whether decision-making, leadership and communication styles have been rescued from their hierarchical past awaits to be seen. The preliminary study was undertaken at an early stage of the reform process, hence few, other than holders of the new management posts, reported much change yet in their own jobs. However, it was evident that staff were more nervous about the impact of the reforms upon their conditions, workload and future job responsibilities, than with other aspects of the reform. There was a great variety of individual concern and speculation, from worries about new accountability relationships to more positive appreciation of better management training opportunities. Apart from staff anxieties, the Hospital Authority also has yet to prove that the Hospital Governing Committees appointed to supervise the management of individual hospitals and the Regional Advisory Committees can form effective entry points for wider public participation. There is also tension between the formerly government hospitals and subvented hospitals, now categorized as schedule I and II hospitals respectively. Ex-subvented hospitals are under the impression that the Hospital Authority's top management, being dominated by ex-government staff, continues to treat them as "second-class citizens." In July 1994, doctors from four such hospitals openly accused the Hospital Authority of showing favouritism to former government hospitals when it came to staffing numbers and funding levels.

It would not be fair to write off the potential benefits of the management reforms so readily. Most reforms, particularly of a scale as the Hospital Authority that involves about 38,000 staff and some 40 institutions, take time for their full impact to be felt and for their benefits to trickle down to all layers of staff and clients. However, even if the Hospital Authority reform is successful, this will only mean the entrenchment of a restructured public hospital care system which offers little role for the private sector. It can even be argued that a stronger and more expansionist Hospital Authority with its new-found managerialist mission will be more threatening to Hong Kong's private hospitals which for the past decade have seen little growth at all. Integration of the public and private sectors in hospital care remains an empty goal. The more the government focuses its attention on the reform of the public sector, the less importance it attaches to the provision of a proper institutional framework in which private hospitals can play a constructive part and "compete" with the predominantly government-financed Hospital Authority.

☐ Health Finance

When the government considered the report of the Provisional Hospital Authority, the only recommendation it did not take up was to give the new Hospital Authority the power to determine fees and charges in public hospitals. Earlier, the Provisional Hospital Authority had proposed a 15 to 20 per cent cost-recovery level following the lines of the Scott Report. The severe public outcry over the issues of fees and cost-recovery might have been the main reason for the government's reluctance to give up control over fees and charges. As a result, the Hospital Authority continues to be a government-funded organization no different from the pre-reform days. Despite whatever management innovation being introduced in resource allocation at the hospital level to promote cost-effectiveness, the major and probably still most effective means to induce budgetary discipline in the Hospital Authority remains to be the government's control of its annual financial allocation. In that exercise, bureaucratic budgetary politics are the rules of the game.

Some people would have hoped that the 1993 health finance reform debate, following the publication of the *Towards Better Health* consultation document, could lead to a constructive breakthrough in the system of health financing in Hong Kong, which could concurrently address issues of health access, affordability as well as integration of different sectors of care provision. However, the consultation exercise has proved to be redundant as far as policy innovation is concerned. Basically, the health financing arrangements are back to square one.

The consultation document considers that the present public sector "has too narrow a financial base and there is not enough interface between public and private sector providers" (para. 3.3). For the financial base, the commonly used argument is that the government, given its low taxation policy, is unable to increase spending on health care beyond the average 8 per cent of public expenditure. Public expectations are on the rise, while advancement in medical technology is rapid, resulting in escalating health care cost. In the 1980s, it was suggested that the setting up of a hospital authority with more emphasis on efficient resource management could curb costs and make the public sector more cost-effective. This is largely wishful thinking. The answer to the financial problem does not lie in a "managerial" strategy. Efficiency savings of 5 or 10 per cent are insignificant in terms of the long-term growing demand for resources. This demand is more induced by producers than clients of health care. The most cost-effective approach to take in containing demand and cost in health care still rests with a "supply-side" strategy. To this extent, how the health service is to be financed by the society, through taxation, insurance or fee-payment, is a less crucial factor in ensuring cost control, although one can argue that competition and group provider supervision (e.g., through large insurers) can help to check excessive supply.

Health finance should not therefore be narrowly construed as a matter of public expenditure control. Instead it should be considered more as an institutional framework to facilitate people's affordability for health care given their different levels of economic means. Historically, Hong Kong has a health care system which is practically free for all citizens: attendance charges are more or less nominal, while in-patient fees basically only pay for catering cost (which people have to bear anyway whether they are in hospital or not) and do not cover medical services. In terms of health care philosophy, Hong Kong has a "national health system" which does not discriminate patients on grounds of class or economic means.

The establishment of the Hospital Authority, because it merely amalgamates the government and subvented hospitals in organizational terms, does not alter this philosophy. On the other hand, the government has time and again reassured people that the existing policy to prevent anybody from being denied adequate medical treatment because of a lack of means will remain paramount. Whether this policy is good or not is a separate debatable issue, but it is clear that if we are to depart from this system, this involves a basic philosophical shift and requires full arguments which not only address financing parsimoniously, but can convince people that a new funding regime when linked up with other elements of the overall health care system can work better and provide our citizens with a greater degree of affordability, access and even choice. As it happens, the government offers no vision of any kind in its consultation document, and clearly the general public is not persuaded that the existing nominally "free" system should be changed. The government has lost both the argument and an opportunity for innovation.

In fact, although the consultation document offered five options for reform, the government's mind has already been focused only on finding some acceptable means to make patients pay more. The five options are:

1. the percentage subsidy approach;
2. the target group approach (comprising semi-private rooms in public hospitals, itemized charging and target waiver groups);
3. the coordinated voluntary insurance approach;
4. the compulsory comprehensive insurance approach; and
5. the prioritization of treatment approach.

Both the government and the Hospital Authority, with the backing of medical professionals who tend to think that the public is not sufficiently cost-conscious, are in favour of the percentage subsidy approach which will render health care no longer a "free" service. However, because of the enormous public opposition, the government has finally decided to drop this idea. It is not that the public has been "negatively biased by incorrect press reports" as the government alleges, but in the absence of any convincing argument as to how citizens can benefit from the proposed scheme whether collectively or individually, it is understandable that the public will feel threatened by the proposal, particularly those who are elderly or chronically sick.

In presenting its options for reform the government has not addressed the question of affordability or how to enhance people's ability to pay for health care. Hence any suggestions aimed at generating more income for health providers are bound to be one-sided considerations which can easily (and perhaps justifiably) be perceived as a curb on the government's commitment to universal health care. Given that the government has at the outset identified options (1), (2) and (3) as its preferred combination of approaches, in the end when (1) could not be pushed ahead, the government simply settled with (2) and (3) by deciding in January 1994 to introduce semi-private rooms in public hospitals with higher cost-recovery charges and a coordinated voluntary insurance scheme.

There are inherent contradictions within the government's overall health reform strategy as practised. What the new Hospital Authority tries to do is to encourage its hospitals to "improve" service so as to attract more customers (in line with the "internal" market approach pursued in the British National Health Service), both as a means for performance evaluation and in order to justify more bids for government funding. The Authority also wants to avail itself of new ways to raise income so as to be less dependent on the government. Thus it has supported percentage subsidy and also advocated a "managed interface model" which is somewhat akin to the American Health Maintenance Organizations (HMO) concept. Semi-private wards represent a way to generate additional revenue as well as to increase the Authority's share of the health market, which should place it in a good position if health insurance (whether voluntary or compulsory) becomes the norm. However, the more successful the Hospital Authority is in its service improvement and semi-private rooms, the more patients will be drawn away from the private sector hospitals (though this possibility is discarded by the government). As a result, the government may turn out to actually pay more (because even semi-private wards are subsidized, up to 40 to 60 per cent) and private hospitals will have even less room for level-field competition.

The government's main motivation for reform is financial; it does not possess any long-range vision on how to make the best use of health finance as an empowering institution for the consumers of health care. Its hope that voluntary insurance can rapidly develop to provide a new source of health financing for public hospitals is highly optimistic and not borne out by substantive evidence. As the consultation document admits, "[f]or those who could not or did not wish to take out insurance, heavily subsidized public services would still be available." If the public hospitals are going to improve their service within the existing nominal fee framework anyway, one would ask why there should be an incentive for people to take out voluntary insurance. Unless public health fees and charges are to be increased significantly, there is limited economic incentive for people to resort to voluntary insurance. Even so, a "rational" demander-strategy might still be to fight against fee increases politically (lobbying Legislative Council, street action) rather than to accommodate them economically (through insurance). If the purpose of voluntary insurance is to augment patients' ability to pay for more expensive semi-private rooms, then this is tantamount to helping those "approved" medical insurance plans to boom by guaranteeing there is some attraction for people to join them in order to take advantage of the semi-private service that is still substantially government-funded and considerably cheaper than private hospital beds. The government remains blank in policy as to how to integrate the public and private sectors in the context of health finance.

The way to do away with the anomalies of the present dual system of public and private sectors should not lie with either pushing people from the public to the private sector or creating a quasi-private sector within public hospitals. What should be considered, for the sake of providing more consumer choice and ensuring better cost control and quality of service through competition, is to absorb both sectors into an integrated system of production. Now that Hong Kong has already moved forward, in the Hospital Authority reform, to separate the provider function from the producer function, it is perfectly logical if the provider role can be aligned to that of a funding function so that consumers can be funded adequately to seek care from producers of their choice, be they publicly or privately managed. But such an arrangement cannot be developed if private producers continue to charge at cost plus profit while the Hospital Authority producers are able to charge below cost under a free or partially subsidized system. The solution should lie with some form of central insurance system which is community-based rather than risk-rated as in private insurance. Under a central insurance system, all citizens will be covered in health risks and their affordability will not be jeopardized even if health producers (public or private) are to charge at full cost for allocative efficiency reasons. A large community insurer has far more clout and bargaining power to negotiate a cost-effective deal with producers. Only by integrating public and private producers in the same "market" can fair competition be obtained which can promote productive efficiency. Compared to the government's unusually bold proposal recently to introduce a compulsory contributory old-age pension scheme in Hong Kong, it is incomprehensible why it is not equally prepared to push for a compulsory central health insurance at the same time. Perhaps the policy-makers' enthusiasm for reform was over-stated after all.

The "managed interface model" advocated by the Hospital Authority has some features of vertical integration (providing comprehensive coverage of primary, secondary and tertiary health care) and horizontal integration (through entering into contracts with various health care producers/practitioners within all sectors of the health care industry, private or public, on a pre-paid community-based capitation). If adopted, it can go some way in enhancing sector interface to improve consumer choice, producer competition and allocative efficiency. The Hospital Authority puts forward the model as a variant of coordinated voluntary insurance, claiming that it "has in-built flexibility and can be incremental moving either to a more market-oriented direction or a more regulated environment." There is certainly a lot of innovation behind this managed interface concept, however the question remains how such a model should be widely implemented. The Hospital Authority envisages the setting up of one or several purchaser agencies to formulate suitable "product packages" of comprehensive health care to enter into contracts with service producers. But essentially these purchaser agencies would operate on a voluntary, though not-for-profit, basis. The uncertainties about people's incentives to take out voluntary insurance as argued earlier apply equally here. The managed interface model will only work effectively if it is extensively adopted. Only a compulsory insurance system or a market-based health care system (where there is no safety net, thus forcing people to look after their own selves) can ensure that. If the model can be implemented through a single purchasing agency, there is no reason why this cannot and should not be construed within the concept of a central compulsory insurance approach outlined above. The Hospital Authority suffers the same constraint in vision as the government in not daring to contemplate a more fundamental change to the existing system.

☐ Primary Health Care

The 1989–1990 review of primary health care has for a time raised some hope that the government has finally felt it necessary to do something about primary health care in Hong Kong. Historically, primary health care has been placed in secondary importance because the public health care system was biased towards curative medicine. In the old Medical and Health Department days, hospital consultants divided up the largest chunk of the departmental budget and hospital doctors monopolized promotion opportunities. The separate corporatization of hospital services in the form of the Hospital Authority was therefore welcomed by "health"-side doctors who saw an opportunity to free themselves from the domination of the surgeons. For the first time, the Health Division, having been upgraded to become the new Department of Health, has its own budget. It was also very much the advocate for the establishment of a primary health care authority of a similar model as the Hospital Authority (since endorsed by the 1990 review report).

Almost four years have passed but the government has not acted on the recommendation for a new health authority. It is understood that due to the changing political climate (when any government restructuring could be seen by China as part of a British conspiracy) and the costly exercise in setting up the Hospital Authority, the government is reluctant now to attempt another corporatization. This is going to disappoint a lot of reform-minded health workers. But it would be simplistic to assume that problems can be easily solved by reorganization alone. There are two crucial questions which must be addressed directly. The first one is how to integrate the public and private sectors in the provision of primary health care. At present there is no institutional framework in which to bring private general practitioners into a comprehensive health care improvement strategy. The private sector's role is rather obscure despite the fact that some 70 per cent of the population depends on its service. The second question is how to integrate primary health care and hospital care, not only for reasons of medical effectiveness, but also in order to secure a better use of society's resources given that successful primary health care can reduce the demand for more expensive hospital-based curative care. Unless the government takes a major concrete step in the right direction, the goal of "Health for All in the Year 2000" as set out in the review report is likely to remain empty rhetoric.

☐ Conclusion

If the government's picture of Hong Kong's achievements in health are to be taken as facts, then there is nothing alarming in the territory's present health care system. However, as the above discussion explains, there are inherent structural problems in the system which need to be properly dealt with in order to promote better health in a more integrated and affordable context. The past decade should have presented a good opportunity for some fundamental rethinking and regeneration of the system, given that reform has already started in public hospital management, by default if not fully by design. Unfortunately, there was simply a lack of vision as well as determination on the part of government policy-makers whose aim in reform was largely confined to a fiscal one. Despite repeated calls from the medical profession and others concerned about health care policy for a new White Paper, the government has thus far failed to produce one. This is not so much because it does not have a policy as it lacks a new comprehensive strategy to breakthrough the perimeters of the existing policy.

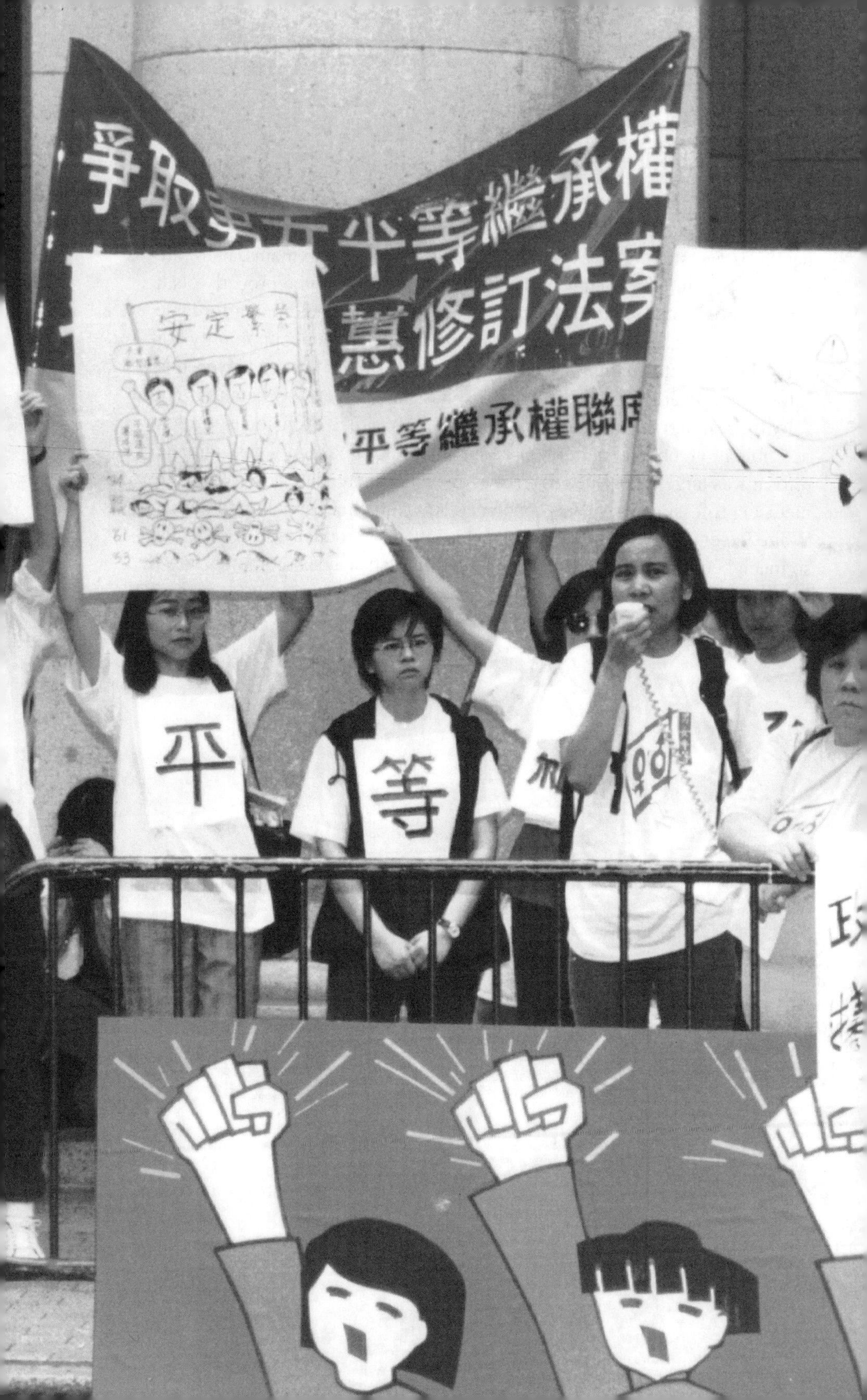

爭取
平等繼承權
慧修訂法
平等繼承權聯
安定繁榮
平
等

Women

Irene Tong

☐ Introduction

The past year has been an unprecedentedly eventful year for the women's cause in Hong Kong. Not only has the government taken the initiative to publish a Green Paper on gender equality, but it has finally been persuaded to adopt the United Nations Convention on the Elimination of All Forms of Discrimination Against Women (CEDAW), for which women's groups have been fighting for more than a decade. Of no less importance is the granting of the legal right to inheritance to "indigenous" women of the New Territories, though achieved only after much hullabaloo. While the government and women's groups are busy at the moment negotiating the terms of reference of an Equal Opportunities Commission due to be set up by the end of this year, the vast majority of women in Hong Kong are still confronted with age-old "women's issues" such as age and wage discrimination in employment, sexual harassment and sexual violence, and the lack of political clout. It is the latter to which I would turn in greater detail, after briefly recounting the "success" we have had during the year in raising the women's agenda to a visibly "public" level.

☐ The Green Paper on Equal Opportunities for Women and Men

Whatever intentions were behind the government's publication of the

---

Irene Tong is a lecturer in the Department of Politics and Public Administration, the University of Hong Kong.

Green Paper on Equal Opportunities for Women and Men (hereafter referred to as the Green Paper) in August 1993, gender equality was, for the first time, formally raised on the political agenda for public debate. Even though the government put in very little effort to publicize the 56-page document (excluding annexes),[1] a total of 1,161 submissions were made and 52,610 signatures were collected when the consultation period ended on 31 December 1993.[2]

Most of the attack on the document came from women's groups, which saw the exercise as too half-hearted, aiming at too little and too late. This was because the document quite complacently claimed that Hong Kong women compared favourably with their counterparts in the rest of the world, *despite* the incomplete evidence and statistics produced, and omissions in various important aspects. It was also over-cautious on the issue of extending to Hong Kong the CEDAW, (to which both Britain and the People's Republic of China were signatories), *in spite of* the fact that the Legislative Council (Legco) voted unanimously for it on 16 December 1992. Thus, the Green Paper provided a convenient focal point for mobilization and lobbying among women and men who believed that sexism was alive and well in modern, industrial Hong Kong.

Various opinion polls were conducted in response to the Green Paper, including one commissioned by the government itself. The findings of all these polls "proved" that an overwhelming majority of the population believed that sex discrimination existed and that there was a need to take measures to facilitate gender equality.[3] A coalition of fourteen women's groups was formed to respond to the Green Paper, and signatures were collected with a view to push for the extension of CEDAW and the establishment of a Women's Commission to monitor its implementation. With

---

[1] In an opinion poll conducted by the Social Sciences Research Centre, the University of Hong Kong, more than half of the respondents were not aware of the release of the Green Paper and two-thirds were totally ignorant of its contents. See *Eastweek*, No. 47 (15 September 1993), p. 92.

[2] See *Express News*, 4 June 1994.

[3] See, for example, surveys done by the Bauhinia Association and by the Hong Kong Policy Viewers, *South China Morning Post*, 31 December 1993; a survey undertaken by the City Polytechnic of Hong Kong, *Hong Kong Standard*, 16 January 1994; and the government-commissioned survey done by The Chinese University of Hong Kong, *Express News*, 4 June 1994.

regard to the latter, it is worth noting that a Coalition of Councillors for the Equality of Women and Men was formed, which successfully gained support from 143 incumbents of important public offices such as the Legco, the Urban and Regional Councils, and the District Boards.[4]

Given the backing of public opinion, the government announced in June 1994 that it would accede to the introduction of CEDAW to Hong Kong, as well as the setting up of an Equal Opportunities Commission, which was likely to have China's support.[5] However, there was already discontent among legislators and the public that the equal rights legislation that the government had in mind was too narrowly conceived,[6] and that the Commission would likely be "toothless" in the sense that it could only play a mediatory, as opposed to a judicial, role.

☐ The New Territories Land (Exemption) Bill

The controversy over female inheritance rights in the New Territories, which the British leased from China in 1898 for 99 years, typified the case of the subsumption of women's interests under the political interests of the powers that be. To appease the indigenous population in the New Territories, the colonial government at the turn of the century introduced the New Territories Ordinance, under which the courts were given the powers to enforce any Chinese custom or customary right pertaining to the land there. In essence, it meant the continuation of Qing Dynasty laws which prohibited women from inheriting property, and to which the rural organization, Heung Yee Kuk, adheres and defends up to this day. The issue had been publicly debated as early as 1990 when the government was drafting the Bill of Rights. At that time, public opinion was already in favour of replacing such archaic legislation with ones which could better reflect societal change.[7]

The recent controversy arose when the Housing Authority admitted late

---

[4] See *South China Morning Post*, 4 November 1993.

[5] See *Hong Kong Standard*, 4 June and 8 June 1994.

[6] For example, it excluded discrimination in age, marital status, or pregnancy, and exempted the small house policy which currently privileges indigenous men in the New Territories. See *Far Eastern Economic Review*, 7 July 1994.

[7] See, for example, the opinion poll conducted by the Asian Commercial Research Ltd., *South China Morning Post*, 30 July 1990.

last year that all property developed in the New Territories under the Home Ownership Scheme were not exempted from the New Territories Ordinance. The government subsequently sought to introduce the New Territories Land (Exemption) Bill with a view to exempt the "urban dwellers" in the new towns from those outdated customs. However, an appointed legislative councillor, Christine Loh, took the opportunity to table an amendment to the Bill in the hope of exempting *all* New Territories land, except for *cho* and *tong*, from section 13 of the New Territories Ordinance. Since granting women the right to inherit land was interpreted as a threat to the integrity of the lineage system, and more importantly, to the economic interests of indigenous men who had been selling the land for profit in recent years, this move was met with violent opposition from the male-dominated Heung Yee Kuk and many indigenous men, who resorted to physical violence outside the Legco in March this year.

The incident sparked off public awareness about the issue, and provided women's groups with another focal point for action. Eleven organizations, including the Anti-Discrimination Female Indigenous Residents' Committee (formed, for the first time, by indigenous women themselves), staged a prolonged campaign to lobby the government as well as legislative councillors to pass Christine Loh's amendment bill. However, alternative, less "radical" views soon came to the fore, among which was an amendment by another legislative councillor, Peggy Lam, who represented the views of the newly formed, popularly perceived as pro-China, Hong Kong Federation of Women. Meanwhile, the Heung Yee Kuk leaders actively sought China's support, claiming that any amendment to the New Territories Ordinance would contravene the Basic Law. An issue of gender equality was then further politicized. For fear of touching too many sensitive nerves, the government remained undecided for many weeks, until the announcement of a compromise solution in June, which marked a hard-won victory for women.

☐ Employment Discrimination, Sexual Harassment, and Violence Against Women

Not only was the issue of equal rights to inheritance omitted from the Green Paper, the diverse forms that discrimination could take place in the area of employment, and the various forms of sexual abuse women have had to put up with in our society were not mentioned either. Nor were they addressed in the *National Report to the Second Asian Pacific Ministerial Conference on Women in Development*, which was submitted by the Hong Kong government in Jakarta this June.

In the area of employment, it was increasingly clear that discrimination existed against women aged over 30. This was substantiated by research done by pressure groups as well as academics. For example, the Women 30 Action Group surveyed local job advertisements and found that most employers discriminated against women aged over 30.[8] In-depth interviews with more than 30 women workers aged 35–50 revealed that middle-aged female factory workers were not only displaced by the relocation of light industries to southern China, but were also barred from re-employment in the service sector other than in those jobs which were considered most obnoxious and offered the least pay.[9]

The government-sponsored retraining schemes were criticized as ineffectual, since the content of those programmes were considered either too irrelevant or too basic to help secure a job after the training period. What was most likely to happen, however, was the use of trainees to fill short-term vacancies: since the Employees Retraining Board subsidized one-third of the employees' wages for the first three months,[10] unscrupulous employers would not hesitate to take advantage of the scheme.

For the rest of the women in the labour force, they have to put up with differential wages which stand at 77 per cent of male wages, and risk being sacked once they apply for maternity leave, for existing legislation proved insufficient to protect them from such abuse.[11]

It would not be too exaggerating to say that sexual harassment and violence against women were "the flavour of the year," to use Michael Sze's "poor taste joke."[12] Public attention was once again drawn to the issue of sexual harassment when in December 1993, the former high-ranking

---

[8] See *South China Morning Post*, 8 March 1994.

[9] Conference on "Economic Changes and Problems of Middle-aged Women in the Labour Force," Centre of Asian Studies, the University of Hong Kong, 1 July 1994.

[10] See *Eastern Express*, 18 April 1994.

[11] See, for example, *Eastern Express*, 6 June 1994.

[12] The Secretary for the Civil Service, Michael Sze, made a blunder when he referred to sexual harassment as the "flavour of the month" during a Legislative Council meeting this May. Women's groups attacked him for trivializing the issue. See "Poor Taste Joke not Meant to Trivialize," *Hong Kong Standard*, 26 May 1994.

officer of the Independent Commission Against Corruption (ICAC), Alex Tsui, made allegations of the mishandling of a sexual assault case in the ICAC. A Coalition Against Sexual Abuse was formed, but it could do little to prevent the rape and murder of a 19-year-old women in Tuen Mun in May. The latter event raised widespread public concern about safety in housing estates, as well as fear and anger among residents of Tuen Mun, who formed voluntary escort groups in some of the estates. Meanwhile, it was revealed that 18 cases of sexual harassment complaints had occurred within the civil service in the last three years,[13] and the government was urged to enforce stricter in-house regulations to deal with it.[14] This summer, a debate on what ought to be the appropriate penalty given to pre-meditated rape-and-murder criminals was kindled when the court decided to imprison a rapist and his accomplice for a mere eight and seven years respectively. It seemed that the Hong Kong public was beginning to see that sexual harassment and violence against women, including age-old wife battering, were more than just "personal" and "private" matters.

At another level, women's groups continued to oppose beauty pageants, which were seen to objectify and degrade women's body and intellect. However, the opposition from women's groups to this year's Miss Hong Kong beauty contest was given unprecedented media attention, all because the chairperson of the Hong Kong Federation of Women and the Women's Affairs officer of the United Democrats of Hong Kong accepted with clear conscience the invitation to adjudicate in the contest!

☐ How Much Political Clout Do Women Have?

If "[f]reedom from discrimination is one of the cornerstones of our open society,"[15] what guarantees are there for the realization and preservation of such freedom? Legislation helps, but that is not sufficient in itself. The picture painted above tells us that unless our society (including women and men in all walks of life, senior civil servants and organizers of women's groups) develops a greater sensitivity towards gender inequality, women will continue to be victims of overt and covert forms of sexism. The Green

---

[13] See *Hong Kong Standard*, 19 May 1994.

[14] *Eastern Express*, 28 March 1994.

[15] Governor Christopher Patten's address to the 1993–1994 Session of the Legislative Council, 6 October 1993, paragraph 114.

Paper and the issue of succession rights in the New Territories had already played an educational role. It is hoped that the Equal Opportunities Commission would at least transmit appropriate messages, even if not possess the power to see them enforced.

For cognitive acknowledgement of the need for change to translate itself to actual social change, physical *and* ideological access to institutionalized political power is necessary. Here, one cannot ignore questions regarding the numerical representation of women in our power structures on the one hand, and the level of representation of "women's voices" in these structures on the other. Furthermore, one needs to assess the potential size and characteristics of the "women's lobby" before statements could be made about the future of the women's movement.

Numerical Representation of Women in Formal Governmental Structures

Women's participation in formal governmental structures has been a relatively recent phenomenon. No female unofficials were appointed into the Legco until 1966, and it was as late as 1976 when the first female member was appointed to serve in the Executive Council (Exco). Prior to the mid-1980s, one could at most find two or three women in each of these bodies at any one time (excluding the clerical staff).

The Legco

The situation in percentage points has not improved much in the last ten years in the case of the Legco, the most important law-making body in Hong Kong. In 1994, 8 out of 60 councillors, or 13.3 per cent, are female, compared to 6 out of 47, or 12.8 per cent, in 1984 (see Table 1). It is interesting to note that women constitute almost 29 per cent of the non-elected seats while they only represent 5 per cent of the elected ones (see Table 2). To account for this phenomenon, one has to look at the channels of political recruitment to this Council.

Until 1993, no women had ever been appointed to the positions of the Chief Secretary, the Financial Secretary and the Attorney General, which constitute the three seats allocated to *ex-officio* members. Anson Chan was the first female, and Chinese, to become the Chief Secretary. This office entitled her not only a seat in the Legco, but in the Exco as well.

The 18 appointed seats were allocated at the discretion of the Governor.

Table 1. Female Representation in the Legislative and Executive Councils

Year	1984 No. of women	1984 No. of seats	%	1994 No. of women	1994 No. of seats	%
Legco	6	47	12.8	8	60	13.3
Exco	2	17	11.8	4	15	26.7

Source: Association for the Advancement of Feminism, *Report on the Survey of Women's Participation in Public Affairs in Hong Kong* (Hong Kong: Association for the Advancement of Feminism, 1985), pp. 110–11. *Hong Kong 1994* (Hong Kong: Government Printer, 1994), Appendices 2 and 3.

Table 2. Channels of Recruitment to the Legco, as at January 1994

	No. of women	No. of seats	% of total	
Ex-officio	1	3	33.3	28.6%
Appointed	5	18	27.8	
Elected (functional)	1	21	4.8	5.1%
Elected (geographical)	1	18	5.6	
Total	8	60	13.3	

Source: Calculated from Appendix 3 of *Hong Kong 1994* (Hong Kong: Government Printer, 1994).

It was no coincidence that all the women appointed possessed either a business or professional background. This means that the non-elite, or grassroots women, would have no chance under this category.

From the point of view of women's groups, functional constituencies are most detrimental to the political recruitment of women. First, each of the constituencies represents either an economic, social, or professional sector. Homemakers or full-time housewives would never be represented. Second, the election system allows for one company one vote, as opposed to one person one vote. As women are generally less likely than men to reach top decision-making positions in an organization, women tend to exercise less influence in returning candidates in this category. Third, of the 21 seats, two are allocated to the rural (represented by Heung Yee Kuk) and the Regional Council sectors. However, women are grossly underrepresented in these two organizations. The Green Paper clearly admitted that at present, all the 27 Rural Committee Chairmen in the New Territories were male, and that there was only one female Village Representative, out of about 690 villages, mainly due to the fact that women were not considered "Head of Household" for election purposes. About one-third of the villages even barred women from standing for elections.[16] As regards the Regional Council, there is only one woman out of a total of 35.

Councillors from geographical constituencies were returned through direct elections, which had never occurred in Hong Kong's history before 1991. Of the 94 candidates who ran for the elections in 1991, only 7 were female, one of whom (Emily Lau) succeeded in winning a seat. Despite the fact that female electors accounted for almost half of the registered electorate, and the fact that there was no significant difference between the sexes in voter turnout,[17] the paucity of female candidates and their low success rate have to be accounted for and not assumed. This will be discussed under the "women's lobby."

The Exco

Referring to Table 1, the more-than-two-fold increase in the percentage of women in the Exco, where most policies are initiated, is quite misleading. If one excludes the *ex-officio* seat held by Anson Chan, there was only an increase of *one* woman over the past ten years. Again, what was said above about the appointment system also applies here.

The Urban and Regional Councils

In the 1991 municipal council elections, a total of 8 out of 61 (13.1 per cent) candidates were female, and only 2 were elected (see Table 3). Again, the low level of participation and election of women compared to men has to be accounted for.

The District Boards

The District Boards are largely non-political organizations which allow public participation at the local level in matters which affect the immediate concerns of the residents of a given district. Studies elsewhere have shown

---

[16] See *Green Paper on Equal Opportunities for Women and Men* (Hong Kong: Hong Kong government, August 1993), p. 9.

[17] See the Green Paper, p. 4.

Table 3. Female Representation in the Municipal Councils, 1993

	Appointed		Elected	
	No. of women	% of total	No. of women	% of total
Urban Council	5	20.0	2	13.3
Regional Council	1	4.2	0	0

Source: Calculated from *National Report to the Second Asian and Pacific Ministerial Conference on Women in Development* (Hong Kong: Hong Kong government, June 1994), Annex I.

that this is the level where we could expect the highest number of female candidates, due to the relative apolitical nature of local level elections, the greater number of seats available (and therefore less competitive and intimidating), and a closer mapping of women's concerns with the nature and requirement of the office.[18]

Female representation in the District Boards has been quite varied over the past decade. The overall percentage has slightly declined from 11 per cent in 1982–1985 to around 10 per cent in 1991–1994 (see Table 4). The overall average for urban areas seemed to have declined, whereas there has been a moderate increase in the rural average. This might be explained by the increase in younger, and probably better educated, age cohorts in the New Towns. From the average age of female candidates for the 1994 District Board elections shown in Table 5, one can see that younger women are relatively active in contesting seats in Tsuen Wan, Tuen Mun, Kwai Tsing, Yuen Long and Tai Po. Overall, it is encouraging to see an increase in the absolute number of women contesting the seats, from 50 in 1991 to 97 in 1994, including eight whose occupation was "housewife."

The Civil Service

The Hong Kong government employed a total of 182,099 civil servants in 1993, 31 per cent of whom were female. However, almost 54 per cent of them were concentrated between points 1–25 of the Master Pay Scale,

---

[18] See, for example, Mark Neylan and Jacoba Brasch, "Women in Local Government," *Current Affairs Bulletin*, Vol. 69, No. 4 (September 1992), pp. 4–10.

Table 4. Female Representation on the District Boards

District	1982–1985	1985–1988	1991–1994
Islands	5.9	5.6	5.0
North	0	0	4.5
Sai Kung	0	8.3	7.1
Sha Tin	11.8	8.3	6.7
Tai Po	0	5.9	4.5
Tsuen Wan	7.8	5.9	14.3
Kwai Tsing	N/A	0	0
Tuen Mun	0	8.0	13.8
Yuen Long	5.3	4.3	8.0
Subtotal	4.2	5.0	7.1
Central & Western	23.1	15.0	10.5
Wan Chai	33.3	23.5	20.0
Eastern	16.7	9.7	8.3
Southern	7.1	15.8	16.7
Kowloon City	15.0	10.7	8.3
Kwun Tong	17.9	14.7	19.4
Mong Kok	8.3	17.6	6.7
Sham Shui Po	9.1	9.7	11.1
Wong Tai Sin	21.4	14.3	10.7
Yau Tsim	10.0	14.3	16.7
Subtotal	16.4	13.8	12.6
Grand Total	11.1	10.1	10.0

Sources: Association for the Advancement of Feminism, *Report on the Survey of Women's Participation in Public Affairs in Hong Kong* (Hong Kong: Association for the Advancement of Feminism, 1985), p. 109; *Civil and Miscellaneous Lists, Hong Kong Government, 1st July, 1993* (Hong Kong: Government Secretariat, 1993).

while the figure for men was only 36 per cent or so.[19] Only 0.2 per cent of the female civil servants were able to reach the apex of the bureaucracy, compared to 0.7 per cent for male civil servants. There had indeed been a substantial increase over the years in the number of female civil servants at the directorate level (see Table 6). Yet one may wonder if women at this

---

[19] Calculated from *Civil Service Personnel Statistics, 1993* (Hong Kong: Civil Service Branch, Government Secretariat, 1993), p. 12.

Table 5. Female Candidates in the 1994 District Board Elections

District	Seats	Number of candidates	Female candidates	Average age	Percentage of total
Central & Western	14	31	3	43	9.7
Wan Chai	10	25	3	53	12.0
Eastern	34	75	12	40	16.0
Southern	16	35	7	40	20.0
Yau Tsim Mong	15	47	7	42	14.9
Sham Shui Po	20	41	3	44	7.3
Kowloon City	21	46	5	47	10.9
Wong Tai Sin	22	41	3	52	7.3
Kwun Tong	33	65	7	40	10.8
Tsuen Wan	15	30	8	36	26.7
Tuen Mun	25	49	11	38	22.4
Yuen Long	19	42	3	37	7.1
North District	11	24	1	29	4.2
Tai Po	17	40	4	37	10.0
Sai Kung	11	26	1	49	3.8
Sha Tin	31	71	10	41	14.1
Kwai Tsing	26	60	8	38	13.3
Islands	6	14	2	42	14.3
Total	346	762	98	41	12.9

Source: Calculated from *South China Morning Post*, 16 August 1994; *Wen Wei Po*, 16 August 1994.

Table 6. Female Civil Servants on Directorate Pay Scale*

Year[@]	No. female	Total	Percentage female
1985	49	900	5.4
1986	53	939	5.6
1987	63	997	6.3
1988	78	1,057	7.4
1989	74	883	8.4
1990	92	972	9.5
1991	106	1,032	10.3
1992	113	1,006	11.2
1993	135	997	13.5

Notes: * From 1989 onwards, the figures include Directorate (Legal) Pay Scale.
[@] As at 1 April of the respective year.

Source: Calculated from *Civil Service Personnel Statistics* (Hong Kong: Civil Service Branch), respective years.

level are more likely to be placed in charge of "soft" areas, such as education, social welfare, health, and the like, which were deemed to commensurate with the female "nature."

Government Advisory Bodies

The Hong Kong government, which claims to govern by consultation and consensus, has always had an elaborate network of advisory boards and committees. As at August 1993, there were a total of 313 advisory bodies, involving 2,433 people. Women constituted only 15.2 per cent of all board and committee members.[20]

Chinese Government Advisory Bodies

To facilitate the transition to 1997, the Chinese government in Beijing has been appointing Hong Kong people to be Hong Kong Affairs advisers and members of the Preliminary Working Committee (PWC) in 1992 and 1993 respectively. The former was seen as a stepping stone towards the latter. The Hong Kong Affairs advisers were supposed to act as a bridge between the Mainland and Hong Kong, to take part in discussions on special topics, and to provide opinions on matters relating to the transition. With access to insider information, these people are seen to be influential in shaping future policies for Hong Kong.

However, there is a numerical under-representation of female members on these advisory bodies. Of the three batches of Hong Kong Affairs advisers totalling 143, only 13 (9.1 per cent) were female. Of the 43 members of the PWC appointed in June 1993, only 4 (9.3 per cent) were female. Of the 13 additional PWC members appointed in May 1994, none of them was female. A survey of the background of the female Hong Kong Affairs advisers shows that service in the now-defunct Basic Law Drafting or Consultative Committees (BLDC or BLCC), or membership in the Chinese People's Political Consultative Committee (CPPCC), was useful for recruitment into the current positions (see Table 7).

"Women's Voice" in Existing Power Structures

It can only be hoped but not assumed that there is necessarily a relationship

---

[20] *South China Morning Post*, 10 December 1993.

Table 7. Profile of Female Hong Kong Affairs Advisers

Name	Batch*	Age	Occupation	Background
Chan Yuen-han	2	48	Vice-chair of Federation of Trade Unions	unionist
Cheng, Alice	1	?	Vice-chair of Chinese Chamber of Commerce	CPPCC delegate; member, One-Country-Two-Systems Economic Research Institute
Chung Kei-wing	3	74	Vice-Chancellor of Shue Yan College	ex-member, BLCC
Fong Wong Kut-man, Nellie@	1	45	accountant	former Legislative Councillor
Ko Siu-wah	3	70	educator	CPPCC delegate; ex-member, BLCC; President, HK Women's Foundation Association
Lam Pei Yu-dja, Peggy	3	66	appointed legislator	CPPCC delegate; Chair, Wan Chai District Board; Chair, HK Federation of Women
Leung Oi-sie, Elsie	2	55	lawyer	National People's Congress (NPC) delegate; member, HK Federation of Women; member, Democratic Alliance for Betterment of Hong Kong
Liu Yiu-chu@	1	59	lawyer	NPC delegate; ex-member, BLDC
Pao Pui-hing, Anna	3	49	Chair of World-wide Shipping Group	daughter of Sir Yue-kong Pao; wife of Dr. Helmut Sohmen
Tam Wai-chu, Maria@	1	48	barrister	founder of Liberal Democratic Federation; ex-member, BLDC; former Executive and Legislative Councillor
Tu, Elsie	3	80	supervisor of Mu Kuang schools	Legislative Councillor; Urban Councillor
Wu Suk-ching, Annie	2	46	General Manager of HK World Trade Centre	CPPCC delegate; ex-member, BLCC
Yuk Tak-fun, Alice	3	43	social worker	general secretary of YWCA

Notes: * Batches 1, 2, and 3 were appointed in March 1992, March 1993 and April 1994 respectively.
@ Member of the PWC for the HKSAR Preparatory Committee.

Source: *South China Morning Post*, 12 March 1992; 30 March 1993; 24 June 1993; and 12 April 1994.

between female office-holders and their representation of women's interests. Conversely, male incumbents of political offices need not be seen as opposed to the women's agenda. Therefore, in the pursuit of numerical representation of the female sex in the formal power structures, women's groups have not been oblivious of the need to raise gender consciousness among female and male power holders, in the hope that transformation could occur from within.

During the 1991 elections, local women's groups had put in much effort to educate the female electorate, as well as to persuade candidates to include women's concerns in their platforms. While such efforts were commendable, it would be naïve to believe in immediate positive results. According to a study published by a women's group early this year, nearly half of the legislative councillors were found to be unresponsive to women's issues. Most of them were male, appointed, or elected through functional constituencies. On the other hand, all the female legislators had either taken part in the debates on women's issues, or taken the initiative to raise questions concerning women's rights. Even so, it was quite disappointing to find that only one per cent of the over 1,000 questions raised between October 1991 and December 1993 was about women's issues.[21] In the current District Board elections, only half of the 97 female candidates can be said to have included women's concerns in their propaganda material.[22]

Another testimony to the weakness of the female voice among people with influence within the establishment was the cool response towards the call to extend CEDAW to Hong Kong. When 14 female District Board members initiated a petition in favour of CEDAW last September, only 143 signatures were collected from the 550 incumbents of the three tiers of representative government. Only 32 out of a total of 58 female incumbents showed their support. Even more surprising was the fact that only one-third of the legislative councillors responded, given that they had already unanimously voted in favour of the issue.[23]

With regard to the civil service, it remains to be seen whether having a

---

[21] *Hong Kong Standard*, 7 March 1994. See also Association for the Advancement of Feminism, *Mid-term Evaluation of the Work of Legislative Councillors* (Hong Kong: Association for the Advancement of Feminism, February 1994).

[22] *Hong Kong Standard*, 16 September 1994.

[23] *Hong Kong Standard*, 4 November 1993.

female Chief Secretary would lead to substantive change for women inside and outside the civil service, or whether having female policy secretaries and administrative officers would help bring about changes in the style and emphases of policy-making. Conventional wisdom tells us that unless the rules of the game are fundamentally altered, women in power are likely to play the game the male way.

A Possible Women's Lobby?

If directly elected legislators were found to be more responsive to women's concerns when compared to other forms of political recruitment, and if political parties had shown more support for women's issues than independents,[24] then the natural conclusion would be to encourage the aggregation of women's interests via political parties, which would then be channelled into the power structure through the mechanism of elections. For this to happen, two factors must be present concurrently. One is the readiness of political parties to be persuaded to adopt the women's agenda as part of their party platform, and to even actively encourage their female members to run for office. The other is the readiness on the part of the female and male electorate to recognize the presence or absence of a women's agenda in a given platform and to cast their vote accordingly. Without having satisfied these two conditions to a certain degree, it would be difficult to envisage a strong women's lobby.

At the moment, we do not have sufficient evidence to make concrete claims. But tentatively, we can suggest that the major political parties are already well aware of the importance of the female vote. Therefore, the United Democrats, Meeting Point, the Democratic Alliance for Betterment of Hong Kong, and the Liberal Party all have spokespersons on women's affairs. However, it takes another major step to go from there towards actively recruiting female members and supporting female candidates, especially in constituencies that are regarded as highly competitive. Judging from the relatively low percentages of female candidates fielded by various political parties in the current District Board elections, political parties are still not well prepared to "give women a go" (see Table 8).

The second condition, the presence of an equality conscious electorate,

---

[24] These were the findings cited in Note 21.

Table 8. Female Candidates Fielded by Major Political Parties in the 1994 District Board Elections

Party	Total candidates	Female candidates	Percentage
United Democrats	105	11	10.5
Meeting Point	27	2	7.4
Association for Democracy and People's Livelihood	41	7	17.1
Liberal Party	90	14	15.6
Democratic Alliance for Betterment of Hong Kong	83	12	14.5
Liberal Democratic Federation	28	1	3.6
123 Democratic Alliance	17	1	5.9

Source: Calculated from *Hong Kong Economic Daily*, 16 August 1994; and *Wen Wei Po*, 16 August 1994.

is the more important of the two. This is because one could safely assume that with sufficiently clear messages arising from the electorate, political parties would be forced to rearrange their priorities. But just how mature is the current electorate on issues of gender equality and why? The question cannot be answered satisfactorily without further research. By observing the fact that women's agenda have never featured prominently in past elections, nor in the legislative debates, and given the low success rate of female candidates at *any* election, the Hong Kong electorate cannot be described as having attained a high level of gender consciousness. At the individual level, the lack of desire of women to contest the seats at the three tiers of representative government has never been seriously questioned or problematized. Such silence bespeaks the existence of insurmountable barriers to women's empowerment to run for public office.

Figure 1 would be helpful in visualizing the multiple factors which come into play in shaping gender consciousness (see the direction of the solid arrows). The latter in turn impacts on politics, the domestic and the international environment (see the direction of the dotted arrows). The size and characteristics of the women's lobby will to a large extent be determined by the dynamic interplay of these factors.

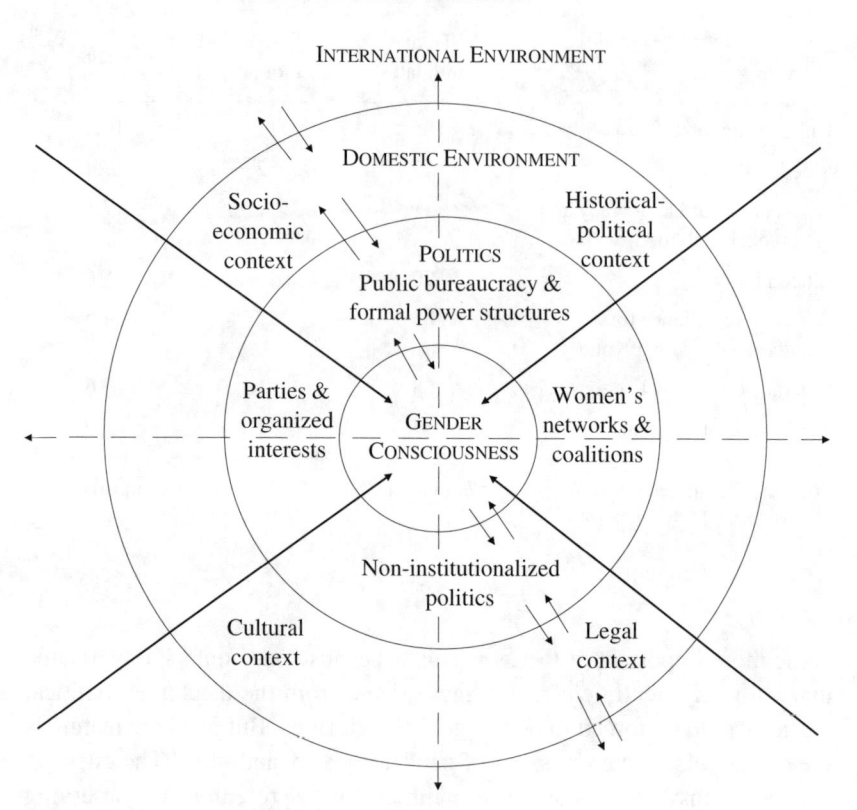

Figure 1. The Relationship between Gender Consciousness, Politics and the Environment

INTERNATIONAL ENVIRONMENT

DOMESTIC ENVIRONMENT

- Socio-economic context
- Historical-political context
- POLITICS: Public bureaucracy & formal power structures
- Parties & organized interests
- Women's networks & coalitions
- GENDER CONSCIOUSNESS
- Non-institutionalized politics
- Cultural context
- Legal context

☐ The Future of the Women's Movement

Owing to the flux and uncertainty associated with the run-up to the change of sovereignty in 1997, remarks made here could only be tentative and speculative. Yet one could still study the women's movement from the vantage point of the interaction between gender consciousness, politics and the domestic and international environment.

At the macro level, the China factor has entered into Hong Kong politics,[25] and it is there to stay. The changing historical-political context

---

[25] See Choi Po-king's discussion in "Women," *The Other Hong Kong Report 1993* (Hong Kong: The Chinese University Press, 1993).

has given rise to opportunities for change. For example, women's groups seized upon the moment of the drafting of the Basic Law to demand that gender equality be written into that constitutional document. That falling onto deaf ears, they took the opportunity provided by the amendment of the New Territories Ordinance to demand legal guarantees of women's inheritance rights. However, that move led to invited intervention from China by those with vested interests, and to debates about the congruency of any legislative change with the Basic Law, and finally to the division among women's groups into the "pro-China camp" and "the rest" with regard to the most suitable way of legislating for change. In retrospect, the whole issue might typify future struggles for gender equality. That is, gender issues would likely be politicized and women's groups would likely be further divided along political lines.[26]

Positive and negative movements in the international arena might also affect the women's movement in Hong Kong. For example, being responsible for hosting the 1995 Fourth World Conference on Women has forced the Chinese government to pay unprecedented attention to women's issues. It has also prompted a coalition of women's groups to be formed in Hong Kong, with the aim of taking advantage of the media attention on this high-level event to educate women and men here. Negative examples such as the "backlash" in the United States, the retrogression in terms of women's status found in the former Soviet Union and Eastern Europe, and closer to home, the re-production of conservative gender stereotypes under Chinese marketization efforts, all spell disincentives to reflect upon existing gender relations, and might prove incapacitating in terms of building global solidarity.

Socially and economically, we saw the double-edged sword of rapid economic growth on the nurturance of gender consciousness. On the one hand, widely available educational opportunities have elevated the position of many Hong Kong women. On the other hand, economic prosperity has desensitized middle-class or professional women to the plight of the less privileged. The conscious or unconscious exploitation of 130,000 or so foreign domestics in Hong Kong is a specific case in point. These women

---

[26] Women's groups are already said to be fighting for the limelight. See *Eastern Express*, 4 February 1994.

are paid to facilitate the emancipation of a class of women from the toils of daily domestic work. But they are never treated as sisters in return.

Culturally, "woman's proper place" has yet to be challenged in schools, in the family, in the mass media, and in our ways of living and communicating. Without having first internalized some sensitivity towards gender equality, the reliance on legal provisions would only be futile.

All that was said above provides the backdrop for real politics to take place, in either institutionalized or non-institutionalized form. Key actors here are women's networks and coalitions which are increasingly sophisticated and familiar with the game of politics. Increasingly, they have formed partnerships with other organized interests in addition to establishing links with the international (especially non-governmental) arena. Though women's groups in the past year had proved themselves capable of forming healthy working relationships with each other, it remains to be seen how strong the feminist vision(s) could be in face of increasing centrifugal forces mentioned above.

Mention must be made here of the role of spontaneous actions at the grassroots in contributing to the success of the past year. That is, thousands of women and men who supported the women's cause signed petitions, joined in mass demonstrations outside the Legco, spoke at the radio phone-in programmes, wrote letters to the editors of newspapers, and organized themselves into concern groups. In short, without the support of public opinion, no matter how well-organized women's groups might be, their efforts could prove to be futile.

Parties are likely to play a pivotal role in translating gender consciousness to systemic change. Not only do they provide an increasingly important ground for the political recruitment of women, they can also play an important educational role in their daily activities. At the moment, there is low sensitivity that women's interests can actually form part and parcel of party interests. Therefore, it is foreseeable that in face of keen competition, party politics would easily overwhelm any concern for gender equality. As for the public bureaucracy and its subsidiary bodies, there is little sign, at the moment, of internal value change among occupants of important positions.

☐ Conclusion

The past year has seen major victories in putting women's (or feminist, to be accurate) issues onto the public agenda, and it has been a very educational year for all. Yet these successes were no accidents. They came about through conscious efforts of organizing, mobilizing, and negotiation, often outside the establishment. However, to consolidate and to advance these gains, more has to be theorized and done. To say the least, not only should there be more *physical* representation of women in formal structures of power, but the incumbents of these structures, whether female or male, should also possess sufficient *ideological* commitment to gender equality. All these depend on an increased level of gender consciousness among the public at large. Short of achieving these, women would continue to enjoy little political clout, and their voices would have great difficulty reaching the centre of politics.

捍衛新聞自由
立即釋放席揚
拯救席揚聯合行
立即釋放席揚
香港民主同盟
抗議秘密審判
捍衛新聞自由
立即釋放席揚
抗議秘密審訊
立即釋放席揚
香港民主民生協進會
要求無條件釋放席揚

21

The Media

Francis Moriarty

☐ **The Chilling Effect**

Weather: High-pressure centres rapidly building up on the mainland are causing an extreme cold front to move in the direction of Hong Kong. The long-term forecast is for progressively chilly winds expected to increase in velocity as temperatures along the border plummet to record lows. People exposed to the harsh conditions are advised not to talk about it.

It has not been a banner year for press freedom in Hong Kong. A few encouraging signs have been more than offset by worrying indications that China's design for Hong Kong is limited purely to producing the sound of "jingling" cash registers. Repeated and increasingly strident statements from senior Chinese officials denouncing and rejecting any role for Hong Kong as a "political" city only suggest that the kind of aggressive, independent and vocal news media we have now are sure to face a more restricted role after 1997. China's jailing of dissident journalist Gao Yu[1] and

---

Francis Moriarty is a journalist based in Hong Kong.

[1] Gau Yu, who has written for several Hong Kong newspapers, was taken from her home by local security officials on 2 October 1993, a week before her departure to the United States to take up a one-year research fellowship at the Columbia University School of Journalism. She was accused of providing state secrets to persons across the border. Her arrest came shortly after Wu Shishen, a New China News Agency editor, was given a life imprisonment for providing a copy of a speech by party chief Jiang Zemin to a Hong Kong reporter.

subsequent arrest and imprisonment of *Ming Pao* reporter Xi Yang eloquently served to make the point.

The year showed distressingly little advance towards key legal reforms protecting freedom of expression, as the government continued its inexplicable foot-dragging in amending or eliminating little-used but ominous colonial legislation. A push to give people a statutory right to access government-held information has been rejected by the government. Self-censorship has been on the rise, with China intimidating individual reporters, editors, owners and even media magnates like Rupert Murdoch,[2] who admitted to dropping the BBC from his Asia-wide satellite STAR TV service in April 1994 in an effort to placate Beijing. Local television station TVB (Television Broadcasts Limited) acquired the rights to two shows critical of China, then did not broadcast them, a form of self-censorship which it defended as a "purely commercial decision." At rival station ATV (Asia Television Limited), a half-dozen journalists resigned in a dispute with management over showing several minutes of film shot by a Spanish crew in Tiananmen Square on the night on 4 June 1989. Oddly, the film — which was ultimately broadcast — seemed to support China's official contention that there was no violence in the square itself. Concern over the affair was sufficient to have the Information Policy Panel of the Legislative Council (Legco) invite all sides in for a hearing. The result was inconclusive but the journalists have stood by their resignations.[3]

One of the least-known but more worrisome events came on 30–31 May when a group of Hong Kong editors was invited to Shenzhen for the opening of a new theme park ("Windows on the World"). The event looked like a good time and a basically harmless perk — so much so that many of those invited did not attend. But for those who did go, the affair turned out quite differently. The journalists found themselves one evening in a closed-door, off-the-record session that went on until midnight. Leading the discussion were Li Yuan, deputy director of the State Council News Office,

---

[2] In July 1993, Murdoch's Australian-based News Corporation purchased 63.6 per cent of HutchVision Ltd. (BVI), the holding company of STAR TV, from Hutchison Whampoa and Li Ka-shing and family for US$525 million. The Li family retains 36.4 per cent.

[3] A detailed look at the self-censorship issue can be found in *Freedom of Expression in Hong Kong: 1994 Annual Report* of ARTICLE 19 and the Hong Kong Journalists Association, 30 June 1994.

and another news office official, Zuo Linshu, bureau chief of Bureau Number One in Beijing. The essential message of the meeting was simple: under the principle of "one country, two systems," journalists are not free to criticize or comment unfavourably upon events in China.

To affirm the point, the message was repeated in an editorial on 2 June in the local Beijing mouthpiece, *Ta Kung Pao*, which ran the veiled warning in a leader titled "Harmonious Relationship Between Hong Kong and China is Hong Kong People's Wish."

The choice of location and the proximity of the date to 4 June serve to underscore the point being made: "Criticize your system, do not criticize ours. We have ways of handling such critics." As the single most important litmus test for the freedom of the Hong Kong news media has always been their freedom to comment upon events in the mainland, the importance of this warning should not be underestimated.

Freedom of expression also suffered a blow when the government refused visas to a pair of exiled Chinese dissidents, who were to speak at a June 4 commemoration. Governor Christopher Patten — whose electoral reform bill was hanging in the balance, along with Sino-British near-deals on defence lands and the airport — defended the decision as showing sensitivity and restraint. Exactly why restricting expression was restraint for him, but self-censorship for a reporter whose job was on the line, he did not explain.

Textbooks made headlines when Director of Education Dominic Wong "advised" two school-book publishers to edit out almost inanely bland references to the Tiananmen Square massacre ("incident"), saying the events surrounding that day were too recent to be viewed objectively. Wong suggested a twenty-year rule for history texts; Patten, under pressure from the news media and educationalists, ordered a review of the Wong's proposal. The director then "clarified" his position, saying that he had offered publishers "comments and advice" for "consideration" in choosing the wording. The damage, however, had likely been done; Wong sent out a clear message to publishers that certain subjects are sensitive, if not entirely taboo. Textbook publishers who want their products placed on recommended reading lists, and actually purchased, will not miss the message. Wong denied to reporters that was kowtowing to China or trying to keep his job after the handover of sovereignty. However, to borrow an old American saying, "you can't un-ring a bell."

New publications have continued to appear, mostly in Chinese, the biggest splash made by the *Hong Kong Today* tabloid, published by *Ming*

Pao. The paper is an attempt by the intellectually oriented *Ming Pao* to go down-market. After a surge of initial interest, circulation has sagged badly, most estimates beneath 10,000. The paper's format caught attention with a smart use of colour and the novelty of putting self-contained stories inside boxes, ending the hunt for story-jumps that many readers of Chinese-language papers complain of. In the end, however, the issue is not about boxes, but what is inside them, and it is here *Hong Kong Today* has had its problems. Simply put, readers say they have not found anything remarkably different from what they already get in the best-selling *Oriental Daily News*. Indeed, with its vast sources and readership, *ODN* — as it is often called — seems just too hard to beat. Nonetheless, *Ming Pao* has not yet pulled the plug and is looking at other opportunities in both print and broadcasting.

There were closures as well, most notable being that of the *Hong Kong Times*, ending forty-three years of publication in February 1994. The paper was financed directly by Taiwan, which pulled the plug as circulation dwindled and losses, according to one source, mounted to an estimated HK$10 million per month. Taiwan interests are not all running away, however. Witness the *United Daily* and *China Times*, wealthy private organizations in Taiwan, which respectively own the *Hong Kong United Daily* news and the *China Times Weekly*, both recent additions to the news-stands.

Another closure of interest was that of *Pai Shing*, a bi-weekly magazine with a reputation for running stories critical of China. *Pai Shing* closed its doors when pro-China businessman T. T. Tsui, who bought into the publication in 1993, decided to pull out. There had been fears at the time Tsui acquired the magazine that it would fall victim to a well-known Beijing strategy — clearly outlined in the memoirs former Xinhua official Xu Jiatun — of having sympathetic individuals buy into publications, then shut down what cannot be changed. Tsui's action seemed to fit.

On 1 February 1994 the English-language press saw the addition of a major paper, the *Eastern Express*, a smart-and-saucy up-market daily (except Sunday) with a tendency to list towards the tabloid — not too surprising, perhaps, as its publisher is the Oriental Press Group, which owns the *ODN*, itself a classic tabloid and the territory's largest-circulation paper. The papers are owned by the wealthy Ma family, which has strong Taiwan ties and what is politely termed a colourful past. The *Express* got off to a somewhat rocky start, its eye-catching photographs sometimes accompanying "exclusives" that proved to be not-quite-so exclusive. With its slogan

"A Paper To Trust," the *Express* was sure to draw critical fire for errors large and small; as is inevitable in start-up operations, it managed both. Nagging computer problems were doubtless no help.

Perhaps the paper's biggest image problem has been the perception that Government House played a pivotal, if not seminal role in its creation. The close friendship dating back to school days between editor Steve Vines[4] and Government House Information Coordinator Mike Hanson has served to fuel the speculation. Indeed, Government House itself has done little to dispel the notion, one source there saying: "What did you expect Mike to do, sit back and watch every paper in town get rolled up by the Chinese?" In any event, the highly readable paper has taken the government on over several issues, such as the fiasco at the Whitehead Detention Centre, and produced some hard-hitting editorials (leaders).

News-wise, the paper is steadily finding its way, but no one knows how long a run the owners will give the *Express* if it is not a money-maker. Media analysts say it will need a larger advertising base of its own to succeed in the marketplace. Estimates of its circulation range wildly from 5,000 to 55,000. One unquestioned contribution the paper has made is a decided improvement in journalists' salary structure.

The *Express* also found itself in the middle of the censorship issue when Huang Xinhua, deputy director of the Shenzhen City Propaganda Department, warned Hong Kong reporters during an informal gathering that they should be "wise," "act in line with the circumstances" and "bend with the wind." Toasting a reporter from the Oriental Press Group, Huang said: "Can you take these words to C. K. Ma? Tell him to watch out.

---

[4] Shortly before midnight the night of 9 September 1994, Vines was fired from his position under circumstances that by all accounts were highly unusual and acrimonious. Vines insisted his sacking had nothing to do with editorial interference by publisher Ma Ching-kwan. Sources within the paper said it had to do with a series of memoranda from the publisher containing controversial management directives that were strongly resented by staff and were not enforced by Vines. Two senior members of the editorial staff immediately resigned to protest his firing. At this writing, there were threats of legal action by Vines. The paper had little comment beyond saying the agreement under which he was working had been terminated. Whatever the actual circumstances, the affair was widely interpreted in the journalistic community as harmful to the paper and perhaps to the wider English-language press as well.

Shenzhen officials quickly sought to distance themselves from Huang's statements, while the vice-director of Xinhua's Hong Kong office, Zhang Junsheng, said Huang was drunk at the time and his comments should not be taken seriously. Nonetheless, Huang's statements sparked considerable concern. Legislator Emily Lau warned that Huang was not the first Chinese official to say what he did, nor would he be the last.

Changes have also been occurring at the *South China Morning Post*, with Rupert Murdoch selling out the bulk of his share to Malaysian investor Robert Kuok in late September 1993 — another move he later admitted was made to avoid hassles with China. Kuok's Kerry Media Ltd. bought 34.9 per cent for US$349 million. Murdoch's remaining 15.1 per cent was later sold to another Malaysian interest, Malayan United Industries. Though it was feared Kuok's close ties with China would influence the paper, there has been little concrete evidence of that since the sale, although some media observers say there seems to be a reduction in the number of political stories and the play they are given (to support their view, they point to the decision by well-regarded political editor Fanny Wong to leave the paper, allegedly in a dispute over who should handle certain political stories).

There may in fact be some irony in the Kuok purchases, as Murdoch used the sale proceeds to help finance his acquisition of STAR TV, then went on to axe the BBC from the northern part of his satellite footprint in what appears to have been a failed bid to get Beijing to drop its ban on the private ownership of satellite dishes (Chinese experts say Beijing cares little about individual dishes set up on a house; the ban is intended to control private companies wishing to set up cable services, the place Murdoch would make his money). Given comments by Murdoch regarding the allegedly anti-China bias of his own papers in Britain, journalists at the *SCMP* might well wonder if they are not better off — at least for the time being — under the Kuok regime. The Hong Kong Journalists Association (HKJA) expressed its concern over the sale, saying it highlighted the problem of cross-media ownership (Kuok also holds 33 per cent of TVB) and the lack of legislation to prevent media monopolies. Meanwhile, editor David Armstrong has become responsible for all the Post's publishing operations. Editorially, the paper raised eyebrows when it called for the resignation of Secretary for Planning, Environment and Lands, A. G. Eason, who had held a private briefing for big land developers ahead of releasing the government's plan for pushing down property prices. Calls for resignations do not occur often in Hong Kong papers, even less frequently for one so long identified in the public eye as chummy with the government. Meanwhile, in yet another sign of the post-1997 future, the paper reportedly prepared a dummy issue of the *North China Morning Post*.

Over in Kowloon Bay, the *Hong Kong Standard* has not stood still. Owner Sally Aw Sian (also proprietor of *Sing Tao*) has been busy developing her already good ties on the mainland, signing a joint-venture agreement in November 1993 to publish a financial paper in Shenzhen. It was the first deal of its kind, but as yet no paper has actually been published. In the wake of the agreement, however, *Sing Tao*'s editor-in-chief and assignment editor were forced to step down, both joining *Wah Kiu Yat Po* (now renamed *Overseas Chinese Daily News*), a small-circulation paper owned by the *SCMP*. *Wah Kiu* is now half-owned by a one-time *Sing Tao* director, who also resigned after the Shenzhen deal.

A tumultuous if sometimes colourful era of flamboyant, expatriate editorship ended in May 1994 with the choice of Michael Chugani, a Cantonese-speaking Hong Kong native, as editor. In July, the paper's main news section went from 20 to 24 pages, the editorial page was smartened up and moved inside, along with an opinion page for letters and columnists.

The once staunchly pro-Taipei *Standard* has been perceived as tilting towards Beijing. One foreign correspondent said, hyperbolically, that he buys it every day because he thinks of it as an "English-language voice of Xinhua," the official New China News Agency. While that view is excessive, there are reasons readers might draw the inference. The paper was originally founded in 1949 as an English-language voice of the Chinese community, a role it seemingly wishes to reassert. The paper's business section has introduced a once-a-week front page produced by the official *China Daily*. The financial section has a different masthead, apparently part of its effort to publish the financial daily in China. In September, it became the first foreign-language paper to be printed in China.

The good news for newspaper readers is more choice, more voices, more competition (including ad rates). That competition now includes satellite-delivered dailies like the *Asian Wall Street Journal* and the *International Herald-Tribune*. Whether the future will allow for the clash of competing opinions is of course the overriding concern.

However, the situation is far different in English-language broadcasting. The long-promised corporatization of Radio Television Hong Kong (RTHK), first suggested in a 1985 review but opposed by China in 1992, appeared to be a step that will not be taken in the run-up to 1997. To ease morale problems, some staff members were hired on civil service terms, while at the same time Radio Three went nearly a year without a permanent station director — with RTHK management in the end evidently deciding not to hire one. Over at Metro Broadcasting, changes were also in the works, with the all-news station Metro News deciding in June 1993 to sack 30 of its 45 reporters, editors and anchors, while switching the format to a blend of computer-driven Mandarin/English pop music and cutting back English-language news from 24 hours to about six hours per day. The evening talk shows disappeared, replaced by horse-racing from Macau and Cantonese sob-sister Pamela Pak's call-in programme. Weekend evenings you can hear *Tagalog* spoken as the station goes after the amah audience. In what may be some kind of first, the station also produced three-minute evening news spots that are half in English, half in Cantonese (each story different). Nevertheless, the AM (medium wave) station's main newscasts continue to provide a lively blend of news, business and sports. As if to show less is sometimes more, the name has been changed to Metro Plus.

The self-censorship issues raised its head at Metro as well. Word filtered down to the newsroom that the company's board of directors (the majority owner is Li Ka-shing's Hutchison) was wondering aloud whether the station's news was "too pro-British." The query definitely had the effect of causing staffers to look more carefully at their copy, while redoubling their (often fruitless) efforts to find pro-China sources to "balance" the news. It turned out that the original statement was not posed as a query; it was a statement that the news, in some unidentified person's view, was in fact pro-British. To management's credit, no directive of any kind was ever issued nor was any story spiked for alleged imbalance. However, concerns about the station's future independence have been heightened by strong in-house rumours that Chinese Radio International (CRI) had struck a deal with Metro under which it would pay the station to air three hours a day of news provided by CRI — one English hour in prime a.m. time, two more hours during the day in Mandarin. If the deal comes about, some staffers fear the programming will be little better than propaganda.

Meanwhile, at Commercial Radio — where the entire English news department was axed not long after the arrival of Metro — headline news resurfaced in anticipation of licensing renewal.

On the television side, Wharf Cable began operation in Chinese and English. A 24-hour, all-news local channel was begun in Chinese, while a few hours a day of local news was being blended with the Cable News Network (CNN) on an English-language channel. The cable operator also struck a deal to pick up the BBC after it was axed by Murdoch. To date, however, few people are able to receive the 11-channel cable service. This will change as the operator installs a fibre-optic system, with 40 channels, over the coming year. Three of the channels are to be made available to the government. Discussion has begun on the creation of a government channel modelled after the National Public Broadcasting Corporation in the United States. Some community groups, such as Zuni Icosahedron, are also pressing for eventual public access channels. Public television and public access are different concepts seemingly not well understood within government, much less within the legislature or the community at large. Before a meaningful community dialogue can begin on these topics, it is clear there will be need for considerable public education at all levels.

☐ The Xi Yang Affair

Without doubt the key event has been China's arrest, secret trial and sentencing of *Ming Pao* reporter Xi Yang.

Xi was detained on 27 September 1993; his arrest under provisions of the Chinese State Security Law was not announced until 7 October. On 28 March 1994, he was sentenced in Beijing to twelve years in prison on charges of "probing into and stealing state secrets," an allegation stemming from a series of articles he authored on China's interest-rate system and plans for international gold sales. His family was not told of his sentencing until four days later. The court did not confirm the case until 4 April, even then issuing no printed judgment. An appeal was filed on 13 April and rejected on 15 April. In every way, Xi's case has struck at the heart of concern about the future of a free press in the territory. China's official position — that the case is simply one of theft of state secrets and has nothing to do with press freedom in Hong Kong — is simply neither believed nor believable.

Were Xi a native Hong Kong person, his case doubtless would have been dealt with differently. But because he is a mainlander, the state was able to treat him with a severity it reserves exclusively for its own. Xi's extraordinary treatment includes: detention without charging; prohibition of visits by legal counsel and even family (the sole exception: a half-hour visit by his father at which they were banned from discussing his case);

secret trial; secret sentencing; no publication of the actual charges by the court (a violation of even China's own rules of juridical procedure), and an appeal that was rejected almost literally overnight. What information *was* made public came through the New China News Agency (Xinhua), a most extraordinary way of handling a legal proceeding even by China's unique standards.

The message to Hong Kong reporters was of bone-chilling clarity: Right now you have special protections, but when you rejoin the motherland and are Chinese nationals just like everybody else, these laws so strict and rules so pliable will apply to you as well. There was an added message to Hong Kong publishers: Don't think you can hire mainlanders like Xi and exploit their personal connections in China to your benefit. The jail sentence of fifteen years handed down to Xi's alleged source, Tian Ye, also required no interpretation. The chilling effect of the Xi case has also permeated the business community in China, with people who once freely gave information now clamming up for fear not only of imprisonment, but of damage to their companies' interests. As one businessman put it: "What is normal information elsewhere could be a secret there. No one knows the rules, so the word has gone around investors and analysts — better not talk to reporters." Some analysts say privately they are not even sure what they should put in their reports to clients.

Meanwhile, public opinion polls in Hong Kong show a clear majority of people expect to have less freedom of the press after 1997. Shum Choi-sang, chairman of the Newspaper Society of Hong Kong, told Legco's Information Policy Panel in September 1993 that many journalists, fearing post-1997 retaliation, were already engaging in self-censorship, adding his personal estimate that seven out of ten journalists were worried that they would not have a free working environment after China takes over. His concerns were echoed in the report on Hong Kong and China by the British Parliament's Foreign Affairs Committee, which noted that "signs of self-censorship in the media are now apparent alongside harassment by China of outspoken journalists."

The complexities of the issue certainly extend to coverage of the People's Liberation Army (PLA), especially after its arrival in Hong Kong on — or, perhaps, even before — 1 July 1997. The PLA is far more than an armed force. It is a vast economic entity involved, according to experts, in the production of more than 700 kinds of civilian goods and services, including cameras, tourist shops, guest homes, automobiles, textiles, warehouses, ships, agriculture and even franchises of U.S.-based fast-food chains. There may be as many as 5,000 PLA-controlled companies in Guangdong Province alone, while the PLA's Logistics Department 999 Enterprise Group controls at least thirty-four firms in Shenzhen, involved in pharmaceuticals, motor vehicles, stocks, securities and real estate. One reason the true budget of the PLA is unknown is because of this boggling array of businesses with their hidden incomes and cash flows. Another reason is because the PLA is also involved in a wide range of activities that are clearly illegal, smuggling and providing labour services, to name but two.

But there is a third reason, of particular concern to journalists, why the army is surrounded by mystery: The PLA, when under investigation, can drape itself in the cover of national security, effectively classifying cases of corruption and economic disputes as military secrets. Xi Yang, we will recall, is a reporter imprisoned for allegedly stealing state secrets while doing a series of stories that — in any country with even a moderately free press — would be considered as perfectly ordinary business reporting (in fact, some of what Xi reported was published as well in Beijing's mouthpieces in the territory). What then does the future hold for a Hong Kong reporter who discovers corporate hanky-panky and thinks it is a good scoop for the business page, only to discover the company may be a dummy for the PLA? Will "national security" be invoked to justify censorship if a reporter learns that a chemical spill or explosion is PLA-related (as was the Shenzhen warehouse, illegally storing unidentified chemicals, that recently blew up killing a never-to-be-certain number of people)? Will a journalist who reveals that a joint-venture's bottom line has been jiggled run the risk of revealing a "state secret" of PLA Inc.? What if Logistics Department 999 turns out to be the owner of one of the distressing number of Guangdong factory buildings unable to remain standing under their own power?

These are not hypothetical concerns. The Sino-British defence lands deal, reached in July 1994 in the Joint Liaison Group, promises fourteen of the present thirty-nine military sites will be handed over to the PLA. In a side letter, China promises the lands will be used only for defence purposes; there is no definition of what constitutes "defence" or "military." A reporter checking whether China was living up to its promise — a perfectly good story with legitimate community interest — would be walking into a minefield by publishing that Stanley barracks had been converted into a karaoke bar — yet another of the security-vital businesses in which the entrepreneurial Chinese army is already engaged.[5] At a prestigious gathering in Hong Kong of PLA experts from around the world, Dr. Jonathan Mirsky, East Asian editor for the *Times* of London, asked whether any of the eighty persons present believed the PLA would honour its commitment to use the lands only for defence purposes, as the term would be normally understood. Mirsky said that when the hilarity — some participants were slapping their thighs in mirth — finally died down, they launched into lengthy descriptions of all the ways the PLA could exploit the situation. At the end, Mirsky again asked whether there was any one present who accepted the possibility that the army would keep its word. Not a single scholar raised his hand.

The "state secrets" question has another very important implication. The Hong Kong government is only now getting around to figuring out how to address the Basic Law's requirement that the future Special Administrative Region (SAR) *must* enact laws pertaining to sedition and treason. Moreover, Article 23 of the Basic Law[6] stipulates that the post-1997 legislature must enact a law banning the "theft of state secrets," the ill-defined legal category applied to Xi Yang.

Additionally, the government is also continuing its painfully slow consideration of a number of colonial laws, mostly unused by the current sovereign, that if left on the books (as happened in other former British colonies, notably Sri Lanka, India and Singapore) would present a not-so-benign future administration with Draconian powers enabling it to suffocate any semblance of independent news media.

Little wonder Hong Kong reporters have begun second-guessing their

---

[5] It is worth noting in this context that on 14 August 1993 the Chinese government announced regulations requiring all news conferences to be registered. The order bans the local news media from reporting unregistered news conferences and also prohibits sponsors of news conferences from leaking party and national secrets.

[6] The Basic Law's Article 23 states that the SAR government shall enact laws to prohibit any acts of treason, secession, sedition or subversion against the Central People's Government. It also prohibits the theft of state secrets. Laws shall also be enacted to prohibit foreign organizations from conducting activities in the SAR, as well as to prohibit political organizations within the region from forming ties with any foreign political organizations.

own stories, while a number of editors have openly begun asking their management and owners: What is our policy towards China? The rise in perceived self-censorship, generally assumed to be a fact although devilishly hard to prove, can come as no surprise when journalists are shorn of their protection, left open to laws the likes of which they have never seen, and are working for people whose business interests may not coincide with editorial integrity.

A positive effect of the Xi Yang case, however, has been the mobilizing of journalists to his cause. When Xi's appeal was denied, it became painfully clear that the earlier efforts by *Ming Pao*'s management to appease China had obtained neither fairness nor leniency. Indeed, Xi's position may have been worsened by owner Yu Pun-hoi's apology and controversial admission — even before a trial — that his reporter might in fact have violated the law. Yu was in a difficult position, as Xi's family had been told directly by Xinhua officials that any efforts to make their son's case high-profile would be counterproductive.

With the failure of appeasement, *Ming Pao* workers began a string of protests, including a round-robin of hunger strikes outside the Xinhua offices in Happy Valley. On 17 April, a protest march from Central to Xinhua brought out more than 2,000 people, including a dozen legislators, as well as a contingent from the Foreign Correspondents Club (FCC), an organization that normally stays out of local issues. The FCC's involvement is a measure of the attention that Xi's case has drawn internationally. In a statement issued on 18 April, the FCC expressed its grave concern, saying "the harsh sentence appears intended as a warning to the Hongkong press not to report news or events in China other than that which has been approved or announced in the official media."

The Legco also became involved, representatives of publishers, management and journalists, as well as *Ming Pao* officials, all appearing before a special session in the council chambers to discuss the affair. The Hong Kong government was asked to raise the issue with London to be taken up through diplomatic channels; Governor Patten relayed the request, later informing the Council that it had been raised at the very start through the British Embassy in Beijing. The concern was also raised during talks between British Foreign Secretary Douglas Hurd and Chinese Foreign Minister Qian Qichen. Patten promised the Legco in July 1994 that Xi's case would again be brought up during a visit to China by Minister of State Alastair Goodlad.

☐ The Preliminary Working Committee

The news media have had to deal over the year with the emergence of China's hand-picked Preliminary Working Committee (PWC). China's decision to create the PWC was a unilateral one. Beijing's decision to push ahead with the controversial body was a reflection of worsened Sino-British ties, though no one can say for sure whether China might have seen the need for such an organization even if relations were better.

Even though the PWC has yet to develop into a fully-fledged shadow government, this could yet occur given repeated threats of setting up a so-called "second stove" prior to 1997.

The PWC is doubtless doing work that will be of use to the 1996 Preparatory Committee. While what and how much remain to be seen, the facts are that (1) the PWC exists, (2) it is laying groundwork of some sort, and (3) it contains persons of potential interest in the future SAR government. China has also given the PWC very considerable amounts of face. These are sufficient reasons to generate reporters' interest and to justify coverage.

However, the PWC poses practical problems as well as fundamental questions for journalists.

One basic question is manpower: Editors and publishers keep an eye on resources and staff allocation. A reporter nosing around PWC meetings, virtually all of them closed, is a reporter who could be productively used elsewhere. Moreover, many meetings take place in Beijing, an expensive place to keep reporters.

Despite the costs involved, the news judgement so far is that the PWC must be covered, even though the group has no particular legitimacy beyond Beijing's imprimatur. Indeed, much of what credibility it has it owes to the personal wherewithal of individual members, a number of them key Hong Kong businessmen (such as Li Ka-shing) or former political personalities in the colonial system (such as Rita Fan and Maria Tam).

The decision to cover the PWC also stems from the fact that it is difficult at best to obtain reliable and timely information from Chinese leaders or the bureaucracy. In Hong Kong, where "getting a reaction" sometimes seems like the be-all of journalism, the pressure to get comments is considerable.

Initially, the PWC filled the bill, as members held meetings with Chinese officials, then either walked out and spoke into microphones or leaked information — much of it impressionistic — to reporters.

The Media

But caution has gradually set in. Some statements ascribed to officials have later required clarifications, at times amounting to denials. Reporters and editors have visibly tired of covering an echo of officials words, rather than the words themselves. Moreover, as was inevitable, some PWC members have simply emerged in reporters' minds as more plugged-in and switched-on than others. The PWC is in some respects remarkably similar to how the Legco operated before the advent of open meetings.

Responsible journalists have also had to deal with a major ethical issue — probably unsolvable — raised by the PWC's existence: Does the decision to grant air time and ink to the PWC give the group a stature and credibility independent of its real worth? Are we then just being used by China to float balloons, affect public opinion and cause headaches for the British? The questions might not be answerable, but they must be constantly asked. It should be noted that coverage of the PWC has noticeably sharpened as the newness has worn off. All this will change, however, if China decides to turn on the burners of its second stove.

☐ The Long-term Interest

We have all heard reports of attempts to exert backdoor pressure on the press and the media. People in Hong Kong are concerned that the press here may be less free after 1997.... We have to address those fears. In Government, we have a special responsibility to do our bit. We will not shirk that responsibility. I repeat my pledge; this Governor and this Government will defend the freedom of the press up hill and down dale. To paraphrase Voltaire, sometimes we may not like what you say, but we'll defend to the death your right to say it.

> Governor Christopher Patten
> Inauguration, Freedom Forum Asian Centre
> 17 January 1994

Meanwhile, Governor Patten was speaking at every opportunity about the importance of a free press, waxing particularly lyrical when addressing foreign visitors who were not in Hong Kong long enough to match his performance against his oratory. But despite his occasionally stirring rhetoric, journalists have been left looking — sometimes vainly — for the action to back up his words. Surely it is no credit to the Governor, for all his efforts on the soap box, that the FCC, the Hong Kong Journalists

Association and the Hong Kong Press Photographers Association all joined together on International Press Freedom Day to attack him. In their joint statement, the three organizations linked the Xi Yang case to the repeal of laws in Hong Kong that threaten the news media. The government, they said, "has failed to show leadership in pressing for law reform."

Patten was also under attack for his lukewarm stance towards a proposed Access to Information Bill, co-sponsored by legislators Christine Loh, Simon Ip and J. D. McGregor, and being brought by Loh as a private member's bill. The legislation, which Patten had the right to block from entering the Legco if it would result in a charge on the public coffers, would confer on all citizens a right to know what is in the government's files, save for 14 categories of restricted information. The bill has been supported by a surprisingly broad range of groups, including the HKJA and the Hong Kong General Chamber of Commerce, and has received almost no comment from China, save a rather *pro forma* statement from one official worried about the executive-led government. More than 2,000 people and organizations responded during the consultation period. While some respondents suggested amendments, not a single reply was in opposition to a legislative right to know. A majority of legislators has signed a letter supporting its submission to the Legco, something that would require the Governor's approval if the plan is found to incur a charge on government revenues.

However, in keeping with what was to become a disturbing pattern on other key issues (e.g., establishment of a human rights commission), Patten and his Executive Council (Exco) clearly had a problem with granting people a statutory right, though they had considerable difficulty explaining why. The most likely reason was opposition from the civil service, unaccustomed to operating without the cover of considerable secrecy, a heritage from their British counterparts. Patten himself said as much when, at the opening of the Freedom Forum's office in Hong Kong, he said he was concerned that bureaucrats would respond to a legislative right to know by creating dual sets of records, one public and one private. Loh later dubbed the idea "one government, two filing cabinets."

How deep is the actual reluctance of bureaucrats to seeing citizens armed with the right to know? Difficult to say, as there has been no real consultation by the government. Indeed, asked whom he had consulted on the issue, Home Affairs Secretary Michael Suen replied that he had spoken with other policy secretaries and some heads of departments, but made no reference to the 2,000 responses to the Loh's bill. To answer the question, proponents of the bill were actively considering whether to sponsor an independent, professional opinion poll of civil servants to find out what they really think.

With Patten openly preferring administrative means over a statutory solution, the government opted for adopting guidelines to access, in part following the Conservative government's approach in Britain, in part responding to civil servants' fear that if a right to access were enacted, they could be subject to penalty for non-disclosure.

It seems likely that Patten is not inclined to see a British colony lead the way on issues where the colonial power lags behind — never mind to what fate may await Hong Kong in less than three year's time. Proponents of an Access to Information Bill have pointed out that Article 19 of the United Nations Declaration of Human Rights enshrines access to information as a fundamental right. They also cite Article 16(2) of the Hong Kong Bill of Rights Ordinance (BORO), which reads: "Everyone shall have the right to freedom of expression; this freedom shall include the freedom to seek, receive and impart information and ideas of all kinds...."[7]

The government, however, has other ideas. Secretary Suen, interpreting the BORO (while reminding legislators that he is not an attorney) told the Information Policy Panel that the clause applies only to "willing" parties. The BORO, he argued, does not apply where one party (read "citizen") seeks information and the other (read "government") does not wish to impart it. This interpretation could well end up being tested in court, which — given the administration's apparent strategy on other rights issues — may in fact be what the government prefers.

---

[7] Article 16 reads:
1. Everyone shall have the right to hold opinions without interference.
2. Everyone shall have the right to freedom of expression; this right shall include freedom to seek, receive and impart information and ideas of all kinds, regardless of frontiers, either orally, in writing or in print, in the form of art or throug any other media of his choice.
3. The exercise of the rights provided for in paragraph (2) of this article carries with it special duties and responsibilities. It may therefore be subject to certain restrictions, but these shall only be such as are provided for by law and are necessary:
    a. for respect of the rights or reputations of others; or
    b. for the protection of national security or of public order, or of public health or morals.

The government's resistance to granting a statutory right to know is also rooted in the sorry state of the government's records system. After all, if people seek something, you ought to be able to find it. Bureaucrats worry they may be punished for being unable to produce something they are obligated to produce, and might even be willing to produce, but simply cannot find.

In fact, when the government finally admitted the seriousness of the archives problem, it also inadvertently revealed the feebleness of its argument for preferring administrative over statutory remedies. During the year, the Legco's Information Policy Panel, chaired by Emily Lau, began looking at records policy (an otherwise obscure issue that gained currency with the government's controversial proposal to move its downtown archives to a facility in the New Territories). No one knew how serious the condition of record-keeping really was until administrators came before the Legco to argue *for* money to solve the problem, but *against* a proposed Archives Ordinance that would straighten things out while making access to archives a right.

In stating its opposition to an Archives Ordinance, the government outlined — but made no attempt to refute — the main reasons for a legislative framework: that the administration did not have a "clear and well-defined policy on the management and protection of public records, that there is a lack of an independent records authority with adequate powers and responsibility for the co-ordination of records management and a potential loss of materials of archival value, and that in the absence of a statutory framework, valuable information could not be easily traced or might even be destroyed *at the discretion of individual Government officers*" (emphasis added).

The administration admitted that inadequate attention had been paid to proper records management, with the result that "active, inactive and historical records are often mingled." But despite the embarrassing catalogue of inadequacies, the administration has refused — at least for now — to consider legislating a management policy, opting instead for an administrative Records Management Strategy. Why? Because, it said, "we believe it would be meaningless to enact any archival legislation before a proper records management system has been established, as Government departments will not have the resources and expertise to comply with the requirements of the legislation." Logically, if they could not comply with an Archives Ordinance, they would face difficulty complying with the Access to Information Bill.

Chief Secretary Anson Chan — who seems to have a particular difficulty in accepting statutory rights — has suggested that the government will first try administrative measures (based on Britain's Code of Practice on Access to Government Information) and see how they work before considering legislation. What she seems to be arguing, rather curiously, is that if the administrative measures work, then fine; but if they fail, the government will consider turning the unsuccessful measures into law.

In the meanwhile, work on the code has begun and the guidelines were expected to be ready sometime in the autumn. However, they would only be implemented in early 1995, and then only as part of a six-month pilot scheme involving a handful of departments (it appeared unlikely that the housing department, perhaps the one in which the most people have the most interest, would be in the pilot programme). In making the announcement, the Home Affairs Branch argued that a "flexible and incremental approach is best-suited for our purpose ... bearing in mind our unique circumstances and needs." The code is to apply to all departments and branches; it is promised to set out clearly how the public can gain access to documents and the time frame within which the department concerned should reply to a request. The government estimates that applying this code throughout the administration would cost up to $90 million annually, though it has offered no breakdown of costs or explanation of how the figure was arrived at. The plan also offers little remedy to the citizen who feels his request has been wrongly dealt with, leaving the individual to lodge a complaint with the Commissioner for Administrative Complaints (COMAC). While recent legislative changes now allow citizens to approach the COMAC directly, the administration's access to information scheme does not give the commissioner the power to compel disclosure. Nor would the COMAC have any power to punish a department or individual bureaucrat for bad-faith non-disclosure. Supporters of Loh's Access to Information Bill cite these as some of the key differences between the competing approaches. Despite introduction of the government's code, supporters of a statutory right to know showed no sign of abandoning their campaign.

☐ Legal Reform

With the arguable exception of rising self-censorship, there has been no issue of more enduring concern than the lamentably slow progress in amending laws that threaten freedom of expression and the press. The handover to China is within 1,000 days and counting, yet the government still continues to treat this deeply worrisome issue as if time was on its side. As always, the need to localize the British Official Secrets Act tops the list of concerns, but it is one among many.

In 1993, the HKJA highlighted seventeen laws that needed either repealing or amending, but while a review has been going on — and on — only the Television, Telecommunication and Broadcasting Authority ordinances have so far been amended. A review of a further seven laws has been completed — although two of these involve provisions of the amended Telecommunication and Television ordinances — and seven more are in progress. But while the administration has removed provisions allowing the pre-censorship and prohibition of programmes, it has still kept the power to seek an injunction banning the broadcasting of certain categories of programmes. The administration plans to incorporate the Television, Telecommunication and Broadcasting Authority ordinances into an omnibus broadcasting law, to be brought to the legislature in February 1995, eight months beyond the original target date. The new law contains a provision allowing a court to ban some types of programming. The HKJA has voiced concern that this could be a loophole that could be used to arbitrarily restrict artistic expression. The omnibus bill will probably contain whatever restrictions, if any, the government decides to place on cross-media ownership. The administration's public statements have flip-flopped on the key issue of whether any such regulations would be retrospective; sources in the Recreation and Culture Branch, who once suggested they might be, switched their tune after Patten indicated his personal disinclination towards retrospective laws in general.

Of major concern is the Emergency Regulations Ordinance, an old but potent colonial law granting the Governor vast powers of censorship, suppression of publications, control of essential services (including communications) and amending or suspending laws in the event of a state of emergency or ill-defined occasion of public danger. The law clearly conflicts with the limits placed on the declaration of emergencies in the Bill of Rights (Section 5). The Attorney General has finished his review of the law, as well as its subsidiary legislation. On 21 February 1994, the Security Branch informed the Legco's Constitutional Development Panel that proposals for amendments were in the works and would be submitted to the Exco "in the next few months," but has not subsequently given any indication what changes were likely, beyond saying that the Attorney General had considered whether there was a need for "more defined legislative controls upon the exercise of these powers." There is worry that changes to the law will be relatively minimal, as there has been an evident and increasing reluctance of the administration to take steps that might provoke a hostile reaction from China. This seems particularly so on those changes Beijing might see as encroaching upon the powers and prerogatives of the "executive-led system."

The Emergency Regulations Ordinance is just one of the security-related laws threatening press freedoms. Another is the Police Force Ordinance, defining the powers of search and seizure. Journalists want provisions to protect news material from the kind of seizure that occurred in October 1989, when officers raided the studios of two television stations to obtain raw footage of a clash between pro-democracy demonstrators and police, who wanted them as the basis for laying further charges. The government says it sees no conflict between the law and the BORO. An inter-departmental working group has been examining the Law Reform Commission's report on police powers. Again, the administration says it will take a view "as soon as possible," and will then hold a public consultation exercise — a procedure pushing any decision into the indefinite future. Meanwhile, reporters and editors should not be too hopeful; in a paper to the Legco, the administration notes: "It is doubtful whether journalistic materials should be singled out for different treatment."

Also of concern is the Prevention of Bribery Ordinance, Section 30 of which makes it an offence to disclose either the identity of a suspect under investigation or details of an investigation, until an arrest has been made. Even a person who is under investigation may not disclose the fact. The law is a clear restriction on the news media, but the government defends it as necessary to protect the reputation of a suspect when no arrest or similar action is made, as well to protect the integrity of investigations. The bribery ordinance is a key part of the legislation giving vast powers to the Independent Commission Against Corruption (ICAC). The super-secret agency (which had much of its cloak pulled aside during the Legco's inquiry into the Alex Tsui dismissal) has been made the subject of a special review committee, appointed by the Governor, whose report was due by the end of 1994. The committee is charged with looking into the powers of commissioner, as well as the operations of the agency.

A not-too-dissimilar provision is contained in the Organized and Serious Crimes Bill, a law that has been in the hands of a Legco *ad hoc* committee for more than two years. Although close to passage when the Legco closed its session in July 1994, the bill still faced objection to provisions protecting investigations from disclosure by the news media. Also of concern are provisions compelling unwilling witnesses to provide testimony under penalty of law. The Bill is likely to come before the legislature for second reading.

But perhaps the biggest and most difficult reform will be to the Official Secrets Act (1989) (OSA) and the related Crimes Ordinance. The OSA provides for six areas of information where it can be shown that disclosure of information has harmed national interest. The OSA is not subject to the BORO, though the government claims the two are consistent. As the OSA is a U.K. law extended to Hong Kong in June 1992, but it will cease to apply after the end of British rule. Journalists want the law liberalized and turned into local law well before that time. Meanwhile, Article 23 of the Basic Law stipulates that Hong Kong must enact laws covering the theft of state secrets — the legal catch-phrase used by China for the prosecution of Xi Yang. But when and how should such a law be enacted? Of the options put forward by the government, the one it appears to like most is letting the OSA lapse in 1997 and leaving it for the Chinese. Given the pressures, however, a more feasible option would be to create a local law based on the OSA (some localization would have to be done in any case to rid the law of reference to the Queen). Alternatively, the government could also draft a law, but leave it for the post-1997 administration to enact, or draft a law that would take effect when China takes over. A government spokesman has privately affirmed that the administration has decided to draft an original piece of legislation, but had not decided what form it would take or when it would be brought to the legislature. As any law intended to be in force beyond 1997 would likely require consultation with China, and as it is unclear what China is willing to accept, the entire issue is in doubt.

Additionally, there is the matter of treason and sedition, laws against which are also called for in the Basic Law's Article 23. This is also being looked at as part of the Official Secrets Act review. "The issue," says the administration, with classic understatement, "is difficult and controversial."

One of the several laws the government refuses to change, but is of serious concern, is the Film Censorship Ordinance, which contains a provision (Section 10) empowering the Film Censorship Authority to consider whether there is a likelihood that showing a film would seriously damage good relations with other territories. It became clear during questioning of officials by the Information Policy Panel that the only neighbouring country of real concern is China, a point made evident in 1989 when a Taiwan-produced film about China pro-democracy film was censored —

the only time the law has been applied. The administration defends the law as compatible with the BORO Article 16, providing for restrictions on the right to freedom of expression when necessary for the protection of national security or public order (*ordre public*, which has a broad connotation). The government also says that Article 19 of the BORO must be considered before this restriction can be applied. Nevertheless, Section 10 is strongly opposed by the HKJA and Article 19; Legislator Martin Lee Chu-ming is expected to move a bill in the legislature seeking to eliminate it. In a related issue, the administration proposed late in the 1993–1994 session that the laws governing the Television and Entertainment Licensing Authority (TELA) be amended to give censors the power to restrict films or delete material that glorifies "offensive behaviour and criminality," or contains triad-related slang, ceremonies or "cryptic" poetry.

Among the laws of concern to freedom of expression and freedom of the press, and their status at this writing are:

1. Prison Rules — Amendments to this law are in process which would loosen the restrictions on the information that can be given to news media by staff of the Correctional Services Department; provisions on censoring prisoners' mail also would be amended.
2. Public Order Ordinance — Now in Legco committee, with consideration to resume in the Autumn 1994 session, the bill seeks to balance the right to assembly with the prevention of nuisance and the protection of public order; the issues of prior notice and size of gathering are holding up passage.
3. Summary Offences Ordinance — The government has dropped the provisions on the use of loudhailers, leaving that as a matter for noise control laws; also repealed is a provision banning "assembly at night without lawful excuse."
4. Places of Public Entertainment Ordinance — The law grants the Commissioner for Entertainment and Licensing enormous powers, including pre-censorship of scripts; the government accepts that this likely violates the Bill of Rights. The law also grants police the power to close or temporarily vacate places of public entertainment, but while the government agrees to narrow the provision, it wishes to retain police power to close down shows for reasons of public order and safety. This law has already been under review for at least two years. Amendments are to be submitted by the end of 1994–1995 Legco session.

5. Registration of Newspapers Ordinance — A relatively minor law governing newspapers and news agencies. Some sections to be repealed, others brought into line with BORO. Amendments to go to the Exco in September 1994.
6. Television Ordinance — In addition to the concerns noted above, the law also contains conditions (Section 25) requiring a broadcaster to carry government-produced programmes at no charge (Section 8). There is concern that this could obligate a station to carry government news programmes, although at present licence conditions are restricted to a specified number of public service announcements. There is also no time limit set under Section 38 of the Ordinance for appeals made by a broadcaster to the Governor-in-Council against the prohibition of programmes under Section 35. The government says it does not intend to change these sections.

   The law also contains a subsidiary section that requires the Director of Health to give consent in writing before any advertisements for medical preparations can be broadcast on television. The administration says it is looking into the original rationale and will take action in the omnibus bill.
7. Telecommunication Ordinance — Two worrisome sections provide for the interception of telecommunications and mail, respectively. The government notes criticism that these provisions are "all-embracing and can easily be abused," as well perhaps being contrary to the International Covenant on Civil and Political Rights; however, it makes no promise of any amendments, saying it awaits a report from the Law Reform Commission — "available probably in early 1995" — before making a decision. Elsewhere in the same Ordinance, the section governing pre-censorship of radio broadcasts is to be deleted or amended in the omnibus bill. Another vague section, affecting the transmission of "a message known to be false," will be restricted only to false signals of distress — not false news.
8. Judicial Proceedings (Regulation of Reports) — This Victorian piece of law contains a provision making it unlawful "to print or publish, or cause or procure to be printed or published ... in relation to any judicial proceedings any indecent matter or any medical, surgical or physiological details being matter or details of which are of a revolting or offensive nature or the publication of

which would be calculated to injure public morals...." Even setting aside the highly subjective language, the law would leave journalists completely in the dark over what they could or could not lawfully report. One example would be during a medical malpractice case or the testimony of a forensic pathologist. The government says it wants to keep the law, but its defence before the Information Policy Panel was less than spirited and it has agreed to take another look.

The worry over Section 30 of the Prevention of Bribery Ordinance became real in August when the Publisher of *Ming Pao* and three of its senior journalists were charged under the law for reporting the existence of an investigation into the holding of land auctions, at which there was suspected collusion of participants to drive down prices. Reporters who had been at the event were contacted by ICAC investigators and asked about what they had witnessed. (It is understood that the ICAC did not generally find these conversations fruitful.) After the ICAC spoke with *Ming Pao*'s reporters, the paper revealed the fact, putting it in violation of a law that was intended originally to protect the reputation of persons who were the subject of investigations, even though in this case it was hard to see how the reputation of anyone was affected.

The ICAC's decision to use reporters as their eyes and ears is extremely worrisome to journalists, who feel they would be compromised in their work if they could be called in after any interview or event and asked what transpired; journalists also fear that news sources would be less likely to give reporters information or even allow them access to certain events if they could not be sure that the reporters were acting independently. The event has considerably heightened concern about the colonial laws that could threaten the freedom of the press. It has also placed Governor Patten in a difficult spot, as he has spoken so often on behalf of the press, yet his government is now prosecuting them on charges not even remotely close to the theft of state secrets.

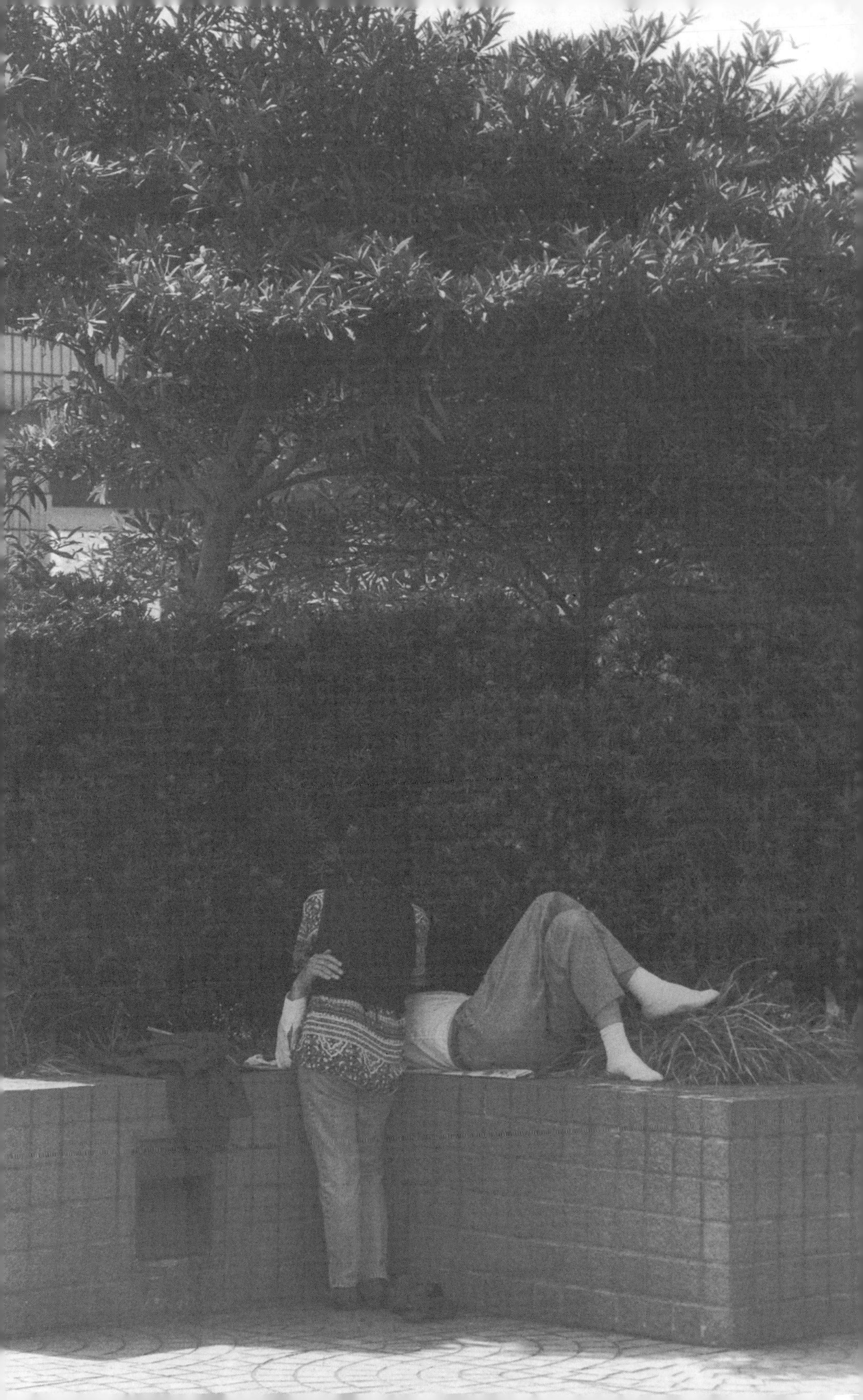

Sexuality in Hong Kong

Ng Man-lun

In Hong Kong, the mass media and the propaganda statements of many social leaders give the impression that Hong Kong people are getting progressively liberal or permissive sexually. Nearly every month, political parties, educational or religious groups alert people of the impending danger of a sexual moral holocaust. They bring out as "evidence" the wide circulation and increasing sexual explicitness of adult movies and publications, the proliferation of sexual contents in books and comics for children and adolescents, the increasing rate of premarital sex and induced abortions among youths, the rapidly rising figures of divorce and the number of horrible rape cases which have occurred in different regions of Hong Kong from time to time. The message seems to be that Hong Kong is among one of the most sexually liberal regions in Asia both in the positive or negative sense.

Sexuality, however, involves many broader and deeper aspects than those mentioned above. Also, some of the "evidence" brought out needs to be examined more closely by longitudinal and cross-sectional comparative data before they can be considered definitive and convincing. It is well known that in nearly any society, official reports and the older generation often interpret the behaviour and belief of their younger generation as getting permissive and corruptive, while in reality, it could just be a sign of the lack of mutual tolerance and understanding. Moralists also tend to exaggerate social problems and the dangers of change in order to promote

---

Ng Man-lun is a reader in the Department of Psychiatry, the University of Hong Kong.

or maintain their firmly held principles and philosophy and they form the group which usually make the loudest noise.

This chapter will examine the direction of change in sexual attitudes and behaviour in Hong Kong in the last few years; reference is made to data collected from a number of different but important sources which have been largely ignored or rejected in many official reports.

☐ Sexual Behaviour

Sex Crime Rate

Much has been said about sex crimes in Hong Kong. Whenever there is a serious case of rape, moralists talk about the increasing number of sex crimes and call for the purging of commercial sexual institutions, prostitutes and pornographies.

While it is controversial that the latter are causes of sex crimes, there also is no reliable data to support the view that the rate of sexual offences in Hong Kong is on the rise. There are only two sources from which reliable figures of sex crime rate can be obtained in Hong Kong, the annual reports of the Royal Hong Kong Police on rape and sexual assault cases and the Family Planning Association of Hong Kong (FPAHK) on rape cases counselled. The police figures showed that in the five years from 1988 to 1992, neither rape nor indecent assault cases, reported or arrested, showed any clear evidence of increase (see Table 1). From the number of those arrested who were below the age of 16, there is also no evidence to support the fear or claim that the age of the sex offenders is getting lower.

Table 1. Annual Sex Crime Rates in Hong Kong

Year	Prosecuted Rape	Prosecuted Indecent assault	Reported Rape	Reported Indecent assault
1992	86 (3)	611 (57)	116	1,099
1991	86 (10)	655 (81)	114	1,101
1990	109 (10)	659 (80)	111	1,078
1989	101 (5)	584 (77)	120	1,019
1988	92 (7)	479 (38)	97	922

Note: Figures in parentheses are the numbers of offenders aged below 16.
Sources: Annual reports of the Royal Hong Kong Police Force, 1988 to 1992.

Sexuality in Hong Kong

The FPAHK figures show that in the same period, the number of sexual assault victims counselled did rise somewhat (see Table 2). However, if observation is shifted to a few years before that period, it can be seen that for many years in the 1980s, the number kept on declining, so much so that the figure of 1990 is still lower than that of 1984. For the recent rise to become a trend, a longer period of observation is needed.

It might be argued that these official figures could not reflect the actual situation since they depend very much on self-reporting which could be affected by a lot of social, legal or psychological factors. However, without more reliable figures or any clear evidence that people are getting more reluctant in reporting sex crimes, it is at least justified to say that there is no proof to show that sex crimes are on the rise in Hong Kong.

Sexual Behaviour among Youths

The FPAHK has been conducting sexuality surveys on secondary school students once every five years since 1981.[1] In each of these surveys, to ensure comparability of data from different years, Hong Kong students of

Table 2. Sexual Assault Victims Counselled by the Family Planning Association of Hong Kong (1984 to 1992)

Year	Number
1992	112
1991	105
1990	95
1989	90
1988	90
1987	68
1986	63
1985	79
1984	97

Sources: Annual reports of the Family Planning Association of Hong Kong, 1984 to 1992.

---

[1] Family Planning Association of Hong Kong, *Hong Kong School Youths* (1981); *Adolescent Sexuality Study* (1986); *Youth Sexuality Study, In-school Youth* (1991); *Youth Sexuality Study, Out-of-school Youth* (1991).

Form 3 to Form 7 (age range 14–19) were sampled with similar methodology and the sampled population was given a similar questionnaire to answer. Despite problems relating to non-response cases and other inevitable technical deficiencies for any sexuality survey, these surveys give the most reliable figures that can be obtained on the sexual behaviour of the youths in Hong Kong. In the 1986 and 1991 surveys, a section on the out-of-school youths aged 19 to 27 was added, making it possible to trace the change in the sexual attitudes or behaviours of the subjects as they grow older.

By comparing the in-school survey results of 1986 to those of 1991, a trend of increasing sexual activity can be spotted. Dating behaviour among the boys increased from 42 per cent to 54.2 per cent, and among the girls from 42.5 per cent to 55.0 per cent in five years. For experience of sexual intercourse, the boys' figure increased from 5.7 per cent to 6.1 per cent and the girls, from 3.5 per cent to 4.3 per cent. The frequencies of other types of physical intimacy increased to even greater extents.

The out-of-school surveys further confirm the sexually permissive behaviour among the youths. A greater number of these youths in 1991 considered their friends and relatives to be sexually permissive, understood in terms of their engagement in premarital sex, and visits to prostitutes or other "vice" establishments. A greater percentage (32.8 per cent in 1986 and 36.7 per cent in 1991) of the boys themselves also had sexual experience. The 1991 survey shows that 16.7 per cent of the males and 15.1 per cent of the females of age 18 to 19 already had sexual intercourse.

However, the out-of-school survey showed that although the Hong Kong youths of 1991 were getting more sexually active, they were also more cautious in many respects. For example, much more of those who engaged in premarital sex did so with their dating partners (52.2 per cent in 1986 compared with 79.8 per cent in 1991) and the percentage of those who had sex with prostitutes (28.4 per cent compared with 10.8 per cent) decreased over the years. The percentage of males who had ever visited prostitutes has decreased, from 16 per cent in 1986 to 11.7 per cent in 1991. When engaged in premarital sex, much more of the youths used condoms too. The percentage of males who used condoms increased from 64.5 per cent to 84.2 per cent and for females, from 50.6 per cent to 76.5 per cent.

With these findings, it would appear that the increasing sexual activities of the Hong Kong youths is more a "perceived" moral problem than a real social one. The Hong Kong youngsters are not as promiscuous or careless with sex as some moralists are trying to portray. It is even more revealing to find the sexual self-restraint of the Hong Kong youths to be stronger than their counterparts in China, who were often thought of as very much subjected to the influence of the sexual repression tradition and conservatism. In 1992, Liu, Ng and Chou did a sexuality survey on 6,092 secondary school students in ten cities in China. They found that in the surveyed population, 8.4 per cent of the males and 20.5 per cent of the females reported to have the experience of sexual intercourse,[2] figures much higher than those reported about the youths of Hong Kong especially for the female respondents. The same is true for the percentages of students who had experienced other types of sexual intimacy.

There are data for comparing the sexual behaviour of university students in Hong Kong and Shanghai too. In 1991, the Hong Kong Tertiary Institutions Health Care Working Group did a sexuality survey on all Hong Kong university freshmen in that year and found that 3.5 per cent of the males and 1.4 per cent of the females had experience of sexual intercourse.[3] In the same year, Hong et al. did a sexuality survey on a random sample of the university freshmen in Shanghai. Their data showed that 6.3 per cent of the males and 2.9 per cent of the females had experience of sexual intercourse.[4] The percentages nearly doubled those of Hong Kong. For those who had sexual experience, 19.5 per cent of the Hong Kong male students had sex with more than one partner. For Shanghai, the corresponding figure was 25.0 per cent, also showing that the Shanghai students were more sexually permissive and active. On the other hand, only 15.0 per cent of the males and 20.0 per cent of the females in Shanghai had the habit of using condoms, while the corresponding figures in Hong Kong were much higher, at 69.5 per cent and 37.5 per cent respectively.

One could therefore take the data which shows that Hong Kong

---

[2] D. L. Liu, M. L. Ng, and L. P. Chou, *Sexual Behaviour in Modern China — A Report of the Nation-wide "Sex Civilization Survey" on 20,000 Subjects in China* (Shanghai: Joint Publishing, 1992) (in Chinese).

[3] Hong Kong Tertiary Institutions Health Care Working Group, "Survey on Sexual Behaviour of Students in Tertiary Institutions in Hong Kong" (unpublished data).

[4] J. H. Hong, M. S. Fan, M. L. Ng, L.K.C. Lee, P. K. Lui, and Y. H. Choy, "Western Influence on Chinese Sexuality — Insights from a Comparison of the Sexual Behaviour and Attitudes of Shanghai and Hong Kong Freshman," *Journal of Sex Education and Therapy*, forthcoming.

subjects are increasingly open and permissive in sexual behaviour to be an illustration of a universal trend in the modern cities, yet the magnitude of change is far less than that of many Western societies and the Chinese city of Shanghai. If this change is inevitable for all modernizing and developing societies, the "falling behind" of the Hong Kong figures could be a cause for perplexity if not self-doubt for those who take Hong Kong to be a very modernized city.

☐ Sexual Attitudes and Values

Like sexual behaviour, the sexual attitudes of Hong Kong youths are also not as open or liberal as many people might think. One has to be specific as regards what sexual attitude or value is being referred to. From the surveys quoted above, although an overall picture which finds the Hong Kong youths increasingly open and permissive in sexual attitudes can be drawn, there are items which show that in some aspects they still subscribe to sexual repression and conservatism. For example, in the in-school surveys conducted by the FPAHK, an increasing percentage of males were found to be unhappy with their masculinity, from 1.4 per cent in 1986 to 2.9 per cent in 1991. In the out-of-school survey, slightly more or at least the same percentage of males in 1991 considered sex with prostitutes as immoral (from 50.5 per cent in 1986 to 58.7 per cent in 1991).

Using and re-analysing part of the 1986 survey data of the FPAHK, Lui *et al.* confirmed that different sexual values in Hong Kong change at very different speeds from the traditional values.[5] They examined three items in the survey which represent three different sets of sexual values: sexual enjoyment, social conformity in sex and sexual equality or inequality. It was found that social conformity in sex was upheld by the greatest majority of the subjects (81.7 per cent) and it was quite impervious to social changes, since convariate analysis demonstrated small contribution of the subjects' social contextual factors to any of its variation. The even more important finding of note is that among these subjects, strong adherence to social conformity went in parallel with their support for the value of sexual

---

[5] P. K. Lui, C. F. Cheung, K. L. Chan, and M. L. Ng, "Differential Erosion of Three Traditional Chinese Sexual Values in Hong Kong," in *Sexuality in Asia*, edited by M. L. Ng and L. S. Lam (Hong Kong: Hong Kong College of Psychiatrists, 1993), pp. 21–32.

Sexuality in Hong Kong

enjoyment which was also quite high (65.9 per cent). The message is that, even though for various reasons Hong Kong youths were increasingly receptive to the enjoyment side of sex, this did not make them less socially responsible in sexual attitude and behaviour. The moralists have been misled or misleading when they sounded out their alarms simply basing on the observation of a changing social attitude towards the function and value of sex.

Despite high acceptance of the value of sexual enjoyment, compared to their counterparts in China, Hong Kong youths still show a much more conservative sexual attitude in general. Of the Hong Kong secondary school students in 1991, 80.4 per cent supported the idea of marriage and said they planned to get married in future.[6] According to the survey on Shanghai secondary school students of 1988, however, only 49.5 per cent had the same idea. For pornography, 39.5 per cent of the Hong Kong secondary school students of 1991 tolerated its presence in the community. In China, the 1989 to 1990 figures showed 63.5 per cent of the secondary school students from a large variety of regions consider pornography as harmless and that they should be allowed to read it.[7]

☐ Sex Education

Hong Kong claims to have started public sex education in the 1950s, when the FPAHK initiated it. Various social service and volunteer agencies joined in afterwards.[8] Late in 1971, the Education Department issued a memorandum to all schools in Hong Kong inviting them to include sex education topics in their standard subjects and made a concise list of suggestions on what could be taught. In the subsequent years, efforts were made to include sex education as part of social education in the junior secondary grades. In 1986, the Education Department issued a *Guidelines on Sex Education in Secondary Schools*. It proposed an interdisciplinary approach to sex education and made further and more detailed recommendations on resources and references. In the same year, a Sex Education Resource Centre was set up by the Department to offer further assistance to sex education teachers.

---

[6] See Note 1, *Youth Sexuality Study, In-school Youth*.
[7] See Note 2.
[8] M. L. Ng, "Development of Sex Education in Hong Kong," *Sex Education*, Vol. 1, No. 1 (1988), pp. 40–44 (in Chinese).

Frequent sex education seminars, lectures and short courses have been conducted for the purpose of teacher training.

These efforts concerning sex education received official applause. Some official statistics also showed that all seemed to be going well.[9] A growing number of schools or teachers were reported to show interest in strengthening existing sex education programmes and increasingly schools assigned teachers as coordinators of these programmes. In 1990, 40 per cent of the schools which responded to a sex education survey conducted by the Education Department felt that their sex education programmes had been successful.

However, a strong rebuttal to these official claims and self-congratulation comes from other surveys. In 1989, the FPAHK did a survey of sex education in schools, which found the topics mostly taught were the topics like "puberty bodily changes" and "menstruation." The teachers were unprepared for more controversial yet essential topics like "contraceptive methods" or "prostitution."[10] In the in-school portion of the sexuality survey of the FPAHK,[11] it was found that the percentage of students who reported having acquired sexual knowledge from their teachers had decreased from 26.4 per cent in 1986 to 21.4 per cent in 1991. The percentage of students who got sexual knowledge from seminars had decreased even further, from 58.4 per cent to 31.6 per cent. Most of them had turned to newspapers and magazines for information. How this drop has affected the students' sexual knowledge was disclosed by the figures in the same surveys. Except for the question on the protective function of condoms, there was on the average a 12.4 per cent decrease in correct response to some simple sexual knowledge questions. The cruel fact is that, despite a lot of statistics and "a lot of work" cited by the educational bodies, they are not meeting the educational needs. How this situation has come about cannot be discussed in detail here. The obvious problem is that the "sex education" efforts in Hong Kong so far have only been superficial, consisting of empty

---

[9] W. N. Pau, "Sex Education in Schools and Its Outcome," in *An Analysis of Hong Kong Education*, edited by the Hong Kong Federation of Sex Educators and Hong Kong Education Resource Centre (Hong Kong: Wide Angle Press, 1991), pp. 377–85 (in Chinese).

[10] Family Planning Association of Hong Kong, *Report on Sex Education in Secondary Schools — A Survey of School Teachers* (1989), pp. 66–67.

[11] See Note 1, the 1986 and 1991 (in-school youths) surveys.

words much more than effective action or support. Memoranda, guidelines, resources, lectures and theories were produced with no concern paid to their practicality or feasibility. Restricted by its status as a "hidden" subject only to be dealt with in the time-slots contributed by other subjects, sex education does not give teachers who teach it an identity, or much psychological or material reward, including additional promotion prospect. Owing to the heavy contents and examination pressure of other "more important" subjects, it is in fact impossible for teachers to insert enough sex education materials into the school curriculum to make their teaching smooth, meaningful or interesting.

The greater blow comes from the official bodies' obstinacy and complacency. In their future plans, focus is still put on the setting up of more resource centres, the publication of more sex education bulletins and the organizing of yet more piecemeal sex education seminars, lectures and courses. The crucial issue of turning sex education into an independent subject, allocated with enough teaching time and given due recognition, is never substantially addressed. Recently, the Education Department has disclosed its latest project on furthering sex education.[12] It will in future produce another set of Sex Education Guidelines which include requiring all secondary schools to set a minimum amount of teaching time for sex education. The actual requirement will be for students of Form 1 to Form 3 to have a minimum of 20 hours of Life Education annually, the contents of which should include civics, social conduct, politics, environmental protection, and so on, and among all these, also sex education! The low requirement of 20 hours per year is bad enough, but the checkmate is the flexibility of subject choice. Since there are so many other things the teachers can teach in Life Education, in view of the special difficulties in teaching about sex, they are likely to use most, if not all the time for the other "more important" contents.

By contrast, despite a late start, sex education in the secondary schools of Mainland China is fast improving and likely to overtake Hong Kong's endeavours very soon. In 1988, a sex education survey in China showed that 56.6 per cent of secondary school students had received or were receiving formal sex education from schools. In 1990, the percentage rose

---

[12] Education Department, "Sex Education in Secondary Schools" (talk given at the Seminar on the Action Guidelines on Sex Education, City Polytechnic of Hong Kong, 23 April 1994).

to 70.1 per cent.[13] The efforts of promoting sex education by the Chinese authorities have been immense. In 1988, the China National Education Committee and the China National Planned Parenthood Committee selected 6,000 schools in different parts of China for a pilot introduction of sex education in secondary schools.[14] After about two years of trial teaching and training of core teachers through special courses and also by correspondence courses, the instruction was to require all secondary schools to set aside special teaching time for sex education. In some big cities like Shanghai, despite difficulties in resources or manpower, the aim has already been met. For example, in Form 1, the teaching time for sex education is specified to be 10 to 12 hours. These teaching hours are compulsory and cannot be occupied by any other topics.[15] Textbooks for the subject have been published and used, and many more are under preparation. A popular sex education magazine, *Ren-zhi-chu*, is widely circulated and is now in its third year and still going strong.

In Taiwan, the Chinese Sex Education Association was set up in 1991. In a matter of three years, the Health Department in Taiwan, in collaboration with the Association, published sex education textbooks and teachers' handbooks for junior and senior secondary schools. Various pictorials for educating younger children in primary schools on the subject of sex have also been published.

One may still be apprehensive of the quality of sex education in China or Taiwan, but it is obvious that they are taking the lead in making the effort to improve sex education.

☐ Sexual Medicine

Hong Kong claims to offer good medical services. It is the first Chinese community in the world to provide good organized service on sexual problems too. The excellence of the general medical service and, more specifically, service in sexual medicine, have been well supported for a long time by statistics on obstetric care, infant mortality, neonatal care, population control, and the treatment and prevention of sexually transmitted

---

[13] See Note 2.

[14] Anonymous author, "Six Thousand Secondary Schools with Sex Education Courses in China," *Sex Education*, Vol. 1, No. 1 (1988), p. 9 (in Chinese).

[15] See Note 2.

diseases.[16] The first sex clinic in a Chinese community was also set up in Hong Kong as early as 1979. It provides the most up-to-date treatments for sexual dysfunctions,[17] sexual variations[18] and other sexual problems and the results have been satisfactory. The first Chinese sexology association, the Hong Kong Sex Education Association, was also set up in Hong Kong in 1985 and it is now the only Chinese sexology association in the membership list of the World Association for Sexology. The Hong Kong Sex Education Association was also instrumental in the organization of the Asian Federation for Sexology, which was established in 1992.

But, with all these in the lead, what is happening to the medical sexology of Hong Kong now? Not much is seen to have improved in recent years. Not counting the clinics run by traditional healers, the first sex clinic is now still the only sex clinic in Hong Kong, and, not counting the gynaecologists or urologists with partial interests in sexual problems, no new medical doctors have really joined the field of medical sexology or sex therapy. The author of this chapter, who has been in the field for a while, might be partially responsible for not having done enough to promote this specialty in Hong Kong. Yet the deep-rooted and strong anti-sexual atmosphere in Hong Kong is not a small obstacle. A clinic cannot exist with just a doctor and a consultation room. It takes nurses, social workers, psychologists, technicians and many other auxiliary personnel to function. It also needs the support of laboratories, and the availability of drugs, reading materials, instructions and treatment devices. And it needs the public's, more specifically the patients', acceptability as well. All these can only come from a sexually enlightened and open social atmosphere. Yet, this is not the kind of atmosphere in Hong Kong, as we have argued earlier on. Like many conservative societies, Hong Kong is hypersensitive to anything about sex. Politicians, social and religious leaders harp on the mythical harm of pornography and may use better sex education as the pretext to brand sex treatment materials as pornographic. They may also control the

---

[16] M. L. Ng, "Sexual Problems in Hong Kong — A Medical Perspective," in *Sexuality in Dissent*, edited by M. L. Ng (Hong Kong: Commercial Press, 1990), pp. 198–210 (in Chinese).

[17] M. L. Ng, "Sexual Therapy for the Chinese in Hong Kong," *Sexual and Marital Therapy*, Vol. 3, No. 2 (1990), pp. 245–52.

[18] M. L. Ng, "Transsexualism — Service and Problems in Hong Kong," *The Hong Kong Practitioners*, Vol. 11, No. 12 (1988), pp. 591–602.

contents and distribution of these materials through the publication laws so as to suit their own sexual idiosyncrasies or beliefs. There is no lack of examples in this arbitrary exercise of "moral" authority. The author has witnessed a case in the Obscene and Indecent Articles Tribunal that a passage in a clearly sex educational article was judged to be indecent simply because it warned youngsters not to use certain dangerous and unsafe means of contraception. Since the message could in no way be seen as erotic, one could conclude that the adjudicators were objecting only because they disagreed with the publicizing of the warning itself. They had that peculiar idea that such a warning can also be a sexual inducement. In another recent case, an acclaimed adult sex education tape produced by a doctor in England which was dubbed into Chinese and submitted to the Television and Entertainment Licensing Authority for permission of release was granted permission on condition that some explicit scenes in the tape would be cut. Obviously, the lay jurors serving in the Authority thought that they knew better than the specialists and that the Hong Kong Chinese were more "intelligent" regarding sexual matters than the British so that they would need fewer and less explicit instructions to understand what was taught.

This kind of ungrounded laymen judgement also controls what sex aids can be put on sale and where. Only recently, a sex shop was prevented from opening due solely to the negative sentiments the tenants in the same building had expressed. The tenants insisted that a sex shop sold obscene objects, not knowing that sex aids are for the treatment or rehabilitation of those suffering from sexual dysfunction or who are sexually underprivileged due to physical illnesses, disabilities or other reasons.

As long as Hong Kong continues to maintain this practice of legally appointing ill-informed laymen to make decisions relating to matters of sexual health for its people, naturally no advancement can be expected in the provision of sexual medicine for members of the public who are in need. At present, sexual medicine books and tapes for the general public in China are more explicit and instructive than the Hong Kong productions. There are more proper sex clinics, sex shops and sex aid factories in a middle-sized city in China than in Hong Kong. In fact, Hong Kong cannot claim to have even one proper sex shop, because even shops that house a satisfactory stock of sex aids shy from categorizing themselves as sex shops and only sell sex aids or related articles along with other kinds of merchandise. Judging from Table 3, we can predict that comparatively, China is heading towards a more prosperous development in sexual medicine than Hong Kong.

Table 3. Numbers of Sex Clinics, Sex Shops and Factories in Different Cities in China

Cities	Sex clinics	Sex shops	Sex aid factories
Shanghai	5	2	14
Beijing	3	2	19
Tienjin	3	1	11
Guangzhou	7	2	25
Nanjing	2	1	15
Changsha	2	0	14
Zhengzhou	3	1	17
Harbin	2	0	13

Source: D. L. Liu, and M. L. Ng, "Sexual Dysfunction in the Chinese," *Singapore Annual of Medicine*, forthcoming.

☐ What Has Gone Wrong?

The sexual attitudes and behaviour of the people in Hong Kong are not as permissive and the moral scene not as hazardous as are often imagined. In comparative terms, they are at the conservative end when compared with other Chinese communities. To some people, this may be reassuring. Yet the kind of stagnation or even regression seen in censorship cases, sex education and sexual medicine should be a cause for concern rather than pride or relief. If the price of conservatism is sexual ignorance, authoritarian control of the media, and underdeveloped medical service in sex, conservatism is itself a sign of social sickness.

One could only speculate on the causes of this trend of progressive conservatism. One important factor, from the observation made by the Hong Kong Sex Education Association, could be the brain drain due to the 1997 issue. The drain has caused the loss of many liberal-minded people, including those who would have been interested in fighting for a more sexually liberal society. In 1986, the Association, in collaboration with the Department of Extramural Studies of the University of Hong Kong, began to run a Diploma Course on Sex Education, which was a one-year course covering comprehensively different aspects of human sexuality and its teaching. It is the most thorough sex education course conducted in Hong Kong so far. However, after two years, because of the emigration of a large proportion of the core teachers, the course had stopped running.

The 1997 issue also tends to make Hong Kong people more conservative in general. Thinking that conservative attitudes in general would be more in line with the future sovereign power, the mass media tend to adapt as much as possible to what is thought to be the "Mainland mentality." The long period of sexual repression and conservatism in China before the 1980s still leaves a strong impression on the Hong Kong people, so much so that as 1997 approaches, restraint on sexual depictions and teachings is seen as the proper line to toe.

A third possible factor is also political. The increased number of elected members in the legislature need to engage in matters which are expected to win support from the general public, and more conservative policies regarding sex is usually seen as one of them. After all, ordinary citizens are more likely to declare publicly that they subscribe to conventional sexual morality than otherwise, and the politicians listen to them.

23

Hong Kong's International Presence

Bernard H. K. Luk

Hong Kong is one of the most important urban centres on earth today. As the world's tenth ranking trading economy, busiest container port, and one of the leading financial markets, it plays host to the consular and trade missions from some ninety countries. Its importance to the present-day global economy is not in doubt.

Hong Kong has been an open city from the beginning of its history. The external and the internal have always been intertwined in its development. It has been widely recognized that Hong Kong's future significance on the world scene will hinge on its post-1997 economic success, institutional health, and administrative autonomy, and vice versa. This chapter examines Hong Kong's international presence, in terms of its international personality, and official as well as unofficial representation of Hong Kong overseas.

☐ Hong Kong's International Personality

The government annual report, *Hong Kong 1994: A Review of 1993* does not focus on Hong Kong's international presence or external relations in any of its chapters. But it does highlight the international activities of senior government officials in the first section of photographs: Governor

---

Bernard H. K. Luk was one of the co-editors of the first edition of *The Other Hong Kong Report*, when he was a senior lecturer in the Faculty of Education, The Chinese University of Hong Kong; he is now an associate professor of history at York University, Toronto.

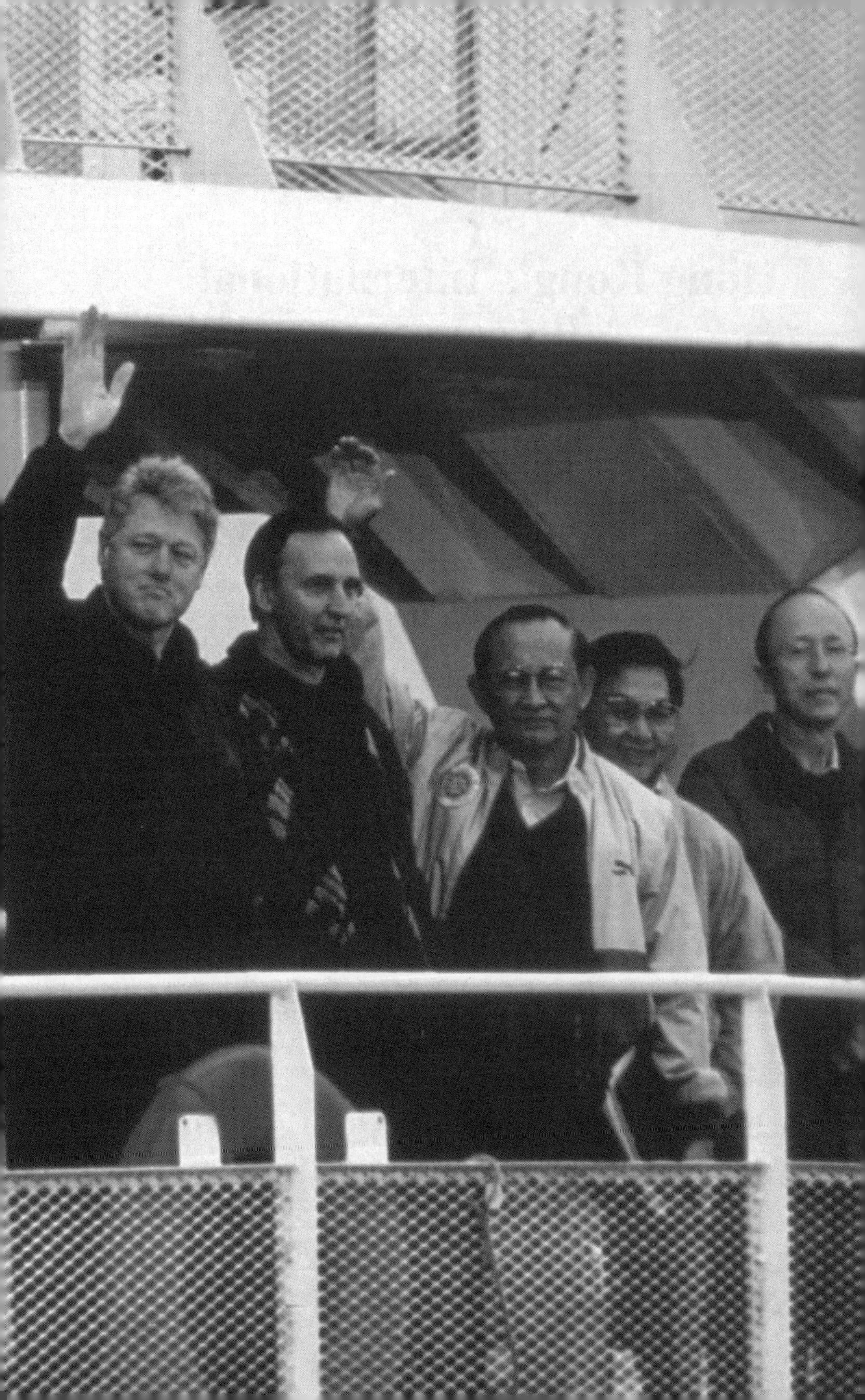

Christopher Patten conferring with U.S. President Bill Clinton in the White House, and playing host to German Chancellor Helmut Kohl and former U.S. President George Bush in Government House, Financial Secretary Hamish Macleod on an outing with Asia Pacific heads of governments during the Asia Pacific Economic Cooperation (APEC) conference in Seattle, and Chief Secretary (designate, as she then was) Anson Chan calling on the President of the French Senate in Paris, and so on. These high-profile visits follow from similar ones during the past few years to Japan, Canada, and other countries. In Ottawa, for instance, both Governor Patten and Governor Wilson had been received as heads of government by the Canadian prime minister during their respective visits in 1990 and 1992.

These manifestations of Hong Kong's international stature befits the territory's economic achievements, well earned by the hard work of all its people, and deserve to be included in the government annual report. However, the report chooses to record them not in words, but in pictures, which should not be surprising. In this late-twentieth century world of sovereign states, Hong Kong is not a sovereign state, nor is it destined to become one. Hence its standing within the "family of nations" is rather ambiguous in international law. Hong Kong's effective autonomy from its present metropolitan power, to manage its international trade, almost all its internal affairs, and much of its external relations, has been a *de facto* working arrangement, not a *de jure* provision, although it does not conflict with existing law. To advertise the international achievements of the government in writing may run the risk of arousing the ire of the future metropolitan power, which has been particularly sensitive towards any "internationalization" of Hong Kong. It is safer to allow the photographs to speak for themselves.

This resort to non-verbal communication in the government annual report underscores the basic tension in Hong Kong's international position, between the facts of the territory's autonomy and stature on the one hand, and the lack of unambiguous legal status on the other. It can be, and has been, argued that the fault lies not with Hong Kong, but with international law — its outdated Roman concepts about sovereignty, and its failure to provide adequately for non-sovereign but significant actors on the world scene. Be that as it may, the very tension, the very ambiguity, is inherent in the notion of "one country two systems, Hong Kong people ruling Hong Kong" underlying the Basic Law of the post-1997 Hong Kong Special Administrative Region (HKSAR).

A legal scholar at the University of Hong Kong has made the following observations about Hong Kong's international personality, which deserve to be quoted at length:

> [T]he high degree of autonomy enjoyed by Hong Kong in the management of its external affairs has been reaffirmed in the Sino-British Joint Declaration, which seeks to formalize its status as a "separate customs territory" that "may participate in relevant international organizations and international trade agreements ..., such as the GATT...." In addition, it is stipulated that after 1997 the HKSAR "may on its own, using the name 'Hong Kong, China' maintain and develop relations and conclude and implement agreements with states, regions and relevant organizations in appropriate fields including the economic, trade, financial, monetary, shipping, communications, touristic, cultural and sporting fields." Also relevant in this context are the HKSAR's powers to issue its own currency and passports, regulate immigration to the territory, and institute official and semi-official trade representation abroad....
>
> ... Evidently, Hong Kong's trading partners, co-members of the international organizations ..., and parties to respective multilateral agreements recognize and respect the separate identity of the territory. The operation overseas of Hong Kong Government Offices and other official representatives (such as the Hong Kong Trade Development Council) and the direct dealings with consular officers of foreign governments based in the territory also reflect ... a recognition of Hong Kong's capacity to engage in international relations.[1]

She concludes that Hong Kong enjoys a "legal proximity to statehood." Proximity, of course, is not the same as equivalence, and Hong Kong is not regarded by international law writers as an "established legal person." On the other hand,

> [a]part from the general waning of [the notion of] sovereignty, it is also evident that states are prepared in practice to admit into the international legal system a broad range of less-than-sovereign entities.... Since claims to international personality are to be assessed in light of the societal needs of the international community, in acknowledging the considerable capacities possessed by Hong Kong (and later by the HKSAR), regard must be paid also to the useful international functions performed by the territory.... As noted at the outset, however, international personality is a flexible and open-ended concept which may mean different things in different circumstances....[2]

In other words, the legal ambiguity will remain even after 1997. The

---

[1] Roda Mushkat, "Hong Kong's International Personality: Issues and Implications," in *Canada–Hong Kong: Some Legal Considerations*, edited by William Angus (Toronto: Joint Centre for Asia Pacific Studies, 1992), pp. 15–16.

[2] Ibid., pp. 23–24.

validity of the international personality before and after 1997, and the willingness of the international community to accept it, will depend on Hong Kong's autonomous performance of its functions.

Hong Kong's international personality, such as it is, is enshrined in the Joint Declaration and codified in the Basic Law. It is beneficial, indeed vital, to both Hong Kong and the People's Republic of China (P.R.C.) for it to be maintained at least for the fifty years stipulated in these august documents. However, legal provisions and political-administrative practice are not necessarily congruent. While during the 1950s to 1980s, Hong Kong evolved its international personality out of the practical conduct of affairs, between Hong Kong and London and other parties, and without much basis in law, in future, the continued viability of the now legally provided, albeit ambiguous, personality will hinge upon the patterns of political and administrative actions between Hong Kong and Beijing and other parties. Most important of all in this context are the manner in which Hong Kong's legislative, executive, and judicial powers are constituted and discharged, and that in which Hong Kong operates with its international rights and obligations.

A pattern that gives substance to the legal provisions for Hong Kong's autonomous personality will reassure the international community of the HKSAR's ability to perform its legal functions. If the formula "one country two systems, Hong Kong people ruling Hong Kong" is to be implemented according to the Joint Declaration, giving the HKSAR meaningful constitutional autonomy, then Hong Kong's international personality will continue to be respected by the international community, enabling the HKSAR to carry on with the functions performed by the present government.

On the contrary, a pattern of subservience will indicate to the international community a withering away of that personality and its inability to function as before, with repercussions on various aspects of Hong Kong's role on the world scene. If the HKSAR government is to be run on so short a leash from Beijing that it could not exercise any significant degree of legislative, executive, or judicial autonomy, no amount of window dressing in diplomatic terms could salvage Hong Kong's international role.

☐ International Rights and Obligations

Negotiations on the post-1997 continued application to Hong Kong of international treaties contracted by the United Kingdom, and of Hong Kong's continued participation in international organizations, is the work of the Subgroup on International Rights and Obligations of the Sino-British Joint Liaison Group. From 1986 to 1993, agreement was reached between the two sides on about half of the multilateral treaties and some thirty organizations.[3] In addition, Hong Kong has been authorized by the two metropolitan powers to sign, in its own name, some ten air services agreements. It has also concluded a number of bilateral agreements with foreign countries, such as agreements with Canada on mutual legal assistance in the control of drug trafficking, on environmental protection, and on cultural exchange.

Talks between the two metropolitan powers on Hong Kong's international rights and obligations made relatively rapid progress during the first three years of the existence of the Subgroup, but subsequently have been held hostage to the deterioration of relations between the two powers over the June Fourth massacre, the Port and Airport Development Strategy, and Governor Patten's constitutional reform package. The stalling of the negotiations of course have not contributed to the confidence of either the local or the international community. While Hong Kong's membership (or associate membership) in most of the more important international organizations have been assured for the time being, the same could not be said of aviation, a vital concern for Hong Kong's future as an international city. In any event, by the autumn of 1994, there are welcome signs that the two metropolitan powers may return to more speedy discussions on international and other matters.

---

[3] The international organizations include the following: the Asian Development Bank (ADB); the Asia Pacific Postal Union (APPU); the Asia Pacific Telecommunity (APT); the Customs Cooperation Council (CCC); the Food and Agriculture Organization (FAO); the General Agreement on Tariffs and Trade (GATT); the International Atomic Energy Agency (IAEA); the International Bank for Reconstruction and Development (IBRD); the International Criminal Police Organization (Interpol); the International Labour Organization (ILO); the International Maritime Organization; the International Monetary Fund (IMF); the International Telecommunication Union (ITU); the International Telecommunications Satellite Organization (Intelsat); the UN Commission on Narcotic Drugs (UNCND); the UN Conference on Trade and Development (UNCTAD); the UN Economic and Social Commission for Asia and the Pacific (ESCAP); the Universal Postal Union (UPU); and the World Health Organization (WHO). Hong Kong is also a member of the APEC.

Countries other than the two metropolitan powers whose vital or important interests are involved have been helpful towards working for Hong Kong's continued participation in international organizations after 1997. The most comprehensive and concrete expression of such efforts is the United States Hong Kong Policy Act passed by the U.S. Congress in 1992. This American law, couched largely in the language of the Joint Declaration and the Basic Law, requires the U.S. government to treat the future HKSAR as an entity distinct from the rest of the P.R.C. in terms of those international functions stipulated in the Joint Declaration, so long as the U.S. government itself was satisfied that the HKSAR does enjoy the autonomy promised to it. Other countries, such as Canada, Australia, and Japan, have also taken steps in similar directions, although not to the extent of putting their policies in legislation.

☐ Official and Semi-official Representation

The governments of some ninety foreign countries are represented by consular missions or trade commissions in Hong Kong. In addition, a number of sub-national governments (provinces, states, etc.) also maintain representative offices in the territory. Hong Kong is probably host to a larger number of foreign diplomatic offices than most countries or cities in the world. However, since these foreign missions are technically accredited to the United Kingdom rather than to Hong Kong, normal rules of reciprocity of representation do not apply.

Hong Kong is represented in most of these countries not by its own overseas missions, but vicariously by British embassies and consulates. After 1997, with the change of sovereignty, the foreign missions in Hong Kong, if permitted to continue, will be technically accredited to the P.R.C., and Hong Kong will be represented in most foreign countries by P.R.C. missions. This has been provided for in the Joint Declaration and the Basic Law, and to be negotiated between the P.R.C. and the other countries involved.

It remains to be seen what mechanisms will be worked out between Hong Kong and Beijing, about: (1) continued representation of foreign countries in Hong Kong, especially those which have no, or only very low-level, diplomatic relations with the P.R.C.; (2) the functioning of relations between the foreign missions in the territory and the HKSAR government; and (3) the representation of Hong Kong interests in international organizations, conferences, and in foreign countries.

The Joint Declaration stipulates in Annex I, sect. XI:

> Foreign consular and other official or semi-official missions may be established in the Hong Kong Special Administrative Region with the approval of the Central People's Government. Consular and other official missions established in Hong Kong by states which have established formal diplomatic relations with the People's Republic of China may be maintained. According to the circumstances of each case, consular and other official missions of states having no formal diplomatic relations with the People's Republic of China may either be maintained or changed to semi-official missions. States not recognised by the People's Republic of China can only establish non-governmental institutions.

These provisions are echoed in the Basic Law. However, some important questions are left open, apart from the issue of countries without formal diplomatic ties with the P.R.C. or not recognized by it, but which have connections with Hong Kong.

At present, a number of Asian and Western countries maintain very large missions in Hong Kong. In fact, some of the consulates/commissions are among the largest of each respective country's overseas missions. This is the case partly because of the importance of the bilateral relations between Hong Kong and the country concerned, and partly because the mission in Hong Kong may be designated as the hub of the country's diplomatic missions in the eastern Asia region. This is part and parcel of Hong Kong's stature as a major world centre today.

When the mission in Hong Kong becomes accredited to Beijing rather than to London, it will be for the P.R.C. to decide whether or not to permit it to maintain the same size and level of activities, and the decision may well be made on criteria different from those of the United Kingdom or of Hong Kong. Beijing might prefer, for instance, for a foreign government to establish or enlarge its mission in Shanghai, Dalian, or Shenzhen while downsizing that in Hong Kong. Whether the foreign government would accede to such a request would depend, in part, on its assessment of how well its mission in Hong Kong could function to serve its needs in Hong Kong and the region.

That, of course, would in turn depend on how the foreign missions in the HKSAR will be permitted to function. At present, the foreign missions deal directly with individual departments of the Hong Kong government, essentially without having to refer to either the British government in London, or the U.K. Foreign Office representative in the Hong Kong government, the Political Adviser. It is yet unclear whether the HKSAR government will be permitted to operate with the same degree of autonomy where the foreign missions are concerned. The Joint Declaration and the Basic Law both assert that "foreign affairs are the responsibility of the Central People's Government." This is, of course, a prerogative of sovereignty. Under this prerogative, the P.R.C. Foreign Ministry would be represented by its officials in Hong Kong. Whether these officials will work out a *modus vivendi* with the HKSAR government like that existing between the Political Adviser and the present government, or instead adopt more interventionist or inquisitive stances, remains to be seen. But if the autonomy of the HKSAR government in dealing with the foreign missions in Hong Kong is seen to be considerably reduced from present standards, Hong Kong's standing in the international community will be eroded, with consequences for its effectiveness as a world centre.

As for the official representation of Hong Kong overseas, there are eight Hong Kong government offices posted to Brussels, Geneva, London, New York, San Francisco, Tokyo, Toronto, and Washington. In addition, there are thirty-seven branches of the Hong Kong Trade Development Council posted to twenty-six countries around the world, which function as semi-official representatives where there are no official government offices. (There are also offices of the Hong Kong Tourist Association in seventeen cities which help to promote certain aspects of Hong Kong's image overseas.)

Apart from the office in London, which is called the Hong Kong Government Office, and which has political liaison as an important part of its brief, the other seven government offices are known as the Hong Kong Economic and Trade Offices. This name is provided for in both the Joint Declaration and the Basic Law. The three offices in the U.S. operate out of the premises of the local British diplomatic missions; the ones in Europe, Canada, and Japan have their own premises distinct from the British ones. In cities or countries where there are no Hong Kong offices, Hong Kong's interests are represented by the nearest missions of the United Kingdom.

The Economic and Trade Offices overseas are more like trade commissions than consulates and do not perform the full range of consular functions. They are directed by administrative officers and staffed by officers seconded from the Government Information Services and the Trade and Industry Department. Hong Kong government officers posted to these offices enjoy, as a rule, "senior official" rather than diplomatic status. Within the structure of the Hong Kong government, they come under the Secretary for Trade and Industry. Matters which are referred home from overseas which do not fall within the Trade and Industry Branch are then directed to other branches and departments of the government. The Overseas Public Relations Division of the Government Information Services also collaborates with the Economic and Trade Offices in their work. Immigration and other consular functions continue to be handled by British missions.

At major international conferences where Hong Kong's vital interests are concerned, Hong Kong delegates often have the opportunity to play an active part, either forming their own team or as part of the United Kingdom delegation. During the Uruguay Round of the General Agreement on Tariffs and Trade (GATT), for instance, where Hong Kong has been a contracting party on its own since 1986, the Hong Kong delegation took an active and constructive role in the negotiations which resulted, at the last minute, in the Final Act of the Round. (The P.R.C. is not yet a contracting party to the GATT.)

At other meetings, the experience was not always quite so positive. The successful snubbing of the Hong Kong delegate to an international meteorological gathering by the P.R.C. delegate in 1990 has been detailed in *The Other Hong Kong Report 1991* and need not be repeated here. More recently, the P.R.C. attempted to stop Hong Kong (and Taiwan) from being invited to the APEC summit at Seattle in November 1993, on the grounds that since Hong Kong is not a sovereign state, its leaders have no place in a meeting of heads of state. APEC was first convened in 1989 as an intergovernmental meeting of the "economies," rather than the "states" of the Pacific Rim. As an autonomous and active economy, Hong Kong has always taken an active part in its deliberations. In fact, Hong Kong, the P.R.C., and Taiwan simultaneously became its members in 1991, the first time all three major Chinese communities were admitted to any international forum together as separate and equal members. After considerable discussion prior to the Seattle meeting, Hong Kong came to be represented at the conference by the Financial Secretary and the Secretary for Trade and Industry. Other participants, from the Hong Kong Trade Development Council, also played high-profile roles in the non-governmental meetings of the conference.

Difficulties with the P.R.C. authorities where Hong Kong representation overseas is concerned are likely to continue for sometime, until a *modus operandi* could be worked out that would take care of both Beijing's sensitivities and Hong Kong's interests. While certain general principles have been laid down in the Joint Declaration and the Basic Law about Hong Kong delegates forming part of P.R.C. teams or their own teams in international conferences, the international community will be monitoring the actual practice and performance in the years after 1997 to determine to what extent Hong Kong speaks with its own voice in international conferences, and to what extent it will simply echo the P.R.C. line. Hong Kong's international personality and stature will be assessed accordingly.

While officers and offices of the Hong Kong government have been performing overseas with credit to themselves and to the territory, there is perhaps a need at home to examine certain broader issues, especially with regard to coordination of external affairs within the administration, and working towards a consensus between the administration and the Legislative Council (Legco) on external relations.

During the past few years, serious questions have been raised on a number of occasions in the Legco over expenditure for the overseas offices or overseas promotion exercises. While the questions have been legitimate ones, they do indicate insufficient communication between the administration and the legislature on a very important evolving area of the government's work. Some prominent Legco members do engage in establishing overseas contacts of their own. It would appear that both sides need to work together towards a consensus on external policies which are vital for Hong Kong's survival as a significant world centre.

While Hong Kong is not, and is not destined to be, a sovereign state, there is no call for it to establish a foreign ministry or a diplomatic service. However, it is an international city with multifarious and complex external relations of a civilian nature, and plays a pivotal role in the development of eastern Asia. To live up to its potentials under the formula of "one country two systems, Hong Kong people ruling Hong Kong," a core of expertise would need to be developed in the Government Secretariat to provide the staff work and the coordination in support of the various departments, overseas missions, and delegations to international conferences. This would be necessary in itself, by virtue of the challenge of the tasks involved. It would be even more so if the Government Secretariat hopes to work on a more or less equal footing with the officials from the P.R.C. Foreign Ministry to be assigned to the HKSAR government, in order to give adequate expression to Hong Kong's autonomous needs and interests. To be able to meet those officials from a basis of adequate staff work would be a big step towards maintaining Hong Kong's international interests and position. Perhaps an office of assistant chief secretary for external relations could be created to head a unit for research, coordination, staff development, and legislative liaison.

☐ Unofficial Representation Overseas

Unofficially, Hong Kong is represented overseas by more than half a million emigrants who have left the territory since the early 1980s. The emigrants come from diverse backgrounds within Hong Kong society. Some are tertiary-educated, professionally qualified persons, bilingual in Chinese and English. Some have had no more than a primary or junior secondary education, but might have made their fortunes from Hong Kong's economic boom or the open door policy of the P.R.C. Some might have both education and wealth, while others might be more moderately endowed with either. In terms of age, they range from small infants to old grannies.

There is no simple way to generalize about them, but most of them have in common Hong Kong travel documents (British Dependent Territories Citizens passports or Certificates of Identity), the Cantonese dialect, attachment to the lifestyle, popular culture, and patterns of work and rest which arose in Hong Kong since the 1970s. In major Canadian, Australian, and U.S. cities where large communities of Hong Kong emigrants have settled, they have transformed the landscape and consumption patterns of certain districts, and brought important changes to the local scene of education and work. They have also brought with them not only Hong Kong-style restaurants serving Chinese and Western cuisine, shops specializing in Hong Kong-style products of all kinds, banks and other businesses, but also Hong Kong daily newspapers as well as radio and television broadcast services. To the host societies, they are the most powerful reminder of the work ethic, the rationality and organizational skills, the economic success, the cosmopolitanism, and the finer things in life that may be taken to represent Hong Kong. The immigrant communities are distinct not only from the "mainstream" of the host society, but often also from the other local Chinese communities.

Members of the host societies have diverse perceptions of this unofficial representation from Hong Kong, depending on each individual's situation and personality, and on the economic and social conditions of the society at any given time. Some might see the Hong Kong emigrant as a bearer of cultural gifts to enrich the host society, or as a potential investor with a good deal of unencumbered capital, or as a worker with skills, experience, and attitudes that local workers could well emulate. Other members of the host society might perceive the immigrant from Hong Kong as a threat or a part of a wave that would bring untold and unwelcome changes to the host society. Whichever it may be, in overseas societies where there are large numbers of immigrants from Hong Kong, the awareness of the existence and high economic levels of Hong Kong, and of the 1997 issue, is quite high.

Since the immigrants are fairly well integrated into the host societies, but not easily assimilated by them to the extent of losing any distinctiveness, Hong Kong could well maintain an unofficial presence in these cities, until 2047 or beyond. (On the other hand, of course, claims also could be laid by rival Chinese authorities to the ethnic allegiance of these communities.)

In some cities, in fact, organizations have been established to help members keep up with developments in Hong Kong, and to help make the society and government of the host country aware of Hong Kong issues. These include the Alliance of Hong Kong Chinese in the United States, and the Hong Kong Forum Society of Vancouver, both of which have been very active.

Less positively, organized crime also has followed the migration. Police forces in the host countries have been worried about a mass exodus of triads from Hong Kong towards 1997, although the increase of triad activities does not seem so far to have been as serious as once predicted. Indeed, a good many of the so-called "Asian crimes" have been traced to "Big Circle Gangs" of Mainlanders, rather than to triads from Hong Kong. Host country police officials must have noted with very mixed feelings the statements by the P.R.C. Minister of Public Security in 1992 and 1993, that he had no difficulty working with "patriotic triads" in Hong Kong.

☐ Conclusion

From the beginning of its history, Hong Kong has served as a bridge for the international movement of goods, people, and ideas. For many decades, Hong Kong's external side had been so much more important than its internal side that it was as if it had only an existence as a bridge for passing, without a personality of its own. During the past five decades, however, Hong Kong has evolved into a distinct society, with a culture that is at once Chinese and cosmopolitan. The internal and external sides of this society sustain each other to an unusual degree. It is this Hong Kong which has developed the international presence which it enjoys today. Whether or not that international presence will long survive the transfer of constitutional sovereignty will be a function of whether its governmental autonomy and its cultural and juridical personality could be maintained in the years to come.

UA

灣仔之虎

True Lies
真實謊言

Culture and Identity

Chan Hoi-man

☐ Introduction: The Winter of Our (Cultural) Discontent

Culture and identity are clearly not subjects restricted to the compass of a single year. Readers of *The Other Hong Kong Report* may also observe that previous volumes of the series, while certainly touched upon relevant discussions, have by and large refrained from broaching this wide-ranging, if also labyrinthine subject. The readers should thus be duly forewarned that the ensuing discussion may differ markedly, in both method and style, from other chapters in this volume. Culture and identity concern areas that are rightly deemed abstract and elusive. The juxtaposition of these areas in composite terms, as in the concept of cultural identity, would no doubt extenuate its ambiguity as well.

These considerations notwithstanding, there is also little doubt that the question of a Hong Kong identity remains very much at the forefront of the collective endeavour of the city, whether along political, cultural, or everyday horizons. Politicians, publics, and academicians alike invoke as a matter of course precepts and generalizations which either presume or seek to delineate, to varying degree of concreteness, the characteristics and spirit of a "Hong Kong culture," as embodied by the "Hong Kong folks," who identify themselves as distinctive and different in cultural, territorial, and historical terms. Hence the intertwining of Hong Kong culture and identity, and hence also the various — as yet inconclusive — approaches to delimit

---

Chan Hoi-man is a lecturer in the Department of Sociology, The Chinese University of Hong Kong.

this Hong Kong identity *qua* indigenous culture, hybridity, otherness, ethos, post-colonialism, ideologies, and other analogous conceptual rubrics. In addition, the even more politically inspired vantage points would demarcate the essence of this cultural identity via its dynamic struggle to hold on to cherished social ideals — and to the framework of society involved — amid the upheavals of transition and transformation. It is in here that the striving for prosperity and stability, for law and order, and for the Hong Kong way of life, enter into the picture as more pragmatic vindications of a presumed, distinctive Hong Kong culture and society.

In even more down-to-earth, tangible terms, the presence of a unique and even autonomous Hong Kong cultural identity is also immensely affirmed by its successful invasion and influence over the adjacent cultural areas. Considering the size of Hong Kong society, the cultural impact it is able to assert on other Chinese-speaking communities must be seen as entirely amazing. Considering also that many of these Chinese-speaking communities have regularly regarded Hong Kong as but a small colonial enclave, a historically created anomaly even, then the magnitude of its cultural vitality is all the more incredible, on a par with the economic miracle that Hong Kong has become internationally renowned for.

The agenda of Hong Kong culture and identity therefore stands at the confluence of three sets of concerns: namely intellectual pursuits that aim to unravel the deeper unity — such as there might be — of culture and society in Hong Kong; political enigma that imputes a more acute contrasting dichotomy of "otherness" and "togetherness"; and cultural impacts upon outside regions that rebound to underline the quality of Hong Kong culture and identity from without. These three sets of vantage points, when pitched together, fairly indicate the dynamic complexity of the formation of cultural identity in Hong Kong. All these as situated upon the historical juncture known as "the late-transitional" phase — or more rhetorically as *fin-de-siècle* Hong Kong, marking in one symptomatic epithet the ambivalence of imminent demise and uncertain regeneration.

At a more obvious and incontrovertible level, this prevalent sense of demise and uncertainty is by and large the joint outcome of the post-June Fourth and the pre-1997 historical syndromes. While the general contour of these syndromes would be familiar for most "Hong Kong folks" and their faithful observers, some of the more salient benchmarks may still merit reiteration, as a backdrop for the discussions to ensue. Thus, the hazards of prediction aside, the 1997 epochal threshold dictates with unyielding authority that in a matter of a thousand days the return of Hong Kong sovereignty to China will duly take place, and that tidings of cataclysmic transformation will overtake Hong Kong both during and after the passover of the threshold. On top of the resigned foreboding which the 1997 tidings may bring, the post-June Fourth political pessimism in addition served as disturbing reminder that to actually believe in the promise of "arresting change for fifty years" can be only so many middle-class pipe-dreams.

At the heart of this "late-transitional" phase is the looming confusion over novel defining political precepts such as "one country, two systems," "special administrative region," "basic law," "maintaining prosperity and stability," "the second stove," and of course the formula "arresting change for fifty years." The ambiguity of these precepts and formula stem not simply from the often jingoistic innocence of their formulation. In reality, public reservation and suspicion are not greatly alleviated by the roller-coaster ride of the rather unfruitful "Hong Kong talks." If the political through-train solution has now been formally killed off once and for all, it naturally raises concerns over related prospects of a reasonably smooth transition. And in this case, the long-standing deadlock over the new airport on the more recent dispute over Container Terminal No. 9 have all been less than reassuring. In this regard, the sometimes wildly fluctuating Hang Seng Index becomes the barometer for gauging the extent of sociopolitical confidence and stability. And the current news has not been good, at least if one looks at the by and large dismal performance of the stock market in the first half of 1994. Whether the somewhat softened position of the Hong Kong government in the newest policy report can help remains to be seen. Amid the agony of it all, both the prosperity and the vulnerability of Hong Kong society inevitably surge to the fore of collective consciousness.

This contrasting sentiment is further complicated by the pervasive love-hate conflict of the Hong Kong folks towards China, as the inevitable target of patriotism and fear. China is herself a country of conflict, caught between economic growth and backwardness, between lofty aspiration and unthinking ruthlessness. Notwithstanding the righteous fury of the June Fourth protests, Hong Kong society must sensibly revive "normal" and stable interaction with China. Yet whether as a gesture or otherwise, Hong Kong still hosts the best-attended and the most elaborate commemoration of June Fourth anniversaries. The Christopher Patten era therefore unfolds upon shaky ground. What was dubbed a new beginning soon enough sank into a long twilight. The substantial political talent of "the last governor" has only occasioned new rounds of debates and anxieties.

The historical foundation of this chapter thus rests upon the interface of both a recognition and a lacuna. The recognition is that, into the mid-1990s, dramatic shifts of cultural sensitivity unmistakably took place, culminated in a general mood of pessimism, confusion, and discontent. Whereas the lacuna has to do with how best to identify and comprehend the human dynamics and meaning that have transpired in this sea change. And here, one returns to the organizing leitmotif of this chapter, namely the formation of culture and identity at a time of unprecedented transformation of Hong Kong society.

As mentioned above, the elusiveness of the twin categories of culture and identity would prescribe that they can only be tackled in a largely conceptual, interpretive manner. The more intricate constitution of culture and identity cannot be directly observed, but only perceived and inferred. And there is little straightforward data or fact that may be seen as conveniently — or unproblematically — spelling out the inner meaning of cultural identity as such.

The implication here is not simply a methodological one, as per interpretive understanding contra quantitative measurements and statistics. Even in terms of the subject matter to be addressed, the considerations above suggest that what is at stake is not so much a question of cultural artifacts and phenomena, seen in and of themselves. Areas such as fine art, custom and mores, mass and high cultures, and so forth, are no doubt relevant. Especially the domain of popular culture, which has unsurpassed impact upon the cultural and identity formation of Hong Kong society. Perceiving the character of culture and identity of Hong Kong, however, goes beyond such artifacts and arenas. What will be furthermore called for is an interpretive reading that rises above individual domains of social life — be they cultural or otherwise — and that probes into the possible cultural common denominators that can be teased out from these widely diverse domains.

Culture, when cast in this light, takes on the more active meaning of being (funda)mental guide-map, which the public in different walks of social life would make reference to, with varying senses of obligation and understanding. This would be the original anthropological meaning of culture, which sees the latter as the encompassing, organizing categories that rendered patterned social life possible. Based upon this by and large holistic conception of culture, one may then enter the connected horizon of identity, as the self-aware reflection, recognition, and allegiance by the individuals within their shared cultural rubrics. And to be really meticulous about it, identity itself can also be underlined along personal, collective, even national dimensions. All of which, again, defies simplistic reading in factual or empiricist terms, because their multifarious formations resonate simultaneously within realms that are psychological, symbolic, political, even philosophical in nature.

Without getting into the somewhat esoteric methodological controversies, what the above discussion signifies is the primacy in constructing certain framework of organizing themes, by way of which more systematic and penetrating insights might be obtained. Such a framework would presumably go beyond simply registering particular cultural phenomena, events, and artifacts; while at the same time must not be so sweeping or unspecific that it bypasses the actuality of the Hong Kong vicissitudes altogether. In this way, benchmark events or trends that have notable bearings on the formation of the Hong Kong cultural identity can be meaningfully interpreted only when contextualized within the rubrics of this framework. The postulation of the latter, to its full analytical order, would of necessity begin with some preconceived conceptions regarding the broad outlook and character of the Hong Kong cultural scene. In other words, there is no escaping the potential irony that a perspective on Hong Kong cultural identity is itself erected upon initial preconceptions regarding the latter. The question is but to delineate and rethink more precisely and self-consciously the nature of such conceptions, to determine if they might be developed analytically into a fully-fledged, empirically significant framework of understanding. Such would be an integrative strategy combining "local knowledge" with analytical protocols, a strategy that will be crucial for the agenda of the present chapter. Two stages of endeavour need to be addressed for this purpose, namely the general attributes of the Hong Kong cultural scene as commonly perceived, as well as its less tangible, constituting cultural discourses that should be more precisely identified and delimited. While the first task will be discharged briefly, the second will form the bulk of this chapter.

The general survey of the Hong Kong cultural scene might begin with the recognition that, at heart, Hong Kong is by and large a society devoid of a unifying cultural foundation. Three socio-ideological spectres haunt her like so many layers of structural straitjacket, namely modernism, colonialism, and Chinese traditionalism. The combined and respective impacts of these, at different levels of tangibility, made up the sociocultural labyrinth that the "Hong Kong folks" have learnt to live with. For these Hong Kong folks, this unlikely amalgamation, being part and parcel of the fabric of everyday life, has been largely assumed and "normalized." Yet others observing from the wider perspective of social and historical development can immediately see the complexity, the schism that must entail for the formation of culture concerned, and all the more marvel at the vibrant sociocultural order being sustained in spite of all.

In Hong Kong, therefore, there is not much unified, coherent cultural foundation to speak of, whether in the sense of a high culture, a national culture, a traditional culture, or even a "borrowed culture." One ventures to observe, the only sociocultural arena that comes closest to providing overarching cultural framework of some form is the arena of popular culture. The latter can take on this function mainly because, by its nature, popular culture does not actively shape or construe the deeper dynamics of cultural imperatives, and thus can paint over but not resolve, the fragmentary ground upon which it also stands. It is this general condition of culture, and of popular culture, that should inform investigations into the nature of culture, society, and identity in Hong Kong. This explains the use of popular culture as privileged exemplars and point of departure in the following.

Furthermore, what gives this programme of understanding special dynamics and urgency is the empirical intertwining of popular and political culture in Hong Kong. On the one hand, the incessant expansion and diversification of the popular culture industry has placed the greatest majority of the "Hong Kong folks" under its spell. While on the other hand, rapid successions of political drama have stimulated outcries for greater extent of participation and expression in the public sphere. Even if the striving for political participation and expression is largely the outcome of political, macro-structural transformation, yet the substantive attitudes, posture, values, and even rhetoric of the resulting outcry are influenced heavily by the popular cultural milieu that the population at large embeds in. This postulation is of course not an excuse for simplistic political reading of popular culture. The sociopolitical impacts of popular culture can be adequately unravelled only by way of the more encompassing cultural-discursive formations that underline the twin spheres of the popular and the political, and of which popular culture, as suggested in the above, is the privileged arena of articulation.

Two observations can hence be made about a more dynamic picture of culture and identity in Hong Kong. Firstly, the seemingly apolitical arena of popular culture, in so far as it stands at the heart of cultural formation in Hong Kong, is instrumental in the moulding of substantive political culture and action. And secondly, on a more practical plane, one must view with scepticism any political claim or programme that recklessly sidesteps the attitudinal or behavioural messages as prescribed in this popular cultural universe. Along both directions, popular culture may act as the key dynamic agent in embodying as well as shaping the social, cultural, and political mentality of Hong Kong.

☐ Culture: Readings of Discursive Formation in Hong Kong

This section postulates an interpretive framework on Hong Kong culture and identity, as a context towards the understanding of actual sociocultural currents and events. Broadly speaking, the postulation in this section is that, by way of — and as articulated in — the arena of popular culture, the formation of cultural identity in Hong Kong can be best conceived in terms of sets of intertwining and contradistinctive constellations of cultural discourses. It would be imperative to recognize that the pervasive cultural condition in Hong Kong is more complex and nebulous than can be conveniently embraced under any single rubric or epithet. Even if the more dominant theoretical schools tend to view popular culture as a homogenizing, levelling cultural horizon, this position may not be readily applicable to the case of Hong Kong. This is not simply to vindicate the sphere of popular culture against its more high-minded, critical theorists. While much of the homogenizing, desensitizing effect of popular culture may be quite real, in so far as Hong Kong society is concerned, popular culture is decidedly also the primary sphere of consciousness and sentiment where the concerns, anxieties, and foreboding of society as a whole find their expression. In the absence of any hegemonic framework of high culture, national culture, and so forth, popular culture in Hong Kong must play the role — set the agenda — of "culture" *per se*.

It is therefore in light of the substantive formations and dynamics of popular culture in Hong Kong that different discourses or constellations of cultural formations can be initially identified. More specifically, the three sets of discourse underlined in this section are also meant to adhere closely to the key thematic orientations within the empirical nexus of Hong Kong culture as such. To this extent, each of these discursive formations, as exemplified by the conjuncture of popular culture, represents contradistinctive rubrics in the essential constitution of the Hong Kong cultural milieu. Their presence, furthermore, is directly rooted upon — contextualized within — Hong Kong's current sociohistorical development. It is in this sense that, in the following, these discursive formations would be designated in more down-to-earth terms, simply depicted as the cultures of affluence, of survival, and of deliverance — *qua* sets of criss-crossing, contrasting parameters epitomized in the cultural formation of Hong Kong. The strategy of the following analyses, in other words, is to start with more tangible, salient orientations in cultural formations, and progressively raise these to the level of an encompassing framework of interpretive understanding. While there is no need to claim any "definitiveness" for the approach and framework here undertaken, the point remains that the culture and identity of Hong Kong can only be underlined by a framework of understanding that addresses both the special sociohistorical conjuncture of Hong Kong, as well as the general attributes of the elusive categories of culture and identity.

Discursive Formations (i): Culture of Affluence

The first constellation of cultural discourse here postulated has to do with the easily visible facade of material affluence here in Hong Kong. It is already common knowledge that Hong Kong is a place of dramatic economic and material advancement, a fine specimen of capitalist success. This material affluence necessarily has its impact on the growth and orientation of cultural development in Hong Kong, and thus merits more precise delineation as the first major constellation of cultural discourse. The sense of material abundance is clearly prevalent from the mid-1970s onward, when Hong Kong sustained a growth rate nothing short of extraordinary. In so far as the popular culture industry is closely associated with entertainment and fulfilment in leisure life, the widening magnitude of socioeconomic affluence is readily reflected in the metamorphosis that the popular culture industry has gone through. Even mainly at the level of institutional forms and development, the expansion of a sense of affluence, of consumerism and materialism, or even of a general climate of individualistic hedonism, is clearly reflected in the exponential growth of mass cultural choices and forms. This expansion of the cultural horizon first took place during the same conjuncture that saw Hong Kong's rise as international metropolis. The rapid accumulation and concentration of resources, whether financial, cultural, or technological, cannot be divorced from this trend.

Furthermore, it is also in this same conjuncture that one may note the initial formation of a more self-conscious indigenous culture. The expansion of the cultural horizon, subsequent to economic and material success, thus afforded more opportunities and resources for local cultural creators, a prominent example being the local talents assembled under television broadcasting in the 1970s. Many of them would later enter the local movie industry and became instrumental in initiating a sustained high tide of local movie productions. To the extent that, almost by definition, the fashioning of indigenous culture was both embedded in and reflected indigenous conditions, one may observe that the emergence of an indigenous culture in the 1970s was closely tied to a cultural discourse of affluence as here depicted. While on the one hand this culture of affluence may focus on the more immediate portrayal of consumerism, materialistic aspiration, hedonistic indulgence, and so forth, in a more general sense it is also connected with the widespread creation and use of exasperating cultural spectacles as a whole. Such cultural spectacles were conducive to the conjuring of more exuberant, larger than life experiences, as befitting an audience no longer satisfied merely with mundane, humble pleasures. These cultural spectacles could well include such diverging popular culture genres as kung-fu movies, TV variety shows, sagas and soap operas, all of which reinforced the formation of a cultural discourse that emphasized the generous, abandoned relish of the spectacular excitement that society has to offer, once the constraints on material existence were greatly loosened if not eliminated.

Associated with this culture of affluence is a sense of greater cultural freedom and potency. This is a result in connection with the easy availability of cultural choices whether in terms of genres, taste, or price range. As well, the consolidation of an indigenous culture as afforded by the culture and the economic reality of affluence, also heightened the feeling of cultural autonomy of Hong Kong. The trajectory of this progressive expansion in cultural freedom can be best illustrated by such institutional development as the shifting fortune of the television industry in Hong Kong. It was after all the initial impact of television broadcasting that first extended significantly the range of cultural choices in Hong Kong in the early 1970s. The glamour and allure of television broadcasting was such that, for the entire decade of the 1970s, the novelty and variety of TV programming dominated the local cultural imagination. It was a time of new-found rejuvenations, when popular culture in Hong Kong could actually rally around local efforts and aspirations, nurturing a cultural outlook that pertained closely to the condition, demand, and imagination of the local society. While cultural productions imported from elsewhere remain important, yet the centre of cultural gravity decidedly shifted in favour of local productions, represented above all by the wide-ranging productions and experimentations in the television industry. The novelty and momentum of what took place was so mesmerizing that, regardless of objective flaw or simplicity when compared with more sophisticated productions elsewhere, what was produced within the cultural orbit of Hong Kong, by this token, was sufficient to occupy centre stage. This would be the time when local TV sagas could become the rightful talk of the town, and local TV literacy a prime measure of cultural awareness.

Yet by the end of the 1980s, the hegemony of the television industry was already heavily undermined, consistently losing in audienceship even up to the present. One may observe that it was actually the same consistent widening of the horizon of cultural choices, as mentioned earlier, that eventually weakened the hegemony of television in the world of Hong Kong popular culture. In fact, the grip of TV programming in the 1970s was largely based on the novelty of much of the entertainment choices offered by assorted genres of TV production. In this golden age of television broadcasting, TV figured not simply as one form of popular culture among others. It was rather in itself a vast collection of glamorous genres and novel choices, the lot of which projected an aura of abundant ambience that kept the audience spell-bound.

Be that as it may, it can be further observed that, into the 1980s the same audience who used to be captivated by TV broadcasting outgrew what TV programming had to offer. It makes no difference that television was instrumental in familiarizing — educating — the Hong Kong audience with a more glamorous and confident cultural outlook. In time, the audience has learnt to demand more than what the local television productions can offer. Or, what amounts to the same thing, the reality of TV can no longer catch up with an audience that has learnt to become even more self-assured and demanding. As of today, watching local television dramas, variety shows, and the like can be easily viewed as an outdated entertainment for less resourceful groups such as housewives or the aged. The affirmation of cultural affluence and potency must be sought elsewhere — in the participatory excitement of karaoke and the pinball parlour, for example — in this unending quest for the ever rising threshold of fulfilment. Such would be the quintessential orientation of the culture of affluence. In this way, if the culture of affluence was originally rooted in a state of new-found freedom and momentum, in time it entered into a state of more mature disenchantment, as indicated for example by the shifting fortune of the television industry in Hong Kong. In this scenario, affluence may yet stand side by side with discontent. As well, this transformation was aided by the growth of other facets of cultural discourse, in connection with and in contradistinction to this culture of affluence itself.

Discourse Formation (ii): Culture of Survival

The above depiction of the culture of affluence maps out the basic overtone of the cultural climate in Hong Kong, especially during the phase of the presumed indigenous cultural formation. It is no accident that, starting with this basic orientation, Hong Kong culture strikes its more critical observers as materialistic, hedonist, self-indulgent, and of course superficial. The point, however, is that, once moving beyond this first impression of a culture of affluence, the facile abundance of generic choices, institutions, and productions, in and of themselves, are still far from sufficient in masquerading the city as but a blatant arena of affluence and wish-fulfilment. The articulation of other less obvious, and yet perhaps more hard-boiled cultural discourses can also be plausibly demonstrated by way of the constitution of the popular culture industry.

Even as in the creative conjuring of subject matter and plots in popular culture, the requirement of thematic and textual varieties is antithetical to any simplistic, abstract feeling of affluence and fulfilment. The presence of the latter is by all means prominent, but must be complemented by more realistic and down-to-earth concerns, thus setting the contrasting background of both the potential promises and setbacks of city life. In more concrete terms, the feelings of affluence that characterized the city of Hong Kong in rapid progress is inevitably counterbalanced by simultaneous senses of uncertainties, anxieties, and other such probable traumas. In the craft of popular cultural formations, especially in genres that rely heavily on textual narratives of various forms, e.g., romance fiction, movies, TV drama, and so forth, the appeal of material abundance would have to be set within specific contexts and given specific plots, and stands out against counter points of contrasting themes and motifs. In so doing, it becomes inevitable to probe beneath the facade of affluence and evoke also the more problematic side of human drama, which probably makes up the bulk of social life for the majority of the Hong Kong folks. What happens is therefore that the culture of affluence can hardly pre-empt the formation of an alternate yet connected cultural discourse of survival, which focuses upon how the problematic vicissitudes of social life must also be embodied in cultural terms.

Empirically speaking, even as varieties of exuberant cultural spectacles dominated popular culture imagination in the golden age of the 1970s and the early 1980s, such cultural movement as the "new wave movies" of the early 1980s did in fact seek to address this more problematic dimension of life in Hong Kong, to various degrees of artistic success. Also the great popularity of romance fictions — mostly authored by women writers — portrayed as much sentimental fantasies as this same stark encounter with surviving in a city of unceasing tribulations. In very broad strokes, this culture of survival manifests itself at both the levels of the individual and of the collectivity. At a personal level, survival and stoicism have to do with the quest of individuals for self-actualization in a seemingly chaotic societal setting. While the affluent society of Hong Kong can be rightly deemed an arena of resources, of possibilities and hopes, yet there is little guarantee that these may be readily realized for everyone even after dire struggles. It is in this respect that the cultures of affluence and of survival can be very much the two contrasting sides of the same societal coin. Affluence, even as the prevalent goal in the endeavours and anticipation of the individual, is not as yet such an all-pervasive reality that everyone can attain. The culture of survival is precisely built upon confronting the frustration of broken promises and of unrealized aspiration. Hence, the culture of affluence deepens the culture of survival, in as much as the latter must also come to terms with the relative deprivation and expanding anticipation heightened by growing affluence of the fortunate ones.

As for culture of survival pitched at the collective level, this of course has to do with the future of Hong Kong society at large. The 1997 threshold is on everyone's mind, and the vacillation between whether to stay or to emigrate becomes a prominent motif in the cultural practice of the populace. The fragility of collective survival, into the 1990s, is for example rehearsed each year in the commemoration of the June Fourth. Notwithstanding the gradual dissipation of democratic movement in China, and notwithstanding retroactive doubts regarding the magnitude or seriousness of the alleged massacre, the June Fourth incident has nonetheless come to symbolize for so many Hong Kong folks the bleak political reality that they might have to live with after 1997. Collective survival, in this way, stands for the survival of the city, in history and in culture.

In contrast to the indulgence of cultural spectacles and other exhibitionist modes, the portrayal of survival takes on much more mundane, everyday outlook. In that sense there is not much fanciful glamour to it, but perhaps mainly feelings of empathy. What the culture of survival articulates into is therefore a far from negligible streak of realism in Hong Kong popular culture formation. This realism can be established in a number of directions. Thus, on the one hand, as in the straightforward depiction of everyday family life, lives of the working people, or of the so-called "little folks" and so forth, realism can be deployed as presumably a more direct and honest reflection of "life as it is" in Hong Kong, untainted by the exaggerated illusion of fulfilment and affluence. However, on the other hand, discourse of realism can also be deployed in a more intense, active manner, as a discourse that seeks to disclose and demystify the hidden side of city glamours. In this case, as in the earlier "new wave movies" of the 1980s, discourse of realism did not simply reflect the configuration of everyday life as it is. In seeking to go beyond superficial, unreflective perception of reality, it would often go to the other extreme and propound an unflinching view of reality that is intense, hardened, and sometimes equally exaggerated. In this way, if the discourse of affluence pertains to fanciful glamour and charm of the growing metropolis that is Hong Kong, the discourse of survival would pertain to hard-boiled realism of varied intensity.

Discursive Formations (iii): Culture of Deliverance

A third formation of cultural discourse arises simultaneous to the juxtaposition of affluence and survival as the master cultural leitmotifs. This third discourse basically addresses the tension that might be present both in the confrontation of affluence and survival, as well as within each of these discursive formations. Such tension is relieved mainly by invoking the facade of enchantment and aura of the city, by means of which existential enigma, whether realistic or romantic, may be temporarily alleviated. Realistic enigma of survival is of course more readily understandable. Yet even affluence is itself associated with unwitting outcomes like competition, relative deprivation, or anomie that comes with increased opportunities for fulfilment and self-indulgence. All these would have to be confronted, resolved, by way of yet other formations of cultural discourse, which might be empowered to lift its audience out of their embedding, exasperating context, albeit temporarily or fleetingly. This alternative formation of culture is here designated as the discourse of deliverance.

In a less flattering sense, what is being alluded to here is the aura of intoxication, of escapism commonly associated with the popular culture industry, which renders the latter heavily suspect by the more highly aspiring critics. Yet it would seem that this sphere of cultural enchantment can be more diffused and multi-faceted than commonly assumed. At this level of cultural formation, the metropolis of Hong Kong is not merely represented as the arena of tension between affluence and frustration, but in a way must also figure as the arena of resistance and comfort as well. In present day Hong Kong, this extensive use of enchantment is best captured in the prevalence of comic genres of all forms, right down into the 1990s. In the raving popularity of comic genres, life experiences can be rendered somewhat more enjoyable, detached and "livable," through the use of jokes, dark humour, or outright farce. In the more extreme instances, essentially all situations can be laughed at, including even the severest obstacles or the most sacred symbols. Hence the resulting mood of resistance, triumph, and deliverance.

One may suggest, it is by way of this discourse of deliverance that the demands for fulfilment and survival attain their delicate balance, coming together to constitute a unique configuration of cultural outlook and practice. The widespread popularity of the comical form is therefore not accidental. Especially in the proliferation of comic movies in the 1980s and the early 1990s, comic defiance can be taken to the pivot of not simply mocking, but even negating, the fundamental senselessness of social life at large. Hence, the transformation of comical form into the absurdist-styled celebration of "mindlessness."

While the prevalence of this "cult of mindlessness" in the late-1980s was most visibly articulated in the movie world, its initial tremor originated by way of radio and television broadcasting, in such area as TV series, stand-up comedies, talk-shows, singing, and — of all things — traffic reports. It was when the movie world sought to exploit the rise of this rap-talk like, unpredictable — because nonlogical — style that the mindless culture really caught on. Fun and whims began where reason is put on hold, more obsessively and arbitrarily than ever before. It is potentially a holistic negation of the "objective" social order and its organizing rationality, thus generating a prospect of deliverance that appears palpable yet desperate.

In actuality, however, the case of the Hong Kong comedies is an inevitably watered-down, diluted version of the absurdist outlook. The particular tactics and manner of articulation must remain in keeping with the constraints of popular culture formations of Hong Kong. This way, in this absurdist, mindless turn is also created the margin of resignation and submissiveness in the comical form, at the threshold of popular entertainment where subversion and defiance can no longer push any further. Hence

Culture and Identity

the intertwining of hard-boiled dark humour and aimless discontent in the genre of comic mindlessness.

Furthermore, the impetus for the prevalence and intensity of comedy in Hong Kong is amplified by the specific historicity of the city. It is perhaps no accident that the spread of comical form coincided with the progressive acknowledgement of the historical fate of the city, and that the more recent petering out of the comical genre is connected with the resigned acceptance of the fruitlessness of the "Hong Kong talks." Into the mid-1990s, the vision of deliverance, whether in historical or psychological terms, may seem but glaring utopian dreams. And the Hong Kong folks once again driven to confront real-life agonies as they are, without the benefit of disguise or delusions, but perhaps somewhat strengthened by the comic overtone of playful cynicism.

Be that as it may, and at the risk of oversimplification, it can be maintained that in the formation of Hong Kong culture, discourse of deliverance asserts itself even as endeavours of fulfilment and of survival must square off in a time of accelerating social change and progress. If the culture of affluence articulates itself in an aspiration of innocent wish-fulfilment, of assertive, self-assured spectacles and indulgence, and the culture of survival in a mood of biting realism, of hardened and tactical stoicism, in the same vein the culture of deliverance manifests itself in a spirit of soothing enchantment, of lifting beyond — rising above — the tension and hazards bound up with life experiences in the enigmatic Hong Kong. Comedy, in its various incarnations, is a major form of this spirit of enchantment and deliverance. While other analogous modes may also be underlined, it is safe to observe that in Hong Kong none attains the same widespread celebration as the comical form.

With the delineation of these sets of cultural discourses then, a threefold constellation of the Hong Kong cultural formation can be put forth. It is perhaps not too wide off the mark to see this constellation as embodying the more fundamental, encompassing cultural parameters which have a major role to play in delimiting the trajectory of sociopolitical development in Hong Kong, and which contextualize the two interactive horizons of popular culture and social life at large.

☐ Identity: The Fate of the Sojourners Continues

This is then the elusive arena of culture that sets the stage for attitudes and expression — for sociocultural strategies *per se* — towards other more pragmatic, down-to-earth pursuits, including of course the pursuit of an acceptable sociopolitical order. From a more dynamic vantage point of cultural analysis then, the social and political culture of the Hong Kong folks cannot be understood apart from its rootedness in this cultural milieu. To put it plainly, political culture cannot go against the tides of cultural milieu at large.

The complication for Hong Kong is, however, that one is immediately confronted with the absence in this cultural milieu of any well-defined, overriding agenda and direction in the first place. The cultural discourses of affluence, of survival, and of deliverance, as depicted above, are essentially discursive strands that stem from contrasting demands, and pull in different directions. And none may be readily seen as domineering in a fundamental sense. Instead, they can only be contained in a precarious, fluid balance of some kind. Hence this cultural constellation must be constantly adjusting, improvising, reshaping itself in order to contain new changes or development. Caught in a cultural conjuncture devoid of clear direction and unified foundation, stable, well-defined sociocultural ideals and programmes would be difficult to generate and to sustain.

This way, the crux of the problem is that the ingrained tension and conflict in the cultural arena of Hong Kong can have no easy, feasible resolution. It is not a question of choice, preference, or priority in one's encounter with the cultural and the practical discourses of affluence or survival. Both are part and parcel of the conflicting necessities of everyday reality in Hong Kong. Whereas the kind of defiance or redemption that might be attained by way of the cultural discourse of deliverance can only be a partial one, effective largely as but an emotional outlet. The real-life interlocking of glamour and predicament remains in place within the structuration of social development, and assumes different extents of urgency under changing sociopolitical scenarios. This would apply not simply to such cataclysmic events as June Fourth or 1997, but in general to the fabric of social life conduct in Hong Kong. The pervasiveness and exasperation of the comical form is therefore itself a key indicator of the relentless intensity in this mingling of glamour and predicament.

The crucial outcome of this surface light-heartedness and ingrained schism is the concomitant difficulty in the generation of positive commitment of one kind or another. Such commitment, whether of a political or sociocultural character, would be futile as realistic constraints go far beyond what individual assertion might accomplish. Commitment will also be seemingly redundant since these constraints are often concealed, or downplayed through invoking cultural enchantment of different forms. This is then the intricate dynamics that flow from the three-way tug-of-war that make up the substance of the Hong Kong cultural milieu. Enthusiasm and emotion notwithstanding, in the absence of convincing and feasible societal goal, even the presence of positive, progressive postures cannot be easily concretized into palpable vision and agenda. At issue is not simply any absence of sincerity, aspiration, or passion on the part of the public, but also for want of commensurate and convincing agenda of intervention and practices.

In the development of the Hong Kong popular culture scene, this dilemma can be readily discerned in some of the more recent happenings. It can firstly be noted that, as subsidiary movie genres of the 1980s, the so-called heroic movies and the "category III" soft-porn movies both — in their more limited way — took their pride of place beside comical genres of various shades. In their contrasting ways, both of these alternative genres may be seen as the quest for tangible, concrete ideals of some form, whether that be the upholding of out-dated and deviant gangster morales, or the satisfaction of elementary, albeit indulging desires.

The so-called heroic movies express in their own violent fashion positive commitment to certain subcultural values. Such quest for positive values, even in its anti-social mode, does indicate a somewhat more steadfast, elevating orientation in the configuration of cultural mentality. Portents for commitment and sincerity are thus not entirely absent from the cultural imagination of Hong Kong society. This quest for personal, positive assertion however must remain entrenched within the sphere of myth-making in popular culture. This is so because in the violent, gangster or assassin infested world of the heroic movies, the kinds of values emphasized clearly deviate from the day-to-day conduct of social life. The feasibility of these values and ideals can only be attained or admired within the insulated parameter of the fictive popular cultural world. While the heroic movies may indeed stand for the genre that injects certain inspiration for the audience of popular culture, they do so only by virtue of their remoteness from the pragmatic, everyday way of life.

Likewise for the prevalence of soft-porn "category III" movies, which in their own way again seek to establish more elementary, persistent quest of some form. In this case, at stake is of course the fulfilment and actualization of sexual desires and fantasies. Moral considerations aside, at least it can be maintained that well defined goals and values are being propounded in this genre. Yet the discrepancy between wish-fulfilment in the popular cultural world and real-life conduct is clearly acute in this instance as well.

In both of these cases, what it comes down to is that the quest for positive values and self-assertion would involve costs and sacrifices which the Hong Kong folks may be unwilling to bear in real life — not for the sake of these more off-beat values anyway. Yet beyond these somewhat vulgar, deviant values, other equally inspiring, largely consensual ideals are unlikely to be generated or sustained, as prescribed in the contrasting, schistic cultural discourses of Hong Kong society. In the actual development of popular culture in Hong Kong, it is therefore no accident that both the heroic and the soft-porn movies stand secondary to the comical genres. The latter blends in much more readily as a general, everyday attitude. In the absence of a recognized, master ideal of whatever kind, essentially any ideal upheld can be questioned, dismissed, or laughed at — including of course the rebuilding of the social and political framework of life in Hong Kong. Laughter and mockery would be the most natural response to a somewhat enlightened, yet post-utopian milieu. The gist of the cultural identity of the solitary Hong Kong folks must be seen in this light.

This explains the difficulties in pinning down precisely the cultural identity characteristic of Hong Kong, because this identity can only be defined in relation to its vacuous centre, to the empty stage in the consolidation of primary cultural values and ideals. To draw the specific boundary of this cultural identity is difficult because it is essentially unbounded by tangible parameters, by a problematic that as yet harbours no ready resolution. While there has been general outcry for political expression and participation among the Hong Kong folks, as yet it does appear that a stable cultural framework or ideal is not forthcoming, which can justify and inspire prolonged struggles and sacrifices in sociopolitical life. After all is said and done, the political apathy of the Hong Kong folks remained evident, a signal clearly sent across by the dismal turnout rate of the landmark 1991 direct elections. The episode was all the more disappointing because it took place only two years from the June Fourth incident, which allegedly aroused the political conscience of Hong Kong from its apathetic slumber.

Instead, what the Hong Kong folks would mostly have to confront in real life remains by and large clusters of often mutually inconsistent, mundane everyday interests that must be tackled in an episodic, pragmatic manner. The unresolved tension among cultural discourses, in the main, dictates that cultural ideals and agenda in Hong Kong would remain incoherent and transient in character, and as befitting the society which is once again plagued by the unsettling fate of the sojourners — the same scenario that did once mark the nascent growth of Hong Kong society.

Between the present and the previous stages of this sojourners society, the main difference lies in that the new sojourners can have no ready actual or psychological homesteads to return to, in their eschewing of Hong Kong. The sojourners of the 1950s and 1960s were defined by their — perhaps misguided — belief in the eventual return to the motherland. Yet the new sojourners, whether in actuality or in spirit, are not taking their leave for any such homeland. They would be forced into a much lengthier and solitary exile, before a sense of "homely domain" can be rebuilt someplace else, all over again.

As yet, it remains difficult for the Hong Kong folks to both agree on fundamental sociopolitical ideals worth pursuing, and uphold political action and sacrifices over a meaningful period of time. Such would be the limits that the cultural milieu has imposed on the social development of Hong Kong. And such would also be the context that rekindled the continuation of the fate of the sojourners. Individuals can always camouflage their predicament in light-hearted, unconcerned laughter — in the laughter of self-conscious cynics, mocking the *a priori* futility of securing durable identity or homely domain in a social world of unceasing itineraries. In Hong Kong, this undercurrent of incipient cynicism already had its root in the imposed ideology and practice of colonialism. With the oncoming of the late-transitional phase, this incipient cynicism inevitably loomed over the forefront of cultural consciousness, via the undecided tensions of cultural discourses. One can almost postulate that, in the case of Hong Kong, prevalent cynicism is the joint product of the colonial original sin and the 1997 redemption-cum-apocalypse.

The foregoing line of thought brings this discussion to an examination of the more recent cultural events of some significance, as both illustrations and exemplifications of the framework outlined above. In this broad survey of the cultural conjuncture of the last years, several controversies and trends may merit special attention.

If the movie industry is once again taken as illustration, it appears that local film productions have gradually ceded to foreign productions in both public acclaim and hence box office return. And the discrepancy has been consistent over time, all the way from "Jurassic Park" to "Speed" and "True Lies." Apparently, the once highly successful "mindless" comic movies, featuring such stars as Stephen Chow and Eric Tsang, have run out of laughs; whereas the heroic or the soft-porn genres, as noted above, never had what it took to become dominant genres in the first place. Local film industry, analogous with society at large, is caught in the agony of transition. If in the past, the impending plunge into an unknown future can be temporarily defused through the novelty of laughter, by now both the wonder and the novelty have worn out. Whatever other gimmicks or themes that the movie industry has turned to — e.g., sado-masochism, androgyny, seedy local celebrities, nostalgic parody, scandalous news stories — the much coveted attention of the audience remained short-lived. If the trend continues, it would appear that after all the smoke and fire, local movie productions no longer intertwine as closely into their embedding sociocultural development, as they had unwittingly done before. Or, to put it somewhat differently, they are caught in a stage of societal development that can no longer be effectively mediated by popular cultural formations. The latter might in fact have reached the limit of their sociocultural impetus. As noted earlier, popular culture in Hong Kong may take on the part of playing culture *per se*. The limit of this impostering make-believe can now be clearly seen. In a cynical society obsessed with its own predicament, not only the quest for meaning, but even mockery and laughter — the most effective gimmick of popular culture in Hong Kong — can be futile as well. Instead, the practice of popular culture inadvertently falls back upon its more elementary role of providing mass entertainment as past-time. And in this capacity, and as already happened in the 1960s and the early 1970s, foreign productions easily override local ones in terms of sophistication, resource, production, and star-studded appeal.

Local productions have receded not only in the movie industry, but in television broadcasting as well. The run of the mill programmes regularly churned out by local TV stations, be they variety shows, drama, situation comedies, and what not, have long been wearing thin in terms of audience appeal. And the surprise success of the year, the "Judge Pao" series, is of course a Taiwan production. Other widely appreciated TV dramas also include such Japanese productions as the "Tokyo Love Story" and the "101 Marriage Proposals." These imported productions are popular for the same reason as foreign movies, that once the local sociocultural context can be legitimately side-stepped, these productions are much better crafted, performed, and produced, and therefore provide more appealing entertainment.

The benchmark case of the "Judge Pao" series, however, merits special attention. The wholly unexpected success of the series on prime time television triggered off widespread speculation on the reasons behind its success. For one thing, Taiwan television production has seldom done well in the Hong Kong market. More often than not, it is the reverse that is the case. Besides, the "Judge Pao" series so clearly built on traditional values, morals, as well as dramatic presentation that it hardly seems congruent with the reckless, cynical Hong Kong society. On top of all these, the historical legends that provided the basic framework of the series also appeared out of place in a society caught in the throes of hyper-modernization. Everything considered, it is indeed intriguing to ponder the source of consonance there might be. And a more positive, hopeful message seems to be that, perhaps Hong Kong society is actually breaking away from its nihilistic materialism and cynicism, and returning to the fold of the great tradition of Chinese culture and civilization. Presumably, because the vicissitudes of history and politics can no longer be denied or camouflaged, the Hong Kong folks become more susceptible to values and norms taken to be permanent, unchanging through the ages. Others also observed that, in the present conjuncture of chaos, injustice, and personal powerlessness, there is psychological need for righteous and chivalrous public figures like the virtuous Judge Pao and his resourceful associates.

The credibility of this line of reasoning cannot be easily established, and it may be pointless to seek definite answers at this time. The key to such possible answers, however, must lie with the actual attitude that the audience themselves adopt regarding the widely acknowledged moral aspiration of the series. A true appreciation — let alone acceptance — of these moral messages as they are, it must be emphasized, must also involve the recognition of their unyielding, imperative nature; that morality is meant to be hegemonic and binding, which figures as the sole legitimate frame of reference of social conduct. While deviations to various degree are to be expected, they are still assessed in accordance with the standards set by the moral framework itself. Morality loses its *raisons d'être* if it loses this binding, prescriptive hegemony. When this happens, observers or audience may then look on simply in appreciation of its long forgotten novelty and depth, but stripped of the moral obligation to act accordingly. This is by and large the same scenario as depicted in the above discussion of cynicism, by way of which everything can be laughed at, admired, or hated at will, yet with but little bearing on actual conduct. In the case of the Judge Pao series, clearly one cannot say that it has indeed reinvigorated for Hong Kong society the moral foundation of bygone days. In a very real sense, the appreciation rendered by the audience, in the absence of any genuine feeling of moral commitment, in effect turns the moral framework involved into aesthetic object, to be appreciated, marvelled at, even envied, but with the unmistakable recognition of its unbridgeable distance from the actualities of contemporary Hong Kong. What accounted for the popularity of the "Judge Pao" series, in other words, is what might be termed the aestheticization of moral persuasion. While it may indeed signify the opening up of Hong Kong society to greater moral sensitivity, by that ambivalent token it can ironically stand for a further devaluation of moral commitment, denuding the latter essentially of its unyielding stronghold, to become an object of detached wonder only.

The ensuing battle of the screening of the "Judge Pao" series between the two TV stations sheds further light on the wider meaning of this cultural episode. The scramble that finally led to the simultaneous screening of the series on both TVB and ATV clearly did not stem from the moral supremacy or messages of the series, but from considerations of its commercial success alone. Here the mass entertainment nature of the episode — behind its facade of high-minded seriousness — reveals itself in glaring light. When it was clear that even morality can sell, the cultural industrialists duly jump on the band-wagon. The aestheticization of morality is hence only the prelude to a more intense form of the commodification of morality. What happens is a two-part story. In the first place, morality loses its prescriptive hegemony to become one option, one vision of conduct among others, and must rely on its aestheticization to gain non-committal appreciation. While in the second place, the aestheticization of morality paved the way towards the more far-reaching commodificaiton of morality as such. And if even morality can be sold in a competitive cultural market like any other commodity, it gives new meaning and depth to the cynicism that Hong Kong society has subscribed to. Such would be the ironic popularity of the Judge Pao stories.

This newest trend to commodify morality, in typical Hong Kong fashion, is also carried on by way of sloppy imitations and spin-offs. At a more limited scale, actors and characters in the "Judge Pao" series were invited to take part in Hong Kong-produced variety shows, or to pursue side line careers such as singing. At one point, there was talk of TVB buying over the production rights from Taiwan. Even more characteristic of the Hong Kong approach is the production of imitations such as the movie "Hail the Judge," which is a free-reined exploitation of the virtuous Judge motif, yet combining the latter with the usual Hong Kong brand of high mindlessness. The starring of Stephen Chow, the uncontested hero of mindless comedies, therefore unwittingly epitomized a complex cultural conjuncture. It is the symptomatic attempt by the "mindless comedies" to reclaim their lost audience domain, both as a genre and as indigenous production, against the current of imported tides. Yet it only does so by succumbing to the leitmotif of its contestant, and thus effectively ceding to the power of the latter. It was therefore a move that largely marks the end of the mindless, amoral comedies wherein everything is for a laugh. In its place, a new note has been struck, which announces that if even laughter is out, then perhaps serious morality play can be sold for a change of taste. This does not mean that it has not been done before, but that now it constitutes a fully justified facet of the cultural mechanism of a materialistic, cynical society.

The morality play and the utopia of justice as newly evoked by the Judge Pao saga ironically also harp on other important recent tidings of Hong Kong culture and identity. Thus, outside of the insulated fantasies of the popular culture world, in the real life social drama of Hong Kong, the case of the imprisonment of the *Ming Pao* reporter, Xi Yang, by the Chinese authorities captured in an all too stark and immediate episode the complexities and tenuousness of justice. The general sequence of events that led to Xi's arrest and subsequent imprisonment was well known among the Hong Kong folks, yet to pinpoint the enigmatic messages of the episode is no easy task. In general, few people really doubt that Xi Yang might have stepped over the line in his hunt for news-worthy information; or that the Chinese government, as a rule, habitually guards jealously over the vaguely defined category of so-called "state secrets." As well, few among the Hong Kong folks would not voice support in the building of legality and legal institutions in China, or in the independent operation of the judicial system in the face of the state or of public opinion. It is generally accepted that the legal framework in China would take a while to mature, yet to value and encourage its operation would be an important first step.

The case of Xi Yang raises immediately the spectre and dilemma of a possibly unjust legal system, as well as the thornier issues of who should define what justice might be, and what to do in one's confrontation with an unjust legal system. The Xi Yang case epitomizes this complex scenario by opposing the theoretical and the practical facets of legality. In a nutshell, one may say that even though the Hong Kong folks are all for the legal-institutionalization of China, they are in fact not as prepared to support at the same time a concept of legal justice viewed as different from their own. In Xi Yang's case, one thus finds members of the community — some of them prominent ones — openly declaring that one must not obey, abide by a legal system that is unjust. In theory and in extreme cases this proposition might seem obvious. The question however is that, in the less clear cut zone of practice, it implies that each person is ultimately entitled to decide for himself the acceptability and fairness of particular legal codes or even the entire system itself. In other words, what it may signify is that people are entitled to take the law in their own hands, and consent only to what they deem just and fair. This would be only a short step from the reinstatement of legal anarchy, a scenario that allows the state and its oppressive machinery to once again step in with good reason. If a framework of social order cannot be maintained by means of imperative, binding legal codes, the only alternative would be a hegemonic order based on brute force. The Xi Yang case, and all the protest movements that come with it, therefore carries the disturbing signal that the elevating support of legalization in China, for the Hong Kong folks, is perceived only in the image of law and sentencing that Hong Kong society has grown accustomed to. When the prosecution and sentencing of Xi Yang contradicts the local sense of justice, public opinion readily refutes the very legality and institution that rendered this sequence of events possible. China, on the other hand, is predictably as adamant as ever towards outside efforts to influence its own framework of values, morality, and justice.

What the Xi Yang incident comes down to is therefore a situation that has increasingly typified the cultural predicament that Hong Kong is facing. In the absence of any integrative, feasible framework of cultural value and morality, the populace is confronted with a potentially nihilistic reality. This daunting scenario can be seemingly resolved in two directions. On a more intellectual, perhaps theoretical level, a cynical world-view can in one stroke both admit to the senselessness of the social world, and yet maintain a certain safety distance for the individuals who must still strive for survival after all. While on a practical level, the absence of an unifying framework of action would imply that individuals can only rely either on their own accustomed, habitual patterns of behaviour, or react to situation with their own gut feelings, oblivious of justification or ramifications. If the "Judge Pao" series does not stand for the reinvigoration of moral values as such, the Xi Yang incident likewise does not simply stand for the apparent upholding of law and justice. The attention accorded to both cases merely reaffirmed a state of confusion in fundamental cultural values, as rooted in the schistic cultural makeup outlined in the earlier section.

The surge of moral fervour in the years 1993 and 1994 was also marked by other culturally significant events. A prominent case in point is the wide-ranging controversy over gender equality, especially as following the amendment tabled by legislator Christine Loh, subsequent to the proposed

Government amendments to the New Territories Ordinance. At issue is both the inheritance right of women villagers in the New Territories, as well as the wider demand for gender equality across the societal board, regardless of presumed historical legacies or political vicissitudes. In the context of the present discussion, this controversy summarized neatly once again the confrontation of principle and implementation in the moralistic pursuit of justice, this time in the domain of gender equality. Both sides agreed in principle to the lofty ideal of gender equality, yet again controversies break out over how such principle may be made practicable under specific situations. For Christine Loh and her supporters, the most opportune moment is always now, and no pragmatic considerations should be allowed to work against cherished values of humanity. Especially for Loh, her proposed amendment appeared to be such a cautious, small step that she did not even see the need to first assess the standpoint of the indigenous residents in the New Territories. One can only assume that if she had intended to play serious moral crusade, she would have been better prepared. Her inadvertent oversight to assess the situation in its proper perspective, one surmises, stems at least partly from firm belief in the moral supremacy and self-evidence of the principle she upholds, which should be grounds enough to overturn any empirical or practical scruples that other observers might privately harbour.

As things unfolded, this was not to be the case. The sometimes violent confrontation outside the Legislative Council, on and around 22 March, thus symbolizes among other things the clash between value and vicissitudes. Both sides claimed to be all for gender equality. Yet the problem goes beyond even the intrinsic ambiguity of such claims, which can readily lead to contradictory interpretations. In addition, the political ramifications of the controversies were greatly extenuated in a volatile context of sociopolitical development. The question of hereditary privileges, as part of historical legacies, is certainly at stake. Others may also harp on the possible political foul-play designed to further upset stability during the late-transitional phase.

What this episode exemplifies is therefore once again the fragility of moral goodness amid criss-crossing currents of interests and real politics. The fervour of moral aspiration is not matched to the same extent by its pragmatic import, not simply because of the inevitable gaps between principle and reality, but even more importantly because vicissitudes of the late-transitional phase would not permit the insulation of high-minded moral pursuit from all-out power play of Hong Kong society as a whole.

While other culturally related episodes may also be included in the present discussion, from the foregoing analysis a distinctive trend can at least be underlined. This is the ironic, partial resurgence of moral concerns in a society that remains as cynical as ever. The commodification of morality is perhaps of the same cynical depth as the politicization of morality. And popular culture and mass media abound with such symptomatic episodes. This latest interplay of facile value commitment and inner scepticism is as yet inconclusive, but fast closing onto the 1997 moment of truth.

☐ Conclusion

All in all, the above depiction of culture and identity in Hong Kong must remain tentative and incomplete. The attempt at a multi-tiered framework of cultural identity as pertaining to Hong Kong, is but another way of admitting the implausibility — in fact the misguidedness — of any uniform, simplistic vision in this regard. The culture and identity of Hong Kong is defined more by a shared problematic than by any common resolution. Thus, the readers who seek straightforward and uncomplicated answers may well be disappointed. If anything, the foregoing analyses have only epitomized and unravelled the complexities of the issues at hand, thereby perhaps unsettling even further any quest for concise and obvious truths.

Be that as it may, it is incontrovertible that Hong Kong culture and society have entered into a transitional phase with no readily foreseeable outcome. The fundamental scaffolding of culture, as articulated by way of the discourses — as well as their related practices — of affluence, of survival, and of deliverance, is further compounded by the wildly fluctuating scenarios of events and impetus. All these may trigger currents of moral outrage among the Hong Kong folks. Yet even such currents are as yet insufficient to consolidate in a more positive and persistent manner into a framework of culture and identity based on shared ideals and endeavour. The cultural cynicism of the original schistic setting remains in place, or is in fact further heightened by moral fervour and outrage that have been consistently frustrated from being translated into action. Such would be the continuing fate of the sojourners — the unwitting protagonists of the Hong Kong epic — who must consign themselves to a renewed voyage into "unhomely" spiritual or geographical territories, even when they had been on the verge of securing their homely domain in the society of Hong Kong.

China–Hong Kong Integration

George Shen

☐ Introduction

The British colony of Hong Kong will become a Special Administrative Region (SAR) of China in less than three years' time. On 1 July 1997, Hong Kong will formally and legally become part of China when political integration will take effect. In the meantime, the economies of Hong Kong and South China, if not the whole of China, have already been integrated long before political integration takes place.

The China–Hong Kong political integration in 1997 will be the outcome of the 1984 Sino-British Joint Declaration, an agreement between two sovereign states, and the subsequent Basic Law promulgated by China's National People's Congress. The economic integration of the two entities would still have happened even without the prospect of political integration because it is an inevitable outcome arising out of mutual needs which diplomatic deals could neither foster nor stifle.

For decades, rising labour costs have obliged manufacturers in the industrialized countries to invest in and shift their production operations to developing countries where wages are low in order to keep their products competitive. Since about the same time, developing countries have sought foreign direct investments, which are invariably accompanied by management know-how and technology transfer, to help their economic development. It so happened that, in the late 1970s and early 1980s, Hong Kong and China were respectively in need of a low-cost production base and foreign

---

George Shen is Chief Editor, *Hong Kong Economic Journal*.

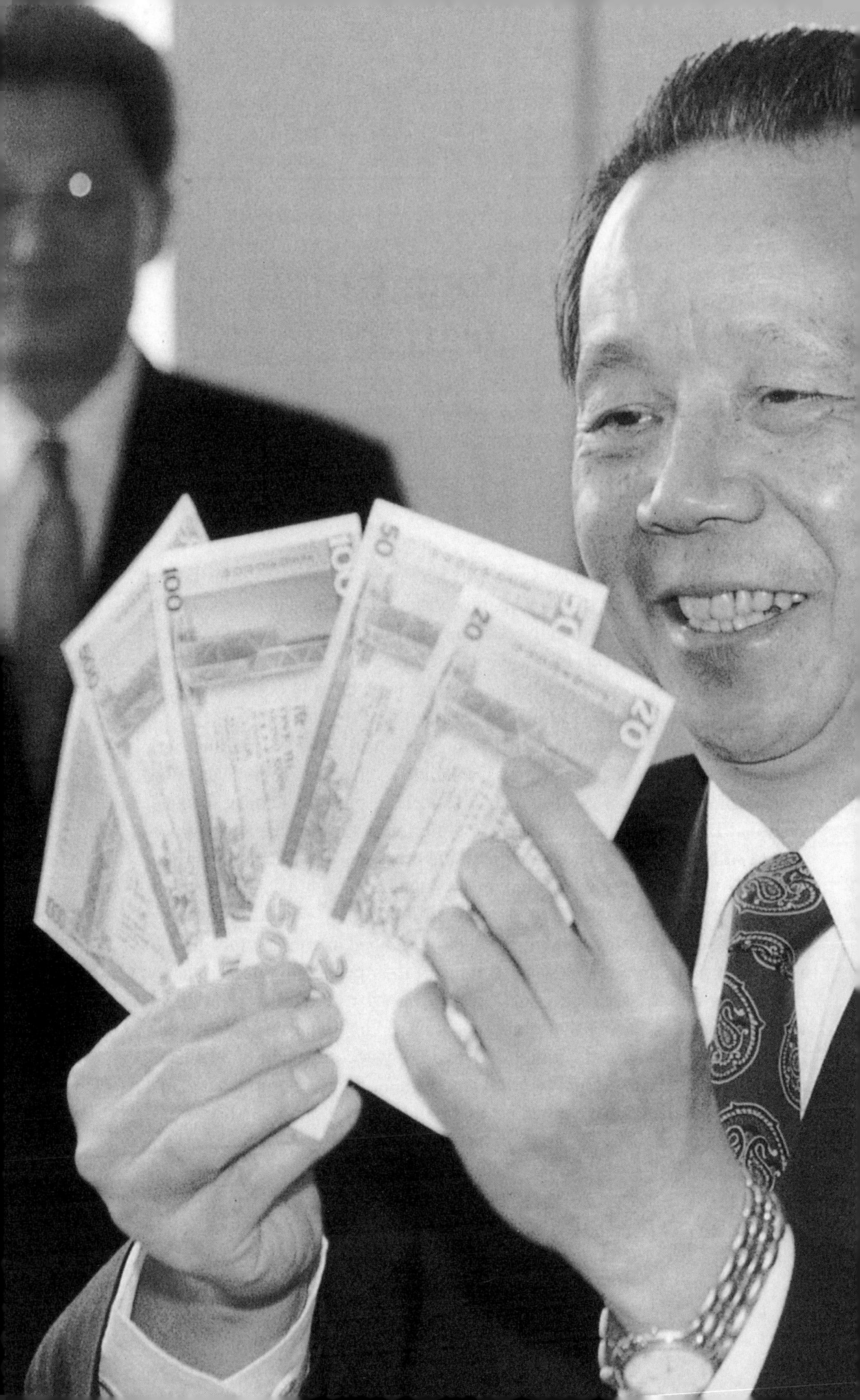

direct investment with technology transfer. Thanks to China's open door policy and Hong Kong manufacturers' profit-oriented decision to take advantage of such a policy, the process of economic integration was started.

Even without China opening its doors and the establishment of Special Economic Zones (SEZs) in Shenzhen and Zhuhai, Hong Kong manufacturers would have to move their operations elsewhere in the face of rising labour and land costs in order to maintain competitiveness and augment profits. China's economic reform merely made investing in China the obvious choice. Nevertheless, China's subsequent decision in the late 1980s to opt for a socialist market economy in preference to its former centrally planned economy added impetus to Hong Kong manufacturers' moving process, because the policy change was tantamount to China taking a positive step to integrate itself into the global economic mechanism.

Before China opened its doors to foreign investors, some Hong Kong manufacturers had already shifted part of their operations or started new ones in developing countries both within the region, such as Sri Lanka and Thailand, and in other parts of the world, such as Mauritius and countries in West Africa. Yet such investments did not lead to Hong Kong's economic integration with these countries due to the quantum of investment involved and, perhaps more importantly, cultural and geographical factors. China's geographical proximity and cultural similarity, plus attractive tax incentives, not only encouraged many local industrialists to take up the China option, but virtually caused a "northern exodus." From Hong Kong's point of view, the ensuing integration was profit-and-need-induced, although China seems to prefer to attribute it to its own "correctness of policy and Hong Kong compatriots' desire to contribute to the building of a socialist motherland."

☐ The Integration Process

Motives aside, the fact remains that what began as a cost reduction step on the part of Hong Kong manufacturers has led to the gradual integration of the two neighbouring economies. This integration has gone through several stages and has involved changes in the roles played by both Hong Kong and China. It all started in Shenzhen, the SEZ adjacent to Hong Kong, later spreading to the Pearl River Delta and eventually to other parts of China.

At first, the Shenzhen SEZ served as a labour-intensive low-cost processing centre for Hong Kong manufacturers. The arrangement was to Hong Kong's advantage, but was not exactly in line with China's objective of setting up the SEZs. True, factories provided employment, but since capital input from Hong Kong consisted mainly of machinery and equipment from abroad, many of which were second-hand or used, capital inflow was limited. Because most operations were labour-intensive, few capital-intensive or technology-intensive industries were being set up. Also, as most raw materials and semi-processed inputs were imported, foreign exchange outflow was considerable, value added was low and transfer of management know-how and technology inadequate. Moreover, many processing operations brought along pollution. Hence, Hong Kong was the party which gained most in the early stages of the integration process, while China actually suffered some disadvantages.

During this earlier stage of China's open door policy, many of Hong Kong's labour-intensive manufacturing industries had been moved to Shenzhen and the Pearl River Delta. These industries included food processing, garment-making, and the manufacturing of radios, plastics, watches and clocks, toys, and electronic products. Had it not been for export quotas held by Hong Kong, the whole textiles industry might also have moved from Hong Kong to China. Hong Kong thus underwent a structural change, transforming itself from a manufacturing centre to a service centre. With most of the manufacturing process being done across the border, former factories became management and design offices, coordinating production, marketing and sales functions by fully utilizing the finance, telecommunications and transportation facilities available locally. China, on the other hand, became a provider of cheap labour and land. Obviously, cooperation with Hong Kong at such a low level did little to help China realize its goal of developing the Shenzhen SEZ or the Pearl River Delta into an economically efficient industrial base.

But this China–Hong Kong relationship changed as time went by. Among the factors that caused such changes, two important ones should be cited. The first was the eagerness of the Chinese workforce to learn and improve, especially those with higher levels of education whose technical capabilities were as good as, if not better than, their Hong Kong counterparts. The second was China's determination to use Hong Kong as a channel through which to induct foreign capital, technology, equipment and knowledge to build up its own industries in Shenzhen and the Pearl River Delta. These led to a more healthy relationship between the two working partners, gradually elevating the level of cooperation. The changing role of China in this process was reflected through Hong Kong's re-exports, consisting mostly of trade with China, which showed a steady increase.

For instance, in 1979, Hong Kong's re-exports originating from China amounted to HK$1,315.17 million; in 1993, the figure was HK$474,007.39 million. These figures imply that the economies of China and Hong Kong became more and more closely integrated during the period, and as Guangdong is traditionally the province leading in exports, the Pearl River Delta witnessed rapid progress in building up its industrial capability alongside Hong Kong's increased investment in the region. Indeed, with Hong Kong's manufacturing sector employing more than three million people in the Pearl River Delta, the division of labour between the two reached a more advanced level. The number of skilled workers and technical staff showed a steady increase, expediting the transfer of technology and know-how, which in turn resulted in Hong Kong-invested manufacturing operations producing higher value added.

Today, the Hong Kong–China tie-up has made the Pearl River Delta the world's largest light industry centre and the world's leading exporter of toys, electronic products and plastic products. In fact, most of the production work of Hong Kong's garment industry was also done in China in accordance with designs originating from Hong Kong and elsewhere, leaving only some essential processes being performed in Hong Kong to meet certificate of origin requirements. With the most-favoured-nation (MFN) issue no longer a threat to China's exports to the U.S. market, it is expected that Hong Kong's investment in China would be increased, and exports from China as well as Hong Kong's re-exports would also rise.

Moreover, there are signs that China's capability in research and development (R&D) has begun to be recognized and utilized, which has also helped raise the technological level and productivity of Hong Kong–China joint ventures in the SEZs and the Pearl River Delta. Here, China's role as an originator and innovator and Hong Kong's role as a catalyst of R&D and commercializing agent for research results originating from China, when further developed, have promising potentials and will benefit both parties.

Expansion into Infrastructure and the Tertiary Sector

China–Hong Kong integration entered a new stage when Hong Kong investors started to divert their investments into sectors other than manufacturing. These have included infrastructure and the tertiary sector. Two outstanding examples of infrastructure investments were the Daya Bay Nuclear Power Station and the Guangzhou–Shenzhen–Zhuhai Expressway, in which the China Light and Power Company Limited and Hopewell Holdings, both public companies listed on the Stock Exchange of Hong Kong, were involved, respectively. The former is already in operation and the latter has been partially completed. Hopewell has recently formed the Consolidated Electric Power Co., Ltd., another listed company, to oversee its investments in this field.

The earliest foreign investments in China's tertiary sector were in hotels and tourism, and many Hong Kong investors are today either joint owners of or management agents for leading hotels in China. Such investments are not limited to the SEZs but cover most major cities in all parts of China.

In the financial sector, many local and foreign banks in Hong Kong have for many years been actively engaged in doing business with China. In the earlier days, they provided funding or guarantees for most, if not all, Hong Kong-related investment projects in China, and China itself utilized on numerous occasions syndicated loans extended by banks in Hong Kong to finance domestic projects. More recently, local Hong Kong banks and foreign banks with Hong Kong as their regional base started to establish agencies in China, some of them upgraded to branches. Today, the Hong Kong Monetary Authority is in close touch with the People's Bank of China to exchange views and ideas on matters of mutual interest.

On the securities side, the Stock Exchange of Hong Kong and the Hong Kong Securities and Futures Commission entered into a Memorandum of Regulatory Cooperation with the China Securities Regulatory Commission, Shanghai Securities Exchange and Shenzhen Stock Exchange in 1993, and many Chinese state enterprises have since been listed on the Stock Exchange of Hong Kong. In addition, China-related companies ranging from central, provincial and municipal-backed entities to those controlled by sons or close relatives of top Party cadres have acquired shares in many Hong Kong companies. Capital from China has also been very active in purchasing residential and commercial property on the local market. All these have made China and Hong Kong more closely knitted together, rendering them economically more interdependent.

China's vast consumer market is always a big attraction to foreign investors and many Hong Kong-based companies are today running operations, setting up branches or establishing direct sale channels in China. They include department stores, fast food chains, brand name outlets for Hong Kong or foreign-made wearing apparel and accessories, duty free shops, and cosmetics and household appliances. A Hong Kong-based company has even helped reorganize South China's domestic distribution channels and developed its own distribution and support facilities.

Real estate development in China is another area where large sums of foreign capital are involved. Major property developers in Hong Kong are today involved in real estate development in Shanghai, Beijing, and Wuhan, to name a few. Most projects involve the development of a whole area, with commercial and residential complexes involving billions of Hong Kong dollars. Since the latter part of last year, as a result of the credit squeeze and the ensuing capital shortage for housing projects in many cities, Hong Kong property developers have been encouraged to build residential quarters to relocate thousands of people so that their former homes could be demolished and the whole area redeveloped for commercial and residential purposes. This, coupled with numerous housing projects financed by Hong Kong capital in cities and suburban areas in Guangdong Province, signifies Hong Kong's increasing involvement in China's effort to ease its housing shortage and to form a property market.

Two-way Flow of Capital

But economic relations between Hong Kong and China are by no means limited to Hong Kong capital flowing into China. China started to invest in Hong Kong from the very early days, and Chinese capital became very active in Hong Kong after China's economic reform. Today, there are many state, provincial and municipal-level companies operating in Hong Kong in a wide spectrum of business. They engage in trading, banking, shipping, travel, hotels and restaurants, wholesaling and retailing, real estate and property development, and so on. As already mentioned, many state enterprises are now listed on the Stock Exchange of Hong Kong, and more are forthcoming. This signifies that Hong Kong's capital market, which has access to international capital, is now at China's service.

On 2 May 1994, the Bank of China became the third bank in Hong Kong to issue Hong Kong dollar banknotes. Although the move was largely symbolic, it was of historical importance because it marked the first instance for a bank with headquarters in China to issue Hong Kong's legal tender.

In fact, the integration of the two economies through Hong Kong's investment in the manufacturing and non-manufacturing sectors, has from the very beginning helped China foster a market economy. Employment opportunities arising from such investments have not only gradually increased labour mobility in China but also helped enhance fair treatment of labour. At first, China had provided foreign invested entities with workers on contract basis, but later foreign concerns were able to recruit workers, especially skilled and white-collar ones, with more freedom. In other words, Hong Kong's investment in China has helped form a labour market, one of the prerequisites of a market economy.

There is no denying that when China first opened its doors to the outside world, the required infrastructure and legal framework to provide an attractive and competitive environment to foreign investors were almost totally lacking. Thanks to the mutual efforts of concerned parties in China and Hong Kong, the situation has since seen much improvement. Today, China is in a position to reassess its policy in respect of SEZs, and there is every indication that China aims to make structural adjustment by discouraging labour-intensive industries in the coastal region. Instead, SEZs are to produce high value-added products requiring higher levels of technology geared for distribution in overseas markets. For this purpose, it is expected that more efforts will be exerted on the part of China to improve the investment environment and to accelerate the speed towards a market economy. This will in turn make it necessary for Hong Kong to upgrade its service capabilities and to make further progress in restructuring its economy to cope with new and changing circumstances. If everything goes well, China's and Hong Kong's further economic integration will bring benefits to both parties.

Negative and Positive Factors

However, recent economic woes in China, such as a high rate of inflation, credit squeeze, unemployment, natural calamities, continued losses sustained by state enterprises, and so on, have become negative factors to economic integration. Also, China's efforts in reforming its tax laws, while a step in the right direction, have caused some concern among Hong Kong investors, especially the introduction of a value added tax which is to be levied on a wide spectrum of business activities, including manufacturing, sales and real estate transactions. On the other hand, China's inability to effectively enforce the laws protecting intellectual property rights such as patents, copyrights and brand names forms a deterring factor which hampers foreign investment. And high inflation leading to increases in property prices and rentals of shops and offices has rendered many retail operations unprofitable. Furthermore, there is a tendency to either control profits or limit the profit margins of Hong Kong investors, such as in power generation and housing projects. How these negative factors would affect further China–Hong Kong integration remains to be seen.

But U.S. President Bill Clinton's decision in early June to delink trade and human rights came as encouraging news, because Hong Kong investors operating factories in China with the U.S. market as their most important source of income would no longer have to worry about the loss of China's MFN status and its adverse effect on their export business. This would in turn encourage further investments not only from Hong Kong but from other potential foreign investors, provided, of course, that China's political and economic climate remained favourable.

☐ Effects of Integration

The China–Hong Kong economic integration has many ramifications. As already mentioned, the process started with Hong Kong moving its manufacturing operations to the SEZs in Guangdong Province. Today, not only has the integration developed into what may be called the core of a South China Economic Region encompassing Hong Kong, Macau, Guangdong, Fujian and Taiwan, Hong Kong investors have also extended their activities to other parts of China. The economies of Hong Kong and the Pearl River Delta are so closely knitted together that a borderless economy has truly emerged. It is now common knowledge that almost 80 per cent of goods produced in the Pearl River Delta are exported to or through Hong Kong, which also supplies about 70 per cent of merchandise imported to the Pearl River Delta. Also, Hong Kong is now the most important source of capital not only to the Pearl River Delta, but to the whole of China.

From China's point of view, such integration, though beneficial to the economy, leaves much to be desired. From the very beginning, China would have preferred to have more overall planning in the development of the SEZs and more control over the type of manufacturing operations to be set up by foreign investors. However, today the Pearl River Delta has an over-concentration of light industries, mainly labour-intensive sub-sectors such as textiles, toys and electronics, with their products duplicating each other and lacking sectoral division of work and coordination. Also, infrastructure is still inadequate, and land and sea transportation between Shenzhen and Hong Kong remains at bottleneck. Over-dependence upon Hong Kong as a trade channel and service centre also worries China, which may be part of the reason why the Chinese government is determined to develop Shanghai in order for it to regain its pre-1949 status as China's most important commercial and financial centre.

On the more negative side, there are Party cadres who view the open door policy with reservations and are worried about the influence of Western bourgeois decadence on China. Their worries are not without justification. Moral standards have changed. Prostitution, drugs, gambling and other crimes have been on the increase. Corruption is rampant. All these, plus the fact that it is almost impossible to control the spread of information. As people living in the coastal regions can have easy access to TV telecasts from stations across the border, the gap between the coastal region and the rest of China has widened.

Hong Kong seemingly has everything to gain from economically integrating with China. Business with China has been flourishing and money-making opportunities are abundant. Many foreign investors are concerned that because of the lack of a clear-cut legal framework, risks are high. They have such an attitude because they do not understand the old Chinese saying that "it is easier to catch fish in muddled water," the meaning of which is appreciated by many ethnic Chinese. In China, *guanxi* is always important, and good *guanxi* with the right people goes a long way in getting things done.

At the time China opened its doors to the outside world, Hong Kong was facing stiff competition from the other "three little dragons of Asia." By 1985, Hong Kong was lagging behind its peers both in terms of gross domestic product (GDP) growth and labour productivity increase, as shown in Tables 1 and 2.

Hong Kong's lower GDP and productivity growth during the first half of the 1980s compared with the other "little dragons" was due to rising costs and lack of R&D which in turn resulted in stagnation in technological advancement. By 1985, China's economic reform had achieved remarkable success, the signing of the Joint Declaration on the future of Hong Kong

Table 1. Comparison of GDP Growth at Constant Prices (1980 = 100)

	1981	1982	1983	1984	1985
Hong Kong	109.42	112.63	119.98	131.68	132.79
South Korea	107.41	113.51	122.92	136.81	143.86
Singapore	109.94	116.92	126.13	136.54	134.05
Taiwan	106.13	109.07	117.47	128.70	133.96

Source: National Accounts published by respective governments.

Table 2. Comparison of Productivity Growth at Constant Prices (1980 = 100)

	1981	1982	1983	1984	1985
Hong Kong	103.81	105.77	110.47	116.00	114.57
South Korea	104.52	107.86	118.90	130.07	132.02
Singapore	106.42	104.41	116.45	125.27	125.14
Taiwan	104.15	104.84	108.18	115.30	118.32

Source: Asian Productivity Organization, Tokyo.

had instilled a factor of stability into China–Hong Kong relations, and Hong Kong had moved and was continuing to move the labour-intensive portion of its manufacturing operations to Shenzhen and the Pearl River Delta, all of which caused the improvement of Hong Kong's labour productivity growth which began to compare favourably with the other "little dragons" (Table 3). However, it should be noted that Hong Kong's productivity grew at a higher rate than the other "little dragons" because of a lower base in 1985.

Table 3. Comparison of Productivity Growth at Constant Prices (1985 = 100)

	1986	1987	1988	1989	1990	1991	1992
Hong Kong	109.33	122.58	130.98	135.69	140.17	141.84	149.48
South Korea	108.52	115.26	124.57	127.31	134.76	142.24	146.29
Singapore	102.31	107.86	115.47	122.29	127.64	142.24	—
Taiwan	107.24	116.13	123.33	130.26	136.49	143.33	149.36

Source: Asian Productivity Organization, Tokyo.

Improvement in Hong Kong's labour productivity may be attributed to structural change in Hong Kong, with employment shifting from the manufacturing to the service sector, resulting in higher value added and higher productivity. Such structural change which started in the mid-1980s was a direct result of Hong Kong moving labour-intensive manufacturing operations to China. Since Hong Kong benefited from such changes, it follows that economic integration with China has had a positive effect on Hong Kong in raising productivity.

But was Hong Kong really the leader in productivity among the "four little dragons" because of its integration with China? The answer is quite dubious. This is because although in terms of absolute level of productivity, i.e., value added production per employed person, Hong Kong was behind Singapore, but much higher than South Korea and Taiwan. Yet when the over 3,000 factories and almost four million workers producing for Hong Kong are considered as actually constituting an extension of Hong Kong's manufacturing sector, then Hong Kong's productivity would be pulled downwards. Table 4 compares the productivity levels of the "four little dragons," Guangdong and China to illustrate this point.

Table 4. Index of Labour Productivity Levels — 1990
(In 1980 constant U.S. dollars, Hong Kong = 100)

Singapore	103.65
Hong Kong	100.00
Taiwan	62.19
South Korea	49.33
Guangdong	8.83
China	6.79

Thus, moving manufacturing operations to China also had some negative effects on Hong Kong. First, for any economy to achieve a higher level of development, it is essential for it to transform its production activities from factor-driven to technology-driven. In the face of competition, Singapore, South Korea and Taiwan all made efforts in the late 1970s and early 1980s to raise their technological levels. Whereas Singapore opted for high-level technology, South Korea and Taiwan established science parks to engage in R&D. Hong Kong's manufacturing sector, however, found a hinterland in China to provide cheap labour and land for its manufacturing operations. On the surface, Hong Kong seemed to have regained its competitiveness, but as a result, the gap between Hong Kong and its competitors widened. By expanding its manufacturing sector to China, Hong Kong continued to rely on production factors, while the others overtook Hong Kong by elevating themselves to the technology-driven stage of development.

Second, although Hong Kong's manufacturing sector compared favourably with the other three economies in terms of labour productivity, the sector's contribution to GDP dropped from 23.8 per cent in 1980 to less than 15 per cent in 1992. Domestic exports of locally manufactured products also showed a decrease in recent years. What remains as the manufacturing sector today in Hong Kong is mainly engaged in design, planning, management and that portion of production process necessary to meet certificate of origin requirements under Hong Kong's "entitled" export quotas. Granted that there are instances of high-technology manufacturing activities in Hong Kong; however, as the vast majority of manufacturing work is now done in China, the overall technological level has not seen significant advancement over the years when compared with the other three "little dragons." It may even be said that because economic integration with China in the 1980s relieved Hong Kong of the need to elevate its technological level, it actually hampered Hong Kong's industrial development.

Third, one of the spin-off effects of economic integration was the wide acceptance of the Hong Kong dollar in SEZs and other parts of China as a *de facto* legal tender. It is estimated that over HK$22 billion, or 30 per cent of Hong Kong's banknotes, are now circulating inside China. On the other hand, many banks and shops in Hong Kong started to accept Renminbi, the Chinese currency, last year when China allowed each outward traveller to bring out a maximum of RMB 6,000. While there is no estimate of the amount of Renminbi in Hong Kong, it is believed to be quite substantial and on the increase. Despite established channels to absorb massive return flows of their respective currencies from across the border, both Hong Kong and China are concerned about the possible impact of such return flows. Assuming that no serious problem would arise, the cross flow of currencies has made it doubly important to maintain a stable exchange rate not only between them, but with the U.S. dollar to which the Hong Kong dollar is pegged. This implies that China would not like any changes to the present linkage between Hong Kong and U.S. dollars. In view of the linkage system's adverse impact on Hong Kong's economy, including negative interest rates which is the direct culprit of speculation in both the stock and property markets, the China–Hong Kong integration indirectly prolongs this undesirable arrangement.

Changing of Development Paths

Nevertheless, economic integration did bring about Hong Kong's structural change and did help quicken China's transition from a centrally planned economy to a market economy. This has been achieved through the changing of the development paths of both entities.

When Hong Kong's economy took off in the mid-1970s, it followed a similar development path as that of the other "little dragons" of South Korea, Singapore and Taiwan and, to a certain extent, that of Japan. That path may be described as "importation of a new product — domestic production — export of the same product." At a later stage, these newly industrializing economies, or NIEs, perhaps with the sole exception of Hong Kong, started to engage in R&D with a view to elevating the level of technology, so that they could improve their domestic product to compete better on the world market. Their development path then became "importation — domestic production — elevation of technological level and export." Later, when their own production costs became too high, they sought investment overseas to have access to cheaper labour and land, thus adding "overseas investment" to their development process.

As Hong Kong was lagging behind in R&D and also faced rising labour and land costs, a shadow of doubt began to be cast on its economic future. Luckily, China launched its economic reform programme at that time and Hong Kong found a way out by investing in China. Thus, Hong Kong's development experience became different from the other NIEs and took the path of "domestic production for export — investment in the hinterland (China) to extend manufacturing operations to adjacent localities — expansion of export." In this process, the technological level of Hong Kong's products did not have the same degree of improvement as the other NIEs and, as mentioned earlier, Hong Kong's economic development continued to be factor-driven instead of technology-driven.

China's development path underwent fundamental changes following its open door and economic reform policies. The most significant ingredient causing such changes was the introduction of the market element. Although even today, the Chinese Communist Party still claims to have communism as its final goal, in practice it is aimed at building a market economy with Chinese socialist characteristics. For decades, China's planned economy emphasized the importance of having a strong heavy industries sector, with the required capital mainly drawn from the primary sector. Also, the economy was biased towards production and state-regulated distribution. Economic reform started in the late 1970s led to the collapse of the earlier economy pattern, which in turn resulted in the emergence of a free market for agricultural products. This helped increase the income of the farmers which in turn created a new demand for consumer goods for the first time since the founding of the People's Republic of China. When economic reform was introduced to the secondary sector in the mid-1980s, the consumer boom also spread to the urban areas. It was at that time that

China's economic reform reached a point of no return, and China had no alternative but to pursue a new development path.

This new path involved the mass import of consumer goods to satisfy domestic demand, making it necessary to export domestic products to earn the necessary foreign exchange. The whole planned production system had to undergo changes to cope with new circumstances. Trade with the Western world, in particular with the United States, the bastion of capitalism as well as the economic locomotive, became essential. Thus, China's development started to fit in the "domestic production for export — investment to expand manufacturing operations — expansion of exports" pattern, albeit with some variance. Domestic production for export was done in the SEZs, helped by manufacturing facilities moved in from Hong Kong, investment was supplemented by the inflow of foreign capital, and expansion of exports was to a considerable degree accelerated by economic integration of the southern coastal region with Hong Kong. Also, like almost all developing economies, light industries became the mainstay of the export trade.

It is interesting to note that changes in development paths of both Hong Kong and China have converged into a pattern with common features. Of course, China is a big country and the SEZs in Guangdong do not represent the whole of China. Yet there is no denying that the economic integration and convergence have made the two entities mutually complementary and have contributed to the economic prosperity of both entities.

☐ Outlook

As stated at the beginning of this chapter, before the political integration of Hong Kong with China in 1997, economic integration has already taken place. With the convergence of development paths mentioned above, the future of China and Hong Kong is closely tied together. The fact that China is one of the major economic powers of the world in terms of GDP, whereas Hong Kong, at least for the present, ranks higher than China in terms of external trade, means that their economic integration is a phenomenon of importance not only to China but to the world community as a whole.

The future of Hong Kong, as spelt out by the Joint Declaration and the Basic Law, is based on the principle of "one country, two systems," one country meaning China, and two systems, socialism and capitalism. But things have turned out that, at least economically, China and Hong Kong are both on a similar development path heading for a free market economy which is characteristic of a capitalist economic system. But politically, when Hong Kong eventually reverts back to China, the Hong Kong SAR will be, again according to the Joint Declaration and the Basic Law, highly autonomous and "governed by the people of Hong Kong." In other words, under one country, there will be two administrative entities, but economically they will function in a symbiotic manner, sharing the same economic system in their mutual pursuance of stability and prosperity. In effect, therefore, when the SAR government is truly highly autonomous, the China–Hong Kong economic integration will lead to "two (administrative) entities, one (economic) system" after 1 July 1997.

Assuming that such a relationship between China and Hong Kong prevails and does not change for 50 years, further economic integration will bind the two entities more closely together. However, the development curves of China and Hong Kong are different. China, starting at a much lower base, is still on the lower side of the curve and has a lot of room to climb upwards, whereas Hong Kong, being at a more advanced stage of economic development, can not expect to continue to grow much further. Moreover, Hong Kong's economic growth is limited by technology shortcomings, whereas China has much better potential in technology advancement. Hence, it may be said that Hong Kong's future is more dependent upon China's economic growth than vice versa, and future development prospects are brighter for China than for Hong Kong.

Index

access to information xviii, 4, 6, 84, 85, 404–7
Ad Hoc Pre-Primary Education Working Group 312
adequate housing 191, 269–71, 282, 283, 288
Advisory Committee on Teacher Education and Qualifications (ACTEQ) 302, 309
Advisory Council on the Environment (ACE) 260
affirmative action against discrimination 163, 164
ageing 315, 317, 319, 327
Agenda 21 255
air pollution 213, 244, 258–60
Airport Authority 215, 218, 221
airport construction xvii, xviii, 77, 218
  financing proposals 218
Airport Consultative Committee xiii
Airport Corporation xvi, 218
Akers-Jones, Sir David ix, xvii, 212

Alliance in Support of the Patriotic Movement in China xi
American Chamber of Commerce xxiii, 26
Anti-Speculation Task Force 189, 207
Appropriation Bill 5
April 5th Action Group 93
Archives Ordinance 406
Armstrong, David 394
Asia Pacific Economic Cooperation (APEC) viii, 431, 438
Asia Television Limited (ATV) 84, 390, 464
Asian Wall Street Journal 395
Asprey, Alistair xiv, 56, 57
asset inflation 129–31, 143, 144
Association for Democracy and People's Livelihood (ADPL) 79, 119, 121, 122, 123
Association of Expatriate Civil Servants 54
Association of Lecturers at Colleges of Education 303, 306

Legend: † place names

Association of South East Asian
  Nations (ASEAN)   145
Attorney General   xv, xviii, 27, 55,
  56, 373, 408
†Australia   53, 63, 168–71, 175, 208,
  435
autonomy   39, 50, 58, 59, 61, 63–65,
  67–69, 71, 72, 74, 75, 143, 145,
  292, 300, 303, 355, 357, 429,
  431–33, 435–37, 441, 451
Aw Sian, Sally   395

baby-boomers   128, 129
Bank of China   viii, xxii, 475
Barma, Haider   55, 57
Basic Law   xii, xiii, xiv, xvi, xix,
  xxxii, xxxiii, 1, 8, 9, 11, 13, 22, 32,
  36, 41, 46, 52, 53, 55, 64–70, 75,
  77, 78, 80–83, 87, 88, 98–100, 136,
  145, 157, 178, 181, 183, 334, 370,
  379, 385, 400, 410, 431, 433,
  435–38, 445, 469, 483, 484
Basic Law Consultative Committee
  69
Basic Law Drafting Committee   65, 69
BBC World Service   xix, xx, 84
Bilingual Laws Advisory Committee
  (BLAC)   12
Bill of Rights   xiv, 3, 54, 69, 85, 163,
  369, 408, 411
Bill of Rights Ordinance (BORO)   7,
  13, 405, 409–12
Biodiversity Convention   254
Blake, Sir Henry   7
Board of Education   301, 305, 309,
  312
brain drain   165, 170, 427
British Dependent Territories Citizens
  (BDTC)   54, 181, 182, 440

British Foreign Office   72
British National (Overseas) (BNO)
  xiv, 181–84
British Nationality Scheme   vii, xxi,
  58, 184
British Official Secrets Act   408
British Overseas Citizens (BOC)
  182, 183
Buckle, Jim   27, 28, 30–33, 35
Buffer Zone   257
Bush, George   431
Business and Professional Federation
  93

Cable News Network (CNN)   397
†Canada   25, 53, 96, 168–71, 175,
  208, 431, 434, 435, 437
Capital Works Fund   293
Castle Peak power plant explosion   x,
  xv, xxiv
central government   25, 61, 63, 65,
  67, 68, 75, 100, 138, 357
Central People's Government,
  Chinese   41, 48, 59, 436, 437
central provident fund (CPF)   149,
  159, 322, 323, 327–29
Certificate of Identity   182
certificate of origin requirements
  473, 481
Chan Cho-chak, John   xii, xxi
Chan Fang On-sang, Anson   vii, x,
  xii, xx, xxiv, 28, 54, 55, 57, 85, 373,
  375, 407, 431
Chan Kam-pui   232, 234
Chan Nai-keong, Nicky   xxi, xxiii
Chan Wa-shek   xxi
†Chek Lap Kok   xxxii, 71, 77, 138,
  139, 174, 211, 215–17, 221, 236,
  245 (*see also* replacement airport)

Index

Chen, Edward xiv
Cheung Bing-leung, Anthony vii, xxii, xxiii, 70, 79
Chief Executive xiv, 25, 33, 36, 41, 46, 56, 68, 70, 337, 356
Chief Justice vii, xvii, xix, 13, 14, 16, 66, 343
Chim Pui-chung ix
China International Trust and Investment Corporation (CITIC) xviii, xxii
China Light and Power (CLP) ix, x, xxiv, 213, 259, 474
China Motor Bus (CMB) 221, 225, 226, 247–49
China National Education Committee 424
China National Planned Parenthood Committee 424
China Securities Regulatory Commission 474
China Times 392
Chinese Communist Party (CCP) xiv, xxxv, 34, 64, 65, 67, 69, 70, 74, 89, 482
Chinese Constitution 64
Chinese government advisory bodies 379
Chinese Radio International 396
Chinese Sex Education Association 424
Chinese State Security Law 397
cholera bacteria 263
Chow Liang Shuk-yee, Selina xvii, 118, 120, 121, 343
Chow, Stephen 461, 464
Chugani, Michael 395
Chung, Sir S. Y. xv, 356
Citibank 142

Citizens Liaison Group 37
Citybus 221, 225, 248, 249
Civil Aviation Department 221
civil servants v, x, xii, xvi, xxi, xxiii, xxiv, 4, 23, 25, 31, 33–35, 39, 41–47, 50, 54, 56, 58, 59, 69, 71, 77, 85, 149, 163, 164, 225, 250, 251, 372, 376–78, 405
  directorate grade, accountability 42, 46, 48, 49
  directorate grade, localization 51–59
  directorate grade, relationship with China xxii, 47–51
  directorate grade, relationship with the Legco 42–47
  expatriate x, xxiv, 54, 85, 163, 164
  females on directorate pay scale 378
  local Chinese 85
civil service x, xi, xv, xvi, xxxii, 6, 41, 50–59, 62, 79, 84, 89, 163, 164, 184, 303, 324, 342, 355, 372, 376, 381, 382, 396, 404
Civil Service Branch 3, 33, 55
Civil Service Regulations 52
Climate Change Convention 254
Clinton, Bill xxiv, 431, 477
Coalition Against Sexual Abuse 372
Coalition of Councillors for the Equality of Women and Men 369
Code of Practice on Access to Government Information 407
Commercial Crime Bureau 30
Commercial Radio 396
Commissioner for Administrative Complaints (COMAC) xvi, xvii, 70, 84, 407
Commissioner for Rehabilitation 346

Commissioner of Police   ix, 55
Commissioner of the Independent Commission Against Corruption   2, 55, 57
Committee on Home-School Cooperation   300
Committee on Public Education in Rehabilitation (COMPERE)   343
common law system   9, 65
community care   315, 320, 335
Community Chest   348
Comprehensive Social Security Assistance (CSSA)   339–42
Confederation of Trade Unions   326
Conservancy Association   255
Consolidated Electric Power Co.   474
Constitutional Development Panel   408
constitutional reforms   ix, xv, xix, xxi, xxii, xxv, xxxi, xxxii, 112, 113, 116, 434
Consumer Council   x, 21
consumer expenditure   128
Consumer Legal Action Fund   21
Consumer Price Index (A) [CPI(A)]   129, 131, 132
container port   vii, 211, 222, 241–43, 429
container terminal   xxxii, 130, 138, 211, 219, 220, 242, 243, 445
Convention on International Trade in Endangered Species (CITES)   xiii
Convention on the Elimination of All Forms of Discrimination Against Women (CEDAW)   367–69, 381
corruption   v, vii, xii, xvii, xx, xxxii, 2, 18, 23, 25–33, 35–38, 55, 62, 86, 89, 225, 233, 372, 399, 409, 478
cost-recovery charges in medical services   355, 358, 361

Council for Professional Conduct in Education (CPCE)   302, 303, 314
counselling service   339
Court of Final Appeal   xix, 11, 16, 17, 22, 66
Cradock, Percy   xv, xxii, 77
Crimes Ordinance   410
Croft, Michael William   27, 30
cross-border freight movement   237, 242
Cultural Revolution   64
culture
  new corporate   357
  of affluence   450–54, 457
  of deliverance   455, 457
  of survival   453, 454, 457
Customer Service Assistance Scheme   295

†Daya Bay   xviii, 90, 255, 473
de Speville, Bertrand   2, 27–32, 36, 57
de-industrialization   132, 144, 145
Deep Bay pollution abatement plan   262
demand and supply parameters   201
Democratic Alliance for Betterment of Hong Kong (DAB)   78, 93, 119, 121, 122, 382
Deng Xiaoping   xii, xxxi, 64, 127, 134, 137
Department of Health   364
Development Fund   189, 292, 293
development path   482, 483
Director of Education   71, 303, 305, 310, 313, 391
discrimination   xxviii, 4, 7, 21, 22, 96, 163, 164, 307, 320, 331, 343, 344, 367, 368, 370–72

Index

District Boards (DB)   12, 78, 79, 89, 93, 94, 98, 238, 239, 251, 343, 355, 369, 375–78, 381–83
divorce mediation   333, 334, 347
domestic exports   128, 134, 480
domestic servants   173, 174
dual system in health care provision   353, 362
Duanmu Zheng   9, 65

Earth Summit   254–56, 259, 264
ease of travel   182, 183
Eason, A. G.   57, 263
Eastern Express   xix, 84, 392
Economic and Trade Offices   437, 438
economic integration   xxxiv, 136, 141, 145, 147, 469, 471, 476, 477, 479, 481, 483, 484
Education and Manpower Branch   309, 323
Education Commission   xiv, 305, 308, 309, 311, 313
  Report No. 4 (ECR4)   307, 309
  Report No. 5 (ECR5)   302
Education Department   299–304, 307, 309, 311–13, 344, 421–23
Education Services Liaison Group   300, 304
education
  funding of   311–12
  language in   303, 306–8
  mother tongue education   306, 307
  pre-primary education   312
  quality in   308, 310
effective demand   201, 206, 207, 283, 284
elderly care and service planning   315, 319
elderly population   317, 318, 322, 323

elderly women   viii, 320
election arrangements   x, xii, xiii, xix, xxxi, xxxii, 1, 2, 78, 82
election committee   1, 78
electoral reforms   x, xv, xxiv, xxv, 1, 70
electricity   209, 213, 214, 219, 260, 270
Emergency Regulations Ordinance   408, 409
emigration   vi, xxviii, 151, 165, 168, 170–73, 176, 177, 180, 184–86, 427
Employees Retraining Board   156, 371
employment tax   149, 161
energy
  energy conservation   258
  energy consumption   256, 258, 259
  energy resources   258, 259
  energy supply   255, 259, 264
Energy Efficiency Advisory Committee   256, 259, 261
environmental
  environmental challenge   25
  environmental impact assessments (EIAs)   254
  environmental problems   212
  environmental protection   205, 209, 222, 255, 263, 423, 434 (*see also* green groups)
Environmental and Conservation Fund   261
Environmental Campaign Committee (ECC)   260, 261
Environmental Protection Department (EPD)   254–56, 260, 261, 263
equal employment opportunity   163, 164
Equal Opportunities Bill   xxiv, 21

Equal Opportunities Commission xix, 367, 369, 373
Exchange Fund ix
Executive Council (Exco) 5, 20, 21, 30, 62, 84, 89, 223, 226, 250, 251, 292, 322, 323, 373, 375, 404, 408, 412
exports 126, 128, 130, 133–36, 211, 472, 473, 480, 483
Express Daily xi
external trade 133, 143, 483

family
  family aide 335, 337
  family care 335
  family carers 320
  family reunification 158
  family services
    family service centres 335, 347, 348
    shortfall of 336
Family Court 333, 334
Family Planning Association of Hong Kong (FPAHK) 416, 417, 420–22
Fan Hsu Lai-tai, Rita xiv, xxii, 30, 34, 70, 402
Federation for a Stable and Prosperous Hong Kong 93
Federation of Educational Workers 306
fertility 151, 154–56, 158, 162, 169, 177, 186, 324, 325
Film Censorship Ordinance 410
Financial Secretary viii, ix, xxiii, 4–6, 55, 56, 373, 431, 438
Fok Lo Shiu-ching, Katherine xxv, 57
Fok, Henry xiv
forced saving 161, 162
Ford, Michael ix

Ford, Sir David vii, xi, xii, xv, xxix, xxxv, 55
Foreign Affairs Committee (FAC) xiii, xvii, xviii, xxi, 68, 73, 86, 398
Foreign Correspondents Club (FCC) 401, 403
foreign missions 435–37
foreign nationals 174, 176
Foreign Office 72, 77, 436
formal political participation index 92
freedom
  of expression 390, 391, 405, 407, 411
  of movement xi, xxxi, 180
freight transport industry
  container storage 241–42
  daytime parking and loading/unloading 239–40
  freight transport policy 236
  freight transport study 226, 235
  overnight parking 237–39
Friedman, Milton xiii
frontloaded pricing strategy (FPS) 229, 230
Fung, Daniel xxiv

Garcia, Arthur xvi, xxi
gas xxi, 209, 219, 256–59
gender consciousness 381, 383–87
gender equality viii, 118, 367, 368, 370, 372, 383, 385–87, 466, 467
General Sympathy Strike 91
global economy 168, 170, 176, 429
Goodlad, Alastair xiii, xviii, 401
government advisory bodies 379
Government House vii, xvii, 33, 393, 431
Government Information Services 437, 438

Index

Government Secretariat   265, 309, 322, 323, 439
green groups   255, 260–63 (*see also* environmental protection)
Green Paper on Equal Opportunities for Women and Men   367, 368
Green Paper on Rehabilitation: Full Participation and Equal Opportunity   342
greenhouse effect   259
gross domestic product (GDP)   125–27, 131, 135, 213–15, 258, 259, 327, 351, 478, 480, 483
†Guangdong   xvi, xvii, 140–42, 145, 177, 178, 243, 263, 399, 473, 475, 477, 480, 483
Guangming Daily   xvi
†Guangzhou   xvi, xxii, xxv, 90, 138, 146
Guangzhou–Shenzhen–Zhuhai Expressway   473
Guo Fengmin   xxiii

Han Dongfang   x, xi, xiv, xxxi, 86
Hang Seng Index   x, xii, xiii, xv, xvi, xviii, xxxii, 130, 445
Hanson, Mike   393
Health and Welfare Branch   340, 356
health care system   352–54, 360, 363–65
health finance   353, 358, 359, 361, 362
Heung Yee Kuk   ix, xx, 8, 89, 90, 369, 370, 374
High Court   x, 12, 14–17
Higher Education 1991–2001: An Interim Report   310
Home Affairs Branch   xiv, 265, 407
home ownership rate   197, 281, 289

Home Ownership Scheme (HOS)   203, 265, 267–69, 275–78, 280–82, 284, 285, 289, 290, 293, 294, 370 (*see also* Private Sector Participation Scheme)
Green Form applicants   275, 284
Home Ownership Scheme Income Limit (HOSIL)   277, 278, 280, 281, 284
HOS/PSPS flats   275, 284, 285, 290
White Form applicants   284
Home Purchase Loan Scheme (HPLS)   275–77, 280, 281, 289
Hong Kong Affairs advisers   xix, xxi, xxii, xxiii, 69, 70, 78, 79, 325, 329, 379, 380
Hong Kong and Macau Affairs Office   ix, xvi, xxxii, 8, 69, 70, 73, 85
Hong Kong Bar Association   14
Hong Kong Boxing Association   29
Hong Kong Chinese Enterprises Association   26
Hong Kong Council of Early Childhood Education and Services   306
Hong Kong Council of Social Service   329, 335
Hong Kong Electric   213
Hong Kong Federation of Trade Unions   122, 326
Hong Kong Federation of Women   370, 372
Hong Kong General Chamber of Commerce   xii, xxii, 26, 404
Hong Kong Institute of Education (HKIEd)   302–4
Hong Kong Journalists Association (HKJA)   xii, xxi, 394, 404, 408, 411
Hong Kong Monetary Authority   474

Hong Kong Polling and Business Research   105, 326
Hong Kong Press Photographers Association   404
Hong Kong Professional Teachers' Union (HKPTU)   302, 306, 309
Hong Kong Securities and Futures Commission   474
Hong Kong Sex Education Association   425, 427
Hong Kong Standard   395
Hong Kong Telecom (HKT)   213, 221, 222
Hong Kong Times   392
Hong Kong Today   391, 392
Hong Kong United Daily   392
Hong Kong's international personality   429, 432, 433, 439
Hong Kong–Guangdong Environmental Protection Liaison Group   263
Hopewell Holdings   474
Hospital Authority   337, 344, 352, 354–64
household size   196, 272, 335
Housing Authority   vii, ix, 189, 265, 267, 269, 272, 273, 275, 281, 288, 290–96, 369
  new financial arrangements   292–94
Housing Department   283, 284, 295, 407
Housing Society   189, 269, 279
Howell, David   xiii
Huang Wenfang   69
Huang Xinhua   393
Huanggang checkpoint   xxiii
Hui Yin-fat   4
human rights   xx, xxi, 20, 21, 56, 72, 73, 85, 86, 100, 151, 163, 405, 477

Human Rights and Equal Opportunities Commission   xix
Human Rights Commission   xxi, xxiii, xxiv, 4, 6, 20, 84, 404
Hung Wing-wah   29
Hurd, Douglas   ix, x, xv, 401
Hutchison Whampoa   xix

illegal immigration   16, 23, 151, 180, 191
immigration   vi, vii, xxviii, 12, 23, 55, 96, 97, 151, 154, 157, 158, 165, 169, 172–74, 176–80, 185, 186, 191, 432, 438
immigration control   165, 185
importation of labour   xxxii, 149, 157, 174, 179
income disparity   135, 147, 329
income eligibility criteria   268, 269
Independent Commission Against Corruption (ICAC)   v, vii, xii, xv, xvi, xvii, xix, xxi, xxxii, 2, 3, 18, 19, 23, 25–38, 55, 233, 372, 409, 413
  Community Relations Department   26
  ICAC Ordinance   27, 34, 36
  Operations Department   26, 27, 30
  Operations Review Committee   28, 30, 33, 34, 36
industrial restructuring   132
inflation   7, 129–32, 135, 143–45, 147, 277, 324, 476
infrastructure   vi, xxxii, 106, 129, 135, 139, 144, 190, 204, 209, 211, 213–15, 222, 228, 235, 253, 270, 293, 331, 473, 476, 477
  infrastructural services   209, 211, 213, 219
  infrastructural spending   213–15

Index

Institute of Language in Education (ILE) 303
integration vi, xxviii, xxxiv, 136, 141, 145, 147, 204, 235, 343, 353–56, 358, 359, 363, 469, 471–73, 475–77, 479, 481, 483, 484
International Court of Justice 73
International Covenant on Civil and Political Rights 1, 72, 412
International Covenant on Economic, Social and Cultural Rights 72, 270
International Herald-Tribune 395
International Maritime Organization xiii
International Press Freedom Day xxii, 404
international rights and obligations 433, 434
International Year of the Family 331, 335
investment in building and construction 128, 129
Ip, Simon xii, 404

Jenney, Brian x, 57
Jiang Zemin xi, 69, 70
Joint Declaration (*see* Sino-British Joint Declaration)
Joint Liaison Group (*see* Sino-British Joint Liaison Group)
Journal of Chinese Law 65
Judicial Committee of the Privy Council 66
Judicial Proceedings (Regulation of Reports) 412
June 4 incident 189, 217 (*see also* Tiananmen massacre)

Kai Tak airport 216, 221, 245 (*see also* Chek Lap Kok)
Kamm, John xiv
†Kau Sai Chau 258, 261
Knight, Nigel 26
Kohl, Helmut 431
Kowloon Motor Bus (KMB) 221, 247, 248
Kowloon–Canton Railway (KCR) xxii, 77, 212, 219
Kowloon–Canton Railway Corporation (KCRC) 212, 214, 220
    KCRC privatization 220
Kuok, Robert xi, 394
Kuomintang (KMT) 34, 89

Labour Department 341
labour force 149, 151–56, 158, 168, 173, 176, 321, 334, 371
    labour force participation 151–56, 160–62
    labour importation schemes 174, 179
    labour market 149, 154–56, 158, 160, 163, 476
    labour mobility 476
    labour productivity 127, 478–80
    labour shortage 144, 149, 151, 156
    labour supply 149, 151–57, 160
labour-deficit economy 168, 177, 185
†Laguna City vii, xvii, 22, 343
Lam, Peggy 370
Land Development Corporation (LDC) 189
land reclamation 211, 213, 253
land use planning 187, 202–4
Language Fund 307
language in court proceedings 12, 14, 22

Lantau Fixed Crossing   217
Lau Chin-shek   118, 120, 121
Lau Wah-sum   xi
Lau Wai-hing, Emily   vii, ix, xiv, 2,
    118, 119, 120, 121, 375, 394, 406
Law Reform Commission   33, 409,
    412
Law Society of Hong Kong   14
    code of practice, amendment to   18
Lee Chu-ming, Martin   vii, x, xi, 5,
    18, 118, 120, 121, 411
Lee, Allen   118, 120, 121
legal aid   20–21
Legal Aid Department   20
Legal Aid Services Council   20
Legal Department   xxiv, 12, 28, 31
Legal Practitioners (Amendment)
    Bill   19
legal reform   64, 407
legal system   v, xxviii, 9, 13, 14, 22,
    64, 68, 432, 465
Legislative Council (Legco)   vii, viii,
    ix, x, xii, xv, xix, xxi, xxii, xxxi,
    xxxii, xxxiv, 1–7, 12, 16, 19, 27, 28,
    30, 32–36, 41–46, 50, 54, 59, 62,
    66, 70, 73, 78–80, 82, 84, 85, 89,
    90, 98, 104, 113, 118, 120, 121,
    163, 223, 244, 250, 261, 307, 312,
    313, 322, 323, 344, 355, 362,
    368–70, 373, 374, 386, 390, 398,
    401, 403, 404, 406, 408, 409, 411,
    439, 467
    Finance Committee   xvii, 4
    Information Policy Panel   3, 390,
        398, 405, 406, 410, 413
    Legislative Council (Powers and
        Privileges) Ordinance   xv, xxi, 2,
        27, 28
    Public Service Panel   54

Security Panel   2, 3, 27, 35
Standing Orders   2
Transport Panel   223, 250
legislative performance   45
legislative representativeness   45
Leong Che-hung   353
Letters Patent   1, 2, 5, 79
Leung Wai-man   xi
Li Fook-sean, Simon   x, 18
Li Ka-shing   396, 402
Li Kwan-ha   ix
Li Kwok-cheung, Arthur   xiv
Li Kwok-nang, Andrew   xxv
Li Peng   xiii, xviii, xx, 70, 255
Li Yuan   390
Li Yuet-wah, Daisy   xii
Liberal Party   xi, xvii, xxiv, 6, 78, 93,
    119, 121, 122, 326, 343, 382
liberalization   28, 213, 216
life expectancy   318, 351
linked exchange rate   201
Liu Yiu-chu   xi, xv, xx
†Lo Wu   xiv
Lo, Vincent   xx
Lobo, Sir Roger   xvi
Local Affairs advisers   78
localization   xxiv, xxxii, 11, 15, 16,
    31, 32, 41, 51, 53–56, 58, 85, 149,
    163, 164, 410
    and adaptation of laws   11–12
    of the Judiciary   15, 16
Loh Kung-wai, Christine   v, viii, xiv,
    xviii, xx, 4, 6, 90, 118, 119, 120,
    370, 404, 466, 467
†Lok Ma Chau   xxiii, 23, 243
Long Term Housing Strategy (LTHS)
    203, 204, 267, 269, 276, 282, 286,
    288–90
    mid-term review   286–92

Index

Lord Howe   xxiii
Lord MacLehose, Murray   xx, xxiii
Lord Wilson, David   xxiii, 77, 116
Lotteries Fund   4
low-cost production base   469
Lu Ping   vii, xi, xiii, xiv, xvii, xviii, xx, xxii, xxiii, xxv, xxxii, 8, 73, 74, 85
†Luk Keng   257, 261

Ma Yuzhen   xviii
Maanshan Iron and Steel Corporation   xiv
Macleod, Hamish   viii, ix, xix, 57, 431
†Mai Po Marshes   205, 254, 258, 261
Major, John   77
†Man Kam To   23
manufacturing sector   132, 155, 473, 480, 481
Mao Zedong   64, 69
market economy   xiii, xxxv, 130, 147, 471, 475, 476, 481–83
Mass Transit Railway Corporation (MTRC)   212, 214, 215, 220, 342
Master Layout Plan   205
Mathews, Jeremy   27, 57
McGregor, J. D.   xxii, 404
media polls
  by broad topics   106
  by research organizations   105
Medical and Health Department   356, 364
Medical Development Advisory Committee   355
medical social work service   337
medium of instruction   vii, 306–8
Medium of Instruction Grouping Assessment (MIGA)   307, 308

Meeting Point (MP)   xxii, xxiii, 70, 79, 93, 119, 121, 122, 123, 306, 382
Memorandum of Understanding   48, 77, 217, 218
Metro Broadcasting   396
Metroplan   202, 204
migration   145, 155, 165, 173, 175, 176, 178, 186, 301, 441
Ming Pao   xii, xxi, xxiii, xxxi, 86, 326, 390, 392, 397, 401, 413, 465
mini-constitution   64, 68, 75
Ministry of Justice   64
Mirsky, Jonathan   400
most-favoured-nation (MFN)   xx, xxii, xxiv, 473, 477
movie industry   451, 461, 462
multimedia services   213, 222
Murdoch, Rupert   xi, xix, xxii, 84, 390, 394

National People's Congress (NPC)   xi, xv, xix, xx, xxxii, 1, 8, 21, 64, 65, 71, 75, 469
  Standing Committee   8, 67
nationality   vii, xxi, xxv, 52, 53, 55, 58, 79, 182–84
Nationality Law   183
New China News Agency (NCNA)   xi, xii, xiii, xvi, xvii, xix, xx, xxi, xxii, xxiv, xxxi, 25, 38, 69, 329, 395, 398 (*see also* Xinhua)
new immigrants   154, 334
New Territories Land (Exemption) Bill   7, 369–70
New Territories Ordinance   7, 369, 370, 385, 467
news media   389, 391, 400, 402, 404, 409–11

Newspaper Society of Hong Kong 398
Ng Hong-min xx
Ngai Shiu-kit xi
Nguyen, Peter xxiv
Non-Graduate Teachers' Qualification Assessment (NGTQA) 302
North China Morning Post 395

Office of the Telecommunications Authority 222
official and semi-official representation overseas 435
Official Languages Ordinance 12, 13
Official Secrets Act (OSA) 408, 410
Old Age Pension Scheme (OPS) 139, 149, 159, 161–63, 315, 323, 324, 326–30, 338, 340
Olympic Committee xii
one-way permits from China 173
open door policy 440, 471, 472, 478
Organization for Economic Cooperation and Development (OECD) 127
Organized and Serious Crimes Bill 4, 409
Oriental Daily News (ODN) 392
Oriental Press Group 392, 393
overcrowding 194
Overseas Chinese Daily News 395
Overseas Lawyers Admission Examination 19
Overseas Public Relations Division 438

Pai Shing 392
Parent-Teacher Associations 300
†Pat Sin Leng xvii

patriotism 69, 100, 445
Patten, Christopher ix, x, xi, xii, xiii, xiv, xv, xvi, xvii, xviii, xix, xx, xxi, xxii, xxiii, xxiv, xxv, xxxi, xxxii, xxxiii, 2, 25, 26, 28, 29, 31, 34, 35, 37, 45, 75, 77, 79, 80, 103, 104, 109, 112–18, 218, 246, 247, 342, 391, 401, 403–5, 408, 413, 431, 434, 445
monthly ratings of 117, 118
Patten's proposals xxxiii, 79, 80, 113
popularity of 113, 116
pay-as-you-go system 147, 159, 162, 327
payroll tax 159, 162, 327
†Pearl River Delta 130, 138, 140, 141, 263, 471–73, 477, 479
†Pearl River Estuary xxv
People's Bank of China 474
People's Liberation Army (PLA) xxii, 398–400
People's Republic of China (P.R.C.) 26, 27, 38, 63, 75, 77, 81, 82, 84, 87, 97, 98, 302, 312, 368, 433, 435–41, 482
Places of Public Entertainment Ordinance 411
planning application 203, 204
Planning Department 203, 205
Po Lin Monastery xvi
police force ix, 30, 31, 164
Police Force Ordinance 409
political
political congruence 136
political culture xxxiv, 109, 448, 458
political economy xxviii, xxx, 136, 137

Index 497

political elite   39
political integration   469, 483
political participation   86, 89, 92–94, 165, 448
political reforms   xiv, xv, xvi, 37, 218
popular culture   440, 446, 448–57, 459, 460, 462, 465, 468
population
  population ageing   315, 317
  population control   177, 424
  population growth   165, 169, 194, 195
  population projection   315, 317
Port and Airport Development Strategy (PADS)   204, 217, 244, 256, 260, 434
port operations   237, 242
Preliminary Working Committee (PWC)   vii, ix, x, xi, xiii, xiv, xv, xvi, xvii, xx, xxii, xxiii, xxxi, 34, 56, 58, 69, 70, 71, 78, 81, 82, 84, 100, 379, 402, 403 (*see also* second stove)
Preparatory Committee   ix, xiii, xxxi, 70, 78, 402
press freedom   xii, xxii, 389, 397, 404
Prevention of Bribery Ordinance   409, 413
price searching   206–8
primary health care   352, 353, 364
private provident fund scheme   323
Private Sector Participation Scheme (PSPS)   269, 275, 276, 278, 280–82, 284, 285, 290 (*see also* Home Ownership Scheme)
privatization   215, 219, 220, 222, 356
professional workers from China   157

property inheritance rights of New Territories women   7–8
property market   xxxii, 129, 187, 202, 267, 285, 290, 475
property prices   vi, xx, xxv, xxvii, 129, 130, 132, 141, 187, 189, 198, 201, 206, 254, 276, 277, 287, 292, 394, 476
proportional representation   78, 79
Provisional Airport Authority   217, 245
Provisional Hospital Authority Report   352, 354, 358
public assistance   163, 273, 318, 321, 339, 341
public corporations   211–15, 220, 221, 222
Public Housing Development Programme   288, 291
Public Officers (Variation of Conditions of Service) (Temporary Provisions) Ordinance   54
public opinion
  monthly ratings of Governor Christopher Patten   117, 118
  opinion polls   104, 106–9, 123, 368, 398
  opinion survey development   107
  policy speech satisfaction   116
  ratings of Legco members   118–19, 120–21
  ratings of political parties   119, 121–22
Public Order Ordinance   411
public rental housing (PRH)   190, 265, 267, 269, 271–75, 277, 280, 282–84, 289, 290, 293, 295, 318
  Waiting List Income Limits (WLILs)   271–75, 277, 278, 280, 281

public retirement protection scheme 322, 329

Qian Qichen ix, x, xxxi, 67, 70, 401
Quality Assurance Unit (QAU) 311

racism 30, 31
Radio Television Hong Kong (RTHK) 84, 395, 396
Rail Development Strategy (RDS) 204, 205
Rating Bill 5
Rating Ordinance 6
re-exports 128, 211, 472, 473
real estate management 220, 475
Regional Advisory Committees 358
Regional Council 12, 374, 375
Rehabilitation Programme Plan review 331, 342
rehabilitation services 342–46
replacement airport 138, 211, 216, 217, 236, 245 (*see also* Chek Lap Kok)
Retirement Protection Scheme (RPS) 323, 327, 329
right of abode xiv, xvi, xviii, xxv, 16, 32, 52, 55, 66, 182–84
Rio Declaration 255
road network 212, 227, 245, 246
Ross, James xiv
Royal Hong Kong Jockey Club 25, 348
Royal Hong Kong Police ix, 416
Special Branch 30, 31, 34, 35
Royal Instructions 1, 2, 5, 6
Rural Committee 374

Sale of Flats to Sitting Tenants Scheme 289

sandwich class 189, 203, 207, 277, 279–81, 285
sandwich class housing scheme income limit 279, 280
School Education: A Statement of Aims 309
School Management Initiative (SMI) 308, 309, 311, 313, 314
Scott Report 352–54, 357, 358
Scott, Tony 25
seabed dredging 253, 254
seaport 211, 216
Second Review of the White Paper on Environmental Pollution 255
second stove xxxii, 70, 78, 402, 403, 445 (*see also* Preliminary Working Committee)
Secondary School Placement Allocation (SSPA) 299, 307, 308
Secretary for Health and Welfare xxv, 55, 57, 352
Secretary for Planning, Environment and Lands 57, 189, 263, 394
Secretary for Transport 30, 55, 57, 225, 247
self-censorship xxx, 390, 391, 396, 398, 401, 407
Senior Non-expatriate Officers Association 3, 54
service economy 173, 178
sewerage 205, 212
sexuality vi, xxviii, 21, 415, 417–19, 422, 427
sex crime rate 416
sex discrimination 22, 368
sex education 421–27
sexual attitudes and values 420
sexual behaviour 416–20

Index

sexual harassment 367, 370–72
sexual medicine 424, 426, 427
Sex Education Resource Centre 421
†Sha Lo Tung 257, 261
†Shenzhen x, xiv, xxiv, 138, 140, 141, 146, 178, 216, 225, 263, 390, 394, 395, 399, 436, 471, 472, 477, 479
Shenzhen Stock Exchange 474
Sing Tao 395
†Singapore xiv, 145, 146, 177, 228, 241, 249, 318, 327, 400, 480, 482
Sino-British Airport Committee xxiii
Sino-British Joint Declaration v, xxv, xxviii, xxxiii, 1, 48, 61–64, 66–69, 71–73, 75, 92, 98, 136, 145, 181, 182, 187, 217, 432, 433, 435–38, 469, 478, 483, 484
Sino-British Joint Liaison Group (JLG) xv, xvii, xix, xxiii, 11, 16, 71, 72, 73, 85, 262, 399, 434
Sino-British talks x, xiii, xv, xxxi, xxxii, 62, 66, 77, 79, 93, 103, 109–11, 221
Siu Kwing-chue, Gordon xvii, 57
So Kwok-wing, Andrew xvi
So Yiu-cho, James xii, 57
Social Sciences Research Centre (SSRC) ix, xxv, 105–8, 110, 113, 116, 118, 119
social security 159, 162, 273, 321, 326, 327, 331, 338–40
Social Welfare Department (SWD) 299, 312, 335, 337, 338, 344, 346–48
socialist market economy xxxv, 147, 471
Sohmen, Helmut xix, 34
South China Economic Region 477

South China Morning Post (SCMP) ix, x, xi, xxii, xxiv, 394, 395
†South Korea 177, 318, 328, 480, 482
sovereignty 1, 36, 53, 62–65, 73, 136, 161, 169, 176, 183, 186, 201, 216–19, 384, 391, 431, 432, 435, 437, 441, 445
Special Administrative Region (SAR) ix, xi, xii, xvi, xvii, xix, xxxi, xxxii, xxxiii, 1, 9, 11, 13, 16, 41, 46, 51, 55, 56, 59, 63–65, 67, 68, 70, 71, 73–75, 77, 79, 82, 85, 99, 136–39, 145, 147, 176, 178, 179, 182, 184, 217–19, 400, 402, 431–33, 435–37, 439, 445, 469, 484
  SAR passport 182, 184
Special Economic Zone (SEZ) 471–74, 476, 477, 481, 483
speculation xx, 130, 140, 147, 189, 190, 203, 206–8, 227, 231, 287, 358, 393, 462, 481
St. Joseph's Anglo-Chinese School vii, xxi, 307
STAR TV xx, 84, 390, 394
Stock Exchange of Hong Kong xiv, 474, 475
strategic sewage disposal scheme (SSDS) 262, 263
structural transformation 144, 147, 448
subvented hospital staff 354, 355
Suen Ming-yeung, Michael xxiv, 57, 404
Summary Offences Ordinance 411
Sun Yat-sen 87
Supreme Court ix, 14, 15
Supreme People's Court of China 65
Swaine, John 5

Swire Properties   xx, xxii
Sze Cho-cheung, Michael   xviii, 55, 56, 57, 371
Szeto Wah   x, xi, 18, 118, 120, 121

Ta Kung Pao   391
†Taiwan   xvi, xxi, xxiii, 53, 70, 92, 143, 170, 171, 175, 177, 302, 318, 392, 410, 424, 438, 462, 464, 477, 480, 482
Tam Wai-chu, Maria   402
Tam Yiu-chung   54, 120, 121
Target Oriented Curriculum (TOC)   310, 311, 313, 314
tax laws   476
taxi services
  fare policy and structure of   228–30
  law enforcement against malpractice   230–33
  quality of   233–35
  taxi licensing system   226–28
  taxi policy review   226–35
Teacher Recruitment Information Office (TRIO)   301
Technical Services Division   34
technology transfer   469, 471
Telecommunication Ordinance   33, 412
telecommunications   33, 140, 209, 213, 214, 219, 221, 222, 408, 412, 472
Television and Entertainment Licensing Authority (TELA)   29, 411, 426
Television Broadcasts Limited (TVB)   390, 394, 464
television industry   451, 452
Territorial Development Strategy Review   202, 204

tertiary sector   201, 473, 474
Thomas, Michael   xviii, 22
through train   xxxii, 75, 77, 80, 104
Tiananmen massacre   71, 77, 168, 169 (*see also* June 4 incident)
Tiananmen Square   85, 91, 390, 391
Tin Sau-kwok, Henfrey   29
Todd, David   xxv
"touch-base" policy   173
touting   18, 84
Towards Better Health consultation document   352, 359
Town Planning Board   257, 262
Trade and Industry Branch   437
trade intermediary   142, 143
Trade Union Congress   326
traffic congestion   212, 241
Tramway Boycott   91
transport   vi, 30, 55, 128, 131, 141, 205, 209, 212, 213, 219, 221, 223, 225–30, 235, 236, 238, 239, 241, 242–51, 270
Transport Advisory Committee (TAC)   221, 223, 226–35, 243, 245, 246, 249–51
Transport Complaints Unit (TCU)   230, 233
Tsang Yam-kuen, Donald   xix, xxiii
Tsui Ka-kit, Alex   vii, xv, xxi, xxxii, 2, 3, 23, 27–38, 372, 409
Tsui, T. T.   392
Tu, Elsie   vii, ix, xi, xxi, 79, 118, 119, 120, 121
Tung Tau Estate   343

unemployment   132, 144, 145, 155, 168, 169, 175, 324, 325, 341, 476
United Daily   392

Index 501

United Democrats of Hong Kong (UDHK)   vii, xxii, xxiii, 6, 18, 70, 79, 87, 93, 119, 121, 122, 123, 372, 382
United Front Department   69
United Nations   69, 72, 73, 254, 367, 405
   United Nations Conference on Environment and Development   254
   United Nations Declaration of Human Rights   405
   United Nations Human Rights Committee (UNHRC)   72, 73
United States Hong Kong Policy Act   435
Universal Declaration on Human Rights   72
University and Polytechnic Grants Committee (UPGC)   306, 310, 311, 313
Urban and Regional Councils   78, 89, 369, 375
urban densities   201, 202

†Victoria Harbour   253, 257, 263
Vietnamese migrants   167, 180
visa applications   172
visa-free travel   182, 183

Wah Kiu Yat Po   395
Wang Juntao   xxii
Watkins, Guy   25
Wei Jingsheng   xii
Wen Wei Po   91
Wharf Cable   222, 396
White Paper on Transport Policy in Hong Kong (1990)   223, 229, 236, 248

Whitehead Detention Centre   xxi, xxv, 3, 181, 393
Wide Angle   xiii
Wiggham, Barrie   55
wire-tapping   33
women
   candidates in the 1994 District Board elections   378
   civil servants on directorate pay scale   378
   labour force participation   154, 156, 160, 162
   numerical representation in formal governmental structures   373
   political recruitment of   374, 386
   representation in the Legislative and Executive Councils   374
   representation in the municipal councils   376
   representation on the District Boards   377
   right to inherit property in the New Territories   7
   violence against   370–72
Women 30 Action Group   371
women's movement   373, 384, 385
Wong Yick-ming, Rosanna   ix, 288, 292
Wong Ying-wai, Wilfred   xxi
Wong, Dominic   71, 391
Working Group on Educational Standards   311
Working Group on Language Proficiency   308, 311
working population   127, 132, 155, 160, 318, 320, 321, 322, 472
World Wide Fund for Nature (HK)   256
Wu Hung-yuk, Anna   xiv, xix, 4, 6, 21, 163, 344

Xi Yang   viii, xii, xxi, xxii, xxiii, xxxi, 86, 390, 397, 399–401, 404, 410, 465, 466
Xi Yang affair   397–401
Xinhua   vii, viii, 69, 70, 392, 394, 395, 398, 401 (*see also* New China News Agency)
Xu Jiatun   392

Yang, Sir Ti-liang   vii, xvii, xix
Yeoh, E. K.   356
Yeung Kai-yin   xii, xxi, xxii, 30
Yu Pun-hoi   401
Yung Chi-kin, Larry   xviii

Zhang Junsheng   xi, 38, 394
Zhou Nan   xiii, xvi, xx
Zhu Senlin   xvi
†Zhuhai   138, 140, 146, 263, 471
zoning   203, 204, 239, 240
Zuo Linshu   391